LET EUROPE HEAR

LET EUROPE HEAR

The Spiritual Plight
of Europe

By
ROBERT P. EVANS, B.D., LL.D.
Founder and European Director
Greater Europe Mission

A survey of sixteen countries of free, western Europe,
stressing the conditions which have made them mission
fields in our generation

 MOODY PRESS
CHICAGO

To My Mother

MRS. ROWLAND HILL EVANS

Foreign Missionary, Faithful Intercessor, Fond Parent

19409

Contents

CHAPTER   PAGE

Preface 9

1. *The Overlooked Continent* 15
2. *Giants in the Land* 47
3. *The Missionary to Europe* 91
4. *France, the Smoldering Fire* 107
5. *The Truth About Spain* 179
6. *The Awakening of Portugal* 231
7. *Italy, the Land of Heartbreak* 245
8. *Blindness in Belgium and Luxemburg* 291
9. *Austria Forgotten* 317
10. *The Enigma of Ireland* 327
11. *Greece's Unknown God* 347
12. *Changing Holland* 361
13. *Whither Germany Leads* 389
14. *Switzerland: No Paradise Without God* 431
15. *Scandinavia in Silhouette* 449
    Appendices 501
    Notes 509
    Bibliographic Essay 521
    Index 523

Preface

Europe a mission field? Until recently this question would have startled the average person. But today, as more facts about Europe emerge, the question is becoming an assertion: *Europe is a mission field!* The twentieth century has returned full circle to the first: the oldest mission field is now the newest. Especially since World War II a mounting prayer interest and a steady trickle of missionaries to the Old World have aroused much curiosity. People are asking, "What is the spiritual picture there?"

This book describes some of the conditions which have turned Europe into a mission field. These underlying issues—the paganism and de-Christianization of the continent—are the basis for what missionary work is being done in Europe. Naturally a study like this must be limited. For this reason our survey does not review missionary activity as such, except to choose certain examples now and then to illustrate the need. The full story of foreign missionary work in Europe deserves another volume.

Since God has declared our whole race to be under His wrath and condemnation, we do not need to justify missionary effort anywhere among the sons of Adam. Rather, this survey is like a photographer's exposure meter, registering the amount of light present. As I have worked on the material my conviction has deepened that we wrongly assume Europe to be Christian simply because it is so civilized. Through lack of information we overrate the light and understanding the average European has concerning God's truth.

As evangelical Christians who believe that only a personal trust in Jesus Christ can save, our whole interpretation of the European religious scene, be it Catholic or Protestant, is conditioned. We make no apology for this. Europe is saturated with the symbols and trappings of religion, but how little Europeans know of the Prince of Life!

Only western Europe is in view in these pages. Of Europe's 460 million inhabitants, over 250 million—including 146 million in the European part of the Soviet Union—are under Communist rule.* Though Westerners cannot permanently reside as missionaries in Communist-

*Figures are from the current *United Nations Demographic Report.*

9

dominated lands, we can intercede for our fellow members of the body of Christ who witness there for His name.

Of the thirty-four nations in Europe, fewer than half are in the non-Communist part. The sixteen covered in this survey are open to foreign Christian workers. With varying degrees of liberty, some open, public witness can be carried on in each, though full separation of church and state, in our sense, is nowhere seen in Europe. Because the sixteen-nation area of 166 million souls is unsurpassed anywhere for strategic importance, western Europe is a prime field for missionary thrust.

Several countries in free Europe are not included in this discussion. Great Britain is one. Though she belongs to the continent geographically, Britain is culturally and spiritually a kingdom apart. Like America she has a redemptive minority capable, if revived and alert, of winning many to Christ.

Then there is Yugoslavia. Tourists are now welcome there, but her attitude toward resident foreign workers has yet to be given a fair test. In an interview with an American evangelical leader several years ago, Marshal Tito hinted that such work by foreigners might be tolerated. When one considers the political scene there, however, very little hope of open activity seems likely.

The republic of Iceland has been excluded not so much because of her isolation from continental Europe as because spiritual characteristics there parallel those in Scandinavia.

With the exception of Luxemburg I have not dealt with the smaller pocket states; Monaco, San Marino, Liechtenstein, and Andorra are spiritually similar to their Catholic neighbors.

Though part of Turkey is in Europe, that nation belongs as a whole with Asia. European Turkey contains only one and a half million people, while the population of Asian Turkey, east of the Dardanelles, reaches 20 million.

In each chapter devoted to a country appears a sketch of the national personality and customs of that country. Every missionary becomes, perhaps unknowingly, an amateur social anthropologist as he avidly studies his adopted people's way of life. The best missionaries are those who best understand their fellow human beings as well as their God.

Some historic background is helpful, especially when one is considering Europe. Every effect in this continent has a cause deeply involved in the past. I have included only brief historic glimpses which throw light on the present scene, but to gain perspective those interested should read all the history they can.

Then there are some brief summaries from the European world of ideas. The theological, philosophical, and political foes of the gospel cannot be overlooked. As one American university professor writes—

For the European to believe in an idea, it must first have passed through the filter of his intellect. This also explains why, in Europe, religions tend to shed their purely devotional aspects and to develop into doctrine (intellect) and into ethics (will). The Christian religion has been no exception to this rule; it too has tended to become a dogmatic and doctrinal construction and a set of principles of behaviour, mostly for social use.

Since the intellectual commands more respect on this continent than in North America, he is an important contact for his own sake and for that of his circle of influence.

During the past fourteen years I have resided in Europe and frequently visited all the countries discussed, some of them dozens of times. Even so, I feel that I know so little about this vast and varied continent. To supplement my own observations I have drawn from the experiences and writings of a host of fellow workers and friends. For their contributions I am deeply grateful. I should add that any opinions expressed are my own and not necessarily those of any organizations I have served.

I want to thank those who were of special help in furnishing material or in critically reading certain chapters of the manuscript. David Barnes of the Greater Europe Mission and Arthur Johnston of the Evangelical Alliance Mission read the chapter on France. Dr. John D. Hughey, Jr., President of the Baptist Seminary in Rushlikon, Switzerland, a former missionary in Spain and an authority on Protestant history there, pointed me to certain background materials on Spain, and Harold Kregel of the Worldwide European Fellowship in Barcelona carefully read the Spanish chapter. Arthur Brown of the Conservative Baptist mission in Portugal, shared information about that country. While I was preparing the material on Italy, Dr. Edwin Jacques, a Foreign Secretary of the Conservative Baptist Foreign Mission Society and former missionary in Italy, encouraged and advised me. In Italy itself I received help from Richard Mosher of the Conservative Baptists in Naples. A special thanks is due Royal Peck, head of the Greater Europe Mission's Italian Bible Institute in Rome, for evaluating the whole chapter on Italy.

During my research on Belgium and Luxemburg, Dr. John C. Winston, long-time codirector of the Belgian Gospel Mission, kindly opened his files to me in Brussels, and all the personnel of this fine mission gave information from time to time. In Salzburg, Leander Penner of the Greater Europe Mission, and Miss Nell Pearson, of the European Evangelistic Crusade, revealed conditions in Austria which otherwise would have been unrecorded. The interviews I had in Dublin with Mr. E. G. Broadstock, secretary of the Hibernian Bible Society, and T. R. Horan, superintendent of the Irish Church Missions, were invaluable for writing about Ireland.

The late Pastor Constantin Metallinos, an evangelical leader in Athens, and Mr. George Kladis, secretary of the British and Foreign Bible Society's Athens branch, patiently answered my questions about Greece. Miss Ruth Mellis, a missionary to Greece, added perspective to our concept of Greece during her furlough. George Papadopoulos, a graduate of the European Bible Institute in Paris, was a perfect guide in Athens.

In Holland I obtained material from Mr. Jan van Capeleveen, a Christian journalist in Rotterdam, Robert Miller, an American Bible teacher who lives in Oosterbeek, Mrs. Gien Kaarsen of the Navigators at The Hague, and a host of Dutch friends.

I owe special thanks to the Office for External Affairs of the German Evangelical Church in Frankfurt, Germany, the Privileged Württemberg Bible Society in Stuttgart and the offices of the German free churches for the information they furnished. Dr. Wilhelm Brauer, an old friend and former director of the Evangelical Church's Berlin City Mission, counseled me many times. I must also thank Bishop Otto Dibelius, former head of the Evangelical Church of Berlin-Brandenburg, and Dr. Hans Lilje, Bishop of the Evangelical Church of Hanover, for insights received from interviews with them. Dr. Martin Niemöller, president of the Evangelical Church in Hessen-Nassau, received me at his Darmstadt office and contributed his views. While these churchmen would not agree with all my conclusions, I appreciated the chance to share their thinking.

Dr. René Pâche, principal of the Emmaus Bible Institute at Vennes-sur-Lausanne, Switzerland, has helped me understand Europe and his country better by many contacts over the years. By attending the campaigns of the Janz brothers of Basel, and through Leo Janz's interpretations of the Holy Spirit's work, my eyes have been opened to the possibilities of wider evangelism in Switzerland and German-speaking Europe. Enos Zimmerman of the Greater Europe Mission, formerly in Finland, filled in gaps of information about his remote land, and Paul Gullans, who serves with the same mission in Sweden, kindly read the entire Scandinavian chapter.

Finally, I am grateful to Dr. Arthur Glasser, North American Director of the China Inland Mission, for reviewing the first three chapters, especially the section on Communism. Dr. Carl F. H. Henry, editor of *Christianity Today*, read the theological section. The whole manuscript was gone over with close attention by Elwyn Davies, Canadian Secretary of the Bible Christian Union, who made most valuable contributions. James Kiefer, former General Director of Child Evangelism Fellowship International, also read the whole book before publication, taking special interest in the chapters on the German-speaking part of Europe he knows so well.

My special thanks are due to my wife for her patient help during my preparation of the material. Miss Geneviève Ariège of France, Miss Sandy Ubbink of Holland, and Mrs. Wendy Hill Miller of England, all helped in the typing of the manuscript in Paris.

Of all the free continents, Europe has the lowest ratio of missionaries in proportion to population. May those who plan, pray, and provide for the evangelization of this world for our Lord Jesus Christ be stimulated by these pages. Best of all, may some who follow the Lamb whithersoever He goeth contribute their lives to the winning of "the overlooked continent" for Him.

ROBERT P. EVANS

Paris, France

Counselors singing in an evangelistic effort in Germany above the sign "I am the Way, the Truth, and the Life."

Credit: Pressebilk Schubert

Chapter 1

THE OVERLOOKED CONTINENT

*"In many sections of Europe an individual has about as little chance
of receiving an evangelical Christian witness as he would have in
many better-known mission fields of the world."*

—DR. HAROLD JOHN OCKENGA
Park St. Church, Boston

Not Considered! The refugee miner working near the Belgian border
is not sure who Jesus Christ is. "Somewhere, though, I've heard the
name," he says. In Paris a professor at the world's largest university asks
for a Bible, "that book we hear about but never see." When a French
Readers' Digest advertisement offers free Scriptures, 5,000 people respond
from all over the French world. Less fortunate millions petition St.
Bernadette at her healing spring in Lourdes, the world's best-attended
religious shrine. In the past, few nations have provided more martyrs
for the cause of Christ than has France. Today no nation pays a greater
price for overindulgence in food, drink, and pleasure. France has more
spiritualist healers than medical doctors to attend to ills of the body, but
neither group can solve life's deeper problem of sin. Meanwhile 1,446
French people enter eternity every day; France has the highest death rate
in Europe.

A German *hausfrau* in Schleswig-Holstein fingers some trinkets.
Charms to protect her family against spirits, she explains, bought at the
village pharmacy. At Bad Kreuznach a shabby pianist spins out an intri-
cate passage from Bach. Asked to trust Christ as his Saviour, this German
hesitates. Every night for weeks he has walked twelve kilometers to hear
a gospel message. "No, I can't," he says slowly. "During the war I was
bewitched and forced to do some dirty work. Please let me alone." The
German parliament, obliged to do something about the spreading professional witchcraft, recently passed a new law against sorcerers. Sorcery
in the birthplace of the Reformation? But many things have changed in

the land of Luther. In a Germany where almost half the people now profess to be Catholic, less than 5 per cent of them actually go to any church at all. Those who do go rarely hear a gospel message.

A Dutch youth worries about death and judgment. One night he wakes up his Reformed pastor to ask about hell. "Forget it," soothes the clergyman; "all that is medieval fancy." Because the young man cannot forget, something snaps inside. Seeking oblivion, he jumps in front of the Amsterdam express. Miraculously the youth survives, and finds the Saviour. But his church had failed him.

In Spain's hinterland a black-clad peasant mother sighs tiredly. God is so hard to please, she reflects, as she toils up step after step toward the lofty shrine of Montserrat. Up there the Black Virgin, to whom she must pray, will surely understand. Behind the woman, on the rocky stairs, winds a trail of blood, for she is climbing on her knees. With similar longing to be free, thousands parade through Spanish streets during Holy Week processions of penitents. Some walk on tiptoe with arms raised to show their penance by their pain. Others stagger along the route under heavy crosses, their feet shackled with blood-splashed chains. Hate their slavery? Yes, but they fear for their souls.

Up in Copenhagen police carry out a sheet-wound body from a dingy hotel room. Next day the newspapers routinely announce that another country girl has taken her life. This is Denmark, which has one of the highest suicide rates in the world. This, too, is the part of socialized Scandinavia that leads Europe in divorce. Few people knew the lonely girl in the gay "Paris of the North." Though the Danes may file her away as a statistic and forget her, to God she is an undying soul for whom He gave His Son.

Down in the province of Umbria an Italian farmer carefully attaches a red tassel to his yoke of oxen. Well worth the trouble, he thinks, to ward off the *jettatura* or evil eye. As he trudges down the hill to his Communist cell meeting, he wonders how many *lire* he should risk on next week's football betting in the village cafe. To better his frugal life he is a weekday Communist. For the safety of his soul he is a Sunday Roman Catholic. At heart he remains a pagan.

In the Peloponnesus a Greek boy reads his New Testament in a treetop, the only place where he can study the book forbidden by his Greek Orthodox family. Suddenly his father sees him and rushes furiously out of the house yelling for him to come down. The man fells his son with one great blow, then kicks him into bloody unconsciousness.

These true experiences may surprise the outsider, for they do not come from the Europe of the guidebooks, but from another Europe, seen on a different level. Isolated, sensational cases? You would be surprised to know how common they are. What is the matter with this Old World where most of us have our roots? Just as many symptoms can point to one diseased bodily organ, so ignorance, superstition, and meaningless religious symbols can reveal one basic illness. While we shall study some symptoms of our patient in this book, sin is the real soul-sickness of Europe. Today, in mid-century, as the old restraints slip away, Europe's spiritual malady grows progressively worse.

Under whatever religious exterior Europe retains, she is turning pagan, much as the body of Naaman became leprous under his general's uniform. Europe is tired of religion. Her great cathedrals—tombs enshrining a dead faith—recall her saddest, bloodiest centuries. The present religious belief, which carries more assent than conviction, is little better than the beliefs of the past. Yet something must replace empty creeds in the heart of man. To borrow a phrase from John Stuart Mill, the average European is "destitute of faith and terrified of scepticism." He is like the wandering star Jude saw rushing alone through limitless space forever. Most tragic of all, "heaven's easy, artless, unencumbered plan" for personal salvation through Jesus Christ is unknown to the man on the street.

Before we go further, let us just glance at some stirring facts:

> *Though Europe contains 15 per cent of the world's population only 2 per cent of North America's missionaries serve there.*
> *More Europeans than the whole population of the United States have yet to see a copy of the Bible.*
> *A Chicago-sized population from Europe enters eternity each year.*
> *There are more evangelical foreign missionaries in Haiti and in Jamaica than in all of Europe.*
> *Over a quarter of a million towns and villages in Europe do not have an adequate gospel witness.*
> *Most of Europe's 73 million children between the ages of five and fourteen have never heard the gospel.*
> *Less than a quarter of the people of free continental Europe profess to be Protestant.*

In a well-known American Bible conference auditorium a missionary map of the world marks Europe as "Not Considered"! But how could any part of this world for which Christ died be "not considered" by His own? Can any Christian fail to see a harvest field in a continent with such needs? Why does Europe stand at the end of the line in missionary manpower distribution? Should we do something about this challenge? What *can* we do? These are questions each reader must answer for himself.

What is a Mission Field? In our day we classify the countries of the world minutely but quite artificially. First, we point out the difference between home and foreign mission fields. Then, in the foreign category we further distinguish between primary and secondary fields. The *primary* fields, we say, need pioneer resident missionaries who must devote their time to language reduction, education, Bible translation, evangelism, and teaching. After some years of effort a national church should emerge strong enough to warrant the missionaries' departure. Naturally most of the primitive races and younger nations fall into this division.

On the other hand, the so-called *secondary* mission fields call for only occasional itinerant visits from foreign Christians. Since these countries supposedly have mature churches capable of giving a total witness to their populations, outside helpers are needed only for periodic evangelism or Bible teaching. In other words, these areas need occasional inspiration rather than evangelization by resident missionaries.

While there may be some justification for such an analysis as a mental convenience, I repeat that it is artificial. Unfortunately Satan is a potent, wily foe who shifts his forces to meet new threats to his authority as prince of this world. What is more, events do not freeze any people into a mould, as we might prefer. Would that spiritual gains once won might be held! History shows, however, that under evil influences, any country or people can become decadent and godless, regardless of past blessings.

Europe is usually left out of Anglo-American missionary strategy altogether. At best this continent is called a secondary mission field, less pressing in her need than other areas. Europe is downgraded in missionary terms because of a vague something known as "saturation point." This phrase concerns the amount of effort which must be put into a given area before the missionary must withdraw. Such withdrawal depends on the educational level, the extent of evangelization, the progress of the national church, the temper of nationalism, and other variables. A wide difference of opinion exists on what constitutes grounds for withdrawal. Anyway, the procedure defies definition, since each case is different. Often the Lord of history forces evacuation of the missionaries whether they or their converts are "ready" or not. Only He knows what readiness really is.

In contrast to our complex theories, what beautiful simplicity shines through the statements of the Word of God! Here the field is a whole world, where every inhabitant is a potential child of God. In the book of Acts no line of demarcation appears between home and foreign missions. Nor do primary or secondary areas, saturation points or withdrawals follow a pattern. Principles can be traced in the missionary work of Paul, but not rigid plans. The apostle did not announce where he was going, because he did not know. He could not state how long he would stay or when he would return, for such things were veiled from his eyes. Paul had no design but to obey God in utter dependence. To do this he remained fluid in his thinking. Look at his record. The Holy Spirit hinders him here, draws him there. Sometimes he retraces his footsteps, sometimes not. At times he revisits his converts for three weeks, at others for three years. Paul withdrew only when His Lord made departure plain, not for any artificial reason. Did all this result in confusion? Everywhere in the apostolic period we see what G. Campbell Morgan called "the glorious regularity of the irregular." Through the mobile, seemingly illogical pattern of obedience was woven a steadfast, divine purpose. How did Paul know when his work was completed anywhere? The Lord Jesus Christ, as living Head of the Church, was in the midst of His people to direct their work by the Holy Spirit. Our day is no different. Flexibility and dependence are still the rule. With Him to guide, it seems perfectly clear that we have no right to dismiss any part of the world as already evangelized. In this there can be no pat answers or closed minds. Only He knows the true situation regarding any land. Only He knows how to meet the need, and when.

Sometimes we are careless about our use of the word "unevangelized." On this Frank W. Price, former director of the Missionary Research Library in New York, has this helpful comment:

> If unevangelized places are areas where the gospel has never penetrated, then the number of such places is becoming smaller all the time.
>
> If unevangelized countries are those where it is difficult to preach and win converts but where the missionary witness is greatly needed, then the Communist world, the Arabic world, and the predominantly Roman Catholic countries should all be included.
>
> The tendency of missionary enthusiasts is to . . . shy away from the hard areas such as Communistic and Islamic countries or countries where nationalism, resurgent old religions and anti-Christian spirit make Christian service very difficult. Yet these too are unevangelized fields in the Christian sense.[1]

What is a mission field? Any area which has no national church, or has a church too small or weak to permit its believers to evangelize the population alone, needs help from abroad. Or again, a mission field is any area of the world where the light of His truth, once strong, has died. I experienced such darkness once in a human sense. A thousand feet down in a winding cave we extinguished our lights for a full minute. The resulting darkness could be "felt" with terrifying realism! No place is as dark, goes the proverb, as one where the light has gone out. North Africa is a good example of this. In the first century of our era this region had a strong church. Yet in the decades which followed certain conditions made North Africa, " the land of the vanished church," more of a mission field than ever. This must resemble the "outer darkness" of which the Scriptures speak.

Such is the case with much of western Europe today. Most people think Europe has had a chance to hear the gospel. Yet even if history verified that—which it does not—we would still bear responsibility for our own generation in that continent. The commission of Christ to reach the world with His message of salvation has new validity and authority for each Christian generation. So there is no such thing as a completed cycle of evangelization anytime or anywhere. The Body of Christ, already united to its Head, will not be visibly gathered unto Him until the last soul has been added.

As we examine Europe we find many places where the gospel is completely unknown. We have said that over 250,000 towns have no gospel witness at all. To proclaim the message once in each town—a new town every day—would take an individual 695 years! Would anyone suggest that Spain, where five-hundredths of one per cent of the population is Protestant,* has been reached? Or Italy, where less than one half of 1 per cent is Protestant? Has France been evangelized, when not 2 per cent is Protestant? Germany can scarcely be considered won, since a bare 5 per cent of her people bother to go to any church regularly. What shall we say of Belgium and Luxemburg, with their scores of unreached cities? Austria, Portugal, and Greece have only a tiny fraction of their people within the family of God. Even Switzerland, Holland, and Scandinavia show a shocking ignorance of the new birth.

No wonder thinking Christians today are beginning to wonder whether Europe was ever truly evangelized. A growing conviction is emerging that a Europe reawakening to the claims of Christ could deeply affect the whole world. More power to such a thought! May it result in action!

Civilized but Lost. In today's scene of competitive missionary presentation we have been strongly conditioned by the portrayal of physical suffering, odd customs, strange people. Indeed, these approaches are deliberately if sincerely used, as some mission executives freely admit, to trigger a spiritual concern they hope will find later financial expression. Why are some of us more moved by the bizarre than by the Biblical? Is a Hottentot "more lost" than a Hollander? How lost *is* lost? Are there degrees of "lostness"? The writer once followed another speaker at one of those marathon missionary conferences where a new challenge is presented every few minutes. "This sword killed over a hundred men!" cried the preceding speaker, suddenly flourishing a machete-type weapon he had been hiding behind his back. The audience gasped. Dropping his voice to a whisper, the missionary leaned forward, "Now its owner, a chief of the headhunters, is a child of God!" To follow this dramatic appeal

*We do not imply that all Protestants are Christians in the Biblical sense, nor vice versa, but only use the term throughout this book for want of a more accurate designation.

with a sober review of Europe's godlessness was difficult. Relatively little in that continent is sensational in a like sense. The smart *boulevardier* who crosses the *Place de l'Opera* in Paris swinging his umbrella is a modern pagan, but unfortunately he lives in Paris rather than Pago Pago. By this accident of birth he may never hear the story of God's reconciling love. He is too civilized!

Why should we expect the artificial device to stimulate true Christian compassion? Are we like Pavlov's conditioned dogs, who salivated whenever a bell rang? Those who would care about Europe's state must do so on the Scriptural grounds that "he that believeth not is condemned already" (John 3:18), rather than for any surface reason. Somehow we accept this for ourselves in North America or England. Yet when we "think missions," we undergo a curious mental shift. Fortunately some recent developments have helped remedy this. The late missionary surge into Central and South America has shown that the densely populated cities of our hemisphere are just as needy as its uncivilized outposts. Only one conclusion can be drawn: Whether in tribe or tenement, all of Adam's sons need Adam's Saviour, the Lord Jesus Christ.

Is Europe Already Evangelized? The question is a common one which this book tries to answer in part. Any reply would presuppose some knowledge of history, a grasp of the matrix ideas that have shaped Europe, and firsthand experience with European church life.

Since the average Christian today knows that the gospel spread into Europe in the apostolic period,* he is puzzled to hear this part of the world referred to as a mission field. Christianity, though early corrupted in form and content, was still vital enough in Europe by the second and third centuries to conquer barbarism and Roman polytheism alike. In a short time it even became the official religion of the Roman empire and a major colonizing principle of that dying civilization. Thus most of the continent was becoming nominally Christian in a relatively few centuries.

But even a superficial study of the Christian faith of this period will show how early it began to change. I have thought of this while exploring early civilization in Pompeii or Athens, groping through Roman catacombs, or visiting the site of vanished Carthage. Pagan concepts such as praying for the dead, the mother-and-child fetish, the use of lamps and candles, processions, mystic signs and symbols, the priesthood, the confession, and even a primitive mass had flourished in the mystery religions of the East long before Christianity came upon the scene. Gradually they infiltrated Christian worship. The step from deified emperor to

*Acts 16:12 and later passages.

directing bishop was but a short and natural one. It was not long before the Bishop of Rome and other church leaders had allowed these absorbed pagan elements to alter the character of salvation itself and the way it is received by man. The gospel which Rome propagated was already a humanized husk of Christianity. Small wonder that the continent of Europe, so widely peopled by Romanized tribes who added their pagan ideas to the mixture, was soon plunged into dark ages. The Roman Catholic Church dominated these centuries of twilight. Meanwhile the truth of saving grace through Jesus Christ burned only feebly here and there. V. R. Edman has described the post-Constantine age in these words:

> The vast majority of "Christians" were unregenerate and uninstructed; the number of hypocrites multiplied enormously; strict discipline had to be relaxed; heathen custom crept surreptitiously into the worship of God until the place of penitence and prayer became as pagan as the smoking altars of Moloch or Zeus.[2]

No case can be made for the evangelization of Europe before or through the Middle Ages. The gospel was present but not predominant, known privately by the few but not publicly by the many.

Finally, in the goodness of God, precursors of a new age appeared like supernovae in the firmament, shining brilliantly, disappearing swiftly. Occam, Wycliffe, Huss, Wessel, Tauler, and Savonarola were among these. Then the Reformation exploded across Europe in the wake of the hammer blows of the Friar of Wittenberg. Once again the basic message of justification by grace through faith alone came to light. To spread this knowledge the Bible was translated into the vernacular from the original languages revived by scholars of the Renaissance. Providentially, too, the printing press appeared at the right time to help the process. Even the hearts of some rulers were prepared by God to champion certain reformers.

Soon Calvin, the great systematizer, produced his Biblical expositions for the French Reform. In Zurich, Zwingli gave his life for the evangelical rebirth of Switzerland. During this period a host of nameless heroes lived and died in faithful obedience to the King of kings. Into Holland, Belgium, Scandinavia, and England the new knowledge spread. During the 130 years of its greatest momentum hundreds of thousands were won to Christ through the Reformation. But still the question persists: Was Europe really evangelized?

Limitations of the Reformation. We must realize that, fraught as the Reformation was with blessing, it did not reach all of Europe for Christ. As one contemporary historian has put it, "The Reformation was along all lines an uncompleted movement whose progress was arrested short of its logical goals."[3] "Evangelization" as we use the term means the winning to Christ of a responsible minority sufficiently strong and influential to present the claims of Christ to the untouched majority. By such a definition of the word Europe has never been really evangelized—at least since the Apostolic Age—except in certain local areas. Because of the limitations of the Reformation, millions of Europeans today, who inherited its effects, have no knowledge of the Saviour.

How was this moving of God limited? First, the Reformation was limited in *spiritual depth*. Only an intellectual or creedal change was made in the lives of millions during this period. As we shall see in our study of Protestant Europe, overnight whole populations were declared to be on the side of the reformers. Some of the rulers who brought such changes to pass knew nothing of the saving grace of the Lord Jesus Christ. When we remember that Luther himself did not give up his hopes for a reformed Catholicism until twenty years after he nailed his ninety-five theses to the Wittenberg church door, we can realize how hard it must have been for the less enlightened to take this step as a matter of conviction. We cannot judge how many of those who became Protestant were really born again, yet the record of the items is not encouraging. For many reasons the age saw multitudes carry into their new religion the half-knowledge, conditioned thinking, and pitiful doubts of their old religion. The spiritual state of the Lutheran and Reformed churches in the centuries that followed—and in our day—testify that though many professed, too few understood, faith in the Lord Jesus Christ.

Second, the Reformation was limited by *political opportunism*. The reformers and the rulers who backed them agreed on some of their goals quite apart from any doctrinal issues. A new nationalism found many champions prepared by Renaissance influences to end feudalism and redress economic wrongs, and, not incidentally, to enrich themselves. When social changes that had been in the making for centuries erupted through the opening provided by the reformers, the end of the Holy Roman Empire seemed assured. Many of the Lutheran princes were genuine believers; others were mere opportunists. The worst were despots, like King Christian II of Denmark, who tried to join both sides. While murdering eighty Lutheran Swedish nobles at a Stockholm banquet in the name of the Holy Mother Church, he was simultaneously inviting Lutheran preachers to Denmark.

A third limitation to the effectiveness of the Reformation lay in the *territorial principle* adopted by Luther himself. By this principle the official religious belief was declared to be that of the majority in a given locality. Those in the minority who did not agree were free to move elsewhere. But moving was not always possible or desirable; so it was much easier to change faiths. In future generations all born into Protestant territory were considered Protestant, while Catholics had their own areas. In his heart Luther knew, Roland Bainton points out, what the Body of Christ was: "The true church for him was always the church of the redeemed, known only to God, manifest here and there on earth, small, persecuted and often hidden, at any rate scattered, and united only in the bond of the Spirit."[4] Yet by 1526 Luther had declared that this concept could not be reconciled with the problems.* Thus he chose for the masses a church based upon geographical areas. As Bainton says, "Luther had unwittingly started down the road which was to lead to the territorial church under the authority of the prince . . . Luther never dreamed that he was subordinating the church to the state."[5] To the end of his life Luther insisted, above all, that the church should not be impeded, thus toning down his earlier views on the separation of church and state expressed in the tract *On Civil Government.* Today the parish system, with its perpetuation of nominal belief, is a great hindrance to true faith in Jesus Christ and to the consequences of such faith in a life of discipleship. European Protestantism in both its Reformed and Lutheran expressions is reaping the fruit of this sixteenth-century seed.

Fourth, *internal strife* among the reformers dulled the cutting edge of Reformation truth. In one instance Lutherans became comrades-in-arms with the Catholics to restrain the Calvinists. Lutheran resistance to the Anabaptists is well known. At the Diet of Speyer, with the reluctant consent of Luther himself, Lutherans concurred with Catholics in subjecting the Anabaptists to the death penalty—then helped impose it. The spectacle of certain Reformation Christians drowning their fellow Christians in the Rhine or subjecting them to hideous torture was not a pretty one. Neither was the picture of Zwingli exterminating Anabaptists in Zurich nor Calvin burning Servetus in Geneva any credit to the Lord. In matters of dogma, disagreement, too, sadly divided and weakened the total effect of the movement. At Marburg, had Melanchthon not dissuaded Luther from agreeing with Zwingli during their great debate on the Lord's Supper (when he was at the very point of agreement), the history of ensuing centuries might have been different.

The *low literacy rate* of the period formed a fifth, less often recognized, limiting factor. Only in recent years has the extent of the literacy of the Middle Ages been subjected to genuine research. According to some of the best scholars investigating literacy in the Middle Ages, the ability to read could be measured almost wholly by the knowledge and use of Latin. Among the *noblesse* or upper class of medieval society the knowledge of Latin has proved to be more widespread than was hitherto be-

---

*He erred here, because in his own time the Anabaptists succeeded without the territorial idea, though with much suffering.

lieved. Yet among the masses the story was different. "The illiteracy of the common people is not open to question"[6] is the way James W. Thompson puts it.

This conclusion also applies to the early modern period. Even though the output of Reformation tracts was voluminous, the peasants and other commoners were unable to read them. Schooling was sadly limited on elementary levels. While it is true that in 1520 there were 72 universities in Europe, the upper classes were the sole beneficiaries of this education.

Finally, the efforts of these men of God were limited in *geographic extent*. Fewer than we realize of the estimated 100 million Europeans of that day heard the gospel of grace. No radio, television, or loudspeaking systems made the task easier. Large-scale public evangelism, great publishing houses, organized personal work and visitation programs were unknown then. Nor did the people know anything like that busy beehive, the modern, Western gospel church. There is almost nothing in the writings of the reformers to show that they cared much about the world-wide spread of their doctrines. Not until 150 years after the Reformation do we see foreign missionaries going from Europe to distant places with the gospel. Not even close to the points of origin did "every creature" hear the message. Very few cities or towns got a thorough coverage of truth even through the splendid medium of personal testimony common at the time. In the country districts, where illiteracy reigned, travel arrangements were slow and primitive. In France, for instance, preachers of the new faith were few, overworked, and often harassed by the authorities. Thousands of towns in Latin Europe were completely unaffected except by the general turn of events. The common man in whole countries like Portugal, Spain, and Italy was completely ignorant of the meaning of the events he heard about. Later the zealous planting of Catholicism by explorers from these lands was to create prime mission fields like Latin America at our very doorstep today. Quickly, too, the Counter-Reformation reacted with measures like the Holy Inquisition, slowing the spread of truth.

We would not minimize what God so graciously wrought. In spite of its limitations the Reformation accomplished the incredible. Because "little is much when God is in it," many of the limiting circumstances I have mentioned were temporarily overcome. The power of God transformed sinners, overthrew tryrants and gladdened many a heart. Unfortunately the common man all too rarely apprehended the gospel, with the result that today his heir, the European John Doe, is likewise ignorant of the gospel. Unfortunately too, the practices of sacramental salvation and inherited religion which grew out of the Reformation are problems in Europe today.

Twelve Reasons Why We Should Seek to Win Europe. Let us turn now from the historical to the present. We see in Europe today a complex of thirty-four countries, only some sixteen larger ones hospitable and accessible to resident foreign missionaries. Europe, the exact limits of which are argued over by geographers, merges into the Asian continent on the Russian side and reaches down toward Africa both at Gibraltar and through the Middle East land bridge. In this Canada-sized continent of almost four million square miles live over five hundred million people, giving Europe more people for its size than any other continent. Ten of the twelve densely-populated countries in the world are in Europe. Why should we make any special effort to reach them? What grounds are there for considering teeming Europe as a mission field? Some of the reasons listed here are amplified elsewhere in this book:

1. Europe is part of the world we are commissioned by Christ to evangelize.

   In the spiritual sense this commission is the only authority we need to go to Europe with the gospel. Each generation of Christians is responsible for the unsaved fellow men of its own time. Thus the commission ever renews its validity in cycles, to end only when our Lord comes. European believers must form part of that body God is taking out of the nations for Himself (Acts 15:14), the multitude which, in the words of the Son to the Father, "thou gavest me out of the world" (John 17:6).

2. Europe's population is less than a quarter Protestant.

   Here, as throughout this book, we use the term "Protestant" for lack of a better gauge of those who may believe in the Lord Jesus. This figure, which applies to the free nations of continental Europe, shocks many who have not looked into the facts. Even though religious statistics are notoriously unreliable, Protestants cannot claim more than a quarter of the population to the west of the Iron Curtain. (Our figures of the whole, based on the most accurate surveys in existence: Roman Catholics, 62.2%; Protestants, 21.4%; Jews, Moslems, the sects, and the religiously unaffiliated, 11.5%; Orthodox, 3.9%). We will further show that according to their fruits relatively few Protestants either know the new birth or are actively winning others. In this sense they themselves are a great field of need.

3. Europe is accessible, literate, and receptive.

   Accessible—The easy approaches to Europe are too well known to need mention. Within the western part of the continent there are very few trackless, roadless regions. Parts of Italy, Spain, Greece, the Balkans and upper Scandinavia pose certain inconveniences for the traveler, but are in turn the least inhabited parts. None compare with those found in earth's wilder regions. Literally "every creature" can thus be easily, personally, and quickly reached.

Literate—Some Scandinavian countries, as well as England, have a higher ratio of bookstores to the population than does America. A number of countries also have more people who can read than does the United States. All European countries except Spain and Portugal require a minimum, compulsory education. Possibly Europeans read and study more than Americans do because they have fewer distractions and less money than do Americans. What a continent for Bible distribution and gospel literature effort!

Receptive—Though we have no single accurate technique to measure the receptiveness of this or any other part of the world, witnesses agree that Europeans decide for Christ as readily as others when they hear the clear message.

4. Europe heavily influences the world through her culture, colonies, and commerce.

Culture—European culture is the basis of our own and of all Western civilization. Unfortunately, in the spiritual realm this influence has not always been good. Much today that is humanistic and inimical to the Bible comes from European antecedents. The French Enlightenment, Biblical higher criticism, liberal theology, secular existentialism, the modern rash of dictatorships (from Napoleon to Franco), materialistic psychology—those are some negative influences. On the other hand, the Reformation, the pietistic revivals, and some sound Biblical scholarship have blessed the world. European culture is thus a mighty force for evil or for good.

Colonies—Though Europe is steadily losing her colonies to spreading world nationalism, her influences in those liberated, but still dominated, is immense. In fact, the very reason for the independence movements is the infusion of European ideas. Sadly enough, in most cases greed was substituted for the gospel as a colonizing principle. Though in some cases the missionary preceded the colonists and helped open Africa, Asia, and South America to the new visitors, it was Mammon who finally ruled the day. Only in this century have the home countries finally realized that the mission-educated, "Christianized" native is an asset. But historically the realization comes too late. Africans, recognizing that education has given the white man status, are avidly pursuing this and all other liberating means. If Latin Europe had itself been evangelized, then Africa, South America, and the islands would have heard the gospel of salvation. Only the Protestant countries did a creditable missionary task, but it is now too late for them too. Taken as a whole, the religious message that Europe exported was mostly that of Rome. Again, what a force for good or evil is Europe!

Commerce—Priests accompanied Europe's great explorers who early probed to the limits of their known world. Through the Indies, the New World, Africa, and the islands of the sea, routes were explored to prepare for the great hours of Portugal, Spain, Holland, France, and England. Unhappily this commerce was, and still is, carried on largely without a witness for Christ. Europe introduced her venerable civilization in earth's remotest corners, but failed to share the good news she scarcely knew herself.

5. Europe's present generation is post-Christian.

Europe's own intellectuals refer to her as de-Christianized, but even that is a great assumption. Was she ever Christian at all? For a thousand years the Roman Catholic Church wove her views tightly through the fabric of medieval life. And today, though dethroned as moral arbiter in most countries, the Roman Church still wields enormous influence. But common people, even many Catholics, are "fed up." They would like to see this church pushed even farther out of politics, economics, and everything but the purely religious sphere. The Roman Church of course blames all the usual influences for this attitude of hostility. . But whatever the reason for the attitude, the unquestionable fact remains—for three hundred years a steady secularization, accelerated by wars, has been eating at her vitals. Protestantism is likewise losing ground to the self-interest that rules modern life. But the faith called "No-Faith" is hardly a satisfying one.

6. Europe's languages are well known and expressive.*

If geographical communications are easy in Europe, so are the linguistic. For centuries most of Europe's languages have been reduced to writing and systematized for study. Many of the chief ones taught in high schools and colleges are easy to learn. Every aid modern techniques can provide is available to help the eager student. Nor do European languages lack the full-orbed expression the gospel needs; in the metaphysical realm some are regarded as superior to English.

It is challenging to consider how few major tongues are needed to reach most of Europe. The thirty-nine languages and dialects spoken in modern Europe fall into seven groups. A few of these languages are close to extinction, and some of the remainder are spoken only in enslaved Eastern Europe. Most of the others fall into two branches, the Romance and the Teutonic, which number thirteen languages and dialects in all. (Romansch, a tongue spoken in Switzerland, may be eliminated from the Romance group because of its tiny coverage.) This leaves the following:

Romance: French, Italian, and three similar languages—Catalan, Spanish, and Portuguese

Teutonic: German, English, Dutch, and the three similar languages— Danish, Norwegian, and Swedish

Now by using the "middle languages" of the similar ones above we have another smaller grouping like this:

Romance: French, Italian, and Spanish (the latter understood largely by those using Catalan and Portuguese)

Teutonic: German, English, Dutch, and Norwegian or Swedish (Swedish would be understood by most in Scandinavia. Ten per cent of the Finns use Swedish as a mother tongue, and most Finns have studied it as a second language.)

*See Appendix 5 for a more complete listing.

Of these seven, the five—French, Italian, Spanish, German, and English—would be the most useful from the standpoint of literature work, evangelism, and travel. With these five languages alone over 200 million people can be reached!

7. Europe is the birthplace of most of the world's religious and political absolutism.

It is not only the birthplace but the home. Romanism is the religious absolutism with the largest following. Though the ideas implicit in Roman Catholicism have their roots in Eastern mystery religions, yet the system as we know it is European: it was conceived in the East but born in the West. Today Rome rules from its European base the spiritual destinies of over 400 million people, about one-sixth of the world's population.

Communist absolutism likewise is thoroughly European. Derived mostly from pagan French and German philosophies and histories, Marxism now controls a third of the people on earth. In our lifetime country after country has fallen to this total world view which has locked God out of its inner citadel.

Now consider the number of people jointly controlled by these two forces: one matriarchal, with the Virgin Mary in great authority, and the other materialistic, with unregenerate man in control. (In only a few places, like Italy and Poland, do they overlap or confront each other to any extent.) Together Rome and Moscow exercise a terrifying power over half of the human race. Both exclude and reject the gospel of salvation through faith in Christ. Are they really sisters under the skin? To the extent that they are the progeny of the same evil one, yes. Because Europe gave them birth, suckled them, and looses them upon the world, that continent qualifies today as one of the world's most needy mission fields.

8. Europe's population is multiplying rapidly through a rising birth rate and a falling death rate.

In spite of wars, United Nations figures show, there are more Europeans now than ever before. With more than seven million births each year as against some four million deaths, the over-all population increase surpasses three million annually. And effective Protestant witness is not keeping up with this growth. The number of Europeans for whom Christ died is growing faster than they can be told about Him. In view of this emergency, which is in keeping with general world overpopulation figures, a whole army of missionaries in Europe could easily be assimilated. An even greater need for the immediate future is revival of the true body of Christ in Europe, with the cleansing that would inevitably follow. Filled with the Spirit, one could "chase a thousand" (Josh. 23:10) and many would be won to Christ.

9. Europe has a culture pattern that easily accommodates Christianity.

This was the first continent outside of Asia to hear the message
(Acts 16:9). Almost everything that is worthwhile in European culture today flows from that original association. Whereas in primitive cultures it is sometimes difficult for the missionary to show the
natives how to begin even the minimum organization of a local
church, this is no problem in Europe. Europeans are capable of a
swift adaptation to everything in New Testament Christianity in
the measure that they are willing to obey it.

Think what could still happen if an evangelized Europe would
take spiritual responsibility for the Middle East, with which she is
contiguous. Or for Africa. The European nations that colonized
Africa could have helped win her to Christ, had they themselves
known His truth more widely. There is nothing in the spiritual
realm Europeans could not do for these areas provided they were in a
right relationship with the Lord.

God frequently uses His cultured children, though He does not
depend on culture as such. When the gospel flourishes in a matrix
of education and liberty, it produces a leadership lacking to the less
fortunate parts of the earth. If Europeans are won, the whole world
missionary cause is that much advanced, and the final drama of the
ages brought that much closer.

10. Europe will play an important part in the final events of this age.

Many serious Bible students believe that the Roman Empire is to
revive within much of its original territory (cf. Dan. 2:40, 43; 7:7, 8,
23, 27 with Rev. 13:1-8). According to these passages a confederation of ten dictators must appear and play their -brief role in the
closing drama of this rebellious earth. A European superman must
reign, variously called the "Little Horn" (Dan. 7:8), "The Prince"
(Dan. 9:26) and a nondescript "Beast" (Dan. 7:7; Rev. 13:1, 2).
Regardless of what details the reader might need for his particular
eschatology (and we need charity with each other here), one thing
is certain—part of the last scroll of prophecy will unroll in Europe.
This being true, we ought to do all we can for Europe while there is
yet time.

11. Europe has a quarter of a million cities and towns without an
    evangelical Protestant church.

This figure of 250,000 churchless towns has been arrived at by
a careful study of all existing lists in Protestant yearbooks and directories. Many, in Latin Europe especially, are cities of over 100,000
people. If we consider the towns in which the witness is either extremely weak or unfaithful to the Scriptures, another hundred thousand towns can be added.

12. Europe receives the smallest share of the world missionary dollar.

Of the seven continents, Europe has been accorded the least missionary financial investment in proportion to her population. Not
included in this consideration are the large amounts invested in

Europe for church construction and relief following World War II. If we compare the strategy of this continent's evangelization with the small investment made in her, we can see how great a mistake the Church of Christ has made in the twentieth century.

Opinion in America. We are living in the American Age. What America thinks and does affects everyone everywhere, just as Great Britain influenced the world a half century ago. Former President Eisenhower may have been a little presumptous in 1953 when he called America "the greatest power God has allowed to exist on His footstool." But America is also the child of Europe, where most of her people have their roots. According to a recent census, 7,160,796 United States citizens were European-born. Other millions of Europeans are becoming American citizens. The best features of our ways and ideas are European. In some ways we have acknowledged this debt. During two great wars of the twentieth century America has come to Europe's rescue, spending blood and treasure freely. Since then western Europe has become increasingly dependent on American leadership of the free world. But to supply arms and funds to people without changing their suicidal ideas is folly. What better gift could we impart than the knowledge of Jesus Christ as Saviour and Lord? Though in the past the United States has failed to give enough spiritual help to Europe, today the interest of evangelical Christian Americans is quickening.

What are American Christian leaders saying about Europe today? A comparison of John Caldwell Thiessen's *A Survey of World Missions* with the earlier standard work by Robert Hall Glover, *The Progress of World-Wide Missions*, reveals the changing attitude of American evangelicals toward Europe. Both books are written from a conservative standpoint; but the latter, even in its latest revision of 1961, makes no mention at all of Europe as an area of missionary interest. But in the former book, which is studied by many in Christian training, Thiessen devotes a considerable section to a quick glance at the Old World. He says in part—

> Conditions exist which call for an increased and intensified preaching of the gospel message throughout the Continent . . . from Europe Christianity was brought to the Western Hemisphere. Yet Europe today is itself a great mission field, with millions of its inhabitants born and reared in a non-Christian environment . . . in general the spiritual life of Europe is at a low ebb. . . . Europeans live and die in the shadows of its great churches and cathedrals without ever knowing what it means to experience salvation or live in daily fellowship with the risen Christ.[7]

This conclusion is shared by a growing number of American leaders in church and missionary circles today.

David Adeney, a former missionary to China, echoes the same thought in *The Unchanging Commission*, written primarily for college students, who have arrived at the age of decision. "Today Europe has itself become a mission field. . . . National leadership within the Protestant Churches is essential, but help from outside of Europe is needed."[8]

Billy Graham, in a network broadcast from Paris, heard by an estimated eighteen million listeners in America, flatly stated, "Europe is a mission field."[9] Previously he had written, "Look at Europe—France, Italy, Belgium, Holland—a great, unreached mission field itself."[10] In a personal letter to President Dwight D. Eisenhower, written from Geneva, Switzerland, on June 19, 1955, Graham said, "The religious interest in Western Europe is growing by leaps and bounds . . . I have never seen such spiritual hunger anywhere in the world."[11] Earlier that same year he told a Washington gathering attended by the President, "All over Western Europe there are reports of tremendous religious interest unprecedented in modern times."[12] Graham did not mention his own contribution to that interest: Since 1946 he had preached to millions of Europeans in the largest available stadiums in a dozen countries. Hundreds of thousands had professed Christ in days of intensified effort. No wonder he was convinced of the responsiveness of the average European!

One of the most experienced American workers on the continent has strong views on the opportunities Europe presents. John C. Winston, former co-director of the Belgian Gospel Mission and veteran of more than twenty-five years in Europe, says, "It is my firm conviction, not only that Europe today is a vast mission field, but that it is one of the neediest fields in the world. . . . Europe needs the gospel not only for its own sake, but for the sake of the rest of the world. The influence of European life and thought on every other continent is incalculable."

Adding that "the Bible is an almost unknown book in Europe today," Winston asks, "Can Christianity survive in Europe? Even secular writers are asking this question. . . . Our answer is 'no'—not without another renaissance, not without a Pentecost which gave Spirit-filled men the power to triumph over a pagan world." A change in attitude toward missions in Europe must come, Winston believes, for Europe itself is changing. "Many people were frankly skeptical about the necessity for missionary work in Europe before this last war. . . . After the war most people agreed that Europe had largely turned pagan, in many places even dropping the pretense of Christianity. . . . It may be objected that Europe was Christianized centuries ago, and so she must be Christian today. But has it ever been possible to inherit vital Christianity, so that the second generation need not be born again?"[13]

As a perennial traveler and a former resident in Europe, the late

Donald Grey Barnhouse of Philadelphia, was well-informed. "Believers must understand that Europe is a mission field," he stated, "but perhaps the most delicate in the world. Pray much for it." Barnhouse put his finger on the basic cause of Europe's problems: "The spiritual plight of Europe is undoubtedly the underlying cause for every other problem of that continent. Europe is made up of millions of free thinkers, the heirs of Voltaire, Rousseau and the Encyclopedists, and millions of skeptics who have abandoned Christianity because they have never seen it and do not know what it really is."[14]

Russell Hitt, editor of *Eternity* magazine, was at one time a journalist in Paris. "Will prodigal Europe return?" he asks. Calling Europe "a complex continent of nearly half a billion souls groping in spiritual blindness," he insists it "must be classified as a mission field." Hitt points out that "in many parts of Africa today there is a greater knowledge of God than in most of the pagan countries of present-day Europe. Probably in no other country in the world, unless it be Indonesia, is there a greater lack of gospel witness than in the decadent lands of Europe." This part of the world, he concludes, "stands today as one of the neediest and most strategic areas of the entire world."[15]

An expert in missionary literature, Harold B. Street, Executive Secretary of Evangelical Literature Overseas, was appalled by the needs of Europe after surveying a number of countries. "Europe is a desperately needy mission field," he says, "particularly as we think in terms of the countries of southern Europe. Our surveys in Portugal, Spain, France, Italy, and Greece revealed that less than one per cent of the population is vitally Christian. There are churches, but they are small. . . . The nationals of these countries are a lovable people, possessed of a tremendous potential, from a gospel standpoint." Street concludes that Europe is "one of the greatest mission fields in the world today."[16]

A frequent visitor to Europe, Harold J. Ockenga, pastor of one of America's stalwart and historic evangelical churches, has had ample opportunity to observe world mission fields. He has strong convictions about Europe's needs:

> Europe is a mission field which challenges the best brains of our American church. Although it was the birthplace of the Reformation and thus the return to New Testament Christianity, there have been widespread defections from the Reformation and experimental Christianity, even in the Reformation countries. France is still suffering from the massacre or exile of the Huguenots, Germany suffers from the influence of rationalism, Great Britain suffers from its liturgical emphasis. The Biblical emphasis of experimental Christianity, centering in the new birth and devotional life, has been relegated to smaller groups and movements. Over against this, a medieval Roman

Catholicism controls nations like Italy, Spain, Austria, and part of Germany.[17]

Kenneth Scott Latourette of Yale, America's distinguished historian of missions, is convinced of the spiritual crisis in Europe. "Many are speaking of the de-Christianization of Europe," he says. "The facts which they adduce to the support of this thesis are sobering. . . . In western Europe, outside the Iron Curtain, the inroads of secularism, modern mass society and, among minorities, of Communism, have been notable." All three of these modern influences, Latourette then shows, are of European origin. He goes on to assert, "In Europe . . . Christians are tending to become minorities and Christianity to lose the place which it recently held of being the avowed faith of the community, supported by the state . . . the trend is toward de-Christianization of a predominantly nominal Christian population." Whereas the faith is progressing here and there, Latourette believes that "in the heart of historic Christendom, Europe, it has experienced numerical losses." Here, the historian writes, "Christianity is ceasing to be a faith professed by the majority and is becoming that of minorities who are tempted to resign themselves to that position."[18]

The British View. Great Britain, so close to the continent and yet so different from it, has had the light of the gospel for many centuries. From her islands for decades Britain's churches have performed a noble missionary task in the farthest corners of the earth. But now a new awareness of the needs of the countries at her doorstep has come to some Christian leaders. Such concern, while slowly spreading, is by no means yet general among British believers. Much more than a few miles of water separates England from the continent. A great gulf of custom, opinion, and history is fixed between the two. Several score of Britishers, though, are already laboring here and there in lands across the channel.

Robert C. Mackie says that in the twentieth century Europe "has been so largely dechristianized" that "the mind of the man on the street, in the factory, or the mine no longer has a Christian framework or content." What about the Protestant witness? "The failure of the Church to make itself felt," Mackie thinks, "will now influence the future of Europe for centuries."[19]

Alexander McLeish, Survey Editor for *World Dominion*, of London, agrees with this view of the professing church. He believes that "great uninstructed nominal Christian communities in Europe need pioneers who will devise a new evangelistic approach."[20] In other words, the Protestants of northern Europe need to be evangelized as well as the Catholics in the south, for many of the former are just as nominal in their faith as the latter.

In an article entitled "The Neglected Continent," a writer in *The*

Christian, well-known London periodical, says, "In the last war this country sent 330,000 men with the British Expeditionary Forces in the defense of our continental allies. Thousands laid down their lives for the salvation of Europe from political enslavement. Yet the spiritual enslavement of sin has called forth no similar heights of sacrifice and effort on any scale from these shores. In precisely the same sector of Flanders fields where hundreds of thousands of British fought for political freedom, our evangelical contribution to the spiritual issue amounts to one lone Englishman. . . . The ratio of 330,000 to 1 is some comment on the degree of importance we give to the spiritual issues of the continent over against the political."[21]

Alexander McLeish again comments on what he calls "the spiritual malady of Europe." He says that "for the vast majority, attachment to the churches has been determined by place of birth rather than by conscious religious conviction. The chief fact to be reckoned with is that there has been a steady drift into nominal Christianity, to complete indifference, or to violent antagonism to all churches. This movement away from the church, which until the first World War might have been described as a tendency, has today become a torrent threatening to leave high and dry all church life in Europe . . . twenty-two percent are recorded as making no religious profession."[22]

Late director of the Spanish Gospel Mission in England, Percy J. Buffard, saw the opportunity this way: "Europe is as needy and as important a mission field as any other continent. . . . Thousands of Europeans have realized the emptiness of political creeds and are groping for light, but they can find none to point them to the true Light."[23]

"In surveying the relative needs of continents, it is impressive to consider how great is the lack of knowledge of true Christianity in the very continent where its roots are deepest . . . today Europe's 400 million people have only a surface knowledge of biblical Christianity and the masses are largely ignorant of the simple message of the gospel. . . . If there is a neglected continent today, surely it is Europe." With these words Dennis Pape, in a recent magazine article, summarizes the feeling of most informed British evangelical leaders today. "At Great Britain's doorstep, only a few hours away, nearer to London than Scotland, lies a challenge to every missionary-hearted evangelical. It is a challenge to our belief in the gospel as a real answer to the acute problem of life in twentieth century Europe."[24] In a brief country-by-country study of the Continent A. J. Dain insists that "Europe is still a needy mission field . . . the primary need of the Continent today would seem to be another Reformation. The work of Luther, Zwingli, and Calvin is as much needed now as in the sixteenth century . . . 400,000,000 are said to be still unevangelized. . . . Great indeed is the unfinished task." [25]

Suiting Action to the Word. In the face of these recent challenges and testimonies about the need of Europe, some young followers of Christ have acted. Since World War II several hundred American, Canadian, and British workers have settled on the Continent to make known the redeeming name of Jesus. Since only a handful had preceded them before 1940, this new help is heartening indeed. The Holy Spirit Himself has sent them forth, for the written appeals of Europe have been negligible and her human advocates few.

More than a dozen missions and service groups, some of them created especially for European work, have entered Europe since the war. Like the missions already established these new works are primarily interested in reaching the untouched masses. Together they are involved in many activities: personal and mass evangelism, Bible and literature distribution, camp and orphanage work, gospel text billposting, children's and youth activities, Bible institutes, correspondence courses, university witness, home visitation, and radio broadcasting. In Italy, France, and Germany annual inter-mission conferences are conducted so that these organizations may view their work on a broader basis, compare notes, and pray together.

Foreign Christians who have invested their lives in this continent have encouraged and sponsored evangelism on a large scale. One of the new American missions has helped plan and organize all the Billy Graham campaigns in Europe in recent years. Foreign evangelists resident in Europe have made their contribution after mastering the languages. The American, Eugene Boyer, in France and the Canadian, Leo Janz, in Germany and Switzerland, have consistently drawn the largest crowds to campaigns in these countries in modern times. Through their efforts a multitude have been turned to the Saviour. Less sensational but very effective have been the personal witness, home visits, and patient teaching of hundreds of other missionaries in Europe who have helped many a cultured pagan find peace with God through His Son. Perhaps the most lasting contribution has been the inspiration given to Europeans to do this necessary work themselves. Some churches, too, have been founded by missionaries in areas where there were none at all, thus providing nurture for the new-born.

Another example of effective foreign activity lies in the training of Europeans who have spiritual gifts for the service of their Lord. Six Bible institutes and two theological seminaries have been founded in Europe by North Americans since the war. Twelve other such schools have either permanent or periodic North American teaching help, some in schools directed by Europeans. These twelve and several others comprise the greatest proportion of evangelical institutions in Europe, all dependent in some measure on North American financial help. A great gap would be left in training young disciples for the Lord's work were these schools not aided by men and money from abroad, for in their halls more than five hundred future witnesses are learning more about their Lord. When one tallies up everything foreign Christians are doing it proves to be all too little in the face of the overwhelming task. We repeat that the number of towns and villages which have never heard the word of life, conservatively estimated, surpasses more than a quarter million. Add to these the great cities, ten of them with more than a million inhabitants each, and almost a hundred with over a hundred thousand people each. In these places life grows more secular, godless, and empty with each passing hour. Here the few centers of witness for Christ are being swallowed up in a tidal wave of population growth that is outgrowing every evangelical effort. What will the end be? Eternal doom awaits those without the Saviour, and shame of heart for us who even unknowingly withhold the truth. Surely Europe is included in the divine goal expressed by the psalmist: "Let the whole earth be filled with his glory" (Ps. 72:19).

What Europeans Think. A weighty argument, indeed, for the evangelization of Europe is the viewpoint of her own spiritual leaders. What do enlightened Europeans think of the situation around them? Those true to the Bible view their own lands as mission fields today. What they express becomes virtually a call for help to Christians outside this continent who may feel led to volunteer.

René Pâche, educator and Bible expositor, is one of the outstanding leaders of French-speaking Europe. The following is the view of this highly-respected teacher whose work is well known among believers in France, Switzerland, and Belgium:

> The 400,000,000 non-Protestants in Europe represent one of the most neglected and strategic fields in the world . . . the masses remain untouched . . . a tremendous task is still before us. . . . If you compare France with Madagascar, Belgium with the Congo, Spain and Portugal with South America, in every case the mother country is seen to be far less evangelized than the new . . . let us pray that many more workers may be sent forth into the harvest.[26]

The whole world's attention was drawn some time ago to the plight of Hungary under Communism. One of the best-known evangelicals in that country is Dr. Ferenc Kiss, of the University of Budapest Medical College. Widely traveled in Europe and America, Kiss sounds this warning: "I am not the only man of my standing who thinks that we are now witnessing the death struggles of European civilization. We are watching to see whether there is any sign of regeneration or not."[27] Dr. Kiss is on record as believing that such regeneration of Europe can only be accomplished by the regenerating of the individual by the Holy Spirit, through faith in Christ.

Probably the most important opinion comes from one of the leaders of Europe's largest Protestant church. With unusual frankness a stirring preacher lays bare the new Europe turned pagan. Dr. Hans Lilje, Bishop of Hannover, is one of the Council of Bishops of the German Evangelical Church and a former president of the World Lutheran Federation. He can speak not only as a German but as one of the most influential men of a major Protestant body. "The era when Europe was a Christian continent lies behind us," Lilje says. "Europe cannot remain what it was if the drift away from Christianity continues; at the moment it appears as though that trend were well-established. Only a dilettante can claim that a new faith strong enough to replace the old has already made its appearance. . . . Europe faces once more the hour of decision."

Bishop Lilje adds this word on the strategic importance of Europe: "Europe has been the battlefield for the intellectual struggles of history. Man's great spiritual decisions have been reached almost exclusively on European soil ever since Christianity began." In this old battleground the church no longer has much authority, Lilje finds. At one time "every member of the European civilization was automatically a Christian," but now the "era when Europe was a Christian continent lies behind us." The church of tomorrow may well be a "missionary church." In the future, "church membership will become more a matter of personal choice than social custom . . . it is no longer a question as to which church one wishes to belong to, but whether one wants church at all." Though some may disagree with Bishop Lilje's view of the church's constitution, role, or sacraments, yet his opinion as a churchman is interesting and challenging to evangelicals.

In the light of an emergency situation Lilje is even willing, it seems, to let go some of the old traditional practices in order to urge Protestantism into becoming a fighting force: "Since the Lord of history has already crushed the last remains of a bourgeois civilization in Europe, the church has been set free from many premises which were once thought indispensable. They are now recognized for what they are: mere scaffolding which the church does not need in order to be a church."[28]

Many in one part of Europe regard some other part as a "mission field." The French-speaking Swiss have done much for France: an estimated three hundred of them serve the Lord in one manner or another there. Italian-speaking Swiss likewise help Italy by radio broadcasts and other means. In Holland and Germany we have noticed a growing interest in Spain. For the Germans this comes naturally, since they had wartime ties with Spain and are highly regarded there. Some French Christians too have shown a burden for Spain. Generally the Scandinavians, who have both the means and manpower to help southern Europe, have lacked the vision.

Signs multiply that spiritual people in Europe are beginning to "think Europe." In the past dozen years we have seen conferences on evangelism held in increasing number, delegates being invited from all of western Europe. Switzerland and the Paris area are favorite places for such conferences, which before the war were scarcely known. A few years ago literature and radio conferences were being conducted in individual countries to survey the ministry of the printed and broadcast word. As helpful as that was, the next step shows greater vision still. Those who concentrate on this field now meet occasionally in pan-European conferences. They have come to see that what one European knows about missionary methods should be shared with others.

Why Europe is Neglected. As evidence of the plight of this continent begins to accumulate, we naturally ask ourselves why English-speaking Christians have not done more before this. These may be some basic reasons:

1. Ignorance in English-speaking countries of the true spiritual conditions beneath the surface of European life.

   What contributes to our ignorance? Tourists and Christian workers traveling through Europe often fail, because of language barriers and lack of time, to get the true picture. Sometimes no competent person is present to point out certain facts. Quick assimilation of a complex continent is not easy at best. Little current writing is extant on Europe as a mission field.

2. Emphasis by many European Christian leaders on the material needs of the people rather than on spiritual needs.

   European Christians traveling outside their continent or writing for the English-language press often overlook spiritual issues in representing Europe. We are partly to blame. After World War II Christians of North America pressed material help upon Europeans, conditioning them to think in terms of the material. But these leaders need new ideas, new methods, new blood for future leadership. Above all they need vision of their own area and what God can do there. When they turn from the *status quo* of their own churches and begin to work among the unreached masses, they are usually glad for any such help they can receive.

3. Nationalistic views which color our opinions, robbing us of compassion.

   It is distressing to hear expressions like "Europe has had her chance" or "God is through with Europe," as though God had a special interest in the New World above any other part of earth. Likewise disturbing are the common cynical allusions to the unstable French political scene or the latent German desire to dominate. We should concentrate on the real issue—lost souls—instead of clouding it with our prejudices and perferences about nations.

4. Mistaken views as to the effect of past spiritual movements on the present generation.

While we recognize that the Reformation, the German pietistic movement, the Scandinavian revivals, the French Huguenot glories, and other similar awakenings have left decades of blessing in their wake, we must realize that the present generation is lost. We are responsible for our generation only, and a needy one it is in Europe.

5. Too few foreign missionaries in Europe to make any sizable impact on Christian workers in the homelands.

The missionary to Europe will almost always find himself in the minority in any American or English missionary gathering. Consequently his plea for his part of the world is given less consideration. Often Europe is left completely out of missionary conferences devoted to the whole world, or out of articles and books covering the same ground.

6. Europe is our continent of origin.

Why should this make any difference? Since the majority of Americans and Canadians are of European descent, they find it difficult to believe that so many who look, speak, and act like themselves are in need of God. As one's own family or home town is often the most difficult spot to acknowledge as a "mission field," so it is easier to think of peoples of other colors and customs as the most needy. On this point Scandinavians, Germans, and Dutch now living in North America have an especially big adjustment to make in their minds.

Europe As One. The non-European Christian would do well to note the essential unity of this continent. The French historian, André Siegfried, once expressed a thought little understood but relevant to the capture of this continent for Christ. He said that one European nation can understand another, even though they are separated by many differences, because they are in a way tenants of the same block. Though made up of various countries, Europe is one. This may not appear obvious at first glance. What do the Swedes and Italians have in common? Or the Germans and French? Animosity seems to reign more often than amity in some countries, while habits differ widely between others.

But a second long look will reveal a unity the casual traveler tends to miss. Anyone who has lived in several countries will testify to a certain European-ness, a substratum of similarity beneath the surface of life:

"A common cultural tradition," one European cabinet minister has called it, "which has never known any national boundaries."[29] Business, tourism, intermarriage, language study, and other factors bring many into contact with each other. Then history, with spear, sword, or shell, has often forced modifications no one wanted but everyone had to accept. As a result the remote valleys and isolated ways of life are now the exception. Fifty years ago peasants born in Swiss hamlets lived and died in their valleys, speaking their odd dialects and preserving their quaint ways. But railroads, highways, and tourists have changed that forever. Some border areas, like Alsace-Lorraine, pass back and forth from one country to the other by generation or century. Here you can find French-born oldsters who have been French all their lives but speak only German. In the northern Italian valleys live French-speaking Italians, but in the south Tyrol part of Italy the Italians speak German and are pro-Austrian. Not all Europeans like this overlapping, but you do not choose the neighbors on your street.

A curious example of this European-ness comes to mind. Most people think of the renowned bas-relief of the dying lion in Lucerne, Switzerland, as a Swiss monument. True enough, the broken lance in the stricken animal's side speaks of the sacrifice of Swiss soldiers. But there the Swiss-ness ends. The lion was created in Italy by a German sculptor named Lucas Ahorn, after a model by a Frenchman named Bienaimé, who got his design from the Danish sculptor Thorvaldsen. All this was done to honor the memory of the Swiss mercenaries who died in Paris before a French mob infuriated by an Austro-Prussian invasion!

The Europeanization of any dynamic idea can be readily illustrated. During the Dark Ages the Roman Church maintained a feudal uniformity throughout Europe with the help of kings who were for centuries vassals of the popes. Renaissance ideas, once expressed, did not remain long in Italy nor in any other one land. Soon all of scholarly Europe was talking of the new learning. Thus the way for Luther's insight into the Word of God was prepared. In its turn the Reformation swept Europe. We have seen that the penetration was not deep enough, but the reach of the Reformation was quite wide. Scandinavian, British, and Flemish Protestantism soon sprang from what was at first only a German reform, while Calvinism became Swiss and Scottish as well as French. Later the same principle can be seen at work through the thinkers of the French revolution, as the writings of Rousseau and his contemporaries were devoured by all who longed for new political expression. In a twinkling, historically speaking, these French ideas and others which followed became European—and they still are. At a later day Marx, who had founded his movement on German, French, English, and Italian sources, soon saw his Communism continentalized.

In our era of faster communications, the process of assimilation is speeded still more. In every sizable city in Europe there are newsstands carrying newspapers of the different countries. Most Europeans can also tune in on broadcasts in several languages on their radios. More recently there has appeared an all-Europe television network called Eurovision. The protests of France's Pierre Poujade are echoed the very next day by every Italian or Spanish small shopkeeper with a tax-burdened life. All of Europe rushes aid to Holland's flood victims because, after all is said and done, all Europeans are neighbors. When the cauldron of Hungarian wrath boils over onto Russia, Europe feels Hungary's pain more keenly than America can, for she had an iron heel on her neck more than once. Though brotherly feelings in a thousand similar cases may vary widely, they still exist, even among the most traditional rivals. Europe is like a body whose many dissimilar organs are all linked with a single nervous system. The last two world wars and the present economic and political pressures they produced have intensified that oneness. Even neutrals like Switzerland and Sweden can no longer remain isolated. Colonial troubles, for instance, have beset Britain, Italy, Holland, Belgium, Portugal, and France in the last generation. The troubles of one are often the troubles of all.

Barring more wars and other unforeseen obstacles, the old continent may soon give birth to some kind of true federation. The kingdoms of Charlemagne, Napoleon, and Hitler were based on greed and force, but the present concept of federation rests on sheer necessity. Statesmen like Spaak, Monnet, Schumann, and Adenauer saw quite early that survival tomorrow depends upon closer co-operation today. In western Europe after World War II, the lone-wolf attitude began to die in the face of dwindling trade markets and political instability. The several experiments in joint effort undertaken after World War II—Benelux, the Council of Europe, the Coal-Steel Pool, and the European Defense Community—led to bolder plans. On January 1, 1958, programs were launched to share industrial atomic power (Euratom) and to pool economic resources (The Common Market). The possibilities of the latter, which includes most of western Europe, are especially immense. A market of over two hundred million people will gradually eliminate tariffs, guarantee free labor and investment, equalize taxes and currency exchange. This undertaking has already rejuvenated the European economy and boosted the standard of living. Many European statesmen feel that such arrangements will surely lead to common citizenship, elimination of frontiers, and final political union. Herr Franz Etzel, former Minister of Finance of the Federal Republic of Germany, says, "In the last few years, the term 'Europe' has universally come to stand for the close community formed by the people living in the free part of Europe. Though the various sovereign States continue to exist, the boundaries separating them have become less of a barrier and, in some respects, even have vanished."[30] While all this may only prove to be another human dream which leaves God out, its implications for the preaching of the gospel are suggestive.

What is the meaning of a federated Europe for the world program of Jesus Christ? First, every missionary society or individual serving Europe must study and recognize these inter-European ties. Otherwise missionary vision may become localized. A missionary to Italy, in addition to "thinking Italy," must also "think Europe." As we have said, many of the frontiers of Europe are basically meaningless. The Swiss who live on the southern slopes of the Alps near the Italian lake district have little in common temperamentally or linguistically with the French Swiss in Montreux. These latter may have a deeper fellow feeling for the people of France just across the lake from them than for the Italian-speaking Swiss. By the same token the Swedish-speaking Finnish minority—ten per cent of the population—still remain culturally and sentimentally tied to Sweden. Many of the Bavarian Germans are more like their Austrian neighbors than like northern Germans.

Second, our God surely does not see a compartmentalized Europe from His vantage point. Every great spiritual movement Europe has ever known has crossed the frontiers of the country where it began. That is the inherent nature of the gospel. Revival fires are spreading fires. We have often seen this principle at work in the hearts of European Christians. When French believers lose their stiff nationalism at the foot of Calvary, their vision becomes filled with a lost Europe and a lost world. Henceforth they are transformed people. The same is true in every land. Could we pray for the winning of America by limiting our intercession to New York state? Or for Britain by confining our praying to Sussex? Those who would evangelize Europe cannot be frontier-bound. They must see these millions as God sees them. Europe is one.

A Lull Between Storms. The frequency and duration of wars in European history suggests that this continent is now enjoying an interval between wars. But what does the present era of peace in Europe portend? First, that if such a parenthesis is to be short, there is all the more urgency to preach Christ now. Second, the European himself must be prepared to carry on Christian work if and when outsiders and their aid withdraw.

Someone has observed that between 1946 B.C. and 1861 A.D.—a period of 3,358 years—there were only 227 years of total peace in the world as over against 3,130 years of war. That works out to thirteen years of war for every year of peace. When we narrow this down to Europe, we learn that in the last three hundred years she has had 286 wars. It has been estimated that from 1500 B.C. to 1860 A.D. there have been 8,000 peace treaties between nations. But the average duration of these treaties was two years! France has spent almost half her history since 1100 A.D. fighting wars, while Russia has spent three-quarters of hers.

Europe is perhaps the only continent where war has been scientifically studied by the finest minds and reduced to chilling effectiveness. One of its great theorists who fathered the Prussian war machine, Karl von Clausewitz, called war the prosecution of politics by other means. Hence Germany and her allies, having justified war philosophically and planned for it scientifically, could terrorize western Europe three times during the last eighty years.* During these recent conflicts Christian activity has been greatly reduced. Wars, taken as a whole, have devastated church properties, decimated their leadership, and reduced their resources. A let down in morals has followed. Paradoxically, though, God has remained the victor.

There is much to sociologist Pitirim Sorokin's thesis that as modern western civilization progresses, the probability of war increases. Intervals between wars are growing shorter. During the nineteenth century, for instance, there was a continual cycle of eight years of war—called by one writer an "incubation period"—followed by the thirteen to seventeen years of peace. Though this cycle concept is only a theory, it serves to remind us that Europe has known wars on small or large scales since time immemorial. The nature of man being what it is, another conflict should come in time. Then too, our Lord prophesied that in the end time wars and rumors of wars will multiply.

If we assume that the peace we are now experiencing is provisional, our outlook on the conquest of Europe for Christ must be affected. Since time is running out, several strategies for our day suggest themselves. One is a "saturation attack" on the common man through the twin means of literature and radio. There is little vision in Europe along lines of reaching a whole city, an area or a country with gospel literature. Some evangelical radio broadcasting is being done through Europe's few commercial stations, but the need for a gospel transmitter has been the subject of much prayer for years. Although an evangelical short wave station is now on the air, Europe remains the only continent without a long and medium-wave evangelical radio voice. Such a station would permit the sustained and intensive sowing of the seed of the Word.

Conserving our fruit is another facet of strategy. By training young Europeans in the Scriptures, we impart to them responsibility for their

---

*The bellicose spirit is not exclusively German, except in recent history. Other nations have had their turns at dominating Europe. For instance, France, for over a thousand years, kept in check the people of the region that is now Germany.

own people. If European Christians learn to follow New Testament methods, they will carry on intensive evangelism and church-planting. All these advances must be carried on, in their fullest sense, during the lulls between wars.

Jehovah's Witnesses gather for a district rally before large auditorium in Paris.

Credit: Bible Christian Union

The cemetery of the Capuchins in a vault under a church in downtown Rome.

Credit: Vera Fotografia

Chapter 2

GIANTS IN THE LAND

"And they told him, . . . the people be strong that dwell in the land, . . . And Caleb . . . said, Let us go up at once, and possess it; for we are well able to overcome it."
—Numbers 13:27, 28, 30

Europe would not be a mission field today if most of it were not controlled by spiritual forces opposed to our God and to His Christ. According to the New Testament, the true foes encountered in Christian service are not familiar ones of flesh and blood. Rather, we wrestle against principalities and powers ruled by the prince of this world. On the surface Europe looks civilized and progressive, its standard of living rising every day. But beneath the surface, in the hearts of people, the Christian worker finds giants very much present. Some of these foes are fearsome in aspect. Fortunately our Lord has assured us of ultimate victory in the desperate combat for men's souls.

These giants the Christian witness faces in Europe differ in stature and strength. Romanism, the oldest and largest, is the proponent of paganized Christianity. Communism, which is at heart only atheistic materialism, assures men that they *do* live by bread alone. A third enemy is everyday Protestantism, too often offering religion void of a personal encounter with Christ. In the realm of the mind, secular existentialism, Satan's latest prophet of despair, reigns over the continent's intellectual life. Latest to arrive, the militant cults constitute a young and lusty antagonist. Now let us look more closely at these five.

1. *THE GRIP OF ROME*

Rethinking Romanism. Before facing this oldest and strongest opponent of the gospel in western Europe, let us review some of our conceptions about Catholicism. This is a system with which it is not easy for

47

evangelicals to differ. Even in the circles most loyal to the Bible the condemnation of Catholicism is not always popular. Though we may realize that the Roman Church "runs counter to the American tradition," as André Siegfried wrote, it is still a familiar part of the American scene. We Protestants prefer to think of Catholicism as just another, though wholly wrong, denomination. We have Catholic friends who are fine, decent people, with nothing sinister or foreign about them at all. They go their way and we go ours. So, long as we do not argue about religion all goes well. To be tolerant is American, we say. The only adverse thing we feel about Catholics is a vague uneasiness we cannot even define. At the worst, their faith seems to be an irritating mixture of mumbo jumbo, Latin, and strange rules; at the best, it seems to contain some truth, however garbled. The least we can do, we reason, is to live and let live in the good Anglo-American spirit of fair play.

In the face of such attitudes, the missionary or minister who speaks out boldly about this "giant in the land" will find a sure reaction from Christians. Even when he describes this church in terms of the Scriptures, using only Catholic sources for the opposition and speaking with com-passion, many misunderstand. Christian people too often feel that rehearsing the alarming facts about Roman Catholicism is a form of bigotry. But the price we pay for desisting from such rehearsal is high, for thousands of Protestant adults pass into Romanism yearly. We should love Catholic people and treat them kindly, seeking their reconciliation to God. But we are wrong when we fail to examine their doctrines, using the Scriptures as the court of highest appeal. We err in maintaining silence about "the Church we are afraid to mention."

If the review of Catholic belief and practice is unpopular within the fold, outside it is not even safe. Let us face the fact that we are silent partly because of the certainty of Roman Catholic public reaction. Catholics are far from wearing a gag, and we are glad they do not. Our Protestant forefathers fought for Catholic beginnings in this free land. Yet today Catholics maintain a string of offices, newspapers, publishing houses, and apologists whose sole purpose is to answer Protestants and convert them. Clipping services pour everything considered anti-Catholic into these offices for study. For fear of being cut off the air by such opposition, even Protestant radio stations caution speakers not to refer to anything even vaguely anti-Catholic. In the matter of schools, Protestant parents and teachers, rather than create division or appear contentious, give in, letting Catholics set up their own separate schools with both Protestant and Catholic taxpayers' money. Sometimes reaction is more personal. In one large California church an unusually brave pastor advertised in the paper that he would devote his broadcast Sunday night sermon to the subject, "Catholic Persecution I Saw in South America." The result? A rock through his window and a series of threatening telephone calls. Political pressure, local discrimination, character assassination, and even personal violence can await the individual or groups who dare to speak the truth.

The Same Old Deceptions. There is little excuse today for a Christian's ignorance of Vatican political designs. European history is a commentary on them, and America is becoming their greatest arena. Many volumes, some of which can be bought in any bookstore, outline these aims with care. The Papacy's use of the state has been scrutinized for centuries by friends, enemies, and neutrals.

What do the statements of the Roman Church herself show? The pronouncement of Boniface VIII in his *Unam Sanctam* encyclical of 1302, which has never been retracted by any other pontiff, serves as a good example:

> By the words of the gospels we are taught that the two swords, namely, the spiritual authority and the temporal, are in the power of the Church. . . . The former is used by the Church, the latter for the Church; the one by the hand of the priests, the other by the hand of kings and knights, but all at the command and permission of the priest. Moreover, it is necessary for one sword to be under the other, and the temporal authority to be subjected to the spiritual. . . . We therefore declare and affirm that submission on the part of every man to the bishop of Rome is altogether necessary to his salvation.[1]

Within the scope of this book we cannot examine the Catholic thesis of the temporal power (authority in secular or civil affairs) as restated by popes, cardinals, and bishops without number. But these statements are not medievalisms at which to smile. Note that in the bull quoted above, Boniface VIII said *"submission on the part of every man."* The hierarchy has never repudiated its "two swords view" that the state should be the servant of the Church for the conversion of men—by force, if necessary. Its encyclicals against Protestantism have been restated for each generation. In some parts of the world standards reminiscent of the Inquisition are still viciously applied, in keeping with the view that error has no rights. We agree with Paul Blanshard when he says that "the philosophy of Church and state espoused by the Vatican is the most important thing in the whole Catholic system."[2] Through the manipulation of political powers, the church finds the means to force its soul-destroying beliefs upon millions. In a recent article *Newsweek* speaks of "the vast extent and formidable power of the Roman Catholic Church," and adds that "the Church has never been stronger—in numbers, prestige, and spiritual force. It has won the allegiance of nearly one-fifth of the world's people and is the largest single religious faith around the globe."[3]

The average American Protestant would be appalled to live long in a wholly or heavily Catholic country. He would soon agree with Hilaire Belloc, himself a Catholic, who said that "the Catholic Church is in its root principle at issue with the civic definition both of freedom and authority."[4] The words of William E. Gladstone, a prime minister of England, would have new meaning: "Romanism is a perpetual war against the progress of the human mind. . . . Its influence is adverse to freedom in the State, the family and the individual."[5] But much more than civil liberties is at stake. The ultimate evil is that, by enchaining whole populations to herself, Rome keeps the masses from the One who is Truth, while insisting that she alone has the truth. Thomas Jefferson, one of the fathers of American democracy, saw that danger when he said, "The care of every man's soul belongs to himself. No man has the power to let another prescribe his faith. . . . History, I believe, furnishes no example of a priest-ridden people maintaining a free civil government."[6] Luther expressed the same thought in pointing out that men have no right to force a faith upon others when even God, with all His power, refuses to do so.

Our greatest obstacle in reaching Catholics is our mental block, our own prejudice. The individual follower of this faith is not himself a problem. Though Roman Catholics in Europe may be prejudiced by their priests against the truth, they can still be won. Once given the wonderful message of salvation, they are often surprisingly open. A Catholic may live near a bustling European airport, where the whole world can get to him within hours. To reach him missionaries do not need an expensive voyage, a special outfit, a jungle training course, a knowledge of phonemics, or malaria medicine. Nor do they have to hack their way through the bush—they can just drive up to the door in a car! Can it be that this Catholic, so beloved of God, remains lost, just because he is not remote enough? Or—I tremble to ask it—will he die eternally because we believe he is *not quite lost?*

Half Saved or Wholly Lost? Many who know the Lord Jesus Christ as Saviour are ill-informed about the nature of Roman Catholic dogma. Catholics' use of expressions similar to ours, their profession of some of the same truths, and their diligence to perform their duties all veil the extent of their error. Some who should know better even express an envy of the tangible ritual, the pomp and ceremony which make most Protestant worship seem almost colorless by comparison. Others will point out an individual Catholic who seems so sincere, so obviously trying to be a Christian. But let us not confound the individual with the system. The individual may indeed be saved, but if so, he has found the truth elsewhere, not in the official teaching of the Roman Church. He has learned to know Christ in a saving way not because of the Church, but in spite of her disapproval. Thus we should not condone the system in which this person was reared, but strengthen him to abandon it altogether in order to fully obey the Lord Jesus Christ.

The fact that the Roman Church is based on some half-truths does not mean that even its most sincere followers are thereby half-saved. Pure Catholic dogma does not lead to a knowledge of salvation, nor is it intended to do so. Rather, it is meant to bind the conscience while soothing it with the pretension that any final hope of salvation lies only in the Roman Church, its sole and rightful dispenser. True, Catholics are required to believe in sin, the deity of Christ, His shed blood on the cross, His resurrection, and other Biblical facts. However, the faith they are asked to exercise is not saving, effective, appropriating faith. Nor are these doctrines taught in their Biblical sense. Sins, for instance, are minutely classified and indexed, and various penances set for their forgiveness through the allegedly stored-up merit of Jesus Christ. By this means sins are actually multiplied rather than restrained. What a travesty of both sin's nature and the soul's Redeemer! The work of Christ, rather than a complete act for our redemption (Heb. 10:14), becomes an incomplete sacrifice perpetuated by the mass. The individual begins his religious life with faith and continues it with works. Yet he is never sure of his salvation. No priest, nor even the Pope himself, can be sure that his policy is paid up in what amounts to an immense insurance company against the risks of after-death.

Half-truths are more dangerous than lies because they are more believable, more readily grasped by needy souls. What would an ideal religious deception for the ages teach? Not that man can save himself through his own goodness. In most cases he cannot accept that. A salvation wholly of grace, on the other hand, has no appeal because it utterly condemns him. But a man will accept a system whereby God and he work out salvation together, a solution that leaves his ego intact. This, the height of self-delusion, is the teaching of the Roman Catholic Church, masterminded by the Great Deceiver. The European Catholic is the more pitifully entangled in that Galatian error of faith-plus-works because he knows nothing else.

Behind the Purple Curtain. How much of the continent of Europe is Roman Catholic?* According to the most recent Vatican figures there are 241 million faithful in Europe out of a claimed world total of more

*See Appendix 3 for proportionate Roman Catholic strength in Europe, and Appendix 4 for the statistical picture.

than 500 million. But this figure includes Catholics in Communist-controlled Eurasia. In free Europe—the area covered in our survey—Rome claims over 186 million people, or 57.3 per cent of the total population. Presiding over their worship in 247,545 European churches is an army of 264,916 priests. Not only do almost half of the world's professing Catholics live in Eurasia, but the papal seat is found in a continent which serves as the principal recruiting ground for the church's missionaries. In Europe, says one American publication, the roots of the Catholic Church "are so deep, its influence so subtle and profound that it is taken almost for granted. . . . Despite Communism, the Church has grown stronger."[7] Consider the numerical impact of 5,814,499 European children attending 41,904 parochial schools. Or think of 117,796 monks and 596,421 nuns in 61,336 institutions—all controlled by 57 cardinals, 119 archbishops, and 726 bishops. The figures may mean little, but try to picture the millions who are born, live, and die in an empire where they never see a Bible, meet a non-Catholic, or hear of full forgiveness. In terms of our own hemisphere, an equivalent empire would embrace an area covering Mexico, all of Central America, Venezuela, and Ecuador. But packed within this space is a Catholic following equivalent to that of the United States and South America together! Because of its stature alone the Roman system is the most powerful "giant in the land," a prime reason for evangelizing this continent.

Let us look at this predominance in another way. In Portugal, Spain, France, Belgium, Italy, and French Switzerland, there is a combined population of roughly 128 million people. But in this group are only 1,600,000 Protestants. Omitting France and Switzerland, the total number of Protestants in the remaining four countries is only 114,000 in the midst of a sea of 86 million Catholics! Stewart Herman, responsible for the calculation, makes this observation: "Multiply the latter figure (86 million) by two and you obtain approximately the present United States population; multiply the former figure (114,000) by two, and you can imagine how much impact 228,000 Protestants would be able to make on the whole of the United States if it were solidly Roman Catholic."[8]

How much padding is there in Catholic statistics?* Obviously very much. All children and minors are included. Also all who have ever been baptized, even though they may never have practiced their faith or have openly left it. The inclusion stems from the scholastic reasoning which is the basis of Catholic theology. In the chapter on Italy we note the very obvious tampering with religious statistics which seriously underrates the Protestant strength of that country through Catholic-slanted census-taking. The same could be said for Spain and other so-called

*All Catholic figures we give are from the *National Catholic Almanac*, 1961.

Catholic Countries. Protestant converts are still counted as Catholics many years after they have been excommunicated for leaving the church. Even if we use the common measuring device of halving adult Roman Catholic figures in any given community, over 100 million of this faith still remain as ignorant of the true way of salvation as they would be in the interior of remote Tibet.

Generally speaking, Roman power predominates in southern Europe, while the Protestants occupy the northern countries. France, Italy, Spain, Portugal, Belgium, Eire, and Austria must be counted as a Vatican bloc. The five pocket states of Luxemburg, Liechtenstein, Monte Carlo, Andorra, and San Marino, belong with it. Almost half of Germany, Holland, and Switzerland are likewise within the purple orbit, with their Catholic minorities growing. Greece is, of course, mostly Greek Orthodox. Only Scandinavia remains virtually untouched by Rome. For most of the postwar years the prime ministers in almost all countries south of Scandinavia have been Catholic.

Profession and Practice. In evaluating European Romanism, we must distinguish between the active and the passive followers. A far wider gulf separates the practicing Catholic from the lapsed one there than in America or other "Protestant" countries. In the heavily Catholic countries of the Continent, great numbers of people do not even keep up the minimum observances—the merest appearance of piety. When asked if they are Catholic, many reflect a moment before replying in the affirmative, often with a deprecating gesture or shrug. A majority sheepishly admit that they are "religious," meaning in the least sense of the word. Some observers have tried to apply the following rule of thumb to the typical Catholic country: one-fifth of the population are actively anticlerical and another fifth strongly Catholic. The other three-fifths may be said to waver between the two extremes, now throwing their weight on one side, now on the other. Whether this is valid or not, one thing is sure: anticlericals remain for the most part mentally Catholic. Chained as they are from childhood to the seven sacraments, their ultimate subservience to the favor of the Holy Mother Church is imbedded in their subconscious. Whether serious or flippant, those are rare who do not want to die in grace.

Now let us look at the loyal practicing type. In investigating loyalty, much depends on the class of people, their sex, and the area of the continent under consideration. Most regular in attending mass and confession are women, whose faithfulness is constantly stimulated by the image of the Holy Mother and her indirect influence over the destiny of their children's souls. Usually country people, even in their superstitions, are more observant of religious duties than people in the cities. Most in the working classes, alienated by Marxism and economic troubles, are cool to Rome. Italian and Spanish intellectuals tend to have little use for the church, but the French and Belgian aristocracy and *littérateurs* are by and large more true. In the increasingly Roman countries, like Holland, Switzerland, and Germany, the individual practices his faith more than his opposite number does in wholly Catholic lands. For centuries Holland has been under the influence of Jansenism, a purer strain of reformed Catholicism.

Some work hard for a new political Roman bloc based on the dream of Charlemagne, a medieval Europe where a *Pax Romana* would reign and all states bow to the supreme pontiff. A number of very able, dedicated statesmen and their parties passionately believe in and promote this revival of an empire like that of Pope Innocent III, but their opponents are mighty. Such leaders, whipped on by Jesuit persuasion, regard the Church as the great white western hope to stem the red tide from the east. Though their number is inferior and their motives are mixed, the dedicated Catholics must never be underrated as a force in Europe. They are often in key positions in politics. The Vatican has used such men in forging postwar concordats with five countries: Austria, Germany, Italy, Portugal and Spain.

Faces of the Faith. Naturally there are many national differences in the observance of the Catholic faith. In the Latin countries Catholicism is quite ignorantly and emotionally followed, while in the Teutonic lands there is a more intelligent, less superstitious observance. But such a generalization has its dangers. The French, wrongly labeled as a wholly Latin race, are genuine intellectuals, whose emotionalism is mostly a surface matter. For this reason, and because of their revolutionary principles, most French people are careless about their church duties, a matter of great concern to the Vatican. The Spanish and Portuguese, on the other hand, are mystics, and the Italians a people of elemental instinct. Differences in temperament thus separate the Latins from each other, making any classing of southern European peoples together a mistake. The lines of demarcation are not always clear. For instance, the Belgians, a progressive Teutonic people, seem almost as ignorantly superstitious about their Catholic practice as those in southern Europe, a characteristic not wholly shared by their Dutch Catholic neighbors a few miles away.

We might risk another general comparison. In Spain, Catholics are mystically medieval, in Italy political, in France largely nominal, and in Belgium heavily traditional. Holland has a virile, disciplined church. Switzerland bans—yet tolerates—Jesuit activity, and is witnessing a spreading Catholic influence from Fribourg, its "little Rome." Portugal uses the Church as a state instrument, or as others have put it, is itself a creature of the Vatican. Enslaved Poland is still predominantly Catholic, with the present, less rigidly Communist regime treating her prelates more gently than before. The Republic of Eire is an intrenched stronghold unique in its own way. Within all these countries appear further local areas of Catholic strength and weakness on many levels.

A World to Win. The vigor of any religion can be well evaluated by its missionary force and overseas outreach. Though increasingly short of new priests, the Catholic Church is still able to maintain an average of one priest for every 938 Catholics in Europe. Beyond this the Roman Church can boast a surprisingly large army of workers sent to regions beyond. European Catholics alone furnish about as many missionaries to other continents as all the world's Protestant churches put together. Above the support of their quarter of a million priests on the continent, these Catholics have sent abroad over forty thousand workers.*

Any faith strong enough to seek converts in such a large way must have some vitality. Thus the strategy of preaching the reconciling grace of God in the homelands of this militant religion should be obvious. Were this area evangelized, the Roman Church's grip on South America, French Canada, Asia, Africa, and the islands of the sea could be that much lessened. By winning people to Christ in this dark corner of the world, we indirectly help evangelize the rest of the world. But despite its occasional cries of alarm, Rome has had little to fear from a relatively weak Protestant witness in its European strongholds. Were spiritual awakening to come to the tiny flocks of the Lord's own in Catholic Europe, a glad witness would result. For this we must pray, so that Catholic peoples, beloved by God, may come to know Him in spirit and in truth.

Now for a closer look at the Catholic missionaries Europe sends elsewhere. Strangely enough, France, a nation only partially—and almost reluctantly—Catholic, has provided more personnel for this effort than any other nation in the world. Her contribution surpasses fifteen thousand men and women! When we consider the ratio of missionaries to Catholic population, though, France is not ahead. Little Ireland, with only three million Catholics, has dispatched an amazing seven thousand missionaries abroad. Holland's hearty Roman Church has contributed about the same number out of about four million Catholics. Even tiny Belgium has sent eight thousand priests and nuns to other continents. It is significant that much larger Italy, out of its heavily Catholic population of fifty

*In contrast to this, European Protestants have sent out 6,097 missionaries, almost half of them from Scandinavia.

million, has given to the Church fewer missionary sons and daughters than little Belgium?

Outside of Europe the Vatican has two major objectives. One is to win the United States, its heaviest financial backer and leader of the West. With amazing rapidity this goal is being achieved by the American hierarchy, helped by many European priests sent to occupy key posts in America. The United States is now a major Catholic country, ranking in fourth place in its number of Catholics. In 1790 there were only twenty-five thousand American Catholics among her four million inhabitants. By 1890, a century later, Catholics accounted for a growing 9.9 per cent of the population. But in less than seventy years this proportion has doubled to 19.9 per cent of the inhabitants. In the last decade alone more than a million new members have come into the Roman Church. America doubled its Catholic workers sent abroad between 1940 and 1950. Whatever American evangelicals may think of Catholic Europe, that area certainly regards the conversion of the United States as a primary missionary objective. Strangely enough, Europe may yet help make America the most Catholic nation in the world!

The second world goal of the Vatican is to win the awakening nations of the Orient and Africa. More than forty national seminaries in Rome help prepare priests to reach the missionary areas of the world. Most of the countries whose people are non-white have a large number of European missionaries. Though the powers of Europe may find their colonial possessions slipping away, the Roman Catholic Church manages not only to survive, but to grow, in those same colonies. How does she do it? By training a local clergy and giving them some autonomous fields of action. On a higher level Rome is hard at work, by concordats, coercion, and compromise, to convert these nations whose destinies are now being shaped. Money contributed by simple Catholics in Europe makes this intensive foreign program possible.

The Catholic Mind. We have seen that many millions of careless Catholics in Europe have little to do with the church throughout their entire lives. Why do such people remain mentally Catholic? Even Protestants in heavily Catholic lands will often evidence Roman Catholic views both in their church work and in everyday life. Christian workers discover that it usually takes years for a convert from European Catholicism to de-Romanize his thoughts with the help of the Sword of the Spirit. A former nun in France told us that twelve years of Bible study and prayer were needed to uproot the pagan from her life and replace it with the Biblical. Our observation of ex-priests has confirmed that statement.

Most surprising of all is that Catholic conditioning of the mind prepares a person to accept Communism. How can Europe's largest Communist party of two million flourish in an Italy which the Roman Church wholly claims? There is little doubt that if the Church were not even stronger in Spain and Portugal, this materialistic philosophy would be popular in those countries. Catholic training has conditioned people for the dictatorships of Franco, Salazar, and Mussolini as well, for an extreme rightist government is often useful to the Roman Church, which is herself absolutist.

What is the source of Catholic mentality? From childhood the mind is cast into a mould of which dependence is the key. All of us have heard the saying attributed to the Roman Church: "Give me a child until he is seven and he will always remain mine." Although the church would say that this loyalty rises from truth, we know that it comes from dependence based upon feelings of insecurity and fear. The whole sacramental system of salvation keeps the worshipper off-balance with the ever-recurring mass, the perpetual sacrifice of Christ, and the endless penances. On the disciplinary side of the system, the confessional plays a special role, for men are the slaves of their inner selves. Whoever knows their secrets and their guilt can become their master. Since the priest holds as it were the keys of salvation, he can and does sometimes use the threat of damnation to force people to act against their own convictions. Anyone who has ever worked in Latin countries can furnish many illustrations: Spanish Catholics, for example, have to be roused by the priests to react against the Protestants whom they usually like and respect.

The dependent souls made pliable enough can then be led in many directions that are not strictly religious, for the Roman Church claims the whole man and his whole life. Among other things, he is told where to study, whom to marry, how many children to have, how to instruct his children, what to read, how to vote, which labor union to join, and where to amuse himself. The true child of God would expect God himself to exercise His lordship over his life in all these matters, but the Roman Church replaces the authority of God by its own human, totalitarian power. Catholic jurists, doctors, and politicians all have a church-imposed course of action to follow on every point. This terrible dependence and its bitter fruit in the life of Catholics is what makes missionary work in Catholic lands a difficult task.

Double-mindedness, another aspect of the Catholic mind, is carefully instilled by the Church's experience through the ages. There are rules for everything, and exceptions to all the rules. Few have expressed this better than the celebrated French novelist, Frédéric Hoffet. In a book written in French for French people, he diagnoses the basic ills of

France and how they were acquired. Regarding the moral elasticity of the French character, he says:

> The Catholic man, accustomed by the legalism of the church to regard law only as exterior to himself, has learned to twist the law. . . . Catholicism persists in this course by an extremely supple moral system which never puts forth a rule without multiplying exceptions thereto.[9]

Of the lack of a selfless national spirit in his own land, he further writes:

> It is Catholicism which has dominated the development of the French nation and has given the Frenchman his psychological and moral character. . . . Catholicism explains, alas, our vices and weaknesses . . . . and that enfeeblement of civic spirit which is perhaps the gravest symptom of illness the country suffers . . .[10]

M. Hoffet goes on to say that this kind of background has—

> created in Catholic countries a diluted moral climate which makes possible the closing of one's eyes to a thousand little dishonesties which are later accepted as normal. . . . France suffers in the highest degree from this excessive practice leading, in present circumstances, to such a weakening of public morality that one wonders how the country will ever emerge from a crisis that threatens her very foundations.[11]

Like many another onlooker, Hoffet has remarked the failure of people in Latin lands to make even those changes they know are for the better: "The popular conscience has not reacted against practices which would draw immediate condemnation elsewhere. This conscience has been formed by centuries of Catholicism . . . the weakness of Catholic ethics only ends by demoralizing people."[12] Elsewhere in his penetrating study the novelist notes that the word "integrity" does not even have a French equivalent, so he turns to the German word *Zuverlässigkeit* to describe what is generally found in Protestant countries but lacking in his own. "In Italy, Spain and France they promise so much more quickly things they scarcely dream of being able to do."[13] In France especially, Hoffet says, there is the casuistry that results from "the habit of playing with the law and bargaining with the conscience."[14]

Under the Fourth Republic many Frenchmen considered tax-collecting as an unwarranted invasion of their privacy, and thus kept double books—one for the government and one for their own information. But a certain new convert to Christ, wanting to please the Lord by providing things honest in the sight of all men, insisted on declaring his entire income honestly and paying his taxes in full. An unheard of thing, this! Even the government clerk at the tax window called him a fool for such naïve conformity to an unpopular law. Some weeks later the new convert had occasion to return to the same tax window. The same official handed him an envelope. "There you are, my slow-witted friend," he said blandly. "This is part of your money back. Since you didn't have enough sense to fib about your tax returns, I did it for you!"

2. THE COMMUNIST THREAT

Communism Is European. "A spectre is haunting Europe—the spectre of Communism." With these words the Communist Manifesto of 1848 unknowingly uttered a prophecy. More than one hundred years later Europe is still pursued by the same ghost. The largest mass movement in history since the rise of Christianity was not conceived or defined in Russia. Communism is the product of the spiritual bankruptcy of "Christian" Europe. Its philosophy came from Germany, its social and revolutionary outlook from France; England provided the economic theory for its principal thesis. The predecessors of the Marxian philosophy, as well as the contributors to it, were European—men like Adam Smith, Sismondi, Ricardo, Saint-Simon, Sorel, Hegel, and Feuerbach. Paris' left-bank cafés, the gloomy galleries of the British Museum, Munich's beer halls, and the quaint streets of old Zurich were all locales for the genesis of this new movement. On one occasion a Brussels flour mill was the rendezvous for forty-four revolutionary delegates to meet with Lenin and discuss whether they should use bullets or ballots to implement this idea of ideas.

But Communism is a judgment upon the western world as well as a product of it. Like the ancient Assyrians, Communist power has been allowed by God to scourge many countries where Christians live. Perhaps in His plan this neophyte may be permitted to harass Christianity and mankind for some time before it, too, passes to its doom. Perhaps a Communist triumph in Europe might even set the stage for the rise of Antichrist there. Especially significant to the world is Communism's origin in Europe. Not only does the Kremlin message have a large following there, but the conditions that produced it still exist to produce something else equally evil. As the homeland of Communism and a hundred other ills, Europe must become more than ever a target for alert missionary work by Christians. This is particularly true in the light of a recent warning by J. Edgar Hoover that the Communist leaders will not wait forever to execute their plans.

The Gospel According to Marx. Karl Marx is a symbol of what is wrong with Europe. Though a child of the religion of his day, he repudiated its meaningless symbols to venture out into the unknown. Since he had fed his mind on the festering humanism of eighteenth-century Europe, it is small wonder that he fathered a godless system. Marx was born in 1818 in the German Rhineland town of Trier. Though his grandfather was a rabbi named Levi, Marx's prosperous lawyer father expediently chose to Germanize the family name and baptize his children as Protestants. Expelled from the University of Bonn, Marx settled in England after studying and disputing for a time in Berlin and in France and Belgium. In the British Museum the founder of Communism did most of his research for his principal work, *Capital*. As an arrogant, self-centered scholar, fighting poor health and creditors, he was kept alive mostly by the patronage of his collaborator, Friedrich Engels.

Of the four apostles—Marx, Engels, Lenin, and Stalin—whose writings are alone considered canonical, Marx occupies chief place. With *Capital* as a Bible and the *Communist Manifesto* as an Apostle's Creed, he and Engels laid the foundations of dogma. In the years that followed, Lenin and Stalin were to add their own contributions to the doctrine of economic determinism and its world-wide application. Anyone who has ever read these works has detected in them a note of sincerity and of almost religious fervor. Buttressed by what they believed was the scientifically inevitable dialectic of Hegel, these architects of Communism were bursting with zeal and optimism. So are their Kremlin heirs today, who are just as sure that they will win the proletarian war on capitalism.

Of course there are many fallacies in this too neat solution for all of life's problems. Marxist adaptation of Hegelian dialectics is pseudo-scientific and lacks demonstrable proof. Just as Hegel's disciples in other fields failed to make his dialectics apply there, Marxists cannot make it work in society. Then, too, enlightened capitalism has moved in other directions than Marx imagined. Even for the great part of our world which is materially miserable the villains are not always Big Business and Wall Street. Because Marx's knowledge of history was especially weak, he developed a warped, one-sided view of yesterday's lessons for today. But his biggest mistake lay in his incomplete concept of the nature of man. The genius who said, "I detest all the gods," could only think of man as a "tool-making animal." Ignoring men's spiritual hungers and their creation by God, he taught that they *can* live by bread alone.

What is the core of Marx's belief? According to the classic view, this system aims at creating a classless society in which the means of production, distribution, and exchange will all belong to the community. On the surface this looks like a noble, if not almost Christian, goal. Communist leaders were not motivated by compassion, however, when they originated the idea. Out of their experiments has risen a new class system of commissars and party bosses dedicated to self-interest rather than to national interests. The progress of working-class people has taken second place to the political ambitions of a handful who neither consult them nor consider their rights and interests. There has followed a more ruthless exploitation of the masses than any that the Communists profess to find in capitalism. According to Marx, capitalism, which represents only the bourgeoisie class, obtains its profits from the surplus value of proletariat labor. As a result of this exploitation, an inevitable tension must arise between these workers and the capitalists. A fight to the finish is to occur. Though capitalism is self-doomed and must fall, will its overthrow come peacefully? Marx and the other Communist writers insist that force will be needed, though the present regime talks of peaceful coexistence. Only as the ownership of productive property, the sole real means of exploitation, is removed will competition die and the old order collapse. But violence must be used because the vested interests are intrenched and will not give up without a fight. After the overthrow of capitalism, a period of socialism called the dictatorship of the proletariat must follow. In this whole process the synthesis, or union of opposites which Hegel taught, must always issue from mutual challenges. Later socialism, and even the state apparatus itself, must be discarded as pure Communism emerges, a goal not yet reached anywhere.

An Elastic Morality. To true Communists, lying, stealing, cheating, and murder are all legitimate means by which to shape a better world. Everything is permissible which is consistent with the announced goals, for there is no moral law to say otherwise. Such standards of conduct and principle as do exist in Communist countries are introduced for their worth to the regime rather than for fear of any thou-shalt-nots of a capitalist god. "In what sense do we repudiate ethics and morality?" asked Lenin. "In the sense that it is preached by the bourgeoisie who derive ethics from God's commandments. . . . We repudiate all morality derived from non-human and non-class concepts. We say that it is a deception, a fraud in the interests of the landlords and capitalists. We say that our morality is entirely subordinated to the interests of the class struggle of the proletariat. . . . We do not believe in an eternal morality. . . . All religious ideas are an unspeakable abomination."[15]

What a pity that the once nominal Protestant Karl Marx spent so many years extracting so little of value from the minds of other apostate Protestants! Is not this a commentary on the terrible toll exacted from eighteenth-century Protestantism by the philosophers? Though in modern Europe it has not always been easy for Communism to erase moral standards from even vaguely Christianized minds, yet two generations of propaganda and brainwashing have affected many. Today the true Communist is ready to deny his materialistic faith, denounce his family, and desert his country if the party commands.

Nikolai Lenin, whom we have just quoted, observed the decadence of this Christian morality during his ten-year sojourn in western Europe. He had seen the honest, well-ordered lives of the Swiss, for example, who pay at least a lip service to Christianity. But, after all, he looked at that world through eastern glasses and reached what some might suspect were eastern conclusions. Friedrich Engels was, on the other hand, a westerner, a poised and cultured university product of Germany, Europe's leading power. He had lived in Manchester and other parts of England where he had had firsthand contacts with the Christian faith. But Engels, too, came to the same conclusion: "We therefore reject any attempt to impose on us any moral dogma whatsoever as an eternal, ultimate, and forever immutable moral law."[16]

In practical terms what has all this meant to several million European Communists, their fellow travelers and sympathizers? It has given them the excuse to call white black, and black white, and to break the commandments of God in the interest of their views. One has only to browse through the leftist bookstore on Amsterdam's Leidsestraat, read the Paris paper *L'Humanité* and its Italian cousin *Avanti,* or scan one of Jean Paul Sartre's political plays to see the extent of the influence. And those who make moral accommodations in the political realm will make them in other realms as well: "A double minded man is unstable in *all* his ways" (James 1:8). Christianity's greatest rival matches her theology point for point on a materialistic basis. Such a challenge cannot be ignored, for "Christianity can never concede to any ideology that absolute value which Communists claim for their own," says R. N. E. Hunt, "since by its transcendent standard every human achievement must stand condemned."[17] On moral issues Karl Marx and Jesus Christ stand embattled in the twentieth century.

Dimensions of the Danger. A little over five hundred years ago Constantinople fell to the Ottoman Turks, and Europe was partitioned between Christendom and Islam. As a result, millions were to endure several more centuries of misgovernment, ignorance, and fear behind that Muslim curtain to the east. Today the partition of Europe is again as absolute as it was then, but Communist expansion has surpassed that of Islam and represents a far greater threat to Europe than did the armies of Suleiman the Magnificent and Kara Mustafa, camped before the gates of Vienna. Then there is the added internal threat of the Communist fifth column within the free Western nations themselves, an advantage the Muslims never had.

It is true that most Communist parties in free Europe have declined in size and significance since reaching their peak just after the war. This world conspiracy does not think, though, in terms of size and public acceptance alone. Even in Russia herself there are fewer party members than one would expect. Indeed, the party sometimes purges its own ranks to eliminate the weak and disloyal, for it is far more concerned with blind devotion than with numbers. How much strength is needed for a *coup d'état?* Czechoslovakia was taken over by a bloodless revolution in 1948 while the party's parliamentary percentage and popular vote still numbered less than forty per cent. For the time being, the Kremlin has decided that constitutional methods rather than open revolution are the best means to advance its aims in this part of the world. Should the situation warrant, however, a violent change could occur very quickly in some places in Europe. Undoubtedly world Communism is prepared for this eventuality in just the same way it was prepared for China, Greece, and Korea. The huge stockpiles of weapons in the hands of European Communists prove this.

In free Europe there are roughly three million Communists and several million sympathizers. Only five countries—Spain, Portugal, Greece, West Germany, and Turkey—ban the party altogether; but in some of these there is an underground movement or a front party with Communist intentions. We will now look briefly at the remaining countries where Communism has any influential following.

Italy—Europe's largest party of more than two million is also the third largest in the world. Italy has two-thirds of Europe's total Communists, while France has half of the remainder. Though the Italian party has suffered periodic setbacks in its encounter with the leading Christian Democrats at the polls, these can only be considered as temporary. Very likely American influence and funds have helped save this country from a Communist coup. The Italian Reds are especially noted for their party wealth and their ability to strike profitable alliances.

France—Communists here emerged from World War II with a fine underground record and were thus able to draw, with their allies, as high as 5,500,000 votes at that time. By 1951 they had dropped a million votes, and party membership fell to half of the previous high of 800,000. The past decade has seen a powerful party bloc at work in the national assembly, stirring up strife, strikes, and staged demonstrations. With the launching of the Fifth Republic under General Charles De Gaulle came further losses. Under his new, centralized executive powers De Gaulle curbed the party's power. Defections of top leaders further divided the ranks. Nevertheless the Reds of France will remain a potent force even if forced underground. On local levels there is still growth and interest.

Germany—Since the war Germany has been the scene of the Communists' most ignoble defeat. In 1932 Germany had the largest party outside Russia, with six million votes and one hundred seats in the Reichstag. The present party had been reduced to only about 80,000 members when the government declared it unconstitutional on August 17, 1956. Though illegal and forced underground, authorities estimate that a large network of agents function behind at least 150 *Tarn* or front organizations. Fortunately most labor union leadership is non-Communist, but there remains intense party activity at the workbench level in the factories.

Austria—This little land has never shown a party strength of more than 150,000 in spite of its experience during the Soviet occupation. Or perhaps we should say that because of that experience fewer than five per cent of the electorate have ever voted for the party.

Switzerland—With her high standard of living, Switzerland is not fertile soil for Communism. Banned during the war, the party resurrected afterwards. Its hold is largely confined to intellectuals and unskilled workers. No support comes from the Federation of Swiss Trade Unions. Membership is less than 8,000.

Spain and Portugal—Though the party is illegal in both these countries, a fairly well-organized illegal party deserves mention in Portugal. With 4,000 members there, and the help of some front organizations, the movement is far from dead. Most Spanish Communists are either jailed in Spain or living in France. The French police keep close watch on these latter and deport their leaders from time to time.

Holland—About half of Dutch Communist strength is in Amsterdam, but Rotterdam, the area around Zaandam, and the provinces of Groningen and Friesland have some support. There is a Communist-run trade union. Much resistance comes from both Catholics and Protestants. There are perhaps 25,000 active party members. More followers may come out of Holland's growing secularization, but the governments since the war have been strongly opposed to Communism.

Belgium—Here too is a sensational loss, as in Germany. The postwar membership of over 100,000 has fallen to less than 25,000. Heaviest support comes from French-speaking Walloons in the Liège and Hainaut provinces. The prominent socialist party repudiates Communists.

Sweden—Somewhat fewer than 30,000 party members are especially influential in the metalworking and mining industries. These members and their sympathizers inspired and led a big metalworkers' strike in 1945. There are strong cells in the northern state railways, in the navy, and to a slighter extent in the army.

Norway—The number of active members has fallen from a postwar high of about 22,000 to no more than 8,000 at present. The Communists control one small union.

Denmark—An extremely active party of about 27 per cent of the parliamentary strength controlled many key union positions at war's end, but there has been a sharp decline in the Danish party's political fortunes. Communists still control many stevedores in key ports, where they sometimes organize crippling strikes.

Finland—This country suffers by its proximity to Russia. While there are probably not over 50,000 party members, mostly in the extreme north and in the few large cities, Communists have recently improved their legislative position in parliament. By trade agreements and economic necessity Finland risks alienation from the West and financial strangulation by the East, though this is against her will. Russia definitely has dangerous and dedicated allies inside this country which is as a whole nationalistic and morally opposed to Marxism. Though Finland was allowed to align with some Western organizations, the Soviets now seek to use the little nation as a buffer between themselves and West Germany.

Why Europeans See Red. Naturally there are reasons why Communism has found listeners to its proposals in free Europe. Some of these reasons are common to all mankind, and others pertain to Europe particularly. Tte Marxist interpretation of life has receded from most minds, for the time being, due to improved material conditions since the war and to the mistakes of the Soviet Union. However, the end is not yet, and the pendulum could quickly swing the other way under other conditions. We summarize a few of the more obvious reasons why Europe has provided an audience for this belief.

1. The Breakdown of Vital Christianity

A principal explanation for the limited success of Communism in Europe is the breakdown of church holds on family life. Biblical Christianity can impart moral fiber to any people, but without this there is no spiritual counterforce to meet Communism. European Protestantism is not as a whole Christ-centered, vital, and evangelistic. Roman Catholicism, unable to combat materialism on a spiritual plane, has organized political parties instead. Communist strength in Catholic Italy is a good example of how a strong materialistic philosophy rushes into a religious void. That situation also illustrates how a Catholic mentality makes a good breeding ground for Communist ideas. Even though much European Protestantism is spiritually sterile, there is more resistance to Communism in the countries where it flourishes.

2. A Revolutionary Tradition

The French Enlightenment which swept Europe in the wake of the French revolution still has millions of advocates. The followers of Voltaire, Rousseau, and the Encyclopedists abominate clericalism and espouse any humanistic cause. The image of man as master of his own destiny and freed from the chains of tradition fascinates a host of people who have nothing better to believe. Especially is Latin Europe open to this kind of thinking, which partly explains Communist success in Italy and France. Only the strong measures of dictatorship have kept Spain and Portugal from following suit.

3. *The Appeal of Materialism*

Economic unrest in our time has led many to consider their material needs as life's most important issue. Existentialism is the philosophic expression of a materialism which "faces the facts of existence." In some countries with periodic financial crises many religious people vote as far to the left as possible to improve their lot. A new prosperity in some countries has made people thirst for the things they have never enjoyed, like a car or a refrigerator. Communism capitalizes on the common human trait of acquisitiveness.

4. *Political Instability*

In countries with a long record of honest representative government, Communism has scant appeal. But the movement has been able to thrive where political upheavals and selfish intrigue produce chaos.

5. *Alliances with Labor and Socialism*

Though doctrinaire Communism champions the working man, the practical Communist course of action ignores his problems and perpetuates the very evils it professes to see in capitalism. Communism has cleverly exploited labor for political ends by offering to lift its low economic standards. The party has also found alliances with socialistic parties which it really opposes in doctrine. With some branches of the labor movement and of socialism as temporary partners in Europe, Communism has been able to win positions it never would have gained alone.

The Winsomeness of Christ. In every European country where Communism flourishes, some party members have become deserters. These have quit the ranks in search of something better, for like all men, Communists seek a faith to live by, a star to follow. Only because the clear gospel of the Lord Jesus Christ is little proclaimed in free Europe have Communists remained unevangelized, for many are ready to listen. We have met former Communists in every leading country of Europe who now know and love the Lord they once spurned. Sometimes in befriending people on trains and in restaurants we have listened long to the earnest talk of party members just to find an opening for a reply. Since theoretic Marxism appeals more to intellectuals than to workmen, a ready opportunity to contact Reds and pinks for Christ can be found in almost any university, and among writers, artists, and other educated people.

An outstanding example of what the Lord can do for a Communist comes to mind. In the so-called Red Belt of the Paris industrial suburbs lie dozens of communities which are Communist-controlled, from the mayor and town council down. In one of these lives a young factory worker named Jean. The young idealist gave in early to the golden promises from Moscow, for what other party offered to improve his salary and working conditions as much? Advancing further, he studied and believed the Marxist doctrines of invincible victory. Jean quickly rose through cell and section responsibility to the leadership of Communist youth and a place on the central committee. When the French politburo pondered which of the younger men should be sent to Moscow for training, their minds instantly turned to the ambitious, dedicated Jean. Giddy with anticipation and joy, Jean arrived in the Russian capital to attend school. In the months that followed, disillusionment came slowly and strongly. Underneath Jean's discontent were memories, stirred by the Holy Spirit, of fragments of gospel truth heard long ago and far away. Jean returned to Paris, and there the Lord mercifully led him to some of His own servants, who told him how God's Son bore his sin on the cross. Conviction of sin deepened and the desire quickened to be free. Deeply stirred to action at last, the professed atheist accepted Christ one night in a tiny gospel gathering on the north side of Paris. Today he still lives in his old neighborhood, but with new drives. Instead of plotting, he prays. Instead of working for a time-limited cause, he serves an eternal one. His dreams of a brave new world have given way now to preoccupation with a Person. Though his material situation remains unimproved, Jean cares little, for he and his family, all redeemed, are content in their fellowship with Christ. Once again the Lord's words have proved to be trustworthy: "And I, if I be lifted up from the earth, will draw all men unto me" (John 12:32).

3. TRADITIONAL PROTESTANTISM

A Protestant Opponent? It may come as a surprise to some to find Protestantism listed as "a giant in the land" along with beliefs like Communism and Catholicism. Naturally we are not classing with this "giant" the genuine believers within Protestantism's ranks nor their all-too-few vital churches. Rather we refer in a general way to the millions who belong to the Reformed and Lutheran bodies, custodians of the glorious truths of the Reformation. Numerically these two comprise 92.9 per cent of the Protestant camp in free Europe, in the following general proportion: *

Lutheran churches	75.2%
Reformed churches	17.7%
Other Protestants	7.1%
	100%

*See Appendix 3 and Appendix 4 for a more detailed, numerical analysis.

Since the Lutheran-Reformed element is so strong, it may be considered representative of European Protestantism. What is the spiritual impact of this Protestant bloc upon free Europe? In the first chapter we quoted many, among them leading Europeans like Bishop Hans Lilje of Germany, who believe that Protestantism is losing, rather than gaining, influence. As we see it, there are three characteristics of the Lutheran-Reformed church bloc which, speaking generally, are turning even Protestant Europe into a mission field. These churches show (a) a confused message, (b) a compromised posture, and (c) a complacent outlook. Let us consider these in order.

a. *The Confused Message*

It would be useless to examine the daily activity of the churches without first considering the message they deliver. If the message is true to God's Word, all sorts of latitude may exist in the means used to get it to the people. But if this message be confused, no means of publishing it will succeed, regardless of how earnest or ingenious its bearers. The message believed and shared, then, is the principal point to examine. English-speaking Christians are familiar with the names of some leaders faithful to the historic, confessional position in Europe. Yet such men and women are few and their total influence upon the majority negligible. These fine servants of Jesus Christ are not the product of, but the exception to, everyday Protestantism in this continent. The average pastor, in our view, is neither thoroughly evangelical nor evangelistic. Consequently the parishioner listening to him is not vitally Christian in commitment and discipleship. Rarely in Europe does one hear a clear presentation of the person and work of Jesus Christ in Protestant churches. More rarely still is the need for personal salvation pressed upon the hearers as an urgent matter needing decision. In America or Canada, and less so in Great Britain, the church picture is much more hopeful. Through constant challenges by orthodoxy, doctrinally weak pastors are more plainly exposed to view. Of course in Europe there have been many cleansing streams of spiritual refreshment, like the German pietism begun by Spener and Franke or the revivals in Scandinavia. These revivals fade and pass; then the old movements to which they gave birth themselves need renewal. Very rarely have the challenging groups left their parent body. As time passes they tend to conform. Even some which separate, like sixty churches which withdrew from the French Reformed Church in 1938 to maintain purer doctrine, reconsider later and begin their trek back to conformity, one by one.

The past three centuries have seen few strong renewals within the churches. As scholars like Kenneth Scott Latourette have noted, the trend of faith in Europe has been downward, beginning with World War I. Too many attacks from intellectual, philosophical, and theological directions have left the churches even weaker and less effective. False shepherds often mislead congregations, not only failing to warn them, but hindering outsiders who do so. To such pastors the unity and continuation of the visible church organization is everything. As a result, some of their parishes have become mission fields rather than missionary bases. A realistic *Time* magazine report puts it thus: "In Europe the state churches—both Protestant and Catholic—that once were a part of the fiber of society, stand cold with empty pews and silent with declining vocations."[18]

Let us reduce the problem for a moment to the individual, where its tragedy can be better seen. A Dutch jurist with a high reputation in international law confided to me that he had grown up in a large Reformed church in Holland. Although his father was Prime Minister then, and he had been reared in the best intellectual and social circles in that enlightened nation, he never heard the message of salvation until later in life. A Swiss businessman, comfortably wealthy and a world traveler, said the same thing. In his reaction to the dead formalism of the National Church he once attended, he wants nothing more now than to share his happy experience of Jesus Christ with others. In his home this man told me that he had even gone to the lengths of earning a doctorate in theology before he stumbled across the truth about the new birth in a simple book written by a foreigner. A last word comes from a Norwegian shipping magnate. Leaning across the dinner table, he earnestly asked prayer for the churches of his country which, said he, "leave out the most important part" of the gospel. Of course, empty Protestant profession is worldwide, but the chance to escape from it into the glad certainty of salvation is much less in Europe than it is in America, for instance. All three of these men grew up in Protestant churches of rich, historic heritage. But all three missed the way to heaven until later, outside influence entered. What message did they hear during all those years in their churches?

On the Theological Fence. In Europe the old modernism so prevalent a generation ago is dead. In its place some form or other of neo-orthodoxy reigns in the thinking of almost all Protestant pastors. As Bernard Ramm notes, Barthian thought is "the prevailing theology" of western Europe today.* We have only space to take the merest glimpse at this innovation

---

*Many in the United States today are talking about the demise of neo-orthodoxy and the rise of the theology of Bultmann. In Europe the pulpits are largely filled by men trained in Barthian thought. Some of the younger preachers are trained in the thought of Bultmann. Europe is now in the last stages of Barthian influence, but the neo-liberalism of Bultmann has not yet won the day—nor can we be sure that it will. Bultmann's views are not held to any large extent outside of Germany.

of our times. Who are its leading thinkers? Best known are Karl Barth of Basel, Emil Brunner of Zurich, and Reinhold Niebuhr of the United States. The main tenets of the new school were conceived in Europe upon European antecedents, then found their way around the world. Besides Niebuhr, other leading American followers are Horton, Tillich, Brauer, Pelikan, and Marcus Barth. Although these men are far from agreeing among themselves on every aspect, yet they have certain common viewpoints which can be summarized.

Unlike modernism, which denies revelation and is essentially humanistic, neo-orthodoxy sets a bridge between divine revelation and human reason. Modernism taught that man was essentially good and God-indwelt; neo-orthodoxy presents him as distanced from God through sin. The older belief also humanized Jesus. In contrast the new thinkers present Jesus Christ as God-man, Saviour, and the hope of the world. Concerning redemption these teachers vary much. By and large most believe that Christ died to reconcile men alienated from Him by sin.

At first glance some elements in neo-orthodoxy appear sound enough to seem acceptable to evangelicals. With these the true believer is sympathetic because he sees in them at least part of the essential message. Thanks to neo-orthodoxy, too, discussion of the great Bible doctrines and of personal Christian experience are again the order of the day. But in another sense this quasi-orthodoxy falls short, and is even more subtle or dangerous than the downright denial of God's Word by modernism. Many of the current philosopher-theologians of this school make strong departures from Biblical truth. Most serious of all, they have changed the grounds of ultimate authority. For the Christian throughout the ages the Bible has always been the infallible source of both faith and service, the last court of appeal concerning man's relationship to God. We do not stand *over* the Bible but *under* its authority. Regardless of different definitions of inspiration, the Bible remains objectively the Word of God.

In the neo-orthodox view, however, "the Bible says" is not good enough. Other criteria must be found to replace what are called "the naïve formulae of fundamentalism" in the matter of inspiration. To back their position these writers turn to philosophers like Kierkegaard, Berdayaev, Buber, and others. With the help of existential philosophers they restate the gospel in their own terms. In their "scientific" approach to the Bible, the neo-orthodox thinkers side with the liberals who so mightily attacked the text of Scripture itself. As Emil Brunner says, "Orthodoxy has become impossible for anyone who knows anything of science. This I would call fortunate."[19] If these men were asked directly whether the Bible was in fact the Word of God, they would all give a careful, qualified answer. This book is, in their view, a commentary on the Word which may *become* the Word to us if we wholly accept it. In other words, it is a means to bring the Word to man.

On the historicity of Biblical events, the theology of crisis (as neo-orthodoxy is also called) is ambiguous. As one critic of the school says of its view, the fall of man "did not actually happen at a certain time to real people in an actual garden, but the story merely expressed the dimension of sin."[20] Yet could "events" which have no historic basis have any real significance at all, even as ideas? Paul King Jewett sees this difficulty and objects, "The prosaic mind can hardly escape the suspicion that an event which did not happen in time and space did not happen at all."[21] Likewise events in the life of Christ are "primal history," as Brunner calls it, and did not occur in time and space. If the accounts in the gospels did not occur historically, then Jesus did not actually say what the disciples reported that He said. Even though we cannot believe this written record, we are asked to retain the truths rising from it. The cross and the resurrection are not important, according to neo-orthodoxy, as actual events; what counts is that we believe in their meaning. But how can there be an Easter faith without resurrection facts?

Charles C. Ryrie summarizes five basic weaknesses in the neo-orthodox view of revelation: (1) It carries with it the idea of error in the Scripture. (2) It leads to "double talk" about the validity of even the witness value of the Bible. (3) It reduces the authority of the Bible to the same level as that of the preaching of the church. (4) It opens the door for other witnesses to the revelation of God outside the Bible. (5) It actually reduces the authority of the Bible to a subjective vanishing point.

The Barthian Blur. The best-known neo-orthodox teacher in the world is Karl Barth of the University of Basel. Analyzing and interpreting the thought of the famous thelogian is not easy, for several reasons. First, Barth's views constantly change as he confronts what he considers different opponents of the Christian gospel. Thus a particular view must be traced from early-Barth through middle-Barth to current-Barth, an exhausting and often inconclusive exercise. What he says on any point depends on when, why, and to whom he said it; nothing irritates Barth more than quoting him against himself without regard for the progression in his thinking. Second, Barth's dialectal and pardoxical approach to theology is difficult to follow. His quest for truth in any area is a flow of affirmations and denials, statements and counterstatements. Often these are like dissonant chords which never resolve into tonic ones, which is quite in keeping with Barth's feeling that at best truth can be only im-

perfectly known. Third, the sheer volume of Barth's output is so staggering and his style often so labored that a clear picture emerges only with
difficulty. Brilliant and beguiling as Barth's mind may be, to the evangelical student his utterances often transmit a blurred impression of this new
orthodoxy.

In spite of these obstacles some very clear convictions are discernible,
for some of which evangelicals can be thankful. Barth's greatest emphasis
is placed on the infinite qualitative differences between God and man,
the awesome, holy "otherness" of God as opposed to the sinfulness of man.
Developing his transcendentalism from the basis of Kierkegaard's existentialism, Barth used it with great effect in the twenties against the
modernists who claimed that man was esentially good because he was
an extension of God's being. Though he has probably taken the point too
far and has neglected too many others, this emphasis has been, on the
whole, a useful one. For his firm belief in the virgin birth, deity, redemptive death, and resurrection of Christ—even though he says these are historically unverifiable—we are also in debt to the Basel teacher. On the
intellectual level, he has helped restrain liberalism by leading people to
think again about sin, redemption, and the person of Christ during a
period when Bible doctrine was unpopular.

Despite these favorable features, there are some great limitations to
Barthian thinking. While condemning modernism, Barth also attacks
fundamentalism, which he regards as obscurantist and not respectable
intellectually.* He does not believe that the Bible is an objective revelation of God. Trained by the German liberals and Bible critics, he shows
incomplete views of inspiration, distrust of the Biblical text, doubt of the
historicity of some scriptural events, and criticism of the miraculous.
With this negative and critical approach, Barth cannot use exegetical
methods to reduce Biblical truth to a system, but must apply philosophy
to Scripture, attempting to impose evangelical conclusions on a rational
foundation. In other words, he uses orthodox terminology built upon
liberal exegesis. To Barth, scientific errors abound in a Bible stripped of its
divinely balanced unity and Spirit-inspired authorship. The Scriptures
are not wholly nor objectively inspired, but they constitute a human
record, a sort of sermon to point to the Word of God. He speaks of the
"inspiringness" of the Bible as over against its "inspiredness." Once believed, however, the Scriptures can become the Word of God to the individual who apprehends truth by an intuitive "flash of faith." Two other
difficulties that emerge from Barth's utterances are his presentation of a
Christ who was a "sinner among sinners" but never sinned, and his appar-

---

*A favorite attack by neo-orthodoxy is upon the dictation theory of inspiration,
rarely held by evangelicals.

ent lack of appreciation of the sanctifying work of the Holy Spirit in giving the believer daily victory over sin.

As a halfway house between liberalism and orthodoxy, this position may seem inviting. But with all its doubts and half-truths it reveals itself as another clever, satanic ruse to dull the Sword of the Spirit and render God's servants ineffective in the face of the enemy. If the Christian worker in Europe is to rescue lost souls, he must have clear convictions about the redemptive plan. In contrasting Barth's blurred conclusions with the clarity of Martin Luther's "Here I stand!", the Swedish theologian David Hedegard says, "Barth sometimes seems to stand nowhere and everywhere."[22] The dependence of Protestant Europeans on neo-orthodoxy is largely to blame for the absence of any note of authority in their Christian message. No theology—liberal, orthodox or otherwise—can replace the use of the Scriptures themselves and the exaltation of their great subject, the Lord Jesus Christ. If Europeans would learn to study the Bible, letting it speak as the Holy Spirit directs, there would be more power in their lives. Evangelism, personal and public, would follow meaningful Bible study and replace the fruitless formalism of today.

Everybody Will Be Saved. The very old hope that all mankind can expect final restoration to grace is widespread in Europe. René Pâche of Switzerland says, "Universalism is a very widely accepted doctrine."[23] Karl Barth is at least partly responsible for this (though he denies outright universalism) through his teaching of a present justification of our whole race through Jesus Christ. The mind of man naturally revolts, not only against the condemnation of the unreached heathen, but against eternal punishment for anybody. To Barth the preaching of the gospel is a declaration of God's overpowering love rather than an offer of pardon which can be rejected. Even the most recalcitrant sinner, despite his rejection of the gospel, is eventually to be saved through God's irresistible grace. Universalism is an attractive view because it does not eliminate the necessity of atonement but only widens its application. There are various degrees of restorationism among European pastors. Some hold that our whole race is reconciled to God through Calvary without the need of any personal decision for Christ at all. Others teach that believers can be sure of eternal life now; eventually unbelievers, in the after life, will also bow to Christ and be accepted by Him. This is Emil Brunner's view.

A very large number of Protestant leaders and people hold that God can punish eternally only those who have categorically rejected His truth. This means that the great masses who have never heard a clear gospel presentation, or who failed to grasp it completely, are covered through the atonement of Christ in the same way that unaccountable infants are redeemed. To many, the word "believe" in Scripture has a broad connotation: one does not need to have assurance of conversion or to confess Christ openly. These leaders feel that God, who sees the heart, will count the merest assent, or even mere lack of hostility, as saving faith. Belief in one or the other of these theories has much to do with lack of evangelistic zeal in Europe. Worse still, those who hold these views interpret what God has plainly said in terms of what man would prefer to hear.

Baptism for Salvation. We turn for a moment to one of the worst features of European Protestantism. Martin Luther, the great advocate of justification by grace through faith alone, had some difficulty relating faith to baptism. In his earlier writings, between 1517 and 1520, Luther seems to emphasize belief as the one all-important issue. Faith alone (*sole fide*) is required by God, and on occasion may even replace the need of the sacraments altogether. Without the Word of God behind it, Luther taught, any sacrament is useless. By 1525, however, Luther was presenting strong sacramental views in his tract, *Against the Heavenly Prophets*. We must remember that Luther was a man entirely subjected to the Word of God as he understood it, even when some particular teaching was personally repugnant to him.

Although Luther's central belief was justification by faith (Rom. 3: 28), he also stretched his credulity to take in another point. As Charles Hodge said, "He understood our Lord in John 3:5 to teach that baptism is essential to salvation. Thus he asserted its absolute necessity, although sorely against his will. To reconcile this with his doctrine of the necessity and sufficiency of faith, he held that new-born infants, when baptized, exercised faith, although he meant by faith the intelligent, voluntary and cordial reception of Christ as He is offered in the gospel."[24]

How could Luther really believe that all people who underwent baptism, including babies, were necessarily doing so in faith? By 1530 the need of baptism for salvation had been written into the Augsburg Confession, as well as into the Smaller and Larger Catechisms, as official Lutheran doctrine. Many Lutherans have had misgivings about this strange solution to the dilemma. Gennrich asks, "Did not Luther inject a magical and physical element into baptism, i.e., into infant baptism, by connecting the new birth with baptism?"[25] Werner Elert also senses the inconsistency of Luther's position: "The assertion concerning the saving necessity of baptism, a ceremony that can only be conceived as an external matter, seems to be in utter contradiction to the most important concern of the evangelical position, according to which salvation eventuates exclusively through the gospel and through faith."[26]

What Luther actually did was to appeal to Scripture for his views of faith and to tradition for authority on child baptism. Roland Bainton points out that Luther was forced to turn to what he called unbroken church tradition in defense of this baptism, since he could not justify it with Scripture.

Where did all this lead? William A. Mueller sums up the evidence by saying, "After 400 years of the history of the Lutheran Church in Germany it has been proved beyond the shadow of a doubt that the idea of a *Volkskirche** and its correlate, infant baptism, works to the detriment of the deeper interests of the church."[27] Luther was right in heart, but mistaken in working out his problem. The result? Millions of Lutherans, who comprise over 75 per cent of Europe's Protestants, are trusting baptism and other "works" for salvation because the church teaches that baptism is an essential. Would that they could trust in Jesus Christ alone!

Myth or Manna? Although, as we have observed, most Protestant pastors in Europe are heavily influenced by neo-orthodoxy, an increasing number read the essays of Professor Rudolph Bultmann of the University of Marburg and follow the heated controversy over them. These are causing the liveliest theological discussion carried on in Germany since World War II. Over a period of years this trained scholar produced many essays, the best known of which are collected in the volume *Kerygma und Mythos,* roughly translatable as *Message and Myth.* Here Bultmann presents his *Entmythologisierung,* or demythologizing, theory. The New Testament, he says, must be stripped of its mythological overlay if the true, inner message of the gospel, the *Kerygma,* is to reach modern man. Jewish and Gnostic encrustations over the original Christian gospel, Bultmann declares, must now be removed. The reasons are many. He points out that the world did not end apocalyptically, as the New Testament writers expected. When modern science arrived, acceptance of the older mythology became impossible. Demon possession in Christ's day, for example, might be called epilepsy or schizophrenia today. "It is impossible," avers Bultman, "to make use of electric light and the radio, and, in case of illness, to claim the help of modern medical and clinical methods, and at the same time to believe in the New Testament's world of spirits and miracles."

Bultmann says that he does not want to destroy this mythology—only interpret it. The process of interpretation he uses is borrowed from existentialism. Language and thought processes in the essays are clearly derived from atheist Martin Heidigger, the chief systematizer of secular existentialism.† In interpreting the New Testament, we must think in

*This word is difficult to render in English. It means a people's church in the sense of a community or regional church into which one is born.
†Even though Bultmann attacks secular existentialism as unredemptive, he depends on it for his system.

terms of the existent: What is the writer saying about himself? This pre-occupation with man leads one French interpreter to ask if "this theology, to such an extent centered upon man and his salvation . . ., has not become simply an anthropology."[28] Indeed, when demythologizing is applied to the person and work of Christ, and to anything supernatural, there is little spared from the scalpel of dissection. "Under the caption of myth," Bernard Ramm points out, "Bultmann would list such items as the in-carnation, the virgin birth, the miracles of Christ, the resurrection, the ascension, the exaltation of Christ, the second coming, and all statements about demons and Satan."[29]

Rudolph Bultmann is continuing the old traditions of German liberal theology and criticism under new expressions. In fact, his use of Christian terms for essentially non-Christian thoughts is typical of the older, nine-teenth-century liberalism. Says Ramm, "Here is a man who seems to deny what the gospel teaches, yet stoutly affirms the gospel." Though Bultmann uses the old terms of historic Christianity, "he labels all such previous understandings of these terms as mythical."[30] The conservative theologi-an, G. C. Berkouwer, of Amsterdam, in discussing Bultmann's influence and pointing out its antecedents, concludes, "In Europe . . . the struggle still centers around the same basic questions raised by the modernism that has influenced theology for a century now."[31]

b. *The Compromised Posture*

Second, let us consider *the compromised posture* of European Prot-estantism. As the result of shaky beliefs, many church bodies have sought governmental alliances. René Pâche links the two by saying, "Europe was the birthplace of Biblical criticism and is still greatly under its influence. It is extremely difficult to find a professor of theology who upholds the full inspiration of the Scriptures." Then he adds, "In most of the Protestant countries there is an established church . . . practically every person who does not belong to some independent group has been baptized and confirmed in the established church and tends to consider himself a real Christian."[32] A confused message can only lead to the adoption of props. Lacking God's authority, the churches turned to human help in the form of a government alliance.

We saw earlier that Luther's problems regarding church leadership led him to the state-church plan. Most of the Reformation churches, the Lutheran and Reformed, continued the practice of hereditary church membership. Everywhere in Europe where Protestantism became ascend-ant, state churches were established under government sponsorship. Up to World War II this practice continued, with the two exceptions of the nominal, legal separation of church and state in France in 1901 and the optional, cantonal system adopted in Switzerland. As Herman points out, "There is not a single country in Europe where complete separation of church and state prevails."[33] France probably comes nearest to holding our American conception of religious liberty. But wherever Catholicism, Eastern Orthodoxy, Lutheranism, the Reformed faith, or the Episcopal Church are involved, the state church concept seems to lead to nominal, hereditary Christianity. Though today a growing dissatisfaction with the system is evident, leaders are reluctant to confront the world without some sort of official help. The educational and financial consequences alone would be great and frightening. Meanwhile the man in the street suffers from a defective version of the gospel of grace. What happens to free churches in this process? For a long time they were persecuted by the state churches, but that period is now over. Unfortunately many have started their long upward climb to recognition, subsidy, and the smile of the state, thereby weakening their testimony.

c. A Complacent Outlook

Out of these first two characteristics rises a third—*a complacent outlook*. Evangelism is born only of burning convictions about God and man. It is not enough just to believe, as do the neo-orthodox, that an abyss separates an infinitely holy God from our wholly godless race. One must also accept everything else God has recorded about His redemptive plan, whether modern science or philosophy can be brought into line with it or not. "All the words that I command thee to speak unto them," said the Lord to Jeremiah; "diminish not a word" (Jer. 26:2). The world will still listen to men of conviction: preaching is effective only in the measure that the message is believed by the evangelist himself. Naturally when the church permits alliances with governments, world-conformed conduct, and dependence on human resources, she loses her evangelistic passion still more.

European Protestantism has always been intellectual in cast. In our times evangelism has been only a passing phenomenon—never the main thrust of the church's effort. Nor has evangelistic work ever become wholly respectable. As a fringe activity, soul-winning engages only a tiny fraction of Europe's Protestants. To many Protestant leaders an open, avowed effort to win the public, if it be bold in concept, brings only embarrassment. To most pastors evangelism consists in collecting the dispersed or disinterested Protestants who move into a given parish. All Lutheran or Reformed territory has been divided on maps into parishes. Everyone is always in a parish wherever he is. Instead of thinking in terms of towns or individuals without witness, the leader tends to think of his parish as the Protestant farmework into which the interested may fit if they so desire. It is obviously easier to speak of some foreign pagan country as a mission field than to see the mission field in one's own region. This rationalization is not confined to Europe!

Some European preachers do have evangelistic gifts. But those gifts are rarely recognized, respected, and directed into the denomination's program. Few fulltime, itinerant evangelists are in use in Europe. Some of the larger church bodies could easily find these gifted ones were they interested enough to look for them. Nor would financial support of the evangelists pose any problem. There is just not enough interest. When non-European evangelists arrive on the scene and enter into such a ministry, they are usually successful, showing that the masses are interested in their own spiritual welfare. But by and large the established churches evidence no concern.

On the laymen's level personal soul-winning activity is exceedingly rare. Many true Christians who would like to testify about their experiences with Christ just do not know how. Nothing in their church program stimulates or helps these regenerated people to witness. I once helped set in motion a program of brief, intensive training in personal work for 25,000 Europeans. The Navigators, who taught the classes, were experts and the hearers eager. Lasting results in many lives were striking. One can imagine what unlimited power would be unleashed if more believers in Europe were so taught. The unsaved church members in "Protestant" Europe would soon be won to Christ by instructed laymen whether or not the pulpit ministry to them was clear. Not much later the darkened, Roman Catholic two-thirds of Europe would receive missionary witness from the revitalized Christians now awakened to responsibility. Instead of depending on foreign missionaries from other continents, Europeans would become missionaries to other Europeans. This is, of course, the only way the task of reaching Europe can be completed. Until it happens though, outside help will still be needed to proclaim the redemptive word in Europe. Otherwise how is this generation to hear the gospel? "Oh, Jerusalem, that bringeth good tidings, lift up thy voice with strength; lift it up, be not afraid; say unto the cities of Judah, Behold your God!" (Isa. 40:9).

4. EXISTENTIALISM—THE THRILL PHILOSOPHY

Where Whirl is King. No solutions please man so much as those reached by his own reason. Since he cannot banish God, he is tempted at least to rival Him by trying to work things out for himself. Though he may be as frightened as a lost explorer hacking his way through the jungle, still he likes the adventure of trusting his own wits as far as they will take him. Nowhere is this exciting loneliness more evident than among European intellectuals. Materially disinherited time and again, they have now become spiritually disillusioned as well. Whistling in the dark, however, has not helped, for when the whistling stops the darkness is still there. What about God? Since the intellectual will not accept the divine self-revelation in Holy Scripture, only institutionalized Christianity remains. He rightly analyzes most of this as the husk without the juices. Gyrating between faith and scepticism, he sometimes stumbles upon solutions which he thinks are new. Actually they are just the same old delusions with different labels. All the alternatives he can devise have been tried before, but he fails to see them all as variations of the same error. The currently popular European panacea is existentialism, a system of thought that raises more questions than it can answer. Although this gilded gift of Europe to the world has already become tarnished and tawdry, it is still widely accepted. Hence the Christian would do well to investigate this system of thought which is the most significant philosophic trend in Europe.

Some ill-informed people regard existentialism as a form of escapism with intellectual overtones, largely confined to the antics of the long-haired students in the left-bank cafés of Paris. Others consider it a closed enigma with little content. One interpreter feels that adult children are playing with these concepts as with bright and shiny toys, soon to be thrown aside. But no such opinions do justice to this well-knit, clearly expressed system of thought read and seriously discussed in every university of Europe and the world. Beyond the classroom existentialist influence ranges wide. Prize-winning plays, popular novels, paintings, and all other forms of art are being saturated with its meanings. Some manifestations are political in character. Dialectic masters like Sartre have made existentialism as readable and gripping as a novel. Only a fringe group use these theories about life as a springboard to escapism, and these are the type who would use any other convenient excuse to do so.

The Leap into the Abyss. Someone has called existentialism "a philosophy for thought-adventurers . . . a way of thinking for an age of experiment, tension, and stress."[34] Guido de Ruggiero suggests that it is "philosophy in the manner of a thriller."[35] Ussher called Karl Jasper's view a "philosophy of night,"[36] whose supreme experience *scheitern*, or shipwreck. Here, he adds, we are in the climate of Einstein, Picasso, and Freud, exploring strange new worlds. This view of life "varies from the feelings of a prisoner on the night before his execution to the sheer zeal experienced in thinking and living dangerously . . . a dangerous philosophy when taken 'neat.' "[37] In the extreme, such thinking could become "something like a state of mind of a man who throws a bomb just to see what will happen, or to show that he is not afraid."[38] Unlike the passive resignation of Schopenhauer, existentialist pessimism imparts a heady and "bracing sense of the menace and challenge of existence."[39] These comments, taken together, portray a kind of intellectual intoxication followed by a headache.

Without doubt Europe's most fashionable life-answer has risen out of the dilemma of our times. Expressions like "leap," "crisis," "dread," and "abyss," used by the movement's high priests, reflect the uncertainty felt everywhere today. How this system can bring peace to anyone in a chaotic world is difficult to understand, for existentialism, being fluid by its very nature, holds that nothing can be final or complete. What comfort does this bring? It is the very opposite of the Christian faith, in which bewildered, erring man finds forgiveness and fulfillment in the Absolute and the Infinite God. Jean Paul Sartre says that any set of values can be adopted only for a particular individual in his own situation, and are valid for him alone. Even Plato knew better; he asserted that the problem of philosophy is to find, for all that exists conditionally, a ground unconditional and absolute.

European and Anglo-American philosophies of our day differ widely. While we have been examining the tools of logic and concept, Europeans have been probing the objects of experience. After all, the world's stark realities and brutalities have been closer to European lives than to American. Europeans who reject the Marxist way have been trying to interpret experience in other terms. In an atmosphere of intense excitement they are reviving classic philosophy and adding their own innovations to it.

Leaders of the Movement. The Christian existentialism of Sören Kierkegaard has been adapted to twentieth-century needs by many thinkers. Outstanding leaders of modern existentialism have been Martin Heidigger and Karl Jasper, of Germany, and Gabriel Marcel and Jean Paul Sartre, of France. Others, like Ortega y Gasset, Reinhold Niebuhr, Paul Tillich, Rudolf Bultmann, Nicolai Berdyaev, Karl Barth, Emil Brunner, and Martin Buber have all been influenced by Kierkegaard, adding their own ideas to his and thus influencing others. The four leaders first named have taken up many of Kierkegaard's assumptions, leaving out his Christian core. Like him, they are interested in radical empiricism—the examination of the concrete data of existence. Like him, again, they are resolved to reject all artificial or theoretical solutions. Nor can they accept the idealistic view of man as an individual absorbed into the whole. All reject materialism on one side and idealism on the other, seeking insight into the individual being of man. Heidegger, for instance, created categories as modes of existence in order to investigate man better. Good and evil, all these leaders agree, are not fixed qualities. To Heidegger they are existentials or modes only.

Stumbling in the Dark. Since we cannot survey the whole range of existential thought, we choose here only several glimpses from the ethics of some chief writers. Conscience is spoken of as commending as well as accusing, but not working according to fixed forms. Though it may speak different things to different people, its voice is nevertheless personal and inescapable. Guilt follows the condemnation of conscience even though there are no absolute moral rules. The way out of guilt is to face it and learn its full meaning. Only then will we be able to exist with real awareness even in the light of an inevitable death. Much is made by existentialists of the freedom of this decision in the face of guilt. Man is "condemned to freedom" of choice whether he likes it or not. Men settle their own destiny by all-important free choices which divide them into "authentic" or "unauthentic" kinds of existence. The decision to face guilt rather than avoid it, for example, would be an authentic choice. Similar decisions cover the whole range of life and determine one's ability to exist in the full sense of the word. Though some of the language and the terms employed in this system of thought are used in Christian thought as well, there is no resemblance at all between the meanings of the two systems. Modern philosophical existentialism is utterly void of any Christian content, though in its origin it had Christian content.

Born for No Reason, Going Nowhere. Probably Sartre is the best-known, most popular existentialist, but it is Heidegger who has laid down the most carefully thought-out system. Although Sartre has not yet written his ethics, he implies that it is cowardly for anyone to justify his actions on moral grounds. First,—and here all existentialists agree—such moral grounds are not absolute. Second, by justifying his actions through moral reference, man is only attempting to evade responsibility of choice. It follows that such appeals to moral absolutes are useless. Morals are relative, and life is a puzzle to be worked out in loneliness by those who will not shirk the decisions. Organic society is rejected as of no help in this struggle. Man is alone with the consequences of his life; "I am my liberty," is Sartre's phrase.[40] God, human love, and friendship cannot be understood. Heidegger does not fear God, but he dreads nonentity; while Sartre dangerously says: "If God is dead, then all is permitted." Only a morbid, suffering individualism remains. Each one of us lives in his own world, where he sets up a tension with all aliens who enter his life by attempting to rise above them. Life, in short, is an absurd nihilism. "Existence," says Sartre, "is reasonless, causeless, and unnecessary. We are born for no reason, go on living because we are weak, and our death is decided by chance."[41]

Passport to Perplexity. Existentialism is especially popular in Europe because it is a protest and a challenge to both the worlds between which Europe now lies. Many want neither the capitalism of the West nor the Marxism of the East, but are looking for some new path. They regard Christianity as harmless, decadent, and useless, like an old man in a rocking chair. The sad solitude of this negativistic way of life is strikingly drawn in one of postwar Europe's best-sellers, *The Twenty-Fifth Hour.* In this novel Virgil Gheorhiu represents his hero as chewed up by both East and West, his life the mere pawn of pitiless, warring powers to whom the individual means nothing. Any European whose existence was disrupted by the war could identify himself with the thesis: You are on your own in life; come to terms with your problems without depending on others—without depending upon God, even. Another realm existentialism challenges is that where science is king. People in Europe often express their weariness with the false optimism of a shiny new world of material good which lacks any real meaning. In this realm, too, they find the arms manufacturers and nuclear despots who do not care for the individual.

Existentialism is a keep-your-chin-up philosophy, which appeals strongly to modern man. But of course there is a limit to every person's endurance, and this philosophy shows no way out. As David Roberts has put it, this view "offers a particularly poignant exposition of the predicament of modern man. Here we see individuals facing tragedy without any hope of salvation. We see them standing in utter loneliness and staring at bleak emptiness." He adds that existentialists speak "for millions of our contemporaries for whom God is dead."[42] This is why it constitutes a powerful enemy of the gospel of Jesus Christ in the realm of the mind. Mingled with neo-orthodox theology, it is offered to university and theological students who hunger for certainty. In their hands, in turn, rests the spiritual welfare of a host of souls of the next generation. In many other fields those affected by the new nihilism are on a similar diet. In contrast to such poor fare the Son of God spreads a feast for His own that satisfies the mind as well as the heart.

5. *A SALIENT FOR THE CULTS*

The Eager Rivals. In Europe Christianity's marginal movements which we call cults, are not only the opponents of evangelical Christianity but its rivals as well. In English-speaking countries Protestantism is so large that when the sects collide with it, there is an alert reaction. Since most militant sects originated in America, American Protestants know about them. But the field of opportunity for both in Europe is so vast that, except in certain places, Protestantism and the cults rarely clash. This means that the false cults are less understood and less resisted by Protestants in the Old World than they are in the new. Roman Catholics seem almost better armed than Protestants to resist them. The finest studies of these cults we have yet read in Europe have been written in many languages by Catholic priests who, at the request of their superiors, have procured the needed information from America.

It is an indictment of our evangelical Protestant bodies that we have allowed the messengers of these cults to outnumber our own missionaries to the continent. They have also outspent and outworked us. Some day these groups will confront genuine European believers with a problem, for they have moved surely and swiftly into postwar spiritual vacuum. In the last decade a number of movements that entered Europe years ago have consolidated their gains after heavy offensives. According to a senior official of the Evangelical Church in Württemberg, Germany, the sixty-five sects in Germany number 900,000 in membership, which indicates an increase of 200,000 in the last four years. Only thirty-five of these sects are German. Eighteen of them, the larger ones, are of American origin.

The present successes of the cults, which we will briefly evaluate, are based on three characteristics which apply to all: (1) complete fearlessness in presentation; (2) constant propaganda by word and pen; (3) careful training of converts. Since the cults do not worry about whether they will be "accepted" by the religious *status quo* or not, their approach may be likened to that of a bulldozer. Usually they make no attempt to establish *rapport* with either Protestants, Catholics, or those of any other religion, being convinced that all need the new revelation. Nor can they be intimidated, even by governments. Propaganda-wise they owe not so much to subtlety as to shoe leather. Like every other nascent movement, they make their share of mistakes, but they profit by them and plod on. Then they are wise enough to create leadership, with both formal and informal training, from the local level up. Having made these general observations, let us look at some of the individual sects at work. Unfortunately there will not be space for more than a few glimpses.

European Beachheads. The *Mormons* or Latter-day Saints began their expansion into Europe very early. By 1837 they had entered England, by 1840 Germany, and by 1849 France, Scandinavia, Iceland, and Italy. In 1861 Holland became a Mormon field. Since many Mormon young people are expected to spend a period as missionaries abroad, it is difficult to obtain accurate figures of their strength at any given time. Most stay about thirty months, and are then replaced. It is certain that there are more American Mormons in unpaid short-term work here than there are American evangelicals of all origins. According to recent authoritative reports, there are 3,500 American Mormon missionaries in Europe. Their presence has proved to be enormously productive in results. By 1960 Mormon membership had doubled in Great Britain; 1,200 converts were baptized in the month of July, 1961 alone. In France the Latter-day Saints reported 1,000 conversions in 1960, with 2,500 as their target for the following year. In the past five years the number of Mormon missionaries in France has zoomed from 140 to 250. A reported four hundred serve in Scandinavia.

West Germany has 16,000 Mormon Church members, and West Berlin, 1,400. Because of intensive effort by missionaries, the number of Berlin converts has doubled in the last three years. Some fifty-six Americans between the ages of nineteen and twenty-two (and all but four of them men), serve in the beleaguered city. The number of Mormon churches is soon to be doubled. How has this quick success been achieved? For one thing, the missionaries begin work at six in the morning and sometimes put in as many as seventy hours a week. For another, they systematically divide up the city and ring scores of doorbells every day.

Two missionaries, Craig Colton, 22, of Los Angeles, and Gary Harris, 20 of Taber, Alberta, Canada, recently invaded the southern French city of Nîmes, which has a population of ninety thousand. In this predominantly Protestant city the two young men talked with fifty to one hundred people a day. Some prospects were attracted through English language lessons and a softball team. Monsieur and Madame Zannelli were Roman Catholics before the two young Mormons knocked on their door. Marceline Zannelli told them to come back later and talk to her husband, a head waiter. They visited the Zannellis repeatedly over a period of two months. Then the wife was baptized as a Mormon in the local swimming pool. A year before she had never heard of the Mormons. All together Colton and Harris made a dozen converts in nine months—the nucleus of a church. The regional newspaper *Midi-Libre* called them better recruiters than the Communists.

Mormon young people in another typical beginning set up a teaching chart on an easel in a central French city park. There they began to explain their doctrines daily to a handful of people who gathered. For a time no response came. Persistence paid off, though, for today a vigorous church flourishes there. Recently in London a large temple was opened as a showplace for the Latter-day Saints, with special guides and lecturers on duty at all times. On the Continent itself the same church opened its first temple* in 1955 in a suburb of Bern, the capital of Switzerland. About fifty thousand Mormons are reported for all of Europe, but the present strong missionary thrust will surely increase this number.

The *Seventh-day Adventists* entered more than fifteen European countries between 1860 and 1929. Today three of their twelve world divisions encompass Europe. Since the beginning of their missionary effort they have laid heavy emphasis on literature, with "every member a missionary" to distribute it. Several of their European monthlies, for instance, with covers in color and many illustrated pages, have circulations well over the 100,000 mark. Usually no mark indentifies this material as Adventist. In Italy the Adventists send postcards to persons listed in the telephone directories offering Bible studies—"with optimum results," says one Vatican source. Education is another feature of the Adventists' advance. One of many schools is a seminary with several hundred students, located in the Haute Savoie section of France. In 1949 a well-equipped recording studio was opened in Paris to record the "Voice of Prophecy" programs broadcast over Radio Luxemburg and Radio Monte Carlo in Europe's principal languages. The approach to the listener is usually made through a moral talk with some current and personal application. Literature is then offered.

Not much impact is made in America by the *New Apostolic Church*, but it is the strongest sect in Germany. Here in the land of Luther about three-quarters of the church's 300,000 members live. We have often noticed the new, modern-styled churches erected in Germany and other countries by this growing minority group. Of the twelve apostles or leaders who claim to exercise the delegated authority of the early, apostolic church, nine are in Europe.

One of the most aggressive of the sects is *Moral Rearmament*. In 1946 Swiss converts of the movement purchased a huge hotel in the town of Caux, high in the Swiss Alps overlooking Lake Geneva. Here at their headquarters, called Mountain House, the leaders of MRA established the nerve center for their European operation under the leadership of the late Frank Buchman. Today MRA owns twelve more hotels in Caux, which has become one of the largest conference centers on this continent. On any summer day one can see thousands of delegates from the chief countries of the world strolling around the grounds.

Ordinarily, close followers of the movement donate all their financial resources to it, and serve it for their expenses only, without salary. Not a few millionaires have come to Caux to lay all they have before their companions and follow the vague, powerless idealism of MRA. These men

*There are many churches in Mormonism, but few temples. The temples fulfill a special function limited to the baptized inner circle.

sincerely feel that the world's problems can be solved by preaching their four "absolutes"—honesty, purity, unselfishness, and love—though without the new birth and the dynamism of the Holy Spirit to create a genuine change in individuals.

Moral Rearmament has published 73 million copies of the book *Ideology and Co-existence* for distribution in Europe. The distribution took place first in Switzerland, Holland, and Scandinavia. Right now 52 million more copies are being distributed in France, Germany, Italy, and England. To make this possible, MRA followers gave $2,500,000 in 1960.

One Cult in Many Countries. Perhaps a third of all the members of *Jehovah's Witnesses* are in Europe. A half of the world total of organized groups is also in this continent. Thus this cult must be recognized as successful in terms of missionary effort. With 2,201 "pioneers" (missionaries) at work in Europe during 1955, there could hardly be failure. According to the 1956 yearbook of this faith, there were likewise 110,824 "publishers" (active witnessing members) serving free Europe during the same year. These are the people who patiently sell *The Watchtower* on the street corners of the principal cities of Europe and around the world. Aside from the "publishers," who are directly committed to propaganda work, hundreds of thousands of others are studying the material and attending classes.

The primary method of this group is to publish and distribute literature. They operate large publishing plants in Germany, Switzerland, Sweden, Finland, and Greece. During 1955 the 110,824 "publishers" we have mentioned distributed the phenomenal total of 7,098,975 pieces of printed matter. Each individual, in other words, averaged a distribution of sixty-five pieces that year. Does such effort succeed? As a result, 42,549 people were enrolled in correspondence courses.

As the national body of Witnesses increases, the investment of "pioneers" can be reduced. In 1951, for instance, Belgium had 104 "pioneers" preaching the Witness doctrine. In 1955 there were only 81, a reduction of 23 during five years' time. This fact is advanced by the Witnesses themselves as proof of the growing number of "congregation publishers" in Belgium. In 1955 an increase of nine hundred more subscriptions to *The Watchtower* than during the previous year was also noted.

West Germany is the most heavily attacked country and the most successful field. The Jehovah's Witnesses are the second largest of the sects in that country. In 1955 with 949 "pioneer publishers" and 48,446 "congregation publishers" the Witnesses disposed of 3,781,175 pieces of literature in West Germany. This netted them 20,163 Bible study enrollments and 30,982 public meetings. Witness broadcasts have often been aired over five German stations. Scandinavia was the second most successful field during the same year. Sweden had 200 "pioneers," Finland 196, Denmark 117, and Norway 70—a total of 583 missionaries in these Protestant lands. Distribution of literature totalled 1,823,737 in Scandinavia— a job handled by 22,796 of the faithful. Even little Denmark could marshal 8,101 individuals to participate in this. In order of Witness strength the four countries rate as follows: (1) Denmark, (2) Sweden, (3) Finland, (4) Norway.

Sometimes a concentrated effort is made over one short period. One year the Witnesses divided Rome into zones and sent out 75 workers into these zones on daily visitation for a month. During the month they distributed 250,000 sample magazines and 1,450,000 leaflets. Naturally there are permanent results from such an effort. Led by 111 "pioneers," almost three thousand Witnesses carry out such propaganda in Italy in a regular way.

Other successful activities are the congress and the major rallies. In 1955 more than five thousand delegates from North America paid their own way to attend the "Triumphant Kingdom" assemblies in England. Afterward, simultaneous conventions were held in Paris and Rome. But the most spectacular success was the rally in Nuremberg's Zeppelin-Wiese Stadium. After a Sunday morning meeting of 80,145, and afternoon rally of 107,423 featured the baptism of 4,333 new members. Thirteen other rallies in other cities like Stockholm, the Hague, Helsinki, and Berlin drew 403,682 people in public stadium meetings. Almost 14,000 were baptized into the new faith, and immeasurable public attention was secured through the press, radio, and television.

It is challenging to note that Protestant Europe has been singled out for the most attention by the Witnesses. Realizing the similarity of some of their terms and traditions to those of Protestantism, they have concentrated on these Protestant nations. Germany is the center of the work because that country is the key to leadership in western Europe. How much we have to learn from those who labor in a wrong cause!

Many Cults in One Country. Having glimpsed the activity of one sect in many countries, let us now examine the work of several in one particular country. In tiny Holland, as elsewhere in Europe, the sects are militant and growing. Their success is more than ever assured in a land where Calvinistic tradition has lost much of its evangelical zeal but provides a tolerant climate to all faiths. We will mention here only the Dutch sects with these three characteristics: a growing constituency, a national character, and a planned proselytism.

1. *Moral Rearmament (Morale Herbewapening).* The world-wide movement of Frank Buchman finds much sympathetic support among Dutch Protestants. Since Holland has always been especially open to British and American cultural influence, it is quite natural that Buchmanism should penetrate certain circles without much difficulty. In 1938 Queen Wilhelmina lent royal prestige by devoting a broadcast to the message of the Oxford Group Movement, as it was then called. Since MRA is a movement rather than a church with membership, figures are difficult to obtain, but its influence is reaching into most Protestant and nonreligious groups and penetrating the upper classes. National headquarters are in The Hague.

2. *Jehovah's Witnesses (Jehovah's Getuigen).* On Saturday afternoons Dutch Witnesses appear on the street corners everywhere to sell the bimonthly *Watchtower (Wachtoren).* Although their share of the immense two million world circulation (forty languages) of this magazine is small, steady sales have gained a large following over a period of thirty years. As some other sects do, the Witnesses split up large churches into units or cells, where each person can be stimulated into systematic study and aggressive missionary work. The Amsterdam church, for instance, has fifteen such units. No individual member can remain inactive. Witnesses in Holland have had the usual scrapes with the government over compulsory military service, all of which have only served to publicize and strengthen their cause. The 150 churches in the country are administered from Amsterdam.

3. Mormons *(Kerk van Jezus Christus van de Heiligen der Laatste Dagen).* In Holland the disciples of Joseph Smith claim only 3,500 members in twenty-three churches, but their pattern of growth is strong. More than one hundred missionaries of several nationalities (some American) constantly circulate under the direction of the headquarters in The Hague.

Distinct divisions carefully group new converts to the Latter-day Saints into potential churches after the usual literature campaign, personal visitation, and other forms of witness have achieved any success. Dutch Mormons are continually stimulated by periodic visits of some of the 10,000 world missionaries of this sect. Many are Americans on the short-term missionary stint Mormons have made famous. On occasion these personable young men have attempted to benefit by other evangelism too, following up converts of campaigns held by Protestant churches.

4. *Seventh-day Adventists (Zevende-dags Adventisten).* Since entering the country in April, 1898, the Adventists have had a quiet but an extremely solid growth. Their forty churches have 2,500 members. National headquarters, as well as a seminary, are near The Hague. *Tekenen des Tijds (Signs of the Times)* is the principal monthly organ with a family appeal. Literary activity is supervised by the Hague bookstore-library,

called *Veritas*. One of the most interesting aspects of the work in Holland is the Ond-Zandbergen seminary at Huis ter Heide. Thirty pastors currently leading churches have been trained here. Ministerial students whose previous education is inadequate are given five years of pre-university training. This is followed by the five-year theological course, of which three years are spent in Holland and two in England. Insistence on such high standards of training undoubtedly accounts for both the solid indoctrination passed on to converts and the general stability of the work. As a means of evangelization, the weekly broadcast, *De Steder Hoop*, Dutch version of the familiar *Voice of Prophecy*, brings heavy response through Radio Luxembourg. Follow-up literature of all kinds is sent out on a big scale, so that interest is much higher than membership figures indicate.

5. *Christian Science.* The Amsterdam First Church of Christ, Scientist, built in the Richard Wagnerstraat in 1937, was followed by other churches in The Hague and Haarlem. Though church membership is not over three thousand, Christian Science practitioners are dealing with thousands more, while the usual Reading Rooms interest still others. No expense is spared to bring full, expensively printed explanations of Science doctrine and *Science and Health* before the general public. As is true elsewhere, wealthy and intellectual classes are attracted to Science while the ill are looking for mental release.

In addition to the cults we have mentioned, the Humanists, Buddhists, and Muslims are all active in Holland. Theosophy, Bahaism and Rosicrucianism have small followings too.

Missionaries of the Greater Europe Mission plan future moves at their annual conference.

Kermit Zopfi (left), director of the German Bible Institute in Seeheim, welcomes Harry Liu, of the Pocket Testament League, to chapel.

Chapter 3

THE MISSIONARY TO EUROPE

"Europe needs missionaries, and we Europeans will do what we can to help them. I am unable to list all the American missions and groups that are working in Europe with success, but we do appreciate them. Missionaries should know the Word of God thoroughly, be able to teach it, and be willing to lose sight of the fact that they are from North America. European Christians will generally accept foreign missionaries on this basis."

—Dr. René Pâche,
Principal of Emmaus Bible Institute, Switzerland
Congress on World Missions, Chicago, 1960

Unparalleled Opportunity. "If I could live my life over again, I would be a missionary to Europe." With these words, the head of one of America's best-known spiritual movements wistfully gazed through this wide-open door. Over a cup of black French coffee, he spoke of what he had seen and felt during four months' travel through the overlooked continent. A year or two later we were lunching together near the Arch of Triumph. This time he had an earnest young man with him, the fruit of his representations about Europe to Christians at home. In leaving the first American representative of his movement in France, he was beginning to pay off his spiritual debt to Europe—and that of the American church.

The leader of a mission with almost a thousand workers stationed around the world stood on the runway at Orly airport in Paris, having just come from the Orient. "I am appalled," he said. "Hongkong, Singapore and Calcutta have more of a gospel witness than I have found in some cities in France." As he clung to his hat in the brisk wind, he asked for help in entering this land with missionaries. "Pray that young people will volunteer," were his final words before the big silver airliner winged toward America. He was true to his new vision. Over twenty missionaries are in France today because of what this man learned about its plight.

91

Just a few years ago a young man came bounding up the stairs of our Paris apartment clutching his camera case and other tourist paraphernalia. Yet he was more than a tourist. While still a college student, he had come to Europe on a summer gospel team trip. When he left, we thought we had seen the last of the energetic redhead with the infectious laugh. But, back in the States he could not forget his experience of soulwinning in half a dozen countries. When he finished his schooling, he contacted us again to ask, "Where is the need greatest?" Today he is in Italy directing Rome's Italian Bible Institute. And he would not be anywhere else for all the world.

A Strategy for Winning. When answering the Lord's call to serve in Europe, the missionary candidate must ask himself: What will be my goal there? What do I want to accomplish? The average missionary never considers this question before leaving for a foreign field. But could any question be more pertinent? Such a person would naturally respond, "I will do Christian work, of course." What he means is that he will do "Christian work" as he has seen it done at home with the particular methods, programs, specialties, and all the rest, used here. He will win souls, teach converts, and form an organization. Very well, the Word of God never changes and the human heart everywhere is the same. But does the missionary know what is the *ultimate* goal?

There are missionaries in Europe and elsewhere who are exceedingly faithful in witness. They contact people, distribute tracts, lead seekers to Christ, and in other ways keep commendably busy. Such people seldom ask if this is missionary work in its best and most lasting form. What could be more scriptural than winning a soul? Is not this the principal task of a missionary? Yes and no. According to the New Testament, the Apostle Paul and his fellow workers never won souls, in countries they visited, just to make converts. They saw beyond this. By applying the "teaching them to observe" of Matt. 28: 20, they made disciples rather than mere converts. To them each soul was a potential disciple and missionary—a means to reach others (II Tim. 2:2). In each group of converts Paul saw, in embryo, a witnessing cell which would ultimately be responsible for a whole area (Rom. 15:19-25, 28). This cell, which he called a church, was the basic unit in eventually winning a whole country. The planting, edification, and growth of the local church were therefore of utmost importance.

The missionary to Europe, if he is to succeed in his task, must keep his eyes on the region, the area, the whole country in which he serves. Does he not want to evangelize the whole country? But how can he, or even an army of missionaries, accomplish this? He concludes that as a missionary he is not an end in himself, only a prime mover of others. He must believe that the European can become, under God, a better soul-winner, teacher, and leader than himself. In the long view of things, he reasons, only the European can win Europeans. In a way, the missionary is an expensive, inefficient, and temporary alien whose presence can be justified only if he is able to get the European saved and started on the road toward spiritual responsibility for others. Only as he places trust in the European individual or group he has trained will the work go forward. He could not serve anywhere in the world where nationals are more intelligent, better educated, and more ready to move into eventual independence than in Europe. To bring this goal about, the missionary to Europe must carefully study the growing literature on the indigenous church on the foreign field.

Spiritual Requirements. The fact that Europe, in most places, does not abound in snakes, ferocious beasts, or ignorant savages does not mean that the missionary to Europe will not be exposed to trial. True, the exterior side of life will be more comfortable here than it is on many other fields, even if the missionary seeks to live, as is preferable, on a not-too-foreign basis. Yet the attacks of Satan on the Christian worker here are vicious. Generally they take the subtle form of pressure on the inner life. Among the reasons why missionaries have left Europe we have noted these through the years: inability to follow mission directives; unwillingness to co-operate with other missionaries; adultery, homosexuality; nervous breakdowns and physical collapses; marriage outside of God's will; loneliness; fear of failure; and offers of supposedly better situations at home. Some of these may be effects rather than causes. The first two reasons for failure are the most common. From this list we can see that missionary life in Europe requires deep inward commitment to the Lord, obedience in outer things, steadfastness, and courage. In some of the Latin countries the pressure upon mind and body is very great, and can be borne only by the total dependence on the grace of God. Some of these countries have been under Satan's domination for centuries, and he will not cede them without a fight.

Academic Preparation. What kind of missionary does Europe need? In discussing this we can too easily become idealistic. Actually, the Lord uses all kinds of people in His service, and those of every type and gift can be His instruments in Europe. A person ministering to almost illiterate Spanish villagers would not need the same background as someone working among students at the University of Paris. As I write, I have two people in mind who are doing these very two things. Radically different in training and gift, neither could do the task of the other, yet neither is superior to the other. Both are needed in a continent teeming with ordinary people but led by a superior few. The Head of the Body can easily fit into His service any truly called of Him. He knows in advance where each one can best serve.

In the United States one common misconception prevails about European education. A recent wave of American reappraisal of elementary and high school training has resulted in much favorable comment about European school systems. The early training of European children is indeed more intensive and serious, if less practical, than equivalent American training.* This period of study in Europe is especially directed toward helping the child express himself well in his native language. By and large the results in that realm are superior to those in America. For instance, the European child, at any given elementary age, knows and uses more words than his American counterpart. We must never make the mistake of thinking, however, that *the average European adult* is so much better educated than an American that he can be reached only by missionaries who are college graduates or have even more advanced training. The percentage of college graduates is much higher in America than in any country on the Continent or in England. Nevertheless, the minority in Europe who do go into the nationalized university or graduate school are probably better educated than students on the same level in America. At least they specialize more deeply in one field. The picture that emerges in Europe shows (1) masses whose formal education rarely passes the twelfth or fourteenth year, and (2) a small percentage of people educated superbly by the state for leadership along a particular line.

What academic background will be needed by those intending to serve Christ in Europe will therefore depend on what class of people they hope to serve. We use the term "class" advisedly; there are distinct social classes in most countries. The laboring class is the largest single neglected group. In some countries there is almost no middle class; in others the middle class is large and important enough to be strategic. In all countries the upper classes and the educated constitute an unreached mission field. In order to win the latter, college graduates and people with advanced degrees are in the best position to help. Those who have a thorough theological education in a sound seminary would prove useful in Europe's growing number of Bible institutes and theological seminaries.

On the other hand, Bible institute and Bible college graduates can work acceptably in evangelizing the middle and lower classes. Preferably such workers should have some college background, too, although this is not essential. In general, all classes of Europeans tend to respect edu-

---

*Only Spain and Portugal do not have compulsory elementary schools.

cation and art for their own sakes. A writer or an artist is a king even to the peasants of France, Italy, or Spain. On the European side of the Atlantic the successful business man, that paragon of American life, gets scant attention. The most highly respected profession in postwar Germany, as a recent poll revealed, is that of the college professor. In France, the intellectuals and writers of Paris occupy life's center stage—not film stars.

The Sina Qua Non. Good sense suggests that a prospective missionary should get a good basic education, especially in Bible, without making a fetish of the Book. General education is a tool needed to make a Christian worker more effective. But in Europe, as elsewhere, the fullness of the Spirit is our Lord's sole condition for power. "Be filled with the Spirit" (Eph. 5:18) is a command as well as a provision. Let a worker come to Europe directed and controlled by the Holy Spirit, and he will succeed. Every facet of his personality and product of his mind will then serve one end—the exaltation of Jesus Christ. He will be an integrated, mature person, Christ-indwelt and God-glorifying.

No missionary can love the people among whom he works without God's grace and help. Natural affinity and even similar national roots have little to do with the kind of love he must demonstrate. Scripture teaches that the love of God is shed abroad in our hearts by the Holy Spirit. Superior education and knowledge may well lead to pride if they are not tempered by this divine love. Like everyone else, the European needs to feel that God—and we who are God's—love him. This will impress him much more than a display of knowledge. Once a heart is made receptive and open through the ministry of love, whatever understanding of the Word we missionaries have begins to take effect.

Love always includes respect, too. If a missionary is working in the Spirit's fullness, he will never look down on the European from superior heights. He will respect and appreciate everything he can in the national culture, realizing that what counts is a person's relationship to God, not his reaction to America. When the Holy Spirit is loving people through us, those people will never feel degraded or inferior when they are with us. They will tend to forget our nationality because of their interest in Him who sent us.

A Word About Language. Everyone feels complimented when a foreigner speaks his language well. But our goal as missionaries is greater than making people react favorably to our fluency in the language. Life-and-death issues—the very salvation of souls—may hinge on our ability to express ourselves well. Further, the progress of young Christians under our care may largely depend on it. So we cannot afford to fail in language study. In the first chapter of this study the language problem in Europe was discussed, and the appendix contains a complete table. The theoretical side of language training can well begin before the missionary ever leaves home. Since Europeans study other languages from childhood, and many speak several, they are sympathetic to all the problems. Once in Europe, the Christian worker should put his mind to the task with vigor. The mastery of a language is a speedy highway to the heart. To help in this we recommend the use of Dr. Eugene Nida's book, *Learning a Foreign Language.**

A Good Thing Perverted. Love of country can take several forms. Everyone realizes that a simple devotion to one's native soil, language, and customs is a natural, commendable feeling. Such an emotion the foreign missionary must accommodate and use for the furtherance of his work. He realizes that the more national every phase of his work is, the better he will succeed. After all, he reasons, only a locally-rooted testimony can serve the goals of total evangelization. There is no problem in this, for the gospel of Christ can fit any culture-pattern.

But another form of nationalism, political in nature, can be viciously *antiforeign.* Here pride of country is sometimes inflamed with the fires of hate and prejudice. In many parts of the world the press and other media of information either are government controlled or represent a partisan political viewpoint. The pictures painted of America's- foreign policy and way of life are often grotesque. Deliberate falsehood and exaggeration are used to indoctrinate the mind and produce a calculated reaction among the masses.

In 1958 former President Herbert Hoover spoke to a European-wide radio audience from the Brussels World's Fair about the dangers of exaggerated nationalism. Hoover scored the "false legends, misrepresentations, and vicious propaganda" about America as a country where "we live under the control of wicked men who exploit our economic life . . . grind the faces of the poor . . . exploit other nations." Summing up Mr. Hoover's speech, one of our national magazines deplored "an infectious nationalism which has developed even among our allies, a feeling partly the result of errors in U. S. foreign policy, but compounded too of ignorance, envy, frustration, and Communist propaganda."[1]

Balance Sheet of Prejudice. The more the missionary knows about the charges leveled against his country, the less they will upset him and the more free he will be to concentrate on his real mission. We summarize

*(Friendship Press, New York, 1957).

the general over-all attitudes of Europeans rather than dealing with the shifting ground of American foreign policy.

1. *Americans are materialistic.* Misunderstandings of this sort do contain a grain of truth, of course. America is the one country in the world which has openly glorified big business. Her own immigrants from Europe helped to spread the incredible rags-to-riches story of the New World. Our national hero-type has successively been the frontiersman, the self-made Horatio Alger boy, who climbs from office boy to president in the big city, and now the soft-spoken executive. In the minds of the world's humble and poor we stand for incalculable wealth. In our country you can gain more money for less work than anywhere else on earth. With this advantage comes grave responsibility, to which our awakening nation is only beginning to turn. But it is largely America's own fault if she has conveyed the impression that *things* matter to her more than the life of the spirit. That is the acquisitive image we have wrongly projected abroad through our books, films, magazines, business operations, and tourists. Now we are paying the price, and though we protest, our consciences hurt.

Of course this basis of truth has been distorted out of all reason. Perhaps it would be best to let a long-time European resident of America answer the charge that we are materialistic. Jacques Maritain, professor emeritus of philosophy at Princeton University, is a native of France known throughout the world of letters. He writes:

> I have already said that the American people are the least materialist among the modern peoples which have attained the industrial stage. . . . I would like to insist on this point, because few things, to my mind, are as sickening as the stock remarks with which many persons in Europe, who are themselves far from despising the earthly goods of this world, reproach this country with its so-called materialism. The power of this fable is so great that sometimes you yourselves are taken in by it . . . all this talk about American materialism is no more than a curtain of silly gossip and slander.[2]

Dr. Maritain finds no avarice in the American cast of mind. He points out that the very lack of hypocrisy about money which characterizes Americans makes Europeans, who associate the accumulation of money with avarice, uncomfortable. We add that materialism is a failing of the human race, not just of Americans.

2. *Americans are culturally shallow.* This view is a corollary of the first. According to the European, Americans are technological giants but cultural pygmies. The charge is hardly fair. Sometimes the nations of the Old World forget how young the New World really is. We are not yet two hundred years old as an independent country. Our first intellectuals came from Europe, which remains even today the source of many of our best minds in numerous fields. But a change is taking place. Today

a true American culture is emerging, a culture which is increasingly less dependent on Europe. Now the United States is beginning to export the intangible side of her life and thus to convince the world that she cares for art, music, literature, religion, and other things besides the sciences.

3. *Americans are conformists, not individualists.* Europe is convinced that Americans are the victims of massive and clever advertising, which forces them to buy in spite of themselves. Again, there is a partial truth in the picture. Because a large country invites a mass market, many of our products are identical. We dress much the same. We do not like to be alone; we are joiners. We talk over the back fence to our neighbors, and we like to be liked. On the other hand, most Europeans fight for privacy, deliberately limit their circle of close friends, cultivate individualism, and care less whether they are liked. There are so many notable exceptions, though, on both sides of the Atlantic, that generalizations are dangerous. Be that as it may, the stereotyped European view of American ways is far from accurate.

4. *Americans are chauvinistic.* This view applies more to the country as a whole than to the individuals which comprise it. Europeans harbor suspicion of America's motives in rebuilding Europe after the last war ("to provide yourselves a market"), a conviction that America is not so altruistic as she likes to appear. Our bounty toward Europe, for instance, is sometimes construed as veiled self-interest. Of course there is nothing essentially new in this view. As the rich man has grown richer, his poorer friends are sure that he gives out of his plenty, but not from the heart.

Part of this attitude rests on injured pride. The proud nations of the Old World do not like to think of themselves as weaker, since they are much older. This reaction is understandable. The American nation is regarded as an upstart, a boy among men. The galling truth is that Europeans have been dependent on this stripling, this Johnny-come-lately among countries. At this point in history western Europe can survive only by economic and defensive partnership with America. Even the pouring out of huge sums of money in aid and our intervention in two world holocausts have done little toward affecting the injured pride which arises from this dependence.

"Fifty years ago," an American publication recently recalled, "Europe's statesmen determined world policy, its bankers controlled world commerce, its fleets ruled the seven seas. But by 1945 Europe found itself dependent on America for protection, on its colonies for food, on the Middle East for oil. The old continental alliances had disappeared and no nation alone could guarantee the safety of its people."[3] An American can understand Europe better if he takes into account this psychological factor of inferiority. To make matters worse, since the above words were written Europe has lost still more colonies and has had her oil and mineral supply threatened more than once. No one can blame the Europeans if they show less dependence upon America in the years ahead.

Christians are Affected Too. In every country of the world where nationalism is an issue there are Christians who partly believe the allegations made about other nations and allow this to affect their fellowship with believers from those countries. Even though our new relationship with each other in Christ is one "where there is neither Greek nor Jew, circumcision nor uncircumcision, Barbarian, Scythian, bond, nor free," some Christians put national considerations before the truth that "Christ is all, and in all" (Col. 3:11). The verses that follow describe the communion that should flow from it: kindness, humility, meekness, longsuffering, forbearance, forgiveness. Such is the realizable goal God leads us to pursue. "We are citizens of heaven" (Phil. 3:20, Phillips), a citizenship more desirable than any on earth.

In Europe, sadly enough, some genuine believers in the Lord Jesus resent having foreigners serving side by side with them in the work of the Lord. The missionary would do well to be prepared for a less than enthusiastic reception by some individuals and groups in Europe, depending on where he is. As Alexander McLeish of England has put it, "The feeling of the European nationals is such that direct, personal help from foreigners will be difficult. . . . a strong feeling exists everywhere which resents Europe's being referred to as a mission field."[4] One would expect this to diminish in Latin countries, where Protestants are only a handful, facing another religious Goliath. Yet here, sometimes, definite anti-missionary feeling may exist.

The writer remembers a case in western Europe in which a large, important co-operative effort along evangelical lines was held up for months because one of its outspoken leaders was opposed to the participation of American missionaries resident in Europe. As these missionaries—who do not call themselves missionaries—searched their hearts in the matter before the Lord, they could find nothing in the nature of pride to explain such a reaction. They had approached this united effort by invitation of the Europeans with all humility, having something distinctive to offer. It was the view of the other Europeans in the project that the one person concerned was affected by nationalistic prejudice.

At a recent conference of foreign workers of German-speaking countries several outstanding German Christians were asked to speak to the American, Canadian, English, and Swiss audience. All these Germans made the same point about the foreign workers' relationships with German

Christians. They said that a new reaction about such help has risen among Protestant leaders in German-speaking Europe. When Germany was prostrate after the war, her leaders were more open. But as conditions improved and Germany regained her place among the nations, national pride reasserted itself. Henceforth, these workers prophesied, it will be increasingly difficult for foreigners to work with German leaders. These views are being confirmed as German co-workers of foreign mission organizations in Germany find themselves in an increasingly delicate position with their own people. Fortunately no such attitude is met among the German masses.

In a similar conference, this time in France, a French leader was asked to spell out frankly to the foreign workers of French-speaking Europe the errors of their ways. These workers were amazed at the pettiness of criticisms. At the same time they realized after genuine heart-searching, that little things, such as those outlined by the leader, can hinder what is always a sensitive fellowship. Many French Christians link their own faith, perhaps unconsciously, with the problems of France. In spite of themselves they believe some of the vicious things they read about America in their biased press, even though their foreign brethren have nothing to do with the political issue under attack there.

Some of this nationalistic Christianity asserts itself in an astonishing smugness, a conviction that the local way of doing Christian work is the only one possible, and cannot be improved upon. While not an outright criticism of foreign contributions, such an attitude is not receptive to anything that comes from abroad. On a practical level nationals may resent translated Christian literature (even if nothing local is available and the printing itself is done locally), messages interpreted by foreigners, (even messages by transients of unusual gifts who do not know the language), foreign gospel music (even though the words may be in the local language). While a mild insistence on national standards is normal, a harsh exclusion of all foreign influence betrays spiritual immaturity and failure to understand the oneness of the body of Christ.

A Two-way Street. We have spoken of nationalism among Europeans and especially among European Christians. Is it possible that the missionary to Europe, though called and dedicated to God, can be tainted with this same disease? Can he bear the prejudices of his homeland abroad and nurse them there for years? It is our observation that he can and sometimes does do this very thing. Nothing can queer him with his foreign brethren more quickly than the expression, "Back in America we used to . . ." Even to call himself a missionary when talking to a national may imply a certain feeling of superiority. Americans can easily

1940

display a nationalistic spirit without knowing it. Many young Christian workers have never before left their large and modern country for a foreign land. Never having conformed to another culture, they face an entirely new and humbling experience. Few are prepared, through the study of geography, history, language, and the arts, for residence in the Old World. The shortcomings of Americans in this realm can sometimes be serious. Not to know the names of Racine, Molière, or Corneille—and not to care to know—offends the type of Frenchman who makes a cult of the intellect. Then why does William of Orange mean so much to the Dutch? Or Garibaldi or Mazzini to the Italians? We should also show the deepest respect for the history, achievements, customs, and sufferings of the local Protestants. In addition there are the thousand and one tiny conformities to customs of everyday life to be learned. Can we drink a cup of southern European coffee, black, strong, and sickly sweet? Some declare they cannot drink it and never will. Others learn, and are surprised to discover that they even like it—by the grace of God!

We tend to be nationalistic in other matters than clothes, customs, and coffee. Must we import our whole structure of Christian work, cell by cell, into other countries? This is foolish, because with all our efforts we can never provide a background for our friends abroad that approximates our own. After all, is that really necessary or desirable? Do we need to Americanize the European before he can become an effective servant of Christ? Surely the New Testament teaches that the standards of discipleship for one age and race will succeed in all. Indeed, we have known European Christians whose saintliness and fruitfulness surpassed that of many of our countrymen. God is no respecter of persons.

As we divest ourselves of the idea that our home-grown evangelistic and organizational methods are indispensable to win Europe for Christ, a new understanding dawns. We begin to drop off the foreign mannerisms which are unessential to our message and offend local people. In this our approach is like that used to launch space satellites: initially-needed but finally-useless pieces are dropped away in the interest of getting the pay load—in our case, the gospel message—aloft. Adaptation is the only way to avoid foreignness in the Lord's work. Of course our message itself need never be modified, being eternal and unalterable.

Differences of Perspective. One strong reason for the national leader's attitude can be just his difference of perspective. The Lord Jesus commands his own to go to other countries with the gospel partly because the foreign viewpoint is a valuable one. Should the European visit our country, he would notice many unchristian aspects of our national life which would lead him to classify it as a "mission field." Yet these same

aspects we, as residents of our own country, may rationalize away or fail
to see at all. If that European should decide to become a missionary to
America, then *we* would need to swallow *our* pride and admit that things
are not what they should be in *our* country. Fundamentally the difference
is this: the European pastor tends to see things in his homeland through
his own conditioned eyes. History, tradition, local difficulties, and a
hundred influences enter in. Deeply involved in the *status quo*, he reflects the attitudes of intrenched Protestantism. The foreign missionary,
on the other hand, sees not so much what is already being done as what
remains undone. Yet let him beware of attempting to prove his case
for evangelizing unreached towns and multitudes by scorning the local
believers. Let him, instead, help national believers with one hand while
ministering to the unreached with the other. While a helpful, constructive
critique of the local Protestant situation has its place, it can never be
critical or abusive in spirit. Judgments will result in hurt feelings and
counterjudgments, thus hindering the advance of Christ's cause.

Another point involves the nature of the true Body of Christ. In the
Word of God the true Church is regarded as indivisible. Within it are no
racial barriers—neither Jew nor Greek. Nor are there cultural barriers—
neither Greek nor barbarian. Then it is interdependent. No member of
the Body can cut himself off from the others whom he needs. All are
accountable to the Head, the Lord Jesus Christ. If these things be true—
and they are—the foreigner must feel himself a part of the inner Church
even though he may not be indentified with its outer forms. He belongs
to every European brother or sister in Christ. The bond which holds
together this international, interracial, interdependent body is not an
organizational one. We are one in Christ, who enjoins us to love one
another. The foreigner with an open, loved-filled heart will almost always
be welcome in circles of true believers in Europe.

Slaying the Giant. What can those who are in the Lord's work do
when confronted by the giant of nationalism? They must do what David
did. He believed Goliath hindered the Lord's work, so he resolutely set
out to destroy him. In doing so he did not weigh himself down with
the bulky, conventional weapons Saul sought to press on him. Rather
he attacked with his shepherd's staff, his sling and stones, and above all
"in the name of the Lord of hosts, the God of the armies of Israel, whom
thou hast defied" (I Sam. 17:45). The result was inevitable: the Philistine
giant perished and God's honor was maintained.

Icy nationalism can melt in the presence of a soul whose spiritual tem-
perature is high enough. Love and humility have ever been the ultimate
weapons of the Christian confronted with resistance in any form. Edwin
Markham put it well in his verse, "Outwitted":

He drew a circle that shut me out—
Heretic, rebel, a thing to flout.
But Love and I had the wit to win:
We drew a circle that took him in.

Better still is the inspired counsel of Paul, the most successful missionary—
"I am made all things to all men, that I might by all means save some"
(I Cor. 9:22). A compassionate sensitiveness to the heart and mind of
others, when Spirit-directed, will win many of any culture, anywhere and
any time.

Kinds of Work. One of the first questions a prospective missionary
asks is, What kind of work shall I attempt? The following list outlines
the types of Christian work now being carried on by foreigners in Europe.
Others may be introduced in years to come. All are useful if we bear
in mind the ultimate long-range purpose—to leave leadership, churches,
institutions, and other activities in the hands of Europeans on a basis
which they can continue without foreign help.

Evangelism—Tent and hall campaigns, personal witness, telephone
evangelism, door-to-door visitation, home Bible classes, teen-age
rallies and school Bible clubs, businessmen's luncheons, high school
and university meetings, witness to special groups, such as Jews,
refugees, gypsies, etc.

Church-planting—Instruction of converts with a view to establishment
of local indigenous churches.

Teaching—Seminaries, Bible institutes, converts' classes, home study
groups, etc.

Literature—Bible distribution through bookstores, market sales, bookmobiles, expositions at fairs, newspaper ads, correspondence courses,
publication and distribution of tracts and booklets, editing of magazines, books, and special newspapers.

Radio—Program production, technical help, construction and maintenance of studios and equipment.

Gospel Billposting—Systematic posting of gospel text posters and
permanent road signs bearing offers of free Scripture and correspondence courses.

Music—Teaching of music theory in institutions, and performance
for evangelism, radio, etc. (A Christian conservatory of music is
needed in Europe.)

Children's Work—Preparation of materials (original and translated),
children's classes, teaching of teachers, free lending library of
flannelgraph materials, camp work, leadership training, etc.

Orphanages—Staffing and maintenance of orphanages with the specific
purpose of winning and holding children for Christ.

Bible Conferences—Deeper life training for pastors and leaders among
laymen, as well as for the average Christian.

Camps—Evangelism and teaching, for youth especially.

In determining what missions or organizations in Europe are engaged
in these activities, the reader may find the list of addresses in the appendix
helpful. By writing the missions concerned, an interested person may find
where he can best serve.

The Nonprofessional Missionary. God sometimes calls people to serve
Him abroad, either permanently or temporarily, by earning a livelihood
in some other way than in full-time Christian service. An estimated
175,000 United States citizens are overseas on federal payrolls (exclusive
of the armed forces proper). During an average year, another 500,000
are in other countries doing construction work. Other thousands of students and teachers are abroad, as well as businessmen at work with private
concerns. Then an army of tourists travels outside America each year.
Travel experts estimate that a million tourists a year will visit Europe in
the decade ahead.

A nonprofessional missionary, realizing that his first call and obligation is to make Christ known, deliberately seeks study or work abroad
which may open doors of witness closed to the foreign missionary himself. He has a unique opportunity to contact foreigners in a natural,
friendly manner. If he is to be in Europe only a short time and does not
know the language, he will still find many there who speak English,
especially among young people.

Two kinds of jobs are obtainable abroad: (1) those with United States
organizations which pay in dollars on an American wage scale; (2) those
which pay in foreign currency at a local wage scale. The former jobs
are crowded and harder to find, though better paying. While the latter
pay less, they offer greater opportunity for contacts with nationals. According to one source, there are as many as a million overseas jobs available. Even if a small percentage of those were filled by Christians, what
a help that would be!

Most positions with American organizations abroad call for some
particular skill. About half, we understand, require either college graduates or specialists of some sort. The girl graduate of a teachers' college,
secretarial school, or nurses' training has no trouble getting a job in her
line. The technician, stenographer, plumber, bricklayer, journalist, sales-
man or accountant can usually find his kind of work. Almost every American government agency sends people abroad. For jobs within the national
economy of a country, one must usually have a permanent or temporary
residence visa, even though most countries in free Europe can be visited

by touring North Americans without a visa. If possible, a prospective worker should get the residence visa before he leaves for Europe, as it is usually harder to get there. It is best to check with the embassy or consulate concerned in one's home country beforehand. Except for certain transient labor, most countries in Europe require the foreigner to have a work permit also. Usually the rule is that such a permit is granted only if a national cannot be found to fill the position. Yet there are loopholes. For instance, a foreigner can pick grapes in France or Switzerland or wait on tables in Norway, temporarily, without such a permit. Another interesting opportunity lies in the international work camps, where one gets little money but makes many contacts.

Some initiative is required for the nonprofessional Christian worker to go abroad. Almost certainly such a person will know everything about his work in advance. Yet if his heart burns to impart Christ to others and he is not afraid to venture, his opportunities for witness will probably amaze him.

One word of counsel. It is often wise for one who expects to work in an international youth camp, or even to study, to find a Christian friend of the same sex and approximately the same age to go along. This person will be a prayer partner and fellow witness. This is not essential, but helps on trips of a year or less.

A word ought to be added about the limitations of nonprofessional Christian work. Only a small percentage of time outside of one's work hours can be given to the Lord's service. This means that the primary witness must be limited to the few people contacted at work. Travel is likewise restricted, except during vacation periods. It is difficult for the nonprofessional missionary to form an accurate picture of a country's needs, because he moves within a circle restricted to a few people in one area. Of course this does not mean that a vital, successful ministry in such a field cannot be carried on by anyone truly called of God.

Bedfast pilgrims wait for miraculous healing at the grotto of Ste. Bernadette in Lourdes, the most popular religious shrine in the world.

Chapter 4

FRANCE, THE SMOLDERING FIRE

"It is one of the marvels of history that, while evangelical Christian doctrine has been so utterly deformed in France as to become un-recognizable superstition, yet a latent evangelism has never ceased to exist and manifest itself from time to time by outbursts of light which have astonished and frightened the lords of ecclesiastical power."

—REUBEN SAILLENS

"Humble yourself, impotent Reason! Hear from your Master your true condition, of which ye know nothing. Listen to God!"

—BLAISE PASCAL

"The Reformed must be taught to appreciate the Reformation."

—ALEXANDER VINET

1. *THE NATION AND ITS PEOPLE*

Beachhead Encounter. The year was 1944. Throughout the night our mighty invasion fleet silently edged closer into position for assault. Few of us aboard the landing craft had slept much. I had alternately prayed, consulted a Testament, encouraged my men, and studied the skipper's thick attack plan. Now, with the first hint of dawn, came H-hour. I gazed out across the choppy sea, straining to see the shore. Somewhere there ahead slept unsuspecting foes. Or did they know we were coming? If so, guns might open fire at any moment. Hours earlier bombers and gliders had winged over us, headed inland to destroy communications. Now the strain of not knowing what to expect, or when, grew almost unbearable.

Suddenly the whole world seemed to explode at once. Sound pounded with a fury that stunned the senses. Tracers and flares crisscrossed wildly. Instinctively we all pressed down against the deck. The first wave had just landed, meaning that we were due ashore in exactly eight minutes.

I clutched my gear—two musette bags filled with Scriptures and first aid equipment, pressed my helmet down tighter, and committed myself to the Lord. Minutes later I was in the water to my waist and felt the soil of France under my feet. We were to be on that soil for some time— or such was the plan. Little did I know that very shortly I would be gravely wounded and lie unconscious for three days before being flown back to America.

Soon after the landing I met my first Frenchman, a peasant dressed in typical faded blue, with a beret on his head. He was crossing himself fervently as he looked down at the endless lines of tanks, dozers, and trucks surging out of the sea and up over the sand. "Why do you cross yourself, *monsieur?*" I asked. "Wouldn't anybody—" he snorted, "to see, well—*this!*" He pointed to the amazing scene before us. "Oh," I ventured "I thought you might be a pious Catholic using the sign of the cross as a prayer." He stared incredulously at the naïve American who would make such a remark. Then, with an inimitable French shrug, he spat contemptuously. "*That* is what I think of all religion," said he. Suddenly he frowned as an afterthought struck him. "What has crossing oneself got to do with the church anyway?"

This irreligious Catholic, using meaningless religious gestures, was my introduction to a French phenomenon. Was he inconsistent? Not from his point of view. That I expected him, a rational individual, to reveal any such weakness as dependence upon God astonished him. Naturally I was surprised too. But then, so much about the French is unpredictable that I have had to revise my views about them countless times, and am still doing so. As someone has said, "Nothing is quite as it seems in France, where every valid generalization has its opposite, which is equally valid."[1] But from all my contacts with these unpredictable people, one impression lingers—the French need the Saviour, whether they admit it or not.

A Nation Waits. That first day in France raised a host of questions in my mind. Why does France, one of the world's leading powers, remain so ignorant of personal salvation through Jesus Christ? Why are her few Protestants, free at last to evangelize after centuries of persecution, so slow to seize their opportunity? Is it God's will that the biggest, most accessible country in western Europe should never hear His message? What can we who see the problem do?

These questions persist as the spiritual poverty of France becomes more fully understood. Just a few hours' flight from New York lie 36,000 French towns and cities without any organized Protestant witness for Jesus Christ. There are more unevangelized people in this country than the total American population west of the Mississippi. Only one hour by plane from London over forty million lost souls are almost overlooked by Great Britain's Christians. To win them, France's tiny Protestant force —two per cent of the population—seems inadequate. Bewildered by a changing world, the French masses seek something absolute. Most look to Rome or Moscow, rather than heavenward, for some personal meaning to the riddle of life. In this land the gospel is almost unknown by the common man.

One cannot travel widely in Europe without visiting France, which borders eight other countries.* Since the Second World War, thousands of missionary leaders, pastors, and Christian laymen have passed through this crossroads-country of Europe. Because their eyes are often on other destinations, like the Asian or African mission fields, few bother to investigate the local need in France. Maybe these are not to blame for failing to see the ready harvest fields around them: they have heard little and read less. France has few human advocates to represent her in missionary circles, for not many know the truth about her spiritual condition.

Across North America we have asked church people if they had ever before heard a direct report of the plight of France. Few had. "How many of you have ever prayed for France?" Almost none. In the face of such neglect, how can the Holy Spirit brood over the face of this deep? He works when and where we intreat His help. A nation which lacks intercessors will edge ever nearer the brink of moral collapse. France has long tottered there, unknowingly awaiting some nameless Saviour. Meanwhile foreign Christians who could pray, plan, and provide seem hardly aware of the problem. At best they have some vague idea that the Reformation settled everything. ("Wasn't John Calvin a Frenchman?") Even in tidy Switzerland next door some Swiss Christians are surprised to find that their French neighbors are so bereft of light. How localized we all are!

I grew up in a French African colony where my parents were missionaries. As a boy I saw the growth of what is today a husky, independent African church. Many years later two pastors of this native church telephoned me in the Paris suburbs. My father, they said, had led them to the Saviour while still youngsters. Naturally I asked them to speak at the European Bible Institute. Their impassioned words startled our French students. "We expected to find our French colonizers more Christian," they said. "But France is a pagan land, almost void of the knowledge of God. In our country it is easier to find the Lord than here in France. Our

*Spain, Andorra, Italy, Monaco, Switzerland, Luxemburg, Belgium, and Germany.

Christians in the African forest are more dedicated and burdened for souls, too. Why don't you evangelize your own mission field right here?"

Why not indeed? Of course they were right. As graduate students at the University of Paris, the largest concentration of students in the world, they had seen the tragedy at firsthand. In those ancient halls where half a million foreigners have studied, they had heard less about the Lord of life than had the students of 1530. For during 1529 John Calvin, while at the University, had come to Christ and let his joy be known. Soon all Paris was discussing his conversion. True, the school and city were smaller then. But 400 years later these Africans could find only a handful of real Christians among the 65,000 students from seventy nations. What do young students at this great university learn beyond their studies? Generally, the refinements of sin. To converse and carouse in Left-Bank cafés is part of the do-as-you-please way of life students traditionally follow.

Fortunately my African friends saw life beyond the university, which is hardly typical, after all. They traveled widely through the land, questioning, observing, and assimilating impressions. Was their conclusion— "France is a pagan land almost void of the knowledge of God"—justifiable? Is the claim that France is a mission field defensible? That is what we will investigate here.

Fire in the Ashes. Probably there have been Christians in France continuously since the first two centuries after Christ. We know that a Christian church existed in Lyons in the middle of the second century. Even during the Middle Ages, pre-Reformation Protestants, such as the followers of Peter Waldo, kept the truth of God's Word alive. Then in the sixteenth century France's own Reformation arrived. The movement under Calvin, one of the most profound thinkers of Christian history, was typically French in that it was original in expression (naturally God Himself was the true originator) and owed little to foreign influences. Throughout succeeding centuries, French Protestants were executed or tortured or exiled; the record of their experiences adds a glorious chapter to the history of martyrdom. This continuous, unbroken witness is the theme championed by Reuben Saillens in *The Soul of France*. He contends, rightly, that the light never failed completely in France, but was maintained across the centuries by what he calls a "latent evangelism."

Since a redemptive remnant, often weak and tiny, has continued some vital Christian witness across the years, we believe France's potential testimony for Christ to be significant. On the surface of French Protestant life lie gray, lifeless ashes of tradition, fuel previously consumed and now largely used. But put your hand to these ashes, and you will feel some heat. Stir them, and a weak red glow will appear. Breathe patiently on the embers beneath until they emit more light and heat. Now add fuel quickly while the little flame revives. The result? A blaze limited in intensity and extent only by the amount of fuel provided.

The analogy is obvious. Divine principles which govern revival are the same for the individual as for the church. God is always ready to meet the seeking heart more than halfway. Herein lies hope for this talented but soul-sick people. In a downtown Paris room on a dark side street, a little group prays every week for the spiritual awakening of France. Its composition changes now and then. Sometimes foreigners drop in. At other times a few French people carry on alone. For more than fifty years the prayer meeting has persisted, like the undying flame of the unknown soldier's tomb under the Arch of Triumph. Even war, strikes, and the upheavals of the nation have failed to kill it. God must heed the cry of His people in France for an ingathering, just as He once heard His captive Israel: "I have surely seen the affliction of my people . . . and have heard their cry . . . for I know their sorrows . . . and I am come down to deliver them" (Exod. 3:7, 8). France needs the breath of prayer to blow her embers into flame.

What the Gallic nation could become if her Christians would again begin to witness! At one time almost a quarter of the nation professed to be Protestant. When the Edict of Nantes was revoked in 1685, there were twice as many professing Protestants as there are today, even though France was only half as populous then as now. But for the next hundred years, to be openly Protestant usually meant death, exile, or a lifetime in the galleys. An ingathering of souls could move across today's France, we believe, with amazing speed and matching depth. The conditions for an awakening of conscience are there. As this nation has often and inexplicably revived in the political realm, she can awaken spiritually under the quickening power of the Holy Spirit. The perceptive French could quickly embrace the truth of salvation if they once heard it. A country which has sent out 15,000 Roman Catholic foreign missionaries—the largest contribution of any Catholic nation—could send out men on a far wider scale for the King of kings.

A Question of Attitude. France is an enigma to many. "Why do the French have so many political troubles?" people ask. "Are they really immoral? How can a people so creative and logical be so unpredictable? Why cannot the French discipline themselves, or develop their fine resources?" "The brilliance, yet the waste of its genius, makes France the most bewildering, provocative and irritating of all countries," declares David Schoenbrun. "No other nation has so won the affection and suffered the contempt of all the world."[2] Finally, there is that baffling but winsome, headstrong but charming Frenchman himself to mystify all foreigners.

A brief visit to France only heightens the puzzle. Because of lack of time and the barriers of different language and mentality, Christian visitors from abroad learn little about the people. Some who are curious about spiritual conditions find it difficult to get the facts. They see few, if any, Protestant churches and little of what is called "Christian activity" in Anglo-Saxon countries.

Although the French character has been often described by foreigners, rarely is it discussed from the Biblical standpoint and with accents of love. We Christians have no right to share in the attitude of worldly cynicism toward any land. So much has been written about France's problems that God's people, too, are in danger of viewing her after the flesh. Someone has said that "deeper discernment is always a call to intercession, never to criticism." Intercessors, not detractors, are what this key country needs today.

"France had the gospel and rejected it, so God is finished with her. Christians waste the Lord's money if they invest in that country." Thus spoke one of America's great industrialists as I sat in his spacious office. He went on to recount all the familiar, plaguing problems the nation has faced since the last war. Though a Christian, his attitude toward this country was warped and shallow. Christ, I pointed out to him, did not criticize Jerusalem as a disillusioned tourist, but wept over her as a compassionate Saviour. Yet this "holy" Jerusalem had once out-sinned Sodom! (Ezek. 16:48, 49) Compassion is what lost people anywhere need, and lost Frenchmen are no exception. Our attitude toward France may need the Holy Spirit's cleansing and clarifying.

Is France a twentieth-century mission field largely because Christians elsewhere have not cared enough to help her before? In one sense God is through with a city, nation, or continent only when *we* are through with it. How blessed it is to know though God considered Sodom's sin "very grievous," He still permitted an intercessor. "Abraham stood *yet* before the Lord." Faced by an advocate who cared, how could God fail to deliver "just Lot," though "as by fire"?

Europe's Largest Country. The French people, who are as much attached to their homeland as any people in the world, have every right to be proud of France in a natural sense. The country has been blessed of God by several extraordinary advantages. First, it is large enough to accommodate its population easily. Few countries of the continent have this advantage of uncrowded space. Since the postwar partition of Germany, France has become the largest nation of Europe in area; she is about 600 miles long by 550 miles wide, with almost 2,000 miles of coast-line. Nevertheless, the whole country would fit inside Texas!

Second, the geography of France has an unusual variety-amid-unity, similar to that of the United States. Two thousand years ago Julius Caesar compared France to the human anatomy, in which little is missing and nothing is superfluous. This balance between mountain and plain, pasture and woods, resembles a garden provided by God for man's use. Five massive mountain chains—the Alps, Vosges, Jura, Cevennes, and Pyrenees—determine the natural geographic divisions. Four principal river systems—the Seine, Loire, Garonne, and Rhone—with their tribu-taries and canals, form 2,500 miles of navigable waterways.

A third blessing is the bounty of farmlands, forests, and minerals. France is one of the few countries in Europe that can fully provide for her people's needs. With sufficient space and manpower to grow her own food, there is still enough left over for export. Other resources, like the recent oil discoveries in the Sahara, give France great potential stability, provided she can solve her political problems.

A negative side to this perfection is the average Frenchman's too-pat satisfaction with his own country. He is neither so curious about other places as most Europeans, nor has he as much "travel itch." He knows that he can find in his homeland fine ocean beaches (which the Swiss cannot), breath-taking ski trails (the Dutch lack these), desert, forest, and all the rest. "Why should I go elsewhere," he reasons, "when I have everything here?" While this is largely true, it does not help to broaden the French outlook.

Cradle for Civilization. Thomas Jefferson once called France "the second country of every civilized man." When the Romans invaded Gaul 2,000 years ago, it was divided, as every school child knows, into three parts. Ever since Julius Caesar defeated Vercingetorix at Alesia and began to Romanize Gaul, France has had a distinct mission as a great civilizing power. Someone has said, "Wherever the French flag goes, there goes a schoolhouse." I recall the dignity and civilizing graces the French admin-istration brought to backward natives in the African colony of my child-hood. Today that former colony is a free nation, with France as her sponsor.

Anyone who would bring the gospel to France must respect her culture and history even as he will learn to love her people. The adult foreigner may never become mentally French, but he can assimilate, with much profit, the language and learning of a wise and ancient people. He should remember the venerable contributions of France to world culture. For example, the University of Paris was already world-famous by the year

1200. (Oxford University, itself so ancient, is its child.) Between 1233 and 1289 the universities of Toulouse, Besançon, and Montpellier had been founded, the latter teaching anatomy, medicine, and surgery as early as the fourteenth century. At the time Columbus discovered America, France already had nine universities and thirty-nine printing presses!

But why emphasize these things if our interest in France is purely spiritual? Because love and respect are indivisible. What one writer pens about the attitude of Americans should never apply to Christians: "Like the British, Americans look down upon the French as an inferior race, lazy, immoral, and inefficient. France, for most Americans, is a land of bad women and bad plumbing."[3] While the foreign Christian faces the realities of French life, he must do so with love and understanding, knowing his own wayward heart.

A foreigner should fully acknowledge the debt the world owes, in terms of human accomplishment, to France. How tactless for a Christian worker to ignore what is good and worthy in the culture he serves! What would an American think of a Frenchman who lived all his adult life in America without being able to identify Alexander Hamilton or the Boston Tea Party? Or the New York Yankees or Custer's Last Stand? To the Frenchman, history is the life-stuff of his nation, and the foreigner does well to learn this. Schoenbrun's remarks on this attitude are worth careful review:

> To Americans, all history is ancient. America is the country of tomorrow. France, however, is the land of yesterday, and to the French all history is contemporary. The past, for the French, is one with the present, in a continuous stream of life. . . . You cannot escape from history in France. It is all around you, in the newspapers and on the billboards and boulevards of Paris.[4]

Whenever we turn on an electric light, we owe something to a French physicist named Ampère. Whoever drinks a glass of pure milk acknowledges Pasteur. Thanks to Louis Braille, the blind can read with their fingers. We even measure our intelligence by an IQ test for which Binet set certain standards. The list of France's greats is long and impressive in both the arts and the sciences. One sure way to the French heart is through genuine appreciation of what they have contributed to the world. I recall an evening visit with an old gentlemen in Toulouse. He spent an hour and a half explaining certain aspects of the Second Empire, using some of his faded heirlooms as signposts to point us through the maze of history. I was intrigued and showed my interest. The result? An open heart God could bless.

The Recurring Nightmare. Throughout her whole history the verdant French paradise has always been vulnerable to invasion, especially from the east. Many rulers have coveted the rich price so easy to reach by several routes. From the fourth century on, hordes of Goths, Vandals, Huns, and Franks poured into Roman Gaul through the cleft between the Alps and the Jura called the Belfort gap. The Arabs came around the flank of the formidable Pyrenees from Spain, as did Wellington in 1814. Both Norsemen and Englishmen boldly sailed into ports and up rivers. Spaniards, British, and Germans used the Low Countries as a northeast passage. Of course, by these same routes the French themselves went out, under Napoleon Bonaparte and others, to ravage other countries.

Though a Frenchman talks little about the threat of war and deprivation, it is always on his mind and forms a facet of his character. With good reason, too. During the last thousand years, almost every adult French person has known war intimately, either as a civilian or soldier, at home or abroad. In the last 856 years France has spent 400 years in formal wars! This does not include innumerable local "brush-fire wars" in the provinces, especially during the Middle Ages. In the last 200 years alone, seven great wars and numerous revoluions have ravaged France. Three of the more recent attacks have come from the same enemy within three generations.

The First World War cost France the staggering casualty rate of 73 per cent of all her men mobilized over the whole period of conflict. One out of five adult French men either died or was gravely wounded as a direct result of the war. A million were permanently maimed. In the Second World War the dead and missing totalled 1,345,000. (A comparative loss for America, percentagewise, would be fifteen per cent more than her actual casualty rate.) Over a million homes were wrecked by war, 360,000 of them completely destroyed. Six million acres of farmland were devastated, and 80 per cent of the industrial production was either destroyed or vandalized. Many people do not realize that France was, until the Algerian war ended, the only nation in the world which had been continuously at war since 1939. The deep moral blows to individual and family can never be fully known. But the resulting state of national nerves, which we will now consider, is a part of French life the foreigner must view with sympathy.

Are the French Anti-American? Though World War II is now some years past, we are living in its immediate backwash. Of course France has completely recovered from the war economically and has gone on to break all her own previous records for expansion and production. But the friend of France must realize that she is still suffering otherwise from defeat and disaster. Because of the quick, ignominious downfall in 1940, and regardless of its causes, the French suffer a national inferiority complex. Psychologically, they are still touchy about being beaten so easily by the same old enemy. To be rescued a second time by America and the allies is humiliating in itself, since France considers herself a world power. The further step of accepting Marshall Plan aid was necessary for survival, but who enjoys being forced to accept charity and then acknowledge it afterwards? No one likes to admit he ever stood in a breadline.

Much of what might be called "anti-Americanism" is just this injured pride. Prolonged, costly wars, loss of colonies, and reduced sphere of world influence have complicated the situation further. As for American life and ideas, the average Frenchman is very ignorant of them—a situation worsened by heavy Communist propaganda, which cleverly plays up certain weak points. But the French are not so much anti-anyone as they are pro-French. Who can blame them for wanting to see their national glory and leadership restored? Yet when either the United States or France is in a corner, traditional friendship reasserts itself: the French owe much to America and they know it. Besides that, America and France are the only major powers in the world which have never waged formal warfare against each other! A distinction must always be made between French words and deeds. The deeds count more. The French prefer to show their debt in their own way, from a position of restored strength and prestige rather than from a state of weakness and dependence.

The foreign Christian working alongside the French can find the path to their hearts if he tries. The secret is to treat them as equals (which they surely are), and to find what is praiseworthy (there is so much!). Above all, he must never indulge in the bad American habit of boasting. The activated love of Christ always opens doors, and France is one of the easier places in our present world in which to manifest that love sincerely.

Living the French Way. The body exists to be pleasantly nourished, conversation enlivens the mind, and the family circle satisfies man's craving for affection. Add to this simple credo a touch of religion, café companionship, and a seasonal vacation, and you have the Frenchman's basic life-pattern in a few words. Of course there are exceptions.

The intimacy of home life deserves further comment. Usually a house outside urban areas is surrounded by walls, to protect a person's property from pillage and the prying eyes of neighbors. What a Frenchman does may be his own business, but his neighbors try to make it theirs. Though their curiosity is veiled (direct personal questions are taboo), they are observant enough to know much that goes on behind the walls. In city apartment houses the *concièrge* or guardian carries on this silent investigation. The home-dweller, who regards his house as his castle, is extremely jealous of his privacy. Here one sees little of our over-the-hedge chatting with folks next door, for self-reliance is a byword to the French. Yet there is something pathetic about such lonely self-sufficiency. The "mentality

of the walls" mirrors a deep heart need of a God who can free from
suspicion and fill one's heart with love for others.

The outside of a house is plain and unpainted, and the landscaping
negligible, since the government heavily taxes what it calls "the outward,
visible signs of wealth." Inside, the cozy atmosphere exudes a lived-in
feeling. The furnishings are usually unimpressive. Antique rather than
functional furniture predominates. Only the living room is open to the
casual visitor. No Frenchman, and for that matter, few Europeans, would
show anyone more than he needs to see. Modern conveniences, though
they are arousing new interest now, are relatively unimportant to the
French. For one thing, they have known repeated lootings of hearth and
home for centuries. For another, they are experts at making do with
little. They can improvise, patch things up, or make unworkable equipment run with amazing ingenuity. But this has its bad side as well. The
conviction that they can always "muddle through" sometimes keeps the
French from doing things neatly, thoroughly, and with dispatch.

The French think of home more as a place to relax than as a place
to entertain outsiders. The wife spends a great deal of her time on food
preparation. Probably the most familiar sight in the land is the women
coming home from the *boulangerie,* several times a day, with long loaves
of bread in hand. Since few families have refrigeration, the average
woman must often shop at least twice a day in the neighborhood market.
Children are cherished and indulged from birth. The sons are especially
close to their mothers. Even after marriage a son commonly consults his
mother, rather than his father, on matters which puzzle him most.

Getting to know the neighbors is not always easy at first. Most of
the French are not backslappers, hail-fellows-well-met, or borrowers of
their neighbors' lawnmowers. But they can be reached with prayer and
perseverance. One way is through their children. By starting children's
Bible classes in our own home, we slowly began to know our neighbors
in suburban Paris. Any kindness to children is an open highway to the
heart. Then there is the emergency. We live just beyond a sharp,
somewhat blind curve, where accidents are likely to happen. Once a half-
drunk motorcyclist failed to make the turn and smashed into our wall.
We picked him up, treated him for shock, and called the police ambulance.
When the neighbors congregated at our door, we found them strangely
warm, congenial, and talkative.

The 445,000 cafés in France (one for every thirty-four adults) fill the
need for social life. They are primarily for conversation, which is induced
and sustained by liquor or *café noir.* Here every man can expand his
ego with knowing comment on sports, politics, or current complaints.
Normally Frenchmen do not humbly ask questions of each other or qualify

their statements very much. They give strong opinions in incisive words barbed with Gallic wit and punctuated with gestures. Yet they reserve for others the right to be equally dogmatic. Most cafés are stopping points for men or women on their way to or from work, or while awaiting someone. But they are also places to talk over business deals, write letters, or read papers. Usually a person patronizes favorite cafés which suit his personality and pocketbook. There are workman's cafés, literary cafés, sport club cafés, student cafés, sidewalk cafés, and tourist cafés. Usually a meal can be ordered at the back table, and a cold snack is available at at any hour.

Vacation time is a fixed concept which cannot be altered short of death or war. When the summer vacation comes, the small business is closed down and its owner heads for the country and fresh air. In August, over a million Parisians leave, while the foreign tourists arrive to stare at each other in bewilderment ("Where *is* everybody?"). A Paris quip claims that "a person who dies in the summer cannot be buried until the fall." At this season the knowledgeable Christian worker seeks to evangelize where the people are, in camps, at the seashore, or among the mountains.

Class and Caste. Although France is known for her ideals of "liberty, equality, and fraternity," all social levels are quite firmly fixed. Americans and others may move upward from class to class, with corresponding rises in opportunity. Not so in France. In almost every case an individual remains frozen in the class in which he was born, no matter how much he dislikes it. As one report has noted, "France is a land of rock-bound social strata. Her younger generation is locked at birth into firmly built cell-blocks from which escape is virtually impossible and even temporary parole difficult. . . . Class boundaries in France are often as rigid as Hindu caste lines."[5] No dentist's daughter would ever elope with a mechanic's son. Nor would a shoemaker's boy achieve a Sorbonne professorship. Business people usually remain in business, and government employees in government. To be sure, there is a limited changing-over of jobs, but usually within the same category. On top of the pile are the two hundred families of the snobbish, inbred upper caste who have lived for centuries on inherited wealth in the same great estates. The marriage of a Rockefeller to a foreign housemaid does not happen here. Sons of the great families go to exclusive schools, marry into the right circles, and are carefully prepared for positions of power and leadership.

The Peasant Profile. France, the last major European power to industrialize on a large scale, remains primarily a rural nation. Half of the people live either on small farms or in towns of less than two thousand population. How did this come about? At the time of the Revolution the government seized land from the church and the nobility (which between them had held most of it), and parceled it out to the people. As a result the peasants have an unusual attachment to their land. Three-quarters of the farms are owned by those who work them. Usually they are farmed with little outside help, and are passed from father to son, century after century. Only 25 per cent of the farmers are *metayers*, or tenants; these sharecroppers receive both livestock and equipment from the landowner, to whom they return a fixed proportion of the total income as rent. Widespread land ownership gives the French farmer much more independence than his counterpart in Italy, Spain, or Portugal. France also surpasses the other Latin nations in the fertility of its soil; only 15 per cent of the country is entirely unfit for cultivation. But there are drawbacks too. Often a man's holdings are divided into a crazy quiltwork of strips miles apart. Only by hard work can the peasant turn a profit, but at least he is quite self-sufficient.

Since the peasants are many and enjoy economic independence, they naturally have a powerful political voice. Every government courts them, but they are difficult to handle, not being organized as a party. Each man is on his own, and rarely does he join the others in common action. Yet peasant revolts are traditional. In the past decade there have been at least seven; in 1953 and 1961 for instance, farmers barricaded roads and paralyzed communications in some counties.

Though the peasant is often sarcastically caricatured in French literature, it is important to understand him. By tradition frugal, fiercely protective of his rights, and conservative to the point of narrowness, he reigns over his twenty-five acres from his 300-year-old stone house.* What happens outside his own fences is secondary to him. He refuses to be coerced by "those rascals from Paris," and will defend his home and land with shotgun, pitchfork, or his own hands, if need be. Rather than lend money to the government or entrust it to a bank, he buries it in the ground or hides it under a mattress. Distrustful of strangers and of progress in many forms, he watches like a hawk for the hated government tax-collector, often his sole contact with authority in any form. This hard-drinking, quick-tempered farmer brews his own moonshine and argues with his neighbors over boundaries and prices. Almost daily the national press reports murder, suicide, or violence among the peasants. This son of the soil shrugs off the jibes of city-dwellers, as his ancestors did, with sardonic wit.

With all his eccentricities, the peasant can be won to Christ. Some families have remained steadfastly Protestant for centuries, even though

*Many houses are this old. The average size farm is only twenty-five acres. Only a quarter of the agricultural area has farms of 250 acres or more.

surrounded by a sea of Catholics. The Christian worker will find the average peasant nominally, but often superficially, Catholic. Superstition and provincialism are large factors in his life. His suspicious surliness toward outsiders will sometimes melt into kindness when he becomes convinced of another's sincerity. Of course the best person to win him is another French person, preferably a farmer like himself who can win his confidence. But wise is the man who realizes that there is a little of the peasant mentality in every Frenchman, whether he lives on the farm or not. As a matter of course he resists collective authority and thinks for himself.*

Paris is a World. For several reasons Paris deserves unusual attention from any who hope to help evangelize France: (1) It is the capital and administrative center. (2) Over 16 per cent of the people of France live in its metropolitan area. (3) The Catholic hierarchy considers it the most irreligious spot in the country. (4) It dominates the life and thought of the French in a marked way. (5) Europe and all the world are influenced by it.

For some years we have collected expressions about Paris which attempt to epitomize the city in a single phrase. Together their brush-strokes paint a picture which may help the foreigner to understand the importance of the city on the Seine. Charles Morgan, the renowned English writer, characterizes Paris as "the heart that pumps the blood of civilization." Others have called it: the most brilliant visitor-city in the world . . . the great lodestar of travelers . . . the glittering gem of all Europe . . . the fashion center of three continents . . . the playtown of the world . . . the city with everything for everyone . . . the capital of taste and vice . . . the world center of art and culture . . . the world's liveliest carnival of ideas . . . a paradise for fun, food, and fashion . . . the greatest concentration of learning on earth . . . the last redoubt of the individual.

Henry IV (1589–1610), the Protestant king who turned Catholic, rationalized his conversion by the phrase, "Paris is well worth a mass." Robert Browning wrote lyrically of "fair, fantastic Paris." Later, successive generations of Americans and English discovered that fairness and fantasy for themselves. The inter-war expatriates and writers like Ernest Hemingway, Scott Fitzgerald and John Steinbeck planted the desire in American minds to visit the city of sparkling café conversation. Since World War II thousands of soldiers and students have had their look and left. Today travel writers make a visit to the City of Light sound like a pilgrimage to some Mecca where the restless traveler will supposedly find himself at last.

*Those who desire to learn more about French peasants should read the account of an Englishman who lived among them for twenty years: *The Generous Earth,* by Philip Oyler (London: Hodder and Stoughton, 1950).

Perhaps Louis XIV, the Sun King who ruled France for seventy-two years, was right when he said that "Paris is not a city, but a world." One thing is sure: since the many-sided city is the fulcrum of France, the country cannot be fully evangelized without it. Look at any road, rail, or air map of France. All transportation radiates out from the city like spokes from a wheel. On a larger scale, most of the great European trains originate or terminate in Paris, and every major European airline serves it. In international *élan* the city-that-is-a-world excels. As Donald C. McKay writes in a Harvard University publication:

> Paris has long been the intellectual capital of the world, and one of the surest indications of this is the variety and importance of the work that has been accomplished there by intellectuals of other countries. . . . Paris is an international city in the full sense of the word, a possession not merely of the French but of all men to whom the western tradition is vital.[6]

Some will say, "You cannot judge France by Paris. Paris alone is not France." This is true in one way. But then, is any other country of comparable size so dominated by one city? Though there are twenty-two French cities with more than 100,000 people each, all are lustreless beside the capital. For instance, Marseilles, the second in size, is a great seaport. Yet in culture and influence it is not even a worthy rival. Someone has rightly stated that, Paris being what it is, "France has only one city." By comparison the others are quite provincial.

The two-thousand-year-old metropolis, once called Lutetia by the Romans, contains about one-quarter of all French factory workers, salaried business employees, and civil servants. Over half of the bank and financial workers and 71 per cent of all insurance employees live and work in Paris. The concentration started long ago. The Revolution abetted it and Napoleon Bonaparte, with his passion for centralization, perfected the system. Problems arising in the swollen city, which is slowly suffocating the country, recently triggered a government study by French engineer Robert Gondouin. In his report Gondouin calls the city a bottleneck retarding national Progress. He urges the dispersion of French industry and government offices, and wants more provincial universities built in order to break the near-monopoly of Paris as a seat of learning. As Herbert Luethy remarks, "Paris has turned the rest of France into an intellectual desert."[7]

For evangelistically-minded Christians, the centrality of Paris is significant. Any idea, to capture the nation, must win support in Paris. In politics, a revolution germinated in Algiers had to explode in Paris in order to influence the national scene. A Poujade may stir up tax-burdened shopkeepers all over France, but Paris will have the last word. A business in the provinces will never be on the map nationally without an office—or better still, its head office—in the capital. "The empty and impoverished life of most French villages and provincial towns . . . is the result of this centralism," says Luethy. "All France is laid waste and her vital energy sucked into Paris."[8] Half of the national income is concentrated in the nine counties around the capital, though they comprise only one-ninth of the country. To feed omniverous Paris, the countryside is slowly depopulated in a process comparable only to that experienced by Ireland. Every provincial looks toward this giant sponge for survival and renewal. For instance, France has only one real food market, *Les Halles* in downtown Paris, to which most farm products must come for resale, then return to the areas where they originated—at many times the original price.* Politically, the state's apparatus of bureaucracy directs the destiny of the common man from Paris, regardless of which government is in power.

2. *INSIDE THE GALLIC SOUL*

The Moral Sag. Experts abound who can tell us "what is wrong with France," but few spell out these problems so well as the thinking Frenchman himself. With his renowned clarity of observation, the French leader, who loves to "see things as they are," spells out his people's difficulties with candor. His conclusion? France's long-standing problem is moral.

Napoleon Bonaparte, the country's greatest military hero, once said that "France has always had plenty of men of talent, but is always deficient in men of action and high character."[9] This view is often echoed today. Marshall Pétain, who in spite of his World War II treachery loved his country, spoke of "our moral laxness and our pleasure seeking" as reasons for the 1940 collapse.[10] "We no longer respect each other," cried Premier Schumann after the war; "we know not how to command or obey."[11] Guy de Carmoy, the distinguished French economist, agrees that "in great part the French crisis is moral."[12] In *The Taxis of the Marne* Jean Dutourd writes bitterly of a France "lurking on the back stairs for years, half asleep, its mind a blank, incapable of reflection, merely able to repeat, as it goes down the steps that lead to hell, 'But I do not intend this . . .' "[13] André Malraux, a leading intellectual, concludes that "France is saturated with lies, hypocrisy, and empty promises . . . the image of man as it existed in Christianity has lost weight."[14] Nobel prize winner François Mauriac wrote thus of his countrymen in the Paris newspaper, *Figaro:*

*Paris city officials are now studying the possibility of relocating *Les Halles* at the edge of the city and reducing its role to only one link in a new national system of food distribution.

We must conclude that their bad political habits are linked with their bad character. The saying that character is destiny applies to nations as well as individuals. Institutions do not change because men do not change.[15]

Foreign observers agree with the French. The perceptive Swiss, Herbert Luethy, describes France as convinced of its own greatness as well as pitilessly self-critical. Yet these two insights, says he, "very seldom come into contact with one another." He finds a moral paralysis at the heart of things: "France finds it easy to pass laws but difficult to take action, even when she wants to." He believes that this is "in many ways the most disordered and inconsistent country in the world," for "French laws are formally passed and policies adopted which are never put into practice. . . . Frenchmen are quick to recognize the ideal course of action and pass laws proclaiming it . . . they are particularly adept at pretending that a proclamation is just as good as, if not infrequently better than, action."[16]

This moral lapse finds national, collective expression in politics and economics, but its true cause is veiled to the natural man. From the standpoint of the Bible, France's problem is that her people need Christ as Saviour and Lord. Only He can provide the strong moral fiber missing from private and public life. There is nothing wrong with France that Jesus Christ cannot right.

Spiritual Poverty. Many who know the Lord here are aware that France's need is fundamentally spiritual. "The French drama is in fact a moral drama," says Dr. André Lamorte, a well-known Protestant leader. "The meaning of the words reaches beyond the framework of frivolous morals, of which France no longer has the monopoly. The moral revolt of France is largely written in contemporary life. Evidences may be found in the widespread religious indifference and atheism, in social evils, in the increase of mental illness and in other aspects of the national life."[17]

In the nineteenth century Adoniram Judson, the pioneer Baptist missionary to Burma, was forced to spend six months in a French jail. Even from this vantage point, he could see the problems and possibilities of the nation: "An evangelized France would stimulate all intelligent classes in Europe."[18]

Mr. Barrington Tatford, British layman, author, and editor, feels that his countrymen must do more to help:

France needs a thousand missionaries. How near it is to the coast of Britain, yet new missionaries pass it by to travel thousands of miles to fields which are no needier! Only twenty miles from the shores of so-called "Christian England" lies a country whose missionary need is perhaps greater than that of any country of the world.[19]

Mr. Eric Hutchings, Britain's Hour of Revival radio evangelist, who periodically leads evangelistic efforts in France, is convinced of France's need: "You ask me: Is France a mission field? Emphatically and unequivocally, Yes!"[20] Dr. T. Christie Innes, of the American Tract Society, calls on Christians to "witness the continuing spiritual desolation of the French people—a whole century and a half after atheism swept the nation in the seventeen nineties."[21]

Between Red and Black. The French people are not in profound spiritual darkness, as some imagine, because they surpass others in rebellion against God. They are lost for the very reasons their fellow human beings are—because they do not know Jesus Christ. Many Frenchmen show humanity's universal subconscious longing to be free from the tyranny of sin. Yet there are some historic reasons why the gospel of Jesus Christ has not shone clearly here in modern times.

In France a basic dualism is always at work. The Frenchman is a product of the ideals of the Revolution on one hand, and of his traditional religion on the other. Understand the connection between these two influences and you go far toward understanding the French mind. Usually both ideas exist in the same person: those whom Pierre Maillaud calls *blasés.* To be sure, occasionally one does meet the rabid revolutionary or the convinced Catholic whose views are mutually exclusive. Once I spoke with a steelworker outside a gospel tent in the Paris suburb of St. Denis. There was no doubt where he stood: he was red all the way, cursing the church and God. Another time I sat in the office of a *notaire* in Boulogne. This lawyer-notary was at the black end of the spectrum, a pious Catholic who dreamed of restoring a prodigal France to the arms of the Holy Father. He spoke feelingly of a coalition of Latin Catholic nations who could rebuild the Vatican's strength in Europe.

Of this dual French personality Thomas Kernan says, "If I were constrained to describe it in a phrase I would use the title of Stendahl's novel, *The Red and the Black.* The red personality of France may be said to be progressive, revolutionary, anti-clerical, Jacobin . . . the black personality is conservative, orderly, Catholic, classic, aristocratic, Latin."[22] Kernan goes on to point out that this distinction is not restricted to class or economic standing. Generally the Blacks are provincial, agrarian, and interested in traditional ways. In contrast, the Reds want real "liberty, fraternity, and equality," as well as more progress in industry in the cities where they tend to gather. The Blacks are not always exclusively Catholic, but retain much church thinking; nor are the Reds always Communist, though many are socialists who stem from the same antecedents. Today's Blacks are personified by the priests, with their authority and obscurantism, while the real revolutionary leaders are the socialistically-minded state school teachers who shape young minds. In Luethy's words, "Teachers of history are the priesthood of the republican faith. The teaching staff of the lay schools, centrally organized in hierarchic fashion like the priesthood of an anti-faith, has assumed functions on the behalf of the republic which the clergy exercised on behalf of the *ancien régime;*[*] they are the militant priesthood of the republican regime."[23]

Reason's Bankrupt Heirs. The black Catholic we shall consider later, but what of the red, reactionary-minded person? Or more precisely, what of the republican streak found in almost everyone's make-up? The Frenchman cherishes his personal liberties won at such cost through the Revolution of 1789. He remembers his deliverance from decadent absolutism and medieval oppression, and especially from religious tyranny. Every Frenchman prides himself on his ability to think and act for himself, and knows whence this freedom springs historically. Even professing Catholics express the republican attitude by keeping the Vatican—and especially the Jesuits—at arm's length. "Let the Church take care of our souls," they say, "but we will take care of the rest." These red-tinged people traditionally vote to the left, oppose Catholic schooling, and espouse more-or-less radical causes.

We who desire the salvation of French people can be glad that they once reacted against Roman Catholic tyranny over their souls. All the ideas behind the Revolution, which occurred only 174 years ago, have yet to work themselves out in time, but their influence over the French mind is as fresh as though expressed yesterday. No political speech worthy of the name omits emotional references to the birth of the republic. The president is pointedly called the President of the Republic. But did the free-thinking philosophers of the eighteenth-century French Enlightenment lead the Frenchman closer to God? No, they led him *out* of one evil *into* another. New demons entered to torture the swept and garnished soul as never before. A god named No-God replaced the contrived god of Rome. This helps explain why most French people make poor Catholics and are basically irreligious today. It also interprets that startling Frenchman, the sceptic with a religious veneer I met on the beachhead in 1944.

A brief glance at the pre-Revolution thinkers will fill in the background. Voltaire, Rousseau, d'Alembert, Montesquieu, Condillac, Diderot, and others laid the groundwork for the tremendous social and political changes which rocked the world. Under Diderot's leadership they worked together to produce a comprehensive encyclopedia of all human ideas.

ancien régime refers to the pre-revolution monarchy before 1789.

The series of thirty-five volumes, produced between 1751 and 1780, became a testament of the philosophers on the new freedom of mind to which man was heir.

Enlightened, but Unredeemed. The Age of Enlightenment was not exclusively French, but the French dominated it. Locke, Newton, Pascal, Hobbes, Descartes, and many others had been its forerunners. Now the philosophers of Nature, Reason, and Man had their day. Naturally they differed in approach and often quarreled. Voltaire was an active cynic, Montesquieu a detached observer, and Rousseau a sincere reformer. Not all were outright atheists; each was in some degree a self-styled naturalist, materialist, or deist. One thing they did agree upon: man, who was naturally good, could become supreme over his world provided he cast off the chains of tradition, religious superstition, and fear. A new age of optimism had dawned.

Charles Louis de Secondat, Baron de Montesquieu (1689–1775) heavily influenced those who wrote the American Constitution and was quoted in *The Federalist*, the commentary on the constitution written by Alexander Hamilton, James Madison and John Jay. In his *Spirit of Laws* Montesquieu said that "law in general is human reason." Of course that left out any responsibility to God and His laws. Amazingly, in his *Persian Letters* he even got away with calling the Pope "an old idol worshipped out of habit." Then La Mettrie published *Man is a Machine* in 1748, asserting that man is a biological being governed by the same laws which apply to animals. This was followed in 1754 by a volume on materialism by Etienne de Condillac entitled *Treatise on Sensations*. In the same year Diderot gave the public his *Interpretation of Nature*, which declared man's independence of a supreme being. D'Alembert's *Treatise on Dynamics* followed a similar theme. It soon became fashionable to be "enlightened." In fact, rulers like Frederick the Great of Prussia and Catherine the Great of Russia became "enlightened" despots.

Voltaire, whose real name was François-Marie Aronet), by living to the age of eighty-four was contemporaneous with all others (1694–1778). His satire and cold mockery were directed at any form of tyranny, but especially at the Roman Catholic Church, which he felt was the supreme tyranny of all. His watchword, *ecrasez l'infame* (crush the infamous thing), applied to all forms of tradition that darken man's mind. In the *Philosophic Letters* and other works, Voltaire, in short, blunt sentences, acidly attacks hypocrisy and humbug. But his fight for tolerance and reason had no faith in God at its base. A professed deist, the brilliant Voltaire died in nominal adherence to Rome, though denying the deity of Christ.

But the Man of the Century was undoubtedly the Genevan, Jean Jacques Rousseau (1712–1778). He was a true revolutionary, who "broke away from every French tradition, either intellectual or spiritual, on absolutely fundamental principles."[24] Napoleon Bonaparte stated that without Rosseau the French Revolution would never have occurred. The impact this genius made on world thought in the eighteenth century was incalculable. Like the scholastics, he reasoned by postulates and axioms, but toward a different goal. His system championed man, not God. He asserted the fundamental goodness of man under the benign smile of nature. For almost a century Rosseau's social and ethical teachings powerfully influenced the French mind. Unlike Voltaire, he showed some feeling for religion and even some appreciation of it, though he was a deist.

The Geneva watchmaker's son was an eccentric social misfit. For many years he lived with an illiterate servant girl whose five children he sired and turned over to an orphanage. Though he failed to educate his own illegitimate children and had little formal education himself, he expressed bold new ideas about what naturalistic education could accomplish. Turn loose a child after some basic instructions, he recommends in his novel *Emile,* and natural development will do the rest. Conscience is a safe enough guide for man, who is inherently good. Politically, the *Social Contract* (1762) continued the same thought. Man is socially involved with other men; he can shape his own destiny apart from any imposed, outside authority. What is good in Rousseau's concepts probably came from his Protestant upbringing. What is bad stemmed from his attempt to hold Christianity's principles of human dignity without accepting the Founder of Christianity. Though Rousseau admired Jesus Christ, he did not worship Him.

This kind of thinking led to what is called the Age of Reason. During the second, more violent phase of the Revolution, the leaders installed the Goddess of Reason on the high altar of the Cathedral of Notre Dame. Human reason replaced revelation from God in any form. Naturally the established church was the first and principal sufferer. The half-conscious resentment of the people throughout the centuries now reached full expression. The holdings of the Catholic Church, estimated to exceed 10 per cent of the country's land, were seized. One of her chief sources of income, a rough third of the sale of all farm and dairy products, was cut off. It was not safe to profess any sort of religious belief during this period. "Thousands of priests, and most of the ministers that were left, were constrained under pain of death to bring their sacred things— vestments, chalices, etc.—to the altars of Reason, declaring that they renounced all superstition."[25]

French National Traits. Of course human nature is basically the same wherever you find it. This is especially true when we study man, as we always must, from the Christian perspective. If a foreign Christian looks at this history-conditioned Frenchman today through the eyes of His Lord he sees only the reflection of himself. All the sinful desires and habits which the French manifest are his as well. As Scripture reveals, there are no priviliged people who deserve salvation. So any difference we note here between other nationalities and ours are only surface ones, useful though they may be.

Is there a French national personality? The French say so, and so does every competent observer. After residing in France for more than a dozen years, I agree that some basic characteristics stand out, always allowing for the exceptional person. We will point out certain French traits and viewpoints to guide those who are meeting these remarkable people for the first time. Christian workers forearmed with some knowledge of these will be better prepared to win French people. But we should approach the French psychological make-up with some reserve. Recall first that the average Frenchman's dual republican-Roman Catholic conditioning (the Red and the Black again) determines in great degree his entire outlook on life. Then there is the weight of tradition which surrounds him from childhood in a way inconceivable to an outsider. These qualifications help those of Protestant birth and heritage to interpret anything that seems strange in the Frenchman as calling for compassion, not criticism.

1) *We Do as We Please.* Probably the most noticeable French personality trait is a *strong individualism.* One astute definition of French freedom of mind comes from a European commentator:

> Private liberty, the supreme imperative of individualism, is fundamentally liberty to behave in an a-social fashion . . . to do with one's life on every day of every week exactly what one wants to do, and to act, not in accordance with any social standards of behaviour, but in accordance with one's own standards, conscience, and abilities.[26]

In the French conception man is an intelligent and sovereign being responsible only to himself. The Gallic educational ideal is "the formation, not of a useful member of society, but of an intellectually complete man."[27] This emancipated man "has the most complete liberty to go his own way, even the most eccentric way, with the most complete ruthlessness and the utmost unconcern for anyone else."[28]

Where does such passion for personal destiny originate? Apart from its deep philosophical roots, which include independence from God as well as from other men, individualism is partly the common man's revolt against centuries of over-centralized government under kings and generals. French history is for the most part dominated by the rule of the extreme right. The school system is as responsible as any other influence for keeping individualism alive. Children are not taught community responsibility or joint effort. Rather, the emphasis is upon individual achievement through competition. The mastery of the subject at hand is secondary to the child's standing with his fellow pupils. The pitting of each against the other issues in either distinction or disgrace—there is no middle ground. As a result the bright few are lionized into intellectual snobs, while the many average (and therefore supposedly inferior) sink into mediocrity. An American reporter put the results this way: "This constant competition among them . . . can only result in the bitter rivalry, jealousies, and discord which I find to be characteristic of French society."[29] From the jungle of the competitive school arises the multiplication of political parties and the thousand-and-one other splintered expressions of national life. Even France's most exciting sport, the great cycling endurance race called the *Tour de France*, exalts individual stamina above the importance of the team. There are few organized sports or team activities which do not feature a solo performance of some kind. The schools themselves admit their failure in developing group spirit. In 1954 M. Brunhold, head of secondary education for the Ministry of National Education, wrote in a Paris newspaper, "In general we French are little inclined toward cooperation. . . . It is deplorable to note our failure to develop a community spirit among our youth, whose activities are motivated by selfish individualism."[30]

In teaching young French Christians the Word of God in the European Bible Institute, we encountered the same problem. Examination time, instead of being a test of the students' knowledge of the subject (as we insisted), was at first an occasion for rivalry between each student and his classmates. The result? Tension, tears, and nervous depression, which sent some to bed. Only the patient and persistent teaching of the principle of I Cor. 10:31 changes the student's attitude. Once he learns that he must please his Lord more than compete with his neighbor, a genuine change generally comes. In contrast to Christian thought, excessive individualism is really a personal anarchy which leaves God out. One of the pitiful results of being "on your own" in French terms is that you are bitterly alone whether you fail or whether you succeed.

Some might point out that the cult of the individual has its good points too. It has produced great lone researchers like the Curies and Pasteur, as well as writers, composers, and painters beyond compare. Then, too, it has kept France from the evil of the mass-mind, so fatal to the Germans. However, these benefits do not counterbalance the basic weakness in French individualism, for the republican tradition that fostered reason puts man in the center of the French universe, a usurper declining to bow to the God of creation and redemption.

2) *A Missing Sense of Sin.* Second, since most of the homes of France do not have the Bible, her people show *little sense of sin.* Without God's law, which gives the knowledge of sin (Rom. 7:7), the French are little aware of offending that ultimate sanctity known to others as God. Of course Scripture reveals that all men have a sense of wrongdoing through the voice of conscience and the light of nature (Rom. 1:20). Man clearly sees and understands the things of God (Rom. 1:19), and acknowledges God's right to judge; but still he rejects Him. Aside from this general human acknowledgement of sin, however, "Europe's most civilized people" are amoral.

Public misdemeanor or private misconduct do not call forth any breast-beating or soul-searching here. The culprit caught in wrongdoing is not so much evil as stupid. At best, eyebrows are raised, and the comment is passed that the unfortunate one should never have allowed himself to be caught. Under the headline, "French Deputies Laugh at Social Scourges," Alain de Lyrot wrote in a Paris daily that "the French National Assembly, turning its attention to vice, has discussed wine, women, and their abuses and appeared to find the subject rather hilarious."[31] Self-doubt before God seldom touches the man on the street. To attribute national or personal troubles to neglect of God would startle him to no end. Yet as someone has said, the God we put out our front door always comes back through our window in other forms. The French national problems bear this out. Drink, demonism, delinquency, and delusion are only a few.

But does not Roman Catholic law produce some sense of sin here? Not of sin in the Biblical sense. Since the mirror held up to the sinner by the Roman Church is faded and cracked, the child of the church fails to see his true image. In Rome's system redemption is promised bit by bit to people who sin little by little and confess their sins one by one. Since Catholics receive no total forgiveness for total depravity, the disturbed soul deeply aroused to search out God is a rarity today. Only occasionally does a lesser Augustine or a minor Calvin voice a *mea culpa* of utter misery, which God graciously hears.

3) *A Shrinking from Commitment.* In the third place, the Frenchman is brought up to *suspect total commitment* to any one idea, movement, or religion. While an Anglo-Saxon may see two sides to a situation or problem, the average Frenchman, as a Cartesian, sees perhaps ten. With Descartes, he is taught to doubt everything he cannot fully understand. Consequently numerous subpoints, and even footnotes to subpoints, mark his thinking. The idea of unreserved, personal involvement in anything

is abhorrent. The Frenchman usually makes a poor zealot or fanatic; he believes he has too much good sense and too many reservations to carry his enthusiasms that far.

One common expression is *je ne voudrais pas m' engager,* "I don't want to commit myself." True, a chat with a Frenchman about spiritual matters is usually lively. He loves the intellectual exercise and may even become interested. But getting his name and address, for instance, is often difficult. He is suspicious of that, not wanting to get involved. Similarly, the shop-keeper hastens to assure you that you may look around freely or try out something *sans engagement.* Only the Holy Spirit, ploughing deeply in the heart, can reverse this in the French mind. When He does, a great victory often follows. Like anyone else who accepts the yoke of the Saviour, the Frenchman finds His bondage surprisingly easy and His burden delightfully light. Some of the most faithful disciples of Jesus Christ anywhere are French people in whom God has wrought this miracle of full discipleship.

Even among Christians quite fully taught of God there is a reluctance to go too far in asking others to commit themselves. On one occasion I shared a train compartment from southern France to Paris with a Christian couple I knew. I was praying silently for opportunities to witness to others. But I also wanted to show this couple how to fish for souls, since they had said, "We don't wear our faith on our sleeve; we just try to live the gospel." (This excuse is not confined to the French!) Whenever any individual would enter our compartment, even for a short time, I would offer him gospel literature and a witness for Christ.

One of our fellow passengers was a young soldier undergoing his period of military service. After chatting with him briefly, I outlined the plan of salvation. Since that plan includes commitment to Christ, I asked him if he wanted to believe then and there. Confused at the prospect, the soldier said he would think it over. I then warned him that there could be no middle ground: Jesus Christ says, "Come after me."

After he left, my Christian friends remonstrated with me. How un-French, they said, to ask anyone to make an open commitment. Surely this was such a personal, private affair that insisting upon a decision before others could only embarrass everybody. I then took the occasion to show, from the Bible, not only that God demands commitment to Himself, but how other human beings are in the picture from the start. Disciple-ship involves immediate confession of Christ, renunciation of self, and even renunciation of other human loyalties. There can be no true disciple-ship without paying a human price. God used the long Bible study to help this couple enter into lives of active witness.

4) *No Togetherness Without God.* A fourth trait we have already

alluded to briefly is the *lack of community or group spirit.* The French
are not joiners. They distinctly oppose togetherness. Ten men of some
other nationality who form a committee may begin with compromise in
their minds. Each knows that he may be forced to modify his position a
little, but is quite willing to do so, for in each person's mind is the thought,
"We must get something done, at all costs. Let's work for that." Ten
Frenchmen meeting in a like committee never dream of compromise at the
start. Each one will agree to a united position only as a last resort, and
will refuse to fight for a "peace at any price." As a skilled tactitian the
individual enjoys maneuver and only approaches *rapport* with his fellows
under pressure.

A French author thus further illuminates this contrast:

> While a Frenchman is only at ease in the absolute, the American
> accommodates contraries. He prefers the synthesis which combines to
> the analysis which divides. . . . The American submits to things that
> would exasperate a Frenchman. He likes to agree with the majority
> which we love to defy. He thirsts for unanimity, has faith in the wis-
> dom of nations, and respects all established customs.[32]

The only kind of genuinely spontaneous group solidarity in France
obtains within families, and among students, or among colleagues closely
linked in some common enterprise. Here good will and a reconciling mood
reign on a very small, tight level. Even in such groups to arrive at
agreement is difficult without a prolonged, satisfying meal and mellow
wine to round off the sharp corners of opinion.

David Schoenbrun comments that "the French do not believe in the
commandment, 'Love thy neighbor.' They say, 'Keep a sharp eye on your
neighbor, for chances are, he is up to no good.' "[33] Why this selfish,
suspicious view? Any Christian knows, but André Tardieu strikingly
expresses it thus:

> The underlying cause of their opposite reflexes is the antagonism of
> two civilizations. The one—ours—the daughter of pagan antiquity;
> the other, daughter of the Reformation. The one, descended from
> Greece and Rome; the other, from the Bible. The Bible is the vigorous
> trunk from which spread the boughs of the American oak. The Refor-
> mation was a reaction against that mating of pagan culture and Roman
> hierarchy which was, under Julius II and Leo X, the Renaissance.[34]

It is clear that only ignorance of the gospel among the French (not any
biologically inborn stubborness) keeps them from the unmerited blessings we enjoy in Bible-saturated lands.

In founding a French community of believers or getting French Christians to work together, this lack of a group spirit again poses a problem.
To be honest, this is no easy task anywhere in the world. The goal a

spiritual leader must strive for is to bring that cell of the body of Christ to praying together in the Spirit. Under His melting, unifying influence individuals can feel their Christian oneness, perhaps for the first time, while they pray. Prayer has a lateral, horizontal action as well as an upward, vertical one. French Christians who achieve a loving awareness of their fellow members of the body are few. But when the Holy Spirit unites, how glorious! Individualism, nationalism, and all the other hindrances magically melt away.

5) *More Gallic Traits.* We now list together other qualities for which the French are known, some of which are amplified elsewhere in this study. The preceding two national traits create another: *distrust of collective, national authority.* But the Frenchman carefully distinguishes between his country and its government. Sometimes he sounds unpatriotic when he derides the current administration, but he deeply loves *la patrie,* his native land. A more pleasing attribute is *mental alertness.* Not many are as well educated as they deserve to be, due to the policy of training fully only the few young people who survive rigorous examinations. The average person attends school only through the age of twelve or fourteen. Yet the French are wonderfully alert and intelligent, a boon for the preaching of the gospel. In these people *lies a strong sense of realism or insight.* The French are obsessed with the desire to see things as they really are—to delve analytically to the heart of any issue. They possess this perceptive gift more than any other people in Europe. Another trait is *attachment to form, principle or ideal.* For instance, the French are more interested in conceiving an ideal government, such as the democracy initiated by their Revolution, than in making it work. (Though the French Revolution was a purer democracy than ours in theory, as Edmund Burke pointed out, it has never been implemented fully to this day.) So there appears a congenital *weakness in putting principles into practice.* Sometimes the insistence of other countries on practical solutions angers the French, who dearly love the theoretical.

Above perhaps any country in the world, France treasures *the traditional values of civilized man.* These include artistic creativeness in any form, individual and political freedom, and many other values. For instance, all Frenchmen traditionally have a *high regard for private property.* They practice a careful use of money or its equivalents, partly inspired by the wars and inflation they have known. The tightest social tie is *the family circle,* which is the freest place of all in which to practice the beloved *art of conversation.* At this the Frenchmen are past masters— probably the most stimulating, if the most exhausting, conversationalists in the world. Because a French person guards his own privacy he also *respects the privacy of others.* These are not a people of quick and easy confidences. They consider it impolite to ask personal questions about a man's job, address, or income, unless he gives some sign of compliance with the idea. Lastly, the French have an unusual *affection and sympathy for children, the blind, the lame, and the unfortunate.* They have suffered themselves, though they may not always show it, and so they commiserate others who suffer—though again, more in principle (mental) than in practice (action).

Morality is Just a Word. We consider now the national morality. The French and other Europeans like to point out that their basic moral problems are the same as ours, which is true enough. But they add that America treats her moral issues hypocritically rather than realistically. They themselves are more honest, they claim, in openly admitting the weaknesses of human nature and even sometimes providing for their outlet. Take the matter of *gambling.* People like to gamble, so why prohibit them? Instead of making gambling illegal, simply control it through a state lottery arrangement. There the people have a chance to win tax-free prizes, and the government profits instead of the racketeer (as in America). All European nations with national lotteries think it ridiculous to condemn gambling on moral grounds. Their solution simply ignores the right and wrong based on divine law.

Prostitution is another item. According to recent government estimates, France has about 230,000 girls who earn at least $100 million a year in this way, tax-free. In Paris there are supposedly nine thousand "regulars," and perhaps three times that many more clandestine women, who have been using four hundred hotels for their trade. But in March, 1959, the de Gaulle government put into effect Ordinance 58-1298 of the Fifth Republic's new penal code. This prohibits "prolonged loitering in the street and equivocal attitudes." (Under the old Fourth Republic, "soliciting" or *racolage* was the softer word.) In reaction to the new laws, 300 prostitutes in Marseilles marched in broad daylight to protest at the City Hall, while in Perpignan, Toulouse, Carcassone, and Sète, the girls went out on public strike to protect their "jobs." The new restrictions, like the 1946 ones which abolished the bordellos, do not aim at eliminating this evil because it is intrinsically wrong. Rather, there are the loss of tax income and a bad name before the world to consider. Today the French are permitting prostitution to continue under tighter controls. For them no moral issue is involved.

When it comes to *sex standards among youth,* the same rule applies: the cult of individual freedom ignores God and His laws. "By Anglo-Saxon standards French youth is immoral. By French standards French youth is realistic," says a widely read report.[35] In this, accepted practices go far beyond the public necking which shocks foreigners in France. "Among workers and emancipated intellectuals, living in sin is acceptable. In the middle class there may be attempts to observe the forms of morality, like the insistence that a young girl come home at night. . . . In rural areas premartial relations are common, . . . and pregnancy is a usual prelude to marriage."[36] Catholic reports insist that in most large cities the number of couples who simply set up housekeeping together is double the number whose marriages are duly registered. The closely-chaperoned girl is becoming increasingly rare in France, although the very strict Catholic family can still be found. The increasing freedoms of the postwar world are evident everywhere—in the easy morality of camping parties, the shared vacation, the stolen weekend. The presence of the Catholic Church seems to make little difference. "Except for a small fraction of fervent youngsters, religion has not interfered with sexual morality. In true Latin fashion, the soul and the body are two distinctly different spheres that may touch briefly behind the curtain of a confessional box."[37] Gaston Racine, a faithful Bible teacher, speaks of such living as "complete amorality under the guise of religion."[38] One of the more painful effects is a high rate of illegitimate births. Just under 10 per cent of births in Paris, for instance, are of unmarried parents.

In the book, *Love and the French,* Jean Claude Ibert and Jerome Charles give the results of a survey of opinion taken among 200,000 men and women of all walks of life and levels of society. When asked whether love was possible outside their marriage, 73 per cent of the men and 56 per cent of the women answered, "Yes." Perhaps the most cynical and blasé quotation in the book, one which characterizes our jaded generation, is this: "My most beautiful memory is of dancing with my husband on the day we got divorced."[39]

Another facet of the moral scene is *illegal but tolerated abortion.* A Paris lawyer told an international crime prevention congress in 1959 that there are more illegal abortions in Paris than births (150,000 to 95,000 over an unspecified period). M. Dourlen-Rollier, in quoting these official figures, stated that 75 per cent of the woman hospitalized for complications following abortions were married women who underwent abortion in agreement with their husbands. Such a calloused attitude toward human life and parental responsibility is shocking in any civilized nation. In France it is indicative once again of a people without God actively at work in their midst. Of course some French observers blame the stand of the Catholic church on birth control, indirectly causing the practice of abortion. Equally sad is the spectacle of govermental indifference toward a situation which could be controlled. Like so many other evils, abortion is tolerated though illegal.

More Healers Than Physicians. Today sick French people are turning as never before to nonreligious, nonmedical healers. The number of these healers, writes M. Noel Bayon in *Miracles at the Healers*, surpasses forty thousand. Generally the nation's press seems to support this figure. Since there are only 38,000 medical doctors licensed in all of France, the demand for such help would seem to be enormous. M. Maurice Colinson insists that there are all of fifty thousand healers. Dr. Gladys Medina, in her *Essay on the Causes of Success of the Healers*, estimates as many as seventy-five thousand.

Who patronizes the healers? Not only the uneducated lower classes. Students of the phenomenon point out that cultured, upper-class people also are clients. In his work, *When Doctors are Silenced*, M. Robert Toquet reports that he has observed among the patients of M. Maurice Messequé, one of the best-known healers, important political figures, business tycoons, judges—and even doctors of medicine. University professors and Roman Catholic clergy were noted in the waiting room, too. Like thousands of his colleagues, Messequé has a richly-furnished office, regular office hours, and a high reputation in the community.

Why do people seek out healers or sorcerers instead of doctors, especially when they are largely reimbursed for medical expense through Social Security funds? Natural reasons might include curiosity, fear of examinations and operations, a thirst for the miraculous, and the desire for a quick, once-for-all cure. Certainly some have no other resort, being medically hopeless cases. But French writers, with their usual analytical approach, find deeper reasons. Usually the healers claim to possess psychic powers, though they do not do so in the name of a known religion or a God. Most claim to have some personal radiation which flows out of them to the sick, energizing and healing. The mystery in all this intrigues the masses. Other healers use some object as a medicating agent— a powder, plant, root, or like substance. Those of still another class employ old magical formulae and incantations, corrupted Christian prayers, or even a mixture of the two. Of these, Jesuit Father Brouillard notes, "There is a whole residue of secular superstitions in the country traditions of our land which are of pagan origin with deformed Christian elements added."[40]

Though the Roman Catholic church co-operates on a practical level with such superstitions and has never condemned the healers in principle, it is sometimes uneasy about the non-Christian element in them. As Abbé Jacquement says, "For some time secular healing in certain areas has had an aspect openly hostile to the church and has even become a polarizing element for anti-Catholic sects."[41]

In summary we might note that the success of the healers demonstrates once more a basic lack of confidence on the part of the French people toward the Catholic faith and their quest for help from the occult, in which they show great interest.

Traffic with the Devil. The spiritual ignorance and moral slavery of many French people almost surpasses belief. Underneath the surface of millions of lives lies a fear of unseen powers and a compulsion to somehow propitiate them. In January, 1959, at Le Mans, site of the famous auto races, a Madame Ida Guilloneau, 32, was sentenced to prison for five years. This farmer's wife had killed her brother Marcel on his eighteenth birthday by suffocating him in a basin of salt. After her father had been kicked to death by a horse seven years before, she had become convinced than an "evil eye" threatened their farm near Le Mans. A local sorcerer whom she consulted made incantations over some salt in order to lift the curse. Madame Guilloneau was instructed to see to it that every member of the family ate some salt. So she forced her mother, her four-year-old son and her husband to eat the miraculous salt. But Marcel, her brother, refused. Desperately the woman pushed his head down into the salt basin, crying, "The devil is here and will get us! Scare him off with the salt! We must purify ourselves!" The lad's mother, grief-stricken by her son's death, hanged herself the next day.

"The devil is at Vanosc!" recently reported *France-Soir*, a leading Paris daily. Vanosc is a little village in the Ardèche, on the edge of the Cevennes mountains. Two local girls, Marie-Paule Jurdic, 18, and Monique Perrier, 15, were walking to the neighboring hamlet of La Rivière, when they were enveloped, they said, in a terrifying black cloud. Stones were thrown at them by some unseen hand. That evening in their room, logs reportedly leaped from the fireplace toward the ceiling, and kitchen utensils sailed up the stairs. Neighbors confirmed that wine bottles danced in the cellar of the girls' home. By midafternoon superstitious neighbors and tourists visiting the scene numbered into the hundreds. To lend these mysterious happenings a dread meaning, Monique's brother was killed the same night on his motorcycle while on his way to bear the news elsewhere. In the minds of the simple villagers some diabolic curse had come on the town. Satan himself was named the murderer of the boy and the instigator of all the strange events. Who had displeased his dark rule in the town? What local agent of his had cast a spell on the unlucky home? The newspaper report concluded by noting that the whole town trembled with disquietude because of the *poltergeist*.

In France a huge literature on demonism intrigues the public. Some bookstores are wholly devoted to occult works. On the Left Bank of Paris certain large auditoriums are rented more often to spiritualists and their ilk than to any others. In spite of a professed disinterest in the metaphysical world, the French are fascinated by the strange and the supernatural. Public interest in these matters has been intense for centuries. During the time of Louis XIV the leaders of satanism introduced the Black Mass, still observed with various modifications by peasants today. This obscene and grotesque parody of the Catholic mass has been described by eyewitnesses. Usually a group of peasants observe it in a deserted wood in the dead of night. Called the "offspring of anticlericalism and sexual license," the pagan mass is essentially devil worship—an antimass to the antipope, Satan. Many characteristics of the debased and sensual worship of Babylon and Egypt are incorporated into it.

The old province of Normandy, lying northwest of Paris toward the English channel, is one of the most progressive in the country. Here farmers and traders, considered by some "the Yankees of France," are shrewd bargainers and successful salesmen. Lush fields surround the best dairy farms in the land. Normandy is also heavily Catholic, leads the country in heinous crimes, and is popular with tourists. Yet who would suspect that an area like this, known only lately to hundreds of thousands of Allied soldiers, is steeped in pagan ideas going back a thousand years?

More than three hundred chapels in Normandy specialize in spiritism and healing. Each town has its sorcerer; this man or woman is thought to be a medium in touch with unseen powers. The sick, worried, or depressed patronize these sorcerers and sometimes make a pact with Satan. Of course the prince of this world exacts a terrible price from those whom he controls. Here, an hour or two from Paris, despair and despondency drive more to suicide than anywhere else in the nation. American missionary David Barnes wrote of the Normans, "These people, possessing the education, culture, and civilization which are the rich heritage of a France once enlightened, are as ignorant of the things of God as the uncivilized, unclad natives of one of the world's darkest continents."[2]

In Normandy old Scandinavian tree worship and Roman Catholic faith strike a truce. In the forest of La Londe, nera Bourgtheroulde, stands a gigantic beech tree many centuries old, nearly twelve feet in circumference, which bears in a niche the Virgin Mary's image. Again, near Bosquerard-de-Marconville is an oak known as the Virgin of La Mesangère. Its trunk is some thirty feet in circumference. The statue of the Virgin is set high among the branches of the four-hundred-year-old tree. In La Haye de Routot's churchyard are two gigantic yews, one thirty and the other twenty-four feet in circumference. The larger one houses a small chapel scooped out of its center. Tradition says the trees are between 1,300 and 1,500 years old. The many tree shrines of Normandy originated in the Druid tree cults and the sacred groves of Scandinavia.

Norman Sorcerers. "Is this the man who deals with magic?" asked a brusk voice on the other end of the telephone Pastor X held to his ear. "For six months my cattle have given no milk. I have been to fifteen sorcerers and many veterinarians, without success. Can you help me?" "No, I'm not a magician," replied the pastor, "but I'll do my best to help you." This faithful evangelical minister has labored for fifteen years in the midst of a French paganism comparable to that found in the heart of Africa.

Pastor X realized that the call was the direct result of a lecture he had given the evening before in a rented hall on the subject of "spirits." A crowd of 150 persons—large for a religious service in this part of France— had attended. Learning the telephone caller's name and address, he agreed to meet the farmer. In his search to locate the man's farm, he stopped in a little town to ask directions of a passerby. "Oh, he's one of my clients," the stranger said. "I'm the village sorcerer!"

The farm proved to be substantial for that area, seventy hectares of land and many cattle and horses. But the fields remain unproductive and the animals sterile. The farmer had even gone to the trouble of attending a spiritualist séance in Paris to seek some solution for his trouble. The medium had correctly told him everything that had happened on the farm, but could do nothing to help. Veterinarians said there was nothing organically wrong with the cattle, yet they would not give milk nor reproduce.

Pastor X explained that he himself had no power, being only the servant of the One who has all power in heaven and earth. Minutes passed into hours as he read the Word of God and prayed with the farmer. Though no decision for Christ resulted, the man's interest in the Bible was aroused. Later Pastor X and the farmer met again. With great rejoicing the latter began to unfold the happenings of the days since their first talk together. The cows were normal again, and he himself was recovering sight in one eye. Now Pastor X prays that this prosperous farmer will have his blind spiritual eyes opened.

Such stories of sorcerers and spiritism in Normandy could be multiplied many times. As in the Le Mans incident, many grisly murders and suicides in Normandy can be traced to mediums who cast a spell, for satanic activity there is very real indeed. It is not unusual to see actual healings by these sorcerers, whose appeal to evil spirits in worship and prayer is common. In the city of Evreux a large temple to spiritism is one of many in the region.

Though outwardly condemning all of this, the Roman Catholic Church still plays along. The annual Fête de St. Jean is a good example. During this festival the center of a large tree is burned in Druid style. The village

priest, invited to the ceremony, comes to bless the burning log. When
the fire is almost out, village boys take the still warm brands and sell
them as magical charms. These fetishes are put in stables to protect
cattle from the foot-and-mouth disease. Some farmers lead their cattle
through the ashes to give added protection. Thus paganism from the
forests of Scandinavia is blessed by the Roman Church in modern France!

The pagan faith of the Norsemen who invaded and conquered France
over a thousand years ago mingles today with a nominal Catholic faith.
In the minds of the Norman peasants of yesteryear, the priest with
his magic sacraments is just another form of the Nordic sorcerer with his
mystic ceremonies. Today the attitude of the Normans is little changed.
Thousands of farmers consult the village sorcerer concerning every problem of husbandry and health. These pagan practitioners do not stop with
animal and human healings, but deal even with domestic and personal
problems. They are the spiritual leaders of the community. Pastor Emile
R. Dallière of Evreux thus summarizes the conditions in Normandy:

> Twenty-five years of ministry in Normandy, permitting contacts
> with hundreds of people in different classes of society—in remote vil-
> lages as well as cities—convince me that the paganism of the Vikings
> of old is still alive today . . . under an outward Christian clothing,
> deep heathen beliefs and practices are as active today as a thousand
> years ago.[43]

Through an Alcoholic Blur. We turn now to a problem which has
brought international disrepute to this land. France is the most alcoholic
nation in the world. True, one does not always see here the staggering
drunk completely out of control. Another worse type of drinking, steady
tippling, is more typical. This form of alcoholism, in which a person loses
mental but not physical control is common in France. Especially in
the late evening, between the closing of offices and stores and dinner time,
millions of French people in cafés and bars are in a semi-intoxicated condition. Many others who have wine bottles handy are in a daze all day
long. Even a fourteen-year-old child can buy a drink in any bar.

Let us look at the stark facts of alcoholism before weighing their significance in spiritual terms. The World Health Organization is the authority
which calls France the most alcoholic nation on earth, and French doctors
agree. A third of the population drink to an excess not considered medically safe. Altogether a million people, or 15 per cent of all adult men and
5 per cent of adult women, are full-blown alcoholics. Every thirty-three
minutes someone dies of acute alcoholism—twice the national death rate
for tuberculosis. Thirty per cent of deaths between the ages of thirty-five
and fifty are related, directly or indirectly, to this evil. In an average year
one out of every twenty-five men will die as a victim of love of drink.

Per capita consumption of pure alcohol runs to 37 quarts a year, the equivalent of 106 bottles of 88-proof whiskey. (Comparable figures: 15 quarts in Italy, 9 in America, and 6 in Great Britain.) Ten per cent of the family budget goes toward the liquor bill, as compared to 5 per cent for health, 4 per cent for education, and 3 per cent for rent. France has Europe's highest incidence of cirrhosis and other liver ailments. In early 1960 the Academy of Medicine flatly stated that drinking was responsible for half of the annual 150,000 traffic deaths. The volume, *Crime in France,* shows that drinking figures heavily in 60 per cent of all murders and 40 per cent of arson cases. A Ministry of Justice survey of prisons indicated that 14.2 per cent of all crimes stem from overindulgence.

In answer to the question, "Why do the French drink so much?", a born-again French doctor says, "Our national appetite for drink is an attempt to compensate for our failure as human beings. Man was born for fellowship with God, but rejecting this, he seeks other solutions. Faced with no answers, he is then driven to drink or drugs. Our capacity for drink is an index to our need of God."[44]

The Quick Way Out. A Frenchman, cap in hand and distress written large on his spectacle-mounted features, one day stood in the entry of the European Bible Institute, near Paris. Clad in the anonymous light blue of France's working-class millions, the man poured out his despair to the sympathetic staff of the Greater Europe Mission's school. His "wife"— who turned out to be his longtime unwed companion—had deserted him with their children. Was he to blame? Oh, partly, he admitted, by his frequent alcoholic sallies into senselessness. But, he murmured with worried frown, he would do anything—yes, anything!—to get his family back. As it turned out later, the missionaries could not trace the family, since his "wife" had covered her tracks well. But they spoke to him warmly of a better way, of God and heaven, of the comfort of an always-present Christ. Yet this failed to sink in, even during several visits to his littered home. Again and again he came and went, woebegone and crushed by the unbearable burden of life. Then one day the missionaries saw the casually-phrased newspaper item, "Police, smelling gas emanating from. . ." Frenchmen are not as wisely casual as they would have each other believe. As a hoped-for escape to oblivion, suicide looms large and friendly in the contemporary mind. During the year this man died by his own hand, over six hundred other Parisians attempted self destruction.

Teen-Age Revolt. As in so many other countries, France's teen-agers are restlessly exploring the possibilities of life. All together 100,000 delinquents are known to the authorities. A recent survey of juvenile lawlessness by Paris Police Chief Maurice Papon revealed that 10,000 young people aged from eight to twenty are organized into eighty gangs in greater Paris alone. The French Teddy boys are called either *les tricheurs* (the cheats), after a film of that name, or *blousons noirs* (black wind-breakers). At first these youths and their girls confined their activities to rock-and-roll, scooter riding, and inter-gang wars. At this stage their mischief involved only fighting, stone-throwing, and minor thefts. Then stealing branched out to automobiles, and pedestrians were assaulted. Finally one hundred *tricheurs* in blue jeans and black leather jackets assembled in a Left-Bank area to carry out a "rumble" against a rival gang. Unable to find their enemies, and keyed up for some knd of action, they began to molest passers by with blackjacks, bicycle chains, and heavy belts. Soon they were attacking a café, which they nearly wrecked. After a long chase, officers caught and arrested twenty-six youths between fourteen and twenty years of age. The police said that the young people arrested averaged six film-goings a week; most of the films featured action and violence.

Paris is not the only place where the revolt of the young is taking place. Almost at the same time at Bandol, near Toulouse, fifty *tricheurs* attacked tourists near the local casino. In a few minutes three tourists had been seriously injured and others were cut up with bicycle chains. A car was overturned and wrecked before police arrived on the scene. A similar occurrence at Pont-de-L'Arche, near Louviers, say thirty-six delinquents (of whom sixteen were less than eighteen years old) arrested for attacking two policemen, besieging a police station, and taking over a town. For two years the gang had terrorized the Rouen suburbs.

The Paris gangs are organized in both poor and elegant neighborhoods. In its particular quarter a gang will often roam the streets tingling with suppressed excitement. Outlets for this energy come by breaking a street bench, smashing a window, molesting a girl, snatching a purse, or picking a fight. Headquarters is usually a jukebox and pinball hangout.

Such young people have absolutely no contact with the Christian gospel. Most Protestant churches are too few, too bourgeois, and too ivory-tower-like to be of much help. "Youth missionaries" who could win their confidence, and lead some of them to Christ would be an immeasurable blessing. Otherwise, the teen-agers of France, who learned many of their ways from American films, music, and magazines, will never hear of the Saviour some Americans know.

University Mission Fields. France, which yields to no nation in her respect for the intellectual, enrolls Europe's largest number of spiritually ignorant students. On the Left Bank of Paris lies what is probably the greatest concentration of learning in the world, centered in the various colleges comprising the University of Paris. Ancient buildings and tawdry hotels line the maze of narrow streets of the Latin Quarter. Like most European schools, this one has no real campus and few dormitories. Of 65,000 university students (out of France's total 160,000) only about 39,000 can find rooms either through the University or at home. The 31,000 luckless ones must live in squalid, unheated attic rooms, many of them tiny *chambres de bonnes,* the maids' quarters atop apartment houses. Often there is no running water, and only one filthy toilet to a floor; but the rent still comes high. Hard conditions like these lead three out of four students in the university's leading colleges to quit after only one year.

To find warmth and companionship, most of the footloose 31,000 scatter through hundreds of cafés and bistros to read, write, and talk. To sit in the Café Dupont on the Boulevard St. Michel and listen to the chatter is to understand why serious postwar observers are struck with the frivolity, lack of intellectual curiosity, or, for that matter, any motivation among these students. More saddening to the Christian is the utter pointlessness of living without God. There seems to be no goal here except to escape, eagerly but briefly, into uninhibited living. This means extreme dress, behavior, and speech. Women and sports dominate the conversation of most of the men, unless they are paired off with girls with whom they live temporarily. Laughter and light talk provide the student ambiance for which the cafés are sought out by tourists. But look well, and you will soon see that not all faces are so animated as the circumstances should warrant. Many are slack with boredom, bearing haggard, troubled eyes. As Stanley Karnow reports, "Life on the Left Bank is not gay and carefree today . . . students spend their lives plodding between overcrowded classes, cafés, and tiny rooms, eating minimal meals in canteens and occasionally treating themselves to a movie."[45] One of these joyless students wrote in a letter to the Paris daily, *La Figaro:* "We have given up everything. We believe in nothing. Our sole interest is the struggle for our personal subsistence."[46]

Among these students are several thousand Americans having a fling at the bohemian life.* Not all, of course, are immoral or capricious. But the average man grows a beard, learns French slang, and tries to slouch around the cafés in the accepted manner. The girls will often ape the continental coed's tumbled hair and nondescript sweater and slacks. Sometimes these Americans will clutch a rumpled copy of the Paris-published *New York Herald Tribune* as a badge of nationality. With little local *savoir-faire,* they feel prepared for that thrilling "experiment in international living" they came for.

*A recent report estimated 15,000 foreign university students and an equal number of foreigners in other schools in Paris.

3. *FRANCE'S RELUCTANT CATHOLICS*

A Double Answer. As everyone knows, the correct answer to some questions is sometimes both "yes" and "no." This double answer is the only possible one to the question, Is France Catholic? Traditionally and mentally the French people *are* Catholic. Yet in practice the French church is the least faithful of all the major national churches of the world. As Blanshard phrases it, "A nation is not necessarily a clerical state because the majority of its people are Catholics; France is a 'Catholic' country, but it is not a *Catholic* country."[47] Herein lies a curious contradiction which begs for explanation.

France is called "the eldest daughter of the Church" because by decision of King Clovis in 496 she became the first large population grouping in Europe to enter the Roman Church. The process of national conversion had been a long one. At the time the Apostle Paul was in Rome, the Roman settlement of Marseilles already had benefited by five hundred years of Greek civilizing influence. Inland, Roman colonies like Arles were flourishing as well. It was only natural that such trade and cultural centers should quickly hear of any movement spreading throughout the empire. We know that a primitive church flourished in Lyons as early as the middle of the second century. By the third and fourth centuries the church of the conquerors was quitely firmly intrenched.

I have visited the oldest church ruins known in France. Since the unmarked site at Metz is not preserved by the government as a tourist center, even local people, for the most part, are unaware of its existence. Finding the location in the modern city takes time and patience, but it is worth the effort. As one stands in the fourth-century ruins of the church of St. Pierre-aux-Nonains, the question naturally comes: Had the truth of God already this early become encrusted with falsity and formalism? When Clovis, the first real King of France, was baptized at Rheims at the end of the fifth century, he decided to continue the earlier policy of the Emperor Constantine. Romanization of the barbarians included their Christianization. Co-operating chieftains who wished to get along with Rome became "Christian" along with their tribes. Of the emptiness of that conversion and its consequences, V. R. Edman says,

> France had received the Church, but not Christ; the sacraments, but not salvation; the bishops, but not the Bible; the monks, but not the Mediator between God and men. . . . If Martin of Tours and his successors had brought to France the Scriptures, whose entrance brings light . . . the place of France in world history might have been different.[48]

The Gallican Church. But France, once converted, did not remain a docile child of Rome. Throughout her history she has developed a strange phenomenon called the Gallican church. Gallicanism is national French Catholicism which, though still tied to the Vatican, remains very independent in spirit. To be sure, many leaders have tried to orient the church's path more strongly toward loyalty, but the general tradition of Gallicanism runs to rebellion rather than conformity. Keeping the French church in line has been a papal problem for centuries. Many dramatic scenes from history illustrate the tendency. We shall choose just two examples, one ancient and the other modern.

In August of the year 314 a general church council was called in the city of Arles to consider the protests of the Donatists to the appointment of Caecilian as Bishop of Carthage. A very wide representation of church officials was present, including British prelates. In effect, the council was rediscussing something upon which Rome had already pronounced. Sylvester, Bishop of Rome, had his own agents present, who apparently did not protest the council's findings. After condemning the Donatists, the council made important pronouncements on church discipline. One letter to the Pope shows how far from present-day obedience to the Holy Father the thinking of the delegates lay:"What we have decreed in common council we signify to your Belovedness that all may know what in future they ought to observe."[49] *They instructed* the Roman bishop!

An up-to-date instance of defiance occurred during the recent worker-priest movement. In 1944 Abbés Godin and Daniel persuaded the late Cardinal Suhard, Archbishop of Paris, to launch a special mission to win back the dechristianized working classes in France to the church. After obtaining papal permission, the leaders established a special seminary to train priests to work alongside men in the factories, wearing the same clothes and sharing their hard lot. The experiment seemed successful for a time. Then several priests were arrested in Communist raids, and others protested against the jailing of Communist leaders. Disturbed, the Vatican closed down the Lisieux seminary by 1953. Soon afterward the papal nuncio in Paris forbade all worker-priest activity in the name of His Holiness. Negotiations with Rome by prominent French clerics brought no compromise. By the end of that year Jesuit priests ordered out of the movement had obeyed, but in January, 1954, a bitter manifesto, almost Marxist in tone, was signed by seventy-five worker-priests, some fifteen of whom had either joined the Communist party, married, or stopped saying mass. Seven prominent Dominican theologians and publicists were removed from their posts on February 10 for support of these rebels. On February 29 over one hundred priests were forced to obey the Vatican order to withdraw or face the consequences. A number remained with the workers. During this time controversy raged in every café in France as the press and radio kept the issue alive. The ten-year experiment of the militant Catholic left had failed, but it had afforded another example of the independent character of the Gallican church.

Rome at Arm's Length. After almost 1,500 years of close acquaintance with Rome's ways, the French people are understandably distrustful. The Vatican, they know, will interfere in state affairs whenever it can, in order to achieve its own ends. They recall, for instance, that the most ruthless and absolute ruler of their history was not a king but a prince of the church—Cardinal Richelieu, soldier, patriot, and priest, whose very name stands for cunning, intrigue, and power. By manipulating King Louis XIII, one of the weakest of the Bourbons, Richelieu (1585–1642) was able to build a strong France. He fought Protestants and destroyed their last armed cities. He opposed every enemy of strong centralized authority. With his vast network of spies and his thirst for power, Richelieu made France dominant power of Europe. Though he became a national hero, the French do not forget that he was the militant cardinal of Rome.

Another unforgettable group comprises the disciples of Ignatius Loyola. Historically, the favorite land for Jesuit activity has been France. Previous to the Revolution the "soldiers of the Pope" were especially active. The whole country was aroused during the dialogue between the great philosophers and the Jesuits. Blaise Pascal (1623–1662), one of the earlier converts to Jansenism, had written the *Provincales,* probably the strongest indictment of Jesuit casuistry ever penned. Now Voltaire and other philosophers joined the offensive against Rome. When the *Parlement* of Paris published three volumes of Jesuit quotations, public opinion demanded that the order be expelled. As a result, in 1763 the Jesuits were temporarily forbidden in France.

Ever since the French Revolution of 1789 weakened the Roman Church and led to disestablishment, Rome has fought with all her wiles to win back her former power. Against this pressure even Napoleon Bonaparte, who made a concordat with the Vatican in 1801, was defiant in his own way. One of the dramatic episodes of French history occurred on December 2, 1804, during the coronation of Bonaparte as Emperor in Notre Dame Cathedral. Emil Ludwig describes the scene thus: "When the appointed instant has come and all are expecting this man, who has never bowed the knee to anyone, to bow before the Holy Father (Pius VII), Napoleon, to the amazement of the congregation, seizes the crown, turns his back on the pope and the altar, and standing upright as always, crowns himself."[50] In a way the incident typifies every Frenchman's attitude toward Rome.

Especially after 1870 tension built up between the church and the state. Following the Associations Act of 1901, many religious orders were suppressed and thousands of schools were closed. In 1904 the government ordered all teaching congregations to be closed within ten years—a move which marked the end of their schools. In 1905 the 1801 concordat was annulled, state support of the clergy was abolished, and church edifices were transferred to state ownership. Yet the church found a way to continue to use these buildings through the formation of voluntary associations. After disestablishment, candidates for the priesthood fell off by 50 per cent. On the positive side, the church was now free of state interference in the appointment of bishops, and could direct her own dioceses.

Beginning about 1914 the supple Vatican found ways to live with republican France. In 1920–1921 diplomatic relations were restored between the Vatican and France. Yet the Roman Church hates the role of equality with other religions in this secular state. She dreams of an earlier day when she dominated throne and people alike, doing as she pleased. The temper of the Holy See on this subject can be seen in a statement like that of Pius X, uttered just after the new French laws regarding separation of church and state had been passed. In his letter of February 11, 1906, to the bishops of France, the primate said, "That it is necessary to separate church and state in a thesis absolutely false, a most pernicious error.[51]

In recent times the French recall the duplicity of their great war hero, Marshal Henri Pétain. In a series of moves too long to relate here, Pétain plotted to effect an early surrender of France's armed forces to Nazi Germany in exchange for Hitler's promise to restore the supremacy of the Roman Church in France. The Vichy government took quick steps after the French collapse to increase Catholic control of education, which brought wrathful reaction from the watchdogs of republicanism. After the Germans were expelled, Pétain was imprisoned, Cardinal Suhard was confined to his palace, and several bishops were arrested.*

The Dearth of Priests and Nuns. Though there is a ratio of more than one priest for every thousand people in France, the hierarchy feels that a shortage of priests is a chronic problem. In 1940 Adolf Keller stated that there were more than twelve thousand parishes without a priest: "In the diocese of Amiens only 450 priests are presently serving 836 parishes."[52] According to a recent edition of the *Catholic Encyclopedia*,

*Even though a good Catholic himself, General De Gaulle tried, unsuccessfully, in 1945, to bring Cardinal Suhard and other ecclesiastical leaders to justice.

In the last half-century the number of secular clergy has been diminishing. This condition exists in all dioceses. There has been an estimated deficit of 250 priests a year. This has had two results: (1) an insufficient number of priests, especially now that sacerdotal and pastoral duties are more arduous; (2) a greater proportion of older priests than younger ones. The average age of French priests is 50 years. In several dioceses more than 50% of the priests are more than 60 years old, whereas the normal proportion would be only 21%.[53]

The number of priests in training being close to nine thousand, the church should expect about 1,200 new priests annually. But these would only replace aging priests, with no advance made. In his book on the subject in 1950, Abbé F. Boulard estimated that 15,416 parishes were vacant. Even the huge archdiocese of Paris has today but 1,600 priests to serve a population of more than five million. Though the average country priest may take care of about 1,000 parishioners, in some of the smaller towns (there are 15,000 with less than 300 population) certain priests may serve as many as eight small parishes.

No doubt increased secularization, Communism, and general anticlericalism have all had their part in causing the shortage of priests. But that shortage will grow as France's birth rate continues to inch higher. Of course some maintain, with Abbé Godin, that there is not so much a shortage involved as a wrong use of priests. He writes, "France contains in city areas some 18 million inhabitants, of whom more than 9 million belong to the pagan proletariat. Our Catholic colleges employ several thousand priests and nuns (some entirely on the business side). If half of these were working as missionaries, France would not revert to paganism, and the recruitment of priests would increase."[54] In urging priests to give up secondary administrative duties for missionary work, he quotes the *Divine Redemptorist* encyclical of Pius XI (1937), "Let the parish priests reserve their greatest strength and the larger share of their energy to win back the masses of the workers . . ."[55] Abbé Godin likewise feels that since the methods existing priests employ are out of date, the church's grip has been weakened. The postwar defection of priests has compounded the problem. In 1954 the Baptist paper *Croire et Servir* reported (though without documentation) that more than two thousand priests had quit the Roman Church during the seven years previous. Though the annual loss today is an ecclesiastical secret, strong rumors in France give credence to a continuing problem.

Urban Indifference. Comments of French Catholic leaders about their own failure in the cities are revealing. Urbanization poses a sticky problem. In 1846, for instance, 75 per cent of the people lived in the country. Now only half do. One aroused priest scores big cities "where the institutions are pagan, the moral atmosphere is pagan, the people are pagan, and natural law itself has become so diminished that consciences react to it only irregularly."[56] In 1950 Adrien Dansette reported that each church in Paris served between 25,000 and 100,000 parishioners. In certain proletarian quarters a full fourth of marriages are remarriages of divorcees. A Paris suburban parish reports that only a few children partake of first communion, and not a single man goes to church. In Lens, a northern city, between a fourteenth and a twentieth of the laboring class ever go to mass, according to a report by Daniel-Rops. The city church is called by its own leaders "a sick and enfeebled faith, buried beneath the dust of superstitions, pushed away into the subconscious."[57] Neglect of religious practice is blamed for the almost complete lack of maternal instinct in women over thirty. In one office where forty women worked, seventeen unmarried ones, over a period of eight months, had abortions. In dechristianized big business the tycoon who amasses a fortune by dubious means is considered dishonest only if the police pry into his affairs and expose him. Other conditions are unearthed: many unknown, unloved charity patients die alone in crowded city hospitals because people have grown calloused to death and suffering.

Peasant Superstitions. Abbé F. Boulard, a country priest, says of rural Catholicism, "The peasant religion is a religion of fear, consisting of prohibitions. It is as if God forbade happiness. . . . Religion is not truly personal. . . . My Christians consider God a faraway God to whom one should submit as much as possible, not out of love for Him, but out of fear of going to hell."[58]

While faithfulness to church practices is thought to be better in the country (Boulard: 38%) than among the urban proletariat (Godin: 2%), and in excess of the national average (10%), one Catholic writer characterizes country worship as "only a few steps from superstition or complete indifference. . . . Parents have only a ritualistic religion colored with superstition. . . . Children when they grow up, hasten to escape from the coercion of a religion which consists more in keeping one's accounts square with God than with being alive in Him."[59]

Naturally such observations are subject to regional differences. Some areas, like Brittany, La Vendée, Flanders, the Basque regions, and Normandy, are strongly Catholic in observance.* Processions and ceremonies are more common there than elsewhere, and crucifixes abound. But none of the French Catholics who decry the peasants' alienation attribute the cause to their own church, which gives them stones in place of bread.

---

*Brittany is also reported to be one of the three areas in Europe with the lowest standard of living; for the past decade an average 18,000 a year—many of them young people—have left the region for economic reasons.

Those who have made religion a sad bondage are unable to see where their own folly and blindness have led.

Abbé Godin summarizes the picture by writing of "vast blanks in the map of Paris indicating whole lost areas . . . country districts where no Christian tradition is left—love of money has devoured it, politics have ravaged it, absence of the clergy has let it all die."[60] During the Middle Ages the parish formed the center of rural life, but today it serves mostly as a mere territorial unit.

"Evangelical" Catholics. One of the strangest phenomena on the French scene is the wooing of Catholic leaders to Christ by the Holy Spirit in spite of the obstacles in their way. When "the wind bloweth where it listeth," some who hear the call of the Saviour through unusual means respond to His call. Jansenism, the greatest single pietistic movement to rise and persist within the French Catholic Church, owes its name to Cornelius Jansenius, professor at Louvain University and later Bishop of Ypres, Belgium. After Jansen died in 1638, the Catholic hierarchy tried to erase his name from history by placing a blank, unmarked stone over his grave. Because Jansen's teaching resembled Luther's and Calvin's in its emphasis on saving grace, it has been called "Catholic Protestantism" or "Roman puritanism." Though the Vatican condemned Jansenism in 1653 after a ferocious attack by the Jesuits, the movement survived. Finally in 1713 Pope Clement XI issued the bull *Unigenitus*, which condemned this "false" theology, so like that of Paul and Augustine.

Many Jansenist priests and nuns have been genuine believers in Christ, whose lives bore evidence of an inner transformation. Although Roman watchdogs have fought the movement for over two hundred years, it is still not extinct today. France has always had pockets of Jansenist clergy, though much of the leadership today has passed into Dutch hands. When the papal pronouncement was issued, thirty French bishops, as well as many Sorbonne professors, refused to abandon their Jansenist views. But under pressure most submitted; by 1760 only six bishops remained rebellious.

The great Blaise Pascal (1623–1662), a genius who lived for only thirty-nine years, was a Jansenist who gave every evidence of true knowledge of and love for Jesus Christ. (Today you can still see the Tour St. Jacques, that beautiful medieval church tower in the heart of Paris which is all that remains of Pascal's parish church.) The Arnauld family, Le Maître, Saint-Cyran and other great Jansenists kept the flame burning through the Port Royal Abbey movement and by their writings. And the Jesuits, who hated and attacked Jansenism, trembled before Pascal's thunder as before no other Frenchman.

Converts from Clergy and Cloister. Fortunately priests and nuns, in a constant trickle, are coming to know the Lord Jesus personally. Sometimes whole groups of Catholics leave the Roman Church together under the leadership of their priests. A few years ago an Abbé Massin and some forty members of his St. Severin parish in Paris decided to break with the church. They issued a clear manifesto, which said in part:

> We reject the imposition of a third party as mediator between the two parties formed by God and his creatures. . . . We reject any church whatsoever claiming to be the exclusive dispenser of communications from God to man, and to define and control man's contact with God. . . . We reject "the infallible authority" of any church. . . . Because we believe that Jesus is God, we hold that all those who live by Him through faith are one. . . . We believe that this constitutes the one holy, universal, and apostolic church of God, the mystical body of Christ.[61]

The conversion of a priest named Henri Dubois, former Abbé of Lège, is a shining example of the power of God at work in an individual heart. I have before me as I write copies of the complete exchange of correspondence between the thirty-seven-year-old Dubois and the local hierarchy. The file is remarkable. When asked whether one could not continue to live the true Christian life within the Catholic Church, Dubois replied, "For a time, yes. I did it for a certain period. But if you want to live this life fully, and if some day you want to proclaim openly what you have dared say in confidence to your friends, you cannot remain in the church for long, especially if you are a priest."[62] For talk like this Dubois was excommunicated by Cardinal Saliège, Archbishop of Toulouse. Two American missionaries who interviewed him were convinced that Dubois' conversion to Christ was sound, and that he was growing in grace.

Not all make such progress. One of the problems confronting priests who leave the Roman system to follow the Lord is how to insure subsequent growth in Him. A former priest wrote another who had also just quit the church:

> I was much moved and interested by your letter, for your problems have been and still are mine. Protestantism is not a sure refuge, and one must be led by God in order to meet those who have remained faithful. The first Protestant pastor whom I sought out stated that he believed everything that Rome taught; the second only knew enough to ask me if I were married; the third wrote that he could not help me; the fourth taught that Jesus only became the Son of God at His baptism.[63]

The ex-priest goes on to tell how he was finally led by God to some true evangelical Christians when he encountered the Salvation Army preaching on the street one evening. In the message given he discerned something parallel to his own experience. How sad that a seeking soul like this, trying to find his way out of the Roman maze, should get so little help from French Protestant pastors! Of course this does not mean that all these pastors are untrue to the Bible.

Nuns, too, sometimes find their way out of darkness to light. Mademoiselle Léone Shigo, one of the best-known ex-nuns in the Paris area, spent the first seven years after her conversion in servitude within Catholic walls simply because she knew no better. "During the seven years which followed my conversion," she says, "I led a more and more devoted Catholic life. I went to mass and communion each morning."[64] Yet she felt an indefinable rebellion deep within, not daring to imagine for an instant that this was the voice of the Holy Spirit. Did ardent obedience to Catholic regulations satisfy her heart? Mademoiselle Shigo adds, "I say this while weighing my words carefully: to learn the counsel, thought and will of God is something completely unknown even to the most dedicated Catholic."[65]

Behind the Veil, a Void. The outward façade of French Catholicism is impressive enough in itself. Within seventeen archdioceses and eighty-six dioceses, 43,000 church edifices raise their steeples in 38,800 parishes. This means that virtually every town in France has at least one church. The parishes, with their numerous institutions, are manned by 51,000 priests, 42,500 of them from the lay orders. Some 8,500 theological students prepare for the priesthood in ninety-three seminaries. One seminary is attached to a state university, while the church maintains five free universities of its own. In Catholic secondary schools 334,000 children study, with 912,000 more in the primary grades. For social and charitable institutions, like hospitals and orphanages, 17,000 nursing sisters and other workers are provided. There are 100 publishing houses, 39 newspapers, and 488 other regular publications to reach the reading public.

Despite these impressive personnel and property statistics, the church is worried because it does not hold the loyalty and love of the average Frenchman. The working classes are almost entirely estranged from Rome. Increasing secularization of city life alienates millions from active participation. In the country districts superstition and indifference bring sincere priests to despair. No wonder that one Catholic leader has said, "We have never really *been* in France during the past hundred years, we have only *camped* there in our clerical ivory tower. . . . of all the great adventures of our country in the nineteenth century, the church inspired not a single one."[66] In their postwar best-seller, *France, A Mission Field?*, Abbés Godin and Daniel stated, "We had all observed the diminishing Christianity of France and even began to fear that positive paganism was upon us. Then we found the formula: France is a missionary country."[67] Today the official view of the Roman Church is that France *is* a mission field. Measures used in other mission fields must now be taken, the Vatican has decided, to win back the lukewarm and indifferent. Among moves the new formula inspired were the ill-fated worker-priest movement, and dozens of others. How strange that Catholics, with all their preponderance, use the term "mission field," while most French Protestants, a tiny minority, almost resent the implication that their land is a mission field!

What Surveys Say. A few years ago the French Institute of Public Opinion was asked by a popular magazine to carry out a survey of national religious beliefs and habits in response to the 1952 statement by the then President Dwight D. Eisenhower that France is "fifty-percent atheist." The survey discovered that about 85 per cent of the population are baptized adult Catholics. (France has roughly 800,000 Protestants, 350,000 Moslems, and 250,000 Jews, as well as members of other religions.) Surprisingly, this French version of a Gallup Poll revealed that 15 per cent of those who had been baptized did not consider themselves Catholic at all. Further, 43 per cent admitted freely that they were lukewarm or inactive, and 40 per cent claimed that they never go to confession. Only 14 per cent of those polled called themselves devout. A full 10 per cent disavowed belief in anything supernatural. Religious services bore 20 per cent of French Catholics, the survey said; 30 per cent deny any need of an intermediary between themselves and God; and 15 per cent would not call for a priest even if they were dying. Figures like these seem to support the former American President's statement to some extent.

In a *New York Times* survey in 1954 top correspondents discussed the hold that great world religions have on their members. From France it was reported that while 85 per cent of the people profess to be Roman Catholics, 60 per cent of these attend mass very irregularly, mostly on special occasions. Forty per cent take no part in church life at all. Only 57 per cent of professing Catholics in France believe that God exists; 15 per cent think His existence only probable.

Professor Gabriel Lebras of Paris and Abbé F. Boulard have set up a rather elaborate method of determining the extent of religious practice. Under three headings the religious observance of the public is classified thus: (1) Occasional: baptism, marriage, burial. (2) Periodical: Sunday service, Easter Communion. (3) Continual: regular mass and communion. Within each classification are numerous subdivisions, with allowances made for geographical regions, particualr social frameworks, and may other variable factors. One conclusion Lebras draws through use of his own yardsticks is that, at most, only 4 million, or 10 per cent of the population, are periodically faithful Catholics of the second classification. The really devout, or those of the third category, would number fewer than this. Between ten and eleven million more have the merest nodding acquaintance with their church. Small wonder that Abbé Godin voices the hierarchy's despair over the fact that, "setting aside the great cities, of the adult population of France only one-tenth practices the faith."[68] According to official mass attendance figures, in only nine of France's ninety counties (*départements*) can the Roman Catholic Church be considered healthy and hearty. Paris shows the worst record of all.

Revival Amidst Lethargy. In spite of low religious practice by the masses, there are signs of Catholic awakening on a small but impressive scale. Many of France's best thinkers are Catholic. Their writings attract millions disaffected with the church but longing for something meaningful in life. One example of the public's response to a better-stated faith can be seen in the audience won by M. Daniel-Rops (whose real name is Henri Petiot). Daniel-Rops, was is called *Le Bestseller* by the press, has sold more of his books than any other author in postwar France. This would be more understandable if he wrote fiction or the sex-and-violence trash so much in demand all over the world today. But most of his seventy published volumes are purely religious—many of them about Catholic history. His sales of almost two million have earned him about half a million dollars in the last decade. The French Academy member is also frequently decorated by the Vatican for making Romanism more readable. Currently he is working on a massive 150-volume encyclopedia of the faith called *The Encyclopedia of Catholicism in the Twentieth Century.*

How can we explain such interest? Part of it may stem from the French tendency to divorce the spiritual ideal from its implementation. But underneath must lie another reason for the success of this man who "has contributed much to the new stirrings of religion in anticlerical France."[69] Daniel-Rops is matched in other fields by other writers pursuing the same end through archaeology, psychology, philosophy, and art. In Daniel-Rops' own words, "There is a new kind of Catholicism afoot. It's not organized, but deep."[70]

Roman Catholic novelist and Nobel prize-winner François Mauriac urges French youth, through the pages of Paris newspapers, to accept Christian social thinking. He thus continues the three-hundred-year-old dialogue between Faith and Reason, between Pascal, Bossuet, and Chateaubriand on the one hand and Descartes, Voltaire, and Rousseau on the other. For twenty-seven years Paul Claudel, a faithful Catholic, carried on a correspondence with the late writer André Gide, the Protestant back-slider, on the same subject. Rome always has its spokesmen to the French mind, who get some hearing.

Revival can be seen in other directions too. Aging churches and mush-rooming housing developments have pushed the hierarchy into a huge, new program of church-building. A thousand new churches are planned for France, with 150 for the Paris suburbs alone. A third of the latter are already under construction in the new middle-class, apartment cities springing up everywhere. In the diocese of Versailles, for instance, sixty churches are to be built in less than three years. Such activity shows the diligence of the church to take its message to the people where they live.

But the church makes its most urgent moves in quest of its lackadaisical youth. Since the war numerous organizations have been formed, all aimed at recapturing the young. Some have had a measure of success, but somehow the French grow more skeptical as they grow older, regard-ing their youthful piety as a part of adolescence. To see the crowds of happy, priest-herded youngsters at Lourdes one might think that the church is recruiting solid followers. Anyone watching the thousands of students taking their annual forty-mile pilgrimage afoot from Paris to Chartres might conclude that these will some day be staunch Catholics. But few keep their youthful ardor for what later becomes a decadent, empty faith.

The School Uproar. One subject that drives almost all other news off the front pages is the school controversy. Every Frenchman has violent opinions either for or against Catholic moves to recapture the state schools. Ever since the Revolution, when Rome lost control of public education, the Vatican has hated and combatted the secular schools of the dechris-tianized republic. Forced to set up its own system, the hierarchy presses ceaselessly for state aid. But the battle is not easy. Less than 50 per cent of the state system's teachers profess any religion, and a majority tend to view religion as a blight on thought and progress.

Recent history has taught the French some harsh lessons on this point. After the German victory in World War II, Marshall Pétain and his Vichy government determined to deliver the schools to Rome. In the course of the struggle the Ministry of Education changed hands many times. For the first time in many years the long republican tradition of refusing sub-sidies to Catholic schools was broken under Jacques Chevalier. Chevalier clericalized the schools, opening teaching posts to priests and even expect-ing the *instituteurs*, teachers of the public schools, to give religious (Cath-olic) instruction to their pupils. Many of the latter who refused to do so were fired. So violent was the public reaction to this that Pétain was forced to replace Chevalier with the more neutral Jerome Carcopino, who later wrote of the Marshal, "He was haunted by the dream of restoring in France the forces of (Catholic) Christianity, and if he had not been stopped, in time he would have crushed the church under the enormous weight of his favors."[71]

By the notorious Barangé laws of 1951 the church was given some subsidies by the state, raising new accusations in the National Assembly that France was returning to early Vichy conditions. Then in 1956 came a reverse, when the Ministry of Education suddenly withdrew government help from six hundred Catholic schools on the ground that these schools had not conformed to laws on the number of teachers of each staff required to have university degrees. Now it was the turn of the Catholic leaders to react.

When Charles de Gaulle came into power in 1958 the world wondered how soon he, as a loyal Catholic, would reopen the question of the schools. In the National Assembly the left favored strict separation between church and state, while the right, of which the Gaullist leaders were a part, advocated state aid to Catholic schools. Premier Michel Debré's government maneuvered very cautiously, but by September, 1959, it faced a stormy controversy. (Though there are more than seven million students in the state or *laïque* schools, the Catholic educational system enrolls a million and a half—the second largest church system in the world, after that of the United States.) Most of de Gaulle's deputies had pushed earlier for debate on financial allocations to private schools, attempting to force a government decision. On December 24 Premier Debré scored a victory by winning a vote of confidence in the legislature, staking the life of his government on the issue. But the night-long legislative fight cost him his Education Minister, André Boulloche, who resigned in protest. The bill passed specified more aid to private schools but also some government control over how the money was to be spent. The amendments of control attached to the bill disappointed the church but were permited by de Gaulle, who compromised in order to save his regime.

By April, 1960, a widespread campaign was under way to repeal the government-sponsored bill altogether. Hundreds of thousands of posters deplored the spending of sixty million dollars of taxpayers' money on "private school" support, while canvassers circulated petitions calling for massive protests. Catholic bishops angrily replied that "to sign is to dishonor one's faith." The long school war appears still far from solution in a France which is both black and red.

Lourdes: Shrine of the Hopeless. France has one great Catholic distinctive in Lourdes, the most-visited religious shrine in the world. Over a hundred million people—the equivalent of more than half the American population—have found their way to the little town in southwestern France. From over a hundred countries two million pilgrims a year, including thirty thousand sick, make the trip to the magic grotto of the Virgin Mary on the river Gave. During the centennial year of 1958 some eight million arrived to pray or partake of the healing waters in the Pyrenees' foothills. What has drawn an average of a million human beings a year, for a full century of time, to this town which has never numbered more than sixteen thousand inhabitants?

It began 105 years ago. In 1858 a fourteen-year-old shepherdess, Bernadette Soubirous, was gathering firewood near the tiny hamlet of Lourdes. According to her story, she saw a vision of a beautiful lady in lustrous white who instructed her to dig for water at an indicated spot, where no spring was then known to exist. When the child did so, first a trickle, then a stream of water appeared. Today, this is the celebrated grotto with its healing waters. Altogether there were eighteen apparitions of "the girl in white whom I saw opening her hands in prayer just like the Holy Virgin does." Naturally Bernadette and the townspeople identified the white lady with the Virgin, who gave a series of commands. Bernadette later became a nun. She died at the age of thirty-five in Nevers, where her preserved body is on view today. In 1933, fifty-four years afterward, the Catholic Church made her a saint. Today at Lourdes she vies with the Virgin herself for attention, with millions praying directly to her.

The real heroes of Lourdes are the sick. Two thousand leather-harnessed stretcher-bearers are on duty from dawn to midnight, meeting the twenty-two pilgrim trains which arrive on a typical day. Activity erupts along the platforms as the bearers and three thousand blue-caped nurses get to work. The very sick are transferred, under the direction of their pilgrimage leaders, to the long lines of waiting hospital ambulances. Meanwhile the well pilgrims are herded into groups and, complete with identifying banners and badges, are escorted to their hotels. Other thousands pour into the area by plane and car, with great tent cities rising for miles around during the summer.

Lourdes is like no town you ever saw before. All day, every day, throngs crowd the streets, wearing various garbs and speaking many tongues. Here is a Belgian priest shooing his schoolboy flock along; there English clerics line up their group for instructions. Italian *monsignorini*, Irish bishops in colorful purple, French peasants, stolid Germans, American crew-cut collegians, Scots in their kilts, Dutch sailors, children in provincial costume—all struggle up and down the narrow streets. Away from the churches and the grotto there is anything but a devotional atmosphere. One sees prostitutes openly solicit their customers on the streets. A gay, carnival air reigns in the streets and shops, and in the six hundred hotels. For young people this is a fling, for adults a release, and for the local merchants a gold mine.

With brazen tastelessness, the shrine's fame is exploited by the town to the extent of nearly $200 million a year, much of it spent on so-called "holy objects." On my last visit to Lourdes I listed these: glow-at-night neckties bearing Bernadette's image, washable plastic virgins (including life-size ones), corkscrews topped by Bernadette adoring the Virgin Mother, fountain pens with peepshow virgins, and three-minute hourglasses embossed with the inevitable Bernadette. Then there are Bernadette-imprinted soap bars, plastic bottles for taking home the miraculous water, throat lozenges, cakes and candy "made from the water blessed by the Holy Father." Of a total of 710 businesses, 580 deal solely with these souvenir gimmicks, lending an air of trashy commercialism to the town. Lourdes has lately put hinges on its street signs to reroute traffic through a different part of town each two weeks, so as to give each merchant a chance.at the pilgrims!

Worship and water are the two key words for Lourdes. A church was built on the huge rock atop the original grotto, but because the crowds grew so great, first a second, and then a third were added above and below. The latest basilica is the world's largest underground church, dedicated by the prelate who is now John XXIII. Here at least 30,000 people can surround a foursquare altar, where mass can be said by four priests at once. Torchlight parades, penance at life-size stations of the cross, and praying before the many statues are all part of the pilgrim's day.

"Go drink at the fountain and there wash yourself," the Madonna told Bernadette. Following this command to the letter, the sick nowadays drink and bathe in the magic water, which flows to faucets and private tubs. The church has officially recognized only fifty-four cures out of reported thousands, yet hope lights up the eyes of the invalids wheeled before the grotto for 7:30 mass each morning. Expectation mounts as the crowd chants "Ave, Maria" hour after hour. Some spectators weep, others sigh, and almost all turn away saddened. Despair is the real winner here, where there is more disappointment than deliverance. Millions have left Lourdes broken-hearted and hopeless. Even some of the French themselves are sceptics. In a recent national survey of religious practice, the French Institute of Public Opinion asked, "Do you believe in the miracles of Lourdes?" Just 57 per cent of the Catholics asked answered "Yes," while 26 per cent were undecided, and 17 per cent denied belief.

Happily, in this pageant of pity the Lord has His own. In 1957 a young girl who found Christ as Saviour in a summer camp returned to her home in Lourdes. Through her changed life her parents, proprietors of one of the religious souvenir shops, were saved too. Soon they had turned their shop, full of the trappings of a human religion, into a grocery store. Now Bible texts adorn the walls and a witness is given to the customers. In this family the Lord—not Lourdes—worked a miracle!

4. PROTESTANT EASE IN ZION

The Gospel Comes to Gaul. We have already mentioned how early the apostolic message of Jesus Christ came to the Roman colony of Gaul. History tells of a letter from Irenaeus in Lyons in 177, addressed to the churches of Asia Minor and Phrygia, and giving a list of martyrs in his city. A bishop of the Lyons church, Irenaeus was an eyewitness of their suffering. (This was the same Irenaeus who was a disciple of Polycarp, follower of the Apostle John in Smyrna.) In the bishop's words, the Lyons martyrs were "strengthened by the fountain of living waters from the heart of Christ." The comment was sigificant, as France's church seemed destined to need more grace to suffer than most of the national churches of the world.

By 220 a Christian church was reported at Arles, and shortly thereafter others were established in Toulouse and Rheims. In 250 Gregory of Tours sent seven missionaries to Gaul from Rome. As a result, Paris and Metz had churches by the fourth century. One of the seven missionaries, France's patron, Saint Denis, is said to have been martyred on the slopes of Montmartre in Paris,* and walked up the hill with his head in his hands after his death. When Clovis, the King of the Franks, was baptized in 496, a new era of nominal Christianity was ushered in; but even before this, French Christianity had become formal and largely fruitless.

Europe's Original Protestants. As the first millennium of the age came to a close, the gospel light which had often faded now blazed again in southern France. A group called the Cathari, or Albigensians (after the town of Albi) preached against the abuses of Rome and practiced purity of life. They objected to the immoralities of the priesthood, the practice of pilgrimages, and the worship of saints and images. Though tinged with Manichean dualism, the Albigensians had, it seems some understanding of spiritual truth. They so filled southern France with their doctrines that Pope Innocent III, the most powerful of pontiffs, ordered a crusade against them in 1208. A bloody attack followed, without parallel in church

*Montmartre means "mountain of the martyr."

history. Under the brutal Simon de Montfort, the king of France moved to exterminate the sect, which had been sheltered under the tolerant rule of the counts of Toulouse. Town after town Simon put to the sword, and murdered the inhabitants, without regard to age or sex. When Béziers, one of the strongholds, was taken, a subordinate remonstrated with Simon de Montfort that there might be good Catholics among the captives. The commander's fierce reply was, "Kill them all. God knows those who are His!" Finally in 1229 the Council of Toulouse, acting on the conclusions about heresy reached at the Fourth Lateran Council (1216), organized the punitive work of the Dominican order into what became the Holy Inquisition.

Another more scriptural movement was that begun by Peter Waldo in about 1176. The Poor Men of Lyons, or Waldensians, giving away their property, as their once-rich founder had done, preached the true gospel and resisted church substitutes for it. Gradually they were pushed back by the Inquisition into the Alpine valleys of northern Italy, where later popes tried to exterminate them. Today the Waldensians are Italy's largest Protestant body.

Aftermath of Reformation. The story of the French Reformation under John Calvin is a fascinating one. In 1523 the New Testament had been translated into French by Lefèvre d' Etaples. When Calvin himself was converted in Paris in 1523, a chain reaction of events began. Robert Olivétan, Calvin's cousin, put the whole French Bible into the people's hands in 1536, the same year that Calvin published his famous *Institutes* in French. After the first Protestant church was founded in 1555 in a Paris of less than a half million inhabitants, the growth of the faith was startling. By 1560 over 400,000 professed to be Protestant in a national population of sixteen million. Two years later Admiral Gaspard de Coligny could report 2,150 churches. Naturally Roman Catholic reaction was swift and bloody. All of France was divided into armed camps during the Catholic-Protestant wars of 1562–1592. For almost forty years the two faiths were embroiled in political and military clashes, symbolized by the infamous massacre of St. Bartholomew's Day, 1572, when at least 10,000 Huguenots were murdered.

Finally the Edict of Nantes (1598) gave Protestants freedom of worship and political rights. But these rights slowly vanished under constant Catholic attack until only 806 churches in sixteen provinces remained open. With victory in their grasp, the hierarchy plotted a death blow. The Revocation of the Edict of Nantes (1685), a result of long Jesuit pressure on Louis XIV, was to have the most tragic consequences for France herself. Within a few weeks 2000 church buildings were razed to the ground and thousands of pastors and laymen were fleeing the country.

Pastors were given two weeks' notice either to abjure their faith or leave the country. As soon as the king discovered that over 300,000 of his country's most useful citizens had gone into exile, he banned Huguenot emigration. Already the city of Geneva in nearby Switzerland had increased its population by a fourth through sheltering the refugees. A suburb of Berlin and many centers in England, Holland, and America benefited by the sad exile of the saints.*

The Steep Ascent of Heaven. Now began a century of terrible persecution. Reading the Bible was prohibited under the pain of death. Anyone caught doing so, or worshiping or preaching according to Protestant tenets, was tortured on the rack, hanged, or sent to the galleys. History has preserved the names of 2,224 of these heroic galley-slaves, the last of whom were freed only in 1775. Galley convicts were automatically sentenced for life, but it was made easy for them to recant. By simply removing their caps during mass, they could be freed. One of many who refused to deny his Lord wrote a book called *Fifty Years a Galley Slave for Jesus Christ*. All over France, Protestant villages were burned, and peasants were forced to sign affidavits of loyalty to Rome or take the consequences.

Naturally the true believers went underground, seeking to maintain their faith at all costs. Deep in the Cévennes mountains, where the Albigensian Christians of an earlier age had hidden, Christians would assemble by night to worship. The very few pastors who remained became fugitives, moving at night from one location to another. Leaders of the *camisards*, as the resistance was called, were young men like Pierre Laporte, the shepherd's son, whose code name was Roland, later caught and executed. A teen-ager, Jean Cavalier, son of a baker, led a group whose watchword, *Résister*, was defiantly carved into the walls of their prison cells. Meanwhile heroic pastors like Antoine Court did risky preaching and organizing. Court set up a divinity school in Lausanne, Switzerland, to supply pastors to the secret church.

One of the purest, noblest, and most zealous of Huguenots was Claude Brousson, who was born in Nîmes in 1647. Devout from his youth, he earned a doctorate in law, preaching as a layman for over twenty years. But in 1683 Brousson had to flee to Switzerland because he had attended a clandestine committee meeting in Toulouse. From Lausanne the lawyer wrote fiery letters to leaders in and out of France, especially urging some of the exiled pastors to return to their persecuted flocks. Between 1687 and 1688 Brousson dispatched an incredible 7,000 letters from Switzer-

---

*It is only fair to state, as Saillens insists, that evidence shows a goodly number of the Huguenots weer not born again. Some later testified of finding the saving grace of God while suffering for His name.

land. Finally one emigré pastor, stung by Brousson's insistence, wrote him, "Why don't you go back yourself?" So back to France Brousson went. For the next nine years he preached and taught in a perilous ministry, hunted like an animal. Often he lived in woods or caves, preaching in secret and writing fiery tracts. Through his life and words a powerful revival broke out in the Cévennes and lower Languedoc. Finally the manhunt ended when, through an enormous price set on his head, Brousson was betrayed and arrested on the Spanish border. Though he was sentenced to be broken alive on the wheel at Montpellier, his judges so admired the fugitive pastor that they secretly ordered him to be strangled first. To the priest who tried to the last to win him back to Rome, Brousson addressed these last, Christlike words: "May Almighty God reward you, sir, for your great charity toward me and grant that you and I may see His face together in Paradise."[72]

The Fresh Air of Freedom. After centuries of persecution like this, the liberties of today are almost too good to be true. Most French Protestant bodies are free from the state's control in conformity with the law on separation of church and state and enacted in 1905. These churches have organized themselves into *associations cultuelles,* or worship organizations, as that law provided, and enjoy complete freedom of worship. In fact, French Protestants have less interference from the state than any others on the Continent, even those in so-called Protestant Europe. The only things which are forbidden, such as holding street or open-air meetings, are prohibited for political security rather than because of any prejudice against them. In strong Catholic areas they may undergo some discrimination and delaying action, due to priestly pressure on officials and the public.

In Alsace and Lorraine, whose representatives were unable to vote on the separation issue in 1905, the churches continue to operate under the Concordat of Napoleon. The older statute does not provide as complete a break from the state, which still subsidizes the churches here to some extent. By the disestablishment clauses of the treaty covering the return of these areas from Germany to France, the churches can separate completely from government control whenever they wish. However, most seem to prefer the arrangement they now have.

The tragic truth is that the French Protestants are not taking advantage of their climate of freedom. Except for a tiny evangelical minority, a lethargy toward Biblical evangelism seems to have gripped the leaders. Whereas their forefathers, many of noble blood, died for distributing the Bible, today such work is not pressed by the leaders. With due respect to the wars and political upheavals of recent decades, the church of

Jesus Christ has not grown as it might, though freedom to do so exists as never before. A massive sowing of the Word, so much needed, is neglected. This is not altogether the fault of the French; the body of Christ elsewhere has prayed little and done little for France.

Variations of Belief. The less than one million Protestants are about equally divided between Reformed and Lutheran followers, with a small percentage belonging to other denominations. The following churches are grouped under the Protestant Federation of France, and are largely, though not wholly, interested in current continental theologies and an ecumenical point of view: The Reformed Church of France, the Reformed Church of Alsace and Lorraine, the Independent Evangelical Reformed Church, the Union of Free Evangelical Churches, the Federation of Baptist Churches, and the National Alliance of Lutheran Churches of France. The latter is further divided into two branches, one of which follows the Augsburg confession, and the other is called simply Evangelical Lutheran. Denominations not attached to the Protestant Federation are the Independent Reformed, the Free Lutheran, the Union of Evangelical Churches, the Methodists, Evangelical Baptists, Mennonites, Quakers, Pentecostals and Plymouth Brethren.

The *Reformed Church of France* in its present expression was formed in 1938 at Lyons by a union of what were hitherto independent synods and denominations. Altogether 650 churches joined: Methodist (23), Free Churches (49), Evangelical Reformed (381), Reformed (164), and others, with the notable exception of a few militantly evangelical Methodist churches and some congregations of the Evangelical Reformed Church. Like many other Protestant denominations in France, the Reformed has two types of members, the *responsables* who share the responsibility and administration of the church, and the *paroissiens*, who attend but cannot vote or be elected to church offices. In most matters the Reformed Church has taken the lead, due to its historic origin under John Calvin, as spokesman and guide for united French Protestantism. This denomination today has about 368,000 followers, of whom possibly 200,000 are members in the full sense of the word.

The *Independent Evangelical Reformed* denomination includes those churches which did not vote to join the larger church in 1938. They have been reduced in number to about forty churches, however, as some congregations have voted to return to the larger body. This group began a seminary in Aix-en-Provence, which was heavily subsidized by Americans after the war. Dissatisfaction and division have attacked the denomination of about 18,000 members, which contains, nevertheless, many believing pastors and people.

The main strength of the *Lutherans* is in Alsace, where about 85 per cent of all Protestant churches are of that persuasion. In Alsace-Lorraine are perhaps 300,000 Protestants altogether, with a genuine spiritual life and influence in some centers. Alsatian German is widely used instead of French, and a strong ecclesiastic (though not political) tie is evident with neighboring Germany. Strasbourg has an especially large concentration of churches. The second large division of Lutheranism, the Lutheran Church of France, is concentrated in Paris and other parts of France. All together the Lutheran community may number as many as 310,000, but actual membership again is lower.

Baptist origins in France are interesting. From the twelfth century on there were always advocates of baptistic principles, but cruel persecution long prevented any real growth. In the year 1810 a farmer named Ferdinand Coulier found an old Bible somewhere in his house in Nomain, a town near the Belgian border. He read it with his wife and shared it with his neighbors, all of whom were Catholics. In 1815, after the battle of Waterloo was fought only forty-eight miles away, some British soldiers were billeted in the village. One of these, a devoted Christian who spoke French, opened the Word to the people, who inaugurated a little chapel. In 1819 the Swiss evangelist, Henri Pyt, arriving there, found 140 born-again people. Thus the first Baptist church in France was founded. Between 1820 and 1870 Baptists were persecuted by the Huguenots after all Protestants were organized into a state church; churches were closed, pastors imprisoned, and evangelism hindered by the police. With the freedom of today the three groups of Baptists in France have grown to a community of about twenty thousand, about a quarter of whom are baptized and are thus actual members.

In *Brethren* circles are found some of France's most Biblical Christians. There are more "closed" Brethren than "open," but the latter are difficult to number, due to their exclusiveness.* *Pentecostal* churches may have as many as 20,000 followers, the *Mennonites* 10,000, and the *Salvation Army* about 45,000.

Advantages Protestants Have. We list now several reasons why we believe French Protestants can hope for an effective witness, providing the Holy Spirit is given more direction in their work.

1) These churches were born in a Biblical milieu. Ever since Peter Waldo had the Latin gospels put into French in 1170, the Word of God has been somewhat known and always loved. One of the few great New

---

*The expressions "closed" and "open" refer to the extent that Christians outside of Brethren fellowships may attend or participate in services. Some assemblies might be altogether "closed" to outsiders, others may have some or all services "open."

Testament Greek texts, the *Codex Ephraemi Rescriptus,* which contains 145 pages written in the fifth century, is kept in the Paris National Library. The same library has sixty editions of Bibles, all dating from the thirteenth and fourteenth centuries. France has always had leaders, including Catholic ones, who did scholarly work on the Scriptures. We even owe the chapter and verse divisions of our English Bibles to scholars working in France. The French must now distribute and teach the Bible, a book almost unknown to the common man. This the Bible societies are doing their best to accomplish, though limited in funds and personnel. Only a handful of colporteurs sell the Bible aggressively to the people.

2) The French Reformation gave the world one of the greatest systematic formulations of divine truth ever written. John Calvin (1509–1564), who first published his *Institutes* in 1536, said of the Scriptures, "The full authority which they ought to possess with the faithful is not recognized unless they are believed to have come from heaven as directly as if God had been heard giving utterance to them."[73] If the French church today would heed this call by the father of the Reformed faith, a great deal more could be accomplished for God in spite of obstacles.

3) A glorious tradition of martyrdom and suffering honors France. No members of Christ's body have ever surpassed the French Christians in the length, variety, and savagery of their persecutions. This record of endurance should inspire rather than lull the church.

4) The already-noted Roman Catholic retrenchment among the masses is a great advantage. The follies and failures of Rome leave millions open to some other message dynamically given.

5) The general respect of the public for Protestants is something to build upon. Though most French do not know who Protestants are, since few have met one, they respect their reputation for integrity, patriotism, and alertness. Here is a foundation for further acceptance.

6) Access to the best of foreign influences should be a help. Since French Protestant leaders are world-oriented, they learn of new evangelical movements whenever they arise, and are exposed to the best of helpful literature.

7) A growing remnant senses needs and opportunities. The truly Biblical and evangelistic element, though tiny, has a sense of destiny and a growing unity. This remnant, the hope of the country, believes France can be evangelized and is eager to help bring in the harvest.

8) Almost complete religious liberty reigns here. France's relationship between church and state is closer to that of America than that of any other European country. With guaranteed constitutional liberties, the French Protestants, once revived and guided by the Holy Spirit, could recapture the masses for Jesus Christ.

Problems Facing the Flock. If the churches are truly to represent Jesus Christ to their country, some honest consideration must be given to failures in belief and emphasis, among which are the following:

1) Weakening effects of liberalism and neo-orthodoxy can be seen. The late Donald Grey Barnhouse, who knew the French scene well, said, "In the larger Reformed church there are a few evangelicals, many semi-evangelicals, and a strong group of extreme liberals." Barnhouse defined a semievangelical as "one who accepts the great Biblical truths as divinely given, but through a Bible which is human in its source and contains the frailty of the human touch." This group have been weaned on neo-orthodox theological concepts. The Philadelphia leader reported that several Reformed pastors of his acquaintance were certain that "the larger church would not welcome the existence of an evangelical seminary fully recognized and capable of turning out evangelical pastors."[74]

Dr. André Lamorte, who served for fifteen years as dean of the faculty and professor of theology at Aix-en-Provence, has this to say to Protestantism as a whole:

> Today, with the exception of a few centers authentically Calvinistic and Biblical by tradition, the Protestant mass has well accommodated itself to the moral, political, and social standard of the nation. Its leaders seem more inclined toward "Reformed clericalism" than toward a return to the principles of the Reformation. The nostalgia for church union has silenced all problems of doctrine.[75]

Most French pastors are deeply under the influence of the writings of Rudolf Bultmann, the neoliberal, or Karl Barth, Emil Brunner, and the other writers of neo-orthodox persuasion. While the great majority of these leaders are persuaded of the deity of Christ and the centrality of His redemption, they do not hold to a fully inspired Bible or an eternally lost race. Some form of restorationism is common to most: very few teach that all who do not know Christ as Saviour will be eternally punished. Naturally such belief in God's overpowering love as opposed to His justice reduces the urge to evangelize and the appeal for Christian commitment.

2) Lack of contact and communication with the masses is a problem. Lucien Fèvre says that the public tends to think of Protestants as "an obscure group, half-secret, somewhat occult, in any case mysterious. What is a Protestant? The average Frenchman does not know at all."[76] Historian Emile Léonard, in his authoritive book, *The French Protestant*, notes "a loss of contact between the nation as a whole and French Protestantism."[77] With only one-fiftieth of the country professing to be Protestant, many Frenchmen can only speculate about this strange faith. Nor is enough done by Protestants to spread God's Word and establish contact. True, regular Protestant radio and television programs and oc-

casional articles in the press help, but here gospel distinctives are often set aside in favor of discussion of social and moral issues. Generally, French Protestants of the Reformed and Lutheran faiths—the vast majority —prefer the barracks to the battlefield: it is easier to wear the Huguenot cross than to be crucified with the Christ of the Huguenots.

3) The clearest, most consistent evangelism is not carried out under official church endorsement. Within Protestantism, individuals and groups devoted to soul-winning often have skirmishes with their own leaders. In too many cases tacit approval of evangelistic projects replaces whole-hearted support. Foreigners like Billy Graham and Eugene Boyer have held preaching missions by enlisting the help of foreign missionaries and true believers within the churches, but these churches withhold full official endorsement from the best French evangelists. "Billy Graham's message is too childish and simple for a cultured people like the French," remarked a leading pastor. In spite of this the Graham efforts have drawn large numbers of both churched and unchurched alike, with hundreds of conversions nightly. On this point two more observations remain. First, advancement in group status means more than evangelism to some churches which have lived for centuries "outside the camp" of acceptance and recognition. Second, most pastors conceive of evangelism only as a means of collecting and indoctrinating dispersed Protestants. An estimated 200,000 such "floaters" fail to identify themselves with the church in any way. Sometimes their claim to being Protestant is based on ancestral faith or is simply a way of expressing their independence. "If I were religious at all, I would be Protestant," some say, by which they mean they are non-Catholic at heart. Of course, most do not know at all what a Protestant is.

4) Today a cautious approach to Rome is popular among the clergy. Lamorte scores "certain churches which pretend jealously to maintain Calvin's conception but remain bound to the sacramental practices of Rome. For fear of alienating a vast number of Protestants of Roman Catholic tendency, their heads, though evangelical, disapprove of pastors who refuse to baptize indiscriminately the children of the faithful and the children of unbelievers."[78] Then Roman Catholic priests are sometimes too easily brought into the pastoral body without proper training, because it is felt that they are already familiar with much of Protestant truth. In some churches, worship lacking in genuineness is starched with sacramentalism to make it more acceptable.

Still more grave are the open moves toward rapprochement with the Vatican. Occasionally Protestant leaders confer with French cardinals on some social problem. There seems to be almost a yearning in certain Prottant circles to "maintain conversations with Rome," as one leader told me, "in view of something more close someday." Open moves in this direction are sometimes made. In the fall of 1960, for instance, sixty Reformed pastors met with six Roman Catholics at Taizé, the monastery of Protestant monks, for conversations on common points. Out of this came an amazing agreement not to proselyte each other. Obviously the overwhelmingly larger church had everything to gain and little to lose from such an agreement, while for the Protestants the reverse was true. Worse still, the arrangement is contrary to scriptural commands.

5) That French Protestants are ancestor worshipers was a pet criticism of the late Emile Léonard. The cult of the past traps many Protestants into self-adulation during an age when millions around them are perishing. While there is much to admire in the history of the martyrs, our times call for action, not reflection on yesterday's heroes. With their love of history, the French overproduce monographs on the past, without realizing that the present generation is their responsibility.

6) Overemphasis on the doctrine of election can chill church life. One of the lingering effects of Calvinism—and perhaps a less important one theologically—has paralyzed much soul-winning activity. If the great reformer's views were taught in their full scope and grandeur, one could wish for little more. But this particular truth, magnified out of all proportion, becomes almost a pretext for not doing more to rescue the lost.

7) The parish system discourages the winning of the nation as a whole. Both Lutheran and Reformed faiths have conveniently divided up the country into districts and consistories. Every Protestant within the little squares on the map is expected to go to his parish church. But such divisions are unrealistic, masking the real problem. Of about 38,000 cities and towns in France, only 2,185 are listed in the Protestant directory as having some sort of witness.* But just 895 have a resident pastor (1,240 are annexes). Another 1,076 towns have no church buildings, yet they are considered accounted for through the parish system. In reality only 1,059 towns have a Protestant church. That so few of the 38,000 communities have Protestant churches does not seem to stir the average Protestant leader very much, neither does the fact that less than 2 per cent of the nation's people profess his faith. He resents the implication that his country is a mission field, and wonders why foreign missionaries consider it so.

5. *THE FRUIT OF WITNESS*

If Thou Knewest. Do French people listen when the gospel is given them? Those who testify of Jesus Christ in France speak of the hunger for truth which many people manifest. Often such soul-winners are surprised by the deep ignorance common people show about Jesus Christ,

*The current annual, called *La France Protestante,* lists fourteen denominations but does not include the Plymouth Brethren, the Pentecostals, or the Salvation Army.

the Bible, and the things of God in general. Traditionally the French police do not hinder the distribution of any kind of free literature on Bastille Day—July 14. On a recent Bastille Day American missionaries James Mulkey and Earl Sandifer, of the Greater Europe Mission, decided to give out tracts on the world-famous Champs Elysées in Paris. In Mulkey's words, "We gave tracts to two women who were tending an ice cream stand. While talking to one, I noticed the other repeating the words of the tract title, 'The Incomparable Christ.' With a bewildered expression on her face she asked, 'Christ, what is that?' 'That concerns the Christ of the Bible,' I responded. 'What is the Bible?', she asked. I then explained that the Bible gives us the life story of Jesus Christ, the one born of the Virgin Mary, who died for us on the cross. I suppose it was the mention of Mary that finally enabled her to identify Jesus. She hastened to add that she was very, very Catholic, which she obviously was not."

The French public is not so much opposed to the gospel as ignorant of it. Another missionary's report involved an offer of a free Bible to a shopowner. Puzzled, he asked if "Bible" were not a new kind of hair tonic! It turned out that there is a hair tonic with a somewhat similar name, yet the man failed to identify the Bible, the world's best-selling book.

British missionary David Cole told of discovering similar ignorance in a printer's office. He was ordering a gospel poster quoting Romans 6:23, "The wages of sin is death." The printer, whose business was communication through words, failed to recognize *péché*, the word for sin. He argued long with Cole, and even called in his brother, who agreed that there was no such word in French, adding that, as an educated man, he should know his own language better than a foreigner. Though Cole failed to convince the two men, he was sure his insistence on *péché* would prevail. Yet when returned to the shop some hours later, he found that the text of thousands of posters read "The wages of sin is *fishing*." The printer insisted that *pêche*, a word spelled the same with different accents, was the word the foreigner really was thinking about rather than a nonexistent one.

During World War II Pastor André Boegner was permitted for a period to read the Bible without comment on the national radio network. The then dictator of occupied France, Pierre Laval, did not like some of the imprecatory psalms he heard read, and called in Boegner for a dressing down. "But I am only reading the Word of God," objected the pastor. "What has reading the Word of God to do with the Bible?" retorted the angry Laval.

Missionary John Rudy of the Greater Europe Mission ministers in the

Nord area of France, where he lives in a working-class district. One day a workman came to his home and said, "I have been looking at your window display for some time, because I pass by here every day on my way to work. Excuse me for bothering you, but I just had to ask—what does it represent?" Surprised, Rudy explained the meaning of the Easter scene, with its flannelgraph figures of the open tomb, the angel, and the three crosses on the hill behind them. "I never heard of this before," exclaimed his visitor wonderingly. Rudy had assumed that in a heavily Catholic area such figures would be recognized.

Such experiences remind us of the words of our Lord to the woman of Samaria at Jacob's well, *"If thou knewest* the gift of God . . . thou wouldest have asked of him, and he would have given thee living water"* (John 4: 10). As a first step toward being saved, a person must learn from the Bible the facts of the death and resurrection of Christ. But if people can be found on the Champs Elysées, the smart Fifth Avenue of Europe, who do not know this first truth, how ignorant must be the peasant high in the Pyrenees, or the shepherd in the bleak Massif Central?

One Tender, Loving Word. "My heart is crying like a tired child," said the poet, "for one fond look, one tender, loving word." In France, as in other countries, many people live alone, forgotten, almost friendless. One such person was old Fernande, the former opera singer. When young and pretty, she had been the toast of Paris, her golden voice and laughing gaiety creating an unforgettable Carmen. But now Fernande was in the last stretch of life, with dust lying thick on her fading mementos— the books, the old papers, the photos. One of these photos I have before me as I write, showing the great star whom France made an *Officier de l' Académie* for her exquisite performances. Mercifully time had cushioned her descent from the peak of fortune to the sixth-floor, cold-water flat— where she now lived. At eighty-five she was poor, ailing, and lonely. Five years before, a dislocated shoulder had immobilized her to final lone- liness. Enthroned in her great chair among her few possessions, she felt solitude close in on her like a fog. Here she learned how wretched it can be to outlive friends, fame, and usefulness.

But Fernande was no senile creature dozing her way to death. Still alert, she remembered that at the age of sixty-seven she had embarked on a search for peace. Something had happened that year which had driven her to seek a Bible, the book where one was supposed to find in- sight into life. Sad to say, none of her few friends knew where a Bible could be found. One of them, more concerned than the rest, had visited fifteen bookstores in vain. On the surface of things it looked as though God did not care at all what happened to the old lady.

One day one of her friends, a Jewess, absent-mindedly watched the market lady wrap up her vegetables in an old newspaper. Suddenly her glance sharpened and settled on something she saw on the paper. An offer in *Paris-Presse* of a free New Testament to anyone who would write for it! Wasn't the New Testament part of the Bible? Yes, the ad said so. She glanced at the date of the paper, and her heart sank. A month old! But maybe the offer was still open after all. She hurried to tell her old friend Fernande about it.

When a strange knock sounded on the door, Fernande stirred. A short lady stood in the doorway. "I have come to bring the Testament you wrote for," she said. In a moment the British missionary was at the old lady's side with a warm greeting. Fernande stared unbelievingly at the book placed in her hands. Was this really the Bible she had sought so long? For two full hours the missionary read the Word of God to a hungry heart. When she returned a few days later, she found that the elderly singer had read to I Samuel 17 in the Old Testament and I Corinthians 6 in the New. A torrent of questions was loosed which the missionary answered as fast as she could. When her visitor left this time, the grateful old lady kissed her impulsively on both cheeks.

Eight days later the dawn of understanding broke as the Holy Spirit slowly dissipated years of darkness with His pure light. Fernande saw Christ revealed as her own Saviour. Now she eagerly awaited each day in order to learn more of this wonderful Person. The quest of decades had been answered; now for the first time Fernande learned why she had been born.

An Avalanche of Letters. In Scripture-saturated America, an advertisement offering free Bibles and Scripture portions might draw scant attention. But in France conditions are different. An advertisement inserted in the French *Reader's Digest* by one foreign mission read as follows:

> The Bible, the world's most widely-read book, is offered to you free of charge. It is called "the incomparable Book" by famous writers and celebrated men of science. Multitudes have found in it consolation, peace of heart, and eternal certainty. The first 100 who write will receive the complete Bible; the next 200, the New Testament. Others who write will be sent one of the Gospels which recounts the life of Christ. Write the European Bible Institute for your copy.

The response to this notice, exceeding the hopes and prayers of the ad's sponsors, revealed an amazing hunger for the Word of God. Unbelievably, those replying told of searching in vain for copies of the Bible, some for many years. Still other revealed that they had never even heard of the Book so widely distributed in other parts of the Christian world.

Typical of the hunger expressed in the 5,000 replies was this letter: "You can never know how much your offer pleased me, because for a long time I have tried to find the Holy Bible. Each time I tried there was some sort of hindrance. I do not even know where to inquire for a Bible. This is why I rejoice in your ad. I hope with all my heart that you will be able to send me, by return mail, a Holy Bible."*

People from all walks of life responded to the ad—mayors of French cities, members of the national police, doctors, engineers, lawyers, military officers, and a number of soldiers. Some sixty-seven were public school teachers, notoriously irreligious as a group.

"Even if I am not in the first one hundred," one of the teachers wrote, "would you make an exception for someone who wants to believe?" And a student wrote, "Please realize that even if my request is too late, you have given me a call to make an about-face in my life, and one that is not shallow."

One of the mayors wrote, "I would like to make the Bible known to the people of this town, isolated in a mountain pass. Would I be abusing your generosity to ask for free New Testaments?"

For several years the teachers of the European Bible Institute had been planning to insert an advertisement in the *Digest*, offering free Scriptures to those who would write in. They spent months preparing a new correspondence course in the Gospel of Luke to follow up prospective inquiries. Institute students from twelve countries concentrated in prayer for the new project. When funds began to come in to underwrite the venture, it was prayerfully launched.

Not only from France, but also from Italy, Spain, Switzerland, Belgium, Holland, Yugoslavia, Germany, Egypt, Israel, Turkey, Africa, Madagascar, Vietnam, and Canada, responses began to pour in. The letters revealed an amazing eagerness for spiritual understanding, considering the usual French reluctance to discuss personal problems.

After receiving a Bible and other literature, a stenography teacher wrote, "I have just received what you sent. All of it moved me profoundly. I just loaned it to a friend who has a like need and would appreciate it if you could send me another." One soldier wrote, "I believe I have found in the Bible you sent what I have been looking for so long, a guide for our disturbed times. This book will surely bring me much help." But the most astonishing letters came from Catholics.

Six nuns, including the Mother Superior of a convent, asked for Scriptures. Seventeen priests responded. One elderly Carmelite nun said,

*All letters in this section are from the files of the European Bible Institute (Greater Europe Mission).

"During my twelve years of continual sickness I have hoped to find a Bible, for I know that all it teaches would bring me consolation. I want to read it before leaving this cheerless place." Another striking response came from the Roman Catholic publishers of a daily newspaper with 500,000 readers and a monthly magazine with 250,000 readers, who suggested that the offer of free Scriptures be inserted in their publications!

A woman from Moselle wrote, "I am studying your correspondence courses with joy and ask your help in my problems. I am Catholic but have not practiced my faith for years. The Jehovah's Witnesses visited me and only increased my confusion. Searching for God, I have battled courageously but am now perplexed to the point that I doubt everything. My thoughts oppress me night and day. I seek the truth with all my heart and want to teach my children the truths of the Bible."

Probably the deeper significance of this large response to a single advertisement lies in its value as a demonstration and encouragement to French Christians. Those who know something of the French quest for reality are convinced that some day it will be expressed on a much larger scale.

Mass Evangelism, Too. We have noted elsewhere that it is a French characteristic to consider a matter acted upon as soon as it is defined. Nowhere is "the paralysis of analysis" so evident as in the implementation of evangelism. To talk about the need of reaching the man on the street is one thing, but to attract and reach him with the gospel is another. One of the unique contributions of foreigners in France has been to help their French brethren put their own Spirit-born desire for public soul-winning into practice. The initiative of these foreign Christian workers made possible the two large evangelistic efforts of Billy Graham and of Eugene Boyer. Again, foreign missionaries from abroad have taken the lead in introducing such special techniques as poster evangelism, winning of children, correspondence courses, the training of counselors, and gospel radio. Sometimes the French surprise themselves with their own zeal once an idea they accept is applied in a practical way.

Realizing how much the winning of France depends on the nationals themselves, missionaries always hope that local evangelicals will show more and more initiative. In France, mass evangelism in tents and halls is not easy, since in most cases there are few believers to help the evangelist and his team. Often preparation must be carried out by the evangelizing group from the very beginning, and mostly alone. Saddest of all is the absence of trained individual Christians to follow up converts and the lack of strong churches to receive them. For all that, such work is not impossible. At the moment France seems poised on the threshold of a new era, when she may well listen to the voice of God.

Salvation for Sodom-on-the-Seine. A newspaper reporter is supposed to have been the first to characterize Paris in these words. As a matter of fact, France's capital has a greater reputation for wickedness than it deserves, due to the desire of certain circles to capitalize on its legend. People here share the same fears, desires, and sins as their fellow men elsewhere. Although Paris has surely not outsinned all other cities in Europe, it is still one of the neediest.

We have already mentioned the importance of Paris to any plan for winning the French to Christ. Just what is being done here for His name? Excluding mission points, annexes, Protestant institutions, and foreign churches, only seventy-five organized Protestant churches serve over five million souls in greater Paris. These are subdivided as follows: Reformed (32), Independent Reformed (1), Evangelical Lutheran (23), Free Evangelical Lutheran (1), Baptist—of various groups (9), Methodist (2), Reformed Home Missions (6), Mennonite (1). Then there are several Plymouth Brethren assemblies of both "closed" and "open" persuasions, as well as a number of Salvation Army halls.

How many of these churches are evangelical and evangelistic? Very few, in our opinion, give out a consistent, clear message of saving grace. As a result, this teeming metropolis, with its 150 suburbs, many of them predominantly Communistic, hears less of the gospel than most similarly-sized cities. Hong Kong and Calcutta are better served. Even Tokyo has more of a vital witness for Christ, according to some who know both cities.

The Twofold Foreign Contribution. Are missionaries really needed in France? We have shown the great scope of unmet need. Ultimately, of course, French Christians themselves are responsible to tell their own people the good news of the gospel. Only they can carry out an extensive witness which foreigners, even in large numbers, could never accomplish.

To implement this, two steps are necessary. First, more French people, as potential reapers, must come to know the Lord as Saviour. How can the foreigner help to gather this body of reapers? The work of the Englishman, R. W. McCall, is one good example. Visiting France quite late in life, McCall began to work in 1871 in the working-class districts in Paris. By 1888 the preaching halls he established numbered 126 in Paris and elsewhere. Support came from English, American, and French sources as McCall broke tradition by going to the man on the street in a "storefront" type of evangelism. Within a quarter-century of its start, the McCall Mission had progressed so rapidly that "it reported a million hearers in its halls and ten thousand scholars in its Sunday Schools."[79] Though the present work of the mission, today called the *Mission Populaire de France,* is considerably reduced, it is now wholly French. It accomplished much during its best days. The same can be said for the Salvation Army, which was launched a little more than fifty years ago in the Paris slums by three English lassies, under the leadership of General Booth's daughter. Today the Army, now thoroughly French, maintains fifty halls or preaching posts. Many more examples could be given of foreigners who have evangelized and inspired the nationals to do the same.

Second, French leaders must be taught in the deeper things of God. In edifying new converts, the foreigner can be especially helpful. Robert Haldane, a Scot who knew how to set orthodoxy aflame, was the chief instrument in France's nineteenth-century awakening. In his biweekly Bible classes in Geneva Haldane so profoundly opened the Epistle to the Romans to a handful of students discouraged by liberalism that revival came. What apostles his men were! Merle d'Aubigné, Frédéric Monod, Louis Gaussen, Bonifas, Guers, César Malan, Henri Pyt, and Ami Bost —all helped France heavenward through pen or preaching. But, alas, giants of this caliber are few today.

Training Timothys. If the shortage of reapers and of gospel churches comprises the greatest problem in confronting all of France with a clear mesage from God, then it follows that disciple-training is the fastest and most practical way to evangelize this country. Whether this be done formally or informally is not too important; what matters is the making of disciples rather than mere converts. The foreign worker in France cannot just win men and women; he must also take some responsibility for deepening their lives in Christ. Like the Apostle Paul, he must travail in birth again until Christ is formed in his converts. Such work takes time and patience. But is there any other way?

Only a new generation of French, conditioned to believe the Bible and utterly obey God, can win France. Take the single issue of giving. The lack of money to do the Lord's work which looms as so large a question here is only a problem in the hearts of believers. There is plenty of money in the pockets of ordinary people for coffee and drinks. If Christians were taught to give even this small equivalent amount to their God, all needs would be abundantly met. On this score, no problem should exist that would call for the use of foreign funds. The wrong use of missionary money to build French church buildings and pay expenses for congregations and pastors has resulted in weakening rather than strengthening the body of Christ.

In the lives of the few hundred young people under the personal influence of dedicated individuals or Bible institutes and other institutions lies hope for the future. As evangelists and pastors are trained in the Scriptures, the cause of Christ must advance. Bringing in hundreds of outside missionaries is needful, but there is no substitute for the national, who alone can finish the task. There is just too much to do—there are too many people to win, too many unreached areas, cities, and towns.

Since World War II the Greater Europe Mission has founded the European Bible Institute north of Paris at Lamorlaye. This school joined the older, Biblically faithful Nogent Bible Institute, founded and led by the French themselves in the eastern suburbs of Paris, and the evangelical seminary at Aix-en-Province. Together these schools seek to prepare the French to reach the French. Though more reapers are needed, the results among those trained to win others are already most encouraging.

Unreached Minorities. Traditionally France has welcomed political refugees and racial minorities with exemplary compassion. These groups, some of which are quite large, cannot be omitted from any missionary strategy designed to win France for Christ. Over two million foreigners live here. Of these, 25 per cent are Italians, who tend to concentrate in the Southeast near their own border. Several thousand other Italians enter the country periodically for seasonal work such as harvesting. Twenty per cent of the aliens are Poles, 15 per cent Spaniards, and 7 per cent Belgians. The large number of refugee Spaniards in the Southwest (mentioned in the chapter on Spain) are poor and spiritually needy. Then come the Swiss, the expatriate White Russians, and the Armenians.

Large racial minorities of French citizenship include 300,000 Algerian Muslims, who now comprise 2 per cent of the population of Paris. These are the latest, poorest, and largest of the migratory elements to enter the land. A third of them gather in big cities like Paris, where fifty thousand have habitable quarters, while an equal number live in *bidonvilles* (shanty towns), or even outdoors. In cold weather some greedy landlords take in twenty or thirty sleepers in airless cellars in rotation groups of ten. As a result of such misery, most crime in the *bas-fonds* (the underworld) is led by Algerians and Corsicans. Of the Algerians in France, 90 per cent come from the Kabyle country and preserve many of the racial characteristics of their Berber ancestors. A considerable number of Moroccans and Tunisians live here, too. All these speak dialects of their own, as well as classical Arabic and French.

France has by far the largest number of Jews in western Europe. (Her

350,000 are trailed by Belgium, in second place, with 35,000.) Many, but not all, are French-born and thus not classified as foreigners. These world wanderers, toward whom all Christians should show special love, have little chance to hear the gospel.

The English-speaking community, most of whom live in greater Paris, number more than 25,000 permanent residents. Others who are students and business, and government people, temporarily in the country, total perhaps 10,000 or more. An English-language gospel church would be a great boon to these.

No country in Europe is more prepared for the sowing of spiritual truth than France, the oldest civilization on this continent. No wonder Billy Graham, sensing this in a recent visit to Paris, said, "A spiritual revival could sweep Paris and make an impact on the entire world. I am burdened for this country." France is prepared to hear and God is ready to work. Who will be His spokesmen?

Two Spanish pastors point to the government seal which has closed their church to the public. This is one of more than a score sealed by official action.

Credit: Greater Europe Mission

The parade of the penitents on Good Friday of Holy Week in Barcelona.

Credit: Greater Europe Mission

Chapter 5

THE TRUTH ABOUT SPAIN

"You will find here the same Spain of the fifteenth and sixteenth centuries—the same noble, intransigent Spain. . . . When a nation has received the divine favor of a single faith, concessions cannot be made to error."

—GENERALISSIMO FRANCISCO FRANCO
Greeting to South Americans, 1950

"We must deal without any human consideration against Protestants when they try to spread their errors and heresies, because after all true ecumenicity means only to return to Rome."
—Bishop of Madrid-Alcala
Spanish Catholic Action magazine *Ecclesia,* 1961

"If Spanish Christians can make this kind of progress under persecution, then give us a little of the same back home!"
—An American pastor visiting Spain

1. *THE SPANISH SCENE*

Not Pity, But Insight. If any European country desperately needs the God of salvation, that country is Spain. Unfortunately we must thank newspaper men more than our Christian leaders for our awareness of this. So often has the world press reported the predicament of Spanish Protestants that every informed Christian already thinks of Spain in missionary terms. Presidents, prime ministers, parliamentary bodies, and the United Nations have all discussed the explosive Spanish religious question. Simultaneously books and articles by the score have condemned government intolerance and called for fair play for Protestants.

For us, all this obscures the deeper issues. There is much more to the Spanish scene than the harassment of Protestants, painful as that is. Almost everybody realizes how little official freedom they are given. But people are surprised to hear how much Spanish Christians do accomplish in spite of—or should we say because of?—adverse conditions. On this subject one Spanish leader says,

179

Many Americans come through Spain and generally speak in a tone of pity for believers here. They commiserate with them on the grounds that Protestants are persecuted, bewailing the lack of liberty that exists in Spain. But I say they have misjudged the situation. The fact is that the Spanish Christians do not take advantage of the liberties which they do have. . . . The Christians here are pampered a bit by visiting Americans who give them the idea that they are all martyrs. This lends them the rosy glow of self-pity. With their eyes on themselves they miss the opportunities that do come.[1]

In our survey we do not intend to contribute further to an enfeebling self-pity. Of course, fighting for religious liberty is always worthwhile. Yet such liberty is not promised in the Bible as a guaranteed concomitant of the gospel. The church of Jesus Christ during most of its history has lived under persecution. Resistance from the enemy can always be expected, anyhow, where Christians are a minority and their churches few. When Satan uses an opponent as ancient and wily as the Roman Catholic Church, the conflict is especially fierce. Only when the gospel has influenced a nation for some generations does a climate of freedom seem to develop. Tolerance has been long in arriving, even in our Protestant western nations.

If we have religious liberty, we must use it. Where we do not have it, we must still preach the gospel to everyone, by any means, regardless of opposition. I once heard a leading missionary statesman gently rebuke a Spanish pastor for presenting his country's needs at a Swiss conference in terms calculated to stir pity rather than a deeper, more lasting concern. Instead of stressing prohibitions against Protestants and the reactions of an unopposed Catholic regime, we must take the Lord's viewpoint. He has given us weapons which the enemy of souls cannot match. David's five smooth stones are still mightier than Goliath's strength. We will even be surprised to discover *how much we foreigners can do* for Spain. Toward the end of this chapter appears a summary of the kinds of help Spain can receive from Christians abroad.

Spain's Cry to the World. No country in Europe arouses a Christian's compassion like Spain. In countless municipalities and tiny farms across the land, almost thirty million people live lives of quiet desperation, without God. Every year 250,000 people die; every three years a million more souls are added to the population. In one average American lifetime sixteen million Spaniards enter eternity. Any foreign Christian who has once seen the hidden hamlets tucked back in the folds of the Pyrenees, their inhabitants ignorant of God, will never be the same again. Along the windswept highlands of the Meseta are thousands more, isolated from both God and man. About five thousand such towns have no roads at all leading to them!

Live a little while anywhere in Spain, and you will sense the bitter frustration behind the Spanish smile. To be sure, a kindly cheer strikes the visitor at first. But the Spaniard, by accepting his lot fatalistically, has struck a truce with sorrow. In that somber way inherited from the Moors, he co-operates with the inevitable in life. He is like a man who lives in the bottom of a pit. A cluster of stars looks to him like the whole firmament, for they are all he can see. Without the new birth he is self-aware, but not God-conscious. Ignorant of God, and even ignorant of his ignorance, the peasant clings unenthusiastically to a garbled Christian heresy which promises—but never delivers—peace of soul.

Is city life any better? In the twenty-four cities of over 100,000 inhabitants physical comforts are superior, and the pay better, if you can find a job. Then too, there are Protestant chapels in some of these. Yet even here the Spanish John Doe, his personality shaped by an imposed, unloved religion, is discontented. His deeper problem is unforgiven sin, the curse of Adam. Perhaps that is why black is so appropriate as his color. More black is seen here than anywhere else in Europe. In Spain, if your parent dies, you wear black for three years. Six months is the duration for a brother, three months for a second cousin. Entire families don this mourning gloom for long periods. Remarking that over half of all Spaniards are always in black for clerical or personal reasons, Roy Wyatt, Jr., remarks:

> It is dark in Spain, dark in the churches, dark in the simply adorned houses, dark in the narrow, cobblestone streets. And the most ominous darkness is in the people's hearts and minds. There is nothing to live for in Spain. Life is day by day drudgery, always an uphill fight. Many people's faces are hardened into fixed masks; there is no light in their souls.[2]

What do those who know the country best think about the extent of soul-darkness? "In some central provinces with millions of people not a single church can be found," says one of Spain's best-known pastors.[3] This leader, grateful that "it has been my privilege throughout my life to establish churches in 14 towns in Spain where the gospel has never been preached," insists that "there are whole provinces with one million or more inhabitants which have not one evangelical church."[4] A British missionary, resident in the country for more than a score of years, asserts that "Spain has at least ten provinces without a witness for Christ."[5] Since there are fifty provinces, a fifth of the country has yet to see a single ray of gospel light. This would be like saying that ten out of America's fifty states have no witness at all! In other provinces supposedly occupied by evangelicals only one church, or perhaps a handful of tiny churches, holds forth the Word of Life. With such a feeble witness these could hardly be called unevangelized provinces.

Now let us reduce the problem to single areas. Lérida province is a good example. Some 331,000 people inhabit its 8,000 square miles. Most of the 324 towns have never heard the gospel. Many years ago a Welsh missionary named Frederick D. Jones established a handful of preaching centers in the province, but he and his Spanish helpers were forced out of the country in 1936, leaving the infant groups leaderless. Only in Lérida city, the provincial capital of 52,000, is there a real witness for Christ. Otherwise some scattered families here and there are the only other believers in the whole province.

According to a recent Catholic yearbook, the remote Navarra region bordering on the French Pyrenees is the most neglected part of Spain in terms of Protestant witness. In this annual yearbook's section on non-Catholic churches, only 175 Protestants are reported in the Vascongades area, 160 in Extremadura, and perhaps 175 in Castilla la Vieja.[*]

The tourist who visits only briefly the places he is expected to see cannot really feel the spiritual pulse beat of Spain. Perhaps Andalusia, most familiar of the tourist regions, gives rise to the image of a land full of bullfighters, dancing gypsies, and *flamenco* singers. Many travelers sigh over the breath-taking Alhambra above Granada, or the colorful Seville of Don Juan. Others prefer the mosque of Cordova, Franco's pompous Valley of the Fallen near Madrid, or the El Greco home in Toledo. Bright travel posters seek to capture the sun's warm caress along the white beaches of the Casta del Sol or the idle beauty of Majorca. Judged by natural terms alone, Spain is indeed enchanting.

> Fair land! Of chivalry the old domain,
> Land of the vine and olive, lovely Spain.

But sunshine, color, and music all fade before the sober truth: the Spanish people, despite the charm of their land, are pitifully lost!

In a word, what is the missionary problem here? Each one of the handful of foreign missionaries in Spain has more than a million souls on his hands; so his contribution is almost negligible. What of the Spanish Christians themselves? Alas, they are too few for so large a task. For comparative purposes, triple the population of the state of Illinois so that it will equal that of Spain. Then spread those thirty million people over an area almost as big as Texas. Now thinly scatter 25,000 Protestants—approximately the number of people who live in the Chicago suburb of Wheaton, Illinois—across this huge area. Give every family head among

---

[*]*La Guia de la Iglesia en Espana*, Madrid: Oficina General de Informacion y Estadistica de la Eglesia en Espana, 1960.

these 25,000 a yearly wage of $280 to cover all his own family needs as well as the cost of getting out the gospel. Install him in a miserable, crowded house and saddle him all day with a wearying work load. Just for good measure, infiltrate his worship service with secret police, hem him in with restrictions, and threaten him with police brutality. Do you begin to glimpse the problems he has in winning his country to Christ?

Where Contrasts Abound. Let us take a closer look at the land. The questions raised by Nicholas B. Adams in *The Heritage of Spain* help to convince the outsider that Spain is not simple to know.

> What sort of country is Spain? A desert made to order for the pilgrimage of ascetic and idealistic Don Quixotes? A lush land in which the lurid passion of Carmen and Don Jose reaches ecstasy and tragedy? Is it the land of the emaciated saints of El Greco or of the rich-fleshed *majas* of Goya? A country of castanets, guitars, love and laughter, or a region of the most sanguinary civil wars? The producer of incredibly rich *conquistadors* or of incurable idlers in the sun? Of proud *hidalgos* or of humble though crafty gipsies? Of fiercely independent country folk or of thoroughgoing autocratic rulers?[6]

In *Kings Without Castles* another writer ventures a somewhat facetious answer. To Lucy Crockett, Spain is "a dream world, steeped in mysticism, locked in tradition, charged with violence, inhabited by the most delightful, the most courtly, the most gracious, barbarians."[7] Such a description at least illustrates the problem we face in trying to understand the Spanish.

So many things about them are contradictory that a whole lifetime would be needed to interpret their nature. Spanish people seem either too rich or too poor, their weather either too cold or too hot, their land too harsh or too unbelievably lovely. Though ruled by dictators for centuries, Spaniards are born individualists who insist on their rights. History charges them with exquisite cruelties, but kinder individuals never lived. Professing loyalty to the church, many Spanish Catholics are vociferous critics and hearty backsliders. In spite of a high rate of illiteracy (14%), they have always produced peerless men of letters. Though they have the lowest living standards in Europe, they also boast of the highest skyscraper. While seeming to stand still, they advance. "The Spaniard is in fact a composite of extremes; he is everything that has ever been said about him and he is also its opposite."[8]

In countless ways Spain is unique. She is the only European nation to have lived for almost eight centuries under Arab rule. First to colonize the New World, proud Spain once ran the world's largest overseas empire. Her continental neighbors dreaded the victorious Spanish armies during "the Spanish century." Of this hour in her history a distinguished Spanish scholar wrote in the nineteenth century, "Spain, evangelizer of half the planet; Spain, the hammer of heretics, light of Trent, sword of Rome, cradle of St. Ignatius—this is our greatness and our glory: we have no other."[9] In our times no land has suffered a more savage and costly civil war or a longer, intrenched dictatorship.

Strangely enough, the Spaniards are pioneers of free government, though they have enjoyed less of it than any other nation of the continent. As Cambridge professor J. B. Trend points out, "It is seldom remembered that modern, democratic government began not in England, but in Spain."[10] The principle that a king could not act against a person or his property without due process of law had been stated in Spain before it was incorporated into the Magna Carta. The right of the accused to legal counsel was practiced here long before England adopted it. Plainly the fiction that Spanish people really prefer dictatorship is as false as the claim that they are instinctively, unalterably Catholic.

When we consider Spain's true Christians, we marvel the more at the colorful and unexpected. Theirs is the only European nation where the Bible, except in a controlled Catholic edition, is proscribed literature. Though oppressed by their government, no people give higher allegiance to their state. Pursued, beaten, sometimes martyred, Spanish Christians have inspired the world throughout history. Today these pilgrims traveling toward a fairer world on high are a credit to their Lord and His kingdom. They know that they have here no continuing city, but seek one to come.

The March of Centuries. A brief outline of Spanish history is useful in helping understand the country today. Christianity enters recorded Spanish history sometime during the second century. By the third it was organizing itself within the framework of the Roman provincial system. Then came waves of conquest by barbarians from the east which were to mark the end of Roman power. The last and strongest tribe, the Visigoths, vanquished the rest, gaining control over most of Spain before 429. Under Gothic sway, trade gradually diminished and a serf class arose to serve the great nobles. Though the king of the Visigoths had been converted to Catholicism near the end of the fifth century, the tribe as a whole never fully embraced Christianity.

In the eighth century the Berber Moors invaded from North Africa, and by 718 they had conquered the whole of the Iberian peninsula. The rest of that century they spent in consolidating their rule and preparing for long centuries of occupation. Moslem handling of the Catholics was quite inconsistent and differed from region to region. Both faiths were severe with apostates who insincerely embraced the other religion for personal advantage. But often Christians, by paying a fee, could continue to worship in their own way, and churches could remain open through paying heavy taxes. Friendly, inter-faith relations during the Moorish ascendancy were punctuated by periods of bloodshed. But in general the Moors were fairly tolerant, being realistic enough to see the advantages of flexibility. From their eight-century-long rule, the Moslems left an indelible imprint upon Spanish life and mentality, which is still visible today.

The year 1492 was decisive in Spanish history as well as in American. That year Isabella and Ferdinand, by the subjugation of Granada, defeated the last of the Muslim states and united Spain under Catholic rule. The period called the Reconquest had been long, slow, and bloody, but opened a new era of Spanish glory and power in Europe and across the world. By sponsoring Christopher Columbus, Isabella became founder of the farflung Spanish empire in the New World. In 1519, Charles V, of the house of Aragon and Castile, was elected Holy Roman Emperor, thus becoming the most powerful ruler in Europe. During his rule the Reformation exploded across Europe.

Charles V vacillated in his treatment of the German reform, but later stiffened his opposition through the Counter-Reformation, the Council of Trent, and the Inquisition. Philip II, his son and successor, oppressed the Low Countries, thereby precipitating the birth of Dutch nationalism. The same king is famed for his disastrous Armada attempt against England in 1588 and his intervention in the French religious wars. During succeeding centuries the monarchy declined. A first republic briefly appeared from 1873 to 1874. In 1931 the monarchy collapsed with the downfall and exile of Alfonso XIII.

A Cruel Civil War. In historic terms the Spanish Civil War of 1936–1939 is so recent that Christians seeking to help Spain must know how it occurred and why. Almost every adult Spaniard either fought in it or lost loved ones through it. The most brutal and senseless civil war of modern times blighted every life and family, leaving marks on people's minds and souls. More than a million died, and other millions were maimed or jailed and tortured.

In 1931 free elections were held for the first time in Spanish history. The people voted for a republican form of government, thus bringing into being the controversial Second Republic, destined to survive for only eight years. For forty-eight hours after its launching the Republican ship of state sailed on calm seas. Then the Roman Catholic primate at Toledo suddenly called upon the population to repudiate the new regime. In an overflow of popular indignation at this intervention on the part of the hierarchy (which was afraid of losing many cherished privileges), the public turned against the church with fury. Priests were killed and churches burned as pent-up anticlericalism burst forth. In Malaga not a single priest survived. Over two thousand of the clergy, all together, were killed during the war that followed. Many Catholic Basques and country priests were loyal to the Republic, but the Jesuit hand in the rebellion was obvious to all the clergy.

With the support of the Vatican, most of the nobility, the army, and several fascist fronts, General Francisco Franco and other generals in Morocco began their rebellion in 1936. For some time the issue hung in balance. Then as reinforcements came from Italy and Germany, the survival of the government grew doubtful. The casualties were appalling, with untold devastation in property and economic potential. Atrocities were committed on both sides, but the rebel side excelled at mass civilian murder, execution without trial, and deliberate cruelty. While the whole world watched what later proved to be an Axis proving-ground for European war, the situation for the Republic deteriorated rapidly. At times mob rule, a collapse of all law and order, produced a total chaos never seen even in as cruel and lawless a period as the French revolution.

Refusing to provide the elected and legitimate Republican government with arms, as they were free under international law to do, the western democracies betrayed Spain to fascism.* Had they supported Spain then, they would not now need to pretend that the present regime in Spain belongs to the free, western world. Their desire to placate the Vatican and the dictators proved the death-knell of free Spanish government. Franco tried to characterize the Republicans (called Loyalists) as godless and communistic. Seeing an opportunity, the Soviet Union intervened on the Republican side—but only to dominate it. Although in the later stages of the conflict there was a Communist and anarchist element, many authorities (like Claude Bowers, then U.S. Ambassador in Madrid) have shown that the charge was generally untrue. By the spring of 1939 Madrid had fallen to Franco. On April 1 Pope Pius XII sent the following telegram to Franco:

> Lifting up our hearts to the Lord, we give sincere thanks with your Excellency for Spain's desired Catholic victory. We express our hope that your most beloved country, with peace attained, may undertake with new vigor the ancient Christian traditions which made her great. With affectionate sentiments we send your excellency and the most noble Spanish people our apostolic blessing.[11]

Within eight months all of Europe was ablaze in World War II, with Franco on the side of the Rome-Berlin Axis.

*The reasons behind the refusal were complex, but Vatican pressure was a strong factor.

Franco's Spain. When Generalissimo Francisco Franco (called *El Caudillo*, "The Leader") assumed power at the end of the Civil War in 1939, he set up a government which rested upon three separate, but interrelated, forces. The first is the Falange, the only legal political party in Spain.* The members, agencies, and secret police of the Falange comprise the body, of which Franco is head. Though small in number, Falangists on every level maintain control of the land. Theoretically civil rights were given to the public in the Charter of 1945, but they are limited in practice. Freedom of speech and press also exist only within the confines allowed by the party. At the moment, most censorship of the "tolerated opposition" is suspended, but the controls are still there. Publications and films are watched, and any real anti-government activity is forbidden. Academic freedom is restricted, too, and students are politically indoctrinated (though the indoctrination is not always successful).

The second force is the Roman Catholic Church, which enjoys a favored place as a ruling partner in the country. The Vatican has demanded, and received, almost absolute power over religious life in Spain, as well as a host of other, practical privileges on lower levels. Under the primate, the Archbishop of Toledo, ten metropolitan and sixty-four suffragan sees operate. Spain has more than 23,000 priests to serve a very-well-supervised Catholic public. Some 22,000 young men are currently studying for the priesthood. Another church prerogative is compulsory religious education in the schools. About 150 million pesetas a year are given the church by the state as a subsidy. Listed Roman Catholic periodicals total 1603—an enormous share in any country's reading matter. Politically, Rome tied herself to the state more closely than ever with a 1953 concordat by which she gained more advantages than she gave. Through Toledo, the seat of the church and its second capital, much of the state's business is actually run by this ecclesiastical partner. The official attitude of the Roman Church toward the present regime is that the country's form of government should be decided by its people, and will be supported by the church (unless it is communist or socialist). Yet when the Second Republic was voted into existence by the people, the hierarchy opposed it and sponsored Franco. The Jesuits, who have been twice expelled from Spain in the last century, are back in their usual role of intrigue and maneuver. Some of the younger priests are now backing the demands of the workers for better living conditions.

As a third element, the armed force of almost a million men is potent. The party, however, manipulates the army, navy, and air force

---

*Currently the Falange, now known as the National Movement, is seeking to get rid of its right-wing label. Elements within it are trying to adopt a forward-looking program of "Spanish Socialism" in order to meet a rising left-wing sentiment among workers, students, and certain Catholic leaders.

with such care that there has been no revolt in recent years, though the thirst is always there. Lately America is helping modernize the military arm in exchange for the favors she seeks.

Up to the present an armed truce has bound all three uneasy allies. Each partner needs the others to maintain its position, and each one's ultimate power is curbed by the others. The church needs the Falange and the army to maintain her spiritual dictatorship; the few times when she lost this double support, the people turned on the church in bloody reprisal. The state in turn needs the church and the armed forces to help it hold the people together and cancel out opposition—a very old combination in European politics. Lastly, the military needs the party for survival, and the unifying discipline of Catholicism to reduce dissatisfaction in its ranks.

An Army of Exiles. Whether voluntarily or under heavy political pressure, a huge number of Spaniards have left their land as exiles, never to return. Some find their way to America or England, or more recently to Argentina. The largest exodus occurred at the end of the Spanish Civil War, when 500,000 political refugees crossed over the Pyrenees into France, where they set up a Republican government-in-exile. Many became rooted there, where their children enjoy a freer life as French citizens. For most, in the area of Perpignan, Toulouse, and Montauban, life consists of bleak poverty. A minority are Communists who play a cat-and-mouse game with the French and Spanish police. Recently Pablo Casals, the world's leading cellist and himself a Spanish exile, underscored the plight of his fellow countrymen in a letter to the well-known ex-priest Walter M. Mantaño: "Many of these refugees are today in hospitals, ill with diseases caused by the miserable conditions under which they live. Although some have been able to build new lives, thousands are destitute, in need of food, medical care, and not the least, of moral encouragement."[12]

Here in free France lies a harvest field of several hundred thousand souls for any missionary who knows Spanish or is willing to learn it. What joy to minister to these Spanish refugees, who are usually receptive to the gospel! Older ones are particularly open to any who will visit them, converse in their own language, and show sympathetic interest in their troubles.

Every year about 50,000 Spaniards leave Spain, either legally or illegally, to begin a new life elsewhere. For many, the country is a prison. To leave, one must have not only a passport, but an exit visa, not easy to obtain. In *The Spanish Temper* V. S. Pritchett has expressed the refugees' plight in colorful language:

Spain is the great producer of exiles, a country unable to tolerate its own people. The Moors, the Jews, the Protestants, the reformers— out with them; and out, at different periods, with the liberals, the atheists, the priests, the kings; the presidents, the generals, the socialists, the anarchists, fascists, and communists; out with the right, with the left, with every government. The fact recalls that cruel roar of abuse that goes up in the ring when the bullfighter misses a trick: out with him![13]

In a gospel camp in southern France I heard one young Spaniard's story. Though thin and emaciated, his dark eyes flashed fire. As he told the circle of French young people about his flight, his voice trembled. First came the heart-rending experience of leaving his family. Then his voice broke a little more as he described the desperate climb over the Pyrenees, sometimes down sheer rocks where a slip could have meant death. One terrifying slide at night down an ice-chute ended only a hand's breadth from a thousand-foot fall. Afraid to move, he called upon God. After some moments courage rose in his heart again. Slowly he inched his way down to safety and freedom, miraculously evading the border police. But the greatest miracle was yet to come. By seeming chance he stumbled upon the home of a poor Spanish family. Refugees like himself, they had one great secret to share—salvation through Jesus Christ. The lad sobbed at the end as he spoke the words I jotted down in my notebook that day, "He was watching over me all the time. I never knew it, but He was drawing me to Himself. Loneliness and danger are nothing compared to the joy of knowing Him." The exile had found his true homeland at last.

Uncle Sam's New Influence. The Spain I first visited just after World War II, with its frontiers sealed and its postal and telegraphic connections cut off, had virtually no tourists. Getting a visa was slow and difficult. To enter from the northeast you had to fly in from a neutral country like Switzerland. After landing at the then primitive Barcelona or Madrid airport, you were regarded with an air of steady suspicion and questioned about your business. In town, secret police clumsily shadowed you. All this has changed now. Spain has belatedly discovered the golden river of tourist income from abroad. Today hundreds of thousands of traveling Americans a year are treated courteously and hospitably in this country. Other foreigners swell the growing travel stream.

American economic aid to Spain has helped the situation. Beginning in 1951, negotiations between Madrid and Washington led to the construction of a four-hundred-million-dollar system of American air and naval bases. We have maintained these privileges by granting Spain almost two billion dollars' worth of economic and military credits. Bomber bases, only 1,500 miles from Russia, have risen at Torrejón de Ardoz (near Madrid), Saragosa (northward toward France), and Morón de la Frontera (south toward Gibraltar). Rota (near Seville), Cartagena (opposite Algeria), and El Ferrol (in northwest Spain), are the new naval bases.

When 8,000 Americans arrived to man these bases, official Spanish neutrality of 140 years standing was broken, and a new era was ushered in. As a direct economic gain Spain expects to double her auto output and step up steel and power production. This new alliance, regardless of how obtained, provides four definite helps toward the evangelization of Spain: (1) Spaniards are seeing foreign Protestants, including some true Christians, among tourists and residents, lessening their suspicions of this little-known faith. (2) Some Christian tourists from abroad, among them pastors, are stirring up their friends at home to pray anew for Spain. (3) Contacts with Spanish Christian leaders and churches result in blessing and enlightenment in both directions. (4) The Spanish government usually hesitates to act too swiftly in excluding foreign Christian workers. This fourth point has special importance for readers of this book.*

All over Spain outside influences, some good and some questionable, are at work. In 1959 seven new state-run *supermarcados* (supermarkets) were opened, with more promised. The government also reported receiving 250 applications for self-service markets. Such innovations may some day revolutionize life for housewives, but they have some reservations. The poor, in the little shops where they are known, have always been able to buy on credit in a pinch, but in the supermarkets one must pay in cash. Then, too, the rich do not like to give up their custom of having everything delivered after one telephone call. Meanwhile the six new Madrid soda fountains, known as "Californias," do a landslide business. Sport clothing, jazz, films, hot dogs *(perros calientes)*, the "bye-bye" instead of *adios*, and even the *Superhombre* (Superman) of the comics all herald changing times. The 150,000 university students are especially anxious to meet foreigners and learn about the outside world. Of course, the country areas are less touched by changing attitudes. In recent years English has replaced French as the most desirable tongue to learn, and young people are strongly pro-American. If such influences can ease things for the foreign missionary and Spanish Christians, so much the better.

Tomorrow Was Yesterday. In 1950 a student of Spanish conditions wrote, "In the last 30 years the country and its people have changed less than those of elsewhere in western Europe."[14] Surprisingly, within the

*In 1953 the late Pedro Cardinal Segura, then Archbishop of Seville, fought the entrance of U. S. military bases into Spain on the ground that Spanish Protestantism would benefit thereby.

decade since he wrote those words Spain has progressed more than it had during the whole previous generation! New pipe lines, power plants, hotels, raises in salaries, and drastic inflation remedies are evidences of changes for the better. It is true that today the Spanish economy is better than it has been at any time during the last century. However, unless you are in the area where progress is noticeable, you never know about it. For most of the common people, time stands still.

Mañana is a part of Spanish life. "There's plenty of time, there's always tomorrow," says the Spaniard. In crumbling villages across the land little has changed for centuries. Politics and religion are the twin causes of stagnation. An American magazine put the situation in a word: "Spain is an island in the stream of history. Separated from Europe by the Pyrenees, it is cut off from the twentieth century by poverty, exhaustion, and the frozen rule of Franco."[15]

Whether or not the Spanish have the gadgets of modern western life is secondary in itself. Christians should pray that Spain may be liberated and modernized, mainly in order that she may hear the gospel message. Walls of absolutism have long blocked off progressive ideas from the rest of the world. "Between Spain and its European neighbors," says Fernsworth, "there is a time lag of two or three centuries."[16] To slow down progress Spanish leaders repelled the Reformation, resisted Renaissance influence, rejected what was worthy in the French Enlightenment, and fumbled industrialization. "Left behind by the great thought-streams of the eighteenth and nineteenth centuries, Spain moved from feudalism to confused socialism to fascism, through one of history's most destructive civil wars," notes *Time*.[17] Geographer Norman J. G. Pounds sums up the timeless isolation of Spain thus:

> Spain fits ill into the European community of nations. The fanaticism and conservatism of the Castilian, his pride and obstinacy, his clinging to the outworn standards of medievalism, which not even Cervantes laughed wholly out of existence, all have kept Spain aloof from other nations. Spain is proud and poor, and her poverty is in some degree the price of her pride.[18]

As long as the country remains in the grip of the present state-church-army triumvirate, tomorrow will be little different from yesterday.

Built-in Depression. Since the average Spaniard makes only $300 a year—half of the western European average—he must learn to live with want. Part of the problem is geographical. Spain's climate is the driest in Europe, with too little rainfall in most of the country and too much in a narrow, northern belt. Erosion is general in a soil already unproductive. Land distribution is likewise bad, with agriculture slowed by Franco's emphasis on industrialization. Sixty per cent of the land is owned by

4 per cent of the population. Only a third of the soil is suitable for cultivation. Even though half the people are farmers, the government must spend a quarter of its budget on food imports. The same peasants who accept their situation with stoical hardness hunger as never before for better living standards. From his beautiful but harsh land the Spaniard wrests a living by hard toil, despite the typical foreign conception of the Spaniard lazily sitting in the shade ignoring his work. But the main reason for a debased economy is bad politics. At times the government has spent as much as half of the national budget on the Falange party and the army. The lot of the common man is secondary to the maintenance of power.

The Lord Loves the Poor. Miguel Ferrer works in a chemical plant in the northern town of Bilbao. His $40-a-month wage does not go far in supporting his family, which includes four children. To get extra rent money he starts to work early, ending his shift at 2 P.M.; then he begins another eight-hour shift. But all that work only buys two rooms, which are not enough space. So the Ferrers cook and eat in the same kitchen with two other families. Yet the Ferrers are much better off than the average Spaniards. Some poorer families of the same size sublet one of their two rooms to buy food money. Up in the next block from the Ferrers is a room where *no fewer than thirty-six people* sleep every night in two shifts, changing at 2 A.M. This is the predicament of slum-dwellers in the cities.

One missionary, describing a similar situation in the villages, says, "The writer has worked for over 20 years among the Spanish people in areas where 80% of the people were illiterate . . . where boys of eight years were expected to start to earn their living, going to work or guarding cattle, goats, sheep, or pigs in a village on the mountain slopes." In such places, he says, "people seek to live out their lives of desperate poverty in homes that most Europeans would not put a pig in." Here "food is scarce, the one warm meal of the day mostly a stew of some kind . . . work is handed out by representatives of rich and absent landlords." He goes on to describe village streets where pigs are loosed as scavengers and the usual mode of transport is by donkey or mule. "It is common in many homes for the family to live in one huge room. In the same room live the goats, the pig, and the chickens." The same man describes his own privations thus:

> We missionaries had to live in most inconvenient situations, with poor housing, molested by insects and myriads of flies, tormented day and night by mosquitoes, ofttimes forbidden to buy our daily needs at the local village store. Along with the rest of the people we bought our water at the door from the water carrier who comes around

twice a day with his jars of water strapped to his donkey. Often this water is unfit to drink. All my family suffered infection through bad or poisoned water and were at times very near death through the severity of such disease.[19]

All tourists know about the gipsy caves of Sacro Monte, outside Granada, and have brought prosperity to some of the gipsies. In Spain there are "rich caves" and "poor caves." In some of the former, old prehistoric caverns now enlarged and whitewashed, you can even find electric lights, hot water, radio, and telephones. (Such caves are not as bad as they may look, being cool in the summer and warm during the winter.) Here the gipsies put on a show of their whirling *zambra* dances and haunting songs, accompanied by thunderous handclapping. But there is another type of cave dwelling deep in the hills where black-haired, sharp-faced gipsies live as they have for centuries. Aside from a piled-up cane or brush windbreak, there is no furniture, and the ragged children sleep on bundles of thyme. Here and there in the hills of Gaudix the caves resemble New Mexico Indian pueblos. Poor people in Córdoba, Jaén, Granada, and elsewhere swell the total cave population to thousands. Who will preach to these poor the gospel that maketh rich? Most foreign missionaries work in the cities, and Spanish Protestants rarely contact these people, as few can afford to travel.

A Town Without Jesus. An American tells of his residence in a Castilian village which he calls "a Spanish Middletown." This average Spanish village, located about seventy miles northwest of Madrid—an hour and a half from the capital by car—is reputedly over four hundred years old. Life here is about the same today as it was centuries ago. There are some 11,800 towns of this size, Irving Wallace points out, containing fifteen million Spaniards, or three-fifths of the population. In other words, this particular village of two thousand people may be called typical of Spain. Nueva Tierra* has no paved streets, no sidewalks, no restaurants, no movies, no automobiles. Its homes have no porches, house numbers, mailboxes, lawns, glass windows, or refrigerators. Nor are there any kitchen sinks or flush toilets. Only one house in the town has more than one electric light bulb; only one has a dining room. Pigs wallow down the rutted dirt streets; they and the mules share the one-room houses. The tiny café on the town plaza is the news center, the people's forum. But there are no chairs, stools, or tables inside—only a counter which supports a long pan of water containing wine bottles. The tavern's proprietor, named Gil Luis, has the only radio in town. Arrested education is part of

---

*Wallace gives the town a false name to protect his informants there from political reprisals.

the town's trouble. In all its history no town child has ever gone beyond high school. The few persons who leave the place do not come back.

A dinner served to Wallace in Nueva Tierra consisted of a large bowl of elongated, tasteless olives. Next came a common bowl, containing chunks of red pimento, wild rice and bits of cooked rabbit, all washed down with a goatskin of red wine. His host could not afford rabbit or any other kind of meat, but for the occasion had stolen one from the wooded estate of a noble in the countryside. (Four other villagers who tried the same trick were caught by the Civil Guard, beaten cruelly, and jailed for weeks on bread and water.) Dessert consisted of one orange, divided between five people. This was dinner in the richest home in town.

Sanchez, on the other hand, was of the middle poor and had an average income. His possessions numbered two—an inherited stone house and a mule. The house had clay floors, no rugs, only a chair and a bed as furniture. One electric light illuminated the room Sanchez shared with his mule. Every morning at five he walked his mule fifteen kilometers up into the mountains to haul wood; at eleven at night he would trudge back with a take-home pay averaging sixty-six cents. What did Sanchez eat? Two pieces of homemade bread and a sardine for breakfast. No lunch. For dinner he had soup made of stolen vegetables, two pieces of bread, and two sardines.

Misery from Mismanagement. We have already said that Spain's basic problem, humanly speaking, is religio-political. Because the Spanish people are deeply affected by the policies of the present regime, we shall summarize their situation. Spain was close to economic disaster when aid began to arrive from the United States. Had the two billion dollars given Spain for a financial blood transfusion been otherwise used, the patient would begin to look better today. But for years the government stressed luxury products rather than basic industrial advances. Thousands of luxury apartments, some still unrented, were built. Between 1957 and 1959 the cost of living for the average Spaniard rocketed by 40 per cent. Gold and reserves dried up and a huge trade deficit appeared. The prevailing party siphoned off profits in a shameless spoils economy style. Only in mid-1959 did the government finally make some sensible proposals about the run-away inflation which had nearly doubled the amount of currency in circulation within five years.

The semi-fascist system has been aggravated by a government-directed capitalism which shackles much free enterprise and almost all foreign investment. As the foreign editor of an American news service put it, "The economy is sick with statism and sodden with bureaucracy. Employer-labor relations are shackled in state syndicates."[20]   The state, through a national holding company, owns from 25 to 100 per cent of various industries. The nationalized industries are for the most part inefficient and run on a government-paid deficit. Yet the recent, crippling, two-month strike of the miners in Asturias has prodded the government to boost wages in some industries and otherwise alleviate the lot of the worker somewhat.

One of the painful but natural results of misery is a huge exodus of villagers to the cities. People from the backward mountain regions, dazzled by comparatively high wages and the prospect of better conditions than they knew in their mountain cottages, are moving to Barcelona and Madrid. Fifty thousand persons from the backward areas of Andalusia, Estremadura, Aragon, and Castile were recently reported seeking work in the cities. Madrid's population is predicted to rise by 500,000 within a year or two. In that city some couples delay their marriages by five or six years because they are unable to obtain housing. This peasants' invasion worries officials. "The peasants arrive in a city and squeeze perhaps eight or ten persons into an apartment of one or two rooms, or into an improvised shack," one newspaper reported.[21] One man, who says, "I went to see for myself," found "hill after hill of caves in the shadows of Madrid's towering apartment buildings. Families of seven ate, slept, and bore children in these black holes in the ground. . . . In one cave I found a family of five—father and son killed in the civil war—subsisting on rotten potatoes thrown away in the markets."[22] He reports other families living in abandoned brick ovens and even three which moved into mausoleums of cemeteries but were evicted by the police.

The Spanish Way. We turn from the living conditions to the people themselves. Anyone who deals with Spaniards must remember that they are individualists, with a flair for the dramatic. Many of their actions and words are camouflage for their real feelings, and so must not be taken too seriously. Outward appearances and all matters of form count heavily in Spain, as in Italy. The right clothes must be worn in the right way at the right time. A "gentleman" does not carry his own baggage down the street. A person who has a servant will give up every luxury to keep him, as the prestige involved is important. A woman without stockings or a hat, or wearing shorts or slacks, is not welcome in a church, where she should also wear something to cover her arms. She must also wear conservative black dress. A casually attired man, even though wealthy, would never be allowed in a smart Spanish restaurant.

The youth likewise spend their last *peseta* to keep up a front. On special occasions a young lady elegantly dressed in black, wearing high heels and a *mantilla*, goes out with her relatives for the inevitable stroll. But her home is probably shabby and her pocketbook empty. The same goes for the young man in his blue suit, white shirt, and shiny shoes. Pride prevents the poor from admitting their condition; even the beggar bears himself with dignity.

Though the Spanish seem deliberate and almost lazy, they are not really so. True, time and punctuality are relatively unimportant to them. But to push a Spaniard to further speed is only to slow him down. To judge by the number of people spending hours a day around marble-topped café tables, you would think they are either unemployed or just lazy. But privacy in the overcrowded homes is rare. Then, too, custom demands that business be transacted anywhere but at home. So the café is a cheap office, where a businessman can make a deal or a lawyer can interrogate his client. There engaged young lovers can freely talk and professional men can exchange information in lieu of a club of their own. Many customers, known by name, pick up their mail and messages at the café, write letters there, use the phone and the *chico* (bellhop). Not bad service for the price of a cup of coffee!

As in many Latin lands, the home is not the center of a man's life. You can know a person for years without ever meeting his family or visiting his house. Often the reason for this is his feeling that the house is unfit, or that he must put up the proper front. A restaurant or a café is the proper place for a *charla* (chat). Women are kept in the background. The idea of a woman's pursuing a career offends the Spanish man, who thinks of her as someone to look beautiful, keep house, and stay out of his daily affairs.

A girl is told from childhood that she is *guapa* (good-looking), and a boy is expected to be *valiente* (masculine). Such compliments help explain young people's sense of assurance. Although young men still often hover over a *señorita* saying things she expects to hear about her unique beauty, the ancient courtly *piropo*, or gallant compliment to a woman, is giving way today to a more suggestive and less respectful form.

Foreigners are often perplexed by the Spaniards' daily routine. Though they do not necessarily begin work later than other Southern Europeans do, they retire later. Factories usually open at eight, and offices at nine. But lunch is at about 2:30 P.M. and dinner at 10 or 11 P.M. The government has been trying to get people to work earlier and shorten their lunch hour. The balance-wheel of life is the siesta, needed in some areas during the hottest part of the day. Films, theatrical performances, and often church services begin at 11 P.M. The foreigner would do well to follow this cycle if he is to stay healthy, and fit into the life of the people. In spite of appearances, the Spaniard does get his day's work done.

Woman's Life in a Man's World. With the notable exception of a small group of liberated women in big cities, the average Spanish lady leads a guarded life. While a man can go where and when he pleases, the women of his household are confined in a sort of moral strait jacket. To him this is a black-and-white matter: the "good" woman is sheltered in the family circle; the "bad" one is on the street. A Spanish man is tremendously fond of his children, especially the little girls, whom he loves to spoil, pet, and dress up. Aside from this, his attention is mainly fixed on the club or café. Here, among other men, he finds his real relaxation and entertainment.

Since a woman's husband works all day and spends a good part of the night in a bar, her dreary life seldom extends beyond her doorstep. Unmarried men and women cannot be "just friends," who can talk together in normal fashion about ordinary things. If a married woman talks too often to any man other than her husband, tongues begin to wag. Deprived of the stimulus of male companionship, what does she do? Most women confide in their brothers, quote their opinions, and hold them up as proper examples of the male sex.

No respectable woman would stop at a café by herself or even walk alone in certain quarters at certain hours. She must walk somewhere with purpose, not stroll alone in the plaza or park. Aside from a few of the wealthy and sophisticated type, most women are not expected to do any serious thinking or to have much fun. Instead, a woman should concentrate on her tasks in the home. Even if the father does live his outside life in the bar, the mother believes it her duty to build a family unit in accord with custom. To the credit of the Spanish people, they do create a home which is tightly-knit, though the reasons why they are so may not be the best.

As a result of his self-exile from all but necessary family relationships, and his preference for male companionship, a man gets a warped view of a woman's role in life. Since he has never known one of his own age with whom he could have a normal friendship, he becomes abnormally lonely. Romantic love has never been exalted in his mind as a basis for marriage. "To breed and educate children, Spanish Catholics believe, is man's most important mission on earth," said one.[23] Immoral habits grow out of his isolation from normality. "A 'married bachelor' might tone down his activities for the first few years which see him (God willing) through the start of a family, after which he is ready with renewed zest for the first amorous adventure that finances, opportunity, and initiative make possible. . . . I don't know whether it's hot blood or habit, but a Spaniard with any woman has only one thought in mind."[24] The writer goes on to explain that only rigid rules governing the conduct of "nice" women, plus vigilant chaperonage, preserve the outer moral scene from crumbling. Another student of Spanish customs adds, "Most well-off Spaniards think nothing of having a mistress."[25]

Under such social conditions, witnessing to women about Christ must be primarily a woman's task. Otherwise, the only place where a Spanish woman could hear the gospel from a man, unless he be a close member of the family, would be in a public gospel service. But since comparatively few ever attend such a service during a lifetime, trained women witnesses, both Spanish and foreign, would seem to be the only way to reach the women and their children.

Regional Snapshots. We have dealt in general terms with Spanish temperament and habits. But the foreign Christian would profit by learning a little also, about the differences among Spaniards. There is no one fixed type, even as in our own country many mentalities share the general term "American." Let us begin with the Basque provinces on the French frontier. The Spanish Basques, who number about 450,000, speak a complex language of their own as well as Spanish. Despite their strong reaction to being assimilated into Spanish life, they are extraordinarily progressive and energetic. Basque people (in the Spanish, *Vascongados*) are of somewhat mysterious origin. Probably the most famous Basques in history were Ignatius Loyola and Francis Xavier. The intelligence and single-mindedness of these two men typify these Spartan people who live on the slopes of the Pyrenees and along the Bay of Biscay. The smuggling which many Basques practice provides an income as well as an outlet for their individualism and bent for adventure. Their everyday life is regulated by assemblies composed of heads of families. Often these families are clannish, self-sufficient, and suspicious of outsiders. As far as we know, the Basques have never been systematically evangelized in either their own tongue or through Spanish, though some who emigrated have found the Lord abroad and become burdened for their own people.

In Santander province, westward along the Bay of Biscay, intensive agricultural activity parallels the coast, while pastoral life prevails in the highlands behind. Up in the latter live nomadic people who lead their herds and flocks to the higher grazing regions in late April and down again to the lowlands in October. Asturias province is much like that of Santander except that the Asturians have a stronger sense of independence. They were relatively free from all foreign domination between the fall of Rome and the Arab invasion of 711. Hence their love of freedom, typified today in the attitudes of the strongly individualistic, nomadic cattle-herders. A region in Asturias called Astorga is the home of the twelve thousand or so Maragatos. These people practice a rigid endogamy, disapproving any woman's marriage to an outsider. The fact that matriarchal effects on the life of the people survive in customs and attitudes poses special problems for the Christian worker.

The region of Galicia likewise has coastal and highland parts. There are no large estates in this part of Spain. Instead, small homesteads average from two-thirds of an acre to 125 acres in size. Subdivided holdings are numerous, with even a single tree, a little mill, or a clump of trees marked out for individual use. A hereditary system of tenure laws for property demands that a peasant family make payments, and yield certain rights, to a landlord.

Castile contains the central plateau of Spain, called the Meseta. Red, parched soil under a blue dome of sky typifies a region where you can see women thresh wheat just as it was done in Biblical times. Castilians are courteous, dignified, and dramatic. This is the country of the Cid, Spain's national hero. Castile dominated Spanish history, furnishing many military garrisons in Italy, Africa, and Flanders. Among the grave Castilians the best classical Spanish is reportedly spoken.

In Andalusia Arab influence can be found. Through the grill of the typical square-shaped house the visitor can see the open patio and palms bending over a murmuring fountain. In this region agricultural workers all eat and sleep together in large rooms. Their harvesting time is full of ritual. Squalid villages scattered across a barren countryside are edged with olive and cork orchards. In the vegetarian meals, olive oil, vinegar, and pungent, peppery condiments predominate. In spite of tourist attractions like its seacoast, and Seville and Granada, Andalusia is poor and needy, both physically and spiritually.

The people of Aragon fought the establishment of the Inquisition as well as all foreign invasions. Mountain towns such as Anso and Hecho retain medieval Christian customs, while in other villages distinct Islamic influence is evident, extending to the turban-like headdress and wide, baggy trousers. Here again we see the hard-working farmer on his little holding, serving a landlord.

Catalonia has been called "an outsider within the gates of Spain" and its capital Barcelona, "Spain's least Spanish city." Catalans have always been a discordant element in history. Today they demand and get more liberties—including religious ones—than other Spaniards. Catalans are not as rugged and strong as the Basques or Aragonese; rather they are subtle, gracious, and given to *seny*, a Catalan word which means common sense, or a realistic outlook on life. During the Civil War, the Catalans made a bid for autonomy. The Franco government humors them somewhat but does not trust them.

Madrid is a metropolis which was artificially created as the capital of Spain in the middle of the sixteenth century by Emperor Charles V. Up to that time the country had no fixed capital. The city is not typical of any region but is representative of each. By being equidistant from all the other big cities, it draws people and ideas from them all. Conversation is said to be especially stimulating in this great international center. The *Madrileño* is exceedingly proud of his city. In the summer, when the weather becomes very hot, the government leaves town for San Sebastian until the return of fall. Madrid is overcrowded, having doubled its population during the last twenty years.

Attitude Toward Foreigners. About two million foreigners now visit Spain each year. What kind of reception do they get? Apart from the offense created by the preaching of the cross, what reaction can the foreign Christian expect here? Though sensitive and quick-tempered, the Spaniard is very kind toward strangers. V. S. Pritchett has well stated this in *The Spanish Temper*:

> The poorer and simpler the people, the more sincere the welcome. In some lovely inn, a *venta* of Extremadura—where there are never beds to sleep in, but men sleep on the floor in the outer stables while their mules and donkeys sleep inside just as they did in the time of Cervantes—they will ask if you have brought your sack and your straw. If you have not brought them, they will get them for you. . . . One is treated like a noble among nobles. . . . There is never avarice.[26]

The Duke of Wellington, during his Spanish military venture in 1820, could write, "There is no country in which foreigners are so much disliked, and even despised, and whose manners and habits are so little congenial with those of other nations in Europe."[27] But then he was writing in the midst of a campaign in which two foreign armies clashed on Spain's soil. Today things are different. Normally the chivalric customs assure a foreigner of help in any situation. I have experienced, personally, the kindness of Spaniards during breakdowns of my car in the open countryside or while hunting for accommodations in the city. In the days when visitors were rare, courtesy to foreigners was so common that a traveler could virtually spend nothing. With the modern tourist invasion, this picture is changing. Yet the greed and tip-snatching common elsewhere in Europe are rare here. In the rural areas, a little gift of some kind is much more appreciated than money, since accepting it does not debase a person in his own eyes. Beggars assume, with dignity, that you are doing yourself, not them, a religious favor by giving alms.

A **Key Language.** Of some 2,500 languages on earth, Spanish ranks fourth in terms of widespread use; it is spoken as a native tongue by about 140 million people. In Spain itself the accent and certain expressions differ from those used in Latin America and elsewhere, but little difficulty arises in communication. There are two main groups of languages in the country, the Basque and Galegan Spanish, each with its own sub-dialects. Three of the historic provinces of Basque settlement are in France, where three different dialects are spoken. Farther around the Bay of Biscay and on the Spanish side of the Pyrenees lie the other four provinces—three so-called Basque provinces, and Navarra. Spanish Basques speak the Guiduzcoan, Upper Navarrese, and Biscayan dialects of the language. Having no apparent affinity with other European languages (except some grammatical likenesses to the Finno-Ungric group), Basque is complicated and difficult to learn. Fortunately many of these people speak Spanish or French in addition to Basque. A Portuguese variety of the Galegan dialect is used in the west; the Catalan language is spoken in the east; and the more familiar Castilian Spanish prevails in the center. Then, too, there is the very ancient *Ladino* of the Spanish Jews, and *Caló*, a gipsy adaptation.

2. *A MEDIEVAL ROMANISM*

Ascendancy of the Church. In Spain the Church of Rome is as ideally placed as can be imagined in the present world scene. Franco early stated his conception of the role of the church in the state. In 1937 he told an American reporter, "Our state must be a Catholic state in the social and spiritual sense, for the true Spain has been, is, and will be Catholic."[28] Since his Civil War victory Franco has repeated the same view scores of times, and his actions bear them out.

This assumed position is now spelled out as official policy, too. Article 1 of the Concordat of 1953 between Spain and the Vatican (a partial renewal of that of 1851) says: "The Roman Catholic and Apostolic Faith will continue to be the only religion of the Spanish nation, and will enjoy all the rights and prerogatives that are due to it, in accordance with divine law and canon law." Article 2 goes a little further: "The Spanish state recognizes in the Catholic Church the perfect type of society, and guarantees its right to free, complete exercise of its spiritual power and its jurisdiction, as well as the right to free public worship."

New Goals of the Hierarchy. The new Concordat which we have just quoted signifies several tendencies. First, Franco is worried about political challengers and underground Communism. His power is waning, and needs shoring up. Second, the Church sees the present as a propitious time in which to press its demands for stronger state support. Faced with rising anticlericalism, liberalism, and tiny (but militant) Protestantism, the Vatican, too, has been worried. The Roman Church has largely benefited from this new statement of an age-old alliance; thirty-six of the thirty-eight articles concern the state's obligations to the Church. On marriage and education Rome's position is slightly strengthened; special privileges are given to priests, and grants for free construction and tax exemptions help church institutions.

In one sentence, how could one best describe the mood of the hierarchy in Spain? We have found nothing clearer on this than the statement of Emmet John Hughes, former United States Embassy attaché in Madrid, a practicing Roman Catholic who attended mass regularly during his long stay in Spain. This speech writer for former President Eisenhower, a highly trained reporter, finds in Spanish Catholic leadership "an overriding dedication to institutional self-interest; a tough prideful imperviousness to criticism; a contempt for any kind of education not synonymous with indoctrination; a sharp distrust of and hostility toward any political or social movement that could be called 'radical,' 'leftist,' or 'liberal,' and a respect that approaches reverence for power in any form."[29]

Where Error Has No Rights. The official Spanish attitude toward minorities, including Protestants, is so well documented that it needs little clarification. First we give some examples of general attitudes. One of the most frequently cited statements in Spain is that of Jaime Balmes, the nineteenth-century philosopher-historian:

> Before the birth of Protestantism, European civilization had developed to its highest level; Protestantism caused civilization to swerve from this course and created irreparable damage for modern society; the progress accomplished since the arrival of Protestantism has not been because of it, but in spite of it.[30]

Crusty old Pedro Cardinal Segura, the late archfoe of the Protestants, liked to quote the above Balmes opinion to support his own still stronger diatribes, like this one:

> Recently . . . a campaign of friendliness toward the Protestants has been launched, as if all religions were equally acceptable in the sight of God. . . . Protestants are now proselytizing in our country. Having broken all the bounds of tolerance, they are now fearlessly advancing toward complete religious freedom . . . their intention to convert Spain into a mission field . . . obliges Catholics to demand that the laws be strictly applied . . . Spain can in no way grant the same right to Protestants as to Catholics as regards the public exercise and profession of their beliefs.[31]

The occasion for this outburst was Segura's fear that Protestants would gain advantages through the economic negotiations with the United States then being carried out in Spain.

But resistance to Protestant Christianity has a much stronger basis than nasty words. The state's views are grounded in administrative decrees. The basic statute governing Protestantism is Article 6 of the *Fuero de los Españoles*, the 1945 charter of the rights and duties of the people. As the fundamental law of Franco's regime, the *Fuero* provides what little legal standing Protestants have. Article 6 reads:

> The profession and practice of the Catholic religion, which is that of the Spanish state, shall enjoy official protection. *No one shall be disturbed because of his religious beliefs or the private practice of his worship.* No other outward ceremonies than those of the Catholic religion shall be permitted. (Italics ours.)

As soon as the *Fuero* appeared, Protestants were overjoyed at what looked like—and temporarily was—a guarantee of freedom for them. Some churches were reopened, and until 1947 the atmosphere was better. Soon, however, the old Latin Catholic talent for "interpretation" came into play. On November 12, 1945, four months after the *Fuero* was adopted by the Cortes, the Ministry of the Interior sent a confidential administrative order to all the provincial governors. The order more precisely defines the meaning of "private practice" of worship. In the years since, the words "private" and "outward" have proved to be the keys of the matter. In our discussion on Protestantism in Spain we shall see how the interpretations work out in practice.

Paganism with a Halo. Now for a look at actual practice of the Catholic faith. To the common people, magic and the occult beliefs of past centuries are part of religion even today. We have noticed that in other Roman Catholic countries the church easily makes terms with a heathen shrine or custom by simply calling it Catholic. In Spain this custom is common. Particularly in Andalusia there are countless springs which for many centuries have been considered by the people as haunts of nymphs or elves. These are now dedicated to the Virgin Mary, and each is either called the Fountain of our Lady so-and-so, or is identified with a local saint. British writer Cedric Salter notes, "The features of Pan, Bacchus, and Apollo, and those of even earlier deities, can often be recognized in the figures of local saints—unchanged except for the addition of a halo."[32] Similarly many Spanish Catholic feasts and celebrations, beginning with austere worship and ending with heavy drinking and moral abandon, reflect pagan origins.

Some primitive customs which the Greek geographer Strabo described in Spain during the first year after Christ still linger in Galacia. On nights of the full moon people dance and sing in the streets. Everyone believes in the *Santa Compaña*, those ghosts of the dead who haunt village cemeteries. Some writers see in this a survival of ancestor worship. Peasants here feel they must propitiate possible tormentors among their dead with food, a practice also common in Ireland (cf. ch. 10).

Religion on the Sleeve. How earnest and regular are Spanish Catholics in the practice of their Catholic faith? With her sacramental teaching, the Church of Rome is able to keep some sort of spiritual control over the majority of Spaniards. Even the indifferent do not like to break their last link with the only religion they know. Criticize and ridicule it they may, and do, but most would rather remain bad Catholics than declare themselves out of the church. Having said that, we can sample opinion on the question, in the right perspective, from both Spaniards and non-Spaniards.

Vatican concern over the lukewarm observance of church duties in Spain goes back a long way. James Cardinal Gibbons (1834–1921), the famous Baltimore prelate who was once primate of all North America, remarked near the turn of the century, "In Latin Europe there remain a Catholic heritage and tradition, but individual Catholicism as such is disappearing at an alarming rate. Nations like Spain continue to be Catholic because their forefathers were; but the individual spirit and sentiment of Catholicism exist no longer."[33]

Educated Spanish Catholics themselves echoed the same view. A generation ago the famous novelist, Emilia Pardo Bazán, openly said, "Spain has ceased to be a Catholic country."[34] Señor Ossorio Gallardo, well-known lawyer and Dean of the College of Lawyers in Madrid, once made the remarkable admission, "Spain is a Catholic country without Christians, careful of its liturgy but forgetful of the commandments of the law of God."[35] A foreign missionary in the country makes this comparison: "Roman Catholicism in Spain has been, and still is, of the degenerate type that is prevalent in South and Central America."[36] Some wrongly think that a country which once sent out zealous priests with her explorers to convert the Americas must naturally show some higher, purer devotion to the church. This is what the Spanish hierarchy would like the world to believe.

The difference between inward belief and outward commitment was pointed up by George Santayana, the famous Harvard philosopher who lived so long in Europe, "The Spaniard is an individualist; he can be devout mystically . . . but socially, externally, he distrusts everything and everybody, even his priests and his kings."[37] Does this mean that these perceptive people, so quick to detect humbug and fraud, are "instinctive protestants"—not in their knowledge of God, but in their protest against an empty man-made religion? Similarly Angelo, an employee in a Valencia hotel, told a foreigner, "There are no Catholics in Spain. That is all exteriorization. The politicians claim to be Catholics because that is a political asset . . . I would like a religion to be a reality—not talk, but reality. In Spain there is only the purchase and sale of consciences—not Catholicism." This man, "while still remaining within the fold of the church, insisted on his right to do his own thinking. There are many Angelos in Spain."[38]

Among the intellectuals and professional people much scepticism reigns. A priest who served 50,000 students at Madrid University, said in the mid-1950's that only 1,000 were loyally Catholic. Even the latest *Encyclopedia Britannica* article on Spain, though heavily slanted in favor of Rome, acknowledges that "with important exceptions, Spanish liberalism has been anti-clerical."[39] In 1956 a doctoral dissertation entitled, "Anticlericalism in Spanish Literature, Particularly in the Twentieth Century," was submitted to the Graduate School of Boston University. Its author John J. Devlin, Jr., now teaches at Fordham University, a Catholic school. Devlin, who believes that anticlericalism in twentieth-century Spanish writers differs only in intensity from that of earlier days, says that "the charge that clerical pressure resisted the flow of change, and the reasonable aspirations of modernists, is justifiable." If this is true, then there must be many grounds for intellectuals to react against Roman tyranny of the mind and soul.

The hierarchy itself sometimes speaks quite openly of its people's disaffection. In the 1950's, *Ecclesia*, the Catholic Action organ, declared that the overwhelming majority of Spanish workers do not practice their faith. In a pastoral letter in 1951 the Bishop of Valencia estimated the faithful and practicing element in his diocese as only 17 per cent of the population. In Barcelona in the mid-50's less than 1,600 priests could be found to serve Barcelona's population of 2,250,000. In Andalusia, church attendance was lower than in what had formerly been Castile. The Catholic Action journal *Signo* for January 28, 1950, carried this comment by G. L. de la Torre:

> Geographically, we are witnessing a retreat of Catholicism. The faith has been losing ground in Spain. The great mass of workers has deserted the house of God, and this did not happen suddenly. The suburbs of our larger cities are almost solid blocks of irreligious feeling. The same can be said of the mining and industrial areas. On a much smaller scale, the same phenomenon can be observed in the middle, and even the upper, classes. . . .

In January, 1954, the magazine *Ecclesia* published the results of a national survey of Catholic loyalty. The conclusions? "Workers abstained from religious services as of old; they still distrusted the clergy, still accused the church of political maneuvers, and demanded that separation of church and state be established as under the Republic." This report, too official to be censored, spoke of

> the Marxist virus that rusts the worker's soul; his aloofness from contact with the clergy; economic difficulties that worry his spirit, and a bitter life, especially about spiritual things, coupled with an indifference for any institution, be it the church or the state, that does not solve his most pressing problems.

The comments of travelers and foreign residents of Spain on this matter are almost uniform: "Judged by strict standards of church doctrine I have often thought that at least 95% of Spaniards must be heretics. . . . In traveling about Spain I was constantly encountering evidence of the hostile, indifferent, or independent attitude of nominal Catholics toward their church."[40] Missionaries, travel writers, visiting clergymen, and members of the working press have gathered many such reactions, from which I choose a few:

> *Muledriver:* "I drive my mules over mountain trails for money—just like the priest."
>
> *Devout woman:* "The priest tells me I must go to the church on Sunday. So I go on Monday, and on Sunday I pray at my own little altar at home."
>
> *Urban man:* "When I want a priest I call for him, as I call for a doctor or a lawyer when they are needed. Otherwise I do not allow a priest in the house. Let a priest get his foot in your house and he is soon the master of it."
>
> *Woman on train:* "I am on to the church. I confess my sins to my husband and he confesses to me. That's all the church we need."
>
> *Educated gentleman:* "Soup and education would destroy the church."
>
> *Madrid author:* "The church encroaches on every aspect of our lives until we have a sense of suffocation and must break free."
>
> *Barcelona lawyer:* "Around 40 per cent of the education in Spain is provided by the church. It's a choice of that, or nothing. I don't know which is worse—a preponderance of church influence on education, or no education."

We can conclude that Spaniards seem to be attached to Catholicism not *as a religion,* but only as a framework for life which goes back farther than they can remember.

Festivals for Fainting Hearts. In Spain, religious occasions, as a part of the life of the people, must be studied by anyone seeking to win them to Christ. These are magnificent but meaningless, exciting but empty. They give the people a lift—then drop them down hard. There are different kinds, variously called *romarias, verbenas, fiestas,* and *fallas.* A *romaria,* practiced by country people, is a mass excursion to some Catholic shrine. Best-known of the romarias is that to the miracle-working Virgin of El Rocío, in Almonte (Huelva province), fifty-five miles from Seville. On the Wednesday before Whitsunday (forty-nine days after Easter) the roads leading to the church sheltering the little statue of Mary begin to fill with traffic. Mounted riders escort white covered wagons festooned with flowers and filled with excited women. Every town having a chapter of the "Lodge of the Brotherhood of the Virgin of El Rocío" sends a similar cavalcade. At the head of each converging column is a Virgin's cart covered with gold-embroidered white silk. Singing, guitar music, and laughter form a setting for romance, as the normally strict guard over unmarried women is briefly relaxed. Then comes the parade of the Virgin's statue through the streets. Pilgrims fight for the honor of carrying the statue, since indulgences go with the honor. The Monday following Whitsunday, church ceremonies give place to dancing, drinking, and moral laxity. The next day the trek back to home and reality begins. Here we have an example of how a "unique pageant combining religious fervor and gay abandon" is used as a means of gratifying the lower desires.[41]

A *verbena* is a festival held in towns and cities on the eve of such a holiday. Most verbenas culminate on August 15—the Assumption Day of the Virgin Mary. On the surface, such festivals seem gay. There are ribbons, garlanded flowers, and unusual tapestries draped from the balcony windows packed with people. The excitement of fireworks, fiery street dances, and colorful costumes brings momentary respite from the dull pointlessness of life. But as dawn steals across the city, the music dies and the fun is over. Ahead lies the grim, religious day from which such merriment provides only temporary escape. The prisoners have returned to their cells.

Fallas are particularly a Valencian specialty, the most famous being those of San José, held during the second week of March. In Valencia a great variety of huge, painted papier-mâché figures appears in the squares and central streets, some caricaturing famous people. One onlooker referred to the week's activities as "scenes of revelry that would undoubtedly surprise St. Joseph (in whose honor they officially take place) by their pagan abandonment."[42] On the last night the figures are set afire. In the light of the flames young people in their regional costumes dance until dawn.

The *fiestas* furnish another kind of escape. "Although they include a religious procession, religion seems to be the excuse for, rather than a restraint upon, the holiday spirit."[43] The fiestas of Corpus Christi at Toledo are probably the best known to tourists. Flowers play an important* part, especially as the exposed host* is carried over a carpet of them at the head of a long procession of chanting priests and alabaster saints.

Holy Week Without Christ. Every city, town, and hamlet in Spain participates in the *Semana Santa* with a burst of church-directed piety. Some have called it "the world's greatest celebration of Holy Week." Indeed, this is the most lavish single display of religious pageantry anywhere in the world: "In a thousand Spanish towns and villages the story of the passion is remembered in magnificient processions and dramas which go on from dawn to dawn for six days."[44] The spectacular week, as the most famous feature of Catholic Spain, deserves close examination by all who cherish a living Saviour instead of a dead one.

Seville, the capital of Andalusia, is the tourist mecca of Holy Week. But a more truly Spanish version of the same spectacle can be seen at Granada or Malaga or in smaller towns. In other festivals we have described, fun comes before faith; but during this one week—the Roman Church's own throughout Spain—grimness is the word. Even the pageantry is overshadowed by a somber darkness, an ill-concealed fear. There is something chill and menacing that a child of God can feel in the atmosphere—the pall of the sepulcher. All the precious scenes of the cross are paraded before him in garish trappings of wealth and splendor. Especially revolting—and pitiful—are the public penances paid by sinners seeking to propitiate God. The whole atmosphere of candles, hooded marchers, and gaudy floats smacks of heathenism, with no resemblance to true Christianity.

People sleep little during Holy Week. Usually on the night of Holy Thursday they do not go to bed at all; "nobody slept in Jerusalem," they will say. Palm branches and flowers grace very window in southern Spain. From balconies hang colorful shawls, tapestries, and sometimes mirrors. In the churches pillars are velvet-wrapped, and red carpets cover the aisles. The finest polished silver sparkles on the altar before the pressing throng. From the activity in the churches during this single week you would think that the Spaniards are always diligent Catholics—which they are not. But this is the week to make vows and renew faith.

Thousands of visitors see the spectacle in Barcelona, and over 200,000 in Seville, the city most famed for it. For several days the main streets

*The sacramental wafer used in celebrating the mass.

of downtown Seville are closed to traffic. Miles of sidewalks are crowded with people sitting in rented chairs. Behind are the sweating, jostling poor, fighting for a look. During the week Seville makes over five million dollars from the tourists alone. Prices for hotel rooms and meals double, while the *Sevillanos* themselves spend freely on clothes bought expressly for Holy Week. The sale of postcards and booklets runs into six figures.

Preparations are long and fabulously expensive. They fall almost wholly upon the *cofradías* or brotherhoods, originally descendants of the medieval guilds. Today these have become neighborhood groups which go to great trouble and sacrifice to make Holy Week a success. Each *cofradía* creates and finances its section of the procession with funds obtained by special drives, bequests, and membership dues. There are forty-eight of these in Seville, ranging in membership from 300 to 25,000. We must remember that the Catholic Church does not pay for this spectacle out of its usual resources, contributed by an already poor people. The brotherhoods make special appeal to women throughout the Spanish-speaking world to lend their jewels to the Virgin. From Spain, and from all South America, women send the contents of their jewel boxes. Earrings, brooches, necklaces, and bracelets pour in, and not only from the rich. Wedding rings by the thousands shower into the offering. Why the spontaneous participation? Because jewels which adorn the Virgin during Holy Week are blessed specially with promises of health and happiness for their owners. All loaned jewels are recorded, and none, supposedly, are lost.

A Pageantry of Death. Different customs mark the daily processions of certain cities, but in general they are similar. From noon on Thursday until Good Friday night, the majority of people wear black. Most cinemas, theaters, and other places of amusement are closed, and street lamps are extinguished. Cars, trolleys, and buses come to a halt as Friday night, the climax point, approaches. The processions are unbelievably long. Usually people kneel as the Virgin's image or the host passes by. At three in the morning in Toledo, the people lie prostrate while a group known as The Silent Ones, *Los Silencios*, pass by. In Murcia and other towns the procession visits the city prison and "pardons" several inmates in memory of the penitent thief crucified beside Christ. Black-draped drums roll and trumpets play, but at times there is no music or sound except the scrape of thousands of feet over cobblestones. Hour after hour, and mile after mile, the processions shuffle on, to the accompaniment of muted music. Elaborately carved, very old images are removed from the churches or the brotherhood centers for the occasion. Clergy and local government officials surround these closely, all dressed in their ceremonial robes. In the center of each group of penitents move several floats, or *pasos*, illumined by the light of thousands of candles and bright with flowers. Statues or tableaux from the crucifixion form the top part of the floats. Usually a *paso*, weighing between two and three tons, is carried on the backs of hidden *costaleros*. Though most of these are poor dock workers or other laboring men paid for the job, penitents, too, join in the backbreaking work.

The brotherhoods vie to create the most magnificient floats, spending, on an average, a million dollars each year on preparations. Of one Seville procession a witness wrote, "Image after image moves through the night laden with a fortune in gold and precious stones. So cleverly are these gems woven into the crowns and bodices of the Madonnas, and so bright is the flare of candles, that you might not notice them at all."[45] As a matter of record Seville's Virgin de la Macarena usually wears at least five million dollars' worth of jewels. The Virgin's robe alone requires a year or more to make and, embroidered with gold thread, will cost not less than $10,000. Overwhelmed by the wonder of it all, and faithful to their training, the people kneel or prostrate themselves as the Virgin passes.

The Price of Penance. What of the penitents themselves? Every class of people is represented among the masked, cowled, and brightly robed marchers. With their pointed hats and eyeholes they startlingly resemble America's Klu Klux Klansmen, who also hide their identity. Students, clerks, workers, soldiers, professional men, and the very rich are among them. Male and female, the old and the young take part. Many are barefoot. Some carry heavy crosses or drag chains. I have even seen women, on Barcelona's *Ramblas*, who walked the whole route *on tiptoe, with arms raised,* their faces a mask of pain. Of course there is pride in this, too, for such penance is complimented by the throng.

Beneath it all is the terrible slavery to dead works. One city official swore to God by the bedside of his ailing wife that, should she recover, he would march barefoot for seven Easters, carrying a fifty-pound cross. For a man of sixty the task of many hours was not easy, but no doubt it eased his sore conscience for a time. Illness in the family is a common ground for such acts of devotion, but there are many others. Once a drunk flung a glass at a Virgin's statue, scarring her cheek. As an atonement, he marched in heavy chains for eight Easters. This macabre emphasis on suffering and pain, in image and penitent alike, is typical of the Spanish temperament as distinguished from the Portuguese.

No Sunrise Tomorrow. At midnight on Saturday a sudden cacophony of church bells, striking at the same moment, marks the end of Holy Week in Spain. With this *toque de gloria* the dark crucifixion day draws to a close. Crowds wearily disperse to catch up on sleep and return to normal life. But what of Easter, that glorious day of hope and promise? This Lord's Day, the resurrection morning, is left out of Holy Week altogether. Instead of being the climax of the week, it is only an aftermath. Calvary without the Open Tomb—how symbolic of the Catholic faith! The sacrifice of the cross, uncompleted by the rising of the Prince of Life, is perpetuated in the mass. Of course the resurrection doctrine is a part of Catholic theology and Easter services are held; but the people never experience the joy of it. They are sombered by the Saviour's death, but never gladdened by His triumph. None of this dirge of death they witness has any personal application to the heart. Like a book which lacks a final chapter, or the chord which fails to resolve, Holy Week leaves the Spanish sinner still unsaved at its close.

3. THE REDEMPTIVE REMNANT

The Gospel Reaches Spain. Did the Apostle Paul ever reach Spain, as he intended to do? In writing to the Romans from Corinth he emphasizes that he will visit them only briefly on the way to Spain, his final destination. "Whensoever I take my journey into Spain, I will come to you" (Rom. 15:24), and again, "I will come by you into Spain" (Rom. 15:28). This may have been only human desire, since the promise of Cod at Jerusalem, "Thou must bear witness also at Rome" (Acts 23:11), did not extend further than the city on the Tiber. Beyond recording Paul's wishes, the Scriptures are silent on this subject. Some believe that the apostle may have gone west during the interval between his two Roman imprisonments, when he had both the freedom and the time to visit France or Spain.

It is reasonable to assume, though, that Spain received some witness during the first century. "And there were dwelling at Jerusalem Jews, devout men, out of every nation under heaven" (Acts 2:5). Were Spanish Jews present at Pentecost, and did some believe? Spain was on the Roman trade routes along which the gospel expanded. Roman soldiers, civilian administrators, Greek merchants, Jews—any of these may have, and probably did, carry the message of salvation. Under a Tarragona tobacco factory workers discovered in 1926 a Roman amphitheater where Christians may have been martyred as early as 259. The convening of a Spanish church council of 19 bishops at Elvira in 306 implies the existence of a church of some consequence earlier. At any rate, there is no historical evidence for the presence of Christianity in Spain before the second century, and no present remains of church buildings date from that era. In the first section of the chapter we saw how Catholic Christians were engulfed, first by the barbarian tribes, then by the Moors, before final restoration of their rights during the Middle Ages.

The Reformation Repulsed. Before the Reformation began to threaten Catholic unity in the sixteenth century, the Roman Church in Spain had already repulsed other menaces. Under the 800-year-long Moorish occupation there had been at least limited liberty for both the Jewish and Catholic minorities. But typically, as the Catholics themselves gained strength, they began to use force to restrain the other two religions. In 1478 Ferdinand and Isabella requested and received a papal bull allowing them to set up the Inquisition. This terrible weapon was first used against Jews who falsely professed Christian conversion in order to gain security or privilege. By 1492, with the capture of Granada, the long reconquest of the country by the church was complete. Now the Jews were given an ultimatum: Accept baptism or leave the country. Early in the sixteenth century the Moors were faced with the same alternative. So the foe confronting the first Protestants in Spain was experienced and formidable indeed.

The Reformation never really took hold in Spain, because it was cut off at the roots. Yet the beginnings were promising enough to silence forever the repeated assertion that Spaniards are "just naturally Catholic." One of the earliest to speak up against Roman abuses was Alfonso de Valdés, secretary to none other than the Emperor Charles V, of the Holy Roman Empire. As an Erasmian, he scored the low moral condition of the clergy and openly called for a change. Since his attacks were directed against the vices, ambitions, and hypocrisy of the church rather than against doctrines, he cannot rightly be called a Protestant. But, as a sort of Spanish Savonarola, he started reactionary fires. Though condemned by the Inquisition, he died a natural death in 1532, before the church was fully roused against the new heresy.

His brother, Juan de Valdés, is sometimes called the foremost Spanish reformer, although he too failed to break openly with the Roman Church. One of the finest writers of his language who ever lived, the aristocratic and scholarly de Valdés fought convincingly against church practices and appeared to hold, at least intellectually, the doctrine of justification by faith. After he moved to Naples, de Valdés had greater influence upon reformed ideas there, as we note in the chapter on Italy.

The first Spanish Protestant to die for his faith was Francisco de San Roman, a traveling merchant converted to Christ while in Germany or

Flanders. At an *auto de fé** in Valladolid, then the capital of Spain, this steadfast believer was burned, along with some Jews, in the 1540's. Others soon added their names to the roll of honor through martyrdom or imprisonment. By the middle of the century several Protestant groups had been planted in Valladolid and Seville, each with as many as a thousand (estimated) believers. Elsewhere, too, there were churches, but history records little about them.

But now the opposition grew fiercer, following the decisions of the Council of Trent and the creation of the Jesuits by the Spaniard Loyola. Great *autos de fé* were instituted by the Holy Office, at the insistence of Charles V, and later, of Philip II. Between 1559 and 1562 the records of the Counter Reformation speak of two hundred Spanish Protestants condemned by the church authorities. Had there been many more prominent ones, history would probably have noted their contribution.

Most of the reformers were from the influential upper classes, for only they could read. The Spanish historian Jaime Balmes admits that "distinguished ecclesiastics, members of the clergy, nuns, important laymen, in a word, individuals of the most influential classes, were found infected by the new errors."[46] For example, one of the leading members of the strong Seville Protestant group was Dr. Constantino Ponce de la Fuente, the preaching canon at the Cathedral. Previously he had served as chaplain and court preacher for Charles V. So persuasive was his preaching that people reportedly went to church as early as three o'clock in the morning to get a place to hear him. In his writings the learned doctor called the Pope Antichrist and charged the monks with inventing purgatory in order to fill their stomachs.

Others were among the Lord's stalwarts in Spain. A muleteer named Julián Hernández smuggled in the New Testament and reformed writings. When three years of torture failed to make him recant, he willingly died for Christ. Even the Primate of Spain, Bartholomé Carranza, Archbishop of Toledo, was accused of heresy. His story is fascinating. Though he had served as a delegate to the Council of Trent and had aided in restoring English Catholicism under Queen Mary, Carranza apparently was influenced by Juan de Valdés and others. Although he seemed reluctant to break openly with the Church of Rome, Carranza's bold views were suspect enough to cause his imprisonment in Spain and Rome for seventeen years.

In spite of these giants of opposition to Rome, the Reformation largely failed here. As John D. Hughey, Jr., says, "It is correct to say that after the 1560's there was no Protestant movement in the country."[47] Juan

---

*A Portuguese word meaning literally "act of the faith," used to describe the trial, sentencing, and execution of a heretic.

Orts Gonzalez speaks thus of the longer range consequences of the failure: "By the year 1570 Protestantism was cut off, root and branch, practically all its converts having suffered either banishment or martyrdom, and for the three centuries that followed, the blood of its martyrs was seed in barren soil."[48] Still, we cannot help but wonder what Spain—and Latin America—would be today had the Reformation taken root. One leading Spanish Catholic historian believes that, had the Inquisition been later in arriving, his country would have readily embraced the new faith.

Foreign Missions Enter. Spain is one of the few countries of our survey to which we give space for a missionary review, because a sketch of the reverses and advances of the work has special value for today. Though the Inquisition succeeded in burning out organized Protestant witness through the *autos de fé*, Spanish exiles kept active little cells of faith alive for many centuries. During brief intervals of tolerance in their homeland, some families would slip back into the country to serve their Lord. Now for the first time foreigners joined them. William H. Rule, a Methodist, took advantage of the liberalism of the 1830's to found, in Cadiz, the first Protestant school ever known in the country, but Rule himself was later forced to withdraw. A Methodist Bible Society agent was also expelled. During the same period George Borrow, of the British and Foreign Bible Society, began the famous colportage tours immortalized in his work, *The Bible in Spain*. Both he and another Bible Society agent, Lieutenant Graydon, sowed much good seed, though they were later imprisoned, attacked, and forced to leave the country.

A revolution in 1854 provided another opportunity to evangelize. In 1856 the Spanish Evangelization Society of Edinburgh, which had been formed in 1845, reported that it had already circulated 100,000 Bibles and Scripture portions in Spain. At the same time the British and Foreign Bible Society had printed 10,000 Bibles in Spain, but was forced to take them out of the country several years later without selling any.

During the revolutionary chaos of 1868–1873 and under the First Republic (1873–1874), Protestantism won some slight legal recognition in Spain. Taking advantage of the relative (and often regional) liberty of the time, foreign workers began to enter in larger numbers. From Ireland came Anglicans; from Scotland, Presbyterians; and from America, Methodists, Congregationalists, and Baptists. As a result of their labors and those of returning Spaniards, the first significant advance was made toward establishing churches. Altogether 166 congregations were born during the fifty years after 1869. One reason for rapid growth was the massive distribution of Scripture by the various Bible societies over a period of some years. During the first Republican regime two Spanish Protestants wrote:

> The chapels were always filled with multitudes anxious to hear the new doctrines. Bibles were sold by thousands; the tracts printed were all too few to satisfy the universal curiosity. It is much to be lamented that in those days there were not laborers and funds enough to have opened a chapel in every city and town of importance throughout Spain, for, had this been done, there would this day exist as many congregations as there were chapels opened to the public.[49]

One of the best-known missionaries associated with the Spanish Christian Church, a union of Presbyterian-inclined groups formed in 1871, was the German, Fritz Fliedner. Fliedner was instructed in Berlin to try to work with existing groups rather than begin a new denomination. His work in Madrid has continued to this day under his descendants of the third and fourth generations. He founded a large Protestant school, a chapel, an orphanage, a hospital, a publishing house, and a bookshop. Elsewhere in Madrid a grammar school and a Protestant seminary went up, much of the money coming from German sources.

One of the earlier Plymouth Brethren missionaries of the period, George Lawrence of England, carried on an extensive work out of Barcelona among assemblies he founded, specializing in Bible and literature distribution. In 1869 alone this zealous servant of God sold no fewer than 300,000 Bible and Scripture portions. From their tent pitched in front of the Barcelona city hall Lawrence and his six associates once sold 60,000 copies of the Bible in two and a half days! Though Lawrence and his family were insulted, stoned, fined, and imprisoned, they planted an enduring testimony in Spain.

William Knapp pioneered a Baptist witness in the same era. In April, 1870, he and his Spanish helpers recorded 1,325 professions of faith in seven months. Later he formed the first Baptist church in Madrid, with 33 charter members; another church was born in Alicante, and still others existed in embryo elsewhere. An 1874 report of the American Baptist Missionary Union shows four churches in Spain, and a total membership of 244. Yet there were many discouragements, especially in the development of Spanish pastors. Unfortunately most of Knapp's work in Madrid and elsewhere died out and the churches closed. In 1876 Knapp left Spain quite discouraged about the prospects for anything permanent. Fortunately a Swede named Eric Lund arrived to rejuvenate the American Baptist work, and other Swedish Baptists helped. At about the turn of the century Valencia had 76 members, and the Catalonia region 114, but the Madrid church had not yet revived. By 1955 2,500 members were reported in thirty-two Baptist churches of the Spanish Evangelical Baptist Union (sponsored by the American Southern Baptists), but only three were considered self-supporting.

The American Board of Commissioners for Foreign Missions (Congregational) sent William H. Gulick to Spain in the nineteenth century. He did a good work, especially in the city of Santander, where his audience climbed to as high as three or four hundred a Sunday. But by 1874 this number had dropped to about thirty permanently interested persons.

Let us sumarize the Spanish Protestant strength in 1874. Twenty-seven foreign men and thirty-two foreign women (including three single ones) were at work in nineteen cities and towns. With them, eighteen Spanish pastors and fourteen evangelists were serving thirty-six churches and preaching points, drawing a total average attendance of 1840; 1,783 pupils were enrolled in forty-three Protestant schools. Help was coming, either financially or through missionaries, from the United Presbyterian Church of Scotland, the Presbyterian Church of Ireland, American Baptists and Congregationalists, English Wesleyan Methodists and Brethren, the Spanish Evangelization Society of Edinburgh, and committees in Germany, Switzerland, and Holland. The British and Foreign Bible Society had fifteen colporteurs (not included in above figures), and the National Bible Society of Holland had seven. All together, four publications were in circulation.

As we evaluate the position of 1874, several conclusions emerge. Though there had been a numerical advance, the faith had still not touched the wealthy, aristocratic classes nor had it gained much acceptance among the poor and uneducated. Protestantism, still largely dependent on outside workers and funds, was considered a foreign religion as opposed to Roman Catholicism, called a truly Spanish faith. Only a beachhead had been gained.

Revival and retrogression have succeeded each other in every group of Spanish believers founded through missionary action. The Congregationalists, who entered in the 1870's and won promising victories, saw their work shrivel to 320 members in six churches by 1931—about fifty years later. Spanish Baptists were turned over to the Southern Baptist Convention by the World Baptist Alliance in 1920, but soon found financial curtailment of the work necessary on account of the world depression. The late Percy Buffard, a British Baptist, founded a non-denominational work in the center of Spain which continued to flourish. In general the work was slow and hard. Everett Gill wrote in 1923, "After 50 years of effort by about 10 denominations there are at present in Spain scarcely 4000 evangelical Christians."[50] Of Protestant progress up to the eve of the Second Republic (1931), another historian says, "The various Protestant groups were apparently holding their own or growing slowly. But on the whole, Protestant work was at a standstill."[51]

Under the Republicans. Before the period of the Second Republic (1931–1936) the tiny Spanish Protestant church had experienced very little liberty to expand. During the centuries under the monarchy, the First Republic, and the dictatorship of General Primo de Rivera, there had been a few encouraging periods, but much oppression. We can understand, then, the joy of the Protestants when the new Republic, in one of its first decrees, proclaimed religious liberty on April 14, 1931. One of their number even became a minor government official. But there were more obstacles ahead. The provisional government made only emergency decrees and left the task of writing a constitution to the Constituent Cortes, made up of all kinds of leaders—Catholics, atheists, socialists of the right and left, radicals, and anarchists. After strong debate they succeeded in drawing up a constitution which separated church and state for the first time in Spanish history: Article 3 read: "The Spanish state has no official religion." So high were feelings over the religious issue that the first president of the provisional government, a liberal Catholic, resigned.

Unfortunately the anticlericalism of the people, shown in the burning of churches and later in the slaughter of priests, during the war, marred the achievement of religious liberty.* The responsibility for these radical and regrettable acts has not been determined fully, but it is clear that the official Republican government was not to blame. Yet that government did indulge in much petty and vindictive anticlericalism, which discredited it. Neither was it able to hold in check radical elements in its midst, which led to its downfall.

Under the Republic, says Hughey, "Protestants enjoyed full freedom of action and received courtesies and consideration from officials of the government."[52] Many of the aggravating regulations about the press, marriage, burial, and education were now corrected in the Protestants' favor. But the Cortes went too far in its treatment of Catholics. It banned the Jesuit order, nationalized all Catholic property (though permitting normal services to continue), and forbade religious orders to have any part in secular affairs. The Pope wrote a strong letter of protest, crying persecution. This put the Catholic Church in the unaccustomed role of a suppliant for religious liberty.

During the civil war, which began in 1936, the Catholics were not permitted to worship publicly in most of Republican Spain until near

---

*Hundreds of churches were burned. In Barcelona almost every Catholic church was destroyed or attacked. Mistakenly one Protestant chapel was set afire, but as soon as the people saw their mistake, they extinguished the flames.

the end of the conflict. On the other hand, Protestants in Republican territory had as much freedom as circumstances allowed. Yet in National-ist (Franco) Spain Protestants were repressed. Regrettably, the Repub-lic now began to swing more sharply to the left as Russian agents and Spanish Communists gained increasing influence.

What real progress was made by the Lord's people under their new freedom? For one thing, the Bible was published and distributed freely through Bible vans, and schools were reopened. Naturally the chaos of war upset much outward planning and organization. But the official introduction of religious liberty and the government attacks on Rome did not result in an ingathering of souls by the Protestants. As Hughey writes, "The advantages resulting from the establishment of religous freedom were to a great extent neutralized by the growth of religious indifference and even opposition to all religion."[53] Anarchy and atheism were flourish-ing as well. Then, too, sixty years of work by foreign missionaries had left the churches still mostly dependent on foreign finances. An American and world depression coincided with Spain's new experiment in democ-racy, reducing the flow of funds.

The hoped-for ingathering of souls never arrived. In 1934 a Spanish pastor wrote:

> The moral and religious level of the Spanish people has confessedly descended in an accentuated manner. The campaigns against the Roman Catholic Church have been many times confounded with re-bellion against the very idea of God, and the activity of atheist litera-ture increases the loss of faith, especially among the lower classes . . . the moral and religious spirit of the people is on the downgrade; every kind of violence is the order of the day.[54]

Surely anti-Catholic action is not the secret of evangelizing a Catholic land. Souls are not won to Christ by exposing error alone. Only when the Holy Spirit is free to work in answer to prayer will the Spanish people turn to Christ. As one writer puts it, "It was evident that, however de-sirable religious liberty might be, it was not the open sesame of Protestant growth."[55]

Roll Call of Protestants Today. Most of us have never met a Quaker in America nor visited a Quaker church. A personal acquaintance with Quakers and their churches is rare indeed, because they are not numerous. We mention this denomination because the proportion of Quakers in the American population is about the same as that of the Protestants in Spain. There are only about 25,000 Protestants of every type among thirty million Spaniards.* Congregations number no more than 250. Of these,

---

*The government admitted this figure in an official 165-page mimeographed re-port, *The Situation of Protestantism in Spain* (Madrid: Diplomatic Information Office, 1955), but asserted that half were foreigners.

some find their churches periodically closed and reopened by the government at intervals, and many are very tiny. Not all the 25,000 listed "Protestants" are members of a church, but the estimated figure includes regular attendants at services and those under Protestant influence. Spanish Protestants are much more faithful and less nominal in their participation in church life than most Protestants elsewhere.

The denominations in Spain can be grouped into three categories, according to their beliefs and affiliations: (1) The *Episcopal* (Reformed) *Church* of eight congregations, and the *Spanish Evangelical Church* (Presbyterian-Methodist-Lutheran-Congregational), with fifty-two; (2) The *Spanish Evangelical Baptist Union* (Southern Baptist Convention), with forty-three churches, and the *"open" Brethren* assemblies numbering possibly sixty groups; (3) The *independent Baptist* churches, *"closed" Brethren* groups, *Pentecostal* churches, and *independent mission* churches. Then there are, in addition, small groups of *Adventists, Jehovah's Witnesses,* and other cults. The first group of churches is generally associated with the World Council of Churches and its Division of Interchurch Aid. Some liberalism and theological weakness was prevalent in the teaching of Spanish pastors at the United Theological Seminary in Madrid (closed by police action since 1956). The extent of this deviation from orthodoxy is hard to guess, but its practical result in some of the churches is a lack of evangelistic zeal and outreach to the lost. As in all other European countries, an altered orthodoxy also appears in Spain.

In the second and third churches listed above, we believe, lie the best hope for evangelizing Spain. Not so much because of any denominational distinctives are these congregations likely to grow and multiply, but because of their basic loyalty to the Word of God. Significantly, most of the closed churches in Spain are of this group. A Federation of Independent Evangelical Churches, formed in 1957, under Pastor José Martinez, today includes twenty-two churches. Some measure of orthodox co-operation is possible among those who love the Lord through the fellowship of the Spanish Evangelical Alliance. The fringe cults which proclaim definite error are no more healthy for Spain than for America, their original home.

What Protestants Cannot Do. Under Article 6 of the Charter of the Spanish people, the Protestants can do nothing regarded as a *public* propagation or extension of their faith. Some prohibitions are subject to local interpretation, but in general the prohibitions are these: (1) They cannot have a church-like building with any external signs suggesting its use. (2) They cannot have churches in prominent locations, but must locate in the side streets. (3) They cannot make public announcements of services by signs or by newspaper or radio. (4) They cannot open a new church without permission (seldom granted), reopen a church closed by police action without permission (also seldom granted), move their church to another location, or hold services in a private home, or anywhere else but the recognized location. (5) They cannot publish (print and circulate) any material for use outside of their own immediate church circle, nor operate gospel bookstores. (6) They cannot conduct private schools for their own children. (7) They cannot contract a civil (non-Catholic) marriage unless they can prove that they were never Catholics; or if they were formerly Catholics, they must show to the satisfaction of the local diocesan authority that they are not now Catholic. (But Catholics believe that baptism is irradicable.) If one of the couple was ever baptized in the Roman Church, he or she is expected to marry in the church. (8) They cannot print, import, or circulate the Protestant Bible, or portions thereof. (9) They cannot give out tracts on the street. (10) In many communities they cannot use a Protestant service to bury their dead in civil cemeteries or have more than two members of the family at the grave. Burial in Catholic cemeteries is forbidden. (11) They cannot, under most conditions, receive government social security benefits, even though they are taxed for them. (12) They cannot become officers in the armed forces. (13) They cannot hold positions of any consequence in the government. (14) Generally they cannot advance far in business, law, or the professions, once their belief is known. (15) They cannot, as a rule, teach in public schools. (16) They cannot openly and officially train their clergy. (17) They cannot operate their own hospitals or become nurses in hospitals. (18) They cannot establish homes for old people or orphans. (19) They cannot rent public halls for evangelistic work. (20) They cannot broadcast over Spanish radio stations. (21) They usually cannot obtain satisfaction for their grievances from the highest officials in the land.

Several of the above are more grave than others. One is the ban on the Bible. Another is the law against opening, reopening, or relocating churches, the most serious threat of all to Protestant expansion. Protestant pastors say this is the liberty they would like most to have. There is always a list of groups waiting for permission to reopen churches; the latest report was that there were six of these, all with little prospect of an affirmative action. In any case they usually do not know who gave the order to close the church. Many churches are little isolated pockets of believers sometimes begun by one or two families in a town, or by personal work from a larger, organized group.

Some of the restrictions listed are subject to wide intepretation locally. Ways are often devised by Protestant pastors to marry their people, including the solemnizing of a wedding before a notary public; which at least puts the ceremony on record, though without legalizing it. Catholic prelates are empowered by the 1953 Concordat to be more firm in holding both active and lapsed Catholics to canonical laws on marriage.

The Brighter Side. Now let us consider the things Protestants *can* do, many of which are of basic importance to the disciple of Jesus Christ. Parenthetically, Latins are renowned for writing something into a law, then failing to enforce it. Not only can local authorities interpret laws liberally, but individuals can find ways of circumventing them. Any Latin gets vast experience in such maneuvers. Many Spanish Christians feel that certain regulations can be manipulated in a limited way without offense to conscience. Spanish believers are not lawbreakers, but neither do they take every regulation literally if there is any possibility of a broader view. Sometimes when officials themselves give them a way out on a technicality, they take it. One pastor said to me, "What our police chief wants is some legitimate material for a report which will satisfy his superiors. At heart he is on our side and we co-operate with him to the full."

What can Protestants do under the heading of "private" worship? (1) They can believe in Christ as Saviour and Lord. No Spaniard is regulated by thought police or ordered to abandon his personal belief and adopt another. (2) They can hold as many meetings as they desire in authorized places. In these they can sing, testify, and proclaim the whole counsel of God as long as they do not challenge the government on any issue. (3) They can witness for Christ to others, provided they do it wisely. If they push too hard in speaking to a convinced Catholic who refuses to listen, there may be repercussions. But most people are open to hear, especially when spoken to individually in their homes. (4) They can invite people to church by word of mouth, even though they cannot use other means of publicity. But was there ever a *better* means? Many believers are faithful in doing this. As a result, a high percentage of inquirers attend gospel services. (5) They can give Biblical instruction to their children, though not in a formal way. (6) They can print some things for use within their own group, provided they have local good will. (7) They can pray. With Jesus Christ, the Head of the church, in their midst (Matt. 18:20), Spanish believers dare not be discouraged.

Other things done clandestinely by Protestants to advance the cause of their Lord cannot be published here. They love their country, and are loyal to it. Nothing they do is either morally wrong or hurtful to the present regime, to which they pay almost more respect than can be expected of people treated as second-class citizens.

Are Believers Persecuted? The answer to this depends on what we mean by "persecution." If we mean that Spanish Christians pay a higher price than most of us to follow Jesus Christ, of course the answer is "Yes." But if we mean that they are often physically attacked, driven underground, or forbidden to worship privately, in most cases the answer is "No." One hears the Protestant church of Spain referred to as "the church in the catacombs" or "the underground church." But the Spanish church is not an illegal or clandestine one, living outside the society of its fellow men. If either the state or its Roman Catholic partners ever desired to exterminate or really persecute this church, they could easily do so. As W. E. Garrison insists, "To say that they are persecuted is, as a generalization, to go beyond the facts. . . . When Spanish authorities have really set out to persecute dissenters from their established church, they take no half-way measures. . . . Knowing what a thoroughgoing and bloody business persecution is understood to be when Spaniards put their minds to it, if anyone asks whether Protestants are now being persecuted in Spain, I would answer, 'No.' "[56] Much unnecessary exaggeration on this point clouds the issue.

Bigoted and unfair attitudes toward these children of God are common. Examples abound of frustrations, delays, discriminations, refusals, insults, economic wrong, and occasional bodily harm. Who do these things? Not the common people, except when they are goaded by the priests. The Catholic Church uses the state and its officials to oppose Protestants, and the state complies to further its own desire for power.

Victory Through Dependence. We have said that the state and the church leaders of Spain repress, but do not break, the Spanish Protestant church. But God does more than support them in their dilemma. He uses their bondage, as is ever His way, for their own good and that of Spain. The Lord balances the cross on the shoulders of His own children with infinite wisdom. The dictatorship under which His people live is just oppressive enough to stimulate them but not ruthless enough to destroy them. Like Paul's thorn in the flesh, the opposition only drives them to His boundless grace. Though Spaniards pray about their thorn of affliction much more often than "thrice," their Lord keeps the thorn there. They resemble the Jews under Egyptian rule: "the more they afflicted them, the more they . . . grew" (Exod. 1:12). As Garrison puts it, the Spanish Church "has turned its legal disabilities to good account and has reaped spiritual benefits from its material weakness."[57]

At the beginning of the chapter we decried expressions of pity for Spanish Protestants in favor of something more practical. Why pity a church as fruitful as this? Consider, for instance, these points: (1) Every

Spanish church has greatly gained in converts under the Franco regime, whereas under the freedom of the Second Republic they were losing ground. One Madrid church tripled its membership during the twenty years following the civil war. Doubling of followers is quite normal in Spain over a ten-year period. No American denomination, nor even American Protestantism or Catholicism as a whole, can match this record. (2) Very few nominal members adhere to a fellowship as costly as this. Only deep spiritual conviction would ever lead a person to identify himself with it. Socially and economically it is a bad thing to do. One's children suffer, too. (3) Any pastor anywhere with a church as full as the average one in Spain would rejoice. Here believers do not stay at home on the slightest excuse or attend only if they are in the mood. Of course there are backsliders in heart, too, in this land, and a number fail to stand the pressure. (4) These Christians bear witness, however halting and lacking in finesse they may be in the presentation. They also invite people to services with what is possibly the world's highest degree of faithfulness.

Bearing His Reproach. The restrictions against Christians in Spain naturally cause them to suffer. We now give a few incidents, mostly from the records of French pastor Jacques Delpech, in order to move other Christians to compassion. Compassion differs from pity in that it is "suffering with" another, and can lead to understanding prayer for fellow believers. We must remember three things about Spanish believers: First, suffering has a strengthening, purifying effect upon their lives. Second, God directs them to live under this oppression, for His glory. Third, there never has been a better form of witness than personal identification with Jesus Christ before men.

A Protestant sailor named José Morado refused to kneel before the sacrament during a military mass. His commander ordered him to be beaten, after which he was removed to a hospital in a serious condition. A military trial later sentenced him to one year in prison. Fatally weakened by the permanent effects of violence and imprisonment, he died shortly afterward. . . . A village priest headed a procession to a Protestant house, where he ordered the woman of the house to kneel before him. When she refused, the priest called a policeman, who recorded her name and address. Later the same priest saw a twenty-one-year-old Protestant girl on the street with her Bible under her arm. "You with the Bible," he called, "go to your knees." After her brave refusal, he again called the police. At their trial later, the woman and the girl were both fined $20, which neither could pay. Instead they were both sent to jail.

A young man from a very devout Catholic home spent some months in a seminary, but was disillusioned by his studies for the priesthood.

Upon his return home, he began visiting a Protestant pastor to ask questions. When his sisters learned of this, they refused to speak to him or stay in the same room with him. His mother declared, "I would prefer to have my son frequent taverns and come home drunk than to have him associate with Protestants" . . . A young woman who read the New Testament in her spare time at the store where she worked was dismissed by her employer when the priest learned of it . . . A well-known businessman was warned by his banker that if he persisted in his beliefs, he would suffer financially. . . A Protestant mother who gave birth to a child in a Catholic hospital (all state hospitals are Catholic) was sent home too early, so that her health was endangered, because she refused baptism for the child. . . In southern Spain a very sick Protestant, who had made an official declaration of his faith at the police station, and had requested a Protestant burial service, later died. Two policemen interrupted the service at his graveside, forbidding the pastor to continue. A priest then arrived, accompanied by four policemen, to give the body a Catholic burial contrary to the officially registered wishes of the deceased, his family, and his church.

A Change for the Better? As we write, a change of attitude toward Protestants now seems imminent, due to the new climate of tolerance created by the Second Vatican Council and the desire of Spain to improve her image abroad. Early in 1963 the Roman Catholic hierarchy withdrew its objections to a government bill which seeks to ease restrictions on Protestants. The person most responsible for this has been Foreign Minister Fernando Castiella y Maiz. He seems to have convinced both Franco and the Pope of the necessity to improve the situation of Spanish Protestants. Though still denying Protestants the right to proselytize, the proposed law would grant legal recognition to churches, permit Protestant schools and seminaries, allow distribution of Bibles and literature and the operation of hospitals and cemeteries. Even the right to hold high civic offices may be included. While all this is good news, it must be remembered that the motive behind the proposal appears tactical, based on pressure rather than principle. It could, therefore, be short-lived as a law, or be subject to "interpretation."

Let's Go To Church. If you attend a typical chapel, as gospel churches are called here, you will enter on a side street, probably in the poorer part of town. Without direction or help you would probably never find it, for it is not listed in the phone book, no sign or light graces the entrance, and the building does not look like a church. Inside, the lighting will be poor. Wooden benches, plain and hard, fill the interior, except for a tiny platform at the front. No decorations or frills are to be seen. A Bible verse or two may be painted on the walls. You had better come early, for long before the service begins every seat will be taken. If the meeting is at night, it will probably begin very late and last long beyond midnight. Look around you, and you will be surprised by the number of men present, as well as by the high proportion of young people. They sing in full-voiced, somewhat somber style, many knowing the words by heart. No peppy song-leading or other means is used to create atmosphere. Praying is often aloud and heartfelt. The preaching may be done by a semi-educated, largely self-taught brother. At the end of the service a blessing awaits. Now souls will be given opportunity to stand and acknowledge the Lord Jesus as Saviour. If some respond, immediately those who invited them and know them in the community will crowd around, embrace them, and praise God. In a warm, vital moment they will accept them into the despised but joyous family of faith. You will never forget your visit to a group reduced to the minimal essentials of worship. This is a New Testament church.

Special Needs. Among the Christians of Spain certain weaknesses appear which are largely the result of their restricted liberties. First, these believers need to study personally the whole counsel of God. If some truths the Christian needs for daily growth are neglected, failure is soon evident in the life. Spanish Christians must know victory over sin, through the Holy Spirit, just to survive. Exposed to great pressures as soon as they are born again, some remain constant, but others fall. At first, confession of Christ and holy living seem easy. But as the warmth and glow of the new life begin to fade somewhat, a danger period begins. The new believers discover that their greatest enemy is self. If at this juncture they fail to settle their hearts upon Christ as the sustaining Bread of Life, they will fall back into the carnal life. Satan believes time is on his side, and seeks to wear out those who cannot be forced out of the fellowship. Sometimes when the weary pilgrim sees no let-up in reactions among people, he becomes faint in heart. Now he is "above strength" (II Cor. 1:8)—beyond his own resources—where only the appropriated strength of Another can help. To achieve the stability and stature the Lord would give, the Spaniard must learn to study the Bible for himself, nourishing his soul in the Lord Jesus daily.

Second, Spaniards need more, and deeper, teaching from the pulpit. On this point the late Donald Grey Barnhouse said, "The great need in Spain is for Bible teaching. There is very little of it, and almost no books on the subject."[58] Many Christians, for instance, who love the Lord deeply are at a loss to deal with others from the Bible.

A third problem is basic to these two. Pastors and leaders must have more and better training. Miracles of evangelization have taken place in spite of a lack in leadership, but over a period of years the void in spiritual understanding by men in the pulpit becomes painful. Since the start of foreign missionary work in Spain, the difficulty of training pastors has persisted. With the government periodically closing organized schools for pastors, private, personal training seems an obvious answer. Another, less satisfactory one is for Spaniards to go out to the country for study, returning later. But the obstacles to that course of action are great.

A foreign worker in Spain can aid splendidly in meeting all three of these needs for personal, public, and pastoral Bible study. He cannot work too much in the open anyhow, if he is to remain long in the country and make a contribution. Further, the realm in which he is so fortunate, that of advanced training, is the very area where Spanish evangelicals are the weakest.

As Conversions Multiply. One of the most urgent but in a sense happy problems facing Spanish Christians is—where to put the people! Almost every chapel in the country is full for each service now, and the government rarely gives permission to open a new one. With private meetings in homes forbidden, standing-room-only conditions are likely to continue for a long time.

Some of the stories of the new converts who fill these churches stir the heart. In Medina del Campo Señorita Antolina Prieto found the Lord as Saviour. Not long afterwards her younger sister shared her joy of sins forgiven. Furiously their mother beat the elder girl daily for months, but both new Christians rejoiced to suffer for His name . . . A certain Manuel Diáz so overflowed with the rapture of knowing Christ that he dared to hold a meeting for others privately in his home. When he was threatened with a jail sentence if he refused to pay a fine, he wrote some other Christians: "I am the first in my town to refuse to pay the fine . . . I prefer to suffer in order to proclaim our right to worship God according to our conscience . . . I am not afflicted and do not feel ashamed to go to prison for such a reason . . . I will tell the director of the prison that I am an evangelical . . . I am asking the Lord to give me joy through all tribulation and, if I am sent to prison, I know the Lord will stand with me and that jail will prove to be a place of blessing to my soul."[59]

In Hostafranchs a man who had heard and rejected the gospel for forty years came to Christ at last. His father, who had been a faithful colporteur of the Scottish Bible Society, had steadily prayed for him over many years . . . In Seville a lady who attended the evangelicals' meeting was forbidden by her husband to worship with them. He tore up her

Bible and other books. When he was away from home, she ventured to attend, but once was in a service when he returned. When she went home trembling, after being warned by a neighbor of her husband's presence, he gave her a systematic, sadistic beating. Still she persisted in her confession of the Saviour, praying for her partner's conversion . . . Two young sailors, members of the Brethren assemby at Vigo, who refused to kneel at military mass, were condemned to two years of imprisonment. If they refuse again to kneel after their release, they will get a prolonged sentence of four years.

A church at Villaineuva y Geltru, which was much persecuted, saw souls saved every Sunday for ten consecutive weeks . . . Señora Maria in southern Spain showed special devotion to the figures of the saints in her church. With great care she dressed them with silk, adorned them with flowers, and surrounded them with lighted candles. But a shadow came into her life when her husband became infected with evangelical truths. She began to denounce every Protestant she knew to her priest, who would in turn tell the authorities. Yet the change in her husband baffled her. One day, going through his coat, she found a Gospel of John. After she had read part of it, she agreed to accompany him to the chepel, where people began to pray for her. Not long afterward she herself became a happy child of God.

In one town where the church has been closed by the authorities, people are still coming to Christ. Recently ten converts were secretly baptized in a bathtub moved into a kitchen to provide room for the one hundred witnesses who came, one by one and by different routes . . . A mother who beat her daughter for professing faith in Christ was visited by the evangelical pastor. Fanatical with hatred, she shouted and screamed like a mad woman when she saw him, not permitting him to speak. When she finally stopped for breath, she heard the pastor calmly talk not about her daughter, but of the Lord. Curious in spite of herself, she calmed down, listened long, and finally promised to attend a meeting herself. Her salvation followed soon afterward.

A twenty-one-year-old daughter of a distinguished, very strict Catholic family was preparing to become a nun, when a local woman invited her to evangelistic services. There she made a decision for Christ. When her father learned of this, he brutally slapped her face. Each time she attended church thereafter, a terrible row occurred. This was her reaction: "If I was willing to sacrifice myself, leaving my family, to try to find salvation in a convent, why should I not be willing to do so now that I know salvation is mine through Jesus, my Lord and my Saviour?"[60] . . . In a small town on the border between Jaén and Albacete provinces a young Spaniard from North Africa began meetings secretly in his own house.

When he told the inquiring Civil Guard he wished people to come to the Lord Jesus, a corporal beat him until he himself was exhausted.

Priests Find Peace. The way to heaven seems especially thorny for those Catholics who are trained to mediate between God and man at the altar. Yet marvelous is the grace of God which reaches and delivers some of these men. One of the most renowned conversions among priests occurred in 1951, when the Jesuit scholar, Don Luis Pedrosa, Director of the Loyola Institute in Barcelona, announced his new faith and fled from Spain to South America. His book, *Why Did I Leave the Church of Rome?*, became popular in several languages, and though forbidden in Spain, is circulated there clandestinely. Another priest was given a Protestant Bible to burn, but began to read it instead. After he found the Lord, he was completely disowned by his family. Rejoicing in his salvation, the ex-priest told how he once lacerated his body and wrote prayers for mercy in his own blood.

A young friar still in a monastery began to visit a little church, where he heard the gospel. On New Year's Eve, when all were on their knees at midnight, he opened his heart to the Lord and received eternal life. Another priest used to scourge his body raw in order to please God. When he was converted, he was thrown into financial peril. Even though he had two advanced degrees, he was forced to labor in a factory. As soon as his past became known, he lost his job, but fortunately local union officials took action to compel his employer to indemnify him.

What Foreigners Can Do. We turn to the practical help non-Spanish Christians can provide. First of all, they can intercede. Intercession should be based on information; so the prayer-warrior would do well to keep informed. Second, foreigners can beam most effective broadcasts into Spain. This is one of the most direct methods, since 80 per cent of Spanish homes have radios. Sponsors of programs beamed into the country from European commercial stations and from other continents all receive heavy mail, indicating a large listening audience. Some such broadcasts, mostly sponsored by foreign missions, send follow-up materials and New Testaments to those requesting them, using contacts within the country for distribution. Third, the circulation of Bibles and gospel literature can be paid for and promoted by foreigners who may never enter the country at all. Though this activity is not officially allowed, it is carried on partially nevertheless.

Fourth, missionaries can and do enter Spain and work there, though they are not officially admitted in that capacity by the government. A few Cuban, Swiss, British, and American missionaries have been expelled since World War II, but some have managed to return. In view of America's new influence in Spanish affairs there is less chance of government reaction against citizens of that country. Many of the British missionaries have resided in the country for years. Men and women truly called of God to Spain can and do serve Him there despite opposition. Courage and conviction are essential to enter and remain. For details on the possibilities, those interested should address missions serving Spain or workers already there. All can expect grim Roman Catholic reaction, mostly through prohibitions and harassment. There is little danger of physical attack. Even though the total number of foreign workers never exceeds a ratio of one to a million, the hierarchy still objects. In an article called "Facing the New Invasion," published in Barcelona's *La Vanguardia* on August 11, 1948, the writer said of foreign missionaries, "Here they are in flocks, like bats, cast out by the ironic coldness of their own fellow countrymen, who do not wish to or prefer not to believe anything." At the time this appeared there were fewer than a dozen foreigners actively at work! We conclude with this thought: Let the church of Jesus Christ outside of Spain concentrate prayer and help on this country, and two things will happen. First, those who love Christ will be amazed at the response that will come in lives and at the change in events here. Second, our God will rejoice over the fulfillment of His will among a waiting, weary people for whom He gave His only Son.

Peasant women washing clothes at the village "laundromat" as their forebears did in centuries past.

Chapter 6

THE AWAKENING OF PORTUGAL

"Portugal has often been regarded by those who are unacquainted with her real spiritual condition as a Christian country, and therefore not in need of missionary help. The truth is that the Portuguese people have been desperately neglected. There are few fields in any continent so spiritually needy and so unenlightened."
—ARTHUR INGLEBY
Missionary to Portugal

"Protestantism has a great mission to this priest-ridden people."
—JUAN ORTS GONZALEZ

On the Edge of Europe. Portugal does not get the attention she deserves because of her isolated position. In terms of European life she is not in the center of things. This is true not only in international affairs but in the missionary sense. Her larger neighbor, Spain, compels more interest because an international press closely follows Protestant persecution there. The customary travel pattern also contributes to the neglect of Portugal. The visitor to Madrid or Barcelona is not far from Lisbon, but he usually lacks the time for the trip to that city, or his itinerary leads him eastward. This is unfortunate because it has deprived English-speaking Christians of information about spiritual conditions there. Yet one of the biggest stories of blessing and fruit in Europe today is to be found in this land on the continent's edge.

After one hundred years of missionary work with only scant success, a harvest is coming in at last in Portugal. From the many hundreds of new converts one missionary alone founded seven churches in a recent year. In the Catholic part of Europe that in itself is unusual enough to draw attention. The obstacles have been many. In spite of their Vatican overlords, people are more receptive to the Word of God now than ever before in Portuguese history. Missionaries serving here have not found their task easy. As this is written most of them must go out of the country every quarter—usually to Spain—to renew tourist visas. For some years residence visas have been refused them. In spite of such hindrances the Portuguese story is a thrilling one. On places like this, where the Holy Spirit is at work, God's children should concentrate their prayers and interest, and perhaps even their lives.

The Gospel Unheard, Unread. According to the Evangelical Alliance Mission, today 90 per cent of Portugal's cities and 99 per cent of her six thousand villages have no established gospel witness. "The number of gospel workers is so few that there are whole provinces with populations between 300,000 and 500,000 in which little or nothing has been done to establish mission centers."[1] Is this not a mission field? An experience told by a missionary executive visiting Portugal helps illustrate the point. While traveling along the road between Santiago and Lisbon he stopped to take pictures of huge stacks of cork. An old Portuguese walked over and watched the scene with interest. One of the missionaries in the party asked if he had ever heard the gospel. The old man looked puzzled. "Have you ever heard that God sent His Son Jesus Christ to die for sin?" There was no glimmer of understanding in the man's face. "Have you ever seen a Bible, the Word of God?" "No." "The Bible is God's message to you. Have you never known God had a message for you?" After some thought the elderly man recalled from the dim recesses of his past that a man had once sold him a little booklet, saying it was a message from God. He knew he had the booklet at home somewhere, but he could not read. As the missionaries witnessed to him, he heard for the first time of Jesus' death for him.

Portuguese Profile. Like all Europeans, the Portuguese are a racial mixture of their many conquerors. Today they are generally Iberian in appearance, short and dark. Though the Romans gave them a new language and a start on their present civilization, the Moorish imprint on architecture, handicraft, and language is more evident today. Portuguese in blood, these people are mostly Catholic in religion but Arab in thought and speech form.

Every Portuguese, remembering the past greatness of his country, is at heart a *grandee*. As such he is usually dignified, polite, unhurried, and charming. Yet he can reflect a visitor's attitude with startling accuracy. Rudeness will bring a sharp response from these very sensitive people. Generally the Portuguese are more affectionate in nature than the Spanish. Of course there are regional differences in temperament. In the Minho, people are peaceful and hardworking; in the Douro, more jovial. The *campino* cowboy of Ribatejo sports a bright costume as he herds cattle. Inhabitants of Trás-os-Montes are adventurous but known for their violent outbursts of temper. Beira folk along the coastal regions are brave but reputedly harsh. Melancholy and fatalism mark those in the Alentejo. The people of the Algarve are especially attached to their land and show Moorish influence by their remarkable ingenuity. Here you will see picturesque carts, chimney pots of open fretwork design, donkey saddlebags, and tempting sweetmeats of almonds and figs.

The Portuguese household is austere in its simplicity. Usually there are whitewashed walls, dark, waxed furniture, flowered cotton curtains, carpets of rush, and oil lamps. Cooking is done over a wood fire in the hearth, which also combats the winter cold. The code of hospitality in this home is rigid. Even an impoverished family must serve a full course dinner to the guest, regardless of sacrifice. Such regard for the outsider is sincere, coming from the heart.

A formal barrier between classes is taken for granted. Acceptance of one's standing in life makes for peace of mind and usually eliminates the stress and strain of ambition. In any case there is little opportunity to rise beyond the class of birth. Women, especially, have little education or liberty. Though the chaperone system is declining in Spain, it finds its last stronghold in Portugal. The Portuguese unmarried woman is much restricted in her relationship to men, and she finds life dull and confining. After marriage, custom calls for many children, and they must be brought up in a country whose national health is poor indeed. Often women will be seen staggering along under heavy burdens, or washing clothes by the riverside.

Among the common people a childlike simplicity of heart is characteristic. Generosity is a special feature in this peasant land, where two-thirds of the people are engaged in agriculture. In comparison with the rest of Europe, the Portuguese are not unduly greedy or tip-conscious. Even a beggar will say, "God bless you," if you refuse him! Sometimes when a customer chooses a small article in a shop, the shopkeeper refuses payment altogether.

Though conditions for the normal Christian witness are a little better in this country than in Spain, Portugal resembles Spain in the depth of its spiritual darkness. With a background of priestcraft, ignorance, and superstition, the people live much like their Spanish neighbors. There are the startling contrasts between modern homes with all the latest conveniences and the little primitive houses along cobblestoned streets. Farming methods are almost the same as those used by the peasants of the Middle Ages. Colorfully garbed fisherfolk, picturesque Moorish castles, and an idyllic countryside may alleviate the picture for the aesthetically-minded, but the true Christian sees Portugal as a country bereft of the Lord of life.

Poverty and Politics. Although the national budget is balanced and the *escudo* is stable currency, these advantages have been obtained at the expense of the common man. One report has called the Portuguese workers "among the worst-paid, worst-fed, and most illiterate in western Europe."[2] For the working classes life is a struggle at low wages and long hours. Portugal has Europe's lowest average annual wage of $197, with some wages artifically kept down to 1926 levels. One third of the population live in villages with neither electricity nor paved roads. Of the continental countries the 40 per cent illiteracy rate in this land is the highest; only Portugal and Spain do not require compulsory elementary education. Under a paternal, political dictatorship, reinforced with a 100,000-man police force twice the size of the army), there is little genuine freedom of opinion. The press is censored. For only forty days before each election is the opposition permited to voice its preferences. Even when some have dared to do so, they have not succeeded in over-throwing the present regime of over thirty years' power. This regime considers democracy "a hopeless system."[3] In spite of the suppression of personal liberties, tiny Portugal has become firmly attached to the western allies and has consequently received more than $250 million in United States aid. One positive feature of the present administration is firm anti-Communism, but it is also moving toward the elimination of all elective bodies. Though many Portuguese oppose the regime, they still prefer it to the chaos of the first quarter of the century, when the country had two kings, ten presidents (one assassinated, six unseated by revolutions), and forty cabinets.

Day of Power. Four centuries ago the Portuguese, with the Spanish, were the most powerful rulers of the world. Geographers such as Prince Henry the Navigator systematized the sea knowledge accumulated by an inquisitive people on the Continent's edge. Explorers like Vasco da Gama explored nearly two-thirds of the globe by sea. Hearty seafarers discovered a new route to the Indies around the Cape of Good Hope during the zenith of Portuguese power. What is now Brazil was for twelve years united with Portugal in a mighty kingdom ruled from Rio de Janeiro. The Portuguese tongue is still spoken in countries all over the earth as well as in the colonies that remain subject to the mother country. Of these the Azores, Angola, and Madeira are perhaps the best known.

Rome in the Driver's Seat. Because the Counter Reformation was so successful in the Iberian peninsula, the Reform movement never took real root there. Portugal never had a reformation. From 1540 until 1820 the Holy Inquisition did its dread work of suppression, under Jesuit direction. Up until 1834 the Roman Church had a complete monopoly upheld by the power of the kings. After the establishment of a republic in 1910, strong reaction against the church resulted in the expulsion of religious orders, confiscation of their property, the granting of religious liberty, and the separation of church and state. But the new constitution of 1933 adopted, in the name of public order, a one-party political system sponsoring a restored Catholicism. As late as 1946 the Premier was still telling the world that in this country there were only Roman Catholics and the irreligious, ignoring the existence of at least ten thousand Protestants, as well as other religious groups. Even though the Constitution guarantees freedom of worship, government support of the Vatican's goals is evident. Time and again Protestants and other non-Catholic leaders have been accused of Communism and thus identified with all opposition to the regime. Furthermore, officials often close their eyes to violations of law where Catholic ascendancy is concerned, favoring Rome wherever possible.

Popular Catholicism here, as elsewhere, is a mixture of faith and pagan rites. "In many respects religion in Portugal has, for the masses, degenerated into a gaudy superstition; the flower of Catholic dogma has reverted to the pagan root, and the church has become the *panem et circensus** of the Portuguese poor."[4] In the summer, fairs and pilgrimages, known as *romarias* (literally, "going to Rome") take place all over the country. These religious festivals include not only masses but fireworks. They are a sort of cut-rate entertainment for the poor, in which the religious significance is only incidental to the excitement of the rest. Even though almost all Portuguese are Catholic, at least a third are judged to be anticlerical, even though they dare not manifest it. Privately there is much lightness about religious things. One poor lady we heard to remark of a gaudily decorated statue of the Virgin, "I wish I had her income!"

Here as elsewhere the Jesuits have been the chief architects of state and church identification. The Marquez de Pombal once forced them out, but they made their way back to ride herd on the church's aims. Expelled in 1910, they secretly and individually returned until permitted to renew their teaching in 1933. By 1948 a reported 481 members of the order were already back at work. The fact that the present strong man of the nation once studied for the priesthood and is himself a practicing Catholic renders the Jesuit task easier. Even so, some resistance to this pressure can be seen in Catholic life itself.

Pattern of Persecution. Although in modern times, because of world opinion, the Roman Church has not been abel to risk wholesale repression of Protestantism, the pattern of intolerance continues. Only a few

*"Bread and circuses," i.e., food and entertainment.

authenticated instances are given. A boy twelve refused to make the sign of the cross, whereupon his school teacher beat him unmercifully on head and body . . . A man suspected of having gospel literature in his house had his place illegally searched by the police. Though nothing was found, he was beaten . . . A preacher invited to Colvilha to witness to the neighbors of an evangelical woman was arrested on the false charge of spreading Communism . . . Another preacher refused to close a gospel hall when ordered to do so, rightly stating that he was not violating the Constitution. He too was arrested and threatened with a trumped-up charge of Communist activity . . . A number of converts in the Lisbon penitentiary who professed the Protestant faith requested a visit from a pastor of their persuasion. For years their request was refused.

Pressures are often exerted by priests upon unwilling townspeople to oppose Protestant work. At Gulpilhares, for instance, a hall was opened in 1955 by Vireato Dias Sobral of the Plymouth Brethren. Immediately Sobral was summoned to appear before the mayor. He found the mayor surrounded by other officials, there to listen to their conversation. When the mayor claimed that no permission had been obtained to open the hall, Sobral rightly answered that none was needed. Though momentarily nonplussed, the mayor threatened to do everything in his power to close the meeting place. It seemed obvious that this official was under pressure from his silent onlookers. After some children in the same town professed Christ, the public school teacher refused to take them back into her classes. Since these children were to terminate their courses there soon, their parents were naturally upset. Sobral then wrote a letter to the teacher reminding her that the law forbade discrimination. The teacher took the students back the following day, saying that she had known her action was wrong but had moved at the insistence of the priests.

When Thou Passest Through the Fire. Throughout the whole history of this country Portuguese believers in the Lord Jesus Christ have shown their faith by fearing staunch witness to His name. One quotation from history's annals may serve to illustrate. In 1539 João de Mello, one of the most vicious torturers of the Inquisition, was appointed chief of the Holy Office's activities in Lisbon. Though this man broke and burned the bodies of thousands of "heretics," he was sometimes moved to tears by their steadfastness. A remarkable statement occurs in a letter he wrote to King Dom João II:

> Nothing surprises me so much as that our Lord gives so much patience to human weakness, so that children see their parents taken to be burned, women their husbands, and brothers one another, with-

out hearing one of them speak or weep or make any movement except to bid each other goodbye, with their blessings, as if they were parting to meet again next day.[5]

A Sponsored Superstition. Perhaps the casual traveler sees little of the tragic or empty in the *romaria* (pardon festival), the *fandango* (dance), the *corrida* (bullfight), or the *feira* (fair). As the men gather in dashing sashes and broad-brimmed hats, their women vie for attention in brilliant cotton dresses decorated with gold and silver filigree. Picturesque costumes lend a carnival air, as the mandolin-like guitar strikes up a sad *fado* for the *fadistas* to sing. While haunting folk songs are sung or quick dances spin, nothing may seem out of order. Here is a sunny world of enchanting blue sea, cascading flowers, and a smiling people. But it is also a magic world peopled by witches, werewolves, sirens, and fairies. The peasant of Portugal really believes in his world of evil beings and influences as truly as does the ignorant savage. He is not just having a good time; he is rattling the chains of his bondage.

This superstition has an avid sponsor in the Roman Catholic Church. There are two basic reasons for this. First, the church realizes that tradition is too deeply inbred to erase, and second, she achieves her own ends through it. Even though she thereby cheapens and degrades her own dogma, Rome allies herself with Portuguese paganism. Such accommodation, common in Europe, results only in further disrespect for Rome. But this church needs help to perpetuate herself. Would she get religious observance from this people without their pagan festivals? Knowing the truth, Rome prefers to pay the price for loyalty. Herself pagan at heart, she must assimilate more paganism to make her views palatable and believable.

Every milestone of Portuguese life calls for a festival. Birth, marriage, death, the coming of spring, midsummer, harvest, and the death of the year all come in for this kind of attention. As one authority puts it, "Magic and superstition, based often on a pre-Christian foundation, enter into almost every phase of life among the more primitive Portuguese, showing that the motivation of acquired habit is among the strongest of human motives."[6] Stripping the tough husks from the maize cobs must be celebrated by an *estfolhada* party at every *quinta* or farm. Beating and carding the flax or treading the wine grapes is an equally gay occasion.

The festive year is based on saints' days. Visits to the shrine of a local saint on his or her day are called *romarias* or pardons. In honor of that saint, open-air dances, fireworks, and side shows flourish. Especially during the summer months are *romarias* numerous, the three most popular being those of St. Anthony, St. John, and St. Peter during June. Little of the religious or the mystic seems to enter into the devotion to the saints: "To the Portuguese they are conceived as being heirs to the mantles of Dionysius and Bacchus—with a good taste in wine and an eye for pretty girls."[7] In Portugal, Catholicism has prettified the passion of Christ, eschewing the bloody bitterness of the Spanish penitence processions. The sensuous replaces the stark here. Hilaire Belloc well expressed his faith and that of the Portuguese when he wrote:

> Where'er a Catholic sun doth shine
> There's laughter and good red wine.
> At least I have always found it so:
> Benediciamus Domino.

A quick glance at some of the saints' days is revealing:

São Bartholomeu—The devil's day on earth. The chains by which the saint holds the devil are loosened in Penafiel from sunrise to sunset. Revelry is called for, of course.

Sant' Antão—In the Alentejo the peasant on his way to the fair hangs a sausage or a ham onto a bare fig tree in the church. This symbolizes the pillorizing of the devil incarnate in the flesh of the swine.

São Gonçalo—In Armante this saint marries off old women. As a symbol of fertility, lupin seeds are distributed among the people, a survival of pagan fertility cults.

São Sebastião—Fireworks mark the day of the patron saint of artillery.

São Jorge—As an actual general in the Portuguese army, this saint has full military honors in his procession.

Sant' Antonio—On the day of the patron saint of Lisbon a man offers a pot of basil to the girl he courts. Planted in the pot is a paper carnation and a verse written in her honor.

St. John's Eve—As everywhere in Europe, this is a survival of the witches' sabbath.

São Vicente—Landowners climb a hill to light a resin torch. The year will be good if the wind blows it out; so then an extra hand must be hired for the farm work. If the flame persists, a bad year is prophesied, meaning a farm hand must be dismissed.

São Martin—Chestnuts are roasted on coals and washed down with red wine. "Children made on St. Martin's Day will all be born happy and gay." Again, we see the fertility cult of paganism.

Dominating all the saints everywhere is the Virgin. Among her statues are those like *Nossa Senhora do O*, whose glass belly reveals the unborn baby Jesus, or *Nossa Senhora do Leite*—Our Lady of Milk. Mary's name is painted on carts, burned into pottery, embroidered on cloth, and baked with cinnamon bread. Patron Virgins are in every town as protectresses. When Our Lady of Espichel visits Our Lady of Ericeira every seven years, the route is flower strewn. In Ericeira suckling pigs are roasted and glass charms sold to ward off the evil eye. The two Virgins are placed opposite each other in the church so that they can converse about the flowers and candles they have given each other. Summing up the sad picture, Pastor Eduardo Moreira says that the population are "for the most part in ignorance of the doctrines of the church to which they professedly belong, and are impregnated with superstition and pagan customs."[8]

The Fatima Spectacle. Second only to Lourdes, the little town of Fatima in central Portugal is the most important Catholic shrine in Europe. Here, according to the legend, the Virgin Mary appeared to three peasant children at play on May 13, 1917. The vision reappeared six times on the thirteenth day of following months. Among other things another world war was said to be impending if the human race did not prove obedient. In the basilica now built there, and wherever the wooden image of the Virgin of Fatima appears, there are purported miracles similar to those of Lourdes. Each year, between May and October, more than a million pilgrims, many of them foreigners, make their way to the sacred spot 100 miles north of Lisbon. An immense traffic jam of taxis, luxurious cars, wagons, and donkey carts crawls between lines of thousands of pilgrims hiking to the shrine, a number protecting themselves from the sun with umbrellas. Some even do the last five or ten miles on their knees. Murmuring prayers and responses, a huge throng waits until night, when numberless candles light the scene through the whole Cora da Iria valley. Of the thousands of sick who remain for the masses that follow, some claim to be healed.

By 1930 the Roman hierarchy had pronounced as authentic the visions of Lucy dos Santos, one of the shepherd girls who saw the Virgin. A prophecy of Mary concerning the possible conversion of Russia is considered especially important. Another prophecy Lucy heard is written and sealed, and will be kept by the Bishop of Leiria until some future date. Meanwhile Lucy, now over fifty, lives as a nun of the Carmelite Order in Coimbra, Portugal. Observers today report a growing irreverence at the Fatima masses. One source feels that interest is dropping all over Portugal, with crowds smaller each year. Nevertheless a great following from abroad appears each year.

The Missionary Foot in the Door. Until 1834 Roman domination of Portugal, bolstered by the monarchs, was so absolute that only a handful of people were reached with the gospel in any generation. In 1839 Protestants began a small effort there. Even today this activity, while fruitful, is more intensive than extensive. Only several hundred of the more than four thousand cities and towns have adequate witness. In larger cities, like Lisbon and Oporto, churches naturally came into being earlier, but there are still a great number of quite large communities completely unreached. Especially neglected are the country folk in remote areas.

Since the war, more missionaries have come, and more effective ways of reaching the masses have been devised. The *Conservative Baptists* sponsor a Baptist Theological Seminary in Leiria, where pre-theological high school training is given as well as the regular seminary courses. Other outreaches from Leiria include pastors' and laymen's conferences on the spiritual life, and literary ministry. More than six thousand are enrolled in correspondence courses in a very thoroughly planned program. The handful of American Conservative Baptists at Leiria have been especially aggressive and wise in initiating evangelism followed by church planting. They use Portuguese evangelists they have trained, then follow up a campaign in a virgin area with missionary-taught Bible study for the converts. Often a church which can stand on its own feet in every way grows out of these concentrated efforts.

Portugal has about forty Baptist churches attended by some three thousand people. The work began with one man's obedience. Near the turn of the century a British businessman named Joseph Jones was earning his living in Portugal. After returning to London he was baptized in Spurgeon's Tabernacle, following a message by George Müller of Bristol. Fired with zeal, Jones returned to Portugal in 1908 to help form the first Baptist church on Portuguese soil in Porto.

Missionaries of *The Evangelical Alliance Mission* have been successful with a bookstore, a lending library, their Word of Life press, and radio broadcasting into Portugal from the outside. Evangelistic meetings and Bible studies round out the program of about fifteen TEAM workers from their headquarters in Lisbon. TEAM missionaries also carried out distribution of Billy Graham's book, *Peace With God*. *Presbyterians* number about two thousand, with several American "fraternal workers" attached to what is primarily a Portuguese work. A hospital and school are part of their responsibility. *Southern Baptist* missionaries carry on many activities. The *Brethren Assemblies* maintain links especially with their English counterparts. An effective program of evangelism is carried on, with the emphasis on distribution of literature.

Birth of a Church. A glance at the spirit and method used by the Conservative Baptists in planting one church is instructive. In 1955 the missionaries at Leiria embarked on a program to swell the number of Baptist churches in Portugal. Arthur Brown and Kenneth and Wanda Cummings were set aside in prayer for this work. The first city chosen was Caldas da Rainha, an important center in the middle of the country. During the first week, evangelistic services were held twice a week, which brought about fifty decisions for Christ. Special instruction began immediately for the new converts in order to ground them in the new life. After about five weeks the group of converts had neared the hundred mark and were receiving instruction in baptism and church organization. Three months later the converts had become self-supporting, paying their own expenses and workers. Fifty per cent of all offerings was marked for evangelism, while ten per cent was designated for education. Every convert became a tither in the total sense, giving time, talents, possession, and income freely. Six months later, in June, 1956, self-government was achieved when fifteen of the original converts took charge upon becoming charter members of the new church. At that point seventy more were prepared by instruction for addition to the fifteen. Soon these, too, were baptized and admitted to membership. All 250 converts attended a week-long series of studies on the church, its worship, government, ordinances, and witness. Self-propagation, the most difficult phase of church growth, came last. Over $400 had been faithfully saved by the new group in its evangelism fund—to help start other churches. By this time two gifted men had volunteered to preach the gospel. Only six months after their conversion, the young believers of the church were financially ready to help these two men receive Bible training at Leiria. The idea is that each new church should take responsibility for the towns in its area, leaving the foreign workers free to pick a key center elsewhere and start the process all over again.

Teamwork between nationals and missionaries made the quick results possible. A young, mission-trained Portuguese evangelist did the evangelistic preaching, with the close counsel and help of the missionaries. This gave a national aspect to the work in public. For the Bible teaching, the missionaries took over the converts. More successes followed this scheme. By July, 1956, a second Baptist church was planted. During the first year of this planned strategy, seven churches in all came into being. Arthur Brown, principal leader of this effort, said of the first church, "The miracle of Caldos has sent a wave of revival spirit and new encouragement across Portugal. For the first time many pastors are convinced that their churches can become self-supporting, free from foreign financing. And with this new conviction has come a new spirit of evangelism and a new emphasis on teaching the Word of God."[9] To pass on what he had learned, Brown authored the pamphlet, *How One Church Can Start Another*, which has inspired similar efforts in Europe and elsewhere.

A Priest Cries Out. Sometimes God speaks to a child in a mysterious way, as though marking him out for salvation to be experienced later in life. Such was the case when Luiz Cardoso was twelve years old. Long before that, in his third-grade reader he had read a lesson on eternal life which had stirred his mind. Now he was at the end of his primary school education. Upon an impulse he celebrated the occasion by purchasing a New Testament. This little book spoke so powerfully to his heart that he decided to seek God. The first step was to enter a Roman Catholic seminary. The road through this training for priesthood was long and dark. Though he had entered with the exalted concept of the priest as an *alter cristus*, "another Christ," disillusionment mounted the further he went. "I did not find the life of the gospel within these four walls," he says, "neither in the men, nor in their teaching."[10] At the end of his first year the professors took away Cardoso's New Testament under the pretext that it was Protestant, exhorting him to obey his leaders implicitly from now on. Thus deprived of this one ray of light, he found the next six years of preparatory study very difficult to bear. There followed three years of philosophical research and a four-year course in theology.

This latter period began with a spiritual retreat. Something about the officiating priest attracted and puzzled Cardoso. Because he seemed different from the others, the young seminarian went to him for counsel, hoping for a helpful word. As Cardoso approached him, the older priest fixed a wondering eye upon him, saying in an emotional voice, "The Lord Jesus expects great things of you." Upon seeing Cardoso burst into tears, the priest added, "Luiz, save thy soul." Although the seminarian sought him out later, he never did find this priest who spoke directly to him of Jesus Christ instead of the Virgin or the saints.

Though Cardoso's conscience was stirred, he silenced it to go through with his ordination at Fatima. He speaks in these words of his first mass, "At my ordination, at the very moment I consecrated the mass, the Lord spoke to my heart, making me realize that I had just practiced the most outrageous act of idolatry."[11] Soon after ordination Cardoso was sent to Oporto to teach philosophy, Greek, and Latin. While there he began to realize how incredible was the fable of an unbroken papal authority descending from Peter. As he studied, he saw that the papacy was nothing but the continuation of paganism with a veneer of Christianity imposed upon it.

Deciding to break with the system in which he could no longer believe, Cardoso leaped over the locked seminary walls on the night of October 12, 1958. Then he proceeded to a post office to inquire after the owner of a box number he had heard mentioned over a gospel broadcast. In a few hours he was in the home of a Portuguese Christian, who led him to Christ and peace at last.

Heart Hunger. Many accounts could be given of the welcome given to the gospel by the Portuguese people. Among the most easily won are children and young people. It was Friday night and time for the Evangelical Alliance missionaries to hold another of their weekly meetings in the village of Penedro Gordo. The old kerosene lamp in the little hall was lit, and the missionaries' son began to play the accordion. In a room meant for eighty people, more than 170 adults and children were jammed in to hear the gospel. At one time opposition had been very stiff here, but as first one and then another came to Christ, the enmity of the villagers melted away. At the close of the message a number accepted Christ. While the missionaries of TEAM chatted together at the back, a boy approached them with the question, "Can a boy of ten be saved?" When told that the Saviour died even for him, he excused himself for a minute to find another lad of about the same age. Together they presented themselves to the workers as candidates for the grace of God. Both accepted Christ and went on to live for Him.

In spite of the official views of their church on the matter, many Catholics are curious about Protestants and how they do things. Missionary Luke Boughter of Lisbon tells of a funeral held for a believer two miles from the little Protestant assembly in Algés. Just before her death the Christian woman had requested that a Protestant funeral be held for her as a testimony to others. A procession of friends and neighbors, all dressed in black, followed the simple hearse on foot to the nearest cemetery. During the half-hour walk to the other side of the mountain, the procession passed through other villages, where more inquisitive people, learning that this was a Protestant funeral, joined the group. By the time they reached the cemetery, a crowd of good size was on hand to see what would happen. Naturally the missionary seized the opportunity to tell the gospel story, emphasizing the hope and joy of the departed sister. As a result, a request came to visit another village to present the gospel to some whose curiosity had turned to inquiry.

Despite the restrictions and inconveniences placed upon missionaries in this land, the challenge to bring in the ripened harvest must be met. This is Portugal's hour. Believers in the Lord Jesus everywhere who rejoice in her response can widen it by prayer.

In Rome the Virgin Mary shares the cross with her Son in a walled garden behind a church where priests meditate.

Chapter 7

ITALY,

THE LAND OF HEARTBREAK

"I warn you, O Italy, I warn you, O Rome, that nothing can save you but Christ."

—GIROLAMO SAVONAROLA
Martyred in Florence in 1498

1. *INTRODUCTION TO AN OPPORTUNITY*

Tourists See So Little.   Italy is a land which overwhelms the senses from the start. A riot of sight, sound, and smell assaults the visitor on every side. What a compelling, elemental country this! But beneath her sensuous surface lie grave spiritual issues, for Italy presents one of the most pressing missionary opportunities in Europe, if not in the world. Over 29,000 villages and towns and 100 cities of over 50,000 inhabitants have no gospel witness. Unfortunately this challenge has been little discussed and thus remains unmet. Something must be done for Italy now while doors there remain ajar. Happily much can be done.

Several hundred thousand English-speaking travelers follow the well-worn tourist paths to Oregon-sized Italy each year. Those with brief air stopovers see Rome, with its religious and cultural sights. Art lovers usually choose Florence for its renowned concentration of Renaissance art. Some visitors visit sparkling Venice to see lovely St. Mark's square, the canals, and the gondoliers. Others seek out the sun-drenched Riviera or the Bay of Naples. For special tastes there are the northern ski resorts and lovely lake districts.

Some of these travelers know Christ—pastors, educators, missionary leaders, and laymen. Yet because of language barriers and lack of time only the very determined can make contact with local Italian believers or foreign missionaries. Usually only those armed beforehand with addresses or met by friends succeed in this quest. Most must form their impressions of the country from the hotel personnel, taxi drivers, ticket agents, waiters, and guides—all English-speaking professionals who serve the tourist.

To get behind this polite curtain to the appalling spiritual plight of Italy is not easy. Tourists see so little. Even what meets the eye may have another explanation than the obvious one. Take the typical idea of the carefree Italian, for instance. Is there another side to him? "On thy sweet brow," said the poet about Italy, "is sorrow plowed by shame."[1] The sorrow which lies so close to the surface of the jolly Italian smile is heart-rending indeed. Rarely can Scripture apply more aptly to any country than does Prov. 14:13 to this one: "Even in laughter the heart is sorrowful." Could the Italian masses vocalize their inner need they might well cry,

> No one comes to our dark country
> It's a lone neglected spot;
> No one hears our wail at midnight
> We are those whom God forgot.

So Late, So Few. Why have English-speaking Christians been so slow to recognize Italy as a mission field? Curious about this, I questioned a number of.laymen in vital churches in America and England. Among the answers were these: "Isn't Italy taken care of?" . . . "Italy heard the gospel during the Reformation" . . . "I never thought about it." Clearly the church would have thought about Italy if it had been elsewhere than in the Old World. Situated in the New World—for instance, in South America, Italy would have been a beehive of activity. For proof of this let us compare the situation in Brazil with that in Italy.

Brazil has a population of fifty-eight million, while Italy has almost fifty million.* In her Protestant community Brazil has a reported 1,775,927 people: Italy no more than 250,000. Again Brazil leads with 10,893 places of Protestant worship to Italy's 724. To train the national ministry, Brazil has thirteen theological seminaries and thirty Bible institutes, while Italy can count only three seminaries and one Bible institute. In both countries the predominant religion is Roman Catholicism. Most Brazilians are of European stock, with one small minority of Indians and another of mixed Negro-Indian blood.

What has been the response of the church of Jesus Christ to these two mission fields of relatively similar populations, religions and races? Almost a thousand Protestant missionaries serve in Brazil today—948 according to the prevailing figures—while only about 60 are in Italy! Certainly not one less worker should be taken from Brazil, which could use even more. Italy, on the other hand, is almost bereft of help in spite of its too small Protestant minority, the presence of the Vatican, and the largest Communist party in Europe.

*Most figures for both countries are from the *Occasional Bulletin* (New York: Missionary Research Library), Vol. IX, No. 10, Dec. 8, 1958.

How Italians Live. It is almost impossible not to like the Italians, as there are few more friendly, charming people on earth. Perhaps the most familiar type outside Italy are the southerners and Sicilians. Dark of eye, skin, and hair, they love to talk and laugh with extravagant gestures. But the Italian is also the wealthy urbane industralist from Milan, with impeccable clothes and manners. Then, too, he is the skilled employee of huge firms like Fiat, Pirelli, and Olivetti, or the scion of the "black nobility" sipping *cappuchino* coffee on Rome's Via Veneto. Or again, the Italian is a country woman walking a country road with erect stateliness, an amphora poised expertly on her head. In Venezia Guila her counterpart could well be blonde and blue-eyed rather than dark. The peasant who guides his single-share plow behind the white oxen is Italian too, his farming methods almost unchanged since the days of Virgil. The red tassel around the animal's neck is an ancient fetish designed to keep evil spirits away. Perhaps the only modern touch is that in areas like Umbria his oxen may wear red yokes, a sign that he belongs to the Communist party. Racially these people are just as much mixed as their jobs, appearance, and social class. After 1,400 years of invasions the southerners have Greek, Saracen, Spanish, and Arabian strains in their blood. Northerners owe more to German, Austrian, French, and Slav blood.

The peninsula's "Mason-Dixon Line" accounts for many of the contrasts noticeable in Italian habits. For the two halves of the country there are quite different ways of life. In the north a siesta is rarely taken after lunch, whereas no southern shopkeeper would open his place before three or four o'clock in the afternoon. The northerner is particular about his food and wine, but circumstances have forced the backward southerner to be content with a heaping platter of sauce-covered spaghetti washed down with a half-liter of cheap wine. Northerners believe southerners are shiftless, and in turn are thought by the latter to be pretentious. Even before the new postwar constitution gave women the right to vote, those in the north were more free to enter the professions and mingle with men socially; in the south, women of the upper and middle classes are rigidly brought up, and their marriages are chosen for them. Perhaps the only thing on which northerners and southerners can fully agree is their scorn of Rome, seat of authority and the geographical link between them.

No doubt the family, called by some the most close-knit in Europe, is the most important single unit in the land. Economically every member contributes to the strength of the whole, even those living abroad sending home their share. This interdependent, clannish family believes that most of the problems its individuals face can be met by its own resources; so any one person's need for a major decision calls for lively, decisive debate. Unfortunately foreigners rarely share the intimacy of this family life, which becomes even more impenetrable in the larger towns. Of course if one member of the family is soundly transformed by faith in Christ, a shock wave of influence can be sent into the tight circle. But decisions like choosing Christ as Saviour are doubly difficult for anyone so accustomed to depending on others.

Next to the family, the church holds a large place in the daily life of Italians. They use it as a kind of a second home. Sometimes one will see the poor eating their lunches of sausage and bread in the churches, or mothers breast-feeding their babies there. To many, a church serves better as a quiet, darkened place in which to relax than as a house of worship, for their own homes are usually filled with din. Unfortunately, this is the most that multitudes of the common people can ever expect, in the way of help, from the great colossus that towers over them from birth to death. As in other Catholic lands, the women predominate in church attendance and see that the children pass into the priests' hands. Men are more ambitious, more free from superstitions, and more readily won to the Saviour.

Third place of influence in daily life goes to the coffee shops, usually called bars, where men spend so much of their time. Here they can heatedly discuss politics, drink, gamble, and gossip to their hearts' content. One of the chief interests is the *totocalcio* or football pool, where anyone who can possibly afford it (most somehow do!) will gamble at least fifty *lire** a week on the games. Whether he is writing a letter, promoting a business deal, or playing a game of *scopone* with a greasy pack of cards, the man on the street feels at home here.

Life for the most part revolves around simple pleasures. Very sports-minded, the men avidly follow football, cycling, and road racing. Money is carefully hoarded to buy a scooter, since a car lies beyond the hopes of most. Frequently this scooter will become the "family car," and set out loaded down with several children and camping gear for a vacation. Countless thousands of such vehicles speed up and down Italy's roads, for Italians dearly love to push any vehicle to its limit. Today a growing affluence is permitting more people to buy cars. It is hard to believe that Italy has a language problem. All understand Italian, but many people can speak only their own dialect—one of ninety-four all together. In some southern regions, for instance, a northerner would need an interpreter to carry on a conversation of any length.

Everyone enjoys that universal and cheap pastime, *andare a spasso,* to go for a walk. Men and women stroll separately, except for engaged or married couples, usually once after lunch and again after supper. Arm in arm, they will animatedly discuss politics, pigs, or prices, according to

*The rate of exchange is about 600 lire to one U.S. dollar.

their interests. Conversation is both a habit and an art, accompanied by a wide range of gestures, each having a meaning of its own. For such gesture-language the Neapolitans, who would understand them even without the words, are especially famous. When bargaining is involved, speech reaches its peak of importance, for few articles are sold at fixed prices outside of large stores. Like many Latins these volatile people cherish the lively pantomime that accompanies buying, complete with indifferent shrugs, indignant refusals, and all the ancient play-acting of their ancestors.

Many visitors express their deepest single impression of Italy in the one word "people." People are one commodity of which Italy is not short! Every community seems to have too many of them. In the center of any city or town crowds stand about with seemingly nothing to do. Many of these are a part of the large army of unemployed. In crowded areas children seem to be underfoot everywhere, even late at night in the southern cities. A crashing cacophony made up of horns, shouts, exhausts, and laughter assaults the ears in many cities, while strong smells and odd sights reach the other senses. Any market place or public square is a good spot in which to study this noisy, charming people, so beloved of God but so lost without Him. Gondolier or muleteer, cameo craftsman or Alpine guide, Christ died for them all. While every region of Italy is different from every other one, Christian workers there know that Italians, like sheep, have gone astray, and that the Lord has laid on Christ the iniquity of them all.

Misery in the Mezzogiorno. Because mountainous spines of rock and volcanic matter constitute one-third of the country, there is too little land for cultivation. A population five million greater than that of France is pressed into an argicultural area only two-thirds as large. With an average of 470 people to each square mile, Italy is one of the most densely populated lands on earth. Since emigration elsewhere has been a partial solution, twenty million Italians live away from their homeland. At one time people left at the rate of one million a year; even now about 200,000 emigrate annually. So fast has the birth rate risen that the population has almost doubled since the unification of the country in 1870. In countries like Belgium, France, Switzerland, and Germany Italians are hired to do seasonal work because of unemployment at home.

In the south, living conditions are especially appalling. Even though the government has undertaken land redistribution and irrigation here there is still much suffering in this area which has provided the most emigrants. In a recent *New York Times* report Hanson W. Baldwin speaks of "evidence of deep political and economic problems which are so major as to seem to defy solution."[2] As a Christian views this part of the country, he cannot but be moved by the material suffering and spiritual darkness of the masses.

In the fifties a commission of parliament reported that three million families could not afford the wine they habitually drink with their meals because it was too expensive at fifteen cents a quart. Blood has been shed in the south more recently by police attempting to enforce a small government tax on wine. A recent survey showed that 50 per cent of the eighteen million people in this region are in dire want. Yearly income here averages $227 a year. According to the Turin newspaper *La Stampa,* twenty-seven provinces are listed as "poor" or "very poor," where the average monthly wage is between $10.50 and $16.66. Only the ten "very rich" provinces at the top of the list average as high as $62.75 monthly wage for their inhabitants. The hourly wage average for Italy is about 240 *lire,* or 35 cents, but in the south it is much less. More than four and a half million people do not taste meat once a year, reporters say. One observer writes of "the simple, awesome *miseria* of the people; hunger, disease, and that pitiful ignorance that Stendahl called 'centuries of childhood.' "[3] True, the tourist on his well-insulated rounds may never touch these open sores of poverty and distress. But should he leave the beaten track in the southern provinces, he would have his eyes opened. He would understand why Italy is a tragic land with a smiling face.

Southern Italy is called by the people the *Mezzogiorno,* which means "afternoon." Here where the sun shines unmercifully at noonday there is a zenith of physical trial as well. An English writer refers to Italy as a whole, and to the south in particular, as "Europe's Dead-end Kid." An American speaks of this as an area "where life—with the exception of some urban centers—is on the level of 200 years ago."[4] A missionary who served there writes:

> This work is somewhat strenuous because of living conditions. Most families live in just one room, and then often the mule, the goat, or the chickens share it with them. As a whole, conditions are very unsanitary. A large percentage of the children die before reaching the age of three, and in general they are all very thin. In spite of this the Christians here are very zealous, although they lack teaching. They just cannot do enough for those who come to minister to them.[5]

The report goes on to describe how the woman missionary slept with the wife, while the latter's husband went down to sleep next to the mule on the hay. It is doubtful whether worse conditions exist anywhere in Europe than here, with the possible exception of parts of Spain and Portugal.

In the wild, rugged mountains of the south there are few roads, most

of them very primitive. Some areas still infested with bandits are dangerous to motorists at times. Many peasants in their whole lifetime do not
travel more than twenty-five miles from their birthplace. Schools here are
few. Certain interior sections are turned into dust bowls by erosion,
while in a few coastal areas malaria remains a plague. Often the common
peasants, called *contadini*, live in earthen huts with dirt floors; inside are
a few beds, perhaps one or two crude chairs, and a table. Cooking is
done in the fireplace. Sometimes people here are so poor that they regard
even spaghetti as a luxury. In the summer they may subsist mostly on
bread, tomatoes, olive oil, and garlic, all pressed together in a soggy sandwich. In winter the diet is often just beans and potatoes, with occasional
greens and eggs. Milk is scarce and expensive. In spite of such conditions,
families average seven children in the south. Both men and women in the
undeveloped areas work from dawn to dusk and then go right to bed
after eating, as candles are too expensive for them to buy.

Italians have been called the happiest people in the world. True, to
hear the song and laughter of the southerners one would think that all
is well with them. With their renowned humor and horseplay, their lives
sometimes resemble a vaudeville show. But under this jolly exterior lies
a throbbing worry. How will they fare next year, next month, or even
tomorrow? Many of the landless peasants find work for less than half the
year on the barren, eroded soil of absent *latifondisti*, the landlords who
have sometimes been known to own as many as thirty farms apiece. Just
since 1938 Italy's cost of living has risen 462.5 per cent. The very struggle
to survive offers little joy, hard work, and no hope for tomorrow. Who
will show the love of Christ, for instance, to the thousands of miserable
mendicants who live in the shanty towns on the edges of the cities? Or
who will offer a cup of cold water in the Saviour's name to the rugged
street urchins? Even in some parts of the north poverty is a byword.
In the depressed province of Ferrara are two villages of this type, Ioland
di Savoia, and Massa Fiscaglia. In the first, the *braccianti*, or common
laborers, receive $900 as an annual wage. But this is high! They earn only
$250 a year in the latter village. It almost goes without saying that these
two towns are solidly Communist, as is most of the province.

There is not much of a middle class. In some cities rich and poor
mingle as they have for centuries, scarcely seeming to notice each other.
This paradox has been noticed by the renowned Irish author Sean
O'Faolain, who writes these sensitive lines about Naples:

> Rich and poor, master and slave swarm so heterogeneously that
> ladies in furs and pearls approach a gracious home through pullula-
> tions of dirt and disease, through lanes and alleys miserable enough

to pass for Cut-Throat Gut in Singapore, and nobody will more than glance at them. . . . Misery lies directly behind the thinnest facade of wealth. Enclaves of wealth flower in the midst of misery.[6]

In Naples' *quartiere,* one-half of the city's 1,500,000 people are crammed into an area smaller than a fourth of the city acreage. This cobweb of narrow, winding streets teems with humanity. A visit to the ramshackle quarters in the heart of Naples is shocking indeed. Families here live as best they can, setting up partitions of blankets, or anything they can find, to try to find some privacy. Especially pitiful are the children, their great brown eyes set in pale faces, shivering in the winter dampness. It is difficult to believe that the great National Museum, one of the country's finest, is nearby. Should scraps of lettered marble from Pompeii receive better care than immortal human beings?

Is it not true that we generally see what we look for? The traveler looks for natural beauty and finds it lavishly present here; the Christian regarding the same scene through His Lord's eyes, finds these people doubly poor because unredeemed. No tourist's rapture over magically-poised rock hamlet or sun-drenched beach can soften the awful fact that these people are lost. So much misery is concentrated in so breath-taking a setting. But here the tragedy lies even deeper, for poverty of body and soul go together. For some reason the gospel of saving grace is usually offered to the upper or middle classes of any society first. But the Word of God has much to say for the poor. Communists have pushed into this vacuum with their pat, futile answers, while Christians have done little. Why have we sketched this physical privation? Because in Italy it is the setting and symbol of much of the nation. While some of the poor may go to heaven and the rich to hell, as in Jesus' account of Lazarus and the rich man, do the poor deserve the last chance to hear because they stand at the end of the line? To them salvation is a luxury. Have we made it so?

Sardinian Silhouette. The island of Sardinia, a twelve-hour sea voyage from the mainland, is part of Italy. More than a million people live on this isolated island which tourists rarely see, where hotels are few, and communications inferior. In some ways it is a wild, strange land with a tradition full of persecutions, barbarities, and massacres. In the past, neither the Reformation nor movements of the Holy Spirit in the rest of Italy have touched lonely Sardinia. Never has the gospel of saving grace been widely preached to its people.

Only in two places on the island has a testimony been established. A tiny Baptist chapel in Cagliari, the capital, has a few extension groups in the immediate area. The only other witness is an even smaller Waldensian outpost in La Maddalena, 150 miles to the north. This latter town is on still another island off the north coast. Two evangelists visited there more than seventy years ago, and later their converts asked for a pastor. Too poor to have a regular shepherd, they are visited once a year by a Waldensian worker from the mainland.

Here and there isolated believers are preaching the Word, however. One of the best-known is a man named Raniondo, who left his miner's job to spread the gospel. He is so beloved by the people that even the local Catholic priest expressed regret that "he can never be made a saint." (Of course he is already a saint in the Biblical sense.) Since Protestants are all but unknown on this island there is almost no persecution, opening a marvelous opportunity for the presentation of the good news. A believing British naval officer, Captain R. M. Stephens, who is well acquainted with these people, recently said, "The people of Sardinia are waiting for the gospel. May God send some to take it to them."[7]

Nightfall in Sicily. The large island of Sicily is primarily known for the entrancing beauty of its volcanic coasts and its romantic bandit legends. Sicilians, usually darker than the mainlanders, are friendly and talkative. But nowhere in Italy is superstition deeper and ignorance more profound. A recent phenomenon was the "Crying Virgin" of Syracuse. Daily in this city a human sea flowed into the street called Via degli Orti. At night people camped in the street in front of the house of Antonietta Guisto in order to see the Madonna's face at dawn. Every Sicilian knows the strange story of the twenty-eight-year-old lady who claims she saw a vision of the tear-filled eyes of the Virgin.

Signora Antonietta Guisto was several months pregnant when her sight and other physical complications began to worry the doctors. Concerned herself, the young woman prayed for a long while to the small statue of the Virgin Mary in her room. All at once she shouted from her bed, "I see the Madonna crying. I see again the Virgin's face." Her husband, thinking his wife delirious, turned to look at the statue and he, too, thought he saw tears on the Virgin's face. While Antonietta's mother fell to her knees, the husband ran for the town priest. Soon the whole neighborhood knew what had happened. Archbishop Barazini of Syracuse arrived on the scene and pushed his way through the immense throng. After a commission of doctors certified that the liquid seen was similar to that in tears, thousands of sick and lame began to arrive to seek healing.

In response to the appeal of helpless city authorities, the Italian Red Cross rushed to build a vast campground in one of the Syracuse suburbs. Each day some 15,000 pilgrims headed for the Via degli Orti, where a highly-organized usher system directed human traffic. On a typical day during this period a Swiss reporter counted forty-seven special groups coming from every city and large town in Sicily. Special trains had to be operated from Palermo, the largest metropolis.

Naturally commercial parasites were not long in attaching themselves to the pilgrims. Small boys with hands full of cotton met arriving delegations with the cry, "Buy some cotton to catch the Virgin's tears." As the typical pilgrim pressed through the crowd his question, "*Dove sta la Madonna?*" ("Where can I find the Madonna?") could scarcely be heard above the tumult.

In this midnight darkness spread by Satan, the great deceiver of souls, the light of the gospel is little seen. But here and there across the large island are groups of those to whom Jesus Christ is a living Saviour. Recently there has been an unusual harvest of souls in Sicily, especially through Pentecostal witness. But this region so replete with history could use many missionaries to bring the gospel light to thousands of darkened homes where ignorance and superstition reign.

Sicily is a terribly poor part of Italy. Of its 4,700,000 people, some 900,000 are officially classified as destitute, 1,200,000 more as semi-destitute. A recent survey in Palermo found 498 people (including 74 infants) crowded into 118 rooms. There was only one toilet in the whole area. Village life is little better. In Palma di Montechiaro, in western Sicily, 65 per cent of the inhabitants are illiterate, living mainly in shacks or caves. A depressed society like this breeds criminals. One area of Sicily recently counted up 520 murders, two-thirds of which remain unsolved. Mafia, the international gangster network, was blamed for many of them. In one town, called Licita, which is probably Italy's most debt-ridden town, Mafia money men charge as high as 120 per cent monthly interest on loans. On this island the "protection" payments of shopkeepers and wealthy landowners line the pockets of bandits.

The government is trying to do what it can for Sicily through large loans and a tax-free industry. While industrialization, sanitation, housing and education can do much, the Christian observer prays that Sicily may receive an even larger bounty—the gospel of Jesus Christ.

Youth's Dreary Outlook. Young people hungry for success find little opportunity here. Though Italy has a free compulsory educational system for children up to the age of fourteen, no more than 84 per cent of such children ever attend. A contributing reason for this is the government's failure to provide more than 60 per cent of the classrooms needed. Of those who do begin school, only 35 per cent ever finish the fifth grade. Some of these survivors may then go on to a secondary or "middle school." Choice of manual, technical, or cultural study is offered at this point, but 74 per cent of this age group never enroll in the secondary schools. Only

9 per cent go on to Junior College, and 4 per cent to university. Less than 2 per cent of the University group ever finish the course. Because of economic conditions, even young people from respectable families who do finish university have little chance of getting ahead. "Thousands of students sweat and starve to finish university, finally to find jobs as waiters and trolley conductors," one observer notes.[8]

Why do so few finish school? Facilities are lacking in many places, as has already been pointed out. Elsewhere parents may be indifferent to the opportunity. But an even stronger reason than these is the need for more breadwinners in the family. A thirteen-year-old boy waiter questioned in Perugia told us that he had finished the fifth grade but then had had to drop out to go to work. As an apprentice he works eleven and one-half hours a day, but receives no pay at all during the first year. Beginning with the second year he will earn between 10,000 and 15,000 *lire* a month ($16-$24) which he must contribute almost entirely to family upkeep. Should he plan to be married later, he would probably need to wait six or eight years after he announced his engagement before he could accumulate enough to marry. Under these conditions most young men must wait until they are near thirty before they can marry.

One would never believe that most of the young girls walking along village streets on a Sunday afternoon in their bright, crisp dresses are completely penniless. Nor would the young men wearing their best appear to have only the price of a cup of coffee or so in their pockets. "Face," or *la bella figura*, is so important to these people that it must be kept up at any price. In Bologna I once observed a wedding dinner in full swing. Everyone was carried away with the contagious joy of the occasion. But the crushing expense of providing the meal and the extras, I was told, would keep the newlyweds poor for many months. It would be unthinkable to omit any of the friends and relatives or to fail to bring them to the restaurant in expensive, rented cars. Even if the groom can ill afford this spectacle and has to save toward it for years, yet "it is done" as tradition demands.

On another occasion I shared a *rapido* train compartment with a student from Florence. As we pulled out of Genoa and began to chat, he discovered, of course, that I was a foreigner. This encouraged him to share his problems. I looked at this young man with pity. His earnest, finely-sculptured face and fluency in four languages spoke of a patrician family, university training, and the broadening effect of travel. But he was intensely bitter. "Even if you are educated and have the background and contacts, it's no use," he complained. "This country has narrow ideas and is no place for any one with ambition and vision. I've been offered a job far below my capacities at a salary I could have earned even if

I didn't have all this education." I gave him the only answer I knew to his problem. To those who have little material prospect and thirst for more, life will inevitably become stale and flat, even if they find what they are seeking. But there is a higher dimension in which to move, where earthly gains become dim. In transforming us, the Lord Jesus Christ also replaces our values so that we no longer drive toward our own objectives, but toward His. When the young man and I parted, he was thoughtful and I was praying.

The Moral Morass. Outwardly the relations between sexes in Italy are circumspect. But under the guise of "engagements," easily made and often broken, many young people live immoral lives. While custom dictates that unengaged couples do not have "dates" in our sense, it also condones extreme freedom between engaged couples. One of the excuses given is that these couples are usually engaged for many years while the husband-to-be accumulates money to marry.

After marriage, men in many areas do not go out with their wives socially, preferring to meet other men alone in bars or at sporting events. In some regions men do take their wives out to a limited extent. But when men gather alone, the acquiring of a mistress is often discussed. Since the wife's life is largely confined to her children and work she, too, is sometimes tempted to seek clandestine adventure. All such relationships, while publicly condemned, are a definite part of the Italian scene. Children raised under these conditions naturally become gradually conditioned to imitate the habits of their parents. As in all Roman Catholic lands the woman's status is low, even while ostensibly protected, with corresponding bad moral effects.

Does the Christian gospel, which ennobles women, help this situation? A girl who came to work as a maid and a cook in one missionary family soon noticed how different the atmosphere of this home was. After about six weeks she told the missionaries how much she envied their peace of mind. Not long afterward she accepted Chist. Later she told her story and sought help. As the mistress of a married man, she was deeply involved in an affair that was difficult to terminate, for many reasons. With the missionaries' help she asked the Lord for grace to break free of a tie which dishonored her new Saviour. Afterward she shared her burden for a brother-in-law who had a mistress, for her girl friend involved with a married man, and for her three brothers, each of whom had a mistress. After telling these relatives of her new-found Christ, she replied to their scoffing thus, "You call me crazy. But I wish you could share my love for Christ, who set me free from such slavery."

Legalized prostitution ended only in 1958, when the Merlin Act went into effect. In closing more than 500 houses of prostitution and forcing 7,500 women to seek other employment, Italy has been the latest nation in western Europe to withdraw its protection from this evil, which brought the government twenty million dollars a year in taxes. Of course that does not mean an end to the practice, but only the spreading of it abroad in the land. As in France, a woman headed the attack on prostitution. Socialist Deputy Angelina Merlin, who fought the issue through the legislature, stated that about 30 per cent of all women between fifteen and sixty still engage in prostitution in varying degrees. If this estimate is correct, hundreds of thousands of women are involved. Naturally such a situation poses a problem for millions of young men and women, and tightens the grip of Satan on their lives.

Challenges Without Reformation. Italy had a small gospel witness in the first century before Paul arrived in Rome. By the fourth century Constantine had made Christianity the official religion. But the darkness deepened as the Middle Ages approached. Though the message of salvation by grace survived, it was little known to the masses for centuries. For three hundred years before the Reformation, the Waldenses had opposed the teachings of the Roman Church. But the Reformation, so explosive in northern Europe, made little doctrinal and moral upheaval here. It is not easy to evaluate what was accomplished during this period, since southern Italy was under Spanish rule at the time, while the north was a battlefield for the French and Spanish. Spanish "heretics" fled to Italy, confusing the situation further. True, many celebrated Italians protested against corruption and urged apostolic simplicity for the church. Among these were Arnold of Brescia, the Duchess Renata, Savonarola, Vittoria Colonna, and Gavazzi. Groups like the Albigenses, the Cathari, the Anabaptists and other "heretics" also protested the tyranny of soul practiced by the church, which resulted in the martyrdom of thousands. Many intellectuals, like Dante, wrote or spoke against papal excesses. During the actual period of the Reformation, a reform movement existed within the Catholic Church in Italy, too, but for many reasons did not take hold.

Any consolidation of local reform was either ruthlessly suppressed or its leaders were bought off or banished by the Roman Church. The renowned reformer, Savonarola, unquestionably the brightest light, paid for his protests with his life in 1498 in Florence. But Savonarola was not a crusader like Luther. Many scholars have pointed out his bondage to the theology of Aquinas, his intellectual views of faith, and his desire to die, even as a rebel, in spiritual oneness with the church. Though his language used against the church's abuses is very strong and resembles Luther's in some places, it is doubtful whether Savonarola wanted more than a clean-up of the practices of the church. In this he illustrates the whole Italian challenge of Rome during this period. The historian, G. K. Brown, says that "the chief thing for which the Italian saints strove was moral renewal, not dogmatic precision."[9] Rodacanachi adds, "Italy, which more than any other country has been fertile in heresies, has not produced religious revolts; heresy there . . . always preserved moderation, if not in ideas, at least in actions; it attacked discipline rather than dogmas, the representatives of the Church rather than the Church itself."[10] A British study concludes, "The ideas of the Reformation never gained a hold on the people of Italy."[11] In the words of Albert Hyma, "Many of those who have been designated as Protestants (in Italy) were merely followers of Erasmus or other orthodox Catholics in the northern countries. . . . Recent research has shown that Juan de Valdés was not a real Protestant and that his admirable treatise *Doctrina Christiana* was thoroughly Erasmian."[12]

The fact that Italy was only stirred—never deeply affected—by the Reformation makes her more than ever a mission field today. Like Spain and Portugal she remained largely outside this wave of truth that engulfed northern Europe and England and so greatly affected the present situation in the United States. This is a point to remember for those who assume that the Reformation produced great churches everywhere in Europe. It did not produce them at all in Italy during that period.

2. UNDER THE PAPAL YOKE

The Enthroned Pontiff. "It isn't just that Italy is a Catholic country," a Waldensian pastor once told me, "but we can't get away from the presence of the Pope." As we begin to look now at the oppressive effect of the Roman Catholic system on the lives of Italians, we must note first the individual who is the leader of the world's most powerful religious body. As supreme pontiff of the Roman Church, the Pope is an absolute monarch. In his hands rest the full executive, judicial, and legislative powers of a "vicar of Christ on earth." The Holy Father alone can speak for the church; its other spokesmen speak officially only when and how he wills. Strictly an advisory body as far as their relationship to His Holiness is concerned, the members of the College of Cardinals are appointed by and subject to the Pope. Whenever a new pope is elected by these princes of the church, he then assumes the enormous, dictatorial powers of his predecessors. This leader is almost the ultimate glorification of man by man. Only at a later day, according to Scripture, will such a religious ruler win universal support and acclaim. But looking at the papal throne today, it is not difficult to imagine what final deification of a man would be like. When a pope speaks on church matters, Catholicism teaches, he does so as the infallible spokesman of Christ, even though his life my be utterly unworthy. Likewise the official intermediating power of any priest is valid regardless of his own sin.

It is difficult for American or English Protestants to imagine the absolutism and harsh intolerance of the Roman Church where it is the sole power. Italy, for instance, is not only a Catholic country, but contains, or rather surrounds, the homeland of the faith. Most of the Popes and cardinals have been Italian. It is natural then that Italians, even though they are not all good Catholics, should be especially affected by anything His Holiness might do or say. Communist strength in the country has further helped to impel the masses into Catholic arms. In the face of repeated political emergencies, the Holy Father has often emerged as a Horatius holding the bridge against the hordes of materialism, a role for which he has been carefully groomed. As a Catholic party the Christian Democrats have proved beyond a doubt that Italian Catholic political power can be mobilized when needed. As one prominent Italian Protestant says, "Unquestionably the Vatican has enormous influence on the Italian government."

Anyone who doubts the power of the Pope to rally the Italian people need only watch, as the author has, some of the historic ceremonies staged at the Vatican. Take the rites marking the opening of the Holy Door of St. Peter's for the 1950 Holy Year. More wealth and pageantry were paraded then than most worldly monarchs ever see. An American newspaper described the glory of Pope Pius XII in these words:

> The Holy Door ceremonies proceeded with the pomp and splendor consecrated by centuries. As the Pope, borne high on his red and gold chair, appeared in the entrance to the huge, hall-like atrium of the Basilica, the gold and jewels of his robes and ornaments sparkled in the sun's rays . . . the Pontiff's chair halted a few feet from the white silk-covered throne. The diamond-studded cross on the peak of his jewelled mitre sparkled in the beams of floodlights . . .[13]

How little there is in this of Him who said, "I am meek and lowly in heart"! Whenever the Pope makes his appearances at given times before huge crowds, a fever of adulation grips the hundreds of thousands who cry, "*Viva il Papa!*" (Long live the Pope!). Such ostentation makes its mark on the sensitive, emotional Italian nature, which loves a show and a hero. Indeed, the presence of the Pope himself in Italy makes it more of a mission field than ever.

Papal influence is on the increase outside the land as well, for the recent Second Ecumenical Council has shown that the Papacy is one of the world's greatest sources of news. According to the *Stampa Estera,* The

Foreign Press Club in Rome, about two-thirds of all news dispatches since the war have been date-lined Vatican City rather than Rome. Before the war this was just the reverse. Whatever personal views newsmen hold, most of them will now agree that the Pontiff's actions and utterances rank as news today with those of the President of the United States and other heads of state.

Secretive Vatican City. When the course of Roman Catholicism is finally run, Byron's lines on Napoleon may well summarize this colossus

> Whose game was Empire, and whose stakes were thrones;
> Whose table Earth—whose dice were human bones.[14]

One Christmas night in the year 800, Charlemagne, King of the Franks and Defender of the Catholic Faith, knelt on Vatican Hill in Rome to be crowned emperor of the Holy Roman Empire by Pope Leo III. For almost a thousand years the fortunes of that empire, sprawled across most of the face of Europe, were to rise and fall periodically under the direction of the popes of Rome. When the empire finally expired in 1806, the pontiffs had to be content with their own papal states, a belt of land across mid-Italy. Stretching from sea to sea, these states gave the pontiffs a temporal sway that at one time included as much as 16,000 square miles and 3,000,000 people. Most of the popes of this period were more concerned with the wealth of their state and the extension of their territory than with spiritual things. As a result, poverty and ignorance reigned in the papal states, one of the worst-governed regions in Europe. Finally, in the nineteenth century, a movement to unite Italy came to the fore, led by patriots like Garibaldi and Mazzini. As these idealists needed the papal states to unite their new Italy, they laid siege to Rome. In 1870 soldiers under King Victor Emmanuel II breached the Aurelian wall and took the city, thus dissolving the papal states and hailing the Eternal City as the capital of a new, united nation.

Following the three Lateran treaties of 1929, signed by the Holy See and the Mussolini government, Vatican City was established as an independent, sovereign state, to which diplomatic representatives have been accredited from many nations. Some 108 acres of the new state cover most of a hill west of the Tiber River in Rome, all surrounded by a high, thick wall. This is, in fact, the only completely walled-in country on earth, having just three entrances, each carefully guarded by the Vatican's own miniature army. Only the basilica of St. Peter and its many museums are open to the public. Back of Bernini's magnificent columns, teeming Vatican City hides behind its walls the most clandestine and powerful religious organization in the world.

One of the important scattered branches of the Vatican in Rome is the Propaganda Fide palace in the Via Due Macelli, headquarters of the Congregation for the Propagation of the Faith. This is the organization that controls the missionary efforts of the Roman Church throughout the world. Another important headquarters is the Holy Office, better known in history by the ominous name of the Inquisition. Besides these, there are the College of Cardinals, the Congregations, the Rota and Signatura, the Secretariat of State, the Nuncios and Apostolic Delegates. Forty seminaries train priests from foreign countries. The centralizing of power in the Vatican grows apace. Speaking of the Vatican Council of 1869–1870, the *Encyclopaedia Britannica* concludes ". . . the attempts of control the intellectual and spiritual life of the Church have now assumed dimensions which, a few decades ago, would have been regarded as anachronistic."[15] Lord Macaulay's observation well summarizes this mighty power: "Among the contrivances which have been derived for controlling mankind, it occupies the highest place."[16]

Largest Church in the World. "As far as I can see, Italy, for fifteen hundred years, has turned all her energies, all her finances, and all her industry to the building of a vast array of wonderful church edifices, while starving half of her citizens to accomplish it. She is today one vast museum of magnificence and misery."[17] Do these words come from a rabid anti-Catholic or an embittered atheist? No, they were penned in 1869 by none other than the great American humorist Mark Twain. But it was as a deadly serious reporter that Twain wrote in *The Innocents Abroad* of the "useless trumpery" and "jewelled frippery" of some of the thousands of churches he saw in this "wretchedest, princeliest land on earth."[18]

Though Italy's material situation has somewhat improved since Mark Twain's time, her spiritual state is little better. Multitudes of the pitifully poor are still obliged to support the imposing edifices already standing, build new ones, pay their priests, and help finance the vast bureaucracy of a decadent system. In the Eternal City alone five hundred churches are their burden.

Almost all visitors to Rome, including Protestants, take time to visit the basilica of St. Peter's, called by Catholics the world's largest church. Though not the leading church of the faith (Rome's St. John Lateran has this honor), St. Peter's is undoubtedly the most famous. In front of the church, in the Piazza San Pietro, the Pope occasionally addresses huge crowds of the faithful. Here the curving rows of columns designed by Bernini as an "embrace," hold the audience in readiness for the appearance of the Supreme Pontiff at the balcony.

Inscribed around the base of the immense, forty-story dome of the church, in purple mosaic letters six feet high, are the Latin words, "Thou art Peter, and upon this rock I will build my church." Thirty-five thousand people have been present on special occasions inside the church, all standing of course. Consecrated by Pope Urban VIII on November 18, 1626, just 120 years after the cornerstone was laid, the church is said to rest on the foundations of Constantine's basilica (324 A.D.), which in turn was built on the site of an earlier church. It is said that in the days of imperial Rome, nineteen hundred years ago, the Circus of Nero stood on the eastern shoulder of what is now Vatican Hill. Here, Catholics believe, the Apostle Peter was crucified head downward, then buried in the old pagan cemetery on the hill. During the Holy Year 1950 Pope Pius XII announced that excavations going on under the present Church were likely to produce Peter's hidden and much-sought-for body. If the tomb has been found and the bones inside are really Peter's—as the Chruch now claims, the archaeologists of the world are certainly not in agreement on the verification of the facts.

Several interesting objects and practices in St. Peter's both interest the evangelical Christian and serve as commentary on the predicament of Italy. Among the 434 statues filling almost all the available niches is the seated bronze one of St. Peter, on the right as one approaches the papal altar. The right foot of the statute has been worn smooth by the kisses of millions. I have often watched the crowds filing by this statue, eager to express their veneration. What a wretched slavery of dead works! The Vatican is also proud of its gold, silver, and precious jewels in St. Peter's treasury. But Peter himself said, "Silver and gold have I none" (Acts 3:6). He and John asked God to heal the lame man at the Gate Beautiful —something better than riches. It was also Peter who wrote of "the precious blood of Christ"—infinitely more valuable than "corruptible things, as silver and gold" (I Pet. 1:18, 19).

On the wall of the Hall of Kings at the entrance to the Sistine Chapel are paintings memorializing the massacre of St. Bartholomew's Day in Paris and the French provinces. To celebrate this cold-blooded papal butchery of thousands of Protestants, the Pope celebrated a *Te Deum*, instituted a Thanksgiving mass, struck a special medal, and called Vasari from Florence to execute the paintings. Thus the slaughter of the Huguenots of Paris on August 23, 1572, is openly memorialized on the walls of the world's largest church. Across the passing centuries the paintings have hung there, silently accusing the murderers.

Of the Rome which he visited just sixty years before the massacre, Martin Luther wrote, "I would not have missed being in Rome for any amount of money. . . . Had I not seen it with my eyes, I would not have believed it. . . . Neither God nor man nor sin nor shame is regarded. . . .

Anti-Christ himself could not possibly rule more abominably. . . . Whoever has been to Rome knows that things are worse than anyone can describe or imagine."[19] When these words were written by Luther, the foundations of St. Peter's had already been laid for four years. If stones could speak, what stories they could tell of intrigue, treachery, and folly! Would they confirm the ancient saying, *Quo Romanae propiores, tanto Christiani tepidores,* "The nearer to Rome, the worse the Christians"?

Not far from the sacred doors of the renowned church are a string of religious shops on Vatican City land. For instance, any tourist can buy, at the Naddeo Religious Gift Shop, a blessing dated and printed in English, adorned with a photograph of the Pope and signed by him. Mine reads as follows:

> Most Holy Father, [my name is lettered in here] humbly prostrate at the feet of Your Holiness, begs the apostolic benediction and a plenary indulgence to be gained at the hour of death, on condition that, being truly sorry for his sins, even though unable to confess them and to receive the holy viaticum, he shall at least invoke with his lips or heart the holy name of Jesus.

This full indulgence, sold commercially at the gates of the Vatican, reveals that Luther's complaints against the traffic in souls not only were justified then, but are still valid today. How disillusioned are the thousands who have bought this document, signed by an archbishop and others, as a balm for their sin-laden hearts!

The Delusion of Rites. Besides visiting the four great basilicas of Rome, the Catholic pilgrim is expected to venerate relics and perform other acts worthy of indulgence. Millions of pilgrims from every corner of the earth come to visit this religious world's fair each year. At certain periods, as during the Easter season, crowds of visitors are so enormous that every hotel, pension, and private room in the city is taken, and hundreds of visitors are accommodated in convents, monasteries, and other church properties. On such occasions the Pope appears on the balcony of St. Peter's to address the great throngs. But non-Catholics must realize that duty rather than love attracts these multitudes, since their souls' salvation is involved in their quest of the promised special indulgences.

Mounting the Holy Stairs, or *Scala Santa,* is another way pilgrims may earn indulgences. One recent visitor thus described his impressions upon visiting the famous stairway housed in a separate building near the St. John Lateran Church: "Pilgrims were climbing them on their knees, painstakingly lifting themselves up, women—sweating from the effort—sobbing and kissing each step; crippled old man shaking with the ague; children, their knees too short, raising themselves by their elbows."[20] The Swiss historian Merle d'Aubigné describes Martin Luther's earlier visit in these words:

> One day, among others wishing to obtain an indulgence promised by the Pope to all who should ascend on their knees what is called Pilate's staircase, the poor Saxon monk was humbly creeping up these steps which he was told had been miraculously transported from Jerusalem to Rome. But while he was performing this meritorious act, he thought he heard a voice of thunder crying from the bottom of his heart, as at Wittenberg and Cologne, *The just shall live by faith.* These words, that twice before had struck him like the voice of an angel from God, resounded unceasingly and powerfully within him. He rises in amazement from the steps up which he was dragging his body: he shudders at himself; he is ashamed of seeing to what a depth superstition had plunged him. He flies from the scene of his folly.[21]

Obviously this description is somewhat colored by d'Aubigné's sometimes powerful imagination, yet the fact is that God did speak to Martin Luther that day. Luther had received one more call from the Holy Spirit to trust Christ, and Christ alone, for his salvation. It was this experience that later fortified him to risk his life by objecting to the indulgence system so flagrantly used at the Castle Church in Wittenberg, "The Rome of Germany."

Multitudes still mount the same Holy Stairs Luther climbed, though their location has been changed since then. These twenty-eight steps are said to be from Pilate's palace in Jerusalem. Christ is thus believed to have ascended and descended them several times. They are, the Roman Church says, "sanctified by the blood of Jesus,"[22] for His blooddrops are pointed out through holes in the wooden covering of the marble steps. For each step, a different prayer is suggested by the church, but all the prayers end with these words, "Holy Mother, pierce me through. In my heart renew each wound of my crucified Saviour."[23] Again Mary must serve as a mediatrix to intercede with her divine Son, while Jesus Christ Himself remains as inaccessible as ever. Many indulgences have been offered for ascending the Holy Stairs on one's knees. The present one, formulated in 1819, promises nine years' indulgence for each of the twenty eight steps (also applicable to souls in purgatory) to all who perform the rite with a contrite heart. According to the Church, by observing certain duties, such as this, one can shorten his suffering in purgatory for temporal punishment. But what are 252 years compared with eternity? It is small wonder that thousands have come here, performed their duty, and left with heavy hearts and downcast faces, for so much is required, with so little attained. Nobody in this world, not even the Pope, can ever tell a Catholic whether his loved one is yet out of purgatory. Not only must the faithful ransom their loved ones from purgatory, but they must obtain their own salvation, too. These somber thoughts have crossed our minds during the hours we have watched young and old, the lame and the halt, hopelessly mount the deeply-grooved steps of the *Scala Santa*.

One religious festival where ecstasy and near hysteria reach their peak is that of the liquification of the dried blood of the martyr St. Januarius, patron saint of Naples. Every May and September the two ampullas alleged to contain his blood are carefully taken out of the tabernacle beneath the high altar of the Cathedral. While devout Neapolitans pray, the ceremony slowly unfolds. No one who has seen this can ever forget the pitifulness of the scene. Sighs of anxiety wash across the vast crowds like ripples of water. Later, a breathless expectancy mounts while all tautly wait for the "grace" that is not always granted. When and if liquification takes place, there is great rejoicing. But should it be denied or delayed, some become angry, while others weep disconsolately. The writer has seen black-dressed women collapse in hysterical sobs because nothing happened. Dates are not necessarily fixed for the liquification ceremony, the celebration of the rite depending on what supplication is addressed to St. Januarius, and on whether or not it is felt he will respond.

In the same Campania region hundreds of other observances take place near areas well known to foreign tourists. Easter marks the procession of the dead Christ at Salerno; in October there is the festival of the Madonna delle Neve at Torre Annunziata; and in August the Assumption observances are held at Pozzuoli. But in this region Avellino has the most elaborate rites, culminating in the mass pilgrimage to the Sanctuary of Montevergine nearby. To see the great crowds arriving from long distances with expectancy on their faces is to realize again that a religion of works only compounds the wretchedness of those without Christ and without hope.

In Florence, in the *Scoppio del Carro* ceremony on Saturday of Holy week, human credulity reaches new heights. One can see here a good example of the combination of showmanship, religion, and superstition in which Rome specializes. The "explosion of the chariot" begins with high mass in the Cathedral of Santa Maria del Fiore, second largest in the world. As the music is begun inside the Cathedral, a miniature rocket shaped like a dove flies from the high altar along a wire and out through the door into the jam-packed Piazza del Duomo. A great cry bursts from the large crowd, and fireworks blaze from a large wooden cart in the square. After the detonator has done its work, it returns up the wire to the high altar. Sometimes the fuses do not function. But upon the successes or failure of this experiment, the masses of Tuscany peasants base their convictions each year as to whether the harvest will be good or bad!

Assisi, in Umbria, is the shrine of the well-known St. Francis. The founder of the Franciscan Order of Mendicant Friars was born in 1182 into a family of wealth and repute. After spending some years in the gay life as a young rake of that time, he was taken seriously ill in Perugia. Following much meditation Francis concluded that desire for possessions was the root of all mankind's evils. For the rest of his life he set an example of poverty and asceticism that made him one of the most popular saints of his time and of all time. Women as well as men flocked to join his order. Today the women's division is known as "Poor Claires," after one of his followers, Santa Chiara. In Europe today some of the other men's orders which originated with Francis survive as Capuchins, Observants, and Conventuals.

The tomb of St. Francis, reportedly found only in 1818, is a crystal crypt two floors down in a secret vault beneath the lower church named after him. In the sacristy are preserved his patched, gray cassock, the cruel cord of camel's hair and needles worn about his waist, and the crude sandals he wore in 1224 when he received the stigmata. Up the hill from the St. Francis Basilica is the church of Santa Chiara, his woman disciple. Her body, much blackened by time, is open to view in the crypt, which is adjoined by the shuttered cloisters of her present-day followers. Through a grated window in the cloisters can be seen what Rome considers one of the most famous and best-loved crucifixes in the world. Before this cross St. Francis reportedly recceived his call to a life of poverty. Later his visions of Christ and the Virgin took place here also. The visits of countless pilgrims to this spot give the nuns of St. Claire's cloisters their only contact with the outside world. Inside the cloisters seven centuries of time have not changed the rigorous discipline, self-denial, and prayer of the inmates. Near the bars, as you adjust your eyes to the dimness of the area surrounding the crucifix, an unreal voice will ask in what language you wish to hear the history of the crucifix. This soft voice is that of a nun, heavily veiled in black, whose dark figure is half-hidden in the shadows. Thank God, the story of the cross of Christ is not one hidden in legend, but good news to be proclaimed from the housetops. What a pity that a crucifix and its legend obscure the simplicity of the death and resurrection of the Prince of Life!

The Roman Church is busily creating more and more saints to be venerated. It has been estimated that 20,000 individuals have been called saints by the masses throughout the centuries, but the church, in its list of official saints, recognizes only 4,394 in all. During this century, thus far, more saints (65) have been canonized than throughout the whole nineteenth century (42). Roman Catholics are required to believe that saints can intercede in heaven and work divine miracles on earth through the power of God. Millions in Italy, believing what they are told, plead with various saints for help in life's dark hours; but they receive only silence in return.

Tombs and Relics Without End. By its very nature the Roman Catholic Church requires outward symbols or objects to worship, as a substitute for a missing faith. Lord Byron, who was so sensitive to atmosphere, approvingly wrote, "With shrines, relics, the real presence, confession, the absolution, there is something sensible to grasp at."[24] It seems that the human heart is indeed inclined to worship things, even while sometimes doing so in the name of God and His Son. The twenty-fifth Session of the Council of Trent contradicted the first two of the Ten Commandments with these words: "The images of Christ and the Virgin Mother of God, and of the other saints, are to be had and to be kept, especially in Churches, and due honor and veneration are to be given them. . . . The Holy bodies of the martyrs and others now living with Christ are to be venerated by the faithful. . . . They who affirm that veneration and honor are not due to the relics of the saints . . . are wholly to be condemned."[25] Though Catholic apologists distinguish between "veneration" and worship, the fact is that the simple people of Italy accord these objects the adoration reserved for God Himself.

Rome and Italy abound in the alleged tombs of disciples, apostles, and saints. Here are a few, with the locations given:

> *Peter*—under the Pope's altar in San Pietro, Rome (minus head)
> *Paul*—Basilica of St. Paul's-Outside-the-Walls, Rome (minus head)
> *Philip and James*—Church of Santi Apostoli, Rome
> *Matthew*—Duomo San Matteo, Salerno
> *Mark*—Basilica of San Marco, Venice
> *Andrew*—Church of St. Andrew, Amalfi

Holy objects and relics number countless thousands. The fact that there are many duplications elsewhere seems to bother the Roman Church not at all. We give only a few locations of principal objects of veneration in Italy to show to what absurdity a man-made religion can lead:

> *Christ*—Fragments of His cross (Rome: Santa Croce in Gerusalemme)
> One of the crucifixion nails (same location)
> Two thorns from His crown (same location)
> The sign which Pilate put over His head (same location)
> A fragment of the column of flagellation (same location)
> Part of the sponge of gall and vinegar (same location)
> A shroud in which His body was wrapped (Turin: Duomo)
> His sandals (Rome: Sanctum Sanctorum Chapel, Scala Santa Building)

Part of the Last Supper table (Rome: San Giovanni Laterano)

Part of the veil with which St. Veronica wiped His face (Rome: San Pietro)

The cup from which He drank at the Last Supper (Florence: Municipal Palace)

Pilate's stairs up which He walked (Rome: Scala Santa Building)

His manger (Rome: Santa Maria Maggiore)

The Virgin Mary—Her house (Loreto)
Her girdle (Prato: Duomo)
Her wedding ring (Perugia: Duomo San Lorenzo)

Matthew—His jawbone (Rome: Sanctum Sanctorum Chapel, Scala Santa Building)

Bartholomew—His chin bone (same location)

John the Disciple—Some of his hair (same location)

John the Baptist—One of his teeth (same location)
A piece of his sackcloth (same location)
His head (Rome: San Silvestro in Capite)

Peter—His head (Rome: San Giovanni Laterano)
His footprints (Rome: Santa Françoise-Romaine)
His chains (Rome: San Pietro in Vincoli)

Paul—His chains (Rome: San Paulo Fuori le Mura)
His head (Rome: San Giovanni Laterano)

Thomas—His finger which touched wounds of Christ (Rome: Santa Croce in Gerusalemme)

The Catholic guidebook for the Sanctum Sanctorum Chapel, where many of these relics are located, states that they are "listed on ancient records last verified by eminent archaeologists."[26] Because of the priceless value of this "Holy of Holies," the Sanctum Sanctorum has inscribed over its altar the words, *Non est in toto sanctior orba locus*, "There is no holier place in all the world." At this altar only the pope can say mass. Under it is the holiest relic of all—the Archeopita, "not made with human hands."[27] This is an image of Christ painted on walnut, reportedly begun by Luke, but finished by God Himself. This "only true portrait of Christ"[28] was said to have been brought to Rome from Constantinople during the persecution of the iconoclasts under the pontificate of Gregory II.

The veil of Veronica is considered one of the holiest relics of St. Peter's, along with another piece of the true cross and part of the lance of Longinus. Here the small shred of cloth, about a foot square, is kept in an enclosure high up in the pillar of Veronica—a patron saint of photographers—under a lock with only three keys, one of which remains in the possession of the Pope. Florence is proud of the *Sacro Catino*, the holy cup from which "Jesus drank." It is also claimed that this cup was used by Joseph of Arimathea to catch and hold the blood of Christ. Until Napoleon took it to France, the cup was believed to be made of emerald, but there it was revealed to be only cheap, oriental glass paste. Siena has a special shrine for St. Catherine, whose head is preserved in a reliquary in the San Domenico Church. This was the Catherine, daughter of a dyer, whose indignant eloquence led Pope Gregory XI to bring the papal seat back from Avignon to Rome in 1377. In the same church is the crucifix painted on wood before which she received the stigmata.

Probably the House of the Holy Family in Loreto is the largest of all relics in the world. According to tradition, angels carried it from the Holy Land in 1291, during the Arab invasion. Catholics believe that this is the house in which Jesus Christ grew up. Now the whole town of 7,000 inhabitants is built around the sacred building, center of great pilgrimages for the worship of Our Lady of Loreto.

Down in Monreale, Sicily, the heart and other organs of St. Louis can be found at the Cathedral. One venerated object in Italy has a special interest for evangelical Christians because of its associations with the Reformation. In the Cathedral at Trento is an old crucifix esteemed because before it, in 1536, the Council of Trent ended seventeen years of discussion by condemning the reformer's doctrine, and then launched their Counter Reformation.

Statues inside and outside the churches are supposed to be primarily works of art. But since some are of saints, apostles, or popes, they too furnish part of the pagan atmosphere in which idolatry reigns. St. Peter's Church in Rome has 434 statues inside, as well as the bodies of thirty-five saints. Among them is the tomb of St. Frances Cabrina, first canonized American, topped by her twelve-foot statue. In the Sanctuary of Sacro Monte at Varallo are eight hundred statues in forty-five chapels. But even this profligacy is surpassed by the famous Duomo in Milan, third largest church in the world. On the outside of this Cathedral stand no fewer than 2,245 statues!

Rome, Matrix of Mariolatry. To the person fascinated by external objects, Rome has always been a mecca. "Come to Rome," pleaded Percy Bysshe Shelley in writing to a friend. "It is a scene by which expression is overpowered—which words cannot convey."[29] Indeed Rome and all of Italy are full of things to admire, but especially of statues to venerate. As one journeys south from Paris to Rome, the crucifixes by the wayside gradually give way to shrines of the Madonna. I doubt if anyone has ever counted these thousands of Marian shrines by the wayside and in the villages. Some are elaborate and some simple, many are adorned with flowers. The Virgin Mary is obviously the principal Christian figure in the minds of the simple-hearted Italians. According to a report prepared for the Vatican by Professor Gastone Inabighy, there are now 2,135 cities and towns in Italy named after Mary!

The city of Rome itself provides many a reminder for the visitor that the Virgin Mother is accorded a central place in the worship of Catholics. The Trastevere section of Rome is one of its poorest as well as the most loyal to the church. Here the larger number of the city's 500 churches, convents, and welfare institutions are concentrated. Sacred images are to be found on almost every street corner. The poverty-stricken people who crowd the dark, twisting alleys overhung with tiny balconies live under the shadow of their Santa Maria Church, built between the seventh and twelfth centuries. This was the first church in Rome to be dedicated to the mother of Christ, and it is officially a part of Vatican City. In the Monti region of Rome, likewise created by the Popes, is the Santa Maria Maggiore basilica. One of the four great pilgrimage churches, it is the largest in the world bearing Mary's name. At the time of its dedication Monti, which spans three of Rome's seven hills, was the most evil part of the city.

In the comparatively recent past the several dogmas proclaimed in Rome regarding Mary mark that city as the Marian capital of the world. In 1854 Pope Pius IX announced that Mary was conceived without original sin, a belief known as the Immaculate Conception. Yet the other very old tradition that Mary did not suffer bodily corruption, but was taken up into heaven, had never been officially declared a dogma—a truth revealed by God which must be held under pain of heresy. On November 1, 1950, Pope Pius XII proclaimed the dogma of the Assumption. This was the first new belief added to Catholic doctrine since the popes had been declared infallible in 1870.

It naturally followed that since Mary was free from original sin and freed from bodily corruption by assumption into heaven, she should also be exalted to the position of Queen of Heaven. This latest promotion of the Virgin occurred during November, 1954, when the Pope issued his 4,000-word encyclical, *Ad Coeli Reginam* (to the Queen of Heaven). In it he wrote, "The Son of God reflects on His . . . mother the glory, the majesty, the power of regality which springs from being associated with [Him]. . . . Hence the Church . . . acclaims her . . . Queen of Heaven."[30] Great crowds surrounded the Santa Maria Maggiore Church on the day that the canons removed from its altar the painting of Mary and her Child (reputedly painted by Luke) and paraded it to St. Peter's Basilica. Inside that church, the Pope, in the presence of forty cardinals and two hundred bishops, affixed jewel-studded crowns to the painting of "The Queen of Heaven and all creation."

In sponsoring Mary's exaltation, Pope Pius XII abetted a trend of ancient origin which has yet to reach its peak. As one magazine expressed it, "By this action at the end of the Marian Year, Pius XII strengthened the ancient Marian movement, which is spreading with new vigor among Catholics."[31] Though the encyclical on the queenship of Mary is not yet dogma, will it not surely become so? And if Jesus Christ is King and Mary queen, should they not reign together as equals? This would be the logical end of these centuries of Mary-worship—to proclaim her a reigning co-mediatrix with the Son of God. It is reported in some quarters that the Pope has ordered new commissions to study the possibility of "Mary's universal mediation" which could even promote her to *sole* mediator. Meanwhile a cross in the garden of one church in Rome already bears the image of Christ and Mary hanging back to back, co-redeemers of the world.

In years to come the hundreds of Madonnas in Italian churches, of which we have mentioned only a few, will continue to receive heightened adoration. Enshrined Black Madonnas, with their link to the goddess Isis, will become the object of more prayers than ever across Europe and around the world. Behind all this lie solid reasons. One is very plain. There is no doubt that the Church strives for a stronger hold over Italian women by emphasizing Mary, for on women more than men depends the loyalty which the Church needs. Women influence their husbands and the children of generations to come; they are the indispensable link with the future.

Are The Catholics Faithful? Just after World War I, Monseigneur Belford stated that "some of the Italians are excellent Catholics, but the vast majority have no religion of any kind. . . . They do not receive the sacraments, except baptism . . . they have no use for the church or the clergy."[32] This Catholic prelate was describing a situation which has become a major problem for the church today. Protestant observers in touch with the drift away from the church add, "As far as the people are concerned . . . Italy cannot properly be described as a Roman Catholic country."[33] The same source, a *World Dominion* study after World War II, adds: "There is no disguising the fact that Italy has been very deeply involved in destroying Christian values in modern civilization and is in danger of losing its soul. What we understand as the Christian gospel is not understood by the mass of the people."[34] In 1951 a Foreign Policy Association publication noted that, until its recent reorganization against Communism, "Catholicism had been losing ground as a political factor if not as a religion."[35]

How faithful are Italian Catholics? To be studiously fair, the question has two sides. When the late Premier Alcide de Gasperi declared in the

Italian Parliament in 1947 that all but 177,529 of Italy's 45 million people were Roman Catholic, he was at least partially justified. It is true that the vast majority of Italians are born into Catholic homes and trained in Catholic schools. Italy is "a country," says one writer, "so thoroughly Catholic that even native Protestants, atheists, and anticlericals unconsciously behave according to Catholic mental habits."[36]

Yet these same Catholics can be amazingly perceptive at times. None other than the distinguished Count Carlo Sforza, former Minister of Italy, said, "One must never forget that Dante, the greatest poet in the world, did not hesitate to fling the popes into the third *bolgia* of his *Inferno*— that of the Simoniacs."[37] (The Simoniacs were those guilty of simony, or traffic in sacred things.) He adds that all Italians for the past five hundred years have known by memory the words Dante uses in his meeting with Pope Nicholas III in that third circle of torment:

> Of gold and silver ye have made your God,
> Differing wherein from the idolater
> But that he worships one, a hundred ye?
> —Inferno, Canto XIX

Sforza fails in his attempt to explain away anticlericalism in Italy as mere opposition to the church's temporal interests. What he interprets as merely innate loyalty on the part of the people to the founders of the Republic is actually more: it is a fear of losing the only system that offers them even the slightest hope.

In spite of outward success of the Roman Church with the masses, qualifications like the following have to be made: (1) More than nine million people or 36 per cent of the population, vote regularly for the Communist party and its allies despite the fact that party members who are Catholics come under excommunication. (2) Less than 10 per cent of the professional class in Milan, leading northern commercial city, attend mass regularly. (3) Not more than one third of Rome's people attend its five hundred churches on Sunday. (4) Italy's priests have steadily diminished in number for more than seventy years. (5) Some holy places like Assisi, one of the foremost shrines in the world, have long been Communist administered. (6) According to Cardinal Levitrano of Palermo, 66 per cent of Italians do not hear mass on religious holidays, while only 12 per cent of Italian men receive communion on Easter. (This means that, by strict interpretation of its own rules, about 88 per cent of the church should be disciplined for not continuing "minimum observance.")

An American priest, after visiting Milan, reported his findings on the matter of loyalty in the United States Catholic review, *America*. His sources were mostly personal interviews with Milan's Archbishop, Giovanni Battista Montini, one of the most powerful leaders of the church. This second largest Italian city counts three and one-half million baptized Catholics in its more than one thousand churches, making up the largest diocese in the nation. One would expect to find much loyalty to the church in such an area. But Father Joseph N. Moody discovered conditions quite otherwise among the masses of relatively well-paid factory workers in Milan. Although observing "a residue of faith and good will" among the industrial classes, he is forced to add that "the reservoir of respect for the church is diminishing among the young workers. One can feel a rising wall of separation that may shut them off completely from the church."[38]

This report is important because it came after Cardinal Montini's heralded efforts to win Communist workers back to the Roman Church. Though the world press once reported that the Communist vote has weakened in Milan, it appears that the church still feels she is losing ground. Cardinal Montini himself once stated that in Milan "God was being outraged, disregarded, rejected, silenced, unloved, ill-served and ill-prayed to," and that his own flock showed "moral and spiritual apathy, laziness of corrupted habits, hate, and strife among themselves."[39] The leading newspaper *l' Italia*, on November 14, 1957, claimed that "a large part of the people live in spiritual torpidity."[40] Renato Tulli, an Italian goverment official, adds the general word that "at least a good third of Italians have lost religious faith and have given their support to the materialistic doctrine of Communism . . . about another third, though not quite indifferent to religion, is at least anticlerical . . . only the remaining third is composed of good Roman Catholics, and then only half of these attend mass regularly."[41]

The Weight of the Chains. Anticlericalism in Italy is an old story. As early as two hundred years before the Reformation, Barnabo of Milan greeted papal legates bearing his excommunication by forcing them to eat the bulls—parchment, cords, lead seals, and all! Today Christian workers in Italy sometimes find allies in strange places. Often civil servants and administrators of the government make no secret of how they feel. But whatever political or personal grounds may exist for opposing the church, the average Italian is just disillusioned by receiving stones instead of bread. One young man from Torre Annunziata wrote to a gospel broadcast emanating from Switzerland: "I remember, when I was a child, I went to church and prayed to God with faith. After growing up, I longed to find work and raise a family. But I could not do either because of many vicissitudes, including the war, which hindered my learning a trade. I am now thirty years of age, morally bankrupt, and already feeling old.

I have lost all confidence in myself, in man, and in God."[42] This young man has given up his childhood's faith for—nothing! Only Jesus Christ himself can fill the void. Almost you can hear this man cry with the poet, "I am an emptiness for Thee to fill, my soul a cavern for Thy sea."

In 1947 a London periodical reported that "the time has gone when Rome can claim a whole population as her own. Materialistic sources are as strong in Italy as elsewhere. In the last twelve months there has been an increase in godless anticlericalism."[43] It has been suggested that some of the eight million votes cast for the Communist-Socialist coalition in 1953 (even after due warnings from Pius XII) were more than just an expression of political opinion. Were they not also an objection to Roman Catholic tryranny? Since it was so perilous for millions of Italians to vote for a party whose leadership and membership were under excommunication, was this not a great, silent "no confidence" vote against "the Vicar of Christ on earth"?

There is no love lost between any of the socialist parties and the Vatican; but countless other people besides Communists and Socialists do not like this or that about the church and say so. In Rome, at the end of the tiny street called San Pantaleo, stands the statue of Pasquino presiding over the *Congresso degli Arguti.* Roman citizens love to hang on this statue bitter attacks on the papacy and its abuses of authority, many of them far from political in nature. A saying frequently seen is, "Faith is made here and believed elsewhere." Even more widely quoted is the proverb, *Roma veduta, fede perduta,* "When you see Rome you will lose your religion."

Others prefer to defy Rome by turning to the occult. After the war the press reported that Cardinal Ildefonso Schuster of Milan complained in pastoral letters that organized groups were "trying to get consecrated hosts, which they profane and use for unmentionable purposes during their meetings."[44] This is a reference to the obscene "black mass," a perverted orgy which has plagued Europe since the twelfth century. Though Masonic rites were banned by Pius VIII in the nineteenth century, they, too, still flourish underground and add to the Vatican's troubles.

Another situation in which anticlerical tendencies can be seen is in the slackening off of recruits for Italy's 25,000 parishes. One Italian prelate put it this way: "Many are chiefly interested in movies, football, and girls at the age when they should enter a seminary if they want to become priests."[45] Even fewer, adds the bishop, enter orders late in life. So the hold of the church on youth in Italy is far from as absolute as it would like the world to believe. One hundred years ago in Rome there were fifty-eight parishes for only 200,000 inhabitants; today's shortage of priests allows only 155 parishes for two million Romans. In 1870 there were 150,000 priests in Italy, when the population was only twenty-six million.

Now there are only 63,000 for almost fifty million people. Additions are also needed to the 152,000 nuns, 13,000 of whom are cloistered.*

Casual use of holy names for secular things is another sign of the shallowness of Italian Catholicism. "Bank of the Holy Spirit" is to be seen on many branches of a leading bank in Italy. One can buy "Tears of Christ" wine everywhere. Various wines are also made and sold in churches, some of them in famous basilicas like St. Paul's-Outside-the-Walls in Rome. The listlessness of many nominal Catholics in attending Easter mass in Italy is pointed out by one Protestant pastor as a means the public uses to demonstrate disfavor of the Roman Church. To receive the Holy Eucharist during Eastertime is one of the six precepts the church enjoins on all as a solemn imperative. In spite of the pageantry at St. Peter's, when Catholic Action and other movements spur fresh allegiance by amassing enormous crowds, there is a falling away that worries the Holy See.

Not a few feel that the Vatican is not only antidemocratic but anti-Italian. "Many Italians resent the influence that the Church exercises in national affairs—clericalism."[46] Opponents point to the Vatican's opposition to the very formation of the country in the first place. Many remember that the papal states alone resisted with war the unification of their country in 1870, while most of the other states entered the union pacifically. Many times since then the interests of the Vatican and those of the Italian people have clashed violently. While Mazzini, one of the country's true patriots, was calling the Vatican "a gigantic ruin," the church was busily excommunicating national heroes like himself, Garibaldi, Cavour, and the King of Italy. Here we see a parallel with the French Republic's struggle against the Roman Church: the liberal creators of both modern France and Italy were at odds with the Vatican. Much ill feeling still remains from these memories. Italians also recall that the popular vote transferring the city of Rome from the Pope to the new Kingdom of Italy was 133,648 to only 1,507. More recently, the record of papal opposition to the fascist regime of Mussolini is spotty and its support of fascist adventures abroad very strong. Another point of discussion is that the creation of Italy's post-World War II republic, was opposed by the Vatican in the face of thirteen million votes by the people. A democratic republic is the very last form of government the Roman Church would choose as ideal for its own purposes; for in a land so governed there cannot be coercion, and tolerance gives the Word of God free course. Yet the church will go along with this or any other kind of government which will serve her ends.

*These figures taken from a French publication, *Informations Catholiques Internationales,* dated July 15, 1959.

Finally, some Italians realize that they are getting nothing from an organization which claims to be in contact with God and able to mediate Him to men. At the bottom of all their disenchantment is a craving for reality only to be found in enlightenment by the Holy Spirit. The peninsula so rich in so much else is so poor in spiritual knowledge of the Son of God.

3. DEDICATED DISCIPLES OF MARX

Two Opponents With a Single Aim. One July midnight, in 1949, the bells of Rome's five hundred Catholic churches began to ring the death knell. For twenty-four hours without ceasing the solemn cacophony for the dead continued to toll. Deep inside the Vatican Pius XII, garbed in the violet vestments of mourning, was seated before a Church committee appointed to weigh the attitude of Catholicism toward Communism. Each member had received two yellow wax candles, which burned lower as the Pope spoke. When he ceased, all rose with him, waited while he read the terrible sentence, then cast their lighted candles on the ground. Again bells tolled, while crucifixes were covered with velvet shrouds and altar ornaments were removed. By this meaningful ceremony the Pope had pronounced excommunication upon all Catholics who persisted in following Communism.

But in spite of the threat of excommunication and frequent papal denunciations, two irreconcilable conditions continue to exist side by side in Italy. Or we may say that in the face of these conditions, many individuals are trying to maintain a double loyalty. The Roman Church, on the one hand, claims almost all the people as her children. Yet the Italian Communist party is the largest in Europe and the third largest in the world.

An amusing view of this contradiction was provided in a postwar session of the Italian Parliament. The subject of debate was the Lateran treaty of 1929, which stated that Roman Catholicism is the "religion of the state." After Premier de Gasperi of the Christian Democrats had earnestly defended the treaty and urged its reaffirmation, Palmiro Togliatti, the Communist leader, rose to his feet. He thanked de Gasperi for pointing out that 45,349,221 out of Italy's 45,526,750 people were "Catholics," since this proved beyond any doubt that most of the four million Communist votes in the previous election had been cast by Roman Catholics. Thereupon the Communist party parliamentary bloc proceeded to vote, for reasons of its own, *in favor* of continuing the Lateran treaty provisions!

What has the excommunication actually accomplished? Has the fear of being eternally cut off from the ministrations of the church—and from salvation itself—made any real difference to Catholic-moulded Communists? "The Vatican's forceful excommunication of Communists in 1949 struck with relatively little impact in Italy," said the *New York Herald Tribune.*[47] It is not within the scope of this book to examine in detail the reasons why the Communist party has seemingly overcome this obstacle, but several background reasons for the party's success are of interest to the Christian surveying Italy's needs:

1. The party operates on a budget of about forty-five million dollars a year, far exceeding the resources of other political parties.*

2. All Communists outside of those few in party-paid work are expected to contribute as much as *one third* of their salaries to this huge budget (parliamentary party members alone give nearly one million dollars annually).

3. The party has followed a very clever conciliatory line with the church. Sometimes, as we just saw, the party will vote for what the church wants. Most party members are now convinced that it is all right to remain both a Communist and a Catholic temporarily, despite what the church says.

4. The party provides social life. This creates a sense of belonging, of togetherness, that is warm and personal. Communists have their own clubs, dances, and sport associations.

5. The party exercises tight discipline. The 139,781 leaders, who control groups of ten, call comrades to cell meetings, check absenteeism, assign and supervise work, investigate study, finances, etc. There are 52,481 cells under the direction of 9,993 sections.

6. The party makes a strong appeal to youth. There are 437,240 members in the Youth Federation.

7. Forty-eight weekly newspapers are published by the provincial organizations of the party, giving the current line of belief and practice. A column called "Party Life" strongly criticizes party members who do not carry out their assigned responsibilities the preceding week.

8. Each of the nearly 10,000 sections has an "Agitation Center," furnished right down to movie projectors and other equipment; after indoctrination in "missionary work," members then go out to do visitation and "win converts."

We have thus outlined the Communist offensive only to show that the grip of the Roman Catholic Church on the Italian people is not so absolute as the latter would have the world believe. Both camps clearly need the simple, saving gospel of Christ in all its power. Methods and organization like those described above won the support of about 36 per cent of the

---

*These figures are, of course, subject to fluctuation, but the relative ratios would not change much.

electorate (about one in every three voters) in the elections of June, 1953, when some nine million Italians voted with the Communists (22.6 per cent voted the Communist ticket, with 12.7 per cent support from the Left Wing Socialists). This was a gain of roughly 3 per cent over the 1948 elections. While later local elections show slight reductions of these figures, especially in the industrial north, there is still danger for Italy. Many people who are uninformed think that a nation must either undergo a *coup d'etat* or show overwhelming Communist victory at the polls to "go Communist." They forget Czechoslovakia. Italian Communist strength is slowly nearing the 39 per cent strength by which the Czech party captured national control at Prague in 1948. With a majority of three to eight per cent more, Communists could win cabinet seats and perhaps even the premiership, which under the Italian Constitution derives solely from Parliament.

The War for Souls. The crusading spirit of Italy's Communists should challenge believers in Christ to work equally hard for an incorruptible crown. Even non-Christians see the contrast here. One reporter points out that the red stucco Communist headquarters on Rome's Via della Botteghe Oscure is a beehive of activity day and night. "The men in the big red building," he writes, "work with a fervor rarely witnessed in the Christian world since the Reformation and Counter Reformation." Regarding their burning witness for Marxism, he adds,

> Into the remotest mountain villages accessible only by mountain track, into the dirtiest, dust-choked towns of impoverished Calabria, the tireless party missionaries carry the gospel with all its symbols and promises of salvation, and with a new fraternity, a stirring strength, a vague but exhilarating hope of being able to move history itself.[48]

Of this grim, deadly war for men's souls on the part of both camps, Edwin Jacques, a former missionary in Italy, says:

> Two totalitarian systems are battling it out for the souls of men on the overpopulated peninsula. Historically dominant is Roman Catholicism, which professes to be apostolic, New Testament, and Christian. In Italy it is hopelessly medieval, mythological, and Marian. Then there is Communism, its "equal and opposite reaction" . . . it diffuses a skillful propaganda by radio and the printed page. With millions of her people alienated from Rome and attracted by Moscow, Italy holds the dubious distinction of having the largest Communist population outside of Russia. . . . As long as neither Catholicism nor Communism holds a monopoly in Italy, missionaries of the gospel may expect to continue their work. But the night cometh![49]

Neither a materialistic Marxism nor a ritualistic Romanism can save

Italy's poor souls caught between these two. Both systems are broken cisterns which can hold no water. If the gospel of Christ can be proclaimed now to these sheep without a shepherd, through literature, radio, preaching, or any other method, surprising results may follow. In proportion to the reaper-power involved, the harvest already looks propitious. But only when God's people elsewhere in the world give themselves to prayer for Italy will the heavens open and blessing flow.

4. A CANDLE IN THE DARKNESS

Members of the Protestant Family. It is difficult to arrive at an exact figure for the number of Protestants in Italy, since estimates vary widely. In some cases accurate membership figures are not kept, while in others they are obviously overestimated. Edwin Jacques says, "Estimates of the number of Protestant adherents vary from 50,000 to less than 300,000. A figure of about 215,000 Protestants, counting baptized and unbaptized, would seem justified and defensible."[50]

In one parliamentary speech the late Premier Alcide de Gasperi stated that all but 177,529 Italians were Roman Catholics. While this is an official government statement, it seems to be inaccurate and padded in favor of the predominating religion. Since there are about 25,000 Jews, 15,000 Greek Orthodox followers, quite a few Muslims, and some without religion, too little room would remain to squeeze in several hundred thousand Protestants. Part of the trouble is that the old census report form asked, "In what religion were you baptized?" Although many thousands have left the Roman Church, they must state that they were originally baptized as Catholics. So these are carried along year after year as Catholics, although they may have long ago ceased to be identified with the Church. To the outside world an appearance of solidarity is thus presented which does not correspond to the facts. After much personal inquiry in Italy, we believe the number of Protestants there to lie somewhere between 200,000 and 250,000. As Jacques explains, 215,000 "would be less than ½ of 1 percent of Italy's 48 million people."[51] What a mission field among the millions who are either loyal or indifferent to Rome, converted to Communism, or ensnared in the sects!

The Waldensian Church is the only one really native to the soil of Italy. Its history is long and stirring. There are about 124 congregations, most having church buildings of their own, a few of which are imposing in size. One of the largest the writer has attended is almost in the shadow of St. Peter's in Rome. In their historic northern Alpine valleys the Waldenses are strongest, having 74 pastors and about 27,000 adherents.*

---

*In this section most of the figures used are from the *World Christian Handbook* (1957), published in London by World Dominion Press.

Pentecostals claim the largest following in the land, their membership being estimated at about 60,000. Some 350 congregations meet in church buildings or hired halls, a number having paid pastors, but many being led only by elders. Sixteen churches are related to the Apostolic Church (British) and 277 to the Assemblies of God (U.S.A.); the rest are independent. Virtually all the Pentecostal assemblies in Southern Italy and Sicily are the fruit of the zealous efforts of Italian-American missionaries. Edwin Jacques assesses the work this way, "Of all Protestant groups, the Pentecostals have appealed most successfully to the emotional Italian nature."[52] The writer participated, just after the second war, in the dedication of a large, new edifice of this group in Rome. Of that particular congregation and the denomination in general Oswald J. Smith remarks:

> I have a very high regard for the Pentecostal work in Italy. It is by far the largest denomination in the entire country and is winning thousands of souls to Christ. . . . I preached Sunday morning and Sunday night in a church crowded, with many standing. Several responded for salvation. If groups of personal workers could be trained in each church, and an invitation extended, souls would be saved in scores instead of in one or twos. Italians, like all others, must be brought to a point of decision.[53]

Emerging as a denomination during the first decade of this century, Pentecostalism spread so rapidly that the incumbent Pope overstated its success, "That movement has invaded every parish of our blessed country."[54] After the Vatican appealed to Mussolini, Pentecostals were prohibited from having services, on the basis that the movement was constituted by individuals suffering from "religious mania and mystic excitement." However, this opposition only proved to be a blessing, forcing the Pentecostal church underground. When I first encountered the Rome congregation referred to, they were literally "underground" in an old catacomb. The pastor had been imprisoned on twenty-nine occasions during Fascist days, his congregation several times going to prison with him as a body, and sharing his confinement in order to express their protest and sympathy.

Lutherans have about 4,200 members in twelve churches. *Anglicans* number twelve congregations, and *Presbyterians* or *Reformed* claim five churches. Perhaps there are six thousand adherents in all three of these denominations, with a score or more regular pastors. The assemblies of *Plymouth Brethren* usually begin in homes of believers. There have been reported to be more than 170 assemblies, counting 10,000 followers, concentrated especially in the areas of heavy industry around Turin. But new assemblies have been formed quite recently down through the center and in Sicily, Emelia, Liguria, and other areas. The actual figures may well surpass those known to the writer, as Brethren statistics are notoriously difficult to gather. A few traveling evangelists and foreign teachers circulate among these groups. *Methodists* united their forces in 1935, and now total about fifty-seven congregations and 8,000 adherents, about 4,000 of whom are active members. Half of the congregations have their own buildings, but there are only about twenty-five pastors. Since 1943 a gradually closer organic union between Methodists and Waldenses is being consummated.

In 1923 the British *Baptists* in Italy turned over most of their churches to the American Southern Baptists, which have fifty-seven congregations, and forty-one outstations, about half with church buildings. Fifty-two pastors serve about 4,000 baptized believers—perhaps 12,000 "sympathizers" and members all together. About a dozen foreign missionaries labor with this group, which is now Italian in leadership. One British Baptist group which did not merge is the *La Spezia Mission*, numbering eight congregations, six or seven pastors, and six hundred baptized believers, as well as hundreds more who attend more or less regularly. Most of the congregations in this communion have their own buildings, donated by English Christians. In early 1953 the British withdrew, leaving the work in the hands of the Italians. *Nazarenes* have five congregations with a few hundred adherents. There are about twenty-two *Church of Christ* (Texas) congregations and seven more affiliated with the United States midwestern branch of that denomination. *The Salvation Army*, though not a church as such, exercises a good influence. It maintains a number of posts and has gained some soldiers. Among the sects outside the Protestant pale, the *Millennial Dawn* movement has eight or ten groups, *Jehovah's Witnesses* about the same. *Seventh Day Adventists* claim about fifty places of worship and perhaps 10,000 followers. A few groups of *Christian Science, Spiritualists,* and *Mormons* complete this list.

It is never easy for Christians from Anglo-Saxon countries to put themselves in the place of their brethren in Catholic lands. The former are usually tempted to wonder why the latter are so careful to avoid giving the Vatican offense. Foreigners wonder why Italian Protestants are not more evangelistic, more open to suggestions from abroad. Those who have not lived under the oppressive darkness of centuries of Romanism can never fully grasp what a struggle true believers have just to "keep going" in their own spiritual lives. Since Satan has the field here largely to himself, he uses many forms of intimidation upon the saints of God, which may not be so clearly felt in more prayer-cleansed parts of the world. Thus we must speak and think of Italian believers with sympathy and prayer.

The Bite of the Two-Edged Sword. On one corner of the *Piazza Venezia* in Rome is the Italian Bible Society headquarters, an affiliate of the British and Foreign Bible Society. Some of the thousands who once packed the famous square to hear *Il Duce* used to crowd right against the Bible Society's windows. From here one had an unobstructed view of Mussolini's balcony in the Palazzo. Today the great boaster is gone, but the Bible remains! "My word," said the Son of God, "shall not pass away."

The attitude of the Roman Church toward the Word of God is too well known to need lengthy recapitulation. Just these brief reminders will help us place Italy's distributors of the Bible in their proper setting. In 1229 the Council of Toulouse ruled that no layman might possess any portion of either Old or New Testament. Due to the influence of the Reformation a few centuries later, however, this position was modified by the Council of Trent. Since interest in the Bible was so great all over Europe, that body decided to allow readers who obtained a certificate of permission from their bishop or confessor to read the sacred book. Priests could give this permission only if they were sure the reading would do the reader no harm. The penalty for not giving up Bibles for which no reading permission had been obtained was the witholding of absolution until the forbidden book was surrendered. From these measures we see that the Catholic Church likes to keep the reading of the Word of God under close control. All five popes of the nineteenth century further confirmed this attitude when, incensed by the aggressiveness of the British and Foreign Bible Society, they pronounced against the use of the Bible in the languages of the people.

From the foregoing one can understand that providing the Bible for the man on the street in the mother country of Catholicism has not been easy. Opposition takes subtle forms. Because the Roman church has centuries of authority behind it, fear of the priest's opinion and disfavor is strong. When people do acquire a Bible, or portions of it, either relatives or the priest himself will often find the literature and confiscate it.

Fortunately there is an Italian Bible to distribute. Though an Italian translation of the Bible was made by Brucioli in 1530, history shows that it was not distributed to the people. But a good version translated by Diodate appeared in 1671; since then others have prepared helpful new translations such as the New Testament and Psalms by the late Baptist pastor, Oscar Cocorda. A number of editions of the Word have been prepared in seven Italian dialects. For the Italian language, as spoken in some parts of the mainland and on the islands, is so different from that generally spoken that it is scarcely understood in other regions.

An annual average of 4,790 whole Bibles were sold by the Italian Bible Society during the nineteen years between 1936 and 1954. During that period the highest sale was reached in 1951, with 10,777 copies. Since then, the average annual sale has been between 6,500 and 7,500. About the same number of New Testaments go out yearly, together with about 100,000 Scripture portions. The distribution of the Bible by this agency is gradually but not noticeably rising. Since other agencies, too, sell the Bible, the figures given above do not represent total distribution. A small Bible bookstore in the port city of Genoa operates under the Geneva Bible Society. In the same city the *Bible Christian Union* maintains its *Centro Vita*, which contains a bookstore and a reading room. Most of the denominational bookstores and other small outlets procure Bibles from one of these two sources, so that their distribution figures would be included in those of the others. There are no salaried colporteurs maintained by the Bible Society, but in a recent year a reported 104 volunteers gave part of their time to this work.

Another newer Bible distribution center is the missionary effort in Naples called the *Centro Biblico*, maintained by the *Conservative Baptists*. Here Bibles, Testaments, and portions in various Protestant and Catholic versions have been made available. One successful feature of this aggressive work has been the distribution, through a post card system, of a special edition of John's gospel containing a return card. A number of those who receive Gospels then request the four-lesson correspondence course. Many thousands have enrolled in the past ten years. Upon completion of the simple course, they receive a New Testament, which leads in turn to further Bible studies. Thus many have been led to the knowledge of Christ as Saviour.

Examples of the transforming power of the Word could be multiplied without number. But the following case of "chain reaction" in lives shows what can be accomplished when the Book of books is at work within a group. The secretary for the British and Foreign Bible Society in Italy tells of a young Sicilian prisoner converted by reading a Bible left by chance in his cell. Through the miraculous change wrought in his life by Christ, others were won to the Lord. In less than two months twenty prisoners had asked for and received Bibles. When Easter Sunday came, they had a service of their own. One of this group, transferred elsewhere, founded a similar group of Scripture-searchers in another prison. All this came about without a preacher or any human agency.

Religious Liberty—the Burning Issue. Italy is a country where you must ask as a favor what you are entitled to by law. If you take the trouble to investigate the laws governing religion, you will find out that they can often be interpreted against you, no matter what they may actually say. No liberty for religion really existed on Italian soil until 1848. On February 17 of that year, some six hundred years after their movement began, the Waldenses held their first legal public worship in Turin. At the instigation of the statesman Cavour (who originated the famous formula *chiesa libera in stato libero,* "a free church in a free state"), Charles Albert, King of Piedmont, issued the celebrated Edict of Emancipation, giving civil rights to all his citizens. This independent state of Piedmont, where Protestantism is still quite strong, was thus the first part of Italy to announce local freedom of worship.

Between the unification of Italy in 1870 and the signing of the Vatican-Italian Concordat of 1929, some tolerance existed under what was called the Albertine Statute. Liberal governments preceding Mussolini even tried to reduce the Vatican's grip during an era of bad will toward the church which had opposed the country's founding. But toleration is far from full liberty, and the churches still lived in judicial inferiority. One advantage was that temporarily the Church of Rome was not ascendant.

When Mussolini signed his Concordat with the Pope in 1929 the Roman Catholic faith became Italy's "sole state religion," gaining a higher standing. That concession grew out of the dictator's desire to find a *modus vivendi* with the Holy See. Other provisions of the Concordat put the minority religious groups in the category of *culti ammessi,* or permitted religions. But their legal standing then became even lower than the previous one of toleration. Just a little more than a month after the signing of the Concordat, Pius XI said in a letter to Cardinal Gasparri that in a Catholic state liberty of conscience and of discussion must be interpreted and practiced according to Catholic doctrine and law. Already the newly-widened powers of the church were being exercised as she volunteered to guide enforcement and interpretation of secular law in a sovereign state. It had been made very clear during the Concordat discussion that the Vatican did not like the word "permitted," and would have preferred some other expression of a tolerance more subject to its own authority. The "permitted religions" have only had relative liberty, since the Lateran Treaty discriminates between national and foreign Protestants, between pre-Reformation Waldenses and those "missionary" churches which entered from abroad after 1860, and again between Protestants and Catholics when convicted of religious offenses. There are many sets of standards according to circumstances, a typical Roman Catholic arrangement.

When the new Italian Constitution of 1948 was passed, the Protestants rejoiced, for all confessions were declared in Articles XVII and XIX to be equal before the law. But Article VIII, which regulated the relationship between the state and non-Catholics, shows dependence again on the Concordat of 1929. In interpreting the constitutional provisions, Dr. Roberto Poppi, director of the Rome *Governorate*, supervising office for religious groups, said that religious confessions different from the Catholic had the right to organize insofar as they do not contrast with Italian judicial order. Their relations with the state were to be regulated by law on the basis of their "relative representation." What this legal language means is that the religious freedom promised in the Constitution is subject to devious interpretations by the government on the basis of the numerical strength of the group.

In practical application some of the restrictions are these: no street meetings, almost no access to national radio, approval of the Minister of the Interior for each appointment or transfer of a pastor, and the obligation to submit church constitutions to the Minister of the Interior for approval.

"Recognition" of the church groups has been, until recently, another sore point. As we have pointed out, before World War II the Pentecostal church was forced to go underground when it was banned by the Mussolini government. But after the liberation of Italy by the Allies, this church, and others in the same category, were able to carry on services under the Allied Military Government. After the withdrawal of the military following the war, relative tolerance continued, and Pentecostals continued to petition for "recognition." This was finally granted in a limited judicial form in November, 1954. At that time the Council of State—highest body reviewing administrative decisions—gave this group the right to perform legally binding marriages, to hold services freely, escape excessive taxation, and so on.

Public interest abroad, aided by the press, has centered mostly on the fight for recognition by the American denomination called the Church of Christ. Not having the representation the law calls for, it has been harried constantly since 1947. Americans organizing the work—comprising roughly five hundred members, twenty-two churches, and a single orphanage—have again and again been hindered in securing the necessary permits.

There has even been public demand in Italy for the repeal of the Concordat of 1929. In an article on October 20, 1946, the Concordat was called by a Rome newspaper "a monstrous instrument" through which the papal power wishes to govern Italy. The paper went on to say that the national holiday celebrating the signing of the Concordat—one of ten guaranteed to the church by the state—should be observed rather as a day of national mourning.

Protestants in Italy have organized a Federal Council of Evangelical Churches to push their case for freedom. When the Constituent Assembly of the government met to form a new Constitution for Italy after the war, each member found before him a "Declaration on Freedom of Conscience and Worship" by these Protestants. After the Constitution was formulated and those issues still remained unsettled, further action was taken. A delegation from the Protestant group waited on the then Premier Alcide de Gasperi to ask why their requests for freedom were being ignored. At that time, January, 1949, both de Gasperi and Interior Minister Mario Scelba told them it was the government's intention to grant absolute freedom of religion to Italian Protestants. Later, in 1953, the current Minister of the Interior, Amintore Fanfani, repeated assurances that agreements would be worked out, as called for by Article VIII of the Constitution.

Several observations can be drawn from these instances. Obviously the coalition governments since the war have had to follow the political and religious convictions of the majority, the Christian Democrat party. Premiers and Ministers of the Interior within this party are pledged to practical co-operation with the Vatican on all levels. As in so many other constitutions in the world, including Russia's, religious freedom is promised in the Italian Constitution. But only as much will be given as is politically expedient. For the motto of the Roman Church seems to be that attributed to Louis Venillot, the French writer: "Where we are a minority, we ask you for religious liberty in the name of *your* principles. Where we are a majority, we refuse it in the name of *ours*."[55] One device is to treat Protestant "churches" better than unrecognized "assemblies" in order to divide Protestant ranks and discourage a united front. Only one strategy for Christians, both in and out of Italy, is practical and dynamic: Prayer still reaches the greatest Authority in the universe, and His hand rules this world.

The Trend Toward Freedom. Both foreign and Italian evangelicals agree that the government's attitude toward religious freedom is better today than it ever was before. The legal office maintained by Italian Protestants in Rome has won all sixty-five legal cases it has fought through the superior courts since 1947. In 1956 the Supreme Court called for by the Constitution was finally established. Protestants have already been helped by this body's interpretations of the Constitution. Public meetings may now be held and signs may be displayed by churches (providing taxes have been paid), the Court has ruled. Centers of witness may now be opened without prior approval, provided the organization involved has government recognition. Quite naturally the government fears political subversives, but organizations which have persisted in application have been recognized. This approval has even been extended to several of the older missionary-created organizations, but as yet few postwar missions have full official recognition. The foreign missionaries in

Italy, who meet annually to discuss their problems, have concluded that to fight for religious freedom is not their primary task. Not that they have enough freedom. They feel, however, that they are not yet availing themselves of the liberty that exists. Meanwhile their mood is optimistic and their faith strong.

Do Italians Accept Christ? During a typical postwar year a leader of the Brethren assemblies writes, "During the year, in the goodness of God, 168 souls have testified by means of baptism to their faith in Christ."[56] This report covered the work of almost an equal number of assemblies, showing an average of about one baptized convert per assembly. Doubtless there were many other converts awaiting baptism while undergoing instruction. Another typical year since the war found the Waldenses instructing 581 catechists for church membership. In 1956, reported the Paulist Fathers in a special report to the Vatican, Italian Pentecostals won 475 backslidden Catholics to their belief. Although this figure seems small, the report added that it is about eleven times the number of Italian Protestants in Rome won to Catholicism.

A testimony like the following also refreshes the heart:

> My name is Vito Pietrosanto, and I was born 30 years ago in a small village in South Italy, of Roman Catholic parents. My family was a large one, but poor and unhappy. Hardship and misery was my lot, with little family care or affection. As far as I can recall, my father and mother did not live in one accord. When I was 10, with my father gone, I went astray so badly that when 11 years old I was in a reformatory at Turin. I stayed four and a half years. While there I learned to read and write and was taught carpentry. When released at 15, however, I could not make a living. After working as a brick-maker at small pay, I once again stole, was caught, and sentenced again. After release in 1942 I went into the Italian army as a means to end it all. However my life was spared.
>
> I then went to France secretly, obtained work, but returned to Italy when I was 28, still without God and without hope. The 1953-4 winter was terrible, so in the spring I set out for Rome in one last effort to find an open door. On June 2, 1954, while walking along a street begging for a job and a piece of bread, I was led to enter a meeting hall. A Youth for Christ rally was going on. A man preached about Jesus as the way of life and the only real source of satisfaction. When he finished preaching and made an appeal, I put up my hand, accepting Christ as my personal Saviour. That day I learned what it means to trust in God. . . . My troubles are not completely over, but I have peace in my heart and faith in the Lord's care.[57]

How wonderful are God's ways in leading the weary footsteps of one of Italy's two million unemployed and hungry to Him who is the Bread of Life! Group meetings, too, result in visible fruit. Doctor Renato Tulli, an important official of the Italian government in Rome and a dedicated Christian, writes, "Last night we had a glorious meeting in the Baptist Chapel. It was packed with people . . . when I made the appeal there were four decisions for Christ. There was great rejoicing and the power of God was almost physically felt."[58] Evangelism as practiced in many other countries is little known in Italy, but is successful when tried. As Paul Lehman reported, "Our colleague in Rome has found open doors in several churches for evangelistic campaigns. As you know, this type of work is just not accepted here, and yet is without doubt the greatest need of the churches. We found a team. . . . We have had meetings in Rome, Roncilione, and Grosseto. In each campaign people have found the Lord. Some conversions were so precious that they will long remain in our hearts."[59] In the Umbria town of Marsciano, missionary Royal Peck of the Greater Europe Mission boldly tried a tent campaign, an unusual and untested approach in this country. In this remote village a number found Christ.

Of Italy, where Oswald J. Smith of Toronto has ministered on several occasions, the well-known missionary leader has said this, "Let anyone take an automobile, load it with tracts, and drive through Italy. Just by giving out tracts he will have a ministry that will count for eternity, even if he is unable to preach in the language of the people."[60] Once when the writer drove from Rome to Naples and back with Dr. Smith, we carried on this form of witness. Of all the thousands of tracts we distributed, not one which fell near anyone was neglected. All were picked up and read on the spot by hungry people. Some even got off bicycles or out of cars, or laid down heavy burdens in order to read the story of eternal life through Jesus Christ.

Arthur and Erma Wiens, missionaries presently in Modena, contribute an interesting instance of a man who was the first in the town of Fonanelle (near Parma) to be saved. One day in 1944 this man heard a neighbor, who had returned from France after World War I, say that he had been given a New Testament upon crossing the frontier into Italy. The friendly neighbor urged his companion to read the little book, and ended up by presenting it to him. Though at first he was afraid, he did read the book through, and was convinced of its truth. For five or six more years he continued to read it before he heard of the existence of an evangelical church in Piacenza, about fifty kilometers from his home. Upon attending that church, he found that he could fully agree with everything that had been said; so he invited a member of the group to return with him for meetings in his home town. Immediately he and several of his friends received Christ. It was quite natural then to start meetings of their own, with only an occasional visit by outside believers. Thus a small church was begun almost entirely through the work of the Holy Spirit and His sword, the Word, in the heart.

A zealous pastor of the La Spezia Mission, named Marano, staked off an area around Turin and asked the Lord to give him the strength to visit all the many hundreds of villages there. In eighteen months Marano covered 80,000 kilometers on his little motorcycle, systematically talking to every person he met along the way. Conversions were many and lasting. Once, approaching a farmer in his vineyard, the pastor started to talk to the man's unfriendly back. He was ignored until he asked the farmer if he knew what the Bible taught about vineyards. Interested now, the gruff farmer listened while Marano told him about the vine and branches of John 15. After the farmer accepted the One who said, "I am the Vine," he was able to gather other branches to become attached to the Lord Jesus. Today that convert is an elder in a small church started in a nearby village as a result of his salvation.

Italians Must Win Italy. Every missionary who has spent much time in Italy has reached the same conclusion: Until his Italian contact has been converted, is studying the Word, and has begun to follow his Lord in full discipleship, the missionary's own labor is unsuccessful. The task is not easy. Few enough converts reach the stage of complete obedience and dedication. Fewer still enter evangelistic work or consistently bear personal witness. Missionaries either teach these converts personally by example and counsel or place them within the framework of a nearby gospel church fellowship. The best of these should be trained in a special school of some kind. Until very recently there was little opportunity for such training in Italy. Existing schools were for the most part liberal or strongly denominational, and few were evangelistic in emphasis.

Recently the Greater Europe Mission opened an Italian Bible Institute in Rome along the same lines followed in its other schools, near Paris and at Seeheim, Germany. Under the direction of Royal Peck, this school seeks to give Italians more than a mere academic grasp of the Bible. The object is to teach the Bible in terms of witness, stressing personal and public evangelism. This is breaking precedent in Italy, where the idea of week-end evangelism and aggressive church-planting by such students is still quite foreign. This strategy is the sole answer to the problem of evangelization in Italy. When Italian Christians become strong enough to win their own converts and train them, the Scriptural chain reaction of II Tim. 2:2 will go into effect. Only then can Italy be won to the Lord.

A group of students at the Brussels Bible Institute in Belgium.
The school is run by the Belgian Gospel Mission.

Credit: Belgian Gospel Mission

"Jesus" rides into a Belgian city during a Palm Sunday procession.
On the left and right are some of his "disciples."

Credit: Acme Photo

Chapter 8

BLINDNESS IN BELGIUM
AND LUXEMBURG

"Belgium is one of the most needy and neglected mission fields in the world."

—JOHN WINSTON, former Co-Director
Belgian Gospel Mission

1. GATEWAY TO EUROPE

Unpossessed Land. With its higher ratio of native pastors and missionaries, the Republic of Congo is better evangelized today than its former European colonizer, Belgium. It is strange but true that a child born in the African country so long under Belgian development is more likely to hear the gospel than one born in Belgium, that industrial beehive in Europe's heart. More than sixty Belgian cities of over ten thousand people still have no gospel witness. In the rocky, picturesque Ardennes forest area, so famous as the locale of World War II's Battle of the Bulge, only two Protestant pastors serve 216,000 inhabitants.

Stop a smartly-dressed business man on Brussels' Boulevard Adolphe Max or Antwerp's De Keyslerei; give him a word of witness about the Saviour, and get his reaction. Talk to a trim salesgirl in the Innovation department store, or to a policeman on duty at the Place Rogier in Brussels. In fact, pick out any average Belgian here and there and learn how much he knows about the way of salvation. You will get almost the same reactions from each. Your contact is a professing Catholic, perhaps not very devout in practice. About the gospel he is just as ignorant as a pygmy in the Eastern Congo jungle. Oh, he can talk about sin, the Virgin Mary, Jesus Christ, and even such matters as the precious blood. But these are just words, the merest labels of humanized Christianity. Hidden beneath the attractive promise of peace and fulfillment is the hook, sal-

291

vation through one's own works. Ensnared, unsatisfied, and bewildered, each Belgian is himself a mission field.

Europe's Trading Post. Belgium is about the size of the state of Maryland, but has a population only slightly larger than that of New York City. There are forty-eight miles of coastline on the North Sea, and land frontiers shared with France, Luxemburg, and Holland. Two-thirds of Belgium's people live in large cities like Brussels, Antwerp, Liege, Ghent, Charleroi, and other centers. One of the highest population densities in the world squeezes the people into the small living space left outside the great industrial complexes. Only 17 per cent of the people cultivate the land, while 42 per cent are employed by industry. Farms in the more open areas of the country are necessarily small. As you drive along in northern Belgium, you feel that you are always in a town or city. Because of its processing economy, based on coal mining, iron, steel and textiles, Belgium is able to give its citizens one of the highest living standards in Europe. Much of this prosperity still comes from the immensely rich, newly independent Congo, eighty times the size of Belgium and about four times the size of the state of Texas. The Congo's so-called "Big Five" companies, which produce uranium, gold, diamonds, and other minerals, and chemicals, have greatly enriched Belgium.

Two official languages are spoken in Belgium. French is the language of Wallonia in the south, spoken at Liege, Charleroi, Mons, Verviers, Namur, and Tournai. In Flanders, including the northern cities of Antwerp, Ghent, Ostend, Coutrai, and Bruges, the Flemish language (a dialect of Dutch) is used. The people of Brussels, the capital, are ethnically within the Flemish part, but most speak French. Many Belgians speak both of these languages, but those who do not are numerous enough to warrant the official use of both. As additional languages many know English and German, both useful for commerce and the large tourist trade.

On Everyone's Way. Someone has said that "Belgium is a country on everyone's way everywhere in Europe." This means that the winning of Belgium to Christ has strategic implications. Because of its location in northern Europe, the land is a natural trade center. Within 250 miles of of its great seaport of Antwerp live 125 million of the most productive and prosperous people in Europe. Connected by the Scheldt River with the continent's main water artery, the Rhine, Antwerp during a recent year shipped 21 million tons of cargo in 13,000 seagoing vessels owned by 240 lines from 45 nations. Thus when the gospel of Christ is preached in Belgium, it resounds elsewhere, for these are a trading and traveling people, contacting every civilized nation in the world. Again, the concentration of so many people in one place is convenient for the Christian worker. With a minimum of travel he can sow the seed of God's Word to a vast company. Here an average of 743 persons live in every square mile, as compared to thirty-five persons per square mile in the United States. A stable currency and fairly sound political and social patterns also make Belgium an influential area in and from which to make Christ known.

In more ways than one Belgium is "on everyone's way." When Hitler's generals pored over their maps to find the best route for their armies to strike west, the Lowlands were their natural choice. What is a favorable geography for Belgium's trade is otherwise a snare. Military leaders throughout history have chosen to cross or occupy the tiny, largely flat land scores of times, often turning the pleasant countryside into a scarred, ghastly ruin.

Struggle for Sovereignty. Only since 1830 has Belgium enjoyed national independence. After the legions of Caesar, came the Germanic Franks, followed by the successive Emperors. France next dominated the country under Louis XI and Napoleon Bonaparte. Then Wellington's armies arrived to crush Napoleon at the famous battle of Waterloo, after which the Dukes of Burgundy and the Spanish Hapsburgs had their turns at conquest. By the treaty of Utrecht in 1713 Belgium became Austrian, though retaining its autonomy. Incorporated into France in 1801, Belgium was reunited to Holland by the Congress of Vienna in 1815 as part of the Kingdom of the Netherlands. In this century two world wars have ravaged farms, wrecked the economy, and decimated the population. But with amazing energy and determination the Belgians have come back again and again to resume their place of importance in northern Europe. Today Belgium is a constitutional monarchy.

The Eclipse of Truth. While it is the noon hour of Belgium's material prosperity, her soul is in the darkest midnight. Over a million tourists are attracted to this country yearly. Most come to see the lovely spots in the Ardennes forest, to enjoy the rich Flemish art collections, or to visit picturesque medieval trading cities like Ghent or Bruges. Though British tourists are currently the most numerous and Americans rank fourth, it is doubtful if either realizes the ignorance, darkness, and superstition that lie beneath the glittering surface of Belgian life. But once the Christian visitor turns from the bustle of the national scene to examine the facts, he is often shocked. How tragic that nearby Britain should fail to share the spiritual heritage she has received! Equally sad is the fact that American business interests in Belgium far overshadow her spiritual ones. Most of the output of Belgium's uranium mines in Africa is bought by the United States, while great concerns like General Motors, Bell Telephone, International Harvester, and others have extensive investments there. But the most powerful nation in the world has done too little to evangelize a land that is spiritually bankrupt. As will be seen in the pages that follow, there are legitimate and successful missionary endeavors in Belgium that claim an interest from the foreign Christian. Then we must face the still unfinished task of evangelizing the masses who have never heard that Christ died and rose again for their salvation.

Life's Daily Round. How do the Belgians live? They work hard and are heavily taxed. Politics interests the average man, while his wife is fond of a cozy home. In the shops along the main streets of Brussels or Antwerp, one sees such a variety of luxurious articles for sale that he could almost imagine himself in America. Yet many of these items are too high priced for most Belgians, who obtain them only with some sacrifice. For diversion these people love sports and beer-drinking. To stop in at one of the country's thousands of bars and cafés on the way home from work is the habit of most men. For many couples an evening out, even accompanied by their children, is spent in a café drinking beer. Belgium leads the world in its per capita consumption of beer, with the average adult consuming thirty-seven quarts a year. These are a class-conscious people, too, with a distinct aristocracy. From moneyed class to laboring man all love to observe the important events of life with a flair, whether it be first communion, marriage, or just a party. Putting up a front to others is an important, though often expensive, indulgence.

2. *CATHOLIC DOMINATION*

Two Poles of Influence. Belgium is considered one of the most Catholic countries in Europe and the world. Most writers who describe conditions in this land simply state in so many words that Belgium is completely Catholic. Although we will show that this solidarity is not so total as is assumed, it is still true that Catholicism, though often only half-heartedly believed and practiced, moulds the mentality of the people from birth to death. Today Roman leadership is centered in two Flemish towns, neither of which is in Flanders proper. Malines (or Mechelen) is in the province of Antwerp, while Louvain (or Leuven) is in Brabant. Although French is used both in the Catholic center at Malines and in the Catholic University of Louvain, both towns are really Flemish-speaking.

Malines, where once the court of the remarkable Princess of Austria flourished, is also well known as the seat of the Cardinal Archbishops of the country. Here in a white palace surrounded by trees and gardens are

masterminded the moves of national ecclesiastical strategy. It is here too
that the present struggle against the socialist government of Belgium is
planned. The hierarchy at Malines directs the work of 15,000 priests—one
for every 574 inhabitants—and almost 60,000 nuns, as well as the activity
of hundreds of institutions and organizations. Look at this comparison.
Belgium, with only 2 per cent of the World's Catholics, has 4.5 per cent
of the world's priests. But Latin America, with 37 per cent of the world's
Catholics, has only 9 per cent of the world's priests.* With this kind of
administrative structure, it is not difficult to keep the homeland in spiritual
chains. All together there are about seven hundred monasteries and three
thousand convents. Foreign missionaries sent out by the Belgian church
total more than seven thousand.

But Louvain, as the center of militant Catholic culture, is hardly less
important. Since the Roman Church feels it has a right to mould the
political, economic, and social minds of its members, an indoctrination
center is essential. The Catholic University at Louvain is that mould.
Even though the library of the university was twice destroyed in the two
world wars, rapid replacement of many volumes has made it once again
one of the great documentation points of the continent. Volumes and
publications found only here are almost as important to the Belgian,
Dutch, and French churches as they were in the sixteenth century. Too
much cannot be said about the importance of this center of learning as a
place for incubation of ideas in Belgium and in Europe. By training
most of the men who eventually occupy the highest places in public life,
Louvain can well be called the cradle of Catholicism in this crossroads
country.

Urban Retrenchment. When one turns from Roman theory to its
practice, a much different picture is often encountered. In a report they
called *La Mèche Qui Fume*, "The Smoking Flax," investigators recently
told of the results of their visits to five thousand families in a crowded
quarter of Brussels. Some of their findings about the state of the faith
in the capital city are astounding. Only one fourth of those interviewed
attended mass on Easter, the minimum observance necessary to maintain
any active status in the church. To the question, Who is Jesus Christ?
here were some of the people's answers: "He is on a cross." "He is the
Sacred Heart." In answer to the question, "Will you baptize your new
baby?" one family said, "No, that's not necessary. But of course we shall
have a party and name a godfather and godmother." Another family
defended a Catholic who attended no services with these words: "He is

*In Argentina there is one priest for 4,631 Catholics; in Brazil, one for 6,741; in
Cuba, one for 7,786; in the Dominican Republic, one for 12,701; and in Guatemala,
one for 28,801.

surely a Catholic, because every time he puts on a clean shirt he makes the sign of the cross." The investigators blamed three sources for the growing indifference of the masses: (1) the city schools, (2) Marxism, (3) the cinema. (Is it a discredit to Protestantism that *it* was not named as a problem?) Summing up their survey in these words, the writers said, "Our working men are being de-Christianized. . . . In a parish of 5,000 families, 90 per cent live in complete indifference and ignorance of Christianity. . . . Marriage has lost almost all of its religious character. . . . As for the first communion, the celebration at home is so important that the sacrament is forgotten."[1] Since the Roman Church regards observance of the sacrament at the time of marriage as necessary for salvation, it seems evident that the hold of the church, though still strong, is not what it once was. In publicizing its great spectacles the Roman Church would have the public and foreigners believe it to be an impregnable fortress, but cracks like this are beginning to show in the foundations themselves. Having said this, we must quickly add that Belgium is still formidably Catholic. Only the power of the Holy Spirit can bring either practicing or indifferent Romanists to the knowledge of the Lord Jesus Christ.

The Facade of Festivals. All over the world the pilgrimages and processions of the Roman Church are its greatest means of propaganda, and Belgium is no exception. Its people know nothing else, yet yearn for something better. Spectacles like the Adoration of the Black Virgin of Halle and the Pageant of the Sacred Blood at Bruges are good examples of the facade. On special days as many as 40,000 people arrive at the Halle station to seek the special healing powers of the Black Virgin. Even more watch the Sacred Blood Procession, one of the most famous in all Europe. Bruges is the quaint medieval trading center of 52,000 people, during the fourteenth and fifteenth centuries the most important commercial city in all of Europe. Here the magnificient court of Burgundy favored the arts during the golden era of palaces, guild houses, and cathedral construction. At the same time the renowned Flemish school of painters—van Eyck, van der Goes, Gerard David, and others—were producing their masterpieces in the region.

Beginning on the morning of the first Monday after May 2, the annual procession of Bruges begins to wind through the ancient streets choked with huge crowds of tourists and pilgrims. As the relic containing the magic blood passes by, the faithful often kneel in the streets, leaving unbelievers conspicuously standing. For centuries, failure to kneel meant seizure and death. But today Belgian Protestants considering the procession a fine opportunity to spread the gospel, distribute literature despite the veiled hostility of the crowd. The Sacred Blood Procession dates from the Second Crusade. Derrick (or Theodoric) of Alsace, Count of Flanders, was regarded as having shown unusual bravery during that crusade. In recognition of this, the Patriarch of Jerusalem gave him a vessel supposedly containing several drops of the blood of Christ. When the count brought the relic back to Bruges in 1150, Leo, then Abbot of St. Bertin, put it in the Basilica of St. Basil, where it has been venerated ever since. Held aloft in an elaborate reliquary, the drops of blood can be seen on a linen cloth in a tubular gold and glass receptacle about nine inches long and two inches in diameter. The true believer in Jesus Christ, while thankful for the infinitely precious blood shed for his salvation, is revolted by the thought of pagan worship of what could only be at best a symbol. Ignorant idolatry by those who do not know the cleansing power of that blood calls for Christians to proclaim the truth in this darkened, needy land.

In 1956, at the 806th anniversary of the Procession, the writer observed posters in Bruges offering many indulgences to worshippers of the Sacred Blood relic, among which were one hundred days for each veneration (limited to a single day) during the two-week period in May. Thus Catholics who would perform this veneration daily for the fourteen days would receive 1,400 days' (a little over three years) indulgence from the terrors of purgatory. But what is this little period out of a long eternity? It is by such promises that pressure is exerted upon the seemingly devoted thousands who attend the famous ceremonies. Fear, not love, motivates these pilgrims.

The same can be said of the Procession of Penitents at Furnes, held on the last Sunday in July. Spanish in origin, this festival features black-hooded "penitents" who carry heavy crosses to stimulate in onlookers a spirit of repentance.

Much Made of Mary. "I believe that the Virgin Mary has more to say than God," said a Belgian woman, "because she performs all the miracles, while God performs none." This poor woman speaks for the majority of her countrymen, whose faith may be epitomized by this inscription seen on the wall of the Church of St. Antonius in Ghent: "Mary is appointed to dispense all graces." The adoration of Mary, on the increase throughout the world, is especially noticeable in Belgium. "On the official side," said the late Dr. O. Van Steenberghe, "the cult of Mary is being fostered with all the means at the disposal of the Roman hierarchy."[2] One Belgian mother put the appeal of Mary in this way: "As a mother, she can understand what we women have to go through all alone." Can this partly explain the tenacious loyalty of Catholic women in many countries where their attendance forms the backbone of Roman strength? Indeed, this very claim is made in *The Glories of Mary,* where Rome suggests the prayer, "Through thee, O Mary, we have been reconciled to God," and "O Lady in Heaven, we have one advocate, and that is thyself."[3]

What a tragedy that in this strategic land the mother of Jesus should have more honor than her Son! One has only to watch the Procession of the Virgins at Wavre to be filled with pitying love for the disillusioned who attend. Attracting the very highest Church patronage in the land, this pageant features the statue of the local virgin. But many other virgin statues are brought from every corner of the country too. As the bearers wind through the streets, multitudes kneel in grossest idolatry, ignoring the One who commanded, "Thou shalt have no other gods before me."

Paganism in Catholic Dress. It is difficult to believe that the gateway country to northern Europe, so intimately in contact with every cultural and scientific advance, can likewise be so full of dark superstition. Here is an example. A woman in deep sorrow because of her husband's illness, and seeking help for him, was instructed by a priest to transplant 230 plants to her garden, kneeling at each planting to repeat the prayer, "Lord, have pity on my husband and heal him." She had been told that the transplanting of the plants was something she was to do for God in order to persuade Him to help her husband. Is this not paganism? Is there an essential difference between this scene and the one where the primitive African puts fetishes in his garden to ward off evil spirits and assure good crops? Fortunately for this particular woman, while she was carefully following the priest's instructions, a Christian worker called on her, showed her the folly of her actions, and pointed her to Christ. Later he witnessed to the husband, who also came to know the Saviour.

It is surprising to find here much of the same traffic in holy objects so common in Spain, Portugal, and Italy. People will quickly pay a small sum for the special cords and knots of St. Joseph, made by nuns for the relief of kidney diseases and other ailments. In many places automobiles are blessed in the name of St. Christopher, patron saint of travel. On April 23, St. George's Day, special attention is given to this patron of horses. Since St. George is also the personal guardian saint of the little Brabant village of Grey-Doiceau, all the draft horses in the region are ridden into this town for a special blessing by a priest standing before an altar erected on a farmer's cart. During the Wastia procession, held in June at Wavre, a fifty-five-pound loaf of bread, garlanded with flowers, is paraded through the streets. Though pagan in origin, the ceremony which then follows is supported and blessed by the church. After remaining in the church edifice for a time, the loaf is cut up and pieces passed out to those seeking protection against hydrophobia, while the flowers are kept for good luck.

Especially pagan are the bonfires of St. John's Eve (June 24), when flames gleam across the Walloon countryside. This custom has roots in ancient Babylon, but is now recognized by the church. In one form or another St. John's Eve ceremonies are celebrated across all of Europe. Here in Belgium it is believed that because good and evil spirits are abroad during the night, good children must stay at home, where they will be safe from the kiss of the werewolf. Druid observances, too, introduced centuries before by Scandinavian invaders, still linger in Belgium. Legend says, for example, that during the thirteenth century, on Trinity Sunday at Walcourt, a statue of the Madonna miraculously escaped destruction by fire. It refused to leave its refuge in the trees until a local chevalier promised to provide an abbey ir its honor. The tradition of the Madonna statue of Walcourt accounts for a custom observed annually in the region. Every year a tree is cut down and its pieces distributed to those who desire good luck during the coming year. Ceremonial tree-burning takes place at Grammont, where at nightfall on a small hill the entire population witnesses the signal for the lighting of beacon fires on the plains below. These customs involving trees, Druid in origin, have been taken up by the Roman Church in Belgium and used to blind the common people still more.

Though such observances may seem but innocent folklore practiced for the delight of tourists, they are actually taken seriously by the participants. So carefully has Satan mingled pagan practices, ages old, with his modern half-Christian gospel, that the mixture gives a clever, temporary surcease to those seeking peace. The dependence of the masses on such deceit only pulls the chains of slavery stronger and tighter. Jesus Christ alone can deliver from this twentieth-century delusion. In Belgium "truth is fallen in the street," where people would say if they could, "We grope for the wall like the blind, and we grope as if we had no eyes: we stumble at noon day as in the night; we are in desolate places as dead men" (Isa. 59:14, 10).

New Interest in the Old Book. History has shown that God is always at work even in the darkest situations. Especially is this true when His Word is put in the hands of any people. The late Dr. O. Van Steenberghe, writing of the revival of interest in the Bible in Belgium, says:

> The Roman Catholic Church is now witnessing a growing interest in the Bible. . . . In 1939 I came in contact with two Benedictine monks who loved the Word of God and carried a Protestant version

with them all the time. This first contact was followed by many more. The subject of our conversation was invariably the Word of God. I was able to tell them of a work of the Holy Spirit through the reading of the Bible in a poor community in their very neighborhood. It was easy for them to discover the power of the Word as described in Hebrews 4:12 and manifest almost at the very gates of their abbey. These men came to me later and asked whether the British and Foreign Bible Society would allow them to use the Second version of the French Bible as a test for a Catholic version they intended to publish. I wrote to the Bible Society, which immediately granted the request. Unfortunately the war upset this plan. But another Benedictine abbey took up the work, and the result is the Maredsous Bible . . . in 1950 another version was published by this abbey which by July, 1954, was in its fifth addition, totalling 123,000 sales.[4]

What motive would lead Catholics to place a Book in the hands of their people which could set them free from their bonds? Van Steenberghe says, "It is safe to say that the nation-wide distribution of the Word of God by Protestants has created a hunger which the Roman Church can no longer ignore. Last summer a Bible exhibition was arranged in Brussels by the Maredsous abbey and is now being shown throughout Belgium and France. The main interest of the exhibit centered in twenty-four panels which had been carefully prepared to show the story of the Bible and the human means which have been used to preserve, translate, and distribute it."[5] One of the panels gives eight Protestant leaders out of a total sixteen, including Luther and Tyndale! A second panel honors the Bible societies in the following words: "The Reformed Church, from its origin in the sixteenth century, but mainly during the last 150 years, has given rise to an unbelievable distribution of the Bible in the world. The British and Foreign Bible Society was the first of these. Born in 1804 of the conviction of a number of London business men that the Bible must be brought within reach of every man, this society accomplished a remarkable work. In the Catholic Church the Bible has remained dormant, but in our day it is witnessing a marvelous revival."[6]

In the light of the many papal denunciations of the Bible societies mentioned elsewhere in this book, such compliments are indeed amazing. Equally surprising is the action of Catholics in giving the Bible to their people so freely. But such moves, considered in the light of the past, are not always as altruistic as they seem. It times of declension the Roman Church has sometimes authorized Bible reading, only to condemn it again when the interest of the readers became too aroused. But God can make even the malevolent designs of Him enemies serve Him. The Christian friend of Belgium would do well to intercede for all who read the Bible there, regardless of its version or imprint. Then the Holy Spirit will be able to bring light to those who live in darkness and the shadow of death.

Catholic-Socialist War. A war is raging in Belgium. It is an old one which has continued ever since the country became independent. Between the two armies is the child, pitiful object of the battle. During the monarchial dispute of 1950, and many times since, the clash between Catholics and Socialists has come to the attention of the whole world. Briefly, the issues are these: Catholics in Belgium often attach more political than spiritual significance to their religion. Or let us say that they feel free to use political weapons to gain spiritual ends—or vice versa. In this war all Belgians are either Catholic or anti-Catholic—there is no middle ground. Thus the Catholics violently oppose Socialist attacks on their cherished, fiercely-won school subsidies paid by the state. The *enseignement libre,* as the Catholic school system is called, can be attended as an alternative to the "public schools" run by the government. In recent years organized riots launched by the church in Brussels and other centers have ended in bloody police suppression. Since the Socialists are equally determined that state funds should be used to finance their own projects rather than Catholic causes, there is likely to be more violence in the future. Probably France's example, of remaining nominally Catholic while resisting the church's political aims, has influenced Belgian Socialists. As long as a Socialist regime remains in power, the climate of thought is more free in Belgium. Generally speaking, the Flemish are more Catholic and royalist, while the French Walloons are more anti-clerical and republican.

The Church of Rome naturally seeks to control the entire life and outlook of her people. In Belgium it even maintains clinics, so that a newborn child can be taken either to the state clinic or to a Catholic one run by sisters of one of the church orders. Later, when the child grows up and goes to work, he can join a union associated with the General Federation of Belgian Labor (Socialist) or one in the Confederation of Christian Unions (Catholic). Of course the Socialist argument against Catholics does not rest primarily on religious grounds, since many of its own followers are themselves nominal Catholics. But here is just another illustration of the deep tide of anticlerical dissatisfaction which surges through the heart of every Catholic country in Europe. Anyone who would understand the Belgian scene must study the Socialist-Catholic controversy which divides the people, and which has linguistic and regional overtones as well.

3. *THE PROTESTANT SCENE*

First Reformation Martyrs. The Belgian return to the Bible started
in the days when some men had to pay for their faith with pain-racked
bodies or flesh seared in the crackling flames. One of the first and most
earnest centers of the Lutheran Reform was the Augustinian convent at
Antwerp. Many of the monks there had passed some time in Wittenberg,
where they had met and heard Luther. Thus salvation by grace through
faith began to be taught zealously in Antwerp after 1519. So widespread
was the acceptance, that violent reaction soon set in. By October, 1522,
the convent was closed and most of its monks scattered, imprisoned, or
condemned to death. The few who escaped were pursued by tireless
inquisitors, who scoured the countryside relentlessly for them.

Among those Augustinians captured were three young men—Esch,
Voes, and Lambert. Led into the presence of the inquisitors in Brussels,
the three were offered their lives if they would renounce their Lord.
"Confess that you have been led astray by Luther," demanded their
opponents. The young men's answer was bold: "As the apostles were led
astray by Jesus Christ!" Since they refused to recant, condemnation quickly followed. "We declare you to be heretics," pronounced the court,
"worthy of being burned alive. We are turning you over to the secular
arm." Lambert, terrified at the prospect of a horrible death, asked respite
to consider his decision. In the end God gave him grace to follow his
companions in their triumph.

As the great Brussels square was being prepared for the burning of the
heretics, the condemned men sang psalms in the midst of the tightly
packed throng, pausing occasionally to declare, "We will die for the name
of Jesus Christ!" Such was their exalted joy and peace that even some
of the inquisitors wept. As the four-hour execution ceremony reached its
climax, with the mounting flames choking and searing the life from the
victims, one of the youths was heard to cry, "I seem to be lying on a bed
of roses!" Later the other fell on his knees, clasped what remained of his
hands, and worshiped his Lord with the words, "Lord Jesus, Son of
David, have mercy upon me." Singing the *Te Deum* with their last
agonizing gasp, both men died on July 1, 1523, as the first martyrs of the
Reformation. Shortly afterward the third, Lambert, also sealed his testimony with his death.

The news rocked Europe and strengthened the Protestant cause. "The
executions have begun!" exclaimed Erasmus, dismayed, but fearful to
venture his own life for the cause. "At last," said Luther, "Christ is
gathering some fruits of our preaching and is creating new martyrs."
These words he wrote to those who had escaped: "Your dungeons and
burning piles are mine. . . . We are all with you and the Lord is at our

head." Inspired to write a hymn to the first martyrs for the new faith, all mere youths, Luther sent these words ringing across the Lowlands and Germany, where many were soon singing them—

> No, no, their ashes shall not die,
> But borne to every land—
> Where'er their sainted dust shall lie—
> Up springs a holy band!

This prophecy was quickly fulfilled, for Erasmus tells us that in Brussels great throngs embraced the reformers' Christ as a result of the noble trio's martyrdom. There must have been a fourth with these three in the flames, in "the form of . . . a son of the gods" (Dan. 3:25 marg.).

A Glimpse of the Churches.   The Protestant church in Belgium has known a stormy history. While some six hundred congregations flourished in the country near the end of the sixteenth century, the energetic Duke of Alva almost wiped out the Reformation's success throughout the Lowlands. As the nineteenth century began, only seven churches remained. In 1807 these merged to form the *Union of Reformed Churches*, which had grown from its founding in 1839 to twenty-four congregations and 7,000 members by 1927. Today this group, as a state-recognized body, has thirty-three churches and preaching points. The Brussels seminary, as well as many of the pastors of this group, have shown liberal and neo-orthodox tendencies, although God has His people among them. In 1837 the *Christian Missionary Church* was founded under the influence of the British and Foreign Bible Society, its creed based on the conservative Belgic Confession of the sixteenth century. The group has fifty churches. *Methodists* have twenty-five places of worship directed by a general superintendent. This denomination joins several others in maintaining a small seminary in Brussels. Proportionately the Methodists in Belgium seem to have more strength than their French brethren, many of whose churches were merged into the French Reformed Church before the war.

Independent Baptists have two churches, while the *Baptist Union* has five, one of which is a Slavic congregation. There are only two *Lutheran Churches*, one *Liberal Church*, and one *Evangelical Free Church*. In addition, the *Pentecostal Church* and some foreign language Protestant churches exist. The *Belgian Gospel Mission*, with its more than sixty churches and annexes, represents the largest evangelical Protestant body. More will be said about this American-sponsored effort, which abstains from the Belgian Federation of Protestant Churches in order to maintain its evangelical position. *Plymouth Brethren* of both "closed" and "open" persuasion are also to be found in Belgium. Most Protestant efforts extend to both the Flemish and French districts of the country, some having more strength in the Flemish language areas, since five-eighths of the population speak that language by preference. The *Salvation Army,* though not a church, lends its usual help to the socially disinherited and maintains a witness for Christ in Belgium through seventeen centers.

Belgian Protestants have been beset with the same doctrinal difficulties others in Europe have faced. The theology of Karl Barth, while restraining some from extreme liberalism, has permitted others to doubt the inspired record of the Word of God. Neo-orthodox thought, with its many variations, remains the prevailing theology of the day, robbing many pastors of authority in their preaching while flattering the human intellect. Since not all pulpits are so affected, some laymen wholly believe in the Word of God and live the Christian life. But revival is sorely needed in doctrinally conservative churches themselves if the battle for the soul of Belgium is to be won. Uninformed Christians outside the Continent often mistakenly suppose that a small Protestant group in an overwhelmingly Catholic country is necessarily a disciplined witnessing body. The contrary is often true. Sometimes intimidated by the power of Rome, this minority develops an inferiority complex, which is deepened by other Satanic attacks. Consequently Protestants are often nominal and unregenerate, while many true believers have never been delivered from sin's thralldom and led by the Holy Spirit into a life of joyful witness.

It is not easy to live the Christian life in such countries. Prayer for the Christians and churches of Belgium would greatly strengthen the tempted, the timid, and the tired. If intercessors for Belgium will especially hold up her nucleus of true believers, these can accomplish much in the future. For has God not promised that "one man of you shall chase a thousand: for the Lord your God, he it is that fighteth for you"? (Josh. 23:10) An important subject for prayer is the provision of shepherds for God's people and evangelists for winning the lost. Reduced to a present 250 (some of them liberal) from about six hundred in the sixteenth century, the present proportion of Protestant pastors to the population is one to 37,546 people.*

Bible Distribution Succeeds. The number of Bibles sold today through the Belgian Bible Society is double the 1939 figure and five times that of 1936. The steady rise of sales indicates a growing hunger. Statistics furnished by other agencies distributing Scriptures tend to confirm this trend. Naturally the distribution of Testaments and portions runs even higher.

It is a heartening thing to see the Bible for sale in bookstores, kiosks, and other places in the country. As one Christian worker put it, "It must

*In America there is a ratio of about one pastor to five hundred people.

certainly be a thorn in the flesh of the Romanist to see the New Testament without the *Imprimateur* (Catholic stamp of approval) publicly displayed all over a city where once the sale of a Bible meant possible death at the stake." Because faithful colporteurs have been pushing the sale of the Bible for some years, today's victories are possible.

Anglo-Saxon Christians owe an immeasurable debt to one who died on this very soil to help bring them their Bible. He was the Englishman, William Tyndale, the saintly scholar, the "morning star of the Reformation," and translator of the Bible into English. Hounded out of England by Sir Thomas More, who called him "that beast," the gentle Tyndale labored in Antwerp for several years on his celebrated translation. For a time it seemed that he might survive despite the feeling against him, for the Reformation was spreading rapidly and more tolerance seemed likely. Although he lived under the protection of a group of powerful English merchants in Europe's leading commercial city, around him was acute danger. In October, 1529, Emperor Charles V proclaimed that "the reading, purchase, or possession of any proscribed books, or any New Testaments prohibited by the theologians of Louvain; attendance at any meeting of heretics, disputing about the Holy Scriptures, want of due respect to the images of God and the saints" were to be considered crimes for which "men were to be beheaded, women buried alive, and the relapsed burnt." Still it was the long arm of the English Church which finally reached Tyndale. He was strangled, and his body was burned at the Castle of Vilvorde, near Brussels, on October 6, 1536.

By heavenly design this city of Antwerp, scene of some of Tyndale's consecrated toil to bring us the English Bible, is today the center of Flanders' celebrated "Bible Day" activities. Every May first since 1936 the largest interdenominational meeting of Flemish Protestants has occurred here. On this national labor holiday thousands of believers, from all five Flemish-speaking provinces gather for rallies and the distribution of Bibles and literature. In the past, even the Belgian national radio has helped in announcing the meetings. One year, more than 200,000 gospel magazines, like *Open Poort* ("the Open Gate") and *De Kruisbanier* ("The Banner of the Cross"), were distributed in the homes. Processions of families that know Christ in Flanders march through Antwerp's streets hundreds strong. A high percentage of pastors from the evangelical churches all over Belgium have participated in observance of Bible Day. If William Tyndale, who once walked these same streets, could be in Antwerp on Bible Day, he would rejoice to see what the Bible he loved so much has accomplished. Once again God is having the last word!

In 1955 the Belgian Bible Society and other organizations celebrated the 500th anniversary of the printing of the Gutenberg Bible. The rediscovery only recently of Belgium's only copy of this first printed Bible has aroused much public interest. During one week of that year all Brussels taxis bore a pennant with the words: "The Bible—the Book of Hope." At the same time posters advertising the Bible were put up all over Belgium. From October 29 to November 6 of the same year a Bible exhibition was held in the Fine Arts Palace of Brussels, ending in a giant demonstration in a large auditorium on Sunday night. Under the patronage of the Queen, who attended in person, much attention was drawn to the occasion by the nation's press. Only fifty years before, Bible colporteurs from England had been stoned and savagely opposed for distributing "the Protestant Book." This victory for the Word that "shall not pass away" was resounding. The Belgian Gospel Mission, which has distributed twenty million pieces of gospel literature since 1918, says: "Thirty-five years ago, when our mission started its activities in Belgium, the Word of God was a book unknown and feared by millions of people. Today it is hailed by a growing number as their most precious possession."[7]

The Seed Planted. When asked how he came to found the Belgian Gospel Mission, Mr. Ralph Norton used to answer, "The mission was founded in London in my pockets." Detained in that city in 1914 by the war, Norton began to meet Belgian soldiers as they came into Victoria Station on leave. His pockets bulging with gospels and tracts in Flemish and French, the tireless personal worker would witness for Christ with a special love for these men. In this manner more than one million tracts found their way into Belgian camps. Next, a center was opened in London where many soldiers came to the Lord. At war's end Norton was urged to come to Belgium, where he arrived in December, 1918. After the organization of a home committee, with Dr. Charles Trumbull of *The Sunday School Times* as chairman, the work began in earnest. Dutch, Swiss, British and American workers were added. When Norton died in 1926, he left the imposing headquarters and Bible school building in Brussels, some preaching centers, and sixty workers, who had already distributed thirteen million pieces of literature.

Teaching Them To Observe. Those who minimize the work of American foreign missions in Europe should study the impact of the Belgian Gospel Mission on one little land. Take its Bible institute at Brussels, for example, where courses are given in both French and Flemish. Here more than 200 students have been trained since its founding in 1919. Some one-fourth of the 250 Protestants and evangelists at work in Belgium have studied here. About half of this number are engaged in leading the mission's own churches; still others are at work in the Republic of Congo and elsewhere.

The emphasis on Bible teaching has proved more than wise. By indoctrinating young converts in the Word, this mission has been able to lay a foundation for future generations. Often such work seems slow, and something less than sensational. Those engaged in it are not "harvesting" in an obvious way. But by preparing the harvesters, they are faithful to the divine counsel of II Tim. 2:2, "And the things that thou hast heard of me among many witnesses, the same commit thou to faithful men, who shall be able to teach others also." Not only have there been day school classes through these years, but evening and correspondence courses as well.

Some recent student testimonies are interesting. One young man, who came from a difficult home, says:

> You may remember that a year ago I told you that I was coming here against my parents' wishes. [They are Communists.] I asked you to pray for them, for they had told me never to come home again. This summer I found a job near my home and boarded with a Christian family. When I went to my home, Father relented enough to speak to me. Mother said that she saw a great change in me and that I seemed to be doing well. It was really a miracle, she said. She even mentioned the name of God twice. Keep on praying for my parents.[8]

Another student, a Frenchman, speaks of his conversion and guidance to study at the Institute:

> After painful experiences as a boy in France, I decided that there was no reality in religion and called myself an atheist. Four years ago I came across a Bible in a bookstore. I had heard other people refer to it as a mysterious book, so bought a copy to help pass the time. The Holy Spirit spoke to me as I read, and I became convicted that it was the truth. At this time I was sent to Indo-China for military service. The great danger drove me closer to God and I promised to serve Him if He would deliver me from that situation. Soon after this, I was able to return to Europe. A Christian friend advised me to come to the Brussels Bible Institute.[9]

A traveling Christian dropping in on the Belgian Gospel Mission headquarters will find himself in a beehive of activity for Christ. Almost every conceivable kind of witness is going out from this center, but not all of it can be seen. A staff of seventeen are at work in the large structure of more than eighty rooms in Brussels. On these premises a bookstore sells literature in both official languages as well as in others, the Bible institute carries on its work, mission administrative offices function, and editors prepare written material for publication. The official organs of the mission in French and Flemish editions are published here, and a large church auditorium serves congregations in the two languages. An effective innovation is the trailer church, a mobile auditorium designed by John Winston, Jr. and ingeniously built on a truck chassis, which folds out to accommodate many listeners. Through the use of the trailer church and tents, many evangelistic campaigns are carried on all over Belgium. Souls come in sufficient numbers to encourage the workers, but "what are these few among so many?"

The mission's principal work lies in its sixty-seven member churches and preaching points scattered throughout the nine Belgian provinces. A staff of ninety-six, including wives, serve in this part of the work. Of these forty-six are Belgian, the rest of other nationalities. There are other outposts, too, which will eventually become churches. The Belgian Gospel Mission owns thirty-eight properties and rents eleven halls. To deepen the spiritual life of church members, annual Bible conferences are held each year in Brussels (in French) and in Ghent (in Flemish). A healthy emphasis on indigenous methods is now coming to the fore. These churches are doubly important because each one can increasingly become a center of light and witness for its own area. Only as each is made a self-sustaining witness can "every creature" hear in this country. A transformed life seen and puzzled over by the neighbors is still the greatest human argument there is for the power of the gospel of Jesus Christ.

Salvation for Some. The redemptive Word is bearing fruit in this country, as it is everywhere else where it is proclaimed. We mention just one unusual conversion as an example of the power of Christ to transform sinners in Belgium. After World War II a young Belgian from near the German border languished in his prison cell. He had been tried and condemned to death for atrocious crimes, including murder, treason, and espionage. After joining the German SS troops early in the war, he had been sent into Russia with the Nazi attackers. Later, in Belgium and Holland, he took part in gruesome massacres of his own people upon the orders of his foreign masters. One would scarcely have thought that such a hardened conscience could ever be touched by anyone or anything. Filled with bitterness, this weakling awaited execution and a hoped-for oblivion. But the sight which finally touched him was that of a fellow prisoner praying. A little unnerved but interested, the condemned man was then contacted by a Protestant pastor. "Sir," he said earnestly to Pastor Overdulve, "I know that I shall be condemned to die; but I want to be able to die praying, as this other prisoner will do. Is that possible? What must I do?" Led to a knowledge of forgiveness through Jesus Christ the condemned man rejoiced in a full salvation. "Because the Mediator shed His blood," he testified, "I believe in God's pardon for my sins."

Many others who have found the Lord Jesus have had a whole life to give for His service. The evangelization of the masses, the instruction of converts, and an intensive training in leadership for specially called young people is the triple task to be accomplished in Belgium. Perhaps some may think that the Protestant forces there are sufficient to accomplish this task, though their numbers are few. As has been pointed out, the contribution of some is questionable. And since Belgium has only a few pastors and evangelists, there is legitimate room for much foreign missionary activity in this land. Such ministry is needed for the strengthening and encouragement of the churches and believers who are faithful to the Lord and to His Word.

The Stranger Within the Gates. Only a few of the many thousands of foreigners in the land are hearing the gospel of grace. Some fifty thousand Italians and thirty thousand Slavs live in Belgium, as well as those of other nationalities. Many work in the coal pits as miners to help meet the need of labor manpower. Except for the expatriate Poles and Russians, who have a few churches, there is little opportunity for the foreigner in Belgium to find the way of salvation. The Italians have been responsive, however, where they have had the opportunity to hear the gospel. At Dour, in the heart of the mining district, about twenty are attending Italian meetings at a preaching station of the Belgian Gospel Mission.

One of these Italians has a particularly fine testimony. After falling sick with the dread miners' tuberculosis, he was given six months' leave to recover in his native mountain village in Italy. As soon as his parents learned of his new faith in Christ, however, they asked him and his family to look for other lodgings. Determined to witness in the village, the miner called upon the local priest, who refused to see him. Then he went higher, and called on the canon of a nearby cathedral. For six hours they talked, comparing the Roman system with the Scriptures point by point. When the canon bid the happy miner goodbye, he said, with tears in his eyes, "You are on the right road and may continue to give your testimony in the village. But please do not say anything against the Catholic Church." With this assurance, the miner began to hold a weekly meeting for interested friends and a daily meeting for children. Conversions followed one after the other. When his six months of sick leave were up, the fiery Italian had on his hands a living church of born-again people. Visiting the nearest group of believers at Modena, twenty-six miles away, he put in their hands the responsibility for his new believers. Now he and his family are back at work in Belgium, strengthened by his experience.

Another young man joined the Belgian church in Braine-le-Compte. This one, a Yugoslav, had seen his foster-parents killed by the Germans in his native country when he was fourteen. He was then sent to work in the iron mines of Germany, where the work was very heavy. One day an ore wagon ran over him, crushing one arm so badly that it had to be amputated. While still under hospital care, he contrived to escape to France. But there he was sent to prison when police found he had no passport or visa. For eight years he lived in prisons in France and Belgium. Finally a Belgian lawyer became interested and procured for him a temporary identity card and admittance to a home for disabled soldiers. Now a possessor of eternal life, the young Yugoslav is rejoicing in the Lord in spite of his troubles and taking part in the church activities in Braine-le-Compte.

In the Borinage and other coal-mining areas, multiplied thousands have never heard the Word of God. What will be done for the teeming cities we have already mentioned? There remain the people in the densely populated countryside as well. Who will tell these lost souls of the saving grace of God? Here in the northern part of Europe lies a whole modern mission field needing Christ. How long must Belgians perish because English and American believers fail to pray for them and take an active part in their rescue? "Why do we sit still" (Jer. 8:14) when "the whole land is made desolate, because no man layeth it to heart?" (12:11)

4. *LUXEMBURG NEEDS CHRIST*

Scenery and Steel. It has been said that the Grand Duchy of Luxemburg presents one great problem to map-makers—how to print so long a name in so short a space! This county-sized land in the center of western Europe has a population of only 300,000 people, living in a area of 999 square miles. Luxemburg is famous, incidentally, for having the highest automobile accident rate in the world. But the spiritual need of this country is so great that we are taking more space than its size seems to warrant in order to present the need. The Grand Duchy, which has played a role in history far out of proportion to her size, is chiefly known to outsiders as a tourist mecca. American soldiers came to know its friendly people during wartime service; ten thousand died there, mostly through von Rundstedt's counterattack. Today tourists visit the graves of these soldiers in the large United States Military Cemetery at Hamm, three miles from Luxemburg City. If ten thousand of America's young and strong offered their lives for a corruptible crown in Luxemburg, are there not even a handful who would follow the orders of Christ, their Commander-in-Chief, to preach the gospel to these people?

Along the Our and Sure rivers on the northeast border are rugged, wild highlands dotted with many castles, some a thousand years old. Through the central valleys lie rich farmlands, in contrast to the vast industrial installations of the south. In this latter area are the plants which have made Luxemburg the tenth largest producer of steel in the world. Her cosmopolitan people usually speak several languages, though the most common is Letzeburgesch, a dialect as different from German as it is from Dutch. But schooling in French and German have made the people proficient in at least one of these languages, and many speak English as well. Except for the everyday dialect, German is really the best understood tongue. Though this country is closely tied to Belgium economically and politically, and is skirted by France, Belgium, and Germany, it manages to maintain its individuality and independence. The one large metropolis, Luxemburg City, is the capital and center of the country's culture, as well as its tourist headquarters.

Life Amid War and Insecurity. Since Caesar's legions subdued the Gauls and Germani tribes of this area in 52 B.C., Luxemburg has been invaded countless times. Traded back and forth under local or foreign rulers, her people have never known real security. From 1443 to 1815 these powers occupied the land: Burgundy, Spain, France, Spain again, Austria, then France a second time. Later Belgium and Prussia had their turns at ruling, under the terms of the Congress of Vienna. Only in October, 1868, did the Grand Duchy finally receive the full constitutional liberty it enjoys today. But twice since then has Luxemburg's freedom been interrupted—by German occupation during both world wars. On May 10, 1940, the second German offensive overran the nation in a few short hours. Occupation policies proved grim and pitiless, as the great steel plants went on twenty-four-hour shifts, seven days a week, to produce Nazi munitions. French, an official language for more than eight hundred years, was outlawed.

When Luxemburgers refused to annex their country to the Reich or to serve in the German army, the Gestapo answered by sending more than sixteen thousand to concentration camps or prisons. Other thousands were drafted into work battalions or impressed into the enemy armed forces. Among three thousand of these latter captured in Russia, about 90 per cent have never been heard of since. Finally, on February 13, 1944, the country was cleared of enemy troops, but years of hard work have been needed to restore things to normal.

Catholic Solidarity. To this picture of past and present struggle must be added one of spiritual darkness. Some 95 per cent of the country's population are Roman Catholic. So nearly complete is the domination of the Roman Church that some have called Luxemburg the principal Catholic stronghold of Europe. However that may be, there is, also, the usual high percentage of indifferent Roman Catholics. As one Protestant worker who knows the country put it, "While the proportion of loyal Catholics is high, yet there are few places in Europe where so many who profess the faith are so dissatisfied and openly critical of their church."

Church bells seem to ring unceasingly throughout the Grand Duchy, and almost as many crosses and flower-bedecked shrines are to be seen here as in French Normandy or Brittany. Though the sophisticated person here may seem less superstitious than the peasant who makes the sign of the cross over his bread before cutting it, he is often as truly Roman. Among the festivals, the *Springprozession* at Eternach attracts the largest crowds of pilgrims. Here on Whit Tuesday some twenty-five thousand pilgrims from Germany, France, and Luxemburg gather for the celebrations dedicated to St. Willibrod. (He was the English missionary to the Ardennes who founded the Benedictine Abbey there in the seventh century, and whose remains are buried in the local basilica of Eternach.) On the morning of the first feast day a seven-ton bell, presented by the Emperor Maximilian, begins to toll as the procession winds through the streets. To the accompaniment of music and dancing this prayer is chanted: "Holy Willibrod, founder of churches, light of the blind, destroyer of idols, pray for us." Use of the water from St. Willibrod's fountain in the church as well as the chanting of the prayer itself are supposed to result in miraculous cures. The rocky pulpit of another early English missionary may be seen at Clervaux, in the Ardennes. Here St. Hubert is said to have preached in the seventh century: later he became the patron saint of hunters.

Doubtless the most important shrine in the land is that of Our Lady of Luxemburg, in the capital city. As chief protectress of the Grand Duchy, the Virgin's statue is credited with having saved the city from former plagues, sieges, and famines. Between the third and fifth Sundays after Easter the well-known Octave celebrations begin at this spot. Thousands of pilgrims on foot parade through the streets chanting prayers for the continued help of the Virgin. At the close the Madonna's statue is carried on a flower-decorated vehicle from the cathedral through the streets of the city.

Here is still another country lying in the grip of the world's largest single religion. Few indeed have heard that men can become "the children of God" only "*by faith* in Christ Jesus" (Gal. 3:26). Instead, most of the people are fettered by superstitions little better than the original paganism from which the seventh-century English catholic missionaries first delivered them. No doubt conditions in this country are not helped by the nearness of Belgium and France, but if anything, Luxemburg is more Catholic than either of those countries. Though her people have emigrated all over the civilized world, the homeland has had but little gospel light. Some Luxemburgers abroad have heard the gospel and have been saved, but at home there is little chance to discover the truth. Who will bring the gospel to these accessible, friendly, literate, intelligent but lost souls in the twentieth century?

Limited Protestant Efforts. A tradition of freedom of worship exists here, and the people have a tolerant spirit. Besides, the constitution guarantees religious freedom to all beliefs. The state supports, out of national funds, not only many Catholic priests but also a Jewish rabbi and the pastor of the sole Protestant church (Reform and Augsburg Confessions) in Luxemburg City. According to postal regulations, all mailboxes in the country may be freely used for tract or invitation distribution.

However, Roman Catholic resistance could change all this. Any new aggressive Protestant work would likely meet opposition. A militant public evangelistic program, for example, would probably bring reaction from local authorities backed by the priests. But such a program has never really been attempted in modern times.

It is not easy to learn how many Protestants there are, as some families are in isolated villages outside the capital. One source says that they total only 3,500. The forebears of a few Protestant families, in several different localities, became Protestant during the Reformation. How many of all the Protestants in the country are true believers would be difficult to judge. One foreign observer, an evangelical, put the figure at several hundred. In any case, the nominal Protestants come to only about one-tenth of one per cent of the whole population.

Evangelization by outsiders is negligible, but it has been effective when tried. In 1955 all the 155 reserved poster sites in Luxemburg were twice covered with gospel text posters by a worker of the Greater Europe Mission. Subsequently the proportionate number of requests for free New Testaments, promised on the posters, surpassed those received in France from similar efforts. This indicates a hunger for spiritual understanding among the population. Delivery of Testaments was turned over to the resident Mennonite workers in order to assure personal contact.

The only foreign Protestant missionaries known to live and work in Luxemburg, three American Mennonite families, are laboring in Diekirch, Dudelange, and Esch-sur-Sure. As this is written, the activity of these Americans is limited to Sunday meetings in their own homes, personal witness, and children's work. Those at Esch are teaching children handicraft in weekly classes as a means of contact. Then each year they invite some of these children to a Bible camp held just over the border on French soil. All these workers are using the German language as the one best adapted to their task, although French is also understood by many in their areas.

Luxemburg desperately needs Christ. She must learn of a living Saviour, for the only one she knows is dead on a crucifix. Must these who live in a neglected corner of Europe die without the Saviour? No doubt God would honor and use any who trusted Him for grace to take the gospel to the lost of little Luxemburg.

The city of Vienna seen from the café on top of Hochhaus. In the background are the cupola of St. Charles' Church (left) and the spires of St. Stephan's (right). Vienna contains a third of the Austrian population.

Chapter 9

AUSTRIA FORGOTTEN

"Why don't foreign Christians do more to help us? We need workers more than money. Doesn't anybody care?"
—An Austrian Protestant Pastor

Gemutlichkeit Without Gluckseligkeit. Austria is much like Switzerland in appearance and atmosphere. Here is another of the smaller European states which "has everything" but a widespread knowledge of the Lord. Of German-speaking lands Austria is the most bereft spiritually. But foreign Christians do not think of the Maine-sized republic as a mission field simply because they do not know the facts. They do not know, for instance, that 95 per cent of the people profess to be Roman Catholic. Since only a handful of foreign Christians are at work here alongside the Protestant minority, their missionary reports to the homeland make little impact in the face of other insistent demands on the churches. As a result the mountain-girt state is unthought of, unprayed for, and all but forgotten.

Few non-Europeans can place Austria, either in their minds or on their maps. Only seven million people live here, about one-third of them in greater Vienna. Deep into central Europe the tiny democracy thrusts its mountains and forests. On the east are enslaved Czechoslovakia, Hungary, and Yugoslavia; free Germany, Italy, Liechtenstein, and Switzerland lie to the west. Two-thirds of the country is covered by the Alps, and most of the rest is agricultural. Since 37 per cent of its surface is wooded, Austria is second only to Scandinavia in forested area. Industry is limited, though Austrians produce the world's largest amounts of magnesite and much oil. Essentially this Danube nation is a peasant one, with tourism as a prime business. The Austrian Alps, in many parts, are inaccessible and uncommercialized; some valleys are so remote that hotels there are small and infrequent, rural life is primitive, and contact with the outside world is negligible. But tourist regions like Vienna, the Salzburg area,

317

the Tyrol, Salzkammergut, and Carinthia are known all over the world. Along the arterial highway to Italy and from Germany armies of cars crawl unceasingly down into Innsbruck, then labor up over the Brenner Pass toward the sunny south. Highly regarded on the tourists' map, Austria does not appear, sad to say, on the missionary strategy map of the world.

Who are the Austrians? That is a good question, because until very recently there were none at all in the national sense. Their roots reach back into the great, polyglot Austro-Hungarian Empire of the Hapsburgs. Until 1918, little Austria was just one segment of that mighty monarchy of fifty-three million people. Before the end of World War I, there was no Austrian national consciousness at all. The many Italians and Slavs who lived within the borders of the Austria of that time were just as Austrian as the German-speaking folk there. The brief twenty years of independence before 1938 were too short a period for a sense of nationality to develop. During that fateful year Hitler annexed the country into the Third Reich. Strangely enough, the German occupation stimulated the first feeling of nationhood, largely because the stiff, methodical, and industrious Germans were so different from the easygoing, casual, and pacific Austrians. After the war came the Four-Power occupation, followed by a peace treaty at last. Only in October, 1955, when the last foreign troops left, could Austria breathe freely and recommence her own history.

At one time the country was larger. But Italy, by an earlier treaty, was given southern Tyrol with its 250,000 German-speaking inhabitants. Today this loss of territory is a sore political issue in Austria. Now only a few Slovenes in Carinthia speak a language other than German, which, along with local dialects, is the language of the land. Yet Austria must never be confused with Germany or Switzerland just because German is spoken there. Its way of life is much different, and especially its spiritual problems. As our paragraph title suggests, Austria is rich in atmosphere, but poor in happiness.

Life in Democracy's Outpost. The most notoriety Austria has received in recent years came out of the Hungarian uprising a few years ago. As refugees poured into Austria, Vienna became, for a few brief weeks, the news capital of the world. Most of the time, though, the Alp-ribbed republic is a quiet place in spite of its perilous position next door to Communist neighbors.

Who is the typical Austrian? Perhaps the dowager in pearl-gray lace who nibbles a frosted sweet at Vienna's Café Sacher. Or a stout *stammgast* visiting the nearby Patisserie Demel to sip an *einspanner* coffee would do just as well. Maybe a more nearly average type would be the peasant, friendly and relaxed in his simple mountain hut. One gets an impression everywhere here of that unhurried quality the Italians call *dolce far niente*, a desire just to watch the world go by. This does not mean that Austrians do not work hard, but such things as punctuality, for instance, count less here than with the Germans. Then, too, Austrians instinctively avoid unpleasantness, are eager to please to the point of courtliness. You still sometimes hear, *Kuss' die Hand*, "I kiss your hand," or *I' habe die Ehre*, "I have the honor"—expressions of traditional courtesy. Since this country was once a part of a many-tongued empire, Austrians are international in outlook. Such qualities as these make things easier for a foreign Christian to witness there and to make friends.

Vienna, A State of Mind. After Vienna, the only large centers are Graz, Salzburg, Innsbruck, and Linz. Since every third Austrian lives in Vienna, would-be evangelizers of the country must carefully consider the city on the Danube. What kind of place is Vienna? By tradition it is the romantic city of the fabulous Emperor Franz Joseph and the Viennese waltz. The truth about it is quite different. The city has become an espionage capital, where numerous secret agents from both East and West carry on their intrigue. Beneath a gay and charming surface throbs the unrest of the refugee and the sorrowing heart of the widow. The isolated capital has more police than Detroit has, patrolling its streets from the Innere Stadt out past the Kingstrasse to the suburbs. Problems like a grave housing shortage and the large war-swollen surplus of women plague the government. Out of tragedy and tension has come Austria's least enviable statistic: this peaceful Danube country leads Europe in suicides. The number of self-inflicted deaths even surpasses the number of deaths from auto accidents. Those who have studied this subject say that most people who determine to die by their own hand are not really mentally unbalanced, nor do they usually tip others off to their intentions. The pressure of life's unresolved issues just gets too great, and then something snaps. An environment of beauty, culture, and freedom has given the present generation of Austrians much. But environment fails here just as it did in the garden of Eden. The average Austrian never hears the gospel nor meets the Lord of Life in person.

Roman Dominance Again. Watch the *Corpus Christi* procession in Zederhaus or the miles of Franciscan friars winding through medieval Viennese streets by candlelight during Passion week. Follow the throngs of students, burghers, and housewives who jam the Graben and St. Stephen's Square to hear the cardinal say a special mass. Stop at a wayside calvary in the Bregenz forest and notice the peasants adorning the fancy shrine with flowers. Here by the crucified figure are the robe, the spear, the cock that crowed to rebuke Peter. Lower down are the chalice, lantern, torch, pillar, chain, sponge—even the purse which held the thirty pieces of silver. Can such a people, surrounded as they are with the outer symbols of Christianity, miss the message? Millions can and do. "The Austrians," insists one authority, "are as dominated by the influence of the Catholic church as are, for example, the Irish." Of this church the same writer adds, "In the interest of saving souls in accordance with its own doctrines, it can adapt itself miraculously to ineradicable national characteristics."[1] Cast in the Roman mould, the Austrians show many traits of their fellow European Catholics elsewhere. Here is the same pitiful slavery to dead works, which brings them not one whit nearer to God, while increasing their misery. We have cited suicide as one manifestation of the Austrians' spiritual poverty, even though suicide is a most heinous sin in the Catholic Church. One of the world's highest rates of illegitimate births over many years is another. The pre-Lenten *fasching* merriment, with its sexual abandon and heavy drinking, is still a further sign. But things were not always thus.

During the sixteenth century Catholicism and the new Protestants fought over Austria's soul. The latter won spectacularly. Only four priests were left in all Vienna, for instance, as the masses of people began to embrace the reform. Then in Trent, at that time a part of the empire, the famous Catholic Council met to consider how to withstand the Protestant Reformation. Here in 1546 they reaffirmed their own doctrines and condemned the dissenters. Luther, who lived to see complete separation from Rome after twenty-eight years of struggle, died two weeks later. Now the Emperor called upon Ignatius Loyola and his Jesuit missionaries to swing the pendulum in the opposite direction. After the ensuing Counter Reformation came a resurgence of Roman influence. With Jesuits in power, even the Protestant following in the Tyrol, which had gained some liberties during the Peasants' War of 1524–1526, was cruelly suppressed for the next two centuries. About thirty thousand people were forced to either leave the Salzburg area or turn Catholic. Many were obliged to leave their children behind to be brought up in Catholic homes; some parents remained and falsely professed conversion to Rome in order to stay with their children. A number of these secret believers and their children later reaffirmed their faith after the persecutions died down, thus enabling the gospel light to burn on dimly.

How Heavy Our Yoke. Everywhere in Europe the Catholic Church has a problem with the working class. Austria is no exception. Here, too, the strong Socialist party hates and fights the church's clericalism, which it blames for the economic problems of the nation. (By and large Austrians are poor people. The average wage earner probably does not make more than $600 a year.) How pitiful to note that Catholics, who often fail to practice their faith, still lack strength to abandon it. One Catholic writer complains that "in Vienna's first district 97% of the people willingly pay the church tax, but not more than 25% to 30% regularly practice their religion." Then the sad comment, "By formally leaving the church the slackers could avoid all payments, but this they would not dream of doing."[2] Why not leave, indeed? Because the destiny of their souls rests upon the sacramental help only "the true church" extends. An Austrian Jesuit writer complained in 1953 that Austria could not really be called Catholic at all. As evidence he declared that no more than 15 per cent of the Viennese, 30 per cent to 40 per cent of folk in other cities, and 70 per cent of the rural population practiced their faith.

In spite of the apparent indifference of the people to their own church, brave is the Catholic villager who will openly attend a Protestant service or speak against Rome. Afterward he would find it difficult to get or hold a civil service job, or, for that matter, any kind of good job. Most likely his child would fail in school. Protestants have difficulty getting permission to open Bible bookstores, though the public would gladly buy. There are even modern cases of stoning and Bible-burning ordered by the priests. Burial of the Protestant dead in village cemeteries is often forbidden. Yet people will often listen with interest to the gospel in a meeting until official opposition is ordered. One priest struck a child very hard for attending a Protestant service. Another told Catholic children that if they attended the local Methodist church, they would fall through a trap door into a basement, where the pastor would eat them. In one town a priest ordered his people to stone an American missionary who was trying to start a children's class. Fortunately she escaped serious injury.

A Squabble with the Vatican. Since Austria is one of the five European countries with which the Holy See has diplomatic relations, we should expect Rome to find her quite pliable. The truth is that the Vatican is having a long feud with Vienna over the status of the Roman Church in Austria. The trouble began after Cardinal Pacelli signed a concordat with Austria on June 5, 1933. (A concordat is a treaty between the Holy See and a civil government about rights of the church within the State; in other words, a diplomatic instrument to safeguard the church's freedom.)

When the Socialists gained control of Austria after World War II, they maintained that the Dollfuss government, which had ratified the concordat in 1933, had been "illegal." Therefore they argued that the stated provisions between church and state were invalid. Against this view the

Catholic-led People's Party held that the concordat was valid because it had been signed by two internationally recognized governments. Finally both parties agreed in 1958 to accept the treaty's validity.

Just as the church was sighing with relief over her victory, she discovered that the end of the discussion was not yet reached. The Socialist government informed the Vatican that the concordat could not be enforced because some of its clauses were not compatible with present Austrian law, and suggested new negotiations. To this the Holy See reacted angrily, accusing Austria of bad logic and dishonesty. To leave itself an open door, the church expressed willingness to renegotiate parts of the concordat if Austria would now accept it as an act of good faith. The points of contention are marriage laws and Catholic schools. At this juncture the whole matter is still in the air.

Protestant Advance and Decline. According to the latest census, 5 per cent of the Austrian people profess to be Protestant. Over a period of twenty years Protestants have doubled their membership through a succession of events. At this century's start there were very few Protestants in what is today called Austria. But even before World War I converts from Catholicism were slowly increasing in number. At the close of that war about 600,000 Protestants lived in the Austro-Hungarian empire. When the house of Hapsburg fell, the dominance of Rome was threatened still further. Even the treaties negotiated with Rome by the Austrian Nazis failed to stop the addition of about 25,000 "converts" to Protestantism during the upheaval of 1934. After Hitler annexed Austria, as we have already noted, the influence of Protestant Germany was strong. By 1938 the Protestants had grown to 342,000, including 40,000 from Burgenland, which had been transferred to Austria from Hungary in 1921.

Then came the opposition of Nazism, with its anti-religious propaganda, shrinking Protestant membership to 317,331. After World War II the tide changed again. An influx of eastern European Protestant refugees and material aid from outside brought the figure up to 411,872 members by 1950. This periodic advance and retreat of Protestantism had been due not so much to spiritual reasons as to territorial changes and political influence. There has been no noticeable ingathering of souls through conversion in modern Austria's history. The liberal and other devitalizing influences on Protestantism so noticeable in Germany are to be found here as well. By and large, the Austrian Protestants have not been aggressively evangelistic. Admittedly, if they were, the price in persecution and opposition by Catholicism would be high. At present the official Lutheran position is a safe one of non-proselytism. Other Protestants are discouraged, claiming that a curse of history is upon their country. Much prayer must be concentrated by foreign Christians upon the real believers within Protestantism, as God can always work in and through this little group for the good of the nation.

The major denomination is the *Evangelical Church of the Augsburg and Helvetic Confessions*. Lutheran in character, this body has about 390,000 members. Children and inactive members are included in that figure. The *Old Catholics* follow in size, with 33,000 members. Next largest group is the *Reformed Helvetic Church*, with a constituency of perhaps 20,000. The *Methodists* count some 3,000 followers, and the *Baptists* 2,000. The *Assemblies of God* have 700 members in thirteen little churches. Surprisingly, the *Seventh-day Adventists* have recruited about 6,000 converts in their forty centers through hard missionary work.

One matter that irks Austrian Protestants is the legal barrier. Two old laws deny non-Catholics certain rights. One, the Edict of Toleration, was enacted by Emperor Joseph II more than 175 years ago. The other is known as the Protestant "patent" of 1861. For more than twenty-five years Protestants have sought a new law guaranteeing equality for them in every phase of life. They are especially concerned about spiritual care for Protestants in the armed forces and equal treatment in tax matters for their welfare organizations. While these matters are important, the Protestants must concentrate above all on the unevangelized masses and how they may be reached. Let us look now at the scope of the unfinished task.

A Spiritual Balance Sheet. A recent survey of Austria conducted by the Greater Europe Mission yielded some challenging facts. A number of representative evangelical pastors questioned in various areas agreed that there are probably no more than 5,000 born-again people among Austria's seven millions. Can any country where less than one-tenth of one per cent of the populace know the Lord Jesus be considered evangelized? Does not a conclusion like this qualify Austria as one of the leading mission fields of the world? The same survey, using Biblical standards of comparison, found no more than thirty individual churches in the country which could be considered sound and evangelistic. Of these the Methodists and Baptists were considered the most promising. Considered city by city, the true witness for Jesus Christ in leading points of Austria looks something like this:

> *Salzburg*—Among 120,000 inhabitants three groups, the largest with fewer than one hundred in attendance.
> *Wels*—Two small groups for 30,000 inhabitants, with no resident pastor or missionary.
> *Vienna*—For almost two million people only nine groups, with no more than 2,000 in attendance.
> *St. Poelten*—One small group among 40,000 people.

Graz—Four groups among about 225,000, the largest drawing fewer than one hundred.

Innsbruck—Three groups, none with a pastor, among a population of 100,000. One foreign lady missionary serves here.

Klagenfurt—Two small groups, about thirty in each, out of 70,000 people.

Bregenz—Only one tiny group among 30,000 people.

North of the Danube the spiritual vacuum is especially alarming. "About 30 cities with populations between twenty and forty thousands have almost nothing in the way of a witness."[3] Only five cities have Protestant churches in this large area, though some other points are occasionally visited by pastors. Then the Vorarlberg and Tyrol districts have only six Protestant churches between them, not counting outstations. Only one foreign missionary serves the Tyrol, and he is not there on a full-time basis. The authorities in the Tyrol seem to block the residence permits of missionaries who wish to settle there. Another sorely neglected area is the whole mountainous strip across the center from east to west. Here thousands of mountain huts should be visited with the gospel of grace. Some of the cities and towns may have one or two believing families, but there is no worker or leader for miles in any direction. Countless villages, clusters of two or three houses in the valleys, or lone chalets high in the mountains have never been visited by a Bible colporteur, a personal worker, or any kind of Christian witness. Most of the handful of foreign workers in Austria are from Germany or Switzerland, with a thin scattering of Americans, Canadians, and English. Obviously this help is tiny in comparison with the need.

True Christians in Austria beg for intercession and more workers. Whether or not they will receive help may well depend on those who read these lines about one of Europe's neediest mission fields.

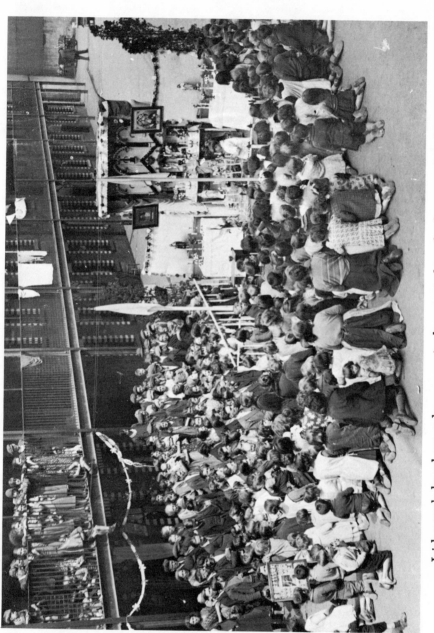

Irish people kneel around an open-air altar erected in a back street of Dublin.

Chapter 10

THE ENIGMA OF IRELAND

"The Irish Republic, the only Roman Catholic country in the English-speaking world, is in practice the most devout Catholic country in the world."

—PAUL BLANSHARD
Author and Lecturer

Cead Míle Fáilte. Whether the Irishman says, "A hundred thousand welcomes!" in Gaelic or "Glad to see you!" in English, he speaks from the heart. Strangers are warmly greeted in this compelling, contradictory island. Probably the heartiest welcome of all awaits Americans, since almost every Irish family has relatives in the United States. In fact, there are more people of Irish descent in America than in Ireland, and New York City has more Irish people than any other city in the world! Though the Irishman's island is not as large as the state of Maine, he manages to make an impact on the world far out of proportion to the size of his homeland. As everybody knows, the Irish are individuals first and foremost. Headstrong and likable, violent but loyal, they are born storytellers, actors, and propagandists, all the way from their prime ministers down to the humblest peasants on their tiny farms. A remarkable, colorful, and kindly people, the Irish easily adjust themselves to life abroad without ever losing their distinctiveness. Irish songs, jokes, and fables have intrigued and entertained every corner of the world, while culture from Ireland has helped on human knowledge.

Why should a child of God be spiritually concerned about Ireland? First, because 95 per cent of the Republic is Roman Catholic.* A second tragedy is that the Irish peasant, in his childhood, receives only a pitiful pagan substitute for a satisfying faith. In the third place, for several reasons, Irish Protestantism is not winning the battle for souls. In the words of one Irish Protestant pastor, "Ireland is becoming increasingly a mission field. We need to be stirred with a vision of this land won for Jesus Christ."[1]

*76 per cent of the island's total population are Roman Catholic.

327

The Two Irelands. Two separate states occupy this one island, each with its own government. Northern Ireland, sometimes referred to as The Six Counties, is a little larger than Connecticut and has only 1,370,921 people. This one-sixth of the island is attached to the crown as part of the United Kingdom, though independently administered. These folk of the north counties of Antrim, Tyrone, Derry, Down, Armagh and Fermanagh are for the most part Protestant, although the Catholic minority of one-third is vocal and militant. The Orangemen, as the northerners are called, occupy most of what was once the old province of Ulster, with Belfast as their capital. The latter city is an active Protestant center known all over the world for its evangelistic and missionary outreach.

In the other twenty-six counties of the south the spiritual need is much greater. These form the independent Republic of Ireland, not much larger than West Virginia and with almost three million people. The republic, called in Gaelic *Poblacht Na Eireann,* otherwise goes by the name Eire. Only in 1949 did this new country break its final ties with its mortal enemy, England, after long years of bitterness and bloodshed.

Though at odds over their attitude toward union with England and over the religious question, the two Irelands are of similar mixed racial stock. In the north some Scottish people settled; so today some people there call themselves Scotch-Irish. Here, however, the resemblance ceases. In the Republic the use of Gaelic, encouraged by the government as a nationalistic expression, is spoken voluntarily by only one-fourth of the population in sixteen different dialects. Most children give up the dying language when they leave school at the average age of fourteen. Though both English and Gaelic are official languages, Eamon de Valera was one of the few politicians to use the Gaelic language in speeches.

The border question, or partition, is the hottest subject in Ireland and the source of tension between the two Irelands. In Northern Ireland almost all Catholics are nationalists, working for a united island under Dublin, while most Protestants support continued ties with Britain. As one observer puts it, the present cold war between the two "would break out into a shooting war if the southern Irish saw any prospect of success by physical violence."[2] Meanwhile there are plenty of skirmishes and incidents along the border, as well as southern agitation in the north. Ulster is determined not to surrender to Roman Catholic rule from Dublin, while Eire insists that The Six Counties are hers by right. The situation of the outnumbered Catholics in Northern Ireland infuriates Dublin. Two of the six northern counties—Tyrone and Fermanagh—are nationalist and Catholic by a narrow margin of about fifty-three to forty-seven. The second city of the north, Derry, is Catholic, though in a unionist county. Here is the emotional center of the conflict, a powder keg located only a few miles from the Republic's County Donegal. Derry, called London-derry by the British, has become the symbol of bitterness, a sort of "world capital of Protestant-Catholic tensions."[3] Aside from war, the best chance for a southern victory is through a higher birth rate. If the Catholics can increase their 35 per cent of the population with a higher rate of repro-duction, they can conceivably capture the north in several decades. Catholics reportedly already have a birth rate double that of Protestants in this part of the island. Because the Republic, or southern Ireland, spells out the spiritual problem of the island better than northern Ireland, we shall concentrate our attention here in this survey.* This does not mean, though, that there is not a harvest to be won in the northern coun-ties as well.

Life in the Emerald Isle. The term "emerald isle" comes from the extraordinary green of the fields, seen everywhere. And this green is produced by constant mists, rains, and drizzles, plus the brief periods of sunshine characteristic of the land. Strangely enough, though green appears everywhere in the world on St. Patrick's Day as the symbol of Ireland, the Irish themselves do not regard this as their special color. To them, the royal blue in their flag represents their country better than the fabled green of their fields.

There are few cities in the Republic of Ireland. Seventy per cent of the population are peasants, who live in town-clusters, of which there are almost seventy thousand in the whole country.** Besides the town-clusters—just little groups of houses, usually approached by *bohereens,* or country lanes, one sees in the countryside an occasional mansion, often dilapidated, belonging to the landed gentry. The humble thatched cottages of many colors, long familiar to the tourist, are now gradually giving way to slate-roofed homes of cement blocks or bricks. In the country air lingers the sweet smell of burning peat, the rural people's substitute for city-dwellers' coal. Inside the peasants' houses not all is so romantic as song and fable imply. The fires glowing in the hearths are attractive, but the houses are often unsanitary and damp from the con-tinual mists and drizzles. In a typical town-cluster life is simple and somewhat austere, by standards of other Europeans, and here everybody knows his neighbors' business. Talk is the great art of the Irish, and they love to indulge it, in the country as well as in the cities.

In the country regions the population is decreasing with alarming rapidity. There are now only half as many people in Ireland as there were a century ago. Depopulation began during the great potato famine

*The term "Ireland," as used hereafter in this study, refers to the Republic of Ireland.
**67 per cent of the Republic's population is rural.

of 1845–1847, when one quarter of the people died, or about two million out of eight million. By 1851 there were only about five million left. Great waves of emigration to America further reduced the number of residents between 1852 and 1914. In the former year alone, a quarter of a million Irish immigrants landed in New York. Today about forty thousand a year seek homes somewhere abroad.

To foreigners, Dublin, the capital, is probably the best-known spot in Ireland, along with Shannon airport at Limerick and Blarney Castle near Cork City. The city is famous for its parks and monuments, wide O'Connell Street, and the sacred scenes of past rebel fighting, called "the troubles." A Minneapolis-sized city on the river Liffey, Dublin dominates the land as "a fascinating blend of a bustling metropolis and one-horse town."[4] The second largest city is Cork. From the fact that its inhabitants traditionally have pleasant dispositions, we get the expression, "He's a corker!" Limerick, Waterford, and Galway follow, in that order, as sizable towns. Strangely enough, five thousand town names in little Ireland begin with *Bally*, which is Gaelic for "home-place," usually a cluster of houses only. *Knock* meaning "a hill," is the prefix for two thousand other town names.

Many of the customs of country people here seem strange to outsiders. For example, the percentage of unmarried people is the highest in the world, and people marry later in Ireland than they do anywhere else. As Father John O'Brien of Notre Dame, one of America's better-known priests, put it, "Ireland is rapidly becoming a nation of bachelors and spinsters; the Irish people will soon become extinct if they do not increase the marriage rate."[5] Only 28 per cent of the population are married; 65 per cent remain single. Students of this phenomenon point out that marriageable young women are leaving the country in great numbers. But there are other reasons for the Irish reluctance to marry, which we shall discuss later.

Marriage in the country districts involves matchmaking, or parental negotiations, and the payment of a dowry. Back of the custom lies the economic control of the family farm, for usually a farmer can afford to settle only one of his sons there. When the father has chosen the son best suited for the place, he passes the word around that he is looking for a wife for the young man. During this looking period there is much discussion of the possibilities in the local inns and at home, with suggestions submitted by all the members of the farmer's family. When the son has found a suitable girl and made his decision to propose to her, he sends a "speaker" to the young lady to find out her reactions. Then she in turn makes her investigation about the man. If he suits, the speaker is told to "draw it down," i.e., draw up the contract. Soon a meeting is arranged between the persons concerned, and the delicate negotiations commence.

A Unique People. What about the Irish character? First, these are a people who tend to see things in black and white. They are usually either strongly for or against an issue, especially a political or religious one. Second, often in the same individual there will be what Charles Duff calls "a lightning change from one frame of mind to its opposite."[6] Yet this does not mean that Irish people are either irrational or unpredictable, for underneath the emotional surface is a logical outlook on life. A third characteristic is what George Bernard Shaw termed Irish flippancy. With their strong sense of the macabre, the Irish love to indulge in "blarney" or exaggerated speech. Often strong speech leads to like action.

At the country fairs, in former times, livestock and goods were sold, but the real attraction lay in sports—especially the horseracing with which they closed. Along with the sports went heavy drinking, bragging, insults, and much violence. Especially famous was the Donnybrook Fair near Dublin, still held in August of each year. Strife, bloodshed, immorality, and brutality made this and other fairs so infamous that the Irish became unjustly associated with unruliness the world over. "The absence of moral restraint," writes a sociologist, "which led to extremes of lawlessness at Donnybrook and elsewhere was a normal and characteristic accompaniment of these periodic folk-gatherings." In them he sees "a lingering fertility magic"[7] underlying the excitement. Rowdyism at these fairs is not as extreme as it once was, nor is men's behavior here worse than that of their fellow human beings elsewhere. The explanation for such outbursts can well be found in the rigid Catholic moral code imposed without the enablement of an indwelling Saviour to make it livable.

The Harvard anthropologist, Conrad Arensberg, believes that the Irish character is made up primarily of patriotic fervor, religious zeal, and belief in fairies. He notes that "a puritanical morality goes hand in hand with the hilarity of a race-meeting. The loyalty too harshly called 'clannishness' runs side by side with the personal acquisitiveness of a peasant proprietorship. Small wonder, then, that the Irish feel no foreigner will ever fully understand."[8] Seán O'Faoláin, Ireland's foremost living writer, also reflects on this odd dualism, "There may be an overlay of stern Christian morality. At bottom there is a joyous pagan amorality."[9] While the study of the Irish personality can help the Christian worker, he already knows the deeper problem. The Irish heart is Everyman's—the heart of a sinful man needing complete fulfillment in Jesus Christ.

Backwardness and Stagnation. The visitor to Ireland is surprised to see there a lower standard of living than exists in Northern Ireland or in

England. He recalls that the Irish overcame tremendous difficulties in obtaining independence, and he wonders why they are so curiously apathic toward national progress now that they are free. "There is one thing that the Republic of Ireland has not become: a modern country," says Duff. He adds the significant comment that a sagging economy is "not due, as many English and Americans think, to sheer apathy and backwardness, but to *a choice of* a way of life."*[10] Like everything else in Ireland, the prevailing way of life is built around the predominant Catholic faith. This fact gives rise to the question: Why should the church want the Irish people to live under decaying conditions?

Fervent Catholic patriots masterminded the whole independence movement. Priests keep it alive, continuing to put pressure on Northern Ireland to join the Republic. But "such a modest country was never meant for complete independence in the modern economic world."[11] Coal and iron are scarce, forests almost non-existent. City slums, slovenly standards of dress, and the depressed condition of the countryside all point to a problem. In more than three-fourths of country homes toilet facilities do not exist, and less than half have a piped water supply. Perennially high unemployment, widespread child labor, and poor diet are other facets of poverty. In buying power the average Irish wage can purchase only half as much as that of the average Englishman. According to de Valera, only 15 per cent of Ireland's agricultural land is tilled, as compared with 40 per cent in the Netherlands. Many blame the shiftlessness of the farmers for the poor conditions. "Rural Ireland," says Cornelius Lucey, Bishop of Cork, "is stricken and dying, and the will to marry and live on the land is almost gone."[12] Part of the difficulty lies in Ireland's relation to Britain. Though now independent, the Republic is still largely, though unwillingly, dependent on Britain for trade. Geography, British imperialism, and other factors may enter in, but the role of Rome in all this has been the decisive one. Even though the church had only periodic support from the masses in the early years of Irish nationalism, and even appeared antirevolutionary by sometimes supporting the Protestant ascendancy, the guidance of the Vatican is unmistakable. Through Rome's compromise and opportunism, "loyalty to authoritarian Rome and loyalty to Irish freedom were fused in the Irish Catholic mind as one emotional value."[13]

A Country of Superstition. Centuries ago, before the Christian era, a Druid priesthood ruled the life of the Irish pagans. When the Scandinavians arrived in the eighth century, however, some forms of Christianity had already flourished in the island for three hundred years. The Danish and Norse invaders brought their pagan religions with them,

*The italics are Duff's.

During their three hundred years of occupation, Scandinavian beliefs in a spirit world became a part of Irish life. These old deposits of pagan superstition are still very much alive in the Irish mind and mingle very easily with Roman Catholic religious magic, as they do in Normandy and elsewhere on the continent.

Most Irish people believe in the baneful effects of curses, black magic, and the evil eye. In some unexplained way men suffer evil from super-natural causes. A St. Bridget's cross, in the shape of a pagan swastika, can protect a house and livestock from harm. No evil spirit dares to pass into a building when the cross hangs above the door. Anyone with an evil eye can blight, maim, or kill a chosen animal or person. A priest's curse can ruin a prosperous farm or strike blindness. Even the shrill imprecations of old men or women are feared for the harm they may bring.

Reality of a Fairy World. An old woman from West Cork, asked if she believed in fairies, replied indignantly, "I do not, but of course they're there!" People refer to fairies as *them*. The pronoun expresses both their nameless power and their immanence. Fairies are involved not only in daily events of harmless character, but in deadly black magic. Sometimes these fairies are called "the good people," or "the gentle folk," out of deference. Every effort is made to please or placate them (*"they* leave you alone if you treat *them* right"). For instance, food and water are left outside the house for them at night. Dirty water is never thrown out of the house in the evening for fear of wetting, and thus angering, a fairy. If *they* are roused enough, a pig, a cow, or a child might die. Even in their daily greetings the people express respect for fairies. "God bless all here," or "God bless the work," or "God spare your health" are expressions not so much of piety as of hope that *they* will be pleased. There is much to fear, people believe, because fairies can co-operate with people, either knowingly or unknowingly, in bringing woe to anyone.

How widespread is belief in these fairies? Arensberg thinks that it is common enough. "The cult of fairies these days is branded as superstition. It is under fire from townsman, school teacher, and priest. But even those who would express no views could be seen to act as if they too were believers."[14] It would seem that the *pisherouges*, or superstitions, are in the country districts to stay.

A visitor to the remote town of Laogh tells what he learned while staying in the west room of a home. Because fairy paths always pass by the west room, food and water left out at night are always placed on that side. No shed, outhouse, or other building can ever be built on the west. Such a move would bring bad luck. "Reluctant as they might be to express belief, my hosts none the less practiced it. No house of Laogh's twenty-six had any shed or outhouse at its western end."[15] Why the west? Ancient sun cults named the west, as the direction of the dying sun, the abode of the dead. In Gaelic *Tir na nóg*, the heaven at life's end, lies to the west. Even in America our cowboy tales feature dying men who talk of "going west." The fairies, then, are the dead of the next world who still have an influence over the living. Actually, there is little difference between this and Shinto ancestor-worship or the African cults which use fetishes to ward off evil spirits from the past.

Life with the Leprechauns. After St. Patrick's Day, which the Irish consider the beginning of spring, leprechauns are much in the minds of the people. These are the shoemakers of the fairies, old men dressed in red breeches, with green jackets and pointed red hats. Said to be black-eyed and ugly, they sit on three-legged stools when at work, and wear leather aprons. Their ancient ancestor is reputed to be the European artisan God, Lugh. All this would be simply delightful nonsense if it were not really believed, and did not reveal fear in people's hearts.

The Irish believe that leprechauns mostly prefer to plague a housewife in her farm kitchen. She must leave out for him at night not the kind of left-over food and drink a dog might receive, but a specially prepared meal. If she fails in this duty, the leprechaun may ride the sheep or gallop the cattle until they are exhausted. He may make the water in the pot boil over to extinguish the fire, or throw the baby on the floor. Other leprechaun tricks are souring the milk or setting the thatch on fire.

Great care is taken not to meddle with leprechaun haunts. "There's not a country man in Ireland who would meddle with a lone tree or a fairy bush," says an Irish writer.[16] Very recently some workmen who were lengthening one of the jet runways at the famous Shannon International Airport belived they had discovered a "fairy fort." They refused to proceed with the work until the government itself ordered that the fairy fort be left unharmed.

While fairies are human size, the leprechauns are perhaps two feet high. The fairies "are really the dead who bring death to the living,"[17] but the leprechauns are supposedly better-natured. Curiously, the ancestors of these spirits, by tradition, were from Celtic Spain and France. In these latter countries similar fears flourish today. For some reason Ireland's leprechauns are a fading legend, while the fairies themselves are more implicitly accepted than ever.

Persons who die before their time or are sinking in health, for unexplained reasons, are "carried" or "in the fairies." Sometimes pitiful excesses are followed to cause the souls of the dead to return to their bodies.

From this sketch of the pagan superstitions of Ireland's masses, we can draw several conclusions. First, Roman Catholicism often flourishes in countries where people already believe in the reality of a spirit world. Second, these people can become Catholics and continue to practice their folklore without straining their credulity. A third conclusion is inescapable if we raise the question, "How can this be?" The answer, as we see it, lies in the very nature of Catholicism itself. As a form of baptized paganism—a pseudo-Christian structure on a naturalistic foundation—the Roman faith can accommodate both sorts of faith.

Sons of St. Patrick. A handful of surprises awaits the person who carefully investigates Ireland's "patron saint," Patrick. First, he was not Irish. Nor is he a canonized saint on Roman Catholic records. Furthermore, many thousands of Irishmen insist he was never a Catholic at all! Patrick came from Britain, in all likelihood from Scotland. His sainthood rests on no papal grounds whatsoever; he "passes as a saint merely by popular usage."[18] As for his being Roman Catholic, the evidence seems solidly against it. Under the avalanche of tradition, legend, and fable about Patrick, only three reliable sources remain: all from his own pen. These are the *Confession*, his letters to Coroticus, and his hymn, "The Breastplate." Taken together, his writings lead many scholars to conclude, from arguments of silence and statement, that Patrick was never an ordained Roman priest, never went to Rome, never recognized the pope, and, indeed, was never a Roman Catholic at all.

As further proof, many of the passages from Patrick's books reveal a warm evangelical heart at rest in the Saviour. No prayer is addressed to other mediators, such as Mary or the saints. Nor is there a single whiff of incense from the altars of good works. None of the practices and trappings of today's Romanism mar what seems to be saving faith on the missionary's part. There is nothing taught about salvation by sacrament. He begins, "I, Patrick, a sinner," and mentions salvation as "the gift of God."

Patrick's father and grandfather were also ministers of the cross, but married rather than celibate. His father, Calprernius, was an ordained deacon, while his grandfather, Potitus, was an ordained presbyter. Patrick, born about 387, was a Roman citizen who grew up speaking colloquial Latin. Sixteen Irish pirates captured the lad and took him to their country as a slave. While tending the flocks of a chieftain in Ulster, he may have become a Christian, perhaps as a result of seed sown in his heart by his parents. A resolve seems to have been born in him to escape and then return, bringing the gospel back to Ireland. He escaped to Auxerre, France, where he spent the next fourteen years preparing himself to return to Ireland. This he did in 432. He began to preach in County Down in the north. For thirty years this missionary labored against tremendous odds. He established his headquarters at Armagh, which is now a hallowed spot. Strangely, "nearly all the scenes of the Patrick story are laid in those six counties where the British writ still runs."[19] When Patrick died in 461, he was buried at Downpatrick, on the spot where he founded his first church. In his lifetime the pioneer had seen much of Ireland turn to Christ. The remarkable zeal of Irish missionary evangelism during the sixth and seventh centuries tends to bear out the belief that Patrick laid a strong gospel foundation. Indefatigable apostles like Columba, Aidan, and Columbanus led an army of Irish missionaries all over Europe. So great was their impact on the Continent that there are towns and counties in Switzerland, Italy and France today which bear the names of some of these men. The very isolation of Ireland apparently meant a purer form of God's truth than was generally known was preserved and propagated here.

With the invasion of the Norsemen came an end to Irish evangelism and a decline in spiritual life. Yet even before this the trend in that direction had begun. "In all gospel work," remarks V. R. Edman, "there has always existed the tendency to substitute form for substance, and the Irish church proved no exception to that distressing, but human, generalization."[20] What is the picture today? Irish Catholics remember Patrick chiefly for the legends and superstitions which grew up around his life. For instance, he is supposed to have cleared the snakes out of Ireland by using the shamrock to illustrate the doctrine of the Trinity. On March 17, St. Patrick's Day, after high mass in the Dublin Cathedral, presided over by the Archbishop, and attended by civic leaders, a parade winds along O'Connell Street. On the final Sunday in July an annual pilgrimage climbs to the summit of Croagh Patrick in County Mayo near Clew Bay. Here pilgrims pray, close to the spot where Patrick supposedly spent many nights in prayer and banished the serpents. On the same day the Archbishop of Armagh says mass in the saint's honor near where his heart lies buried. Anglicans, too, observe St. Patrick's Day at Saul, where the great missionary reportedly landed. Then, the bishops of several counties lead pilgrims to the Cathedral of Downpatrick, where Patrick's bones are said to lie, concluding the day in their Cathedral of Armagh.

The Model Papal State. "Ireland is the last bastion of Christian civilization in western Europe," declares Bishop Fulton J. Sheen.[21] Further praise comes from Rt. Rev. Monsignor James H. Cotter, who describes "Ireland standing majestically among the wrecks of earth" as a "still brilliant apostle among the nations, still model principle before those governments that ignore and disregard all principle."[22] Statements like these could be multiplied from Irish-American Catholics and Irish alike. They add up to a picture of ideal Catholic practice and zeal obviously satisfying to the Vatican. Thus we can think of the average Irishman as a faithful Catholic: "for an Irish Catholic, his nationality is inseparable from his religion."[23] According to the Republic's statistics, 95 per cent of the population are Roman Catholic. Other countries make similar claims, but Ireland comes closest to proving them, for no other Catholic nation takes its faith so seriously. In France, Spain, Italy, or the Latin American countries, there is an obvious, often vocal, anticlericalism. In Ireland, on the other hand, non-Catholics are limited to Protestants, a sprinkling of other faiths, and a very small circle of Catholic sceptics among intellectuals. The rest of the population is quite faithful. This religion is so whole-heartedly accepted as the central reality of life that it is shocking to most Irishmen even to discuss any possible change in his beliefs. "Religion is not really a field of discussion: and since his opinions on all other subjects are conditioned by his religion, there is really nothing the least fundamental which we can discuss with him at all," writes Arland Ussher.[24]

In Ireland the Catholic church claims—and receives—authority over every realm of life. Take the field of education, for instance. More than 97 per cent of all children are in the church's schools, while the rest are in Protestant or other denominational schools. Like Quebec, the Irish Republic has no free public schools in the American sense of the term. Though Ireland is a democracy where everyone pays taxes, the resulting funds meet 99 per cent of the operating expenses of Catholic-owned-and-managed schools. Irish priests are most hostile to the concept of public education as a function and responsibility of government. The national school system thus embodies the whole spirit as well as the letter of Vatican decrees on education. We even see the Ordinary of the Archdiocese of Dublin decreeing it a mortal sin for Catholics to send their children, without his permission, to Dublin University, a Catholic school. To this arrangement the government agrees. So gratifying is the church's position in this respect that the Minister of Education could claim at one time, "I think I am justified in saying that in no country in the world does a national system of education approach the Catholic ideal system as in the Free State."[25] In spite of such smugness, the average Irish child is undereducated. Most leave school at fourteen, and only 3 per cent ever enter university. In England the taxpayers spend at least three times as much on the elementary pupil as people do in Ireland.

How does the church have such rights in a state that is not clerical in the definitive sense? The Irish Republic is a genuine political democracy, which officially grants freedom to both political parties and to all religious faiths. Yet because the population is overwhelmingly Catholic, the Vatican does not need concordats or other instruments to force its way to power. An unofficial alliance binds church and state tightly, with each adulating the other. In the words of Canon Boylan, "The Catholic Church is more favourably placed than it is in even the most Catholic countries of the continent."[26]

From this vantage point the church can control such things as censorship. As a result, most of the books produced in the Republic are strictly Catholic. According to Canon 1399 of church law, the bishops' duty to ban all books on the Index is clear. In this matter, though, the government's Censorship Board chooses the judicious path of banning some books officially while forbidding others unofficially. The official list of censored books and magazines is capriciously compiled, with some two thousand titles in all. Ironically, there is some title or other on the list from almost every living Irish Catholic writer of any note. Books of dozens of other world-famous writers are also under censorship. This situation has aroused much resentment among Irish intellectuals and is widely discussed abroad.

What O'Faolain calls "a disguised Establishment of inordinate power"[27] can use its vast influence over the government almost at will. Which comes first in the thinking of the hierarchy, the welfare of the country, or the advance of the church's interests? O'Faolain, himself a Catholic, puts more abruptly what many other leading Irishmen admit: "The Catholic Church in Ireland as such, does not . . . care a rap about the political nation . . . it watches and waits and bargains all the time . . . whatever power emerges it will follow after—to bargain with it . . . it will condemn the patriot today and do its heavenly business with him tomorrow—if he wins."[28]

Shrines, Wells, and Pilgrimages. Very few people in the world are as fervent pilgrims to holy places as the Irish. In his work, *The Catholic Shrines of Europe*, the Rt. Rev. John K. Cartwright maintains, "I can say that I have never seen such intensity of religious feeling demonstrated on any other occasion, except at audiences with the Holy Father and at visits at the shrine of Lourdes."[29] Father Cartwright could have added that among the most faithful and enraptured of Lourdes' pilgrims are the Irish. I have noticed that in the hotels and restaurants of that city Bernadette's most numerous English-speaking admirers are Irish. In Dublin and other population centers I have also observed how heavily travel agencies advertise their pilgrimages to Lourdes.

Ireland is one of the few countries where little intellectual doubt of religious credibility exists. When the supposed right arm of St. Francis

Xavier was brought from New York to Ireland in 1949, an estimated 100,000 people, headed by their President, thronged the church, streets, and highways to catch a glimpse of the relic. The country has a miniature Fatima or Lourdes of its own in the shrine of Our Lady of Knock, in County Mayo. As many as 25,000 persons at a time make their way to the spot where an apparition of the Virgin Mary allegedly appeared seventeen years ago. At that time fifteen witnesses claimed they saw a vision of the Virgin in white on a gable wall of the parish church of Knock. With St. Joseph on her right, and St. John on her left, the Virgin had supposedly appeared even earlier. For about two hours on the evening of August 21, 1879 she kept local folk in a state of worshipful wonder. This is a favorite shrine for invalids, as are all Marian ones.

If St. Patrick is the unofficial patron saint of Ireland, St. Bridget* is the patroness. On the first Sunday in July, each year, about seven thousand people usually attend the shrine at Faughart, her birthplace, to pray at the stream and holy well there. On this day her relic, a portion of her skull kept two miles away at her church in Kilcurry, is carried in procession to the shrine, where it is placed for public veneration. Bridget, supposedly a woman of great beauty and talent, did not wish to marry or have suitors. To avoid this she prayed that she might become ugly. Her prayer answered, she went to live as a nun under a large oak. Here the monastery of Kildare was founded. February 1, the day that Bridget died, is celebrated throughout the world as her feast day.

One of St. Patrick's shrines is the most popular of all. Between June 1 and August 15 some 35,00 pilgrims visit the island of Sanctuary in County Donegal, on the northwest coast, about 175 miles from Dublin. This is believed to have been the scene of St. Patrick's "purgatory." According to legend, God revealed this spot to Patrick, stating that whoever spent a day and night there would witness both the torments of hell and the joys of heaven. On the island, a narrow strip of rock less than a mile from shore, can be seen the remains of a monastery destroyed in 1632. Now St. Patrick's church stands at the same location as a minor basilica. All-night vigils are kept there, and circuits of the stations of the cross are performed daily by barefoot pilgrims. In the partial fast of this celebration, only one meal a day is allowed for the faithful.

The tragedy of these observances is their utter futility. Irish peasants, who are already heavily superstitious, easily accept any church suggestion about a pilgrimage. Salvation for their souls depends, after all, on the teachings of this demanding religion. Thus they pitifully show their enslavement to a religion of dead works. Ignorant of the joys of faith in a living Saviour, the masses strive for a salvation vaguely promised but unattainable in the end. No wonder this land is a mission field!

*She is also called St. Bride.

Irish Priest—Policemen. More than fifty years ago George Bernard Shaw chided the Irish Catholic for his contented ignorance, his willingness to remain a child before his church. Behind this voluntary childhood stands a father-image in the person of the ordinary priest. Distributed at a ratio to one to every 770 persons, almost six thousand priests chaperone everyday Irish life and thought. Their role in Ireland would seem to bear out James Joyce's jibe of "a priest-ridden, Godforsaken race." What kind of person is this priest? For one thing, he is single-minded and obedient to an amazing degree. In the whole history of his church in Ireland there has never been a native schism or heresy. Though students for the priesthood sometimes drop out, there is no place for ex-priests in this Republic.

The priests did not climb to their mastery over the multitudes without paying a price. King James I persecuted them fiercely, while Cromwell offered a bounty of five pounds for the head of a wolf—or the head of a priest. The social prominence of today's priest is due to his political position. Daniel O'Connell, the great demagogue who organized Catholic resistance to Britain in the early nineteenth century, was responsible for making the priest a representative national figure. Previously the hierarchy had favored union with Britain, but O'Connell gradually showed them where the church's best interests lay. Rome was quick to switch to the nationalistic line when the way became clear. By 1850 the priest in politics was a part of the scene.

The priest sees to it that all answers to moral questions are precisely catalogued. All possible acts are neatly divided into right and wrong, into classes of sin or no-sin. But double standards may also apply—what is usually wrong can be right under certain conditions, or twice as wrong under others. With its age-old casuistry the Catholic Church regulates life for the people from cradle to grave. Lovelife, amusements, voting, education, employment, reading, home life—all these come under the priest's scrutiny. Is such domination popular? Though the Irish accept it, the fact remains that young people are leaving the rural areas—where the priest's hold is strongest—at a faster rate than anywhere else. Spiritual dictatorship is partly responsible.

Of the powers the priest excercises, the worst is to keep souls in ignorance of the true way to heaven through the Lord Jesus Christ. In Ireland the laws governing penance and forgiveness are more widely accepted than among Latin Catholics. A fifty-day indulgence is granted to those who kiss a bishop's ring. One observer calculates that a devout Irish Catholic, by obeying the Dominican Order's rules for use of the rosary, can gain, in a single year, 434 plenary indulgences for sin, 557 years of remission in purgatory, and 47,500 special remission days. With the extra days, total relief in purgatory would amount to more than seven hundred years as the result of one really, repentant day. How pitiful the slavery of endless repetition of prayers! The official handbook *How to Avoid Purgatory* urges the faithful to repeat the little prayer, "Sacred Heart of Jesus, I place my trust in Thee." Those who do so one hundred times a day gain 30,000 days' indulgence. If a person undertakes a thousand petitions, he can have 300,000 days. "Nothing can be easier," urges the booklet, "than to acquire the habit of saying this little prayer all day long, countless times each day."[30]

Moral Relativism. In the face of the claims to high moral principle quoted earlier, one would expect much of this country. Is the praise justified? Outwardly, there is indeed an aspect of decency which could shame some so-called Protestant countries. But if the church really cared about creating the conditions for holiness of life, would she permit certain other practices, when her rule is so absolute? A glance at the national scene reveals the following: the world's largest brewery is in Dublin . . . Only one in seven of the Republic's workers conscientiously pays his income tax, as compared with one in three in Northern Ireland . . . Heavy drinking is one of Ireland's most serious problems, a sign of the immaturity of the people in their religious nursery . . . Under certain conditions, says the Irish Church, a public official may accept a bribe . . . Gambling is universal, being officially permitted by the church. Not only do the churches condone the practice but they sponsor their own gambling establishments in order to support the church.

Ireland's largest single business is, in fact, gambling. The country's four hundred hospitals and clinics are supported by the Irish Hospitals Sweepstakes, called by United States postal inspectors "the greatest bleeding heart racket in the world."[31] The Sweepstakes, operated illegally in the United States, employs 1,800 ticket sorters (3,000 in peak periods) in a Dublin building covering four acres. Its annual income surpasses the country's total exports, and Joseph McGrath, the managing director, is the richest man in the country. A giant government tax slice from the "Sweeps" has brought in over thirty million dollars to Ireland since the business began. The church's official position is that "Gambling on games of skill or chance is lawful, provided that both parties are willing to play, even though one of them realizes that he has no chance of success; that cheating and fraud are absent; and that the money staked is not required for payment of debts or to support themselves or their families."[32]

This is only a partial list of bad practices condoned, if not encouraged, by the church in its model state.

How Protestants Fare. There are fewer than 200,000 Protestants in this Vatican-dominated republic. Among themselves they are divided somewhat by social class and denominational walls. But a still higher, thicker wall separates them from their Catholic neighbors. Protected by the same Article 44 of the Constitution which recognizes the special position of the Roman Catholic Church, these dissenters are allowed free worship. Though the state sees the Catholic Church "as the guardian of the faith professed by the great majority of the citizens," it still extends recognition to the Church of Ireland (Anglican), the Presbyterians, Methodists, Jews, and others.

According to the most recent census, the *Church of Ireland* has about 125,000 members, the *Presbyterians* 24,000, the *Methodists* 9,000, the *Baptists* 462.* There are also some *Lutherans, Plymouth Brethren,* and others. Jews number roughly 4,000.

Why are there not more Protestants in this country? True, during the English ascendancy the Protestants controlled Ireland, bringing in their own churches and persecuting what was then a Catholic minority. But as the Catholics gained sufficient political power to influence the patriots of a hundred years ago, they made sure that their victory would be complete. When the English gentry was forced out, only the ghost of Protestant witness was left. The faith of the Protestants had seemed to most Irish people to be something imported from abroad, foreign to the land.

Even before that, during the Reformation, the story was the same. Though the historic monasteries were repressed at the time, friars were still able to carry on their work. In 1545 the Jesuits arrived and took things in hand. The verdict of historians is that the Reformation "was less thorough in Ireland than elsewhere." The preachers from England and the continent "never secured the allegiance of more than a minority of the Irish people . . . Catholicism retained its hold upon the masses."[33]

The Catholic hierarchy are very fearful of any contacts by their people with Protestants. The latter as a class are still economically and educationally superior. Many own and direct business houses, manufacturing concerns, or large farms. Even though they too are represented in the civil service, no Protestant who criticizes the Catholic Church would ever succeed in politics. Some rise to cabinet minister rank but must remain silent on important issues. A recent mayor of Dublin was Protestant. Protestants also control important Trinity College, as well as the nation's only non-Catholic newspaper, the *Irish Times,* and have contributed heroes to the independence movement.

Unfortunately, not all Protestants, who are heirs of the old English ascendancy, are dedicated disciples of Jesus Christ. Only God knows who are His own, but these are commanded to confess Him before men. This identification goes beyond any earthly bond. The Church of Ireland,

*In Northern Ireland the Presbyterians are slightly more numerous than the Church of Ireland Anglicans.

where much snobbishness and jealous pride remain, must learn the glory of witness and suffering. On a number of occasions this body, which is part of the world-wide Anglican communion, has insisted that it is not Protestant at all, but truly "catholic." Though the leaders themselves may understand this fine distinction in the use of the words, others—both Catholic and Protestants—are confused. To add to their confusion, prelates of the Church of Ireland use many of the same titles as those of the Roman Catholic Church.

Dwindling Congregations. One of the saddest aspects of Irish Protestantism is the loss of opportunity for witness, through emigration of its members and other reasons. In 1959 the Church of Ireland closed fifty churches on the advice of its Sparsely-Populated Areas Commission. Since then many more have been closed. The reason? Worshipers were too few. The General Synod states that the denomination's influence has been seriously affected by the steady emigration from country districts. An Irish Presbyterian pastor also reports that "Protestantism is being slowly extinguished in the southern and western parts of the country."[34] If this continues, and the Catholics are able to boost their birth rate, the day of near extinction of God's truth could come before long. Since Protestants are so much outnumbered, emigration is naturally more preferable to them than to Catholics. This tendency to leave is a serious problem. The only solution is a spiritual awakening which will not only wipe out numerical losses but add many new believers in Jesus Christ.

An Aggressive Witness. Those in Ireland who truly love the Lord are doing much to spread the good news of the grace of God. Their task is not easy. During a recent year the Irish Mission's workers paid 13,464 visits to Roman Catholic homes and sold them 13,198 copies of the Scriptures. Such colportage work, helped on by the Hibernian Bible Society in Dublin, is most rewarding. In the privacy of a home a person alone will often open his heart; with others near, this would be unthinkable.

I was walking down O'Connell Street in Dublin one day, when I came upon three young men selling Scriptures from a pushcart. After watching them for a while, and noting that no one on this crowded main street halted to look over their books, I approached them and identified myself. "Very few stop," explained their leader, a zealous lad from Belfast. "They are afraid to be seen." But as I stood there, a young Irishman *did* stop, probably because he thought I, too, was a customer. "I don't want to buy anything; I just want to look," said he rather gruffly, glancing over his shoulder. But a few minutes later he *did* buy a Gospel, then quickly melted into the crowd. In competition with this witness, the Legion of

Mary had set up its literature stand down the street. "What do *they* do?" I asked. The young men explained that jeering and heckling came from that direction, along with careful scrutiny of any who stopped to buy Bibles. The Legion of Mary is an aggressive organization dedicated to making zealous Catholics out of apathetic ones.

Naturally the Lord's people in Northern Ireland, and to some extent, in England, are deeply concerned about evangelizing the Republic. Their efforts consist of gospel team tours, colportage, evangelistic campaigns, personal work, and Bible conferences. For their pains they are sometimes assaulted physically or get a severe tongue lashing, but it is a glorious work. Some settle down in the south as "foreign missionaries" to provide some sort of witness. Such help from outside stimulates those Christians who were born in the Republic itself. These latter also want outsiders to know the true conditions in their country. "You Americans do not know what goes on here," one Protestant leader earnestly told me. "You hear only fragments of the story." While praying and hoping for their countrymen's salvation, many are doing their best to win the common man. But proportionately, or numerically, they are losing, not winning.

And Some Believed. The words "some believed," from John's Gospel, always make the labor of preaching Christ worth all it costs. Speaking of such victories, E. Rupert Gibson of the Irish Mission writes:

> The greatest thrill of all this week was the pointing of a young Roman Catholic woman to Jesus Christ. As we studied the Word together in her New Testament—which, by the way, I noticed she had carefully underlined in private reading—light began to dawn until the moment when she bowed before God . . .[35]

Even priests are sometimes saved. In County Donegal one who became puzzled and dissatisfied with the teaching about the mass finally made his way to England. Here he saw the gospel's effects and heard its message for the first time. Not long afterward he was rejoicing in the Lord. Another priest from Cork not only believed but later married. Finally he was forced to flee the country. An Irish Protestant leader, asked about his witness to priests, told me he had led four Italian priests to Christ in Dublin. They had come to Ireland for study, and he had been able to deal with them in English. He then added that twenty-five lay Catholics had accepted Christ in his office during the previous year.

How do converts from Catholicism get along later? Not always well, according to Irish Protestant leaders. Under some conditions converts are advised by their new spiritual brethren to leave for England, at least until the storm abates at home. The term "lapsed Catholic" is a fighting one in this country. Even before such a person leaves the church, should he show signs of restiveness, he "is followed up with a persistence that would do credit to the American FBI."[36] The priests work not only on the wavering church member himself, but on his family, employer, and companions as well. Blanshard cites many cases in which food was refused to converts in restaurants or they were beaten up by strangers. Those whose papers are not in order can be forced out of the country through failure of the government to renew one of them. Another common technique is to endanger a convert's livelihood. One country dairy refused to accept a farmer's milk, for example. Naturally our Lord in ways that are sometime extraordinary comes to the aid of any who will confess Him. In fact, the social disapproval faced by potential believers keeps most people from false profession, that curse of Protestant countries.

Here the need is great, the hour ripe, and the cause glorious. Ireland is an enigma only because it remains uninvestigated. Almost unnoticed as one of the world's more pressing mission fields, the Republic of Ireland is a prime candidate for help and prayer.

The temple of Zeus and the Athenian Acropolis to the left remind one of the departed glory and the pagan past of Greece.

Modern Athens, with more than a half million people, stands as a challenge to a modern Paul.

Chapter 11

GREECE'S UNKNOWN GOD

"Gentlemen of Athens, my own eyes tell me that you are in all respects an extremely religious people. For as I made my way here and looked at your shrines, I particularly noticed one altar on which were inscribed the words, TO GOD THE UNKNOWN. It is this God whom you are worshiping in ignorance that I am here to proclaim to you!"*

—The Apostle Paul
Mars Hill, Athens

How Shall They Hear? Little Greece may have a population only equal to that of greater New York, but probably the New York area, for all its indifference, has more born-again people in it than does Greece. How to explain the fact that so few in this little country know Christ as Saviour today? Greece is one of the Bible lands, with names like Thessalonica, Berea, Corinth, and Athens to remind Christians that this country once heard the gospel long ago. The plea, "Come over into Macedonia and help us," Acts 16:9, was a call to the Apostle Paul to bring the gospel to Greece and to Europe. In responding, Paul showed that his claim, "I am debtor . . . to the Greeks" (Rom. 1:14), was more than mere words. He paid his debt by going to Greece. Later, his experience in the land bore out his word to the Romans from Corinth, that the gospel is the power of God "also to the Greek" (Rom. 1:16).

The Greek churches of the New Testament were indeed strong. But centuries of invasion, immigration, despotism, and change have intervened for the worse. Roman conquerors brought in their gods to rival the ancient ones already there. When Turkey reduced Greece to one of her provinces, Islam naturally became the state religion and vigorously presecuted Christians. In the present kingdom of Greece, which only dates from 1832, the Orthodox Church has a favored position. We shall see that this Catholic

---

*Acts 17:22-23 from *The New Testament in Modern English*, copyright J. B. Phillips 1958. Used by permission of The Macmillan Company.

religion is only semi-Christian, and that, over many years, it has followed a consistent pattern of opposition to the gospel of grace.

How shall they hear without a preacher? Only a tiny handful of missionaries are at work today in Greece, although foreign mission societies have made a number of starts in the land since 1830. Obviously the Greeks themselves would make the best witnesses to their own people. Still there is room for the foreigner willing to humbly help these promising people in mastering and proclaiming the Word of God. Men of God in the country testify that only several thousand claim Christ as a personal Saviour. The death rate easily surpasses the number of believers. Every year sixty thousand Greeks pass into eternity—very few to eternal fellowship with God.

When Paul paid his celebrated visit to Athens, he remarked that, among countless altars dedicated to different gods, one was different. He seized upon this one, inscribed "To an Unknown God," to insist that the true God can indeed be known in Jesus Christ. Religion still occupies a very large place in Greek life, but the people's worship remains as ignorant as ever. When Greeks do hear the truth, they often respond with interest. As G. P. Raud says, "Although no widespread work of evangelism has been done in Greece because of ecclesiastical opposition and lack of workers, wherever the Word of God has been preached it has met with response from hungry-hearted people."[1]

The Glory That Was Greece. "Excepting machinery," said Will Durant, "there is hardly anything secular in our culture that does not come from Greece."[2] Probably no country in the world can be prouder of her past than Greece. Her recorded history began in the eighth century before Christ and reached its zenith three hundred years later, during the glorious age of Pericles. Gradually Rome conquered the Balkan peninsula, reducing Greece to one of her provinces by 146 B.C. Until 1204, when Constantinople was captured during the Fourth Crusade, the region remained a part of the Byzantine (continuing Roman) Empire. Latin emperors then ruled it until the fall of the empire in 1453. By 1460 Greece had become a Turkish province and part of the Ottoman Empire. After war with Turkey (1821–1829), Greece won independence, her sovereignty being guaranteed by Britain, France, and Russia in 1827. As a result of the Balkan wars (1912–1913), several Aegean islands and the Macedonian territory were gained. Greece declared war on Germany in 1916. The Republic of 1924 ended in a restoration of the monarchy in 1935. The year 1940 saw an invasion by Italy, which needed Nazi German reinforcement in 1941. The British liberated the country in 1944. Today Greece is a constitutional, hereditary monarchy, with its capital at Athens.

Although the Greeks are now a racial mixture far removed in status from their illustrious ancestors, they still have a fierce pride. Nor is this pride diminished a bit by the fact that their "country," in its modern form, is younger than the United States. Greece may be less industrialized and more backward than many Western nations, but her people have an understandably strong nationalist sentiment. The foreign Christian worker must reckon with this. Though Greece is dependent politically on Western influence, her culture pattern does not follow that of the main stream of continental European life. As a Balkan and Mediterranean nation she has a history and culture drawn more from Turkey and the East. Even though Greece today is quite westernized in her cities, she has an entirely different national personality than that of Western Europe. Doing things as much as possible "in the Greek way" would seem an important consideration in any missionary work done there.

The Country Itself. Greece is about the size of England or of New York state, but its population of seven and a half million is small for such a large area. Only 149 persons live in an average square mile. Still this ratio is three times the average population density of the United States. One reason for the small population is that only a small part of the country can be cultivated, a plight which has caused extensive migration by the peasants. (Most of the emigrants are to be found in Constantinople, the Dodecanese, Cyprus, Egypt, and the United States.) Three-quarters of the populace are engaged in agriculture. Industry is small but growing.

Most of the country lies in the southern part of the Balkan peninsula and on the Peloponnesus, an area connected with the Greek mainland only by the narrow isthmus cut by the Corinth canal. The rest of Greece includes many islands (Crete is the largest), which form steppingstones across the Aegean sea to Asia Minor. Much of the country is mountainous and rocky, where people scratch out a hard living from the unresponsive soil, but there are some plains like of those of Macedonia, Thessaly, and Attica. Winters are long and hard in the mountains, and summers on the plains are often scorchingly hot.

Large cities are few, yet a third of the population lives in towns of 10,000 or more. The metropolitan area of Athens has almost a million and half people, while its seaport, Piraeus, has over 200,000. Including the continuously built-up areas between them, and their outlying towns, the two cities number well over two million people. Thus the plains of Attica around Athens contain almost a fourth of the population of Greece. Salonika (Thessalonica), Volos, Patras, Larisa, Kallithea, Iraklion (Candia) are other cities of over fifty thousand population.

Life of the People. City life is much the same in every country. Athens is a typical, western European city, but with an Oriental mood. In most of the other cities this general pattern prevails, with less modernization evident in the smaller towns. There seem to be many unemployed, or only periodically employed, who are always looking for a few extra coins through odd jobs. Idle young men stand about on corners or in coffee bars much as they do elsewhere in southern Europe. For these there are few prospects of getting ahead. The average young man does not get much schooling; he must serve in the army, then look for a job which does not pay much. The home is closely knit, every member usually loyal and contributing financially. Women do not have as much freedom as they do elsewhere in Europe. Marriages often are "arranged" with financial considerations in mind, as life is hard at best.

Poverty lies at the doorstep of many, like a watchdog which refuses to leave. I was surprised to learn in Athens that three million Greeks—approaching half of the population—carry government "pauper's cards" entitling them to state aid in several forms. Though the Welfare Minister has been reclassifying these "paupers" on the grounds that they are not all eligible, the fact that so many need extra economic help is illuminating. In a way Greece's situation is similar to Spain's, where there are the very rich and the very poor, with few people between. Most Greeks are intelligent, lacking only opportunity for more education. That most would succeed, if given the chance, can be seen in the progress of Greeks in the United States and elsewhere.

Peasants find it very difficult to exist on their bare minimum of food. They often bake their own bread and make their own clothes. The rugged farmers are hard-working, fiercely independent, responsive to kindness, and hospitable to strangers. In the country regions children are not always able to attend school between the ages of seven and twelve, as the law requires. As a result, a number grow up illiterate. Since the farmlands, even the richest of them, have been laid waste by repeated wars and bandit attacks, it requires a perpetual struggle to make them produce. Because of the thinness of the soil, only about one acre in four can be cultivated. Since roads and railways do not serve remote localities of the primitive nation, life in these spots goes on much as it did centuries ago. Ancient customs still continue here and there. On feast days men often wear their short, full-skirted costumes, with long white woolen tights and heavily braided jackets. Women don their long, brightly-colored skirts and full-sleeved white blouses, with chains of gold bangles around their necks.

Greece has always been a seafaring nation because few points in the country are more than forty miles from the sea. From the Athens seaport of Piraeus, Greek sailors travel under the flags of many nations, as well as maintaining a large merchant fleet of their own. Because its coast-line is longer, in proportion to land area, than any other nation in the world, Greece is almost better served by water than by any other means of transportation. This would make a good country for a boat mission, as a missionary could anchor his small boat in thousands of inlets and bays within easy access to towns and cities.

The Greeks Have a Word for It. Perphaps one word sums up the Greek mentality as well as any: *philotimo* is the sensitive self-esteem which makes the common field-hand feel equal to his king or causes a waiter to deliberately delay service when addressed too harshly. Greeks seem to be extroverts, in the main, with warm and open personality. They respond to friendship and are easy to meet. But underneath their open-ness lies a reserve, in the home and family relationships, which allows the stranger to enter in only so far. In business the Greeks are shrewd bar-gainers. Many are tempted into petty dishonesties, so that one has to be careful in the little transactions. Greeks are a volatile people, too. I have seen several furious and bloody fights on the streets, rising out of petty arguments. But the antagonists seemed to calm down just as quickly. Much of the raucous loudness and outgoing manner of this remarkable people masks a sharp intelligence. Once their colorful personalities are put to service for Christ, more devoted and diligent followers of the Lord can scarcely be imagined. The Christians are radiant, and truly a credit to their God.

An Ecclesiastical Goliath. The Greek Orthodox Church is the popular name of one of nineteen independent, loosely-linked Eastern Orthodox church bodies found in Eastern Europe, Asia, Egypt, the United States, and other areas. By far the largest number of Orthodoxy's followers are Russians and other Slavs. Of five patriarchates which arose early as sec-tions of the Christian church, only two remained after intense struggles for power covering centuries of time. But political, racial, and religious rivalry between the survivors, Rome and Constantinople, resulted in a final schism between the two in 1054. Doctrinally, the Eastern Church's disagreement with the Roman Church in the *filioque** controversy seems to have been the main reason for the rupture. Then, too, patriarchs at Constantinople refused to recognize the supremacy of the Roman pope.

After Greece obtained her independence from Turkey in 1830, the Greek Orthodox Church came into existence in 1833. While it is autono-mous, it joins the other Orthodox churches in granting first rank—without control—to the patriarchate of Constantinople. The Greek Church is

*Latin for "and son."

governed by a Holy Synod, presided over by the Archbishop of Athens. Actions of the Church must have the theoretic sanction of the civil government. Since Orthodoxy became the state religion, the church and state have worked very closely together.

What This Church Believes. All the Eastern Orthodox churches accept as general standards the Constantinople form of the Nicene Creed, the Apostle's Creed, and the Athanasian Creed without the *filioque* (they believe that the Holy Spirit proceeds from the Father alone). To this are added the decrees of the seven ecumenical councils. The chief theological authority is John of Damascus and the theologians quoted by him. The Bible is regarded as an inspired book, but since the canon is not definitely set, some apocryphal books are admitted. Thus the Bible is to be interpreted in the light of tradition. What does this tradition include?

Like the Roman Catholics, the Eastern Orthodox believe in praying to the saints, especially to Mary, who is also called "the Mother of God." They do not believe that Mary was free from sin originally (the Immaculate Conception) but hold, rather, that she was cleansed from it at the Annunciation. Images in the form of icons are used, but never graven, carved, or cast ones. In the services themselves the mysticism and passivity of the liturgy are central, to the detriment of the sermon. Actually among the Greek Orthodox, from the leaders on down, there is little interest in doctrine, and Orthodoxy is today theologically stagnant. Proposals for change of any kind meet tremendous resistance.

Seven "sacraments of mysteries" constitute the means by which grace is mediated to the sinner. They are: (1) *Baptism.* This sacrament is necessary to salvation and administered to infants, as in Roman Catholicism and Lutheranism. Original sin is thereby removed in infants and actual sin in adult baptism. Faith necessary for baptism is defined as consent to the teachings of the church. Baptism has an almost magical quality, as obviously infants cannot believe. (2) *Unction with Christ.* As the concluding step of baptism, taking the place of Roman Catholic confirmation, this sacrament supposedly confirms the gifts of the Holy Spirit for growth and strength. (3) *The Holy Communion or Eucharist.* Unlike Roman practice, this chief sacrament of the liturgy is celebrated only once a day in each church. Through priestly consecration, the Holy Spirit transsubstantiates the bread and wine into the body and blood of Christ. The real presence remains afterwards. (4) *Penitence* is much like the Roman version, except that the priest's function is more that of a spiritual advisor than a dictator. The absolution of the priest here, however, remits all temporal punishment due for sin, as well as its guilt. Indulgences are thus unneeded. (5) *Holy Orders* involve laying on of the bishop's hands to ordain a bishop, deacon, or priest. (6)*Matrimony* differs from the Roman form in that it can be dissolved in case of adultery. (7)*Unction.* The difference between Greek Orthodox and Roman practice in this is that here it is used, not for the dying, but to anoint the sick.

Fortunately the Orthodox Church differs from Rome in several other matters too. It rejects the authority and infallibility of the pope, does not aim at world dominion (although it also believes itself to be the only true church), does not deprive the laymen of the chalice (wine in the Eucharist), rejects multiplied masses, as well as indulgences, and purgatory. In the sixteenth century, Orthodox leaders turned down the approaches of Reformation leaders. Melanchthon, Calvin, and later Zinzendorf attempted to impress the patriarchs with the doctrine of justification by faith, but to no avail. Today representatives of the Greek Orthodox Church, a member of the World Council of Churches, sit in many conferences with Protestant leaders. At home, however, this church persecutes Protestant churches. As a doctrinal variation of Roman Catholicism, it is pagan at heart and offers salvation through a mingling of grace and human works. Naturally the church mediates between God and man through its priesthood.

The Orthodox Priest. At one time the local priest occupied an even more important place than he does today. He used to be called upon to "bless" everything, but today people are better educated, somewhat less superstitious. The Orthodox priest seems to have more spare time than his Roman counterpart. He also mixes with the people more. In the typical long wedding parties—which often last several days—the priest will sometimes get drunk with his parishioners. Because he serves as an informer for the police concerning activities in his parish, he in turn gets favors from the police. Hence the authorities often act against Protestant activities even though they might otherwise be inclined to leave them alone. Parish priests may marry, but those of the episcopacy, the bishops, are chosen from monks who are forbidden to marry. In Greece the typical priest wears long black robes. His hair falls to his shoulders and is often fashionably curled and tied. On his head is a stovepipe-shaped, cylindrical black hat with a flat top. Sometimes the priest wears a tremendous cross hung from a chain upon his chest.

Revivals Within Orthodoxy. Across the centuries there have been periodic calls to purity within the Greek Orthodox Church. *Eusebia,* for instance, was one of several such movements of the nineteenth century. In 1893, American-trained Greeks initiated *Eusebia* in Smyrna as a laymen's organization for the preaching of the gospel. In recent years, the

Zoé or "life" movement, has had wide influence. Students at the University of Athens and in other like centers have been affected. The *Zoé* emphasis began fifty years ago through the popular preaching of Eusebius Mathopoulos. Today it is responsible for 1,500 Sunday schools and 150,000 children. A magazine published by *Zoé* has more than 150,000 subscribers. Those priests who are within the *Zoé* brotherhood renounce high church offices, accept no money, do not marry, and live a communal life. In spite of these sacrifices, there are no harsh rules, and one can voluntarily quit at any time. Does *Zoé* know a real spiritual revival? No doubt some of these men are saved by faith in Christ. Yet we must remember that their intense activity is all carried on within the framework, doctrinal and practical, of Greek Orthodoxy. We have already seen that this church does not generally teach, or permit to be taught, salvation by grace through faith.

Attitudes Toward the Bible. Scripture reading on the part of the layman is discouraged on the grounds that he cannot fully understand it. The Confession of Dosithens discourages, and even prohibits, the general and indiscriminate reading of the Scriptures. Only theologians are to have unhindered access to the Scriptures. The laymen ought only to hear selected passages read. When, in the sixteenth century, the Protestant Reformers confronted Orthodox leaders with a challenge to decide for the faith once delivered, they received the following declaration from Constantinople: "We pray you again to receive the scriptures as they have been interpreted by the Church and as they have been confirmed by the seven ecumenical councils and other particular synods. For we must not remove the eternal boundaries made by the Fathers," and again, "We must believe, without doubting, in the scriptures, but not otherwise than they have been interpreted by the Catholic Church."[3] These statements show the same dependence on tradition that the Roman Catholic Church has, with one difference. Roman doctrine is constantly modified, while the Orthodox Church delivered its last authoritive statement in the year 787.

The Scriptures in the popular language have had a hard time in Orthodox lands. In 1903 a Bible translation was the cause for a popular revolt in Athens. Over many centuries there has been relentless persecution of those who read and distribute Bibles. The great missions historian, Julius Richter, noted in 1910 that the sale of the New Testament in modern Greek was forbidden everywhere, adding that this was at the time "the only country in the world in which the reading of the Bible in the mother tongue is a criminal act."[4] Lately, however, there has been a change for the better, so that the Bible is widely circulated and can be sold by colporteurs in the countryside. There is still, however, much opposition by

Orthodox priests on the village level, but at least it no longer has the full backing of the civil authorities. Meanwhile a profound ignorance of the contents of the Bible remains as a challenge to missions.

For many years the British and Foreign Bible Society branch in Athens has distributed multiplied thousands of Testaments and Bibles throughout the land. Sometimes the American Bible Society makes a special grant for some particular distribution. For example, on several occasions it has given 200,000 Testaments to the officers and men of the Greek Army. In a letter to the society, Major General D. Karachristos expressed his appreciation: "Instructions have been given to the agents of the religious service, who personally make the distributions to the officers and soldiers, to accompany them with sermons on the value and the benefit to be derived from reading the Bible."[5] In 1957, the Gideons too did their part toward helping Greece by supplying three thousand Greek villages with New Testaments. Of the hunger in the hearts of the populace for God's Word, George Kladis, the Bible Society secretary in Athens, says, "It is no exaggeration to say that never in the modern history of Greece has there been a greater interest from many quarters in arousing people's attention to the Bible."[6]

True Believers Persecuted. During the last decade there have been hundreds of authenticated cases in which Orthodoxy, usually working through the Greek government, has persecuted its tiny rivals, the real evangelicals. We will cite only one example. Because Mr. Charalambos Agapides of Katerini wrote a letter in 1954 condemning Orthodox persecution, he was sentenced to two months' imprisonment and a three-year suspended sentence. Mr. Agapides, an elder of the Evangelical Church of Katerini, had addressed his letter, about interference with his own congregation, to a Thessalonica newspaper. The three-and-one-half-hour trial on January 12, 1955, drew international attention. In Washington, Clyde W. Taylor of the National Association of Evangelicals, protested to the Greek ambassador. At a convention in Ottawa, the World Presbyterian Alliance voted to ask the World Council of Churches, of which the Greek Orthodox Church is a member, to work for religious freedom in Greece. Freedom of expression and freedom of the press were also involved in the Agapides case. Is there hope for any change of attitude in Athens? As Stewart Herman says, "Time and again the freedom of minorities has been transgressed, and even though the Greek government is sometimes hostile toward the state church, it is unlikely that the Orthodox Church will voluntarily advocate full freedom for all."[7]

A People for His Name. Aside from the huge Greek Orthodox Church, with its 7,500,000 followers and an army of 8,000 priests, there are few religious bodies of any kind. Many of the Lord's true disciples are to be found, however, in the tiny *Greek Evangelical Church.* There are about thirty churches in all, with some two thousand actual members. Under the wider influence of this body, which is Presbyterian in doctrine, are perhaps fifteen thousand people. The *Free Evangelical Church* is similar to the Plymouth Brethren in practice, and has some fine leaders and laymen. There are too few shepherds, however, and a deep need exists for instruction of young people in personal witness. The *Assemblies of God* have about one thousand members in six churches, but Baptists and Methodists, so well known in America, are almost nonexistent here. *Seventh-day Adventists* have five churches for some 250 members.

Among genuine believers in the Lord Jesus Christ can be found some highly-placed government officials, prominent lawyers, university professors, and professional men. For the most part, though, those who know Christ are from ordinary circles. Athens and its suburbs, containing a huge proportion of the country's people, get much more attention from the true body of Christ in Greece than other places. Here, there are half a dozen churches preaching the gospel. In spite of everything these good people can do, "every creature" does not receive a witness even in this densely populated area. More pastors and evangelists are needed, as well as a general plan to capture the present generation for Christ.

Sir, We Would See Jesus. According to the New Testament, the Greeks are a people who "seek after wisdom" (I Cor. 1:22). In this respect the modern Greek fits the picture. He is still seeking the same Unknown God, hearing Christian terminology without meeting Christ Himself. A good example of this endless quest for ultimate reality may be found in an account furnished by George Kladis of Athens. A Bible Society colporteur named Dimitrios Schinas left his Salonika (Thessalonica) home to sell Bibles in Berea, forty miles distant. As a former army officer, Schinas looked up an old army acquaintance who had in the meantime become a Member of Parliament. Schinas pointed out to his old friend that any effort to better the life of the people which did not begin with spiritual work in their hearts, was doomed to fail. "So far," he said, "you who are in authority have been totally indifferent, and stand aloof." Listening intently, the government leader agreed and bought a Bible. He began to read it and to profit thereby.

One Saturday afternoon not long afterward he came to Schinas to invite him to visit the prefect (governor). As soon as they had met, Schinas read Proverbs 1:5 to the prefect, "A wise man will hear, and will increase learning; and a man of understanding shall attain unto wise counsels." Upon request the colporteur repeated the verse, whereupon the prefect issued instruction to his office that he and his visitors should not be interrupted. For an hour the three men sat there with their Bibles open as Schinas explained the plan of redemption. At the close, the prefect said, "This is the book which should be in every Greek family. For many years I passed the Bible depot, but never entered to buy a Bible." A few weeks later the prefect himself was reported to have preached to the assembled population of the town of Barbara, using his newly discovered Bible to proclaim his new Saviour.

Another seeker was reported by Angelos Damaskinides, who found a woman sick with cancer in her home. He spoke to her of the Saviour who brings rest to the soul. "I am a great sinner," she answered. "How can I be saved? I am so sick that I know God is punishing me." As her visitor looked to the Holy Spirit for guidance, he was given the right words. "As I spoke," Damaskinides says, "she opened her weary eyes. Now they were bright with the light which comes from above. She was transformed."[8] "So He has forgiven me. He has forgiven all," the sick woman exclaimed. But she still struggled for complete peace. "Is it really possible? How can it be?" "It is finished," said Damaskinides. "Believe with all your heart. Give yourself to Him." Then suddenly a deep cry left her bosom as though a heavy load were being rolled away. "He *has* received me," she cried. "I thank you, Lord Jesus. You have forgiven me. I receive you now." Tears of joy flowed as the two prayed together. The next day the woman's husband said to a sister, "What happened yesterday? What wonderful things did my wife hear? How happy she is now! She doesn't even seem to feel the pain. She is completely changed." One more inquiring Greek had asked for an interview with the Lord: "Sir, we would see Jesus" (John 12:21).

Help From Abroad. In recent years several American missions have maintained work in Greece. The European Evangelistic Crusade and the Oriental Missionary Society have sent a few missionaries. Probably the best-known societies are the Greek Evangelical Mission and the American Mission to Greeks. The former has helped to build local churches, and to sponsor conferences, evangelism and summer camps, and it has given relief assistance. The latter mission has been interested in such projects as Bible training in Katerini, where it also has an orphanage. Bookstores, camps, and a printing press are other ministries. The Eastern European Mission has done a splendid work in preparing Sunday school literature and organizing Sunday schools with real soul-winning purpose.

All this helpful activity leaves the principal task yet undone. Most of the missions working in Greece do not send missionaries there, but aid local efforts instead. In several personal surveys of Greece the writer has seen a need for more foreign workers to help achieve, along certain lines, the evangelization of Greece. There are amazingly few missionaries in this unevangelized country. The systematic training of young people in an interdenominational Bible institute conducted on a high level would be of untold value. So far such training has been localized and improvised, meaning that the most promising Greek Christians have gone abroad for study. In general the Greek pastors are not receptive to the idea of help from resident foreign missionaries. But the reasons must be considered. Few foreigners have been able to adapt themselves to the mentality of the people, learn the difficult language, or make a genuine contribution. Unquestionably foreigners are needed and should go to Greece. Yet they must be genuinely called of God, willing to serve humbly in the midst of a proud people, and determined to let nothing stop them. There is no doubt that such men and women would succeed, winning souls to Christ and leaving an indelible mark on Greek evangelical life. Our reigning concept in viewing this mission field must be, "How can this land be evangelized in our generation?" Obviously the Greeks themselves must do the greater part of the work. But the foreign missionary can help.

The ornate pulpit in the Nieuwe Kerk of the Dutch Reformed
Church, Amsterdam.

Credit: W. ten Have

Chapter 12

CHANGING HOLLAND

"*The conflict with Rome within the Netherlands, as well as within the United States, is not merely a matter of theology. It is a national problem, which raises the old question of whether or not we are a Protestant nation. . . . The present situation is a period of awakening and of a rapidly developing emancipation of Roman Catholics.*"

—Dr. Gerrit C. Berkouwer
Professor of Dogmatic Theology
Free University of Amsterdam

"*Many people have turned aside entirely from all the churches and live outside any ecclesiastical relationships.*"

—Dr. E. Emmen
Former Secretary of the General Synod
Reformed Church of Holland

1. HOLLANDERS YESTERDAY AND TODAY

Windmills, Dikes, and Tulips. These are some of the things the name *Holland* conjures up in the mind. About one thousand of its renowned windmills still stand, some to drain water, but most to grind corn. As for dikes, often you do not know you are looking at one, so cleverly disguised they are. Tulips of course, are more obvious. Many a tourist, driving through miles of these many-hued flower carpets, feels an intoxication of the senses. Add impressions of traditional costumes, *klompen* or wooden shoes, the mythical boy with his finger in the dike, and you have the foreigner's concept of the Netherlands.

But there is much more to see and know. Since a quarter of this land, about the size of Massachusetts and Connecticut together, lies below sea level, Holland has had to learn to fight the sea as well as her human enemies. Through monumental labor, methods have been devised to block, drain, and channel the waters. Canals, dikes, *polders,*° and pumps

°Polders are units of drained, irrigated land recovered from the sea.

all connect in vast drainage and irrigation arteries similar in complexity to those of the human body. "God made the earth," say the Dutch, "but we made Holland." Elsewhere vistas of an older Holland gladden the eye on every side. Doddering, gabled houses on Amsterdam canals, picturesque island people of Marken and Volendam, removable red mailboxes on the back of streetcars, wide, sparkling windows, Scheveningen's quaint fisher folk, raw herring stands, organ-grinder music—these are only a few glimpses of a fascinating country. In contrast, the breathtaking architecture and lighting of a new Rotterdam emerging from its wartime ruins startle the traveler.

Little Holland is only 120 miles wide and 180 miles long, but here more than ten million people comprise the densest single national population in the world. Almost 25,000 of them are engaged in fishing, and many more in the important dairy products business. Dutch cheese is one of the better-known commodities, with cheeses named after the cities of Edam, Leyden, and Gouda. Boskoop, with its 750 nurseries, is the largest flower center in the world. Amsterdam, the capital, leads in diamond-cutting, while Rotterdam is one of Europe's busiest ports. Everyone has heard of Delft china. Eindhoven is the home of the famous Philips electrical products. About 37 per cent of all workers are employed in industry.

Characteristics of a People. Many of Holland's people are farmers. Half the farms are, in fact, worked by families owning less than ten acres apiece. To make a living under these conditions requires hard work and little play. Though life is somewhat primitive by some standards, yet farm homes in this land are warmed by an indefinable glow of solid comfort—a comfort which rises not from appliances or luxuries but from the nature of the people. The Dutch farmer may seem impassive and austere at first, but longer acquaintance will bring his better qualities to light. He will prove to be honest, thorough, and unusually sound in judgment about his work. Children here are playful, but respectful of parents. The women are more adaptable, gay, and sensitive than the stolid men. A typical Dutch family on a typical farm lacks only one thing. Though the people eat well, are sober, thrifty, and even God-fearing in their way, the new birth is an unheard-of experience to most of them. Many individuals live and die without God, even though the truth has been in their midst for centuries. Jesus Christ is so familiar to them that He remains a total stranger!

Today Holland has more young people in proportion to her population than any other nation in the world. About 37 per cent of all Dutch people are under twenty years of age. Then too, if you were born here you will probably live longer than a person born elsewhere! An average life expectancy of 69.5 years for men and 71.5 years for women is the world's highest. Furthermore, there are more people packed into these 12,850 square miles than there are in any other spot on earth. More than thirteen times as many people inhabit one square mile as inhabit the same area in the United States. Since the end of World War II over 250,000 Dutch people have had to emigrate (mostly to Canada and Australia). Over-population still remains a serious problem, even though the recovery of the Zuider Zee polders from the sea will mean the addition of 10 per cent to the land area of the country.

Hollanders from the nine provinces naturally differ greatly from each other in custom and personality. But city folk, 30 per cent of the total population, are much the same everywhere, more restless and often more superficial. Temptations lurk in the anonymity of city streets that are little known in the country. Thus a "lost generation" of youth in Holland's large cities has grown up without the restraint of their more godly forebears. These new delinquents are the "deadend kids" who are throwing off tradition and growing careless in regard to right and wrong. Some few have become Communists and criminals, while others just drift into the wrong crowd, where they long for still more liberty. But as we shall see elsewhere, a small number are turning to the One whose bondage is perfect freedom.

What qualities mark these people? Dutchmen give finicky attention to trifling details. They love to stress the difference between things that seem alike to the casual observer. But this trait, which is offensive to European Latins, has helped make the nation great. Other qualities are neatness, conscientiousness, tenacity, and caution. There is little spontaneity and imagination; too much enthusiasm in others tends to make Dutch people self-conscious. They are by nature modest and little given to exhibitionism of any kind. Cleanliness for its own sake is a passion: the word *schoon* has the double meaning of "clean" and "beautiful." Every Saturday the people put this to practice in the *schoonmaakdag*, national clean-up day.

Out of the Womb of War. Holland's adults today are not only what wartime evils made them; they are what their own fallen natures have made them. Let us say that war has only intensified and hastened the process. When the SS Nazi troops came looking for Father, children had to be taught to lie about his whereabouts after the enemy learned that children would easily blurt out the truth without thinking. Children were also taught by their own parents that cheating, stealing, falsification of papers, and even murder were justifiable under wartime conditions. But after the war the rules changed. Youngsters then had to be taught that what was right before was wrong now, that morality was no longer relative, but absolute. Some did not care to learn the lesson, and others were never taught it well. Thus the adult of today has emerged from the womb of a war in which everything that discomfited the enemy was legitimate. This is the young adult who is now turning away from the churches to humanism or the cults. He is the man who holds "the truth in unrighteousness" (Rom. 1:18). He and his family are the reason why Holland so much needs our prayer.

Home is Where the Heart Is. To understand the Dutch home is to understand Dutch life, because home is the center and circumference of that life. The much-prized, intimate family relationship is maintained at all costs. Father has somber, patriarchal authority over the others. In many homes Calvinism forms the background for customs which linger long after the spiritual meaning has been lost. In the discussions around the family table one can see the formalities, the deference to authority, the slow but thorough reasonings which form the basis of private and public life. Hospitality and a ready kindness are by-products of these traits, seen in the welcome given to foreigners or to any in distress. Meals in the average family seem almost frugal sometimes, with cooked meat served only occasionally and cold open-face sandwiches accepted as a staple part of the diet. But an outsider is always welcome to share whatever the family has.

This home and its tight circle provide a focal point of contact for the Christian worker. Nowhere is "family salvation" more meaningful than in a country where families are close-knit. In few places in Europe are homes easier to enter than here. Other friends can be freely invited in for a Bible class for example, that could some day become a church. To be a guest in the homes of true Dutch believers gives one a never-to-be-forgotten taste of the oneness of the Body of Christ.

A Quick Glance at Origins. When Julius Caesar invaded the Netherlands in 57 B.C., he found the Belgae, Batavi, and Frisii tribes there. The Romans were followed by the Germanic Franks under Charlemagne. Before that ruler had died, Holland had become almost wholly Catholic. This had been accomplished early by men like St. Boniface, apostle to the Germans, who was later murdered by the Frisians. The several provinces of the medieval kingdom of Lotharingia, which included Holland, became united in the fourteenth century under the French Dukes of Burgundy. This whole area then passed to the Spanish branch of the Hapsburgs in 1506. A few years later the Dutch people in large numbers quickly embraced the doctrines of the Reformation, which had spread through the country like wildfire. Philip II of Catholic Spain was just as quick to begin the bitter persecutions that wrote so dark a chapter of suffering into Dutch history. Nationalism and the new faith became a single cause when the people revolted in 1568. There followed a long, arduous struggle for liberty led by William the Silent, founder of the House of Orange and sometimes called the "Dutch George Washington." Outstanding among his victories were the siege of Alkmaar and the relief of Leiden. In 1579 the seven northern provinces succeeded in forming a coalition called the Union of Utrecht. Independence was declared in 1581 and finally recognized in 1648.

During the seventeenth century Holland came into her own as the leading commercial power in Europe. Overseas territories were extended, and Dutch maritime prowess became a byword. With the eighteenth-century wars, Dutch power declined, and Napoleon's defeat led to the founding of the kingdom of the United Netherlands, a union of Holland and Belgium under William I. Belgium withdrew in 1830, and ten years later the Dutch king abdicated in favor of his son, William II. William III, grandfather of the former Queen Wilhelmina, then succeeded to the throne for a long, prosperous reign. Executive power of this hereditary, constitutional monarchy rests today in the Crown—the Queen and her ministers. Though the Netherlands (the official name) maintained her neutrality in World War I and declared it during World War II, the Germans invaded the country in May, 1940, and held it until May, 1945. Loss of colonies after the war has shaken the country, but thanks to national foresight her economy continues high, providing a good living standard for her people.

Reformation Upheaval. At the time of the Reformation Holland and Belgium were united under a *Stadtholder* (viceroy) as part of the kingdom of Charles V, Emperor of Germany and King of Spain. A strong, free burgher life had developed in many large towns, for the Flemish provinces had long been noted for their love of freedom and highly developed culture. Anticlericalism was especially strong in the towns. There were forerunners of the Reformation in this area long before it came. Among these were Lambert-le-Begue of Liège in the twelfth century and Henri Goethals of Ghent in the thirteenth. Jean de Ruysbroek was still another who paved the way. The society known as "The Brethren of the Common Life" influenced Thomas à Kempis to write his *Imitation of Christ* and made some contribution by training men like Erasmus of Rotterdam.

When the Reformation's first effects began to be felt, Charles V enraged the growing number of Protestants in the Lowlands by discriminating against them. Meanwhile, Calvinism, Lutheranism, and the Anabaptist movement all made headway in Holland. By the 1530's Holland had become the leading center of the Anabaptists, thousands of whom were to die for their faith by some of the cruelest means man could conceive. Menno Simons, one of their later leaders, became the founder of the Mennonites. Here in Holland Cornelius Hoen worked out the symbolic interpretation of the Lord's Supper later adopted by Zwingli in Zurich. By the time Charles V abdicated in 1555, a strong reform was well under way.

In the 1560's a great Calvinist upsurge began to dominate the northern provinces. Meanwhile Philip II of Spain had taken over his father's throne. Unlike Charles V, who had grown up in the Lowlands and knew Flemish, Philip spoke only Spanish—a lack which alienated him from the people. Through heavy taxation, the presence of the Spanish army and officials, and especially by the help of the Inquisition, Philip made it clear that he was using the Netherlands only as a tool of Spanish policy. Included in this of course, was the maintenance of the Spanish faith. As thousands were burned, buried alive, or hanged, resentment flamed into rebellion. The people were forbidden to follow the reformers' writings, read or circulate Scriptures, engage in religious conversation, attend proscribed meetings, or damage the image of any saint. After an attempt to enforce the Counter-Reformation decrees of the Council of Trent, opposition mounted still further. While persecutions raged, trade fell off, work declined, and a pall fell on the land. Finally four hundred nobles presented a "Petition of Rights," which Philip answered by sending an army of ten thousand under the new *Stadtholder,* the Duke of Alva. During this period a great host escaped to other countries, where they settled down and began a new life. A new blood bath now began. The Duke of Alva later claimed that he executed eighteen thousand persons under his own authority, and that 100,000 more were put to death through the Inquisition. In spite of these measures, two-thirds of Flanders is said to have been won over to the views of the reformers. No church was big enough to hold the crowds, who could meet only in the open air. The year 1563 saw the formation of the first Walloon Synod of Churches.

In 1568 the Low Countries rebelled against the Spanish occupation. Extreme means of retaliation resulted. One massacre, called "the Spanish fury," ocurred in Antwerp in 1576 and brought about the death of nine thousand people and the despoiling of large areas of property. The leader who was now to emerge from this chaos had long been in the conflict already. At first only a political and military leader, William the Silent is thought to have passed through a profound experience with God while a hostage in the Court of France. Here, too, he had heard Henry II inadvertently disclose the secret clauses in the treaties between France and Spain concerning the extermination of heresy in their respective kingdoms—including the Netherlands. William, holding his tongue as though he already knew these secrets, was henceforth called "the Silent." Profoundly moved, he resolved to drive Spain out of the Netherlands.

After turning in vain for help to Germany, England, and France, William determined to work alone. Yet he was not alone, for he uttered at this time these magnificent words: "When I undertook the defense of these suppressed Christians, I made an alliance with the mightiest of all potentates, the Lord of Hosts, who is able to save us if He choose." Space does not permit the fascinating story of William's campaigns. Often defeated and discouraged, he nevertheless led Holland to ultimate victory and liberty. It was not until 1648 that Spain finally withdrew, after eighty years of resistance by the Dutch. Throughout the history of Holland, the delivering and protecting hand of God has been very evident. Her peace and prosperity today bear witness to the readiness she once showed to receive the Word of God. Few nations have suffered so much for the Lord, or given Him as many martyrs.

There is much speculation as to why Holland became Calvinist instead of Lutheran. She was closer to Germany geographically. William the Silent, who became in turn Catholic, Lutheran, and Calvinist, was not a man given to the theological niceties. Probably Calvinism was adopted by most of the people because its theology lends itself better to both an underground movement and intervention in state affairs in the name of God. This latter action is still carried on significantly in Holland by the Calvinists of our time.

2. PROTESTANTS UNDER THE MICROSCOPE

Looking Beneath the Surface. It is difficult at first to think of Holland as a modern "mission field" in Europe's heartland. Hollanders living abroad give a deserved impression of integrity, industry, and piety. Every country values the infusion of this racial stock into the national bloodstream, for all the world admires the Dutch people. In Europe they have a high reputation as calculating planners, clever traders, and careful craftsmen. Furthermore, Holland is a land of churches, where the flat countryside shows more than ten thousand steeples lifted skyward. As new land is recovered from the sea, still more churches are added to the scene. The poet speaks of a place "where very prospect pleases, and only man is vile." Such words could very well describe Holland. Are things here other than they seem on the surface? Does opportunity really exist for "every creature" to hear redemption's story? Has Holland become, in this sense, a twentieth-century mission field?

Most of Holland's Protestants hardly think of their country in that way. But the multiplying and militant Catholics do. So do the aggressive sects which are claiming many inactive Protestants. Discerning believers in the Lord Jesus from every church background agree that their country needs intensive evangelization. In this section we propose to show that secularism, Romanism, and Protestant formalism have together created an alarming situation.

The Over-all Religious Picture. The Roman Catholic Church is rapidly gaining numbers. It now claims 38.48 per cent of the population, with the Protestants together retaining 43.69 per cent. Broken down, the proportions are these, according to the latest religious census:

		Members	Per cent of Population
1.	Roman Catholics	3,703,572	38.48
2.	Protestants	4,216,027	43.69
	Dutch Reformed	2,988,839	31.05
	Christian Reformed (5 bodies)	935,956	9.72
	Lutheran (2 bodies)	69,526	.72
	Mennonites	67,420	.70
	Apostolic (3 bodies)	42,964	.44
	Remonstrants	40,044	.42
	Evangelical Free	18,862	.20
	Baptists	15,584	.16
	Salvation Army	15,185	.16
	Old Catholics	11,380	.12
	Smaller varied bodies	10,287	
3.	No religious profession		17.92

The Anatomy of Protestantism. Most of the churches in Holland are either results of, or reactions to, the strong Calvinism which took root here during the fifteenth and sixteenth centuries. By far the largest body is the Dutch Reformed Church *(Nederlands Hervormde Kerk)*, with headquarters in The Hague. About three-fifths of all Protestants, or nearly three million people, are claimed for this church's 1,271 places of worship. Actual adult membership probably does not exceed 800,000, however, since children are included in the larger figure. This inclusion must be considered in analyzing all figures of Reformed bodies, including splinter groups, in Holland. Attendance figures are of course much lower than the adult membership figures suggest.

This large denomination is highly organized into synods, with numerous publications, schools, special institutions, a radio ministry, and missionary activities. Dutch Reformed political influence, too, is great. The church maintains a theological seminary at Driebergen. Greatest strength of the church is in the province of Drenthe, where 60.2 per cent of the population claim membership; the weakest area is the largely Catholic province of Limburg, where only 2.8 per cent are Dutch Reformed. Abraham Kuiper, the intrepid statesman, theologian, and writer, launched the Dutch Reformed Church in its present form in 1885. Doctrinally, several creeds form the basis of belief: the Confession of Guido de Bres (1561), the Heidelberg Catechism (1563), and the Canons of Dordrecht (1619).

Next in size is the Christian Reformed Church (*Gereformeerde Kerk*), which is the equivalent of the same group in America. This group claims 715,936 members, again including the children. Strongest in Friesland province, where it claims 24.4 per cent of the population, the denomination is generally more conservative doctrinally than the Dutch Reformed Church. But many of its pastors are opposed to any open plea to the people to come to Christ, as this would be a violation of Calvinistic views. For a creedal basis, the same documents are used as in the Dutch Reformed Church. Begun through the union of two separate secessions by other bodies in 1837 and 1886, the present seven hundred congregations carry on a vigorous work, maintaining their own theological seminary. There are five other Reformed denominations, which for one reason or another have split off from the two principal churches of the Reformed tradition. Other smaller groups include the *Remonstrants*, an Arminian church formed in reaction to the Synods of Dort, having about 40,000 members. *Lutherans* total 69,526, *Mennonites* 67,420, the *Apostolic Church*, 42,964, *Baptists* 15,584, *Evangelical Free Churches*, 18,862. Then there are the other, smaller churches here, too.

The Baptist Church is a smaller body, with an interesting origin in Holland. Dr. John Elias Feisser, a Dutch Reformed pastor and leader of the nineteenth century, began to insist that members join his church only by personal faith in Christ. When he next proposed a reform in the practice of infant baptism, he was cast out of the Synod. Shortly afterward Feisser himself was baptized, with six others, in Northern Holland by the great Danish Baptist missionary, Julius Kobner. These men formed the first Baptist church in Holland in 1845. From 100 members in 1900, the church grew to its present, still tiny percentage of less than two-tenths of 1 per cent of the population.

Orthodoxy, Semiorthodoxy, and Liberalism. In broad terms, the leaders of the Protestant churches of Holland may be grouped theologically under three headings. In the *orthodox* camp are some Baptists, pastors of the Evangelical Free Church, the Plymouth Brethren, some Reformed League pastors of the Netherland. Reformed Church, the Salvation Army, and other groups. But the Reformed Church based on the Dordrecht Confession is the largest such body. This is the church which goes to some lengths to create church organizations paralleling the secular ones in an effort to wholly influence its people. Then there is the Christian Reformed Church, in which pastors hold a strong separatist ecclesiastical position. In practice this church is opposed to all worldly amusements, keeping a close discipline over its members. "In general, this group of churches is moving away from neo-orthodoxy to increasingly Biblical theology, although many of the pastors are still not what Americans call fundamentalists."[1] A new interest in evangelism animates some of this orthodox group, though those of Reformed persuasion often object to the use of an evangelistic invitation as being foreign to both the creeds and the practice of their churches.

Those in the *semiorthodox* classification have been largely influenced by Karl Barth and the later neo-orthodox thinkers. But we have called them "semiorthodox" since not all are hearty subscribers to neo-orthodoxy as such. Those in the main stream of this group come from the Netherlands Reformed Church, although some leaders are from other segments of other denominations. Within the bosom of the Netherlands Reformed Church can be found almost every shade of belief, from near-Unitarianism to hyper-Calvinism. There are even those whose social views approach those of Communism. Indeed, this church, in its tolerance, reminds one of the traditional variety of belief among rectors in the Church of England or *pasteurs* of the French Reformed Church. Once a great wave of liberalism engulfed it, but now neo-orthodoxy has taken the lead.

Four subgroups can be found among the total of about two thousand Netherlands Reformed pastors. First there are the more than three hundred members of the Reformed League already referred to as belonging to the orthodox wing. These men prefer traditional Calvinism. A second organization is the Confessional Union, with several hundred adherents strongly holding to the Dordrecht Confessioin. A third party in this denomination is made up of those advocating the ethical approach to theology, exalting life above doctrine. A fourth branch of about 35C pastors is said to belong to more liberal circles and movements.

Unfortunately the roughly fourteen hundred pastors (more than half the total) belonging to the second and third groups (Confessional and Ethical) have been under heavy Barthian influence since about 1930. With the governing power of the synods and of the denomination as a whole in their hands, the champions of the new orthodoxy—which so often falls short of genuine orthodoxy—have the strongest voice in this largest denomination. Necessarily much is missing from both preaching and program when the Word of God is not both wholly acceptable and utterly authoritative. The pale, confused message emanating from periodical, radio, pulpit, and classroom leaves many readers and hearers short of saving faith in Jesus Christ. One of neo-orthodoxy's admired theologians, Reinhold Niebuhr, of America, expressed their viewpoint well when he took Billy Graham to task for making too clear a distinction between the saved and the lost, and for being too naïvely Biblical. For those members in this large church who are truly born again, the needed message of growth in holiness must also suffer at the hands of these who fail to preach the whole counsel of God.

In third place are the older *liberals,* now somewhat out of date. Like spinsters who wistfully eye their current beaux but refuse to capitulate to marriage, the standpat liberals of all Dutch churches have waning influence, thinning crowds, and fading aspirations. To be sure, some still have influential pulpits, but the older liberalism is no longer a current trend. All this may be changed if the present interest in the Bultmann theology quickens. Dutch seminary professors have always been under heavy German influence. The Bultmann emphasis, which is only a new form of the old modernism, could catch hold among Dutch theological students and lead to a swing of the pendulum in the opposite direction.

Piety Without Morality. One result of formalism in the churches has been the practice of "a form of godliness" which omits altogether any personal experience with Christ as Saviour. Legalism has arisen in many places—an empty shell without vital, living relationship to God through Christ. This can be seen even in the costumes still worn in some places as a lingering custom from former days. Near Amersfoort, for instance, are the twin villages of Spakenburg and Bunschoten, rivaling Volendam and Marken for their interesting, old regional dress. How did the awkward, ugly clothing of women in Spakenburg originate? These cumbersome dresses were originally designed to deliver men from temptation by shrouding the female form.

In some areas such legalism goes beyond prescribing old dresses to retain its original strict watch over the whole life. Staphorst, in the province of Overijssel, provides such an example. On weekdays this is quite a normal town of some eight thousand inhabitants, who are perhaps only more serious-faced and less tolerant of foreigners than other Hollanders. But on Sundays Staphorst is transformed into a solemn, pious place. Visitors on the Lord's Day are not very welcome; some who have tried to photograph the famous Sunday procession have had their cameras smashed. With heads down-bent and eyes fixed on the ground, the villagers move wordlessly toward the church in separate files of men and women. Dress is strictly regimented in what is probably the only Calvinistic procession in the modern world. Surely it is unique for Europe. In order to discourage observation by strangers, Staphorsters stop automobiles at the village outskirts on Sundays; they themselves do not even ride bicycles on the first day of the week.

While this sober, silent piety seems, at first sight, closer to the Biblical idea of keeping the Lord's Day than the negligence seen elsewhere, is it actually what God desires? Only from a living relationship to Him can true discipleship follow. "The kingdom of God is not meat and drink, but righteousness, and peace, and joy in the Holy Ghost" (Rom. 14:17). To force the whole community to assume the forms of a godliness which is really not in the hearts of many can lead to phariseeism and kindred evils. It is strange but true, that in the pious village of Staphorst trial marriage, which is meant to lead to trial maternity, is encouraged. Local custom dictates that no young man should take his betrothed to wife until she has proved to him by pregnancy that she will be able to bear children. Such reasoning rests on the Bible-based conviction of Staphorsters that farmers should not hire outsiders to do their work, but depend on their own large families. How a stern outer conformity to religion on the one hand can be reconciled with trial maternity on the other, only the people of Staphorst could explain.

Another dour Calvinist community is the former islet of Urk (population 5,500), a fishing village on the Zuider Zee. On Sundays Urkers still separate their hens from the roosters, read only the Bible, turn their paintings to the wall, and walk only to church. To do anything else is sinful. One day ten years ago Urk ceased to be an island. A road was built along a dike, connecting the town to the mainland—and the twentieth century. With the easier contact came the invasion of Teddy boys from the mainland, the introduction of teen-age clothes and habits. One wild night in July, 1959, five hundred youngsters, many of them drunk, rioted on the main street. After this the bars were ordered closed at ten o'clock on Saturday nights. This action only moved the emancipated young people down along the dike, where they continued their drinking and public love-making. Finally the Urk town council was forced to enact a strong law making it a crime to "trudge, slouch, lounge, saunter, flock together" or "to sit or lie" after dark on public roads.[2] The old-fashioned religious people of Urk deplore the change that has come to their town. The blame for actions like those of the Teddy boys cannot be laid on the times, however. Human nature always seems to rebel with some special vigor against a religion that teaches the laws of God but omits to extend His grace.

While the cases of these towns are admittedly extreme and almost unique in Holland, I have chosen them as a symbol of an attitude. Many Protestants brought up in the churches secretly or openly resent the yoke imposed upon them. Especially is this true of today's youth. Without personal experience with Christ as a point of departure, their reactions often begin with indifference, degenerate to cynicism, and end in the severance of all but nominal ties. This can be seen in some of the answers given to the following question in a nation-wide poll: "Do you believe it permissible for young people to have premarital sexual relationships?" Among unchurched people 51 per cent of men polled and 31 per cent of women polled answered, "Yes."[3] Though such a reaction from unchurched people might not be surprising, it was shocking to learn that 29 per cent of *church* men and 14 per cent of *church* women also approved of premarital sex experience. Naturally this approval was based upon the assumption that the young people are in love and intend to marry.

It goes without saying that the older Reformed bodies are concerned about their youth. Sunday schools, usually separate from the church altogether, and devoted mostly to the instruction of the very young, cannot accomplish their potential best in Holland. Most of these have been organized by the Netherlands Sunday School Union of Amsterdam, which in a recent year reported 1,400 Sunday schools and 12,000 students. But since teaching is not often extended beyond the age of twelve, there is little understanding by young people of the reality of faith in Christ. The extensive and thorough protestant school system, with its multiplied thousands of pupils, ought to fill in this gap and prepare for church membership. Here the Bible is taught along with other subjects. But everything depends on the teacher; in many cases personal experience of conversion is not emphasized. As one full-time Christian worker among children expressed it, "I lost my faith while attending a Christian School."[4]

Religious Life in a Dutch Middletown. Since Catholics and Protestants roughly balance each other in Holland's churchgoing population, it would be useful to examine the religious practices of a single community so proportioned. A sort of Dutch "Middletown" in which we could look at people's attitudes in cross section, as it were, would give insight into church life as nothing else could. Sassenheim, a town of about eight thousand inhabitants, just off the main highway between The Hague and Haarlem, is just such a town. Dutch sociologists have made an exhaustive analysis of its people's backgrounds, habits, beliefs, tastes, and prejudices. The soil composition of the Sassenheim area, and the high percentage of underground water, as well as the location near the sea, provide natural bulb-growing conditions. So most of the town's inhabitants work at tulip cultivation in a section of the country which blooms with traditional many-hued splendor during the spring tulip season.

According to the latest religious census, the Roman Catholics numbered 52 per cent of Sassenheim's population, Protestants of several bodies 45.6 per cent, and non-church members 2.4 per cent. Here we notice the Dutchman's habit of claiming some religious affiliation at census time, even though it be hereditary and often nominal. All but 17.92 per cent of the population claim a religion. That figure needs qualification. One of the writer's Dutch friends, upon answering the census taker's question about church affiliation with just the word "Christian," was confronted with a long list of possible denominations to help him be more precise. Under the pressure of long discussion, he chose a denomination just to avoid being classified as "without religion."

These figures, representing almost a whole town's population as church members, need a second qualification. Both Catholics and Protestants of the Reformed tradition count minor children as church "members," since both believe they are under a divine covenant that virtually assures them of ultimate salvation. So the figure representing almost the entire town as Christians in the general sense would be interpreted differently by those who do not agree with these premises.

In a questionnaire about the religious life of individuals, the following facts and percentages of those polled in this *very religious* Dutch community are revealing: (1) 12.6 per cent did not believe that life had any special meaning or purpose. (2) 19.8 per cent did not believe that present conduct would have any effect upon their future state after death. (3) 3.2 per cent were not sure whether they believed in God at all. (4) 24.8 per cent never talked nor thought about religion. (5) 10 per cent never went to church, 3.7 per cent went only rarely, and 2 per cent only once a year. (In other words 13.7 per cent of all those polled rarely or never attended church.) (6) Only 19 per cent had a Bible (even though 45.6 per cent of the town residents claim to be Protestants). (7) 14.9 per cent of the parents never talked about religion with their children. We conclude from the above study of an average Dutch neighborhood, well-churched by both Roman Catholic and Protestant bodies, that there is much nominal profession. As the survey puts it, in past generations "religion, to a greater extent than today, played an important role in the life of the inhabitants."[5]

Weakness Within. Let us now consider three weaknesses in Dutch Protestantism. A first look reveals *a weakness in the message itself.* As is true everywhere else in the world, the failure to emphasize personal salvation has made many Protestants in Holland professors of a creed rather than possessors of a life. Thus the churches have often served more as centers of community social life or guardians of outward decency than as channels of divine truth. This fact quickly becomes evident to all who do evangelistic work with the general public in Holland. The following figures, taken from Billy Graham's Rotterdam meeting at Feyenoord Stadium, June 30, 1955, bear out this point. I quote from the report of the follow-up committee:

> All together, 1,408 people out of a crowd of 60,000 came forward in response to the invitation. Of these who professed Christ, about a third (476) were under the age of twenty. Only eighteen claimed to be Catholic and thirty-seven were without any church, although 132 left the church profession question unanswered for reasons of their own. All the rest (1,221 out of 1,408) were Protestants by profession, the Dutch Reformed church leading with 768 (about half of the total) and the Christian Reformed (Gereformeerd) with 324.[6]

Almost exactly the same percentage has been found again and again in the writer's own evangelistic experience in Holland, covering a span of ten years. In a campaign held at the leading North Sea resort of Scheveningen near The Hague in July, 1956, the following were noted among sixty typical converts: thirty-one (half of the total) claimed the Dutch Reformed Church as their spiritual home, while six belonged to the Christian Reformed (Gereformeerd). The rest came from the following Protestant churches: Christian Reformed (Article 31), Free Evangelical, Lutheran, Brethren, and Liberal Reformed. Only three were Roman Catholics.

If this proportion holds for evangelistic work in general—and there is reason to believe it does, then some link is painfully absent in the teaching of Protestant churches in the Netherlands. Due to the preponderantly Reformed character of the great majority of Protestant churches, failure to evangelize must logically lie at the door of that persuasion. Can a theological system which counts children as "members" impart false assurance of salvation to parents and children alike? Or has Barthian thought so compromised most pastors that they cannot fully believe in an inerrant book? Again, have even thoroughly orthodox pastors in the Reformed communities been themselves lacking in spiritual depth and experience? We raise all these questions without attempting to answer them.

It is sad to hear of a case like that of a young lady in Groningen. This girl was dying, at the age of twenty-five when a godly Brethren laborer told her of a Saviour's love. Later the same evening her *dominie* or pastor called. When she asked about eternal condemnation, he laughed. "Don't worry about that," he assured her. "I have had a theological education and know more about this sort of thing than an ignorant worker like your friend. I tell you there is no hell."[7] So far as anyone knows, though poised on the threshold of a glorious salvation, she never entered in before she died. Today the pastor reportedly occupies a popular and influential pulpit in Amsterdam.

Manufacturer Dick van Katwijk, a prominent and faithful Christian businessman, tells of two young people who decided for Christ in the Billy Graham meeting in Amsterdam in 1954. Directed to a particular minister later, they discovered in a conversation with him that he did not accept the Bible as the infallible Word of God. "The Bible was written long ago by various people in strange languages and has been translated many times since," said the clergyman. "Those people all had different mentalities and habits from ours. So you must not take the Bible too seriously. Just get the spirit of it, the golden rule."[8]

A second weakness concerns *divisions within the churches.* To be sure, some of the older divisions were doctrinal in character and were carried out on the Scriptural grounds of preserving sound faith. These are matters of history. The problem today is that many a Protestant church body in Holland considers itself alone to be the true Body of Christ, and has lost belief in the universal Body of which all believers are members. E. Emmen admits that "great conflicts divide the Christians in the Netherlands. Their separation is typical of the lowlands near the sea."[9] He is referring here to the typical Dutch farms, small and separated from each other by irrigation canals or old dikes. Most of the old dikes once erected to protect the land from sea water are now no longer used for their original purpose. They still stand today only because they make convenient roads or paths at a higher level. The illustration is a good one. The old, unused divisions between the true people of God need to come down if evangelism is to advance. Many of the denominational peculiarities are only empty traditions today, out of date and hindering the work.

Committee work and resolutions will not bring spiritual oneness. Only repentance and obedience to the Holy Spirit can yield the kind of love needed to bring down the dikes of pride. The Dutch people, as we have already noted, love to discuss details with care and infinite patience. This quality, which produced great theologians, has also produced too many pastors and laymen like the ancient Pharisees who placed more importance on the outward matters of the law than on the inner core of the truth. The same stubbornness which led these heroic Dutch people to cling to the Word in the face of savage persecution can lead some to unbelievable harshness over nonessentials. In evangelistic efforts in Holland I have seen clergymen refuse to speak to each other in a meeting because one opposed an open invitation to an individual to come to Christ publicly while the other favored it. Yet both men loved Christ, preached His redemptive work, and championed the teaching of salvation by faith alone. The particular repentant man they differed over got through to God after all, and has been walking with Him for years.

A third problem in Dutch Protestantism is *the chronic shortage of pastors*. The largest denomination, Dutch Reformed, reported 207 pastoral vacancies out of 1,825 posts in a recent year. The Christian Reformed church had 161 openings out of 1,107 appointments. The Baptist Union showed 10 vacancies out of 53 churches. Almost half the Independent Baptist pulpits, or five out of eleven, were empty. Even allowing for the fact that some of the churches reported may be only small preaching stations which can be cared for by a pastor nearby, these statistics are alarming. They remain disquieting even when death, retirement, and normal turnover are considered, affecting as they do more than 10 per cent of the largest church's posts. An average of more than two hundred pastoral vacancies has persisted in the Dutch Reformed church since 1923, or for thirty-three years, having fallen below the average on just three occasions. The most plausible explanation of the pastoral shortage which can be given is that the general spiritual level of the churches must be lower than it once was. Regardless of the highly-organized nature of the church life typical of Holland, not enough young men are being called into the ministry of the gospel or staying with it after training.

3. HUSKY CHALLENGERS OF TRUTH

Catholic Gains. At the beginning of this chapter we quoted statements by two Dutch leaders concerning the growing importance of Catholicism in their country. Let us see to what extent they are borne out by the facts. Several striking traits mark Roman Catholicism in the Netherlands: (1) It is rapidly winning converts. (2) It is carefully indoctrinating them. (3) It is politically ascendant. (4) It maintains a quite pure form and a warm missionary spirit. (5) It receives strong moral support from Flemish Belgium.

It will be worthwhile to consider these points at more length in order to evaluate them.

1) Converts are multiplying rapidly. Such was Catholicism's success that it claimed a 28.3 per cent increase in members during the seventeen years between 1930 and 1947. During the same period the Netherlands Reformed Church, by far the largest Protestant body, *lost* 3.47 per cent of its share of the population. Should the next census show that this trend is steady or climbing, much self-examination would seem in order for the Protestants. Not all Protestant leaders seem concerned that Catholics have now regained almost half of the once wholly Protestant country. Due to a favorable birth rate and to energetic proselyting, about three thousand converts a year are being added to the Catholic church. Looking back in history, we can see that this is the continuation

of a trend only temporarily interrupted by wars. In Holland and Luxemburg, for instance, Catholic population had grown—mostly through births —from 350,000 in 1800 to more than 2,000,000 in 1907. This period is a typical century-long one. Rome's sanctions against birth control are rigorously applied, especially in the south, where big families are proverbial.

In the cities Catholics have gained notably. Between 1930 and 1947 Protestants lost ground in four of Holland's largest cities—Amsterdam, Rotterdam, The Hague, and Utrecht—while Catholics gained in three of the same four during the same period. The gain in Utrecht is a good example of Catholic progress. "In 1853 there were four parishes for 30,000 Romans, in 1900 twelve parishes for 75,000, and in 1955, thirty-three parishes for 175,000 members."[10] While the city was growing, Catholics were steadily increasing, not only in number, but in their percentage of the population.

As we have seen, according to the latest census, 38.38 per cent of the population professed the Catholic faith, 42.4 per cent called themselves Protestant, and 17.1 per cent claimed no religion. In the intervening years since this census the Catholic proportion is approaching 40 per cent and still growing. According to the 1961 *National Catholic Almanac,* Rome claims 39 per cent of Holland today.

How does the church find converts from the more listless fringe of Protestantism and among the religiously uncommitted? Proselyting is carried out in a quiet but persistent fashion. Church appearances and practices, especially in areas where Catholics do not have a majority, tend to be conservative and inoffensive. Even political activity by Catholics is carried out on the local level in a disarming way. Doors are thus opened to the minds of some who might otherwise resist new ideas. The post-war appointment of a Dutch cardinal was trumpeted as an honor to the nation. By radio the Catholic K.R.O. organization in Hilversum has been airing well-planned broadcasts, since 1926. Periodicals and literature written for all levels of society follow up listeners to the broadcasts. Though Catholics have fewer books and libraries than Protestants, statistics show that more books are being borrowed and read from Catholic libraries. Both Catholics and Protestants have youth organizations which are natural recruiting fields, but in 1955 (the latest report available) the government reported that the Catholic youth organization had 52,900 more members than its Protestant opposite number. The social movement run by Catholics has 156,000 more members than the similar Protestant movement.

2) Converts receive good indoctrination. So do all brought up from childhood in the church. In 1957 an amazing 710,455 pupils were enrolled in 3,357 Catholic schools. Separate Catholic education has proved to be a strong factor in the race for supremacy in Holland. For years the

Dutch government fought the parochial school idea but ended up by sub-sidizing both Protestant and Catholic schools in addition to its own. Since the Catholic schools became eligible for this state aid thirty-five years ago, tremendous strides have been made. Under Dutch law the state pays teachers of both Protestant and Catholic schools impartially, school facilities being provided by the community through a proportionate tax arrangement. It has not always been easy for Protestants or Catholics to make their way in town councils where they are a distinct minority, but the law protects them. On the higher level Catholics maintain the Charle-magne University at Nijmegen, opened in 1923, and the Economic University of Tilburg, launched in 1927.

3) The Roman Catholic church has political ascendancy in Holland. In this realm the church is stronger than its proportion of the population would indicate. As this is written, six out of sixteen cabinet ministers are Catholic, while four are Protestant. Out of the second chamber of the States General, which has one hundred seats, the Catholics at the present time have thirty-two seats to the Protestant's twenty-five. In the first chamber they have seventeen, the Protestants only thirteen. In govern-ment civil service the Catholics have 63,898 persons to the Protestants 48,353, or a majority of 15,545. Thus we see that on all the important levels of government the Catholics clearly lead in Holland.

Of course the principal Protestant bodies all have their own political parties. But the Catholic People's Party (*Katholieke Volkspartij*) is often able to outmaneuver and outvote the Protestant parties, which disagree among themselves on many issues. An important ally in this is the new, united Catholic women's movement of 115,000 members. Another is the strong Catholic Trade Union. Solidarity and vigor have won these im-portant concessions for Catholics: (1) the restoration of the hierarchy in 1853; (2) recognition of Catholic schools in 1868; (3) the subsidy of Catholic schools in 1921. If Protestants do not use the spiritual weapons in their hands, such as prayer and the power of the Holy Spirit, it may well be that many souls will be harder to win, or never be won at all, as this situation worsens. The only way to meet the Catholic threat is by a revival among true believers which would issue in more soul-winning.

4) Dutch Catholics have a purer church than that in the Latin coun-tries, and one sustained by a strong missionary spirit. In the Protestant parts of Holland there are few showy processions or outward manifesta-tions of the faith that would offend. More simplicity marks the interior of church buildings too. The Dutch Catholic himself is also more tolerant, less superstitious, than his counterpart in Spain or Italy.

Being a minority has filled Catholics with missionary fervor to win the battle for Holland. In 1948, as soon as war scars were partially erased, a record 2,653 students flocked to the seminaries. Secular and regular priests, now numbering more than 12,000, serve under the leadership of one archbishop and eight bishops. By the close of the war 25,000 nuns were active in 1,184 convents. The foreign missionary force has reached 5,391 men and women working in scores of other countries. If anyone doubts the impact of the Dutch missions, let him visit any remote area of the earth. There he will probably find a Dutch priest or nun. This comparatively small church faithfully contributes 16 per cent of all the Catholic missionaries who have left Europe for other parts of the world. Recently the Church also proudly financed the construction of a huge new set of Vatican radio transmitters near Rome.

5) Neighboring Belgium is very helpful in bolstering Dutch Catholic morale. Flemish Belgium, which uses virtually the same language, is contiguous to the southern provinces of Holland. Thus the more numerous Flemish Catholics help fortify the Dutch Catholics, who are a minority. Frequently the great, colorful processions and pageants of Belgium draw huge crowds from Holland; the Dutch do not often see such things in their own country. Yet a recent Marian Congress dominated life in southern Holland for days. Shrines and festivals, like the annual Procession of the Sacred Blood in Bruges, Belgium, enlist the participation of the Dutch hierarchy as well.

Roadblocks for Rome. Of course this review of the progress of Romanism must be balanced by some of its obvious problems. The new secularization of the country affects Catholics as well as Protestants. Protestantism is by no means the only foe: Socialism and Communism are considered by the church to be special enemies. In trying to win those of the Reformed persuasion, though, the Catholics must get around the whole Dutch experience of medieval popery. Here they need to be at their best.

Then, too, in the Mother Church's own bosom there are inactive members to be taken into account. About 35 per cent of the Catholics of Rotterdam do not observe minimum requirements of the faith. (The Catholic proportion of Rotterdam is 20.9 per cent according to the 1947 census.) Out of all Dutch Catholics, about 10 per cent are thought by the church itself to be inactive, most living in large cities. But when compared to other European Catholic or Protestant figures, this 10 per cent seems a small percentage indeeed. If the figure is reliable, it indicates a very healthy church.

Other opposition lies in some of the Protestant leaders. Certain of the most able of Rome's opponents are roused and exerting every avenue of pressure against her. Steeped in Dutch history, which provides plenty of examples of papal persecution from which to draw, these scholars and writers are doing their best to fight back.

On other than spiritual grounds, however, the battle cannot be won. A political counterattack without the support of the Lord will surely fail. First the psalmist cries, "O God, the heathen are come into thine inheritance" (Ps. 79:1). Then he considers what he should do. He decides to pray: "Help *us*, O God of our salvation, for the glory of thy name; and deliver *us*, and purge away *our* sins, for thy name's sake" (v. 9). The divine order for winning others always puts one's own repentance first. If this were done in regard to Holland, revival would follow, with a new wave of evangelism hard on its heels. Another result would be the raising up of intercessors for those enchained: "Let the sight of the prisoner come before thee" (v. 11). Such intercessors should pray that through Dutch believers and their foreign friends a new surge of God's power may be felt. Only then will those who now live in the twilight of Roman delusion be won.

The Dry Rot of Secularism. Let us go back for a moment to Sassenheim, our Dutch "Middletown." Secularism, or no-religionism, is increasing here in each generation. In the last three generations of Sassenheim's history, membership in the largest Protestant body, the Dutch Reformed, has fallen off 6.2 per cent while the Catholics have been alternately waxing and waning during the same period. Regular church attendance is 10 per cent less among Protestants than it was a generation ago, though the Catholic ratio is slightly higher. There is about 23 per cent less religious discussion between Sassenheim's parents and their children than there was a generation ago, and ownership of Bibles is 5 per cent less.

Dr. E. Emmen, former secretary of the General Synod of the Netherlands Reformed Church, in saying that "many people have turned aside completely from all churches and live entirely outside any ecclesiastical relationships," believed that Protestant forces should act to bring back the drifters.

> The fact that large groups have turned their backs on the church must move us. We find these groups among all classes of people, among workers, farmers, intellectuals. . . . There was for a long time a great lack of penetration by the church into all aspects of Dutch life. . . . Materialism, Marxism, and idealism are movements which have collided critically, and almost totally, with the Word of God.[11]

In the big cities the departure from God and the supernatural is even more evident. The Humanistic League (*Het Humanistisch Verbond*), founded in Amsterdam in 1946, places respect for man alone as its central tenet. Man, humanists say, must not be dominated by class, religion, science, racial prejudice, or any other taboos. He must be left free to fulfill his natural destiny. Thus it is proper to defend human rights wherever they are threatened. The League's seventy branches claim ten thousand adult members, but its influence is even wider. The estimated listening audience to humanist programs on the VARA and AVRO programs of Radio Hilversum reaches 100,000. A bi-monthly paper, *Mens en Wereld* (Man and the World), has a large readership among intellectuals, as does the scientific cultural quarterly *Rekenschap*. Other activities include social work, an orphan's fund, young people's fellowships, an old people's home, and a conference center in Nunspeet. Amsterdam is the seat of the International Humanist and Ethical Union, which has a United States chapter among its many others. This organization stimulates freethinking societies all over the earth. Of all the non-Christian sects in Holland, humanism is the largest and strongest, even though it continues to maintain, strange to say, certain ties of friendship with established Christian organizations.

4. *ECHOES OF GRACE*

The Bible Speaks to Holland. If there is one unadulterated blessing in this land, it is the wide, unhindered, and diligent distribution of the Word of God. Probably more than anyone realizes, the steady, industrious, and honest Dutchman owes his character to the power of the open Book. It would be interesting to know—but we shall never know with any exactitude—what the Bible contributed to the moral fiber of a nation that outsuffered and outprayed Nazi brutality. Nor shall we ever understand as fully as we would like the relation of a Bible-nurtured people to a sound economy and a proverbial integrity in business; God may have His own reasons why He has blessed Holland. But here at least His message to the sons of Adam can be read.

As one browses through the display rooms of the Dutch Bible Society in Amsterdam, he feels an atmosphere of order and work in the air. Secretaries hurry back and forth as though getting out the Bible were urgent business—which it is! Some forty kinds of Bibles are published by this Society, which was founded in 1814, and their styles, sizes, bindings, type, and translations are all of the highest order. It is said that their India-paper Bibles are not considered perfect unless one can hold by a single page the whole weight of the book; I have tried this and have found the bindings and paper strong as iron.

Bibles can be bought in nearly every bookstore in Holland—not just in religious bookshops. Two Bible vans employed by the Society keep the Bibles before the public eye by continually moving about, with brisk sales as a result. "Nobody who wants a Bible, but cannot pay, will go without" is a maxim here; so the poor are served as well as the rich. Probably the Dutch churches could do more to encourage Bible reading, as a Bible on the bookshelf and one being read are two different things. Considered a fetish by some, a nice object to have around the house by others, and the proper book to greet the eye of the visiting pastor by still others, the Word of God is used by all too few even in this land of churches.

When the figures concerning distribution of Scriptures are considered, several interesting facts come to light. In the middle of the war a sudden record figure of 85,778 (1942) was reached, the reasons probably including the uncertainty of life and the sufferings caused by enemy occupation. In 1950 61,344 copies were sold, which was about average for the time. But in 1951 the sales jumped to 132,737—an all-time high. Ever since then they have eased off little by little, though still remaining at 100,000 or more per year. Puzzled about this sudden rise in Bible distribution in 1951, I asked A. W. van Lennep, the Assistant General Secretary, the reason. After reflecting a while, he ventured the answer: "The new translation was completed then, and we first put out the whole Bible in the new version that year."[12] Explaining that the New Testament was prepared and published by the translation committee in 1939, he pointed out that the public eagerly awaited the appearance of the whole Bible. The old translation of 1637 had done its work well, but was in an older Dutch than is now used. Elderly people still like it, but the new version, which is much more than just another translation, is being accepted quite rapidly. One more interesting item was that the disastrous floods of 1953 likewise created a greater demand for God's Word.

Movings of the Almighty. Among a small minority of individuals and groups in Holland the Lord has been powerfully working. Evangelism has come more to the fore during recent days, partly as a result of the Billy Graham meetings in Amsterdam's Olympic Stadium in 1954 and in the Rotterdam Feyonoord Stadium in 1955. A deep and silent awe could be felt in those huge crowds when thousands of these deliberate, careful people responded to invitations to come to Christ. Pastors brought up in a Calvinist theology found that they could not explain away what proved to be a permanent work of grace in many hearts. Follow-up methods were the best, and some whole churches felt the impact. Sales of the Billy Graham books were phenomenal. As a direct result, several "Rotterdam for Christ" campaigns have been conducted under a co-operative church leadership in recent years. Much credit goes to the vision of the Graham committee in the Netherlands, who had the courage to attempt that untried. Because of this example other evangelists in Holland are finding the going easier.

Blessings are not confined to mass evangelism alone. For instance, a Dutch graduate of the Moody Bible Institute who has an interesting newspaper ministry has reached many with a witness. Every week he writes in Rotterdam a full page of news, editorials, and gospel thoughts for the Sunday issue of four newspapers reaching over 100,000 families. Some pastors have written editors of these papers to say that this is the best-read page of the newspaper. It is heartening to think that many who otherwise would never get the gospel are getting it indirectly through a church page edited by an evangelical.

Several Bible conference centers are teaching the Word to believers in a greatly needed ministry. Other Hollanders are concerned because there are so few agencies to sponsor Dutch young people desiring to serve abroad as missionaries. Except for regular denominational channels, there has been little possibility of sponsorships for them, but now steps are being taken to enlist help from God's people. The Dutch branch of the Christian and Missionary Alliance at Wassanaar, near The Hague, has sent out a number to foreign fiields. Another blessing is the number of Dutch people enrolling in Bible correspondence courses, like those prepared by the Navigators at Voorburg.

Christian workers coming into Holland from other countries have made a clear contribution. In the last century the Baptists and the Brethren were among the new arrivals; we have already seen what an important part was played by a Danish missionary in founding the Baptists. Though these movements got little co-operation at first, they nevertheless took root. The Salvation Army and others followed. Since the war, new evangelical movements have entered Holland, challenging the old order of things and bringing in new ideas, new life. The Christian Business Men's Committees International have Dutch representatives, as do the Gideons and the International Council for Christian Leadership, of Washington.

Among the foreign groups here at work are the European Evangelistic Crusade, the Bible Christian Union, the Navigators, Child Evangelism Fellowship International, Baptist Mid-Missions, The Reapers' Fellowship, the Bible Club Movement, and the Greater Europe Mission. Some independent workers are included. Perhaps twenty-five foreign workers in all are serving Christ in Holland. The Youth for Christ Movement begun by Americans in 1947 has become wholly Dutch in character. Summer camps, evangelistic campaigns, and regular rallies in some cities are all part of the program of Youth for Christ. Activities engaged in by the foreign workers include Bible institute teaching, home Bible classes, tent campaigns, children's work, summer camps, follow-up training, and literature work. Though the list of organizations given above and their operations may sound imposing, the total impact made by foreign workers is small because such workers are few in Holland. Probably their greatest contribution lies in the example given by soul-winning and the teaching of new Christians. Here in the Netherlands, as everywhere, the final job of evangelizing must be accomplished by the nationals.

Once Blind, Now I see. Elizabeth was a restless seventeen-year-old girl. Every night she attended a tent campaign at the beach resort of Scheveningen, a suburb of The Hague. What attracted her especially was the lively program conducted by young Americans, with music and testimony. Then, too, there was the chance to hear English, in which she herself was very proficient. Here, a stone's throw from the North Sea, was something new to her. A message of personal salvation was preached, which she had never heard in her Reformed Church. Every night after the service she asked the evangelists questions. Finally, on the last night of the campaign, she could stand no more. That night the evangelist preached on "Eternal Punishment" as the dismal alternative to trusting Christ. After the service another member of the preaching mission led Elizabeth, now deeply convicted, to peace and joy in the Saviour. Long afterward it was learned that she was the daughter of one of Holland's cabinet ministers. More than eighty other persons were saved in this one campaign. Many thousands more have found Christ through foreign evangelists in Holland during the last ten years. A number of these converts are now spiritual leaders in their own country or studying somewhere for Christian service.

Anna Lees was on her way to a dance in a Dutch city. When it suddenly started to rain, she stepped into a nearby lighted doorway in order not to ruin her formal dress. Surprised to hear strange, lively singing, she ventured inside. Here she found a Youth for Christ rally in progress. A long period of conviction ended happily in her salvation that very night. Today she is the wife of an active Christian journalist and evangelist.

Wim was a young Communist in Amsterdam. His mother and father had excluded religion from his life and taught him their empty, materialistic gospel of Marx. But Wim had unfulfilled longings; life for him somehow lacked the flavor he sought. One day he wandered into the edge of a street meeting in the Dam, central square of the city. Interested, he pressed closer, heard the gospel, and was aroused to seek the way to God. Not much later his search was rewarded in his finding the One who had all along been seeking him. In spite of the opposition of family and friends, Wim determined to follow his new Master to the end. This involved going abroad to study, a challenge he was financially unable to meet. But Wim learned to take that step into the void called faith. He found the Rock beneath, and the following year found him in the European Bible Institute in Paris. After learning French, he felt called to serve the Lord by preaching the Gospel in France, where he has a unique ministry with children.

Dutch converts to Christ like the three just mentioned are the secret to the evangelization of this country. Yet foreign movements or people had a part in the salvation or growth of each one. So the foreign worker *does* have a place, after all, in helping Hollanders heavenward.

Teen-age Germans, their country's future leaders, listen to the gospel.

Chapter 13

WHITHER GERMANY LEADS

"We Germans have become completely estranged from biblical knowledge and biblical thinking."
—BISHOP HANS LILJE of Hannover,
The German Evangelical Church

"Germany is like a brave and gallant horse, highly fed, but without a good rider."
—MARTIN LUTHER
in *Table Talk*

1. *MEET THE PEOPLE*

First Impressions. Your plane rolls to a stop at the famous Rhein-Main airport at Frankfort-on-the-Main. Or perhaps you ship docks in the northern port of Bremerhaven. As you step on German soil for the first time, one quick surface impression of the people will come to you. This initial impression will grow stronger as you come to know the Germans and their way of life better. Perhaps it is best expressed in the word "bustle." In every population center you will sense this activity, be it in the crowded Ruhr, the busy Rhineland, relaxed Bavaria, or isolated Berlin. Very early on weekday mornings, trains and buses in every sizable community are jammed and sidewalks are crowded with silent people hurrying to work with a strange intentness. Most are well but plainly dressed, the men each carrying a briefcase (it contains his lunch!) and the women with noticeably little make-up. What is the interest which absorbs these early risers? It is work! The majority of those you see are part of the army of office and factory workers which makes German industry hum, for this is a nation with a passion to manufacture and market things on its ever-expanding world market. Germans are such believers in the gospel of work that even when they are playing, they seem to work at it.

Especially in the country and in the small towns you will soon notice a

389

second characteristic of the German people. For the most part they are
courteous and friendly, even to former enemies. While it is true that their
attitude toward America and the west follows changes in the political
climate, yet German people can usually be counted upon to be personally
helpful. The general openness of the people is a God-send to the foreign
Christian worker. As CBS correspondent Richard C. Hottelet has stated,
"The Germans today are more receptive to foreign ideas than at any time
in the past century."[1] Should anyone have trouble making friends with
the Germans, it will probably be his own fault, as they are most responsive
to friendship. "I believe their friendship is a by-product of their biblical
heritage," said a Canadian serving Christ in Germany. Billy Graham expressed like amazement after preaching in Berlin's badly bombed Süds-
ternkirche. "I am amazed," he exclaimed with feeling. "Here we have
destroyed their beautiful churches and cities, but they receive us so
warmly." Though he was referring to the professing Christians, something
similar could be said of the people as a whole. Anyone who has ever been
sick in a German hospital, in trouble on the road, or just in need of information and help anywhere will testify that these are a kindly people
indeed. Hence the gospel of Christ finds ready entrance into their hearts
when presented with Spirit-led clarity, and power.*

Tenacity is the Spirit. If the foreign Christian is in Germany long
enough, he will notice a third characteristic of the people, one which God
has used before and can use again to give them outstanding leadership in
His cause. Not only do Germans work, but they will usually stay with a
thing—be it construction, philosophy, or the pursuit of pleasure—long after
most Europeans would have quit from disinterest or exhaustion. This
trait, which they share with the Swiss, is *Gründlichkeit* or thoroughness.**
Tourists notice German thoroughness when they buy a Leica camera, a
four-hundred-day clock, or Solingen cutlery. Their passion for detail and
completeness is almost unbelievable. If we can separate the human from
the divine in a man's life for a moment, let us recall the dogged determination at work in Martin Luther at Worms. It had begun years before.
He had prayed many hours and days until he found peace of soul in
Christ; afterward he set his course under the Spirit's guidance and refused to deviate from it in the slightest. This led to that intractable position at Worms immortalized in the words: "Here stand I, I can do no
other, so help me God!" Most Germans are remarkably thorough in everything they do. They have no characteristic shrug of bafflement over their
problems as do some other Europeans.

*We deal with a changing attitude of German leaders in chapter 3.
**Interestingly enough, French and many other languages do not have a good
word for this.

It should be added that efficiency is not necessarily a part of this picture. To the Anglo-American mind the German will often seem to be "doing it the hard way" rather than thinking through the problem he faces. But for sheer determination of purpose, there are few people in the world that can match the Germans. Suppose this single-minded toil were put to the service of the Lord with full surrender to the Holy Spirit. Marvelous things could be done, as has been evidenced time and again, not only in Luther's life, but in the history of God's people as a whole in that land.

Specialization is the Pattern. Germans are moulded into the pattern of specialization from childhood. Home, school, and natural bent all contribute to the average person's desire to master one craft or field of knowledge, or to do any one thing well. Mentally the German finds it difficult to move nimbly around all sides of an issue with the flexibility of, say, the French. Thus at times he seems heavy and unpliable to the foreigner. Allied soldiers noticed during the war how German attacks usually fit certain patterns. Cleverly conceived and thoroughly mounted as they were, the element of flexibility was missing from most military operations. Soon an opposing unit could be typed for its action pattern, which did not usually include keeping the enemy off balance and in a state of perplexity. Probably specialization is an over-rated factor in the German personality, but it is worth knowing about. This tunnel vision, as the oculist might call it, has produced some of the world's greatest leaders and thinkers. It is said that philosopher Immanuel Kant was so punctual in his habits in Königsberg (which he never left in his lifetime) that fellow townsmen would set their watches by his comings and goings. Tradition has it that the only time he ever upset this schedule of concentration was when he first read Jean Jacques Rousseau. Then for the first time he forgot time altogether.

The Surprising Trait. One would not expect the Germans to have a sentimental nature. But they are surprisingly subject to maudlin feelings, not so much collectively as individually. This is more noticeable in certain parts of the country than in others, but is a national trait as well, belying the conception foreigners often have of the stiff, unfeeling, efficient Teuton. When self-pity engulfs the German, he will sometimes give way shamelessly to his feelings, but this does not occur often. On the positive side his kindness to genuine friends is sometimes embarrassingly profuse. Like those of some other nations, the Germans love remembrance of special events, and traditions and festivals of every sort. To make an occasion out of anything important is their custom, often involving long speechmaking and ceremony, which are received with the most solemn attention. Sometimes such ceremony may seem unduly heavy to the foreigner, but it is an aspect of the German nature that one can learn to understand and appreciate.

Lead, But Do Not Push. A much better-known characteristic is the stubbornness of the Germans, a quality which might seem at first glance to be just their famous doggedness carried to its logical conclusion. The expression "hardheaded" soon became attached to early German immigrants to the United States, but respect for them grew when they were found to be successful and honest citizens. It is easy to misunderstand this stubbornness, which is only a desire, after all, to know why a thing is to be done in a certain way. Tradition quite naturally plays a part, too. It has been proved many times that a German can be led when convinced he is on the right track, even though at first he may seen unwilling to change his original view. In the face of tradition, the foreign worker serving Christ needs much patience, love, and tact to introduce ideas. Since World War II some foreigners, moving slowly and prayerfully, have successfully introduced new ideas in the Lord's work. Now, such methods are considered German, which is as it should be. After all, Germans must do Christian work according to New Testament standards, not American ones.

The Gospel Enters. In that part of Germany belonging to the Roman Empire, known as *Germania Cisrhenana,* Christian truth was known quite early. Irenaeus of Lyon, in the second century after Christ, tells of preaching the gospel among German barbarians who "without paper and ink have salvation written in their hearts by the Holy Spirit." This may have referred to the conversion of many who were illiterate but able to rejoice in their faith even without the help of written Bibles. Historians point out that the spread of the gospel message northward in Germany into non-Roman areas had many obstacles to overcome, among which were these: (1) The message itself had lost much of its former simplicity after the rise of the formal visible church. (2) Christianity sought to overthrow the ancient gods of the Germanic tribes. (3) The gospel had been introduced by those subject to a foreign power. (4) Services were held for the most part in Latin, a foreign tongue. (5) Converts were expected to look to the absent Bishop of Rome as their spiritual ruler. (6) Often the messengers, especially the Irish, were ascetic, narrow men. (7) The national independence of these tribes was shaken by the threat of foreign domination.

On the positive side several conditions may help to explain the rapid expansion of the Christian message in Germany: (1) The inner core of gospel truth was probably present everywhere despite the outer changes. (2) The gospel itself has an inherent power through the Holy Spirit to change lives regardless of hindering circumstances. (3) Germanic tribes excelled those of the south in courage, independence, and personal habits. Fischer says that in their pagan worship in the deep woods "the voluptuous and effeminate side of the classical mythology was absent."[2] In that they had no elaborate ritual and powerful priesthood, "the Germans were the 'Protestants' of heathen nations."[3] (4) Some of the best missionaries worked among them, men noted especially for their zeal. No doubt such beginnings laid foundations for the religious people who are today's Germans.

Emergence of Modern Germany. It is profitable to review, even briefly, how Germany became a nation only a short time ago as far as history goes. The first Teutonic tribes, blond and blue-eyed, mixed with the Celts who had moved north from Switzerland about 400 B.C. Roman legions early learned to respect the fierce fighting qualities of the various Germanic tribes—Lombards, Ostrogoths, Visigoths, Franks, Burgundians, and others. After hundreds of years of tribal discord, Charlemagne (712–814) emerged emperor of the Holy Roman Empire, and was crowned in Rome at St. Peter's Church on Christmas Day, 800. In terms of modern nations, Charlemagne's vast Empire included about half of the present Italy, Switzerland, most of Germany, Austria, Czechoslovakia, with parts of France and Yugoslavia. Frederick Barbarossa (1152–1190), Rudolph of Hapsburg (1273–1291), and Charles V (1500–1558) all tried to bring about the unification of Europe, which Charlemagne almost won. But while these rulers were thus preoccupied, they were unable to unite their own Germanic peoples. The dissolution of the Empire was hastened by the Reformation in 1517, Germany thereafter being split into Catholic and Protestant states. The great principalities continued to reign separately, until Prussia rose as the strongest state under Frederick the Great (1712–1786). But it was not until 1871 that Prince Otto von Bismarck (1815–1898) succeeded in uniting all of Germany under Prussian rule.

The Nazi Path to War. Adolf Hitler capitalized on the bitterness, shame, and loss of prestige which followed World War I to organize discontent on a national scale. Having formed the tightly disciplined Nazi Party, he forced President von Hindenburg to name him as Chancellor in early 1933. Democratic government by representation was abolished in favor of rule by decree. Soon absolute dictatorship had paralyzed all the free institutions of the previous republic. Political opposition was crushed swiftly and sometimes bloodily. Jews were attacked as state enemies, on the fiction of Aryan superiority, through the Nuremberg laws of 1935. By 1936 Hitler had re-entered the Rhineland; in 1938 he seized Austria and in 1939 he took Czechoslovakia and the Polish corridor. The consequent attacks on Poland, Norway, and the Lowlands, and the fall of France in 1940 were followed by the conquest of the Balkans and declaration of war on Russia in 1941. Meanwhile England was bombarded but spared an invasion. After America entered the war in December of 1941, German good fortune continued, until, in 1943 at Stalingrad, the tide began to turn. Massive attacks on the Continent by the Allies during 1944 caused the German army to reel backward toward the fatherland, which was itself entered by the victors in 1945. Collapse quickly followed; with Hitler's suicide pointing out the futility of further resistance, the German armed forces surrendered on May 7, 1945.

The Human Price. As a Christian looks at the statistics which represent the German casualities of the war, his heart is moved to sympathy. Though these may seem but cold figures, every one represents a life lost or a body maimed. No records could possibly be kept of the minds and souls blasted by the brutalizing effects of war. Both world wars, which Germany lost, had a profound effect on everyone. Almost every family lost a loved one. Only by sharing their heartache can foreign Christians ever hope to deeply love the German people and labor for their salvation. This is true irrespective of Germany's war guilt. All together there were 6,660,000 Germans killed in the armed forces and as civilians in bombing raids. About 1,500,000 are cripples and 6,500,000 cannot work at all or can work only partially. Some other after-effects have plagued the country. There is a surplus of three million women, and about 10 per cent of the population is over sixty-five years of age. Meanwhile the birth rate has fallen to the second lowest in Europe.

Of course the war did not spare Christian workers and church properties. When Hitler came to power in 1933, there were 18,000 pastors in the Protestant denominations. At the close of the war only 20 per cent of these were in their churches at work. Over 1,000 pastors were killed in the ranks as chaplains or as conscripted soldiers. (There was no draft deferment for ministerial students.) Among the refugees who were pushed into Western Germany were 2,500 pastors who somehow had to be relocated in new posts. In Berlin alone 52 pastors died in the bombing and 28 were recorded as missing. But mere figures cannot tell the story of leaderless churches, from which both pastors and dedicated members were missing for years. This, too, is part of Germany's problem today.

In Nuremberg 30 out of 40 churches were totally destroyed in the inner city's holocaust. The heavy attacks on Hamburg left only one or two churches standing out of 50. In Berlin not one church was left intact of the 187 Lutheran churches, of which 69 were totally destroyed. The area of Baden suffered 136 churches destroyed or damaged as well as 82 parish houses and 135 parsonages. In Essen, where it will take an estimated 30 years to clear away the rubble at the rate of 1,000 tons per day, only 6 churches survived out of 57. These figures are only samples of the material losses of some of the churches.

Moral Damage. As Germany entered the postwar period, the marks of the Nazi teaching of youth became all too evident. Intensified by the initial heady victories of war and the later backwash of disaster, the moral situation worsened. Among the fourteen million refugees from the east, who made the great migration in 1945–1946, were many women and mothers who relaxed their moral standards in order to earn enough to eat and feed their families. Meanwhile some young people who had been encouraged to bear children out of wedlock for the Nazi cause now took to prostitution and other vices. Stealing, lying, and profiteering came naturally to many for whom excuses existed to live thus. As one German writer has said: "Nazidom undermined all the moral laws governing European civilization."[4] Worse still, the breaking of God's laws brought tragedy in its wake. The presence of occupying armies made the moral climate still worse. Of course Germany's problem in this respect was a part of the total European letdown in standards; and apart from these special circumstances, German conditions were no worse than others. Another tremendous problem arose from the paying of pensions to war widows. Today there are reportedly several hundred thousand of these women living in common-law marriages in order to retain government allowances which would cease should they actually remarry. It is difficult to imagine worse conditions under which to bring up children.

What can be said of other scars on the German soul? Many individuals are disillusioned, cynical, weary of life. In spite of their remarkable capacity for work, multitudes have not found in work a refuge from sorrow, nor have they found a faith to replace doubt. More than any other help, the German people need the Lord Jesus. Only He can bring peace and trust to the heart. Only He can forgive sin, obliterate the nightmares of the past, and quiet the guilty conscience. Germany needs the Son of God even more than the sympathy and acceptance of the nations.

Materialism, the New Religion. Visitors to the new dynamic Germany will notice that the store windows which attract the most attention are those of the automobile agencies, appliance stores, and furniture shops.

For many the greatest dream is to have a car and join their neighbors in speeding over their own great land and into other European countries. Now that the war rubble has given way to proud new buildings, the German wants luxuries other Europeans have been enjoying, and he is out to get them with breathless haste. By dint of long hours and hard work, some men have amassed great wealth; these are the new millionaries like the barons of the industrial Ruhr. Just beneath them the management class is newly affluent, and professional workers are prospering with them. But the working-class people, who feel that their share is not enough, can be expected to demand more in days ahead.

Americans have always been accused of being interested in money-making, but many Europeans feel that this desire for wealth now has a counterpart in the new German materialism. While it is impossible to foretell the future, there is little doubt that the Germans will forge far ahead in raising their living standards. Paris reports, for example, that the growing German tourist army spends more there for tips than tourists of any other nation. Meanwhile the Germans are traveling more widely everywhere, for both business and pleasure, than other Europeans.

What is this rising prosperity doing to the German spiritually? Whereas after the war he was easily attracted to gospel meetings, he now has other concerns than survival. Today he wants luxurious creature comforts such as other prosperous nations have. Discerning Christian leaders in Germany are disturbed by this. As one pastor put it: "We dug ourselves out of the ruins and tidied up our houses. During those uncertain times our people were athirst for God. Gospel tents were filled and seats for evangelistic campaigns could not be found in the few auditoriums which still stood. But now we are having a dose of new prosperity. Now we yearn for *things*. God help us!"

2. THE LEGACY OF DOUBT

What Has Happened to Germany? What has made the German people what they are today? Which forces forged the Teutonic soul? Those who wish to win Germans to the Lord Jesus Christ must ask how and why the man on the street has emerged from the nation's past a pagan. Why, for instance, are today's youth a cynical and despairing generation? How was it possible for liberal theological thought to capture the country only 250 years after Luther, and for Nazi barbarism to follow close on its heels? Answers to such questions would help explain why only 5 per cent of the German population attend any church today, though 95 per cent claim a religious affiliation. These answers would also explain the checkered beliefs of a host of Protestant clergymen who embrace a new and altered "orthodoxy." Even the recent replacing of God's authority by that of the State can be understood by observing how the German mind has been moulded in history. Like all of us, this great people are the heirs of their past, and history has bequeathed them, among other things, a legacy of doubt. Fortunately, they need not remain the victims of their history. In every generation God releases captives from the prison house of sin; those the Son of man makes free are free indeed. Each individual may renounce the past through the enablement of the Holy Spirit. With Christ as Redeemer, no German need remain age-conformed; he can be Spirit-transformed by the renewing of his mind.

Since Luther. Psychologists are always fascinated by those discoveries and theories which seem to rise, simultaneously but unrelated, out of a given *zeitgeist* or intellectual climate. In German history enough attacks on divine things have occurred to give these scholars pause, so striking has been the timing of their appearance on the stage of history. Only a supernatural enemy could be responsible for such cunning conception and skillful execution. Who else but Satan, the god of this world, would pluck away the seed of the Word from the hearts of the people? Especially since Luther has the enemy of souls resisted the effects of the liberated Book. Opposition began in Luther's own lifetime, when things began to go wrong. While some Lutheran princes were godly men, others, with their unconverted followers, were only nominal adherents of the new faith. Then came the adoption of the territorial principle and the unwitting retention of some Catholic practices. More trouble came when the Roman Church introduced the reforms of the Catholic Counter Reformation to render error more palatable again. Next came the exhausting religious wars which confused eternal issues with political. But the attack reached a still higher tempo through the philosopher–theologians and psychologists who opened revelation's gates to reason in the twentieth century. Small wonder that, with the enemy within her walls, Germany's daring adventures in our times should call down judgments of fire on her head. We present but a few examples—some leading battles only—of this Satanic conflict. Precious must be the souls of the German people to God, if their possession has driven the deceiver of souls to such excesses.

Kant and Human Reason. Immanuel Kant (1724–1804) differed from most philosophers who preceded him in that he rejected God as the ultimate in the universe. He began with man rather than God. In his theory of knowledge in the *Critique of Pure Reason* he gives a high place to the knowledge gained by experience. But he says that metaphysical knowledge, such as that of God's existence, cannot be so perceived. To

Kant complete devotion to moral duty, learned by experience, is the highest goal of man. But moral principle that "what we ought to do, we can do" gives too much place to reason as guide and fails to explain man's complete failure to attain. How can we, even if we know what is right, do the right without divine help? Kant ignored God's revelation of Himself to man in nature, conscience and the Bible. In so doing his brilliant and original views laid strong foundations for future attacks on the Bible. Especially influenced by Kant was Johann Fichte, who can be considered the founder of that later German nationalism which exalted the state above God. Frederic Schleiermacher, Herman Lotze, and Albrecht Ritschl were others whom Kant strongly affected. These and their colleagues had a part in leaving a legacy of doubt to the present generation.

The Spell of Hegel. Educated at Tübingen University, Georg W. F. Hegel (1770–1831) taught at Jena, Heidelberg, and Berlin. Endowed with a massive intellect that could embrace vast knowledge in the best tradition of German scholarship, Hegel was one of the most influential thinkers in world history. He proposed a dialectic idealism which attempted a broad explanation of everything in human experience. The three steps forming the heart of his dialectic are called thesis, antithesis, and synthesis. An initial fact or action (thesis) is challenged by a second (antithesis); out of the conflict of these two then rises a third (synthesis).

This "union of opposites" Hegel gleefully applied to every realm of life and thought. He could explain, for example, how war was necessary for the creation of power. Then peace was needed as an antithesis to restore the forces which war had expended. Out of these two could come glorious new heights of national power. This exciting new principle gripped the German leaders and thinkers all over the world for generations, and its effects linger still. The magic dialectic could be, and was, applied to politics, economics, history, science, music—and finally to religion.

Hegel's theories contributed to the defense of Darwin's evolutionary views; Marx and Engels borrowed them in order to give pseudo-scientific respectability, under the name of dialectic materialism, to their socialistic theories. Oswald Spengler also built on Hegel and on Goethe's romanticism his monumental but biased work, *The Decline of the West.* In glorifying the state Hegel maintained that it had no obligation to obey moral law: governments did not even need to keep agreements. Thus all the excesses of Nazi nationalism derived philosophic license from Hegel.*
In England and America respectively the philosophers Francis Bradley and Josiah Royce became his intellectual heirs. Royce's views in turn helped shape those of W. E. Hocking, a contemporary contributor to the

---

*Hitler later said, "Law is what is useful for the state."

recent American religious modernism. Sören Kierkegaard was almost the only philosopher in Europe at the time who opposed Hegel's position as anti-Christian.

Biblical Criticism Enthroned. But to the Christian, first in Germany, and later in the whole world, it was Hegel's impact on the Bible and theology that mattered most. His influence here was both broad and deep. F. C. Bauer, founder of the famous Tübingen University school of thought, was a complete Hegelian. So were a host of those who helped found the new Biblical criticism—among others Eichhorn, Vatke, Stade, Wellhausen, Graf, and Keunen of Holland. Vatke studied under Hegel in Berlin, where his own disciple, Wellhausen, later became an influential leader of one aspect of the new thought.

What did these men believe? Many, like Delitzsch in Germany, Keunen in Holland, Driver, Davids, and G. A. Smith in England, were genuine believers, who accepted the Bible as divine revelation. Nevertheless they felt obliged by sheer logic to bow before scientific evidence, which they felt was inescapable. Others of this group put a question mark over everything Biblical, both the text itself, and the progress of doctrine within the Scriptures. Nothing supernatural about the book was to be assumed at the start. It was to be subjected to the same careful tests given any other Oriental literature. Great masses of data were thus made available for synthesis: the authorship of Bible books was probed and the evolutionary growth in the Old Testament plotted.

Then attempts were made to force critical findings into the hypothesis of Hegel about history, using the inevitable dialectic triad. Brauer, to take one example, finds as his thesis in the New Testament the Jewish nationalism of Jesus and of Peter and the other disciples. As an antithesis, he suggests Paul's teaching of the universality of the Gospel. Finally a synthesis is discovered in the second-century Judaizers, the content of the later Epistles, and the rise of the Catholic Church. Similarly Wellhausen in his celebrated *Prolegomena* (1878) divides the Old Testament into the three dialectic phases: (1) animistic, (2) prophetic, (3) monotheistic. Paralleling these he sees the evolution of literature in (1) Hebrew poetry, (2) prophetic writing, (3) legal codes. One can see where such naturalistic ideas must surely lead. Though the Bible itself survived, the common people's faith in it was deeply shaken as their pastors imbibed the new interpretation. In effect, the critics presented man as improving himself gradually while recording his progress in a faulty and primitive book.

So widespread were Wellhausen's ideas that before World War I almost every Protestant Old Testament scholar of any standing in the whole world was a disciple. As such speculations leavened the theological seminaries of Germany, most of the pastors in turn either consciously or unconsciously undermined their congregations' simple acceptance of the Bible as an inerrant Book. Theological leaders of our own day—like Karl Barth—are thus conditioned to the untrustworthiness of the Scriptures, however they may cling to Christ as the Son of God. In the sceptical twenties, when the demoralizing impact of the first world war on Protestantism was so obvious, this startling development was reported—just one of many symptoms of the legacy of doubt: "Eighty-eight Protestant institutions closed in Germany in 1923, while in the five years leading up to that date the Catholic Church opened 100 such institutions."[5] As will be seen elsewhere, similar reports were to come after the second global conflict had done its destructive work.

Enter Psychoanalysis. In any study of the German mentality, the important contribution of psychology must be noted. In this field Germans have produced such leaders as Ebbinghaus (memory steps and nonsense syllables), Wilhelm Stern (I.Q.), and Wilhelm Wundt (experimental psychology). Such schools, too, as the *Gestalt* and the *Verstehende* psychologies (the latter sometimes called intuitional psychology) had their origin in Germany. Not all German leadership in this field has been negative by any means. Though the evangelical Christian would not agree with Franz Delitzsch on all points, his *System of Biblical Psychology* is probably the most thorough study of the Scriptures in the light of psychology ever made, and remains generally true to the Spirit of divine revelation.

But it is Sigmund Freud and his followers who have had the most explosive effect on Germany and the world through their famous theories of psychoanalysis. Freud was born in Moravia, but eventually became professor of neurology at the University of Vienna. Since he wrote and taught in German, the influence of his work in German-speaking countries was both immediate and potent. In 1938, after 50 years in Vienna, Freud fled to London to seek refuge from the Nazi regime. He became a British citizen and died there soon afterward. As a young physician Freud had been stirred by his visit to Paris in 1885. Here, at Professor Charcot's clinic for nervous diseases, Freud had observed repressions in the unconscious minds of hysterical patients. He felt that these repressions must be energized as a center of unrest by the *libido* (nervous energy). By helping a patient elude so-called escape mechanisms in his mind, doctors could bring the suppressed desires to the surface and thus help effect a cure.

Using this method as a basis, Freud then attempted to draw a sort of blueprint of the workings of the mind. The primitive animal urges in the mind's basement he called the *Id*. The drives of the *Id*, particularly the sexual ones, try to break out, but are hindered by the *ego* (personality). This repression is also carried out further by the *super-ego*, a kind of false conscience forcibly imposed on man by his parents, nurses, and social conventions. The lifelong battle to contain the *Id* explained for Freud most neuroses. Following the materialistic premise, he naturally dismissed human will, reason, and moral choice. For him all religions are illusions clung to as mechanisms by adults who do not want to give up their child-to-parent relationships. These infantile adults create a heavenly father to replace the earthly father of childhood. Prayer is equally childish. Freud called religion "the universal obsessional neurosis of humanity."

Out of such views came the popular idea that all repression is dangerous and that self-expression is the only way to mental and physical health. The element of truth contained in Freudian psychoanalysis was thus carried too far and greatly distorted. What effect these views, coupled with theological liberalism, have had upon German students can be measured in part by this generation's disillusionment. Following the first world war German youth were already conditioned to rebel against Victorian "prudery"; Freudian interpretations now gave them the *credo* they needed to interpret life in purely naturalistic terms.

While psychoanalysis has probably contributed something to our knowledge of the subconscious, Freud's overemphasis on the sexual drive and his weird interpretations of dreams are today losing ground. As Dr. Wallace Emerson says, "In some ways psychoanalysis is more a philosophy than a psychology, since much of it has to be taken on faith and lacks experimental evidence."[6] Philosophy or psychology, Freudian theories continue to do their part in keeping multitudes of Germans and others from bowing before the Lord Jesus Christ.

The Strange Imbalance. Because of a historic lack of equilibrium in their nature, Germans easily become fanatical. They tend to become enthusiastic experts specializing along one line, often becoming eccentric and distorted in the process. Is not this lack of balance to be seen in the Biblical critics we have just discussed? In their headlong rush to apply Hegelian explanations to the Scriptures, a kind of Greek *hybris*, or momentum of disaster, can be seen. Many went further than they originally intended, borne along by the magic formulas of dialectics, to hold what now appear to be ridiculous positions. The dynamic seems to come from a sense of duty, or will to power, developed by the philosophers.

Historians have often been puzzled by the willingness of Germans, sometimes, to sacrifice everything decent, even their civilized moral sense, to follow such an ideal. Friedrich Wilhelm Nietzsche (1844–1900) took this already developed idea one step further with his idea of the *Ubermensch* or Superman. Nietzsche's superior being hated weakness, humility, and holiness.

Dreams of Conquest. When this sense of mission, or will to power, is taken up by the masses, it becomes *die Vermassung* or mass mentality. Through its operation unbelievably fast changes have taken place in German history: changes for good, like the transformation of thousands who came to Christ during the Reformation and in numerous revivals; changes, too, for evil, like Hitler's Nazi movement, which rocketed to power so quickly because the moral accommodations for its coming had long been in preparation.

We have already mentioned Johann Fichte (1762–1814) as one of the creators of German militant nationalism. While he was professor of philosophy at Berlin, Napoleon was in control of Germany. Fichte's fiery addresses to the German people in 1807 and 1808 were a large factor in the eventual driving out of the French. Fichte reminded Germans of their destined greatness and their duty to fulfill it. What was called the Not-Self had to become morally identified, he said, with the Absolute-Self in every experience of life. All men are finite parts of an infinite creative power, to which they are obligated to respond. As they realize themselves in the Absolute-Self, a new, common intelligence emerges. While up to this time Frederick the Great, as absolute dictator of Prussia, had forced his people into wars they did not want, there now rose a new national self-consciousness. This national feeling, which had never existed under the Hohenzollerns, now formed the basis for the Prussian conquests which followed. Both Fichte and Johann Herder (1744–1803) were much used later by the Nazi party to appeal to the patriotic duty of the German people. Dreams of conquests like these led count Helmut Von Moltke to say piously, "War is a link in God's order of the world."

Thus not only did the German philosophers attack the Bible, but they laid the foundations of national disaster for their own people. With such conditioning, leaders like Hitler, not wanting to "retain God in their knowledge," proceeded to become "vain in their imaginations, and their foolish heart was darkened" (Rom. 1:28, 21). What a tremendous potential are these talented people for the good or ill of Europe and the world! Whom will they follow in the future—Christ or Caesar? If they remain "without God and without Christ," they will again confess what Hölderlin penned 150 years ago:

Aber weh! es wandelt in Nacht, es wohnt, wie in Orkus
Ohne Göttliches unser Geschlecht.[7]

Christianity Outdated. We have noted briefly how the German people have been prepared through several centuries for national and spiritual disaster. Thus the Nazi regime and the evils it brought were the climax of a de-Christianization program of long standing. A German writer has found four main negative elements in the National Socialism of Hitler: antiliberalism, antisemitism, anti-Christianity, and anti-Marxism. The second and third of these attacks, those on the Jew and the Christian, concern us the most in this study. Probably the worst impression made abroad by the Nazis was their treatment of the 570,000 Jews and two million non-Aryans in Germany after 1933. The tragic liquidation of six million European Jews to satisfy the Nazi race theories shocked the entire world, and is undoubtedly one reason why God permitted fiery judgment to fall upon the nation.

At the start the Nazi party professed to respect the Christian faith, but its brutal treatment of the Jew, after enactment of the law of April 7, 1933, left little doubt as to the real nature of the party's morality. But it was the founding of the German Faith Movement *(Deutsche Glaubensbewegung)* which proved conclusively that an altered Christianity was to be introduced. Ever since 1921 attempts had been made to launch a German national religion based on the "pure" Aryan race. The new faith movement began in 1934 with elaborate attacks on the so-called Jewish element in Christianity. Julius Streicher, as the chief anti-Semitic editor, often jeered at Jesus Christ, and Alfred Rosenberg, as racial philosopher of the movement, presided over the emasculation of the Christian gospel.

Both Catholics and Protestants then entered into a long series of conflicts with the Reich Ministry of Ecclesiastical Affairs and Public Instruction. The Nazis tried to buy off the Catholics with a concordat in July, 1933, which only led to years of friction. Efforts to stampede the Protestants into line also failed. Although many pastors resisted, a surprisingly large number fell into line with the new regime's plans. These were the historic heirs of the legacy of doubt.

The Sheep Join the Wolves. The "German Christians" sponsored by the Nazis were expected to acknowledge the higher authority of the state while remaining within the denominations. But the loyalties of these *Deutsche Christen* were altered as soon as they had taken an oath of obedience to the Fuehrer as head of the church of Jesus Christ. Dropping the Old Testament as too Jewish, these men reworked the New Testament into

*"But alas! Our generation walks in night, dwells as in Hades, without the divine."

a "National Testament," which eliminated the virgin birth, resurrection, and ascension of Jesus Christ. As Bishop Wurm characterized this defection, "These men wanted to be the Storm Troopers of Jesus Christ."[8]

An example of their success was the conquest of Bremen. This city's Lutherans were almost all converted into the new movement after the mayor, a Brown Shirt officer, became president of the Church Council. He appointed Domprediger Weidmann as secretary of the council and later made him a bishop. At the end of the war it was reported that there were not five pastors out of fifty in this city who did not become "German Christians" within Lutheranism. As soon as Bremen was captured by the Allies, the Bishop and his associates were, of course, imprisoned.

Hamburg saw much the same problem. Bishop Schöffel was replaced by a pastor named Tügel, who attempted to run that city's Lutheran churches along Nazi lines, being himself a party member. A Nazi bishop named Schultz was put in charge of the church in the northern province of Mecklenburg, while Propst Meyer took over Frankfurt-on-the-Main. At Lübeck the "German Christians" steadily attacked the city's twenty-five pastors until by 1937 only seven had refused to bow the knee to Baal. These were all placed under house arrest, and though later released, could not prevent the complete capture of the churches there. The province of Thuringia became the biggest prize and later the citadel of the "German Christians," as a majority of the 700 pastors were slowly won over. This was Luther country, with its many shrines to the reformer's memory—places like the Wartburg Castle, where Luther had translated the Bible into German.

How Could It Happen? Professor Hermann Sasse of Erlangen University has put the plight of the church under Hitler this way: "It was not Lutheranism as such but a sick Lutheranism that gave national socialism an open door into the churches."[9] Many of the free churches were equally ill. How was it possible for pastors and people to make such a large surrender to what they knew was morally wrong? We have already pointed out that the faith of everyone had been shaken by the attacks of the philosophers and Bible critics as well as by the demoralization of the first war. It has been suggested as an explanation for their action that many church leaders were deceived into thinking that the Nazi regime would actually benefit Germany. But neither those leaders who surrendered nor the mass of Protestants would have compromised had they been, scripturally speaking, on the grounds of assurance of salvation and conscious guidance from the Lord. Under tremendous pressure many could not stand.

These few examples from the record of the times teach several lessons about Christian believers under persecution: (1) They must be saturated in Biblical truth. (2) They must not only be orthodox, but wholly yielded to the Lord. (3) They must know how to look to the Holy Spirit for discernment between truth and error. These conditions a large segment of the German churches could not meet during the carefree twenties. The door was ajar and the house rested on sand. So when the winds blew and the rains came in the thirties, the faulty structure partly collapsed. Now the postwar generation must reap the whirlwind which their fathers sowed. That is the missionary problem of Germany today.

A Redemptive Minority. As always in history God had His faithful remnant for this hour of peril to the professing church. Perhaps the motives of those who resisted were sometimes mixed—that we cannot judge, but resist they did, and nobly. There were really three courses of action open to the thousands of German pastors of all denominations. The first was to line up with the regime, as a large number did. The second was to try to stay on a conservative middle ground of passive resistance. But it was the third position which came closest to Paul's injunction to Titus to "speak the things which become sound doctrine" (Titus 2:1). This group who followed the third alternative became known as the *Bekennende Kirche* or Confessing Church. The story of their resistance is a glorious one, replete with the suffering of many. In 1937 alone more than 800 pastors were imprisoned for resistance. During the immediate prewar years the Confessing Church secretly trained more than 1,000 pastors in well-hidden seminaries with funds contributed quietly by church members. Later many were martyrs for Christ.* One of the best known was Pastor Dietrich Bonhoeffer who was put to death the week before Hitler died. One of the last things the young author and seminary head said before he died was this: "If you want to know the truth, I am praying for the defeat of my country because I believe that this is the only way in which my country can pay for all the suffering it has caused the world."[10]

3. PROTESTANT STRENGTH AND WEAKNESS

New Catholic-Protestant Balance. Let us turn now to the contemporary Protestant scene. Before the war, about one third of Germany's 65 million people were Catholics, while two-thirds professed the Protestant faith. Fairly definite regional limits marked each group, the Catholics holding mainly the south and west, with the Protestants in the north and east. But population adjustments following the division of Germany into two parts have brought about a new Catholic-Protestant balance in the

*Those who desire to pursue further the story of German Christianity under Nazism would do well to read Stewart Herman's *The Rebirth of the German Church*, which I have largely followed here.

Federal Republic. Ten million refugees from the east were resettled in the west wherever the most room could be found for them. Other hundreds of thousands fleeing yearly through Berlin into West Germany were also assimilated haphazardly. More than half of all refugees were Protestant, many of whom settled in previously Catholic territory. Some half-million Protestants, for instance, moved into the strongly Catholic *Land* of Bavaria, making this the second strongest Protestant state in the Republic. (Among the *Länder*, Nordrhein-Westfalen, Bayern (Bavaria), and Niedersachsen now have the most Protestants, in that order.) At present the highest concentration of Protestants in a single spot is to be found in the area of Stade near Hamburg, where they number 91.3 per cent of the population; the least are in Trier in the southeast. Catholics likewise settled in traditionally Protestant areas, where in the postwar years they have already begun to change some of the old customs and introduce their own. Catholics are greater participants in the pre-Lenten *fasching* season of gay festivals and parties, an annual period of heavy drinking and moral laxness, as well as in the similar *Oktoberfest* in Munich.

What were the general effects of such changes? First, the old regional religious patterns have been broken up into a wider distribution of Catholics and Protestants. Second, the relative strength of the two faiths has been roughly balanced, marking an advance for the Catholics. According to official German census figures, roughly 24 million people now call themselves Protestant, while some 21 million profess to be Catholics. As long as East and West Germany exist in their present forms, it is hardly accurate to call the Federal Republic a Protestant country. But should the two Germanies ever become reunited, this slight present Protestant advantage would soar again, since 82 per cent of the 17 million East Germans are Protestant.*

The value of such an analysis to the evangelical Christian in free Germany is clear. Whereas before the war only one out of every three persons was Catholic; now every other one is. This could make some difference in the approach of the soul-winner to both the individual and the masses. Protestants in Germany are already deeply affected by the shift in numbers, with some leaders searching for new strategies. While the two religions have made common political cause during most of the postwar period, should Catholicism now show a rapid growth, the mentality of Germany could well submerge into that of other Catholic European countries. Not only would it be more difficult to win people to Christ in a new Catholic Germany, but the whole political, psychological, intellectual, and moral climate of the country would change for the worse. In another section we will consider the opportunities and success of the Catholic plan for winning Germany.

*Assuming, of course, that the Church can survive outwardly under Communism.

The Panorama of Churches. Only 142,849 persons in West Germany professed no religious belief at all in the latest census. To put it another way, 96 per cent of the population makes Christian profession. Almost two million people are either Jews (17,116) or members of one of the growing sects, like the Jehovah's Witnesses, Seventh-day Adventists, Mormons, Apostolic Church, Christian Science, and the others. The rest of the population is divided into the almost equal Catholic and Protestant balance just mentioned. Almost all of the Protestants belong to the Evangelical Church, which is predominantly Lutheran. That church claims 23,877,672 parishioners in the west, leaving only 481,122 who belong to the so-called "free churches," such as Reformed, Baptist, Methodist, and so forth. Thus it can be seen that religious profession, whatever that may mean, is very much the mode in Germany. Even in the days of Nazi attacks on Christianity, such profession never fell below 94 per cent of the population. The average German, in contrast to the Frenchman, seems accustomed to making at least an outward commitment to religion in one form or another. Apart from the Evangelical Church, which will be considered separately, several other larger Protestant bodies should be mentioned. Because the average foreigner has difficulty distinguishing between them, we will include the German names too.

The Union of Evangelical Free Churches in Germany *(Bund Evangelisch-Freikirchlicher Gemeinden in Deutschland)* is a federation of Baptists and Plymouth Brethren brought about by the pre-war pressure of the Nazis on the latter group. Baptists claim about 100,000 members in more than 500 churches in the two Germanys. The Brethren who entered this federation were the "closed" group, and since the war some have tried to leave the fellowship. Many assemblies which remained outside are now grouped in a new union of both "open" and "closed" Brethren called the *Freier Brüder.* The Evangelical-United Brethren *(Evangelische Gemeinschaft in Deutschland)* have roughly 95,000 members in 123 places of worship. The Federation of Free Evangelical Churches of Germany, known as the *Bund Freier Evangelischer Gemeinden in Deutschland,* is the German equivalent of the fine church so well known by the same name—Evangelical Free Church—in America and in other parts of the world. There are about 600 churches in this body, with 20,000 members. Assemblies of God congregations number less than 3,000 members, while the Salvation Army has more than 100 meeting places. The Moravian Church *(Evangelische Bruder-Unität)* has 9,000 members in 19 churches. In full communion with the Church of England, the Old Catholic Church *(Altkatholische Kirche in Deutschland)* has 350 churches and 23,000 adherents. Eastern Churches, such as the Orthodox, count 48,000 followers. The Old Reformed Church *(Altreformierte Kirche in Deutschland),* the

Methodist Church *(Methodisten Kirche in Deutschland)* of about 65,000 members, and the Mennonite Church *(Vereinigung der Deutschen Mennoniten Gemeinden)* complete this group.

Evangelical Church Colossus. As has been stated, most Protestants belong to the Evangelical Church—23 million in the Federal Republic and more than 41 million in the west and east together. Up until 1922, each of the state or territorial churches was completely autonomous within its own region. Between 1922 and 1945 a number of unsuccessful attempts were made to unite these separate bodies with their varying degrees of state financial support and organization. Hitler attempted to capitalize on their natural differences, as we have seen, by his German Christian Church, which was resisted by the Confessional Church. In August, 1945, at Treysa, near Kassel, a new united body called the German Evangelical Church *(Evangelische Kirche in Deutschland)* was formed. The pressures of the state during the war had hastened the union, but even then it was not easily accomplished, some churches refusing to join in the merger. A first task was the complete reorganization of the war-ravaged administration. Pastors and church buildings were both in short supply. By July, 1948, a constitution had been adopted at Eisenach and the various agencies of the church set up. Under a council of twelve, the chancellery or headquarters functions in Hannover, where the Internal Affairs Office is also located. Branch offices are in Bonn and Berlin, while the Foreign Office is in Frankfort on the Main. Other governing bodies are the Church Conference, where each member church has a voice, and the Synod (120 members), which meets annually.

Many will be surprised to learn that the Evangelical Church is not wholly Lutheran. Actually, it is a federation of twenty-nine territorial churches, fourteen of which are Lutheran, two Reformed, and thirteen Union. The Moravian and the Evangelical Reformed Churches of Germany also have a loose connection with this large federation. The parent organization exercises very little authority over the groups of federated member bodies, never discussing such things as matters of faith. But it does handle legislative affairs with the state, public relations, relief, relations with the ecumenical movement and so forth. The clergy for the 17,300 parishes are trained at the twelve university theological seminaries or at the theological colleges at Bethel, Wuppertal, and Neuendetteslau.

If an individual registers himself, as most do, as a member of the Evangelical Church, he will then pay his church tax along with his regular government taxes. Amounts and administration of the church tax differ somewhat in the ten states of the country, but the small amount paid goes into the budget which finances church activities. Thus the major part of the operating expenses comes, not from spontaneous gifts of the people, but from taxes traditionally assessed. Since only about 5 per cent of the German people attend church regularly, the taxes paid by the disinterested remainder pay for most of the expense.

With their typical genius for organization, the Germans have created many special agencies of their Evangelical Church which spread across the land in a vast network. The Inner Mission *(Zentralausschuss für die Innere Mission)* is over a hundred years old and employs about 80,000 full-time welfare workers. Some 47,000 of these are trained nurses who work in 2,200 institutions having a total of 150,000 beds. In addition there is the immense work done by the welfare agency *Hilfswerk* along the lines of relief and reconstruction.

Many thousands of Protestant youth have gone into this kind of work as nurses, supervisors, and deaconesses because such participation constitutes their sole idea of Christian service. While it is true that some aspects of such effort are a genuine attempt to win souls, much is simple kindness, in the name of Christ, to suffering humanity. Commendable as this may be, the task of imparting the essential mesage is put to one side. While we should do Christian social work, we ought not to leave the great commission undone. How easily Satan deflects God's children from their one true task, to witness to His saving grace through Christ Jesus! Some young people in Germany are now getting a fresh concept of Christian service through the new Bible institutes and through an emphasis on evangelism by every and all means. Personal work, too, is a lost art, which has so often been replaced in Germany by indirect service for the Lord in relieving pain and poverty.

Profession or Possession? Those in any country who know Christ as personal Saviour are appalled at the difference between their own vital experience of salvation and the empty profession of many Protestants they see around them. According to the Scriptures, here is the very difference between life and death, for Satan cleverly brings people into sight of the truth, where they can examine it, approve it, discuss it, and do everything but embrace it. Of course only "the Lord knoweth them that are his" (II Tim. 2:19), and He alone "calleth his sheep by name" (John 10:3). But the child of God cannot fail to realize, though he is not their judge, that unsaved Protestants are just as eternally lost as unsaved Catholics, Jews, Moslems, or any others. Paraphrasing the Word of God for a moment, we might ask, What advantage hath the Protestant? One of the answers Paul gives to this question about the Jews is in Romans 3:2, "Much every way: chiefly, that because unto them were committed the oracles of God." In other words, a Protestant, like a Jew, is more likely than others to be able to find the Lord Jesus as Saviour because light from the Bible is more apt to reach him.

In the predominantly Lutheran countries of Europe, people born into the church have little knowledge of a true saving experience of faith in Jesus Christ. This is very evident in Germany, where church membership is everywhere thought of more as a matter of family background and geographical location than as the outcome of meeting Christ as a living Saviour.

Baptism brings the infant into the kingdom of God. Then the child, between the ages of twelve and fourteen, is give a course of weekly instruction in the catechism, followed by confirmation. During this period he usually attends the Sunday church services regularly. Fortunately this catechism contains some scriptural truth, which the Holy Spirit can often recall later in life. But negating such help, in large measure, is the teaching of baptismal regeneration. No attempt is made to lead the child into a personal relationship with Christ. Usually the confirmation ceremony, followed by its festive aspects, marks the beginning and the end of many Germans' interest in the life of the church. In spite of family background, baptism, confirmation, communion, and all the other influences through which an individual may pass, the vast majority of even faithful Lutherans never obtain assurance of salvation before they die.

If the faithful church attendants—only 5 per cent or fewer of all Protestants—usually do not possess the joy and certainty of salvation, what must be the condition of the millions who are only vaguely and nominally Protestant? In the light of the casual contact of Protestants with their churches, is not even the statement that 96 per cent of all Germans are church members misleading? If almost half of all West Germans are Catholic, and the majority of the rest do not regularly attend any church, then Germany cannot be considered an evangelized country, although it is indeed a country where the truth of the gospel has been preached sporadically for centuries. The Bible is in almost every Protestant home, but inquiry anywhere will show that it is little read. Naturally the message of the new birth is known to some, but its necessity for entrance into the kingdom of God is not appreciated by most. Hence millions of Protestants are not resting in the sole efficacy of Jesus' blood, as Luther did, nor enjoying the fruits of redemption that were his. Perhaps Sören Kierkegaard's sardonic words about Lutheran Denmark apply here, "We are all Christians without having so much as a suspicion what Christianity is."

Since all the "free" Protestant churches outside the Evangelical Church, including sects, number only about half a million,* their tiny proportion of only 1 per cent of a nation of fifty million people makes little impact.

---

*Some thousands in this number are really in the East, because certain churches still count their membership figures in both Germanies without distinction.

Naturally a strong evangelical testimony within the churches would increase their influence, but this is not always found. The fact that there are outstanding men of God and dedicated laymen in all these Protestant circles, demonstrates again that God keeps a faithful remnant. But like Protestant bodies all over the world, figures themselves have little meaning, since the real issue is whether the members are believing or merely professing. Plymouth Brethren groups in Germany, as everywhere else, hold to Bible truths, but their notorious fragmentation has weakened their testimony. A number of the free church leaders joined the large element within the state Lutheran churches which compromised with National Socialism, thus hurting their postwar testimony and opportunities. On the part of some, too, there has been an obvious attempt to find "a place in the sun" with the Evangelical Church in recognition, political influence, and other so-called gains. But those who have remained true to the Scriptures, and especially the ones who have carried on evangelism, have truly glorified their Lord. Final and accurate judgment of their works, as of ours, awaits the coming of the One "who both will bring to light the hidden things of darkness, and will make manifest the counsels of the hearts: and then shall every man have praise of God" (I Cor. 4:5).

Assurance of Salvation. While Lutheran doctrine contains most of the precious truths of the gospel to which we are all indebted through the Reformation, these truths do not always filter down to the level of the common people. Very wide interpretation of the creeds and confessions is permitted. Perhaps the local *pfarrer* or pastor has been influenced by history's "legacy of doubt" while in his theological seminary. Of course any preaching that stops short of offering the free and full pardon of the Lord Jesus Christ is not faithful preaching. Salvation proffered by God is meant to be accepted by man, and the invitation to trust the perfect work of Christ is extended in hundreds of Biblical passages. But the fact is that much German Protestant preaching and teaching does not include assurance for sinners that God has accepted them in His beloved Son. Few know that "these are written, that ye might believe that Jesus is the Christ, the Son of God; and that believing ye might have life through his name" (John 20:31).

Let us use one example out of hundreds that could be cited by those who carry on evangelism in Germany. This is part of a report by a worker of the Greater Europe Mission: "I told the Lord as I began this day that I would be available for Him, and if He had anything for me to do, I would like to do it to the best of my ability. I had about 200 miles to drive, and decided to pick up hitch-hikers with the hope of ministering to them. The first was a woman; she had been in town and was carrying home the things she had purchased. Not sure whether she was going very far, I opened my conversation, as I often do, by telling her that the reason why I had picked her up was because Jesus had picked me up and made me a child of God. I told her in a few words what Jesus meant to me and then asked her if she were a child of God. When she replied that she was, I then asked her, 'On what do you base that?' 'I'm a Lutheran,' she answered. I said, 'Do you think God would be satisfied with that?' She didn't have any answer, so I suggested that perhaps it would be good if we told the Lord that she wasn't sure of her salvation but would like to be. She started to cry and said she knew that she was not really a Christian. Since I had only talked to her a little while, I didn't like to press the issue too much; but she seemed to be deeply concerned, and I did want to help if at all possible. I asked her if she were willing to make the transaction. Stopping the car and taking up my Bible, I showed her God's simple plan of salvation and had her tell God that she was willing to receive His gift of the Lord Jesus Christ. She then went on her way rejoicing."[11]

Evangelists working in tents or halls to win people to Christ often meet opposition from the leading pastors of the community. These seem offended by the simple presentation of the gospel of Christ whenever it is followed by an invitation to believe. This invitation may include a request for the people to come forward, decide for Christ where they sit, or tarry after the meeting, but decision in some form is urged. The writer himself has more than once experienced such opposition to a decision by clergymen in Germany. Such pastors claim that the appeal to believe upsets their people, who previously felt themselves to be already Christian through baptism and confirmation. Now those people begin to ask questions and wonder whether they are really saved at all. Indignation is then expressed that the church's authority is questioned on this matter, even though the evangelist may have said little or nothing beyond express statements of Scripture on God's plan of salvation. Here the activity of our supernatural enemy can be plainly seen, for he leaves sinners without assurance at the very doorstep of salvation. This is not to say that the gospel is not to be found in both Lutheran doctrine and preaching. In some cases it is preached in its full glory and liberty by individuals, and undoubtedly there are thousands who know the second birth. But it must be said that full knowledge of saving grace and subsequent growth to Christian stature is in most parishes the exception, not the rule.

The Church Within the Church. The Lord Jesus spoke of those Jews whose lips praised Him but whose hearts were alienated from Him (Matt. 15:8, quoting Isa. 29:13). Later Peter wrote of the nurture of "the hidden man of the heart" (I Pet. 3:4). In Germany Pietism, the religion of the heart, has been the salt of Lutheranism throughout the years. Pietism arose partly because many Lutheran pastors of the later sixteenth century were not preaching a clear, pure gospel. As one writer puts it, ". . . their sermons, far from being fountains of living truth, were but homilies learned by rote and spiced with popular pleasantries, having nothing to do with spreading the Word of God."[12]

It was Philip Jacob Spener, a Frankfort-on-the-Main pastor, who conceived the idea in 1670 of carrying on deeper Bible study in church circles. Twice a week he gathered a group together to study the Bible, stressing the neglected truth of the new birth. Soon the idea spread to other areas and leaders, and it dominated German church life for fifty years after 1685. Helpful to the awakening was Spener's book *Pia Desideria*, which condemned the questionable practices of the hour and called for inner holiness. After serving as chaplain to the Elector of Saxony at Dresden, Spener was asked in 1694 to head a new school. The Elector of Brandenburg had created a University out of the Academy at Halle, and here Spener was able to put his ideas to work. Spener was not without opposition; the thelogical faculty at Wittenburg University found 264 "errors" in his book! Together with Professor August Franke, he created in Halle a colony of praying Bible students whose simple sincerity and holy living were to become world-famous. It was from this group that Dober and Nietschmann, Germany's first foreign missionaries since the Reformation, opened a new chapter in missionary history. The Moravian Brotherhood, which influenced John Wesley to seek full assurance in Christ, was in part the fruit of this movement. In the New World a German Pietist pastor of New Jersey touched the life of Gilbert Tennent, who in turn had a major part in America's Great Awakening.

Ever since the period of the Pietists, there has been a small nucleus of genuine spiritual experience within Lutheranism. Early these groups became known as *gemeinschaften* or fellowships. As some have become formal or have lost their clear note of truth, renewals have come from the Lord. Other groups split off of the dying ones or from the Lutheran Church itself, but in general the tradition has been against independence. Throughout the Evangelical and free churches of Germany there is a sprinkling of those who enjoy a heart experience of saving faith in Christ. Sure of their own salvation, these believers joyfully testify to others of their assurance. The Pietistic spirit lives on in groups like the *Liebenzeller Mission* and in the lives of some *Stadtmission* and *Innere Mission* workers carrying on evangelism in German cities. Faithful pastors have been trained at schools like *St. Chrishona* near Basel, Switzerland, and at the renowned *Beatenberg Bibelschule*, in the Swiss Bernese Oberland. In these circles the Bible is fully believed and devoutly obeyed, though a heavy dependence on tradition sometimes dims the vision needed for our times.

God has not left himself without witness in a Protestantism which has largely lost a conception of personal salvation. Today the heirs of the Pietists and the Anabaptists seem more concerned about vital, responsible faith than do the more official descendants of Luther, but this is never an invariable principle. Within all the chief denominations in Germany are pastors and laymen who believe in a personal Saviour and experience a lonely spiritual pilgrimage. Often regarded as odd by their fellow religionists, they remain the Lord's lights within a decadent Protestantism almost returned full circle to the practice of human works. If such men insist upon the full inspiration of the Scriptures, they are considered naïve in belief; if they teach a conscious, unending punishment for the lost, they are literalists; when they preach the message of victorious Christ-centered faith in its fullness, they are dismissed as Pietists. But such has been the experience of their forebears in every land since the age of grace began, and so shall it be until the Head of the Church returns.

Sound Doctrine. By the accepted standards of American or British evangelicals, few spiritual leaders of German churches could be called evangelicals or fundamentalists. It is the exception rather than the rule to find a man whose views of the great verities of Scripture would be considered Biblical by such standards. Moreover it is not considered enough just to quote Scripture to support one's views, as many German pastors reminded each other after Billy Graham's visits to their country. Such a practice seemed almost childishly simple to men who believe Scripture must be supported by other arguments, and is even then always subject to a wide variety of interpretations. How far this is from Luther's declaration at Worms, "My conscience is captive to the Word of God!" At one Bible Conference a German-Canadian speaker stirred up heated controversy when he advanced as a missionary motive the responsibility to evangelize the pagan world "lying under condemnation." How could those who had never heard be under condemnation? In another gathering an Evangelical Church pastor dared to doubt the practice of declaring infants to be subjects of the kingdom of God by baptism. Why, he was asked, raise this question? "Because it is an unscriptural practice," answered the pastor. But he was laughed to scorn. Still another pastor, a noted leader of an Evangelical Church activity, is kept "neutralized" by administrative duties and thus barred from the advancements he deserves. To those in any denomination who are wholehearted disciples of their Lord will inevitably come the resistance of the nominal majority.

In chapter 2 we have considered the theological influences at work in Europe. To a large extent Germany is the focal point of these influences. As the largest Protestant organization in Europe, the German Evangelical Church demonstrates the thesis that local churches are weakened by weak or false theological training.

4. ROMAN ADVANCE

Factors that Favor Rome. We have already seen that Roman Catholics now claim almost half of the population of Germany and that their resultant morale is high. Some Protestant leaders feel that the country's ultimate conversion to Catholicism is now only a matter of time. Such pessimism may rise from the postwar creation of two Germanies and the favorable population increase this gave to the Catholics in West Germany. Among those making the gloomy prediction of an ultimate Catholic victory is the famous Dr. Martin Niemöller. One thing is sure: in the present struggle between the two, aggressiveness may decide the issue. If the Catholics do gain control, a reversion to medieval darkness of soul may sweep the country, denying to multitudes a chance to hear the saving evangel of Jesus Christ.

The enlarged Roman Catholic bloc now senses the possibility of a larger mandate of power. No longer in the minority, it pulsates with missionary zeal to win back the ground lost during the Reformation. When the 1,000-square-mile Saar with its largely Catholic one million inhabitants became the tenth German state in 1957, the dream came one step closer to realization. Currently the 26,265 priests are warning Catholics especially about the danger of interfaith marriages and are attacking birth control practices. About 97,000 nuns serve in 8,209 convents, while 16,293 more are in missionary service abroad. Through the bishops located at Munich, Freiburg, Paderborn, Cologne, Essen and Bamberg, the hierarchy (three cardinals and three archbishops) are trying to create more parishes and dioceses as speedily as possible. The two Cardinal Archbishops are at Cologne and Munich. An encouraging feature for them is the high number of recruits for the priesthood (3,452 seminarians in 1957). The number of such recruits is often a means for measuring the vitality of national Catholicism; in countries like France and Spain, where the shortage of priests is acute, the Church is correspondingly weak. In one area of Germany where Protestants and Catholics are roughly equal in number, a recent vocational poll of one thousand high school graduates is revealing. Protestant youth were inclined to choose technical and commercial employment, but Catholics heavily favored education, medicine, and other professions. Especially did they lean toward the priesthood. Here are some of the figures: (1) Theological students—Catholics, 86 per cent; Protestants, 14 per cent. (2) Teachers—Catholics, 69 per cent; Protestants 31 per cent. (3) Medical doctors—Catholics, 57 per cent; Protestants, 43 per cent. Does this poll indicate a trend toward the priesthood as a result of Church pressure? Commenting on the picture, Protestant Pastor Horst Bannach of Stuttgart says, "These figures speak a definite language. So much so that we can begin to trace typical Protestant and Catholic preferences for employment. We Protestants must examine ourselves in the light of this."[13]

Youth is the Key. German Catholics have a much larger and more militant youth organization than do the Protestants. According to official government figures, the Catholic Youth Organization has 915,000 members, or 15.5 per cent of all the eleven million German youth between the ages of ten and twenty-five. With such significant influence held over the most receptive body in the country, is not the future of the Roman Church in Germany assured? Then too, the publications of this youth movement are better edited and more widely circulated than those of any other in the land. Younger children are not neglected; a goodly proportion of the 600,000 children who live in German public institutions are under Catholic care and guidance. Another 146,111 children of the faith received instruction in 66 Catholic schools in one recent year. Catholics in the Federal Republic have especially set their sights on the uncommitted Protestant young people whose church activity often ceases after confirmation. Since at the critical age of fourteen many German youth are apprenticed to a trade or enter school with a special need of guidance, here is the point of greatest proselytism for the Church. The process of winning converts continues into the university level and beyond. Men's and women's organizations, as well as those in labor and politics, are very strong.

The Stigmata of Therese Neumann. Germany, too, has her shrines and superstitions produced by centuries of Roman Catholic teaching. One of the most popular pilgrimages is that to the little Bavarian village of Konnersreuth, a town so small it cannot be located on most maps. By noon every Friday, the year around, thousands of the curious have arrived to watch a woman seem to relive the agonies of the crucifixion. Therese Neumann, a tailor's daughter, is a fifty-nine-year-old woman who, some claim, lives without food and drink. On Fridays a long line of visitors begins to wind slowly up to the second-floor room where Therese lies on a narrow bed in a simply furnished room. Out of her eyes flow streams of black coagulated blood. On her hands are the stigmata, moist black encrustations, about the size of a penny, which bleed slightly. On Therese's feet are similar marks. As the onlookers stare, Therese begins to writhe in agony and eight crimson spots appear on the head. This is explained to visitors by the elderly town priest as the infliction of Christ's crown of thorns actually felt by the tailor's daughter. Then as, supposedly, the Roman soldiers flog her, she twists violently and groans. In Aramaic, the language Jesus used, she speaks to a young child while she walks in the procession toward Calvary. Now Christ is nailed to the cross, Therese flinching under every stroke of the hammer as more black blood courses down her cheeks. As the thrust of the spear reddens her side, her face turns ashen and she groans with torment. Crying, "It is finished!" she gives a death rattle and a sigh.

Many legends surround this women, who claims to duplicate the suffering of Christ and of saints of the past, like Francis of Assisi. During the coma that follows the stigmata, she supposedly shows an extrasensory perception about unopened letters and events occurring in distant places, and can reportedly speak many languages she has never learned. Most medical controversy surrounds the claim of some that Therese has not eaten any food or drunk any water since 1927. The family doctor of the Neumanns was ordered by the Archbishop of Regensburg to report on a fourteen-day clinical watch over Therese, with four nurses on duty twenty-four hours a day. This doctor reported in the *Munich Medical Weekly Journal* that she had taken no nourishment at all during the period indicated. Her ability to simulate the stigmata allegedly has some connection with an earlier illness which almost took her life. Though the Catholic Church has so far made no official move to recognize her case, high local officials have backed her claims, and she has received the apostolic benedictions of two popes. It seems she is destined to join the 341 cases recorded since the thirteenth century as having one or more marks of the stigmata. Of these, 300 were women, nearly all of whom suffered from extreme physical or neurotic disturbances. Regardless of the explanation, the case of Therese Neumann is being exploited to the full by the Church, which depends on outward, visible objects of faith to stimulate its followers.

Return of the Robe. Like Catholics everywhere, German Catholics pay adoration to sacred objects. One of the most venerated in the country is at Trier, the Romanesque-Gothic city of the Moselle River near Luxemburg. Here, in the cathedral, 'the robe that Christ wore" is guarded carefully. In 1959 the thirteenth annual Holy Tunic Pilgrimage to Trier was Catholicism's biggest event of the year in any country. According to the tradition, Flavia Helena, wife of the Roman Emperor Constantius Chlorus and mother of Constantine the Great, was converted to Christianity in the year 312. Later she visited the site of Calvary and reportedly found there the nails used in the crucifixion, three mud-covered crucifixion trees, and Christ's robe. She gave the tunic to the city of Trier (the *Augusta Treverorum* of the Romans), along with one nail and a piece of the cross. As the centuries passed, the tunic was lost, but the legend persisted. Then in 1196 a seamless cloth was discovered in one of the cathedral altars, but it was walled up again until 1512, when Emperor Maximilian demanded that it be shown. Pope Leo X and the local archbishop then agreed to show the robe every seven years thereafter. In 1810 over 250,000 pilgrims went to the Tunica Domini; in 1933 the robe drew over two million visitors. During the first month of 1959 alone, almost a million people made the recommended pilgrimage, each paying twenty-four cents to see the robe. The home city of this relic (made famous in our day by the Lloyd C. Douglas novel and the film about it) is the least Protestant city in all of Germany.

5. *A PAGAN SUBSTRATUM*

Outlawing the Witches. Superstition broods deep and dark in the hearts of many German peasants. Goethe has expressed its hold in his *Faust,* a dramatic version of the old story of the Black Forest alchemist who sold his soul to Mephistopheles in exchange for the secret of making gold out of dross. But long before this sixteenth-century tale was circulated, the people had feared witches and sorcerers. Even today the exorcism of demons is almost a daily occurrence. Country drugstores sell "devil's dung" to protect farm animals from "the evil eye." Recently three hundred practitioners of the occult arts were turned up in Hamburg alone.

The state of Lower Saxony, with its eerie heaths, is a special stronghold for superstition. When a recent crime wave developed from mysterious incidents there, the state government under the leadership of Dr. Rolf Bunnermann, head of the Health Department, decided to investigate. Bunnermann found that a man had shot his mother-in-law because he thought she had bewitched his family. Later he killed himself. One villager slashed a woman he claimed had put the evil eye on sixty-seven hogs which died mysteriously; the woman committed suicide. A nineteen-year-old boy shot his grandfather because he believed he had bewitched him; still under this delusion the youth hanged himself. Naturally many charlatans move into this kind of situation to exploit the ignorant. According to Bunnermann these quacks have even caused the deaths of some to whom they had promised deliverance from devil-domination. Such men and women are being prosecuted by the Lower Saxony government.

The problem of witchcraft has even assumed national proportions and required federal laws to control it. In 1957 an "antiwitchcraft" law was passed by the parliament at Bonn to protect innocent, suspected "witches" from mental and physical persecution and to speed prosecution of those who prey on gullible rural folk.

Those in the Lord's work in Germany are familiar with this problem, which confronts them during every evangelistic effort. People will unburden their souls to leaders about their fear of being bewitched or about someone who seems to possess uncanny powers. Even more disconcerting is the knowledge that many such people are professing Christians, though Catholics, with their conditioning to magic, predominate. Sometimes genuine believers are involved when someone in their family is so attacked, but they have the advantage of the Lord's protection from the evil one through Christ. I met a student at the German Bible Institute whose spiritualist father prayed that she would die because she was attending the Seeheim school against his wishes. Despite severe depressions, undoubtedly satanic in origin, the young lady in question found deliverance from fear through her living Lord.

Demons Cast Out. Levi and Elizabeth Reimer, Canadian workers in Germany, led a woman to Christ who had been tormented by demons for ten years. In 1944 her son had been killed in the war. In her bereavement she frequently consulted fortunetellers to find out where he was and attempt to communicate with him. At this point demons began to harass her. In her anguish she would tie herself up so that she would not go out and commit the murders she felt in her heart. Sometimes she suffered terrible pains, which the doctors told her had no physical origin but were only from her nerves. In the evenings she would often try to flee the demons or shake them off, but this proved to be impossible. In desperation she would run frantically out to her barn and there roll on the floor in fear and agony.

Elizabeth Reimer began to speak with this woman, but soon, recognizing Satan's powers, called her husband and another German Christian to help. In Mr. Reimer's words, "We united in prayer for her, claiming the good of Christ. In times like this you can really feel the satanic powers in the atmosphere. We felt our utter helplessness but trusted the strong arm of the Lord to carry us through."[14] After much agonizing the woman was enabled to cry out at last, "If there is any hope in Jesus, I ask Him to help me now." Mr. Reimer adds that with her mention of the name of Jesus, the woman began to see her own need. Soon she was facing her own sin and the love of a Saviour. Then came glad testimony: "I have joy in my heart for the first time in ten years." Many are surprised to hear of pagan superstition and demon possession in modern Germany. Only a fraction of this has ever been documented in our time, and that wholly by Germans. If the whole story were ever published in English, we would learn that such beliefs differ little from the fears and superstitions of the ignorant savages in the jungles of Africa or South America.*

Teenager Vows Soul to Satan. Sixteen-year-old Rolf came to Seeheim summer camp from a small town along the Rhine river. Kermit Zopfi, Director of the German Bible Institute, had tried for two whole weeks to win the pleasant lad to Christ. Toward the end of his second week at the camp, Rolf came voluntarily to Mr. Zopfi to talk about his soul's welfare. For an hour Rolf heard the way of salvation unfolded, after which he said he understood everything clearly. Although he had never heard the message of forgiveness before and seemed to feel his need, he declined to accept the gift of eternal life. "I am afraid of my father," he said haltingly. "I want to think it over a little." During the ensuing days Mr. Zopfi and the other camp leaders prayed much for Rolf. Finally the last campfire came, with its radiant testimonies and unforgettable dedications of life. Rolf, obviously troubled, remained silent and depressed. Only after the fire's embers had burned very low, did Rolf finally come to Mr. Zopfi, saying, "Now I want to receive Christ." In the quiet and privacy of one of the Institute rooms, Rolf admitted that he knew what he must say to the Lord. Yet he found that he could not say it. The Greater Europe Mission's account tells of the struggle that now came: "The two knelt together beside one of the beds. Mr. Zopfi suggested he pray, asking simply for the Saviour to come into his heart. After a long period of silence, the Institute director suddenly felt the bed begin to shake with great violence. He looked up quickly to see Rolf's head bent backwards. He tried to form words, but they simply would not come out of his mouth. He was trembling violently as though he had convulsions. He began gasping for air as though he were choking, then flung himself on the bed."[15]

Finally quieted down, Rolf murmured, "The devil will not let me pray. I belong to him." It then came out that his father was one of the leaders of a cult of devil worship in the town where he lived. Rolf himself had participated in a certain ceremony where he and some other youths had promised themselves to the devil in a binding way. (Often such a vow takes place when children are very ill and the parents promise to give them to the devil forever if he will only heal them.) Fortunately,

---

*Those who wish to pursue this subject further will get much help from *Between Christ and Satan*, by Kurt E. Koch (Grand Rapids: Kregel Publications, 1961), or from *Seelsorge und Okkultismus*, published in German only by the same author. An evangelical Christian, Dr. Koch is an authority on Satanism.

Rolf finally did accept Christ some months later, in spite of his problem, and is now living wholly for Him.

6. *THE POWER OF THE BIBLE*

Getting Out the Book. Fortunately for this great people, the production of German Scriptures in many editions and at sensible prices is fully adequate. In spite of their theological and philosophical attacks on the authority of the Bible, the Germans industriously continue to print and circulate it by the millions. Indeed this contradictory action is now very much a tradition, too. Silently and surely the much maligned Bible makes its way into most Protestant homes where, sadly enough, it usually remains an unread fetish. But Germany's massive Bible publication remains one of the greatest of God's blessings throughout the last four centuries. Countless thousands have found Christ as Saviour and grown in grace whether or not the church at the time was a witnessing body. Because God is marvelously faithful to His Word, there has been fruit even during seasons of spiritual drought.

There are twenty-four Bible societies in Germany, all of which have been represented in a Union of Evangelical Bible Societies (*Verband der Evangelischer Bibelgeselschaften in Deutschland*) since 1948. Only two of the twenty-four societies print as well as distribute these Scriptures, the other twenty-two receiving their supply from these. Through all the societies copies of the Word of God are furnished to church groups, organizations, or individuals desiring them. Bibles can be bought in most German bookstores, and of course are available in the many church bookstores as well. Many methods of promoting Bible purchase and reading are used, but some could be improved upon. Especially are Bible reading crusades needed to arouse the interest of the general public. The use of bookmobiles where the Scriptures are displayed and sold would stimulate Bible reading and sales and provide a place for personal work. Though several such mobile bookstores are at work, many more could profitably be used. Posters calling attention to Bible reading might also help. Best of all, pastors of Germany's Protestant churches should continually urge their people to read the Bible already found in most of the homes.

A Giant Society. Largest of all, the renowned Württemberg Bible Society (*Privilegierten Württembergischen Bibelanstalt*) of Stuttgart has been publishing the Word of God continuously since 1812. In more than 150 years of publication, it has produced more than forty million Bibles, Testaments, and portions! Though 80 per cent was destroyed by bombing during World War II, the six large buildings are now completely rebuilt and fitted with their great presses, folding and binding machines, and tons of paper. Hundreds of employees scurry about the downtown compound under the direction of vigorous Dr. Emil Diehl. In the Society's twenty-four page catalogue I counted 413 items—Bibles, Testaments, portions—including the famous Nestle's Greek New Testament, Kittel's Hebrew Old Testament, and a Braille Bible of exquisite workmanship. Dr. Eric North, whose American Bible Society helped put this Bible house back on its feet after the war, praises "the very high printing quality" of all the Württemberg editions of the Bible.

A glance at the publishing figures of this society since 1812 reveals some interesting facts. During the Franco-Prussian war of 1870 the society furnished 103,597 free Bibles and portions to Prussian soldiers. Later, during both World Wars, so many Scriptures were given to soldiers that distribution figures reached heights never since attained. For instance, in 1914–1915, 2,037,149 portions were sold or given away, and more than a million were given out every year thereafter until 1918. Again between 1939 and 1941 the one million mark was surpassed each year. With the bombings and collapse of 1945, production fell to 284,124 annual portions, but is new nearing the million mark again.

The Pulse of Demand. According to the records of the United Bible Societies in London, Germans are buying over a million Bibles a year. Under what conditions are these Bibles bought? In an interview with the writer Dr. Emil Diehl of Stuttgart made these observations:

> Most are confirmation copies given by the churches to children at about the age of 14. Often there is already one Bible or more in the homes of such children. Still another may be acquired at marriage. Though it is impossible to get exact statistics, the assumption that almost every individual Protestant who has passed through confirmation has or had a copy of the Bible seems safe.[16]

If this is so, it means that the Protestant half of Germany—some twenty-four million people—is well supplied with Scriptures. Meanwhile a brisk sale is going on among the ten million refugees who resettled in the West after the war and the thousands of escapees who are joining them yearly. Many of these lost or left everything in their flight from the East. General demand for Bibles seems to be edging up yearly since the war, but not in a marked way. The Pocket Testament League of America has conducted massive distributions in Berlin, among students, and among German soldiers. Whether this indicates a new hunger for Bibles, or simply a recovery of the prewar position, it is too early to decide.

Is Germany "Bible-conditioned"? There is little question that at one time the Luther translation of the Bible deeply affected the population even in the matter of language. It was known, loved, and cherished by the masses after the Reformation, with resulting effects in history. But the "legacy of doubt" left by philosophers, theologians, and scientists has had its dire effects. The securalization and demoralization of several wars has intensified the changes still more. Today's German is *not* "Bible-conditioned"; his mind not prepared for the Holy Spirit's recall of Bible truth. In spite of Protestant church affiliation, he is becoming increasingly paganized. Fortunately, respect for the Bible lingers, and this God can and does use. No one has better expressed this generation's ignorance of the Bible the Bishop of Hannover, Dr. Hans Lilje.

> Modern Europeans, the Germans among them, have become completely estranged from Biblical knowledge and Biblical thinking. All through the nineteenth century British intellectuals retained a much greater familiarity with the Bible than did this same class in Germany. The estrangement started in Germany early in the nineteenth century . . . the men and women of Goethe's day could still speak in the majestic language of the Luther Bible, revel in its vivid imagery, and think its timeless truths. One need not belabor the point that they knew a scource of power and richness which has been lost to our metaphysically impoverished, nihilistic age.[17]

7. YOUTH FACES THE FUTURE

Their Destiny is Germany's. To repeat the old adage that today's youth are tomorrow's adults may seem trite, but the proverb comes alive as surveys in Germany reveal how rarely young people attend church. According to a recent issue of the German weekly religious paper, *Die Kirche der Heimat,* "only 19% of the Lutheran young people between 17 and 28 in western Germany consider themselves regular churchgoers."[18] Ten per cent of the country's young people never attend church, the report added. Only occasional attendance was attributed to 44 per cent, and 27 per cent said they went to church only on special occasions. If the last two figures apply only to those who undergo baptism, catchism training, confirmation, marriage, and burial in the church—as is probably the case, then 71 per cent, or almost three-quarters of all German youth, have only a nodding acquaintance with the church during their formative years. Small wonder that the adult is almost alienated from the life of the church! This poll showed that figures for both rural and urban areas were about the same. Highest attendance by young people was 30 per cent in Baden-Wurtenburg, while the lowest, 7 per cent, was in Lower Saxony and Schleswig-Holstein.

In sharp contrast to this, the poll concluded that 81 per cent of German

Roman Catholic youth are regular attendants at mass. No wonder that Baron F. von der Ropp, writing of the postwar German problem, said, "Most of our youth . . . . are no longer used to the church. They have been enticed against everything that is Christian . . . and the voice of the church does not reach them any longer. If some of them do go to a service, they do not understand the language, the liturgy is strange, and the subject of the sermon unknown. Thus the generation on whom depends the future and faith of our people passes the church without interest."[19]

One significant word should be added here. Young people are the most discerning of all ages in terms of ultimate reality in the lives of others. Is it possible that they see little vital Christian living among the church people, and so reject their empty worship? Can the chief fault lie with the older generation, who pass on to their children the same empty traditional religion they received from their fathers? Religious practice is never a substitute for living faith in Jesus Christ, yet Satan manages so often to make the two look identical.

Home and School as Moulds. The fresh-faced German lad trudging off to school with his booksatchel strapped on his back may well be a great soul-winner in the making. Perhaps he may become the prophet for whom true German believers wait and pray—the man of God to awaken the national conscience and call the population back to the Lord. The merry, pig-tailed girl, with her typical child's dress may become the mother or wife of such a man. But who will win this lad or lassie to the Lord?

So few personal workers witness for Christ in Germany that the chances for these young people to be contacted personally are mathematically very small. The boy and girl both have about 50 per cent chance of being born in a nominal Christian (Protestant) home. Yet even there they may not hear the way of salvation once in a whole lifetime. God never repeats himself in choosing His leaders, yet one wonders if the boy in the peaked cap could become another Luther, dedicated and resolute, or a Zinzendorf, aflame with missionary zeal. Or again he could turn into a *halbstarke*, the German version of our American teen-age delinquent.

In the modern German home there is much more liberty for children than there was in past generations. No longer is the father the stern moralist and disciplinarian he once was. Today mother has a wider influence. In many cases she has had to take over as sole parent, if, for instance, she is a war widow.

The preponderance of sons of husbandless mothers has created new problems. One million war widows and widowers and 1,300,000 orphans live in free Germany today. Between ages ten and thirteen there are nearly 100,000 more boys than girls. In all, 24 per cent of the whole German population are young—between ten and twenty-four. Over 600,000 children must live in public institutions, where few ever hear of the way to heaven.

How is this predominant type of boy, often having only a mother, brought up? With less restraining influence and with more freedom than ever. The mother, baffled and resigned about her son, too often lets him run where and how he will. From this group have come some of the growing army of German delinquents, who are as tough and belligerent toward life as any in the world. Does the German school help? An official American government study has this to say, "The German school has been, on the whole, a thoroughly academic institution, designed to fill the student's head with factual or, in some periods, slanted information; it was not thought of as a means of educating a child *socially and morally** for life within his community or a larger world."[20]

The critical age for young Germans is fourteen; between 85 per cent and 90 per cent of them leave school then to become apprenticed to a trade or to do some kind of work. This is the time when they open a new chapter in life in which decisions must be made and responsibilities will increase. Gone forever are carefree play days. Only a tiny percentage will go on to higher learning and university, and then enter the professions. The German youth is on the threshold of a working life. Can this be a Christ-centered one? Only if more will become burdened to win the lost youth in Europe's most dynamic country. Clubs, camps, and any other means that would help accomplish that goal would be more than worth the effort. We know of a mother of five whose husband *sold* one of their children in a callous move to get money for some selfish purpose. Driven to distraction, the mother kept her sanity only because her Lord stood by.

8. *THE OTHER GERMANY*

A New Country. In 1949 Russia's East German Communist puppets in the amputated third of prewar Germany established what is known as the German Democratic Republic. This area of five *Lander* or states has a population of about 17,500,000. East Prussia, a region of the older Germany once cut off by the fifty-mile-wide Polish Corridor, was divided up between the Russians and the Poles and so is not part of the new nation. Neither is Berlin, though the eastern sector of that city is illegally regarded as the capital. Cities like Dresden, Chemnitz, Halle, Leipzig, Marburg, Rostock and Potsdam have undergone rapid, state-controlled industrialization. Agriculture in what was once the bread basket of a once united Germany is likewise closely regulated. Personal freedoms are curtailed in

*Italics ours.

a police state run along the typical lines of a Soviet-rigged, popular democracy. Has the present regime brought plague or paradise to the land? In a dramatic answer to the question millions of people have fled westward to the Federal Republic since 1945.

The Church Attacked. What has Russian hegemony over East Germany meant for professing Protestantism? At least 80 per cent of the population were nominally Protestant when the Communists took over, with 15 per cent professing Catholicism. At that time there were six thousand Evangelical Church pastors and thirty thousand employed lay workers, such as nursing sisters and teachers. "The Evangelical Church," says one publication, "has stood like a massive roadblock before the Soviet's march to communize East Germany and its predominantly Protestant people."[21] This, the Communists knew, was the Luther country. Other spots, like Halle, were sacred to missionary history. The whole state of Thuringia, which had the best record for Christian resistance to Hitler, seemed to be a hard core of Protestant resistance. How did the Communists proceed to attack this fortress?

Early a pattern of action emerged. Direct methods were shelved for a battle of attrition and infiltration. The East German government promised to pay, in a disarming manner, the traditional subsidy to both Protestant and Catholic churches. Pastors at first were given the usual freedom and guarantees of respect.

Then a subtle campaign began to destroy the grip of the visible church. Among the moves made over the last decade were these: (1) No pastors were permitted to enter from West Germany. (2) Regulations prevented the transfer of pastors from one parish to another. (3) Church revenue from the state was steadily reduced year by year. (4) Funds could not be solicited except during actual church services. (5) Money sent in from the west could be exchanged only at the mark's official rate— 30 per cent or less in value. (6) Pastors' salaries were reduced to a level inferior to those of the working class. (7) Religious education was officially permitted, but its effectiveness was dulled by growing regulation. (8) Church attendance was harassed by the scheduling of compulsory rallies and worker's meetings during worship service. (9) Pastors' children were barred from university study. (10) Higher education was denied children who refused to participate in the Youth Dedication ritual. (11) Pastors and leaders were periodically jailed on one false charge or another. Roman Catholics did not escape harassment. By 1956 their candidates for the priesthood in East Germany had fallen to 336—half the normal number. Annual losses of membership rose from 3,733 in 1948 to over 10,000 in 1955.

In 1955 the Youth Dedication, or *Jugendweihe*, was introduced as a substitute for Christian confirmation and the Roman Catholic First Communion. In a typical ceremony the youth of a village would be assembled in a square, where a brass band was playing before party dignitaries seated on a platform. One at a time boys and girls of thirteen and fourteen would come forward to vow allegiance to the state, kiss the red flag, and receive token gifts. Immediately after the introduction of the *Jugendweihe*, Protestant and Catholic leaders both condemned the atheistic rites. Ever since, there has been a running battle between state and church, with the former exerting more and more pressure. As many as 20 per cent of all youth have been forced into compliance. For many pastors and teachers used by the church the strain proved too great. Determined to break the church's prestige, the only outward bridge between East and West, the German Reds clearly expressed their goal in the words of Education Secretary Robert Girnus, "There cannot be any peaceful coexistence between science and faith."[22]

What We Can Do. It does seem inevitable that the Communists, unless somehow checked, will shatter the facade of the visible church in East Germany and drive its members underground. Of course many who merely profess to be Christian will desert their faith under pressure. Probably only a small percentage are really born anew in Christ. Since the true, inner church is indestructible, we can trust the Lord to protect His own and somehow bring victory out of seeming defeat.

In the past, Berlin has provided a chink in the iron curtain. In refugee centers here, American and British missionaries witnessed for the Lord alongside their German counterparts for some years. During those days a ceaseles flow of humanity slipped from behind the barrier with little but the clothes on their backs. While waiting to be processed and resettled in West Germany by the authorities, the escapees were particularly open to a friendly gospel witness. What a joy it was to preach to young and old alike in their crowded compounds! As they later spread throughout the Federal Republic, their impoverishment and confusion set them apart. Once resettled, a contact by alert believers in the Lord Jesus often proved vital. Some who have been converted have found their way into Bible institutes and dedicated lay discipleship. Other Easterners, after finding the Lord, have deliberately returned to the East just to tell their unsaved families and friends about Him.

In Berlin's odd situation the door of communication with the east remained ajar in other ways. During this period thousands of East Berliners worked daily in West Berlin, returning at night to their homes. All these were reachable. With determination and prayer the foreign worker himself even ventured into the Communist state occasionally. In planning evangelistic crusades embracing both East and West, I was able to visit the East sector of the divided city as well as the East zone beyond. It has always given me an eery feeling to drive through the East Germany corridor from the Berliner Ring to Marienberg and on to the first western city of Helmstadt. On either side I could glimpse the cities Magdeburg and Brandenburg. But to leave the long, white ribbon of the *autobahn* was to risk arrest and detention. Silence and loneliness grip any traveler driving along the deserted 120-mile stretch.

All this free passing between East and West was changed in August of 1961 when the East Germans began to build a wall between the two Berlins. The wall effectively reduced the flow of escapees to a trickle and brought the missionary witness at the refugee centers almost to a halt. The German Democratic Republic seemed determined now to close all escape routes to the West, not only in Berlin, but along their entire long frontiers with the Federal Republic. What will this mean to East German Christians? With what limited contact with the West they had had now virtually stopped, the Protestants may count upon faster, heavier oppression as the Reds move to consolidate their gains.

To recapitulate: In the East, foreigners cannot enter to serve Christ. With refugees they may now have a limited, decreasing ministry in the West. But radio broadcasts, literature, and above all, prayer, *can* penetrate the Communist shield with the story of salvation. In the West hundreds of thousands who need the gospel can be easily reached. Admittedly this fluid situation will probably change for the worse some day. Meanwhile a great opportunity awaits the Christian worker with vision.

The Mormon temple near Bern, sponsored by American
Mormon missionaries.

The Janz brothers of Canada, outstanding evangelistic
team in the German-language areas: Adolph (seated at
left), Leo, and Hildor. The team's base is Basel.

Chapter 14

SWITZERLAND:

NO PARADISE WITHOUT GOD

"The average Swiss citizen does not know that he needs a Saviour, nor how to go about finding Him."
—EVANGELIST LEO JANZ
Basel, Switzerland

Europe's Eden. Writers almost exhaust their superlatives in praise of Switzerland as an island of peace in a stormy European sea. Oasis, Utopia, Eden, Shangri-la, and Paradise are among the terms they use; and in a way the tiny democracy deserves them all: she is indeed unspoiled, idyllic, and superbly serene. In the human sense little is missing from a nearly perfect scene. Here is a country which really lives up to its travel posters. Who can deny the charm of a calm, courteous folk whose homeland abounds with snowy peaks, enchanting valleys, and verdant meadows? In the tourist regions quiet resorts, graceful chalets, and daring mountain railways abound. Tinkling cowbells provide the music, and edelweiss the fragrance for this never-never land. From the carefully stacked woodpiles in the mountains to the spotless city streets you get an impression of order and sense in everything. If environment can make men happy, then the Swiss should be the most contented people in the world.

Much about Switzerland is fascinating to the outsider. She is more than a model state whose citizens make watches, run hotels, own banks, and tend cattle. Here are some aspects few tourists would know about: one out of every five people is a civil servant . . . Swiss women cannot vote . . . men gravely tip hats to each other on the street . . . housewives make a cult of homemaking . . . most German-speaking girls spend a period working in French Swiss homes in order to learn the language (the reverse is not done) . . . the Swiss call their country Helvetia . . . adjoining

431

regions of France and Austria recently voiced a desire to join the confederation . . . watches, cheese, music boxes, and chocolate are the most popular products with tourists, in that order . . . seven hundred square miles of the land are glacier-covered . . . some watch dealers will let you take watches out of the country on the strength of your promise to pay when you get home . . . over four hundred American firms have recently established branches here.

Europe trusts the Swiss. At one time her mercenaries were famous for fighting the wars of foreigners; now she banks foreigners' money and hosts their holidays instead. Among other things the Swiss are industrialists, craftsmen, professional men, and intellectuals. Hence the unfairness of the oft-expressed jibe that Switzerland is a nation of peasants and innkeepers. Since 1848 the confederation has united twenty-two cantons, each with its own independent administration. So autonomous are each of these states that any one of them could secede at any time by simple vote. The federal government at Bern intercedes as little as possible with the internal politics of the cantons. Thus Switzerland approaches the ideal of a pure federal union of states more closely than does the United States. Universal military service helps cement together this loosely-united republic, for common defense has always loomed large in the people's minds. Bonds like this are needed, for the Swiss are quite canton-conscious. Some are provincial to the extreme and very touchy about the rights of their home regions. Locally there are wide differences in custom, race, temperament, and language. Four languages are used officially. About 72 per cent of the people speak German in the regions surrounding Lucerne. French is spoken by 20 per cent of the population in the Montreux-Lausanne-Geneva section. In the Lugano and Locarno areas, two cantons use Italian. The dying Romansch tongue is spoken in the southeast by only a tiny 1 per cent of the total.

One Thing Thou Lackest. This fair land has been marred, like the original Eden, by the shadow of sin. Even in an environment where every prospect pleases human nature fails again to reach God's standards. Sin first sprang forth in a garden, suggesting that places near perfection are the most dangerous for man. In many ways Switzerland is like Scandinavia and Germany in her spiritual problem, though here the rebellion against the old Christian standards seen in some of the northern countries is not so obvious. Instead, a pathetic ignorance and restless dissatisfaction rule. On the one hand one sees a growing secularism, and on the other, an empty religiosity. More explicitly, the spiritual need of this country is marked by (1) an advancing godlessness, (2) a somnolent Protestantism, and (3) an aggressive Roman Catholicism. Let us look at these three manifestations.

Little to Live For. Without God at its center, the life of modern man becomes increasingly meaningless. The closer a person associates with his fellow human beings, the larger his problems seem to loom. The day is over when the Swiss could live and die in their isolated valleys; today the world is much with them. New strains now appear in the midst of apparent tranquillity. Here are a people trained in home, church, school, and army to do their best, take themselves seriously, and find their chosen niche in life. Failure to attain stated goals can plunge even the cheeriest of people into the deepest gloom. Some cannot endure the self-discipline and restraint for which their fellow countrymen are famous. Others feel restricted by what they term a narrow-minded attitude toward new ideas. It is true that the Swiss are slow to adopt new methods without much thought and preparation. This trait has its good side, but the Swiss who have traveled widely are often bitter about the conservatism at home. In England a Swiss girl told me, "A single girl is confined by custom to certain kinds of work in my homeland. Socially her life is limited, too. Here in England there is so much more freedom for women. I am accepted for what I am, and can do what I want."

The Swiss themselves have a number of explanations for their malaise. Many say they are affected by the notorious south wind called the *foehn*.* A warm, dry Alpine wind which blows across central Europe for most of the spring and fall, the *foehn* baffles meteorologists but is even more mysterious because of its depressive effect on people. The *foehn* produces headaches, nausea, faintness, anxiety, and still graver symptoms. Often a collective apathy comes over the population while the wind is blowing. Medical and psychiatric experts agree as to the effect, but cannot analyze the process or suggest any remedy. Many people become short of breath or shaky; others have heart palpitations or falling blood pressure. Irritability, lassitude, and dark depression are common: "I feel as though nothing really matters," say some, of their reaction. Crimes multiply, accidents increase, and the death rates leap during the *foehn*, with suicide as a special feature.

Why should Switzerland have the fourth highest suicide rate in the world? Surely the ordinary frustrations of life or phenomena like the *foehn* are not adequate explanations. Very little poverty exists here. In countries where the comforts of life are unknown, men might have an understandable reason to arrange their own deaths, but why should they do so in a land flowing with milk and honey? Only the absence of the

*Pronounced like *fern* with a silent "r."

Lord from His rightful place in the heart can suggest an answer. A pathetic example occurred in 1958, when novelist Eveline Mahyere, daughter of a strict Geneva pastor, turned up the gas in her parents' home and snuffed out her own life. Just 28 years old, Miss Mahyere reportedly modeled her heroine, Sylvie, after herself in her posthumously published novel, *I Will Not Serve*. One of Sylvie's chief scorns was Christianity; yet without faith, life became unbearable for both the fictional character and her creator. That Switzerland has one of the highest suicide rates in the world should silence those who maintain that man's chief need is a better environment and a higher standard of living.

One aspect of secularization is the growing pursuit of pleasure as an end in itself. Take the city of Geneva as an example. Of the thirty years following the spread of the Reformation there in 1536, the historian Michelet could write, "This city, merry, satirical, and changeable as the lake on which it stands, in which so many fine minds floundered amid medieval superstitions and so many noble hearts were lost in the defilements of dissipation, became an amazing town where all was fire and prayer, study, labor, and austerity, the great school of faith and of the martyrs."[1] What a surprise Calvin would have if he could return to Geneva now! Today the situation is reversed. Rousseau's Geneva, home of godless reason, seems to be vanquishing Calvin's town of faith and worship. With its international atmosphere, throngs of tourists, and proximity to France, the charming city on the lake is sought out for pleasure instead of for prayer. Gambling casinos, bars, night clubs, streetwalkers and other signs spell a worldliness unique in Switzerland. "The only place in Switzerland where you can have a good time," commented one tourist. "The fun capital of the country," a guidebook calls the city. The University of Geneva, where every second student is a foreigner, is surrounded by student *bistros* and a bohemian night life which apes that of Paris. In 1960 the eyes of all Europe were upon Geneva, where a sensational murder case was being tried. Slyly the Paris press jabbed at "the once-pious Genevans who have produced the bloodiest murder of the year." The other big cities of the country, also, including the formerly staid Zurich, are becoming more and more urbane.

Among university students there is a wave of irreligion and ridicule of faith in any form. A certain element of the press specializes in lampooning anything sacred. During the Billy Graham meetings of 1955 in Geneva and Zurich, vociferous newspapers belittled the servant of God and his beliefs with invectives which even surpassed those of the extremist press of Paris. Of course this is a radical fringe in Switzerland, but it did not exist a generation ago. One more piece of evidence, sad to say, that Switzerland is stepping up her rebellion against the things of God.

Protestant Vista. Slightly more than half of the Swiss people claim to be Protestants. Some of the church bodies prominent in America and England are very small indeed here. In the most recent reports the *Baptists* claimed only 16 churches, with fewer than 2,000 members in all. *Methodists* were more numerous, counting 25,000 followers. *Evangelical Free* churches numbered 28, with 2,750 members. The independent Evangelical Free Church of Geneva canton had 16,000 members in 25 churches, while the equivalent church in the canton of Vaud had 5,800 members. (These latter two bodies are not members of the large Evangelical Free Church Union.) *Moravians* have a tiny representation of 283 members in 13 churches. The *Salvation Army* counts 246 centers in the country. There are no accurate statistics available on the "open" and "closed" assemblies of *Plymouth Brethren*, but some of the finest leaders in all phases of the Lord's work are of this persuasion. These free churches listed above and a few smaller ones form only a fraction of the total Protestant strength. The largest group by far is the *Reformed Church*. All together the heirs of Calvin number 2,555,047 communicants. Called the National Church locally, each cantonal body of the Reformed faith is independent.

An Uncertain Sound. Taken as a whole, Swiss Protestantism is beset by three grave problems. First, many of its leaders are theologically unsound or unsure; second, there is all too little evangelistic zeal among church members; and third, a falsely predicated unity weakens rather than strengthens the witness. As everywhere in nominally Christian areas, each of these characteristics grows out of the preceding one. No vital evangelism can grow out of a flabby theology, nor will a workable partnership among denominations succeed without Biblical evangelism. All three failures stem from ignorance of the effective saviourhood and lordship of Jesus Christ. Though the Swiss have superior organizing ability, the presence and power of the Holy Spirit is little felt in the general activity of the Protestant churches.

Let us glance at the theological scene briefly. Because Switzerland is mostly German-speaking, her cultural relations with Germany have always been close. Thus the Swiss have persistently come under the influence—often baneful—of the theological schools in Germany universities. It was not always thus. The original foundations laid by Zwingli, Calvin, and Farel, and buttressed by Lutheran thought, were carefully built upon by Biblical scholars like Godet and Gaussen, pastors like the Monods, and historians like Merle d'Aubigné. But the theories of the French revolution German philosophy, and the higher criticism of the Bible left their imprint, too. In Switzerland a surprising number of radicals have either reworked others' ideas or contributed their own in this direction. Rousseau's rationalism adversely influenced the French part of the country. While much of his thought was negative and destructive, what is good in it can be attributed largely to his Protestant upbringing in Geneva. The German element was affected by Friedrich Wilhelm Nietzsche, who taught at the University of Basel. Nietzsche claimed that the Christian ideal of humility and the democratic standard of equality were contrary to the "will to power," and therefore should be discarded. Though his native Germany responded more to his idea of the *Ubermensch,* or superman, than other countries, the philosopher had a following in Switzerland, and his influence was wide. In the realm of psychology, the Austrian Freud contributed a theory about the basic drive in man which lacked demonstrable proof—a diagnosis without a remedy. Though his Swiss disciple, Carl Jung, modified Freud's views in his own system, much damage was done by their teaching to the idea that man is created by God in His image and redeemed at infinite price. To the psychoanalysts man is basically a superior animal driven by instincts buried in his subconscious.

Karl Barth of Basel and Emil Brunner of Zurich are the world-famed originators of modern neo-orthodoxy. As is pointed out in chapter 2, theology has been helpful in stemming the recent extreme modernism. Neo-orthodox leaders urged pastors in Switzerland to return to Bible study and desert their optimism about human nature. Yet the new orthodoxy has not led to complete confidence in a Bible which has been generally believed to contain much error and to need harmonizing with science. Nor is the teaching of the full counsel of God in Christ forthcoming. On the practical side, assurance of salvation and victory over sin are truths rarely uttered in Swiss pulpits.

Too Little National Evangelism. Since theology is often weak and warped, it follows that evangelism—defined as the clear offer of full salvation through Jesus Christ—is often misunderstood and even combatted. As always, Satan attacks the application of the gospel message to the individual even more than he does the basic message itself. Of this J. D. Hughey, President of the Baptist Theological Seminary near Zurich, said, "In the area around Zurich most of the pastors seem to believe the essential facts about the gospel. Yet many do not offer their people salvation through Christ as an accomplished work to be appropriated by the individual for himself."[2] Actually the offer of salvation is a cardinal point of belief for Christians, without which our presentation is incomplete. Perhaps evangelism, either personal or public, provides an acid test of the average church's *raison d'être*. Will a church permit an evangelist to give an invitation from its pulpit? Hardly, when so many pastors know that this will contradict the view that one "grows into salvation" through the use of the sacraments. Will the church willingly train personal workers? How can it, when so few members are sure of their own salvation? If the goal of the church is to provide a haven within itself rather than a means of rescue for those without, then the hesitation to evangelize is understandable. But if the mission of Christianity is to offer God's pardoning grace to lost souls, then evangelism is an imperative.

On several occasions I have spoken to groups of cantonal church leaders about evangelism. Busy with relief, rehabilitation, and other worthy projects, they have had little time for winning the lost. A number will join an evangelistic crusade, however, because they are desperate about the deadness of their people and the lack of fruit in their own ministry. Underneath the surface a growing hunger for reality and power can be seen. Real evangelicals take the lead, while the professing church as a whole remains unrevived.

One of the most encouraging signs of progress has been the recent interest of Swiss Christians in evangelism carried on by foreigners. The effective campaigns in the German language by the Janz brothers of Canada are one aspect. In Basel, Bern, Zurich, and other German-language centers of the country, they have won thousands to Jesus Christ and brought a measure of revival to some circles. Billy Graham and his associates have had short but large campaigns in Geneva, Zurich, Basel, Bern, and Lausanne. Besides numbers won to Christ there have been blessed effects from the training of several thousand in personal work. Yet one longs to see the Swiss themselves take more initiative in evangelism, mounting efforts of this kind without outside help.

Christ Receiveth Sinful Men. What is the spiritual knowledge of the common people? Almost always the person who exalts Christ in Switzerland will soon be leading people to the Lord, so rare is aggressive personal witness. I have spoken personally to hundreds of Swiss who never heard that sinners can go to heaven redeemed. Though raised and confirmed in the Church, they had no rest of soul in the perfect work of Christ. God-fearing and sincere in their way, they lacked the knowledge needed to share the joys of redemption. Some who do learn the way accept the Saviour, but few become effective witnesses for Him.

Once I spoke to more than 1,500 typical Protestants in a large church in Bern. My message on John 3:16 stressed the word "believe" in the text and explained in whom we must believe and why. When the invitation was given to accept Christ, a stirring could be seen and felt in the audience. Such a procedure was unusual enough itself to create some interest, as most of the churches do not give a direct invitation for Christian commitment. About seventy-five people came quickly and quietly to the inquiry room to claim the Saviour. Fortunately the whole student body of the Beatenberg Bible School and their leader, Frau Dr. Gertrud Wasserzug, were present to deal with the inquirers. In many like services there are few who are sure enough of their own salvation to be able to help others find Christ. Following this meeting several Protestant pastors queried me at length on this strange "American method." There are many ways to give an evangelistic invitation that are little used in America. To some pastors who opposed giving an invitation, the real stumbling block was not an American method, but the appeal to personal commitment to Christ.

After an evangelistic service in Zurich, an attractive girl student at the university came to know Christ. The radiant convert was told of her responsibility to the young man she was soon to marry. Faithfully she witnessed to him of what Christ had done in her life, all unaware that she would never marry him. Nor did she suspect that within a few short days she would see her newly-found Lord face to face. She was killed in an accident soon afterward, but her silenced voice continued to remind her friend of his need by the Holy Spirit's power. Not much later he, too, come to know the Lord.

A busy man near Montreux pursued the affairs of a world-wide business. Though business is a fascinating game to most men, it failed to satisfy his inner longing. In this case the man concerned had sought reality to the extent of spending years in theological study, culminating in an earned doctorate. Finally his prayers were answered on the day he sat down to read Billy Graham's *Peace With God*. Through the Scriptures cited there, the elusive dream of a distant God became personalized in Christ, the very image of the Father. Joy filled this man's life, leading to fruitfulness and fulfillment. Examples could be multiplied of Swiss people who have encountered Christ and have been transformed. Unfortunately, evangelists native to the country and with a solid reputation are few. Evangelistic pastors are a minority as well, with lay soul-winners a rarity indeed. If the lack of evangelism by nationals is any sign of spiritual decline, then Switzerland needs our prayers and help.

A City Divided. Our third observation concerns the weakening of influence. We do not speak of political or ecclesiastical influence, nor of pulpit moralizing. When God is honored and His counsels are obeyed, people are led to seek and follow Him. As an indirect result the whole moral tone of a community or country is heightened. Swiss Protestantism is proud of its leadership in the ecumenical cause and its role as host to the World Council of Churches at Geneva. Yet the oneness for which Jesus Christ prayed in His great prayer of John 17 is not outer uniformity or a union of church effort. Rather it is the purifying, spiritual oneness of the scattered body of which He is head.

Protestantism in little Switzerland is complicated by the regional issue. Each canton has an independent church council as well as political autonomy. The deep differences in language, custom, and temperament are not obvious to the tourist, but are there to rankle. Protestant ranks are torn apart by controversy over many matters, and for good reason. Meanwhile the slow surrender to mammon and to Rome continues. Only God can change lives and transform a nation. The Holy Spirit produces true unity solely among born-again people whom He indwells; even then He can do so only to the extent that they surrender wholly to Him. Any other form of Protestant co-operation is a surface one, ineffective and directed to the wrong ends.

The Blessed Few. Those who know and love the Lord in Switzerland are not many. In their midst, bickering and division are sometimes present as well. But the Spirit-filled handful in this land are a remarkable group. Without their efforts Europe and the world would be much poorer. Missionary work is carried on by them in many countries with heartening success. They support a ministry to gypsies, radio evangelism, a prodigious tract distribution, and many other activities. God's remnant exists in both the national and the free churches. Among them are found institutions like the Beatenberg Bible School, the Emmaus Bible Institute at Vennes-sur-Lausanne, and the St. Chrishona Training School near Basel. Some Christians are active in children's work, gospel publishing, and radio broadcasting over commercial stations. Together the evangelicals sometimes mount powerful evangelistic efforts with encouraging fruit. All of these good people agree, however, that their best is little enough. If Switzerland is ever to be won to Christ, more work must be done by more believers, and with greater power.

A Revival of Black Magic. One of the signs of a religious vacuum is always the invasion of the occult. As we have pointed out elsewhere, Europe continues to practice here and there, and in varying degree, the spiritualism and paganism of past centuries. During 1959 Swiss police imprisoned Paul Baumann, forty-two-year-old "Messiah," and disbanded his cult. Breaking into his secluded sanctuary at Friedberg, police found sixty-eight men, women, and children worshiping in a hypnotic trance "magic white spirits" from behind an electrified barbed-wire fence. Some, including a hysterical fifteen-year-old girl, were taken to mental institutions for psychiatric examination. Occult ceremonies and magic chants had continued in increasing tempo for the previous ten days. A fully-equipped torture chamber was found on the premises. Instruments of torture, magic implements, and symbols, a large amount of cash, and intimate diaries and biographies of each worshiper came to light as well.

Disciples of Baumann swore an oath, while under hypnosis, to obey their leader. The oath was taken on a magic book which emitted an electrical charge when touched. One man was found in a deep trance, hanging upside down in chains in the torture chamber. Johannes Zaugg, Protestant pastor of this secluded farm community, twelve miles southeast of Bern, had this to say, "Many of our people have been shocked by this witchcraft for years, but were powerless to do anything about it."[3]

Strangely enough, the otherwise solid and conservative Swiss seem easily drawn to the bizarre and extreme in religious matters. Divine healers from America and elsewhere have drawn large crowds for campaigns, even in such staid cities as Zurich. Then the slow but solid growth of the various sects has confirmed the trend. While the sower sleeps, the enemy sows tares in his field.

The Continuing Catholic Trend. Switzerland's diplomatic relations with the Vatican, broken off in 1873, were resumed in 1920. In spite of the temporary break, the church continued to grow. In his exhaustive study on Swiss religious belief, Jean de la Compte has shown that during the greatest population increase—from 1888 to 1914—Catholicism grew beyond its normal proportion. An influx of foreigners was partly responsible. M. de la Compte adds that the 1900–1941 period definitely shows an edge for the Catholics. The authoritative Dutch *Katholicke Encyclopaedie* says that between 1850 and 1930 the Catholics increased by 172 per cent to the Protestants' 152 per cent. In 1927 Keller and Stewart wrote that "three-fifths of the population are Protestants, and two-fifths Catholics; that it, 2,230,059 Protestants and 1,585,311 Catholics";[4] but the last census of 1950 showed a Protestant population of 57 per cent while Catholics had climbed to 41 per cent. Differences between the two sets of figures since the previous census show a Protestant decrease of 3 per cent and a Roman Catholic increase of 1 per cent. During the same period the *New York Herald Tribune* reported that "Catholic congregations are increasing steadily, especially in the urban districts."[5] Yet these cities were once the strongholds of Protestant truth. In Zurich, the largest city, which is full of memories of the reformer Zwingli, there are a reported

117,000 Catholics out of 384,000 inhabitants. In 1860 its populace had been only 4 per cent Catholic; in 1900 there were 19 per cent and by 1941 23 per cent. Basel has become almost half Catholic, with 48,786 parishioners out of 104,069 people. Even in Bern, the federal capital and traditional Protestant stronghold, Catholics now have 16,644 followers to challenge the Protestants' 109,925. In 1941, 252 communes out of 2,976 were wholly Catholic and only 76 wholly Protestant. But 2,648 other communes were mixed—1,143 of Catholic majority and 1,505 of Protestant.

The news that great Reformed centers like Zurich and others have again become almost one-third Catholic, is indeed astounding. When Ulrich Zwingli arrived in Zurich on December 27, 1518, he declared to the canons of the Cathedral, "I shall preach upon the whole of the Gospel of St. Matthew, chapter by chapter, according to the inspiration of the Holy Ghost, without human commentaries, drawing solely from the fountains of Scripture, sounding its depths, comparing one passage with another, and seeking for understanding by constant and earnest prayer."[6] It was the power of this Spirit-inspired Word alone that, by 1525, had caused all of Zurich to abolish Catholic rites.

Until true believers in Switzerland are endued again with such power of the Holy Spirit, or unless the Lord intervenes in some other manner, it is doubtful if the Catholic trend will be slowed in the confederation. As cities increase in size, Roman influence grows correspondingly in these cradles of thoughts and action. Increasing numbers of Italian Swiss used for labor in these population centers help the Catholic cause too.

Rome in Switzerland. Fribourg, the picturesque city of bridges, linking the French and German language regions of the country, is the administrative and educational capital of Swiss Catholicism. Here two communities of Franciscan monks flourish amid many other monasteries, convents, and chapels, all dominated by the Cathedral of St. Nicholas. Founded in 1157, the city (and later the canton of the same name) passed into the Confederation in 1481 at the intervention of Nicholas of Flue. Its citizens stubbornly resisted the Reformation, making a stronghold of their canton. Later, in 1580, a Catholic College was founded at Fribourg, and three hundred years afterward, the Catholic University. Here in the only Catholic and bilingual university of the land are trained the future leaders of the faith for every walk of life. Missionaries are prepared for service abroad too. Between 1933 and 1953 the number of Swiss priests serving abroad more than doubled. Many foreigners come to study at this and Fribourg's other schools. Around the sleepy, medieval city can be seen black-robed priests or monks strolling to and fro. On Monday and Thursday of Easter Week the Bishop of Fribourg* takes part in the feet-

*Switzerland has five bishoprics but no archbishopric.

washing ceremonies at the cathedral by symbolically kissing the feet of the pilgrims who enter.

In Fribourg the moves are planned which lead Switzerland further and further into Roman arms. Foremost of all plans is the educational one. In keeping with the principles laid down by the famous educator, Father Girard, Catholic Switzerland's cantons pay most attention to their orphanages, schools, and other institutions. Especially in the Theological College at the University, the Dominican Order has supplied the best-known professors. Long-range concentration on education, a well-known Roman strategy in democratic Protestant countries, slowly but surely challenges the public school systems with the hope of eventually replacing them. On a political level Catholic cantons are represented largely by two wings—the Conservatives and the Christian-Socialists. In 1912 the first Vatican party had been founded; by the mid-1950's it held two of the seven seats in the Federal Council. Naturally these parties aim for better Catholic conditions in the cantons and larger participation in the federal government. Swiss Catholics are steadily increasing their power politically as well as educationally, socially, and culturally.

The Jesuit Power Bid. The Swiss Constitution of 1847, written at the close of a struggle against the secession of seven Catholic cantons, contains the following statement in Article 51: "The Jesuit order and the societies connected with it must not be welcomed in any part of Swiss territory. All activity is forbidden to their members either in churches or schools. By decision of the Federal Assembly this regulation may be extended to other religious orders whose activity is dangerous for the state and makes trouble between denominations."[7]

In spite of this constitutional statement, occasioned by suspected activities of the Jesuits in the secession attempt of 1846 (called by the Swiss the Sonderbund), the government does tolerate some Jesuit activity. There are about 250 Swiss priests of the order. In Zurich, to mention one example, Jesuits publish a magazine and maintain a chaplaincy among Catholic university students. In 1946 a Radical deputy in the Swiss Parliament, named Schmidt, protested against this illegal activity at Zurich. In answer the Grand Council finally shelved the question in 1953 in order not to excite public opinion. The end is not yet. In all likelihood the law will be repealed as it was in Norway recently. For the present, Jesuit leaders in Switzerland are "walking softly," with the knowledge that Article 51 hangs over their heads as a law which can be invoked at any time. The "S.J." after their names is not used. Lay brothers are not addressed by their church titles and wear no cassock. For similar reasons

Jesuits maintain their training school in Feldkirch, Austria—just across the border.

Catholics are fond of crying "Persecution!" over their Swiss situation. In the United States the Jesuit weekly, *America*, thumps for religious liberty in Switzerland. The French Jesuit publication, *Etudes*, in its December, 1953 issue protested against the Swiss attitude toward the teaching order on the grounds that in Spain and South America Protestants do the same thing which they accuse the Catholic hierarchy of doing in Switzerland. But is there not this difference? Swiss Catholics as such have full liberty under the law, only the one order which is famed for political pressure being forbidden. Romanism's rapid growth in the confederation is witness to this freedom. If the Swiss are right—and we do not say they are—in believing that Jesuits engineered the Catholic cantons' revolt, do they not reasonably suspect them of political activity? But on the other hand, Protestant action in many Catholic lands is often wholly forbidden, and no political activity in these countries can be given as the reason for suppression.

Does Switzerland Need Outside Help? Foreign Christians have been of untold blessing here, and can be again. The story of John Calvin's flight to Geneva from Paris is an interesting early example. You can still see the humble, hard chair where he used to sit behind the pulpit in St. Peter's Church. For thirty years the reformer preached here, transforming the city and leaving an indelible imprint on his adopted homeland. Characteristically, the great exile wanted no headstone for his grave, and left no relic for his followers.

Calvin did not bring the Reformation to Geneva, but he helped to establish it there. On August 8, 1535, the new reformers, meeting elsewhere in force cried, "St. Peter's! Let us go to St. Peter's!" The crowd surged toward the cathedral. Out of its doors scurried the frightened priests, some carrying sacred objects. The renowned French reformer Guillaume Farel, another foreigner who did much for this land, mounted the pulpit and began to preach calmly. Very little pillaging followed, as it had elsewhere, though certain statues thought to serve as idols were smashed. By May of the next year the cathedral had been designated the center of the new faith, and by July Calvin himself had arrived.

What Calvin and Farel began, other foreigners have continued, but never without struggle. Even in modern times the deep-seated conservatism of the Swiss has resisted such help. When Catherine Booth, affectionately known in Europe as *la Maréchale*, attempted to plant the Salvation Army in Switzerland, she was met with open hostility. Forbidden, finally, to speak in one city, she was forced to meet her followers in the woods at the outskirts. Shortly afterward policemen stepped forward to arrest and imprison the courageous pioneer, though they themselves were profoundly moved by her message. As a result of this incident, more tolerance toward minorities was won from official Protestantism, and the Salvation Army was firmly rooted to Swiss soil. Through the Army's witness thousands have found Christ. Though now thoroughly Swiss, the movement was born through the labor of the indomitable daughter of Britain's General William Booth.

A Scotsman named Hugh E. Alexander, after studying at Glasgow's Bible Training Institute, arrived in Switzerland in 1906. Without knowledge of French or German, the young man had only a flaming heart of love for Christ to commend him to this country. At the time the land was "sunk in a morass of formalism and liberalism, where nominal Christians knew next to nothing of the things that really matter. . . . The Bible criticism which had spread from Germany had already done unbelievable harm."[8] Ministering at first to children in his poor French, Alexander gradually mastered the language. In 1912, revival broke out following his ministry in the little village of Orvin in Bernese Jura. Next came a moving in Neuchatel so powerful that people sang hymns and held prayer meetings in the tramcars and streets. Vevey, Lausanne, Morges, and Geneva were successively stirred.

The doughty Scot was a fighter, sharp and straightforward in his attacks on the new modernism. When he wrote a pamphlet entitled "Ichabod," exposing the clever enemies of the gospel, bitter reaction was not long in coming. A cunning plot was laid by the Protestant forces to pressure state and federal authorities to expel Alexander. In the end, right prevailed when the missionary found himself vindicated before the law, the authors of the plot publicly denounced, and the judge himself deposed. Hugh Alexander was opposed and misunderstood even by the genuine people of God for his "narrowness." Yet he founded a Bible School, set up fourteen Bible Houses in three continents, and wrote four hundred hymns. Half a million Bibles were printed by this energetic soul, his commentaries on the Word are rich and faithful. Hundreds of his former students serve Christ all over the world, while a small army of trained colporteurs sell Scriptures everywhere. Switzerland owes the austere Alexander a great spiritual debt, so far little acknowledged.

An American Bible teacher who taught classes in Champery a few years ago was expelled from the canton through the influence of the Catholic bishopric of Valais. In Bern in 1950 an American girl working among children had great difficulty winning a permanent residence permit. Only by patiently learning the Bernese dialect of Swiss German and by demonstrating her work was she able to win the gradual respect of the Protestant church leaders. (The cantonal government had required the endorsement of these men in order to grant the young lady's visa. It was finally granted, though reluctantly.) In Basel, the Janz brothers of Canada found their way to broadcasting and evangelism choked with red tape.

I cite these instances only to show that a modern democracy like Switzerland does control the entrance of foreign residents (not tourists) quite closely, requiring a real reason for their presence. Once a cantonal government is convinced of the genuineness and non-political nature of the foreigner's work, no trouble usually ensues. A number of evangelical Christians from other lands have established themselves here and are doing good work for the Lord. Some, like John D. Hughey, Jr., of Rushlikon, teach in seminaries, while others work with children or in radio, public evangelism, or Bible classes. Peter Van Woerden, a Dutchman, has an extensive children's ministry in Geneva.

Mission to Intellectuals. A good example of what can be done by one foreign couple was recently featured in the American press. Americans Francis and Edith Schaeffer have been in Switzerland for more than ten years. Presently they use a unique method to reach some of the intellectual drifters and doubters who are so numerous in Europe. At Huemoz, on the road leading to the ski resort of Villars, the Schaeffers purchased a thirteen-room chalet called *L'Abri* (the shelter), in which, *Time* says, they carry out "one of the most unusual missions in the western world."[9] Every weekend a university crowd of students, painters, writers, actors, singers, dancers, and "beatniks" arrive to discuss with the Schaeffers the meaning of life. By explaining God's truth in terms understandable to such people, Schaeffer has won a goodly number of them to Christ.

The Schaeffers, too, had difficulty with the Swiss authorities at first. Some years earlier they had settled at Champery, a town reached by cog railway from the valley below. In this Roman Catholic canton there were few Christians and there was very little preaching of the redemptive Word. When Francis and Edith led some in the district to Christ, the reaction was immediate. The local police waited upon them with two orders. One stated that they must leave Champery itself, the other that they must leave the country altogether. Later, however, the authorities reversed their decision and allowed them to remain.

In their new location these missionaries now have fourteen fellow workers, who help in Switzerland and in other countries. For some time Francis taught a regular Bible class in Milan, to which he commuted by train. Here an outstanding opera singer was converted, and many others influenced. What draws travelers and students to *L'Abri?* Those who have attended the meetings and have confronted the Lord in person talk with their friends of God's power and grace; thus the Word is spread.

Suffer Little Ones to Come. At a recent Swiss church school conference, a group of theologians laughed at the idea of mentioning sin to children or expecting them to understand the work of Jesus Christ. Two people in their audience did not laugh. Arthur and Agnes Hoffman of Child Evangelism Fellowship International left the conference with a greater burden than ever to win children to the Lord. They knew from personal experience what big dividends spiritual investments in little ones can pay.

Not long before, the Hoffmans had led twelve children to genuine faith in Christ during a week of meetings in Wallisellen. The missionaries were moved to tears by the spontaneous testimonies of these dozen born-again children. In Thun, on another occasion, their rallies were attended by an average 350 children. Many lingered afterward to be dealt with personally. The Hoffmans recently began four Good News clubs in Basel, bringing to fifty-eight the number of these clubs in German-speaking Switzerland alone. A late report from thirty-two of the clubs revealed that during a typical month seventy-four classes were held, with 454 children in attendance.

While foreign workers set an example, some Swiss, too, are doing fine work with children. M. Jean André, a successful business man in Lausanne, conceived the plan of bringing French children (as well as Swiss) to his camp just inside the Swiss border. During holiday seasons, special cars loaded with kiddies leave Paris and other principal points. A large number of city children, some from the slums, have found Christ through the camp witness. M. André also sees that the children and their parents are followed up, through individual contact and in periodic rallies.

Switzerland does need the help of the outsiders whom the Lord sends to her from time to time. This country, though a tourist crossroads, has a peculiar provinciality in many matters. Swiss believers especially need challenge through contacts with foreigners along the lines of broadened vision and progressive methods of getting out the gospel. Those called of God to help win the little land in Europe's heart will find their way smoothed by Him in spite of apparent difficulties.

St. Nicholas Cathedral in the center of Stockholm's "Old Town."

Chapter 15

SCANDINAVIA IN SILHOUETTE

"Of all the parts of Europe where I have preached, Scandinavia has been the least responsive to the gospel."
—BILLY GRAHAM

"The casting off of the yoke of Christianity is progressing according to the prescribed program."
—Editor of Sweden's leading daily newspaper,
Svenska Dagbladet

Why Scandinavia? If any countries of Europe would seem exempt from this kind of survey, the northernmost should. Are they not the most Protestant countries in the world? History shows how quickly and almost painlessly they accepted the principles of the Reformation. Nearly everyone in this combined population of about twenty million people is Lutheran. Furthermore, the human enemies of the truth encountered in southern Europe are negligible here; the militant sects are few, the Catholic Church is tiny, and Communism, except in Finland, is a shadow. If the conditions for successful expansion of the gospel message exist anywhere on earth, Scandinavia would seem to be the ideal place. We shall see to what extent the truth of the Lord Jesus Christ has flourished in this northern Eden.

Some may ask why English-speaking Protestants, with all their faults and divisions, should attempt to interpret Scandinavian Christianity. Our purpose is neither to compare nor condemn, but only to comment on what we have learned. All men are sinners and no nation is altogether righteous. But every country deserves some alert, responsible evangelicals who will provide her people with a clear presentation of Christ. Since Scripture teaches that the field is the world, even Scandinavia—like America—must be viewed in the light of the Great Commission. All such fortunate countries must beware lest, having preached Christ to others in times past, they now become castaways.

449

Outwardly Scandinavia forms what is probably the most upright cluster of nations in the world. All men look up to the hardy descendants of the Vikings for their rectitude, diligence, and moderation; and every nation is proud of its Scandinavian racial stock. How immeasurable has been the contribution of northern European immigrants to the life of America! Few trouble-makers arrived in the New World from Scandinavia. The Scandinavians have been a loyal, law-abiding people, with deep concern for the rights of others. Political parties in this part of Europe have renounced wealth and power to fight for social benefits which they believe everyone needs. Though all this forms a seemingly commendable picture, it is incomplete. No countries can reap the benefits of Christian social concern while ignoring the central, redeeming message of the Lord for the individual. To nations which try to live on Christian ethics without Christian regeneration can come only trouble.

Why a Scandinavian survey? To demonstrate several neglected facts about this area, often considered evangelized:

1) The change-over from Catholicism to national Lutheranism during the Reformation was based more on the political opportunism of the rulers than upon the desires or faith of the common people.

2) The nominal profession of one religion was thereby largely carried over into the other.

3) The form of Lutheranism then adopted does not consistently stress the necessity of the new birth as a personal, conscious experience, even though it includes most of the great truths of the Bible as expressed in the Lutheran confessions and catechisms.

4) As a result, the people have widely demonstrated their dissatisfaction by ceasing to show more than superficial interest, and by seeking other answers to life's problems.

5) The free churches, fruitful in some places, and failing in others, have not proved to be, as a whole, the consistent channels of blessing and truth they could be.

If these propositions are true, much concern by believers all over the world should result. Satan, our mortal enemy, sends men a strong delusion, that they should believe a lie. He would urge men to cling to their baptisms, confirmations, and communions as hopes of salvation, even as he encourages Catholics to cling to their sacraments for the same futile reason. He would lead men up to the door of salvation and then leave them to perish on the very threshold. But our God is surely aware of this situation and seeks men to serve Him in correcting it. Perhaps some who read this will be so called and used.

Things Alike and Different. In this introductory section we shall consider some points which concern the northern countries as a whole. Geographically, our definition of Scandinavia could be broadened to include Greenland, Iceland, the Shetlands, the Orkneys, and the Faroe Islands. But since spiritual conditions in these other areas roughly parallel those in the major four, we will confine our thinking here to Denmark, Sweden, Norway, and Finland. Considered as a geographical unit, Scandinavia is about 1,200 miles in length and some 600 miles wide. Within the four lands, surprising differences as well as many similarities may be found. But a certain Scandinavian-ness—a substratum of history, interests, language, race and society—runs through them all. In topography they are different: Denmark is mostly flat, Norway largely mountainous, Sweden a combination of both, and Finland a lake-and-forest country. Physically the people are quite similar, many with the well-known blond hair and complexion. They are generally husky, fond of outdoor sports like skiing, skating and hiking. In the political realm both likenesses and divergences can be found. All the countries except Finland are constitutional monarchies. In international relations Sweden has clung to neutrality, but Norway and Denmark are loyal members of NATO and other Western alliances. Finland, a democracy headed by a president has been forced to orient herself toward her big neighbor the Soviet Union.

The linguistic pattern is similar in Denmark, Norway and Sweden. Written Danish and Norwegian are very much alike, as written American and British English are. But, on the whole, Danish speech seems slurred and gulped to other Scandinavians. Danes easily understand Swedish, but the Swedes sometimes have trouble with Danish. They like to tease each other about the difference in tongue. "This is not a language; it's a throat infection!" was one Swede's comment about Danish. An old Swedish farmer, having visited Denmark for the first time, was asked how he liked it. He replied, "Ja, it's a fine place, but they speak very bad Swedish there!" Norwegians have both a town language, for scholars and writers, and a country language, and also peasant dialects. Of these three, Norwegian is probably the "middle language." But almost any Scandinavian by training his ear a little, can both understand and make himself understood. Finnish, being neither Scandinavian nor Slavic in origin, is a strange, difficult language, akin to Estonian, and more distantly, to Hungarian. About 10 per cent of the Finns also speak Swedish perfectly, while the rest understand it well enough for some conversation, since they study it at school.

The origins of the people of all four countries are similar. Racially and linguistically only the Lapps constitute any sizable minority. There are about 350,000 Lapps scattered across Norway, Sweden, Finland, and

Russia. The colorful northern nomads have mostly embraced Lutheranism (or, in Russia, Orthodoxy), but retain their own language and way of life. Probably similar Lapp customs, as well as a single bloodstream, have been a big factor in helping Scandinavians introduce progress into the lives of the nomads. Yet they need the gospel of salvation through Christ, which most have never heard.

The Scandinavian Way of Life. A basic simplicity is the keynote of life in northern Europe. Even in the clean, strong design of furniture and in functional architecture, a lack of excess and ostentation is noticeable. In the lives of the people, too, there is less tendency than in America, for example, to overdress or to overdo anything. Isolation from the rest of Europe and a fierce historic struggle to survive have no doubt contributed to this. In the usual frank directness of Scandinavian conversation, simplicity is again the note. One senses in these people little duplicity or evasion, for here is a basic openness of character not usually met in southern Europe. The word of a Scandinavian businessman is usually as good as a signed contract. Naturally there are differences between the temperaments of the peoples. The Danes are the most friendly, urbane, and continental. Swedes have a somber, German-like efficiency, mingled with a sort of British reserve. Norwegians are less stiff, have a greater sense of humor, but lack Swedish polish. Finns are a serious, kind people, living close to nature.

All Swedes love ceremonialism. The long meals where guests are present call for a quite rigid etiquette of toasts, speeches, and profuse thanking of the hosts. Confirmation in the church especially gives opportunity to gather the family and relatives, eat a huge and lengthy meal, give presents, and indulge in endless, admonitory speeches to the young. Even in introductions to each other and in listings in the telephone book, there is a set form. A person's job is always linked to his name: Mr. Truck Driver Peterson or Mr. Laundry Man Larsen. This practice extends to wives, too, who become Mrs. Truck Driver Petersen or Mrs. Laundry Man Larsen! Even a student will be Mr. Law (or Science) Student Andersen. In Sweden we have even heard a milkman who calls himself Mr. Milk Engineer so-and-so! It is always polite for one to repeat his name clearly to everyone he meets, and of course shake hands.

In keeping with their progressive outlook, Scandinavians like to raise their children to be uninhibited. We shall see later that this not the unmixed blessing in practice that the people might think it should be. Women have more freedom here than they do in southern Europe. Scandinavians enjoy a uniformly high standard of education, especially noticeable in the adult training offered to all in later life. They are the most avid readers in the world, with a higher ratio of bookstores to population than anywhere else. Students who have passed their high school examinations are entitled to the special distinction of wearing a student cap when they go out into the streets. Most young people have a burning ambition to be successful students. In between periods of study, compulsory military service claims all healthy young men. Girls often spend a year in England or France learning a new language while taking care of children, and young men sometimes try a year or two at sea.

Winters are long and dark in most of Scandinavia. Months of extended dark give way reluctantly to long, nightless days. When summer's short, sunny weeks finally arrive, they are greeted with joy by these sun-worshippers, and visits to the seasides begin. The midnight sun and the northern lights are seen by people living farther north, such as the inhabitants of the scattered little fishing villages of Norway above the Arctic Circle. Here in the far north, isolation and deep quiet characterize an area of severe winters, few roads, and a taciturn people. As there are few large cities in Scandinavia, life is not primarily urban. The vast majority are country people, like those on a trim Danish dairy farm or a prosperous estate in the Skåne section of Sweden. Again, they may inhabit a tiny Finnish village—a mere cluster of houses so typical of this thinly-populated part of Europe.

Paganism Goes to Church. We consider now the typically Scandinavian expression of the Christian faith. In Old Uppsala, a few miles north of the seat of the Archbishop of Sweden, stands a church which is somehow a symbol. Cherished within its walls are the carefully preserved ruins of a pagan temple. Elsewhere many of the old stave churches with a cross at the top still have pagan dragons carved on their doors—for safety's sake. In the spiritual realm this combination epitomizes the whole problem of Scandinavia: the old superstitions live on in a church that never fully reformed. Indeed Martin Luther would shudder to see what is happening in some of the Scandinavian churches which bear his name today. Until an alarm is sounded, the believing minority awake, and a new evangelism is launched, the northern nations will continue to slumber on to their undoing. There is abundant evidence that Scandinavia cannot be written off the missionary map of the world as an area already evangelized. Many of the well-known revival fires have been burning low for many years, though a few glowing coals can be seen now and then. Even some of the free churches which were once such a challenge are now bedded down for a long hibernation.

To Heaven in a Rocking Chair. Anyone is likely to have an easy conscience about sin if his church requires of him little repentance and belief. If his church leaders say that the grace of God is mediated to Christians chiefly through the sacraments, who is he to disagree? No basic change of life or moral standard is required of him even if Jesus Christ did say, "Ye must be born again" (John 3:7). He professes what he is brought up to believe, and that is the end of it. An official Swedish publication says of the church, "Active participation is not required." In Scandinavia, religion has become to most people a pleasantly impersonal, familiar, but meaningless piece of furniture, like the old family rocking chair. No one would think of dispensing with this old heirloom which has been in the family so long that one almost forgets its origin. It is welcome to stay as long as it remains in its own corner out of the way. Instead of stimulating men to repentance and faith in Christ, the priests* of the state church have mostly administered sedatives to help them repose. Christ has not been able to wield His dividing sword freely where peace is preferable to discipleship and form to faith.

No Reform at the Grass Roots. In Sweden the two chief figures of the Reformation were Olavus Petri, the Wittenberg scholar, and King Gustavus Vasa. In 1540 King Gustavus forced the Örebro Council to accept him as the first ruler of a hereditary line based on the principles of the divine right of kings, a reversal of the elective method of the Middle Ages. At the Diet of Verteras in 1544, the King's plan for embracing Protestantism was accepted by the four States of Sweden. The new faith was therefore introduced by the rulers rather than arising from the will or faith of the people. There was no wave of evangelism, no unusual ingathering of believers. Of course some who read Lutheran and other tracts and books were genuinely converted. At the same period the King transferred huge estates and property from Rome to the crown. The powerful nobility was then restored lands which had been in the hands of the Roman Church since 1454.

Since this event occurred at the time when Sweden was seeking freedom from Danish domination, Lutheranism provided a natural escape from the oppressive and wealthy Roman system which controlled both countries. While it is true that King Gustavus knew Luther personally, had Andreae translate the Bible into Swedish in 1526, and championed the Lutheran cause, yet the pattern of his actions shows that politics, wealth, national independence, and personal ambition were all powerful factors in the "conversion" of Sweden.

Since Finland was at the time under Swedish control, the Reformation

*Lutheran ministers are often called "priests" in Scandinavia.

there naturally followed the same moderate and nominal pattern. Here the leader was Mikael Agricola, who later became the Bishop of Turku. In 1548 Agricola translated the New Testament into Finnish, thus becoming the founder of literary Finnish.

The rulers of an ascendent Denmark also had their political reasons to espouse Lutheranism. Though Norway and part of Sweden were under Danish control, the power and wealth of the nobles and bishops had long frustrated the kings, who sought to build up royal authority. King Christian II, a nephew of Frederick the Wise of Saxony, was the ferocious leader who had subjugated a large part of Sweden under the urging of Catholic Archbishop Troll. In 1520 he had treacherously ordered the infamous slaughter of Swedish Catholic leaders, called "The Stockholm Bloodbath." But on the other side he could be equally zealous. It is the view of most historians that Christian II encouraged Lutheranism in his country as a means of overcoming the power of the bishop and strengthening the crown. The king attempted to get Luther himself to visit Copenhagen; Carlstadt came briefly but had to return to Germany when Luther discredited him. Impatient, Christian II decided to break with Rome without waiting for full instruction in Lutheranism to be given to his people. Although the usual outward reforms took place, the nation was not yet ready. Opposition drove Christian from the throne in 1523, and his uncle and successor Frederick I swore allegiance to Catholicism. But Hans Tausen, "The Danish Luther," returned from Wittenberg in 1524 and began to preach the truth. Finally royal favor was won, and the king became Protestant. Later a son of Christian II took the throne and consolidated the gains of Lutheranism. Redistribution of wealth and land followed.

Norway likewise was in the power of Denmark at the time. Though the powerful Catholic archbishop of Trondheim resisted the advocates of Lutheranism, defeat was inevitable, and the Reformation begun in Denmark was adopted here as well.

From these brief accounts several things become clear. Petri in Sweden, Tausen in Denmark, and Agricola in Finland were all Wittenberg disciples of Luther, and doubtless knew the Saviour by more than profession. But in both Sweden and Denmark strong political motives entered into the Reformation. Rulers who needed the support of the new Church to win power likewise made sure it would become their servant later by attaching it to their courts and directing its every move except in matters of actual belief. The economic gain to the state and the upper classes was enormous.

What of the common people, the masses who now suddenly found themselves Lutheran? Most made the change without further ado. One baptism was as valid in their eyes as another so long as the king and the religious leaders approved. To be fair, there were individuals who knew an actual heart repentance and faith in Jesus Christ. Perhaps the rulers were unknowingly used of God to bring about His purposes. Best of all, the Bible was put into the hands of the people for the first time. But nominal profession of Lutheranism was not difficult for most, for not every Roman vestige had been removed from Lutheran worship, and enough familiar objects remained.

In conclusion we see that personal faith in the Saviour was not required for entrance into the new church; rather, salvation was introduced in baptism and then strengthened by confirmation and communion. Some of the results of this nominal belief were similar to those which followed Constantine's wholesale adoption of Christianity for his Roman subjects.

Sacraments Cannot Replace the Saviour. The following statement is translated from the Swedish edition of *The Small Catechism of the Evangelical Lutheran Church*: "Baptism provides the forgiveness of sins, salvation from death and the devil, and gives eternal blessedness to all who believe what God's Word and promise contain." According to Lutheran teaching, what a child's baptism begins confirmation completes. Faith is required, but also works. The required teaching is carried out at the beginning of adolescence, when the child learns the catechism. To be sure, some of the precepts are very helpful. Fortunately the Ten Commandments once learned are not easily forgotten. Evangelists in Scandinavia testify that conviction of sin often rises when the true gospel is preached against this background. No doubt much of the uprightness of the Scandinavian character arises from the teachings of the catechism and the Ten Commandments. But where does the grace of God in Christ fit into this picture? If baptism, conferred upon one in babyhood, is followed only by memorizing the catechism, where is the living faith required in Scripture for salvation? Presumably faith is exercised when the catechism is learned, and the confirmation ceremony is a kind of confession of faith. But is this not a dangerous assumption? The word "believe" in the above definition of baptism should not refer to mere assent. Faith in Jesus Christ is a conscious, personal vital grasp of His atoning work. But in practice, no one who goes through the motions of piety in the church is rejected, nor is any later transformation of life expected. Confirmation is usually a social affair, complete with dinners and parties. A part of growing up, it is neither a new birth nor even a new beginning. Assembly-line profession of the faith is the pitiful fact, regardless of what good motives may have originally launched the system. Some American believers living in Sweden recently shocked their neighbors by saying that they did not intend to have their children baptized. Some time later the same neighbors were still more incredulous when they heard the same children profess to be "saved"—without baptism—at a still tender age. Such claims were almost as strange to them as they would be to a Roman Catholic, who also trusts in a sacramental system.

Though there are some deep differences in the theology involved, the Lutheran communion does for the unbelieving worshipers much the same that the Catholic mass does for its participants. The misgivings of conscience are salved temporarily by partaking of a sacrament ordained by the church, and therefore presumably by God. Somewhere it has been forgotten that the table of the Lord, given by Him as a memorial of His death and as a promise of His return, can be meaningful and blessed only to those who believe in the Lord Jesus Christ as Saviour. Never intended to become a ceremony to help in one's salvation, the blessed meaning of the communion table has been changed completely.

Small wonder that those Scandinavians genuinely saved and filled with joy and peace of a loving Saviour are saddened about their former ignorance. Such people feel, not without reason, that the truth of salvation is widely withheld and diluted, though perhaps unconsciously, to the detriment of the hungry masses. One can only conclude that the gospel of grace in Scandinavia is confronted by "another gospel" (Gal. 1:6). To all who see the issue clearly, Scandinavia must appear to be a mission field.

Others Enter the Vacuum. While nominal Protestantism sleeps, false teachings have come in. Most Catholic activity in Scandinavia is under the direction of the Vatican's missionary branch, which officially defines it as a "mission area" of the world. Denmark, with 22,000 Catholics, has the largest group. Growing in prestige and power, the Church ordained its first Danish bishop in 1953, raising the vicariate of Denmark to a diocese. The occasion called for the first broadcast ever made by a Pope to the Danes, when Pius XII expressed confidence that the Church in Denmark would some day regain its pre-Reformation glory.

In 1953 Norway also saw its central prefecture raised to a vicariate. When Bishop Johannes Rüth took up residence in Trondheim, he reestablished the See there which had been extinguished by the Reformation eight centuries before. In the same year Oslo was elevated from vicariate to diocese. The 148-year-old ban against Jesuits in Norway was repealed in 1956, aften ten years of Parliamentary debate.

Catholic Swedes have made remarkable strides in the last century. In January, 1952, a broader law on religious freedom went into effect. With this, the ban on convents and monasteries, dating back to 1527, was abolished. On November 7, 1953, the Vatican announced that Sweden's vicariate was likewise to be made a diocese, with the German Johannes Müller as Bishop of Stockholm. Catholic children are now free to attend their own religion classes to match Protestantism's obligatory instruction for its children. The present Catholic population in Sweden is nineteen thousand, an amazing threefold increase over the six thousand before World War II. Finland has only two thousand Roman Catholics, but seventy thousand of the Greek Orthodox Catholic faith.

Other errors are at work in the northern lands. Besides the 400 American Mormon missionaries reportedly going in and out of Scandinavia for short-term service, Muslims are making their appeal. A Pakistani representative of Islam settled in Gothenburg, Sweden, in 1956 to begin a translation of the Koran into Swedish. This city was chosen, he announced, because of its convenient access to all four Scandinavian countries.

INDIFFERENT DENMARK

"Our official Christianity is not the Christianity of the New Testament."

—SÖREN KIERKEGAARD
Danish Theologian (1813–1855)

Awake, Holger, the Dane! In the Danish town of Elsinore, just a few miles across the Kattegat from Sweden, stands mighty Kronberg Castle. Tradition calls this structure the setting of Shakespeare's *Hamlet*. Deep in its dungeons a massive figure sleeps in stone. His name is Holger Danske—a kind of Danish King Arthur. The statue will only awake, the legend says, to wield his sword in Denmark's hour of mortal peril. Though the people of this interesting land are unaware of it, they are in a peril today from which no human being, legendary or otherwise, can save them. Their problem is everyone else's; the difference is in degree. To be lost in sin without a Saviour is the sad experience of most people in our world, but to be unaware of being lost at all deepens the tragedy even more. Most of the four million souls in this small state live jauntily and carelessly for time rather than for eternity, taking their pleasure as they find it. The materialism of our times has taken strong hold upon Danes, whose Protestants no longer provide prophets to call them to repentance.

Denmark does need a delivering sword—the penetrating Sword of the Spirit—to bring the Danish people, now so indifferent, to self-knowledge and trust in Jesus Christ. What child has not loved the delightful fantasies of Hans Christian Andersen? But facts about salvation rather than fables about fairy princes are what Danish children need today. Neils Bohr is illustrious for investigating the nucleus of the atom. Would that as gifted a Dane would delve as assiduously today into the heart of gospel reality! Out of a granite block the great Bertel Thorvaldsen could hew a warm, almost breathing man. Yet the eternal Rock of Ages is scarcely known as a real person in his country. The world has laughed with comedian Victor Borge and hummed with operatic star Lauritz Melchior, but until Danes can rejoice over a personal relationship to Christ, this sort of laughing and singing will not go far. Only after the Lord turned the captivity of His people, says the psalmist, did true joy come. "*Then* was our mouth filled with laughter, and our tongue with singing: *then* said they among the heathen, the Lord hath done great things for them" (Ps. 126:2).

Progressive and Plucky People. Denmark gives a variety of impressions to the visitor. The very mention of the name conjures up the venerated Randers storks, swarms of bicycles, cigar-smoking women, the Tivoli toytown guard, open sandwiches and pastry, and the wistful little mermaid statue of the Andersen fairy tale. The kingdom of Denmark is made up of the peninsula of Jutland, the island of Zealand, and about five hundred other islands, only one hundred of which inhabited. Because of its diminutive size, Denmark has been called "the vest of the Scandinavian suit." Both the flatness and agricultural use of the land remind one a little of Holland. Small, neat farms are everywhere, with sand and sea never far distant. Here you will see tree-lined fjords leading off into slightly undulating country, making unforgettable land and sea scapes. There you will spot charming little houses in provincial towns. Leafy glades, lakes, and old manor houses complete a lovely picture. Denmark has about the same land area as New Jersey and New Hampshire combined, with a population of about four million. Under a constitutional monarchy with a single-chamber *Riksdag* or parliament, six political parties vie for power. Communists are few and weak.

The Danes have always been doers and fighters. At one time their King Canute ruled England, at another they controlled most of Sweden and Norway. So they have had their day of glory, though they are now reduced to a small nation. In our times Danish energy is devoted to shaping an efficient, modern country. About a quarter of the population makes its living by agriculture on tiny farms, half of the country's farms have less than twenty-five acres. A great difference between these and southern European farms is that the farmer invariably owns his own soil. Danish butter, eggs, bacon, and milk are famous for quality. Roughly a third of the working force are in industry, where they have good working conditions. Some are fishermen whose catch totals three times more fish than Denmark uses.

Like the other northern countries, Denmark is highly socialized in every aspect of life. Almost a quarter of a million, or nearly 6 per cent of the whole population, receive old-age pensions. In its health, unemployment, and other insurances, the Dane is benefited by very advanced social legislation. All education is compulsory up to the age of fourteen, and more than 90 per cent of all children attend school. About 25 per cent later enter "examination schools," while the rest continue in institutions which have no examinations. Those who graduate at about eighteen or nineteen from high school (*gymnasium*) wear the white cap, which opens up possible university training to them. Other youngsters begin a four-year apprenticeship in industry or commerce at fourteen or fifteen, some attending evening classes in the field of their specialty.

By hard work and patience the Danes have done well with their little country. Every Danish home boasts a radio, some homes have television, and cars abound even in a land where a car is not as useful as it might be elsewhere. These are a great reading people, too, with well stocked bookshelves in every home. Culturally every advantage is on their side, and in every art they have contributed to the world.

Though it is often said that "Copenhagen is not Denmark," yet the reverse is partly true at least, for in terms of population Copenhagen is one fourth of Denmark. This one large city facing Sweden from the island of Zealand, dominates the land in every respect. "Wonderful, wonderful Copenhagen" is a seaport, clean and picturesque, one of the world's most attractive large cities. Its parks and monuments, fun and food should meet every Dane's deepest need if such needs can be met by environment. But let us look now at the Danish people themselves to discover what they want and whether they are finding it.

Something Rotten in Denmark? "The Danes," says British novelist Evelyn Waugh, "are the most exhilarating people in Europe." By this he doubtless means that they are friendly, courteous, witty, and intelligent, all of which is true. Travel writers vie with each other to describe the peculiar charm of the Danes. Some feel that their facile ease with other people is partly derived from the close peninsular attachment of the country to the Continent proper. Be that as it may, they have a just reputation for humor and kindliness toward all, including foreigners. Danes are more expressive, less introverted than the Swedes, more informal than Norwegians; definitely they are the least inhibited of all the Scandinavians. With their state-subsidized benefits, one of the world's longest average life spans, a stable political situation, and clean, modern homes, they should be a happy people. But are they?

You can find plenty of individuals who fill the happy-go-lucky description. But a closer look reveals several influences at work among them in a different way. One is a soaring divorce rate, with its painful readjustments for adults and children. Another is the rise of a new youth delinquency since the war, with young people leaving home early to savor new freedom. A crisis in many homes is under way, following a breakdown of parental authority. On the heels of these failures a rising lawlessness has appeared, with more than fifty thousand crimes recorded in Copenhagen yearly. This is not the pattern of a happy people. Without the settlement of the sin problem, no gaiety in the "Paris of the North" would ever drown the protesting conscience. "Even in laughter the heart is sorrowful," says the proverb (Prov. 14:13), and no place demonstrates it more than Denmark.

Champions of Self-Destruction. In spite of their reputed love of comedy, life must be a tragedy to many Danes, for to this idyllic little country belongs the sad distinction of nearly leading the world in the suicide rate. In 1956, twenty-two of every one thousand Danes committed suicide, according to United Nations reports. Copenhagen, for example, averages five successful suicides daily, while between twenty and thirty people make unsuccessful attempts, usually using sleeping pills. One writer advanced the theory that the immense talent of these people conditions them for great expectations. Failure to achieve what they feel is their best is said to account for the high suicide rate. While personal frustration no doubt is one aspect of suicide, what is the real reason? Man's moral failure to achieve the highest is one of the Biblical definitions of sin (Rom. 3:23). Falling short and missing the mark in a moral sense can produce a deeper frustration than ever. Sin and its consequences go far in explaining why people become disconsolate. In the light of the truth potentially present in the Lutheran and free churches, there may even be a half-understood conviction of sin, a shame for human failure, to explain, at least partly, so abnormal a tendency.

Sadder still is the fact that many of the suicides are young people. One such case reported a girl named Kirsten. She came to Copenhagen from the country as many young people do, to work and taste the thrills of the big city. Before long drink and loneliness had driven her into a shadowy life of immorality and shame. All the bright idealism of her farm home was soon drained down into the giddy swirl of pleasure. Hardened by sin, Kirsten pitied her earlier innocence, which she now blithely called ignorance; sophistication and cynicism had replaced it.

But these new keys to life apparently failed to open the door to happiness. Motherhood proved bitter when suddenly the baby died. Then money ran out, and the love she had expected from certain people corroded into hate. Faced with closed doors and mounting fear, she took the little convenient side door out, an opening that always promises escape but only brings swifter judgment. Still young, she was found dying in a shabby room, empty sleeping-pill bottles by her side. For Kirsten the way of pleasure was not a way out after all.

A Lutheran Monolith. In Denmark each diocese is headed by a bishop and his deputy, called an archdeacon. Under these leaders are local deans. Any member may vote in church elections by requesting to be registered after the age of twenty-three. But the chief advantage of such a request is to qualify for the ministrations and ceremonies, legal and religious, of the parish priest. For multitudes this service is the only kind the church gives. "I have no use for it otherwise," commented a student. "We should go to church, but don't," added a housewife. Most of the others we approached answered in much the same way.

When 98 per cent of any people are of one religious view, and this faith has lost much of its content and challenge, the results can be disastrous in the lives of the people. The Lutheranism of Denmark is considered by the other Scandinavian state churches to be the least vital. There is more worldliness, less guardianship of moral values, and more political maneuvering in this body than in the other state churches. An example of the latter was seen in a recent visit by Danish bishops to the Soviet Union. Afterward Bishop Berggrav of Norway publicly rebuked the Danish primate, Bishop Fuglsand-Damgaard, for trafficking with the Orthodox church, vassal of a godless state. In replying, the Danish church leaders indicated that they could see no compromise involved.

But how much worse is the dilution of essential gospel truths, like the total corruption of man, his need of a faith-appropriated redemption provided by the Lord Jesus, and the obligations and privileges of a new life in Christ. By making baptism the human substitute for miraculous regeneration, a fundamental error has been mingled with the truth. In practice, there is very little difference between the sleep of death induced upon the masses by such teaching and the similar view advanced by the Roman Church.

A few incidents illustrating this confusion may be helpful. When a truly evangelical group in one town started a neighborhood Sunday school, the reaction of the Lutheran priest was immediate and energetic. He circularized the children's homes, condemning the new teaching because it did not feature baptism as the essential for salvation. An immediate result was a 50 per cent decrease in attendance at the Sunday school. A young lady who found Christ and rejoiced in His Word grew in knowledge of the Lord and decided to exercise her legal right to withdraw from the State Church. Her priest reacted angrily, saying that, in asking this, she had committed the unpardonable sin and had been motivated by Satan alone. According to the representative of Child Evangelism International, a Danish citizen, children are taught in their public school religious classes that the Scriptures are untrustworthy. Recently a foreign evangelist in Copenhagen was proclaiming the truth of coming judgment of sin. As he worked into the heart of his message, the reaction grew intense. Several walked out. Toward the end, one woman stamped down the aisle, slamming the door as hard as she could on the way out. As it happened, this only served to illustrate the very point the evangelist was making at that moment—that when Noah's family had entered the refuge of the ark the door was shut!

Several schools or tendencies have recently marked Danish Lutheranism. The *Centrum* group, by no means the largest, call themselves middle-of-the-roaders who want no identification with anything radical. Another party is named after Grundtvig, the great nineteenth-century leader. His followers emphasize the broader social obligations of Christianity in terms of today's world. The third school is the Inner Mission founded by Vilhelm Beck. Originally the Inner Mission was a revival movement stressing conversion, sanctification, and missionary responsibility. Though there are still some fine pastors and people in this movement, as a whole it now needs renewal from the Lord. There are seven hundred Inner Mission meeting places in the land, where services can be held on any time but Sunday morning. One hundred fifty home missionaries carry on evangelistic and social work. Many believers in Denmark, while grateful for some light within the Inner Mission, feel that its collateral activities and organizational burden have robbed it of power. This branch and the whole church need to return to the new birth as an emphasis carrying highest priority.

We Are All Christians. "We are all Christians . . . besides being in all respects as convenient, as comfortable as possible, the gate is as wide as possibly can be; wider indeed a gate cannot be than that through which we are all going en masse. *Ergo* the New Testament is no longer truth." Though these words were written more than a hundred years ago, they could not more aptly describe the present Danish church had they been penned today. Their author, "the gloomy Dane," Sören Kierkegaard, added, "We are all Christians without so much even as knowing what a Christian is!"[1]

Article 4 of the Danish Constitution specifies that the Evangelical Lutheran Church, or *Folkekirke,* is the State Church of Denmark, supported by and subject to the State. The Law of Congregational Councils adds that the members of this church consist of (1) all who have been baptized into the church and have never subsequently withdrawn, and (2) those who were christened otherwise but were later received into a local congregation. Though withdrawal is permitted, few Danes who have no other living faith go to the trouble of declaring themselves out. Why should they? Salvation is presented as a broad and easy street, and the population which have been born into the church leave their names on the rolls as a matter of course.

Things were not always thus. According to King Christian's code of 1583 the confessional scriptures of the national church are the Bible, the Apostles' Creed, the Nicene and the Athanasian creeds, Luther's Augsburg Confession of 1530, and his Smaller Catechism. If this basis of belief had been preserved for the last three centuries, the church would not be so degenerated as it is today. Though the creeds are professed in principle, in practice they are deserted. As extreme a freedom of personal interpretation of Scripture is tolerated among the clergy here as in the Church of England. In 1955 the Bishop of Aarhus was severely criticized by a majority of the clergy of his diocese when he invited Billy Graham to minister in his city. After the fight was taken up by the press, feelings ran even higher. Graham and his colleagues arrived in an atmosphere of tension occasioned by the view that their beliefs were too primitive and naïve for Denmark. The large Barthian group of state church ministers objected to what they called "the rigid and outworn interpretations of Scripture" held by the evangelist. But their right to differ on this within the framework of the church was upheld by none other than the good bishop himself.

Forced Conversion, Fashionable Conformity. An old runic inscription, dating about 98 A.D., reads thus: "Harold, King, bade this memorial be made to Gorm, his father, and to Tyre, his mother, the Harold who won for himself all Denmark and Norway and made the Danes Christian." "Making the Danes Christian" sometimes proved to be a rough procedure. One writer says of some who resisted baptism, "those who displayed a tepid interest in heaven were sometimes speeded on their way to Valhalla"! The copper plate of the Tandrup Altar shows that the same King Harold of the Felling Stone, so proud of making the Danes Christian, was converted by force. According to the reliefs in the lower row, Harold Bluetooth also was converted through the Hot Iron Ordeal administered by a German cleric, and then baptized.

Although today there are no ordeals to force conversion, modern Danes are born into a nominal Christianity similar to that adopted by all Denmark in about 1000 A.D., at the end of the Viking Age. There was, of course, the Reformation to change the Catholic form to the Lutheran expression. That transformation may have been temporarily meaningful, but replacing gold chalices with copper, destroying images of the saints, and simplifying forms of worship did not produce any lasting change in people. Man so easily grasps at a profession of faith, either Protestant or Catholic or other, ignoring the new birth and its genuine fruits in the life. Changed labels do not guarantee changed lives.

Kierkegaard was right. The Danish Lutheranism both of his day and of ours is not primarily a New Testament faith. The nominal Christianity of Denmark which he characterized as a "monstrous mental delusion" is little better now. This does not mean that there are not tides of truth and blessing ebbing and flowing within the church. Individuals and movements have sometimes been true. But these are slight to influence the millions, clergy and members alike, who are apathetic to a vital personal experience with Christ.

Empty Churches, Hungry Hearts. Only a fraction of the population today in Copenhagen, the largest city, attends any of its several churches with any regularity. Observing this, an American Lutheran theology professor of Danish extraction said sadly, "The great body of the people gives an unexcited adherence to a mild form of Christianity"[2] Church bells one hears tolling in Copenhagen to mark the sunrise and sunset are more useful in this role than to call a careless people to church. The blame for this must lie primarily at the door of a church for which the seemingly rocky, thorny path of discipleship is too great a price to pay. Since the Church Affairs Ministry of the government administers the Church as a state function, it has naturally followed that this body cannot remain the other-worldly, Christ-centered group it was meant by God to be. Government committee meetings cannot replace prayer meetings in determining God's will.

The perfunctory performance of church duties, marriages, funerals, and the keeping of records remain the trappings which have widely replaced the glorious, burning truth of long ago. So it is not enough for foreign believers to abandon Danes to a nominal Protestantism as though they were safe in its care. The masses in Denmark must be prayed for and helped in any way that is feasible and consistent with Scripture. As English and German priests once felt they must convert the Vikings of old to Catholic Christianity, regardles of sacrifice or suffering, so God may yet call out of vital Anglo-American evangelical circles those who will bear Denmark upon their hearts.

Meanwhile the enemy of souls is moving other forces in. In March, 1957, sixteen Mormon missionaries arrived from the United States to join more than one hundred American short-term colleagues already in Denmark. This and other sects are determined to plant their faith here without regard to cost. To this end they publish and circulate literature from door to door or on busy street corners in this truly free land.

Many voices in Denmark confirm the national indifference toward spiritual things. The director of a prominent Copenhagen firm said, "There is a widespread irreligiousness about the people of Denmark today."[3] A deaconess motherhouse leaflet expressed regret because there are few candidates for its ministry. A Sunday school leader reports declining enrollment. Foreign missions leaders cry for volunteers. A dean of the Copenhagen Cathedral writes, "People retain their tie to the Christian church, but in high degree their life is not close to the church. The baptism of their children is the last weak bond that ties many members to the church."[4] Another leader expressed the thought that people would not object to the church so long as it did not raise a voice against their sins.

Christian instruction is compulsory in Danish schools unless parents specifically ask that the child be excused. Few do. Yet this great opportunity for the established church bears all too little fruit because the classes are considered by most young people as something to endure. Back of that feeling are some teachers who lack a vital Christian experience themselves. Can the blind lead the blind?

A Minority Who Care. We have said that God has His own people in Denmark in both state and free churches. From early English missionary efforts the Baptists, for instance, were planted on Danish soil. Only fierce struggles have finally brought them recognition, and they are still few in number. But early Baptist belief was vital, providing missionaries like Kobner and others to bear the truth to Germany and Holland. British Methodism and the Brethren movement also were planted, with their emphasis on a personal experience with Christ. Today empty profession has infected even these and others in the free-church camp, toning down their witness from the joyous sound it once gave forth. Methodist, Mission Covenant, Pentecostal, Brethren, and Reformed bodies all have believers in their circles, but their total number is not significant nor is their influence strong. They, the few Catholics, Jews, and the non-religious must all be classified with the tiny 2 per cent of the population who are not of Lutheran persuasion. Though few, the Lord's people in Denmark are concerned over the obvious need. Their prayers and desires have brought about recent evangelistic efforts, with resulting fruit.

Inter-Varsity Fellowship, the Danish Bible Society, Child Evangelism, Youth for Christ, the Navigators and others are making their contributions. Those really united in Christ above sectarian lines are known to each other, as they are few, and often work together in some common project. British, South African, and American evangelists like Billy Graham, have all stopped through Copenhagen and ministered there with blessing. Unfortunately this city of more than a million people—one quarter of the population—receives the lion's share of attention, as it is easy to reach. But if one should travel through the more than 100 inhabited islands and other cities, like Aarhus, Odense, and Aalborg, he would find hungry hearts everywhere.

Freedom to Preach. Fortunately Article 67 of the Constitution provides that all Danes may worship God freely according to their personal conviction. Article 70 further states that no one may be deprived of his civic or political rights on the grounds of religious belief, a principle buttressed by the guarantee of free asembly in Article 79. It always pays to recall, however, that the statements of national constitutions in this regard mean little anywhere in the world unless they are literally interpreted. Russia and Italy, for example, promise complete liberty constitutionally while denying it in the measure they see fit. As in other Scandinavian countries, equal "recognition"—not to be confused with freedom of worship—has been won only gradually for nonestablished groups. Only much prayer and hard work have won for the free churches some of the prerogatives reserved for the state body. Happy now that the day of imprisonment and harassment are over, free church pastors today push petitions and representations to the *Kirkeministeriet,* the Church Affairs Ministry of the government. Slowly the dissenters have won the right to marry and bury their own members, organize their own activities, and own their own property.

THE PREDICAMENT OF SWEDEN

"Our Swedish State Church is part of the government and so is expected to support the government laws even though it does not always agree with them."
> —A leading Bishop
> The Lutheran Church of Sweden

Utopia Challenges Heaven. Humanly speaking, Sweden is one of the most agreeable places on earth to live. But from the spiritual standpoint this country is in sad condition. In recent years her people have consistently voted into power leaders with materialistic ideas about a heaven-on-earth. To some extent they have succeeded, since there is no higher standard of living anywhere in Europe than here. But what kind of heaven has no God? In this utopia of human devising the established Lutheran church is only a government department, no more or less important than any other state organization. Having paid their respectful nod to religion, the Social Democrat architects of the new Sweden are passing laws and permitting practices which contradict the Ten Commandments and other divine principles. Sociology has largely replaced theology in Scandinavia's leading country. Nor is the gospel of welfare falling on deaf ears. At the grass roots the common people are finding mammon of this world more interesting than manna from heaven. Today it is old-fashioned to be "religious." The emerging generation is savoring a new freedom, reacting from the legalism of the past.

Two generations ago the grandparents of today's youth maintained a strict outward uprightness. Of course, even then there was the usual falling short of the glory of God that characterizes every generation. But strict disciplines ruled almost every home, based on the injunctions of the Lutheran catechism. Unfortunately the law was not always followed by grace, and full assurance of salvation was not always enjoyed. But every child learned by heart some precious words of the Book which could lead him to the One who is Truth. To see how successful such teaching was, one has only to look at the strong churches and many belivers among Swedes who emigrated to other lands.

About one generation ago changes began, as a socialized government started to nudge out church influence and give the schools responsibility for the moral training once received at home. Naturally there were the blessed, exceptional families that resisted such influences and continued to maintain their godly ways. But in the main the parents of the present generation welcomed the enlightenment emanating from Stockholm. These are the parents who now permit and defend, in the name of frankness, the folly of their children.

Wealth, worldliness, and well-being enter into the picture. "I spake unto thee in thy prosperity; but thou saidst, I will not hear" (Jer. 22:21). The best living standard in Europe* has lured the common people to cherish the here-and-now instead of a world to come, even as a similar standard is corrupting America. I shall not soon forget a long press conference I once witnessed aboard the express train between Gothenburg and Stockholm. Billy Graham was surrounded by reporters from Sweden's leading newspapers. "You would be wrong to suppose we are a religious people," the journalists told him. "That is an opinion only held by foreigners. Here in Sweden religion is a surface thing. Underneath we are interested in other matters." These cynical, worldly-wise

*The living standard of Sweden is a shade higher than that of Switzerland.

newspaper people had laid bare the predicament of their own country without realizing it. What they uttered with pride could only be regarded with pity by those who knew the Lord Jesus. But some were still wistful for what Browning called a "lost childhood's faith." One such reporter, a girl, listened with tears standing in her eyes as Billy Graham explained simply "what I preach." The next day in the Stockholm stadium I saw her join the crowd of seekers at the invitation, conviction and longing writ large in every line of her face.

Ike Upsets the Swedes. On July 27, 1960, President Dwight Eisenhower, speaking at a Republican party breakfast in Chicago, criticized socialism in "a fairly friendly European country." He said that "paternalism" in the unnamed country had resulted in a sharp increase in suicides, "more than twice our drunkenness," and a "lack of moderation" all around. The next day Sweden, which has had a socialist government continuously since 1932, retorted with anger. The Swedish newspapers insisted that the President had referred to their country in scoring pressure for federal paternalism in America. In Norway and Denmark, which also have welfare states, people saw at first the image of their own countries in the presidential remarks. Then an Oslo newspaper wrote acidly, "It's a good thing Sweden so readily was willing to be hurt by President Eisenhower's broadside. That saves Norway and Denmark from having to be offended."[5] Later many editorials in the American press agreed that the President was right in refusing to lead the nation into the paternalism, with its attendant social evils, now seen in Sweden.

A Panorama that Pleases. America and Sweden are more closely related than most countries. About the turn of the last century Sweden lost a fifth of her population to the United States, at one period sending as many as a thousand people a week to the Land of Promise. Between 1860 and 1914, a time of severe economic depression for Sweden, more than one million emigrants left for New York. Hence the expression, "America fever," in Swedish dictionaries. Today it is difficult indeed to find a Swede who does not have a relative in the United States. There are supposedly more Swedes in Chicago than in any other city but Stockholm, and New York and Minneapolis are said to follow in that order. All together more than two million people of Swedish blood live outside their mother country.

As the largest Scandinavian country in area and population, Sweden wields a natural domination over the others, not always gracefully accepted by her neighbors. Apart from France and Spain, Sweden is the largest country in Western Europe, occupying three-fifths of the Scandinavian peninsula. Through hard work and careful planning she has achieved what is close to a miracle. Social reforms have made it almost impossible to be poor in Sweden, to remain jobless or homeless, to be physically uncared for or neglected in old age. Children are pampered; their well-being is a national cult. Physical health and body-culture have become all-important. With her high educational standards, progressive social ideas, and emerging industrialization, Sweden has been called a "model for a world" and "the champion of the middle way." Wealthy, worldly, and well regarded, Sweden has passed the mid-century mark with distinction in many fields. But since God looks upon our race with other eyes than ours, we must honestly attempt to appraise this nation as He might see it, using His Word as guide. Unfortunately, in spiritual things Sweden cannot receive so good a grade.

Deep in a virgin forest near Boden a lumberjack fells trees for his country's flourishing wood-products business. High in an ultramodern Stockholm suite a suave, graying executive dials a number through one of the finest telephone systems in the world and chats with a colleague at one of his South American subsidiaries. Out in the remote, glacial valley north of Jukkasjärvi, a red-and-blue-clad Lapp quits his hut to tend the reindeer herd which reduces his demands on the outside world to only coffee and salt. Down in a gaping quarry a workman loads iron ore blasted from the steep slopes of Luossavaara. All are Swedes, engaged in a variety of tasks in different places. Between the fertile, southern places of Skåne and the bleak wilderness of the far north lie startling contrasts. Some ground is stony and unproductive; elsewhere lush fields gladden the eye. One hundred thousand lakes and rivers comprise almost 9 per cent of Sweden's surface. Though it is a surprise to learn that only 10 per cent of the land is under cultivation, enough crops are raised to feed everybody. Half the land is forest-covered; since Sweden's largest income derived from wood products, the forests which cover half the land might be called the basis of her good living.

What is Sweden to us? Nobel prizes, smörgasbord, neutrality, or old jokes about confused immigrants in America? Or perhaps a piece of choice Orrefors glassware, the memory of old King Gustav on the tennis court, and Dag Hammerskjöld in the United Nations? Those who know the country best especially praise her proud, gifted, and sensible people for their many accomplishments. Count Keyserling put it well: "From the point of view of its institutions and frictionless social life Sweden is one of the most civilized countries in Europe."[6] In our times her social advances and political neutrality are the two features which, more than any others, have drawn the world's attention to her. Since 1812 Sweden has been at peace, resting from two centuries of aggressive warfare which made her one of Europe's leading powers. Great contributions in many fields have always been made by this nation. John Ericsson is revered as the inventor of the first practical screw propeller; America particularly remembers him as the designer of the U.S.S. *Monitor*, of Civil War fame. The steam turbine was born in the fertile brain of Gustav de Laval. In the field of botany the name of Linnaeus is a byword. Protestantism was saved, as every history student knows, when King Gustavus Adolphus intervened in the Thirty Years' War. More recently the world remembers Folke Bernadotte, a distant kin of the French marshal Napoleon put on the Swedish throne, who gave his life in Sweden for the cause of peace.

What Is a Swede? A look at Swedish habits may help us understand the typical man, remembering always that exceptions are many. Who is better qualified to define the national personality than the Swedes themselves? In a book issued by the Royal Automobile Club appears this note: "It has often been said that Sweden's long dark winters give its people a heavy character, and the nation's songs well substantiate this statement. Swedish folksongs are generally melancholy and set in a minor key, but in Sweden, as anywhere in the world, all variations of temperament are encountered, from the melancholy to the most vivacious."[7] The Swede, cloaked with a more somber reserve, is usually not an extrovert like his cousin the Dane. Moderation in most things is his natural impulse. He is not excitable and cannot bear scenes; in his country hotheads and rugged individualists do not get ahead. Perhaps Swedes, like Englishmen, appear emotionally cold only through superior self-control and a reluctance to impose their feelings on others.

A Swede usually thinks before he acts. But once his decision is made, he will move patiently and thoroughly into the job. If a promise is involved, he will keep his word. A man of few gestures, he is athletic, industrious, and generally law-abiding. (All laws are contained in one large, well-indexed book, another key to his character.) Though a person of outward integrity, the Swede is also clever and shrewd, as can be seen by his business successes. Accused sometimes of being a "tightwad," he admittedly knows the value of money and saves for a rainy day. He is also called materialistic and acquisitive. Not that this is a new observation; long ago the Roman historian Tacitus (55?–117 A.D.) wrote that "among them wealth enjoys a special esteem." The Swede desires to make a good impression, to have "face" before others. To accomplish this he feels he must conform rather than appear "indifferent," be conservative rather than extreme. Because of his reserve he sometimes loses an opportunity ot make friends, but no one is more appreciative of true friends. These are a people who do not appreciate exhibitionism. At a Swedish business luncheon or meeting you would never encounter any backslapping or devices like name tags. Though Swedes have a sense of humor they do not indulge in the gags and horseplay Americans love. A Swede will immediately introduce himself to you by his last name, but will conceal his first name as long as possible. Often he will sign only with initials. Prestige means much to him, for he covets titles and is fond of formality of address. Here is a land where letters of introduction probably mean more than they do anywhere else in the world. Heavy, ceremonial politeness sometimes seems overdone but is nevertheless sincere. This solemn homage toward others is best demonstrated in the splendid but long entertainment at a formal Swedish dinner party.

Swedes often irritate other nationalities by their air of conscious superiority. Sometimes their Scandinavian neighbors react bitterly to what they regard as a pompous, overbearing, and patronizing attitude.

Swedish people have an insatiable curiosity about other countries which causes them to greet visitors from other countries most warmly. No one who really tries can fail to find a response from these stalwart people. Being neither superficial nor emotional, they are more likely than others to make solid decisions based on reality. There is no closer, more dedicated friend than a Swede whose respect has been won, and the struggle to win it is worth the effort. Perhaps the observation made by Bayard Taylor in 1857 sums it up: "The more I see of Swedes, the more I am convinced that there is no kinder, simpler, and more honest people in the world."[8]

Symptoms of a Sick Soul. We turn now from surface observations to spiritual impressions. In spite of some fine qualities in the people, great changes for the worse have been taking place in Swedish life. Currently the nation as a whole, while professing to know God, is involved in a serious departure from His will. Human rather than divine solutions are being sought to man's ageless moral questions. Few foreign Christians, especially of Swedish extraction, can conceive how far this trend toward godlessness has gone. Unfortunately there has been some careless, incomplete reporting of the scene. Lurid American magazine articles and stories in the British Sunday press have sought out the sensational, ignoring causes and motives. In rebuttal others have hotly denied the drift toward humanism in Sweden, pointing out her towering church organization sponsored by the people's own taxes. Where exactly does the truth lie? The Christian interpreter is bound to summarize the truth he discovers in the light of God's Word alone.

Let us glance at the general scene a moment. Many people are frequent absentees from work, a new practice "rampant everywhere" in Sweden, according to one observer. In the textile industries, for example, absenteeism regularly reaches 11 or 12 per cent on weekends and as high as 7 per cent on weekdays. Tax cheating is a new, growing practice. Suicide has become a major problem in this country, which has one of the highest suicide rates in Europe. In 1955 several leading Stockholm papers discerningly attributed the rising number of attempts at self-destruction to a decline of Christian influence. In two recent years actual suicides doubled even though the material benefits of life continued to mount. Each year more Swedes try to kill themselves than are killed in automobile accidents during the same period. Of about 1,200 annual attempts, many succeed in hastening into eternity to face their appointments with the Great Judge. Some who have studied the unsuccessful tries say that failing marriages and frustrating love affairs are the principal motives of suicide. They add that the modern Swede, freed from the need for decision-making by the state's control of his life, panics in the face of sudden problems. He does not know how to cope with an emergency for which the state has not provided. In other words, he needs God but cannot find his way to Him.

Over 10 per cent of all births, averaging 12,000 per year, are illegitimate. (In the U.S. the rate is about 4 per cent.) Children born out of wedlock are given the same status and care as other children, a commendable humanitarian procedure. But what about the attitude shown toward the mothers? As Joe David Brown in an article in *Time* magazine puts it, "Admittedly it is a Christian virtue to show kindness and tolerance to unwed mothers, but in Sweden they are practically heroines."[9] Controversy recently flared over two teen-age mothers and the boys responsible for their condition. Some objected when their high school principal gave them good conduct grades, but the Swedish Cabinet upheld these marks. In the country as a whole, 62 per cent of all brides go to the altar three months pregnant, notes *Newsweek*. Lack of shame and social stigma in this matter—a reproach to any nation—in Sweden indicates a sad, all too rapid degeneration.

Relatively easy abortion is another sign. Under laws enacted in 1939 the authorities will permit legal abortion for any of four reasons for which adequate grounds can be established. About five thousand such operations are performed yearly, a certain percentage on married women. About one out of every two unmarried women who conceive has a legal abortion. But illegal abortion is also tolerated, and the annual number of such abortions is estimated to reach as high as twenty thousand. No Swedish physican has been jailed for such activity in the last ten years. Naturally there are vigorous protests at home and abroad. American Catholic leaders have branded these practices as "experiments in death." But a professor at Stockholm's largest women's clinic who dared to tell his patient that her coming abortion was equivalent to murdering one of her previous children was officially reported for "cruelty." In Uppsala a doctor who claimed that the country lost through abortions the equivalent of an army regiment each year was called a "fascist" in furious letters to the press. What difference is there between modern legalized fetus-murder and the infanticide of the pagan who abandons the unwanted child in the bush? Only scientific refinement in method. What has happened to the national professedly Christian conscience that will tolerate it? The Swedes would do well to remember one of their own proverbs: "Don't throw gravel at God, for He will throw stones at you."

The Hot Rod Rebellion. Today's international uprising of youth against their elders has given everyone qualms. Swedish young people, who have more money to spend than young people in most countries, are no exception to this phenomenon of our restless times. Juvenile delinquency has risen 30 per cent since World War II, far exceeding what would be a normal rise in a growing population. During the 1950's crimes by children under fifteen trebled. This country holds the world's record for car and motorcycle thefts by minors, with an annual average of seven thousand such cases. Even though a 1957 law required all new cars to be equipped with anti-theft locks, car thefts have quadrupled since 1950. Behind those arrested lies a still larger pool of youth as yet uninvolved with the law, but to whom the dull standards of their fathers have become repugnant. Stockholm and other large cities are seeing the American pattern of casual youthful rebellion enacted in their own streets. Dungaree-clad, leather-jacketed youth, flush with good wages, "hang out" at certain coffeehouses, haunt cinemas and street corners. Stand anywhere on the *Kungsgatan*, Stockholm's main street, and you will see these Swedes of tomorrow daringly darting about with their girls on motorcycles or in cars. Freed from much of the old restraint by parents who themselves have wearied of dead religion, they are now having their own way with life. No doubt American films and magazines have influenced these youth to dream of escape from a humdrum world. Tabloids like the Stockholm *Express*, Scandinavia's largest evening newspaper, have helped on the delinquents at times by championing their cause.

Recently one of the wire services carried a report all over the world of a "raid" on the quiet town of Varberg by two hundred wild youngsters. Arriving in the town of twelve thousand on Saturday night, the "Road Saints," as they were called, parked their American cars in front of the police station on the main square and began to turn the town upside down. For many hours they looted shops, assaulted people, and fought the police with bicycle chains and knives. Only in the early morning hours were the hot rodders subdued. Some returned to Gothenburg, but others were taken to jail or hospital. In August of 1961, the Gothenburg gang and others attacked the town of Kristianstad in south Sweden. Twenty persons were hospitalized and another twenty arrested during the wild weekend battle between police and the invaders. This year the west and southwest coasts have proved the greatest trouble areas, with a number of towns undergoing similar treatment. Every Saturday night a different town is chosen for raiding. The biggest threat occurred when six hundred hot rodders, aged sixteen to twenty years, drove "souped-up" American cars into Gothenburg and threatened to "tear the city apart." Fortunately a counterthreat of force from the police dispersed them, but Swedish authorities are nervous and undecided about how to handle the youngsters.

Sin a Reproach to Any People. Evangelist Billy Graham, after talking to the press and to social and church leaders in Sweden in 1954 and 1955, stated that he felt Sweden's morals were "very low." *Time* reporter Joe David Brown wrote about the same time: "Sexual moral standards in Sweden today are jolting to an outsider."[10] Other leaders and reporters have taken up the cry. Just how do the leaders partially responsible for the new loosened attitude in this country justify their views—people like Mrs. Otteson-Jensen, for instance, who advocated free love in her program for the public schools? The aggressive feminists who have introduced compulsory sex education in the schools feel that the public schools must step in where home advice has failed. Science must replace parental instruction. This in itself is a serious indictment of Swedish family life. Professor Bertil Ohlin, a leading Swedish educator, recently said, "Lower sexual morals have become possible only because the state has taken over many of the duties which used to belong to the individual family." He adds a pathetic question, "But where is our country heading if we go on undermining the family?" Failure in the family, basically on the level of spiritual experience and instruction, has led the state to set up elementary and high school sex-information classes, in which frankness and naturalness are stressed. On a recent show of the state-owned television, two homosexual women discussed their life and love together. This kind of thing is supposed to remove inhibitions and arm the youngsters for life. These pagan advocates of full instruction, in their "enlightened" approach to love and marriage, have left out God's truth. What has been the result? Widespread premarital sex experiments by young people in the name of love and formal engagement. One writer observes that many young people go through three of four such "engagements"; some are engaged as many as ten times. No wonder educators like Dr. Ohlin ask themselves if the state should not return instruction to the family. But with the ignorance of salvation in the average Swedish home, would this be the answer?

Great is the price Sweden is paying for her moral "enlightenment." People are marrying later now, for one thing. The average age for men is twenty-nine, and for women twenty-six. Then, too, the birth rate is dropping: Sweden now has one of the lowest in the world, only 110,000 births annually for a population of seven millions. If such a decrease in birth continues, a real hazard will confront future generations. The divorce rate is rising. One out of every six marriages is dissolved in court, a very high figure when compared with the figures for most other nations. True, the American record is more shameful still—one out of four, but it is sad to see Sweden, a Protestant stronghold, follow suit. Statistics do not always tell an accurate story. Some explain that Sweden's marriage failure is actually as high as America's, but custom and convenience mean so much in Sweden that many couples, dispensing with divorce, simply go their separate ways.

Where Moderates Drink Immoderately. We have already characterized Scandinavians, and Swedes in particular, as advocates of "the middle way" of moderation and good sense. But the heavy drinking of the Swedes is an exception to the rule. Surely this habit is a sign of hunger for peace of heart and failure to find it. From Viking days Scandinavians have had a reputation for such indulgence, art and legend sometimes ascribing it to long, lonely winters in the dark isolated north. And in modern times, before 1917, the Swedes were still known for widespread alcoholism. In that year Dr. Ivan Bratt and others proposed a controlled system of drinking. For forty years the Bratt system of semiprohibition was tried. And for forty years it failed, as it has everywhere, to curb the appetites of people for the releases provided by drink. Finally, in 1955, liquor rationing was revised and liberalized, after long and vocal protest by the population.

What has been the result? Since controls were lifted, the consumption of some types of liquor has doubled, bringing with it the inevitable, sad results. Within the first year after decontrol, drunkenness rose 120 per cent in the country as a whole and 200 per cent in Stockholm. During the years before 1955 the average number of annual arrests for alcoholism while driving had been 9,492. In the last year before decontrol they had risen to 22,000. But in the following year of freer drinking such arrests passed 100,000. Between 1947 and 1957 the number of cases of alcoholism trebled. In 1957 Sweden had the world's highest per capita consumption of hard liquor. Even juveniles under twenty-one, forbidden by law to buy from liquor shops, can get a drink in any restaurant when they order a sandwich. "Many students get roaring drunk several times a month," said a foreign resident in Sweden. My own observation is that it is almost impossible to take a walk in downtown Stockholm, or other sizable communities, without encountering people almost blind drunk. Alcoholism among women rose 80 per cent since decontrol, and cases of *delirium tremens* 10 per cent.

According to the government's Department of Statistics in Stockholm, Swedes drank more heavily in 1956 than at any time since 1913. During 1956 each individual averaged three quarts of hard liquor, three-tenths of a quart of wine, and a quart of beer. Since there are still many who do not drink at all, these figures speak of heavy consumption by the addicts. Spokesmen of the Lutheran Church have said that there is no longer any hope that this is only a passing phenomenon. But the church as a state servant hardly finds itself in a position to oppose state liberalization laws on liquor.

Most serious of all are the hidden reasons which drive people to drink. What fears and frustration must plague the average heart! If only Swedes, as well as others, could understand that in Jesus Christ all desires are fulfilled, all thirsts met, they would spurn all substitutes and drink deep of Him.

Must Christ Serve Caesar? In the face of these conditions in the new Sweden, where does official Christianity stand? Does the State Church, heir of Luther and government-appointed conscience of the nation, dare to cite the moral laws of God? To its credit it has tried, but too late. "They have blown the trumpet, even to make all ready, but none goeth to the battle" (Ezek. 7:14). In 1952 the Lutheran bishops issued a mildly worded pastoral letter against excessive abortion, birth control, and promiscuity. A torrent of indignant reaction instantly followed. Editorialists accused the bishops of trying to dictate moral standards, and citizen groups reminded them that this was none of their affair. Even a few Lutheran priests scorned their superiors for trying to legislate morality as Rome does. "In modern Sweden," says Joe David Brown, "sociology has become a religion in itself, and birth control, abortion, and promiscuity—especially among the young—are recognized as inalienable rights."[11] Though the bishops retreated from the controversy they began, they have not changed their minds. But they face a dilemma. "Our Swedish State Church is part of the government," said one leading bishop; "it is expected to support the government laws even though it does not always agree with them."[12]

Space does not permit a discussion of the involved subject of Christians' obedience to government. But even Luther can be quoted in favor of church resistance to ultimate state domination over the souls of men. As one of the leading Lutherans of the world, Bishop Otto Dibelius, of

Berlin, recently said that the state is not over God, and Christian obedience is still due God, not men. If the church is ordered to bear the message of the Lord, it must be faithful no matter what the consequences. Just here is where the Swedish people have lost confidence in a church which cannot rebuke nor speak with the voice of authority. No longer do they hear the prophetic note. Respect might come if the church were not subservient to and dependent upon the government, of which it has been a part since the sixteenth century. Yet one bishop admitted he had not spoken out against abortion and birth control, even though personally opposed, because he did not think it would be proper as long as they are legal. Did he not know that "Thou shalt not kill" is also a legal expression, from a higher law, that of the living God? To this law, all who minister in His name must be true. Joe David Brown, of *Time*, sums up the matter well: In its efforts to please the government the church has become so watered down as an institution that to the average Swede it has lost most of its spiritual meaning. The Swedes regard the church as a proper place to marry or be buried from."[13]

The Meaning of Deserted Pews. Perhaps unconsciously the Swede shows his lack of respect for the Church by ignoring it most of the time. Since this organization keeps all vital records, however, he must have some dealings with it. But apparently he keeps them to the necessary minimum. "Only a handful go to Sunday worship," says Brown.[14] "Rare is the youth who ever sees the inside of a church except for baptisms, marriage of funerals," adds *Look* magazine.[15] An authoritative writer, resident in Sweden, comments, "Only a fraction of the population attends services regularly."[16] The renowned missions authority, Kenneth Scott Latourette, writing in his *Christian World Mission of Our Day*, doubts if one-tenth of the Swedes go to church. Of course, attendance varies according to communities, areas, and seasons of the year. Through personal inquiry in Halsingborg, fifth largest city of Sweden, with a population of 73,000, I learned that not more than 3 per cent of the people attend church there on an average Sunday. The fact that the country around Gothenburg shows better than average church attendance is due to revival influence of the last century. Here, too, church discipline is more successful. On the other hand, Skane in the south, the most densely-populated and most prosperous area of the land, is reported to be the least responsive. Stockholm, like all big cities the world over, is largely indifferent except on special occasions. According to an American Christian worker there, fewer than 3 per cent of the capital's people go to church.

In olden times, especially during periods of awakening, people did go to church, and probably received something for their souls, too. But this was not a consistent pattern. Almost every sizable Swedish town can proudly point out its old church. Lovanger had a "church town," or *Kyrkstad,* with some 300 church houses, the oldest dating from the eighteenth century. And some other cities had similar "church towns." Here, before the days of convenient modern travel, church-goers from remote parts of the parish were accommodated. In towns like Rattvik, the old *Kyrkstallarna,* or church stables where worshipers kept horses, still stand. In Gammelstad are remains of the largest of church houses. These buildings speak of days when people took the trouble to go to church. Today most "church towns" would easily accommodate, with room to spare, the few worshipers who, even with cars, attend only irregularly. Dr. Carl Rasmussen, an American Lutheran theological professor, summarizes in few words the sad scene of Swedish religious observance: "The Church has not been able to keep in touch with the masses."[17] A comment by the Jesuit journal *America* confirms these views:

> The de-Christianization and secularization of public life in all its aspects may be said to be among the gravest problems faced by the (Lutheran) Church today in Sweden. The Protestant churches have little influence on public life. The average Protestant attends church only on special occasions such as confirmation, Christmas and Easter.[18]

In confirmation of this failure of the church as moral guide, Michal Cabot adds, "Despite the existence of the state Protestant church of Sweden, the people no longer generally accept the ethical standards of the church as standards for everyday behavior. Although the Swedes are a moral people, they are not religious, and the concept of sin in its conventional sense is alien to them."[19]

The daily newspaper *Svenska Dagbladet* recently carried the following information from a poll about Sweden's beliefs and practices as compared with those of other countries:

Belief in life after death		Attended church at least once during past month	
U.S.A.	74%	U.S.A.	62%
Canada	68%	England	44%
Holland	63%	Sweden	23%
England	56%		
Switzerland	55%		
Sweden	40%		

Luther's Established Heirs. Even with its waning influence the *Evangelical Lutheran Church* of Sweden remains a formidable organization. Almost all Swedish citizens are members of it by birth. Taxes, large church-owned forests and businesses, as well as donations, finance the work. All is directed by the Royal Ecclesiastical Department, under a cabinet member. Down through the descending echelon of parliament, synods and bishops the system is divided into thirteen bishop-led dioceses. At Uppsala an archbishop presides over the whole. About 2,500 parishes blanket the country. Many are extremely large, having from 30,000 to 80,000 people. Some of the smaller ones share the same priest.

Much of the priests' activities concern mammon rather than the Master. An amazing amount of time and effort is spent in just keeping routine records for the State. The parish records are the only official ones the government keeps for births, baptisms, confirmations, military service, marriage banns, marriages, divorces, passports, changes of address, death certificates, and funerals. As a result a church often contains offices resembling those of a large business firm. Sometimes whole rooms are filled with files and safes, where government-trained and paid clerks work regular hours. On very short notice any vital statistics can be found on any individual in a parish; often certificates must be copied from these for other purposes. Hence people, in a constant stream, go in and out of church offices all day, atheists and church-goers alike. Other duties of the Royal Ecclesiastical Department include the supervision of art galleries, museums, theaters, schools, libraries, archives, and so on.

The priests who run the vast machine are educated either at the University of Uppsala or at the University of Lund. An average of about three hundred attend the theological seminaries at these two schools. But it is becoming more and more difficult to find interested young men. Because of the extra, state-required activities of the priest, there is no challenge to a young Christian to try to raise the spiritual life levels of others. Parishes do not overlap. Little time is given to winning new members, as 95 per cent of the people are already "members." Confirmation during adolescence covers this question of belonging. Priests likewise have little Christian education responsibility, as the government teaches its views of Lutheran Christianity in the state school system. Raising funds is of little concern either to the individual priest in this tax-supported church. Nor is he expected to call on any but sick people. Since the parishes are large and require a staff of clergy, many priests do not average one sermon a week. Just performing weddings, conducting funerals, calling on the sick, teaching the catechetical classes, and supervising the record-keeping occupies all the time most priests have.

Before 1952 the easiest way to get out of the church was to die, for tedious red tape obstructed those who tried to get out of a group in which they had been born and brought up. Now the law is liberalized, but still not many leave. Nonconformists of the free churches or the indifferent are considered members unless they resign, as little participation is required. Though lapsed Lutherans who declare themselves out of membership escape paying church taxes, they lose some advantages, such as the privilege of burial in consecrated ground.

The flavor of the faith varies with the region of Sweden. In Norrland past revival movements (which remained in the church, rather than separating from it) have given a low-church character to church life. The Gothenburg diocese is known for its discipline. In general, south-western Lutheranism is more conservative than it is elsewhere. Many and varied are the church's organizations: charitable, home and foreign missionary, publishing, education, and the rest. Then, too, there are varying theological trends to be taken into account. One is the Young Church movement, which seeks to introduce a people's church rather than a state church. Its activities are concentrated in Sigtuna, where a number of schools have been established under the Bishop of Stockholm. From this city also emanates the strongest ecumenical emphasis. Common reciprocity of communion and clergy was established with the Church of England in 1922. A liberal movement has espoused wider interpretation of the creeds, while more orthodox, confessional groups adhere closely to the same creeds.

Then there is a new emphasis on sacramentalism, centered at the University of Lund. In Blenon's *Prastambetet*, for example, the priest is pictured as another Christ, whose most important function is the offering of the Eucharistic sacrifice. Strangely enough, all these movements appeal to Luther, who, it seems, can be quoted to support almost any emphasis! Each group feels it presents the true message of Luther, but few appeal to the Bible alone as their first or last court of appeal. Generally speaking, the Swedish churches try to find the characteristic "middle way" between extreme liberalism and fundamentalism.

A Chorus of Dissent. During the middle of the eighteenth century German Pietists and Moravian Brethren spread their faith to Sweden. Even though organized churches never resulted, due particularly to the stiff opposition of the State Church, the country was deeply affected by these movements. Between 1830 and 1860 English Baptists and Methodists entered; as a result revivals came toward the end of the century. Some such awakenings were contained within the State Church but others separated and formed new groups. During this century uneducated laypreachers had great influence and the people zealously built simple wooden meeting houses of chapels, about five thousand of which still stand. The gospel these men and their new movements preached was for the most part the happy Biblical message of salvation through faith in Christ. Because this presentation so differed from that of the State Church, persecution and obstruction continued until the State finally decided, in 1860, to forbid any other faith but that of the Lutheran Church.

From an older, low church tendency developed the *Mission Covenant Church*, today the largest and perhaps most typical free church, with branches all over the world. In Sweden this body now has a following of about 200,000 and owns a reported fourteen million dollars' worth of property. *Baptists* (50,000) and *Methodists* (11,000) form, with the Covenant, the oldest free church groups. About 100,000 *Pentecostals*, and independent *Baptist (Örebro) Church*, the *Salvation Army*, and other small groups total a free church community of about 500,000. Served by 1,600 ministers and other leaders, the free churches together have sent out 600 foreign missionaries. A quarter of a million pupils are in the Sunday schools. Publishing houses, youth groups, and other activities together form an impressive picture.

Should the half million members of these bodies embrace the responsibility for evangelizing the rest of a population of seven million, the rest of the world could seemingly leave Sweden in their hands. Unfortunately it is not as simple as all that! Liberalism, worldliness, formalism, and dispute have all reaped their evil harvest among the free churches, especially the older ones. One Swedish believer dogmatically and sweepingly put it this way, "The Methodists are dying, the Baptists are weak, the Pentecostals are splintered; and the Mission Covenant has lost its first love." While this summary is too general and perhaps uncharitable, certainly tendencies like these are at work in all the groups. Some, striving for "a place in the sun," ape the State Church ceremonialism, including its vestments, and employ similar organization and methods. Others engage in lotteries, or faithlessly sell seats at evangelistic efforts, asking the unsaved to help pay for their own salvation! The large Pentecostal body, a reaction from the vacuum created in hearts by religious formalism, has unfortunately suffered leadership squabbles and splits. It is only honest to say that the free church challenge is spotty; here is a faithful pastor and earnest believing people; there a "dead church," little better than others. Evangelism in the Spirit's power has now become rare all over Sweden.

From time to time revivals have come to these churches, but prayer is needed if they are to become vehicles God can use to call Sweden to Christ. Our Lord is not a respecter of persons. If He cannot find a means here, He will create it elsewhere. Meanwhile His true body within both the free churches and the State Church needs intercession. Sweden is fortunate in having the largest Scandinavian nonconformist groups, but until true holiness of life and a sense of mission grip some here, little will be accomplished. Most of Sweden and the rest of Scandinavia await their help. Even though Swedish believers have sacrificially sent missionaries to other parts of the world, their neglect of needy Europe to the south of them is appalling.

Stirrings of the Spirit. To those who seek God importunately, He is ever nigh. Some of the Lord's people in Sweden have been willing to pay the price of true discipleship, caring nothing for any approval but His. Upon such individuals and groups God has poured out His Spirit of blessing and power. Since space does not permit of a survey of all such movings, we cite only one as representative. In 1954 God began to speak to the hearts of several of His servants within different free churches who put love of souls above denominational activity. As these four young men looked upon the millions of Swedes without Christ, they began to pray that the Holy Spirit would use them to help bring in the harvest. To inspire them at this time the Billy Graham campaigns took place in London and Glasgow. They traveled to these cities, studied the methods, and caught the flame, then returned to plan. When a group of Christian businessmen started a fund for evangelistic work, the AKO (All-Christian Offensive) Team got under way.

Since the team represented several free churches, the co-operation of these bodies in many cities was assured. Later, even some State Churches entered into campaign efforts. After some experience was obtained elsewhere, it was decided to try a campaign in Stockholm. There followed long and careful preparation, including counselor training. Then the meetings began in the old *Blasiehomskyrkan*, with a seating capacity of 2,500. Often during the following weeks the church was packed and hundreds had to stand outside. Overflow meetings were sometimes held in the nearby Immanuel Church, seating 2,200. Even the cynical press of the cold city of Stockholm became interested when crowds came and many conversions resulted. Meetings had to be prolonged beyond the announced closing date. Of the 600 seekers who came forward to be dealt with by 700 trained counselors, about 300 professed faith in Christ as Saviour. Many special rallies for teenagers, older youth, women, and other groups were featured, midnight prayer meetings being the oil of unction to the whole.

Campaigns in other cities of Sweden continue. One feature of the team's work which is especially important has spread blessing to all of Sweden. An office headed by one of the team's leaders sends out Navigator Bible study materials not only to their own converts but to all contacts who desire them. As this is written the 14,000 people now enrolled in the self-feeding Bible study and soul-winning courses constitute a thrilling potential for the Lord if they continue in Him. American Navigator leaders, seizing this opportunity early in the team's experience, found a sympathetic couple to lead their own thrust into Sweden.

From this short report can be seen a little of Sweden's hunger. These are a people who are not opposed to the gospel but have simply been denied it. Nowhere in Europe would Spirit-filled evangelism and Bible teaching have greater acceptance and as much genuine fruit as in Sweden. Foreigners can help by more than intercession. Those whom God may call to prayerful and specialized work in this country will surely find a harvest. Several dedicated American couples are already here. Tactfully but boldly they contribute much even though faced with language barriers and walls of misunderstanding. Sweden is strategic not only because she dominates Scandinavia but because her believers could bless a whole world in need of Christ.

NORWAY IN NEED

"I have a very strong impression that what we in Norway need is a renewal of pastors. If this comes God will be able to send a great blessing through lay witnesses as well."

—Prof. Dr. Thorlief Boman
The Norwegian Lutheran Church

Life Among the Fjords. Norway's people are like her sea and mountains, calm and deep like the one and sturdy and dependable as the other. Reared in the solitude of her deep forests or on tiny farms, the Norwegians are natural, unaffected, living close to the outdoors. Even the city-dweller is most at home in a summer house out by the water or, in winter, on a pair of skis.

Thanks to the Gulf stream, the Norwegians do not freeze to death. Actually, much of Norway has a winter climate warmer than that of Chicago, yet a third of the country lies north of the Arctic Circle. Up here in the Land of the Midnight Sun, the sun shines night and day for two months in the summer, while through two dark winter months sunshine is not seen at all. To the northeast the border touches Finland and for a few miles even Russia. All around the edges of the long, long sea coast are 150,000 islands, some inhabited. If you were to stretch out the tortuous coastline of this slim, New Mexico-sized land, it would stretch from pole to pole!

There is a reason why wild, beautiful Norway is sparsely inhabited. The interior is a high, bare plateau, and three-fifths of the country is mountainous. In consequence, only 4 per cent of the land can be cultivated, and this cultivation makes work for about a third of the population. With 115,000 people employed in fishing and some other thousands in world shipping and industry, there are not many jobs left in northern Scandinavia. Consequently the population ratio is only 26 persons to the square mile. The whole country has only as many people as Chicago.

Norwegians speak two official languages. The older is *Nynorsk,* the rural tongue and a descendant of the old Norse which lingered in country dialects after Danish became the recognized language of the country. During the last century scholars gathered these dialects into the written form of *Nynorsk.* After this it began to develop a literature of its own. *Riksmaal* is the higher Norse speech, spoken mostly in the cities. Although *Riksmaal* is full of Norwegian expressions, it is, in a way, a Norwegian version of Danish, introduced when the Danes ruled. These country and city languages are much alike, though Norway's greatest recent writers use *Riksmaal.*

"Simplicity" is a good single descriptive word for Norway and its people. There is little of the ornate, the gaudy, and the tawdry. Nor are sophistication and suspicion, those twin traits of heavily urbanized life, present here. While Norwegians love their country, they are not excessively nationalistic; they like to travel and enjoy meeting foreigners. Though far from southern Europe's cultural core, Norway has her own "greats," like writer Henrik Ibsen, composer Edvard Grieg, musician Ole Bull, and explorer Amundsen.

The majority of Norwegians live within twenty miles of the sea. Indeed, their national life is tied up with the water. Norway is the greatest whaling nation of all, and has one of the largest merchant fleets in the world. No other country in Europe has as huge an annual catch of fish.

A King's Church. As we look at Norway, we see a contented people in a fair land. But what of their spiritual life? Since the end of the Viking Age nominal Christianity has flourished in Norway. In order to resist King Canute (1016–1035), who also ruled England and Denmark, the pagan, independent peasants rallied around their saint—and former king— Olaf (1016–1028). Under his son came unification of the country. But the Catholic church benefited too, seizing the occasion to build its own power. Because of the opposition of Canute, Norway was placed first under the authority of the Archbishop of Bremen, Germany, then under that of the Archbishop of Lund, Sweden. Finally, in 1153, Norway became a separate ecclesiastical province. During this same year, also, the first dues to the Church of Rome were paid.

Meanwhile the Roman Church gained the opportunity to acquire land and enrich itself. By the end of the twelfth century the church had become a large landowner, and the clergy were on their way to wealth and power. Political influence followed quickly when Rome was able to help seat

Magnus Erlingsson as King, in the first coronation ceremony Norway had ever had. Then followed the centuries-long struggle for power between aristocracy and clergy. After the sweep of the Black Death through Europe, the Roman Church regained power and kept it until the Reformation. There followed several centuries of Danish and Swedish domination, until Norway finally became free of foreign rule in 1905 under King Haakon VII. Thus, as regards self-government, Norway is one of the newer nations of Europe.

Since the twelfth century, as we have seen, the church and throne were allied whenever alliance was convenient to the former. When the nation embraced the Reformation, the king was still recognized as the head of the Lutheran Church. Even though the Norwegian parliament, the Storting, adopted a most democratic constitution in 1814, the state church remained under the same legal power as previously. For more than century a large element of the Lutheran Church of Norway has resisted this absolutism of church government. A minority group even broke away, calling themselves the Lutheran Free Church. Retaining Lutheran doctrine, they gained administrative freedom.

What is the real significance of all this? The Norwegian Lutheran Church, which comprises perhaps 95 per cent of the people, can deliberate, but not legislate, its own affairs. The king appoints, upon recommendation of the prime minister, a cabinet minister as head of the Department of the Church and Education. But neither the cabinet officer concerned nor the party which elected him has any voice in the appointment or its aftermath. Below cabinet level the highest church officials are the eight bishops under the leadership of the Bishop of Oslo, who is primate. Though the king is often guided by the church's preferences in choosing bishops, he is not compelled to follow them. Even in the appointment of pastors through the 1,900 parishes of the nation, the king has the final say, not being bound by the opinions of cabinet officer, bishop, dean, or council. This absolute authority extends even to such details as the choice of a hymnal or order of worship.

The arrangement is stultifying to such evangelical belief and warm spirituality as do exist in the Lutheran Church. Regardless of what form of church government we as Christians may favor, the fact remains that Jesus Christ is our invisible Head. The leadership of His church on earth is not left to a secular ruler, but to born-again men who fulfill the requirements of I Timothy 3:1-7 and related passages of Scripture. Authoritarianism is not limited to the king ruling the Church of Norway. The country's incumbent labor party regulates business with such a strong socialistic hand that Max Eastman has stated, "Norway has gone further in authoritarian state control than any other country this side of the Iron Curtain

. . . . I think they have retained some of Russian Communism's worst traits."[20]

Professional Pulpiteers. As state officials, all pastors in the Norwegian Church are government civil servants. Salaries are set by the Church Affairs Ministry, with regular three-year increases up to a total of six such raises. Naturally, free-will giving suffers in a tax-supported church. There is a shortage of parishes and of pastors, but the church is powerless either to create new congregations or raise the allowable limit of pastors without royal decree. For all practical purposes removal of a pastor is impossible (unless he should break certain legal principles). The average pastor is financially secure, keeps records of vital statistics for the State, preaches once a Sunday, and is not at the mercy of his local church council. Under these conditions many are tempted to enter the ministry just to have a job.

A People for His Name. In spite of the unscriptural practices and the professionalism this system nourishes, God has His own servants among both pastors and people. There have been many memorable movings of the Spirit of God in Lutheran circles in Norway out of which have come much blessing. A periodic deeper life emphasis has been one. A laymen's movement for evangelism and a foreign missionary program are others. Professor Ole Hallesby is one of the best known of modern Norwegian Lutherans abroad because of his books like *Prayer*, *Under His Wings*, and others.

In the theological realm, as well, renewal has come periodically. The Church of Norway bases its beliefs on Luther's Smaller Catechism and the Augsburg Confession as creedal statements of Biblical truth. When nineteenth-century liberalism and higher critical studies of the Scriptures began to influence the nation and the theological faculty at the University of Oslo,—then Norway's only seminary, vigorous protests arose in some church circles. The result was a new, more evangelical school, called the *Menighetsfakultet*, the Independent Theological Faculty. Now, however, the doctrinal distinctions between the two schools have largely disappeared, with graduates of the new one outnumbering the old and some even attaining the rank of bishop.

But revival movements and theological heart-searching to the contrary, most Norwegian Lutherans do not profess assurance of eternal life as promised in the Word of God. Though officially the state is Christian, the population as a whole is ignorant of the joy of full forgiveness in Christ. I have often had occasion to witness to Norwegians, both in and out of their country, using English as a medium. Outside of certain free church and revivalistic Lutheran circles, the average person knows little beyond the fact that he professes to be Christian and Lutheran. What change this should require in his life is not at all clear.

Free Church Challenge. Only about 3 per cent of Norway's people are avowedly outside the *Norske Kerke,* the Lutheran Church of Norway. We have mentioned the *Lutheran Free Church,* which has 83 churches and about 7,000 followers. But by far the largest of the dissenting elements is the *Pentecostal,* with 300 churches and some 40,000 members. As in Sweden and Finland, many believers, in reaction to formal religion, have chosen a church where Christian experience may be heartfelt. Next come the *Methodists,* who count 9,000 people in 200 churches, followed by the *Norwegian Mission Covenant Church,* a cousin of its counterparts elsewhere around the world. This latter body claims 8,300 members in 120 places of worship. *Baptists* are 7,400 in number, meeting in 90 centers. The *Seventh-day Adventists* may be considered a success here, since they already have gained 4,700 disciples and established 72 halls. Counting their posts in Iceland, the *Salvation Army* lists almost 1,900 centers in all —more locations than Lutherans can boast in Norway alone. The laws concerning the Lutheran Church and the state, and the relation of dissenters to them, leave these free Protestants with very few rights. To protect themselves they have formed what is called the *Dissenters' Council.*

Even though the free churches challenge Lutheran doctrines, they do not all succeed in reaching people with their own. A qualified observer from abroad who ministered the Word in Norway writes, "I felt that the spiritual life, especially among the youth, was a little more genuine [in Lutheran churches] than in the free churches, in spite of the presence of form and ritual. For instance, in the free churches those under thirty-five did not attend church on Sundays. The young people had a night during the week when they met, and I can assure you that there is very little Bible study."[21] The same writer, who is not a Lutheran, speaks of organizational walls jealously guarded by pastors afraid of outside, unauthorized influence over their flocks.

Voices from Vanity Fair. The life of professing Christians in Norway today is undergoing the assault of secularism. Hitherto the outwardly religious aspect of society was little disturbed by either mass indifference or downright antagonism. Such is not the case today. Here, a woman from the radical anti-Christian element objects to broadcasts of morning devotions over the state-owned radio. There the opposition publicly attacks compulsory Christian education in State schools. Everywhere the forces of antichrist are at work. Not that the Christian faith is under siege. But the enemy is more active than ever before. "A progressive secularization has taken place," says Iver Iverson. "The masses, especially the intellectuals and labor, are largely dechristianized."[22]

"It is not easy to talk with businessmen about a personal relationship to Jesus Christ," one of Oslo's most prominent industrialists told me. "They believe that it is enough to have a nodding acquaintance with religion. Talk to them about the person and work of Christ and they lose interest. All they care about is outward Christian decency." The same layman went on to say that secular habits penetrate the heart of state and free churches alike in a variety of ways. The raffle is one example of this. Sponsored by the state church to raise much of the money for benevolences (including foreign missions), the operators of the raffle sell chances to people. On the other hand, an earnest Christian girl in Norway would never wear obvious make-up, dance, or attend the theater.

Many in Norway are concerned about sexual laxness, a rising divorce rate, alcoholism, nepotism, and growing juvenile delinquency. The newspapers are full of these matters, of course, some reporting blatantly and irresponsibly. In the rest of Scandinavia, and in shipping circles in particular, it is common knowledge that many Norwegians are heavy drinkers. One press article sarcastically asks why the government conducts its liquor sales at 1500 per cent profit and then in alarm sponsors antialcoholic drives later. In Oslo's main streets, as well as elsewhere, staggering drunks are not an uncommon sight, even though there is so called "regulated drinking."

Juvenile lawlessness is another problem Norway shares with the world. An American magazine carried an article, replete with pictures, under the heading, "Norwegian Hot-Rodders Compete with Way-Out American Cats." In the text the writer spoke of pipestem slacks, pony tails, jeans, black leather jackets, chrome, and motorcycle exhaust fumes. Any visitor to Norway can see by the actions of these young people how little hold the faith of their fathers has upon them today. The very freedom afforded them as a part of their Scandinavian heritage has led many into petty crime, sexual promiscuity, and a materialistic view of life. Real Christians in this land are deeply concerned about the young vikings and their lassies.

Where do the young stand in regard to interest in the Christian faith? Though 1 per cent of a group of young people polled in 1952 registered open hostility to Christianity, only 60 per cent said they were interested. In another area, where church attendance is regarded as above average, only 14 per cent of 680 teen-agers declared themselves to be Christians, and a slim 25 per cent said they were well disposed toward the faith in which they had been born. One source claims that only 50 per cent of all young people believe what is taught them in school about religion. Of course, too, the behavior, as well as the attitudes of young people, raises questions as to the depth of the Christian experience of their parents and pastors.

Jesuit Return. Into this kind of vacuum other forces are moving. The Roman Catholics have quadrupled their membership during the past fifteen years. A major victory for Rome was the repeal in 1956 by the parliament of a 148-year-old ban against the Jesuits. A specific clause in the Norwegian Constitution prohibited the order—as did most European countries at one time—until repeal came after ten years of debate. In that same year Rome officially stated that she had only a single diocese in Norway, with twenty-four churches and forty-six priests. But already there were ten schools with 576 pupils. Though Catholics then accounted for only a tiny fraction of the population and had only four seminarians preparing for the priesthood, there is little doubt that the teaching order of Jesuits will soon produce results on a larger scale.

The Hell Controversy. Rarely does religious news from Norway get world-wide attention, but in 1953 that very thing happened. Because of its deeper significance, the controversy over the Bible's teaching on eternal punishment is worth noting here. Speaking over the radio, Professor Ole Hallesby warned his listeners, "If you are not a believer, be careful! If you were to collapse and die suddenly you could crash straight into hell!" The reaction was instant and enormous. Newspapers bulged with letters taking one side or the other. Bishop Kristian Schjelderup, of the State Church, rebuffed Hallesby's views as "doubtful and imperfect interpretations." In the winter of 1954 the government's Ministry of Church and Education, issued a hundred-page conciliatory document stating that both sides could be right. Theologically conservative Lutherans called for Schjelderup's removal, but the cabinet ruled that a bishop could not be removed because he did not believe in hell. Even today the debate continues.

The sad meaning of the incident is clear to Bible-believing Christians. Only a certain segment of the Church of Norway is true to the teaching of Scripture and of Luther himself on this and other cardinal points of faith. Another larger segment under the leadership of at least one bishop would prefer to explain away the scriptural truth of eternal punishment in a fog of words. No wonder the new birth and the joy of knowing a personal Saviour is the experience of few Norwegians.

Laymen to the Rescue. One of the moving experinces a Christian can have in Oslo is to visit the prison cell where Norway's most famous lay preacher was confined. Hans Nielsen Hauge of Bergen was raised up of God a hundred and sixty years ago when the Lutheran Church was in spiritual sloth. Though an ordinary peasant, the Spirit-filled apostle began to preach on repentance. Arrested and imprisoned because he was not ordained in the State Church and thus had no right to preach, Hauge was provisionally released. He began to preach again. Finally the authorities incarcerated him for eleven years. But his witness had reached the heart of Norway, and the fires of revival began to burn. The whole life of the country was affected, and his followers formed the first missionary society in Norway in 1842. In tribute to this man of God the Oslo University theological faculty recently edited a ten-volume collection of Hauge's writings.

At times laymen cast in Hauge's image have had to contend with both their pastors and the government. It was their protests over liberalism which led to the founding of the Independent Theological Seminary. These men and women likewise carry on other schools as well as various Christian professional organizations, such as the Christian Medical Society. In times of doctrinal vacillation on the part of the clergy, laymen have often insisted on evangelical truths as a base. As laymen early resorted to preaching, a law was passed against this in 1741. (This was the law which imprisoned Hauge.) Now laymen can and do preach, and herein lies one of the great hopes for the country. In free church circles there are likewise some dedicated business and professional men who can and do witness personally to their lost friends day after day. As I have visited and prayed with such men, the future has seemed brighter. Perhaps in answer to prayer the Lord will raise up a common man like Hauge to call Norway back to God.

Other Sheep I Have. One of the most conspicuous blessings to rise out of Norway's revivals has been her strong foreign missionary interest. In proportion to her population, Norway is one of the most active missionary nations in the world. This tiny country has some sixteen missionary societies supporting more than seven hundred missionaries. Especially in central China were Norewegian missions known while that country was open. Many a chapter of heroism has been written into missionary history through the faithfulness of Norwegians there and in Africa, India, and elsewhere. In addition, there are Norwegians abroad under international missions other than their own.

In many cases the message of salvation borne by these missionaries rings true. Yet it must be borne in mind that, as with every nation, the message taken abroad is that learned at home. I will never forget a long conversation I once had with a retired Lutheran missionary to China. He stated quite freely that for fifty years he had taught the Chinese the catechism and had baptized and confirmed thousands. Yet, during all this time he felt he could not assure them that Jesus Christ had forgiven their sins forever and given them eternal life. I left him saddened that such an incomplete message of the victory of Christ should be passed on to pagans, leaving them to trust partially in their works.

Norway has produced great pioneers like Frederick Franson, who seventy years ago helped found the Norwegian Covenant Mission and was also the father of the Evangelical Alliance Mission (known as TEAM), now one of the world's finest. A new Franson is needed in Norway today to stimulate missions in other directions. Norwegian young people of our time could well serve in other needy European countries for instance. The expense of travel would be much less than for travel to other continents, and their training in European languages would help. Yet like so many other Scandinavian Christians, Norwegians show little burden for Latin, Catholic Europe and other needy areas of the Continent. Continued government restrictions on forming new societies and regulations on funds which can be exported do not make the task any easier.

Revive Thy Work, O Lord. The greatest hope for Norway is that the Lord has an earnest remnant of His own here. Revivals do not just happen. They are prayed down by expectant faith. Periodically in the country's history the deadness of ordinary Protestantism has weighed upon one soul, then upon several souls, until praying has begun. In this way God has been able many times to stimulate His people to holy living, bring in a harvest of the lost, and extend missionary vision. We have already mentioned the nineteenth-century awakening under Hans Nilesen Hauge. Several such movings of the spirit occurred before World War II, under such men as Thomas Barrett and the Swedish evangelist Frank Mangs. Oswald J. Smith of Canada, Billy Graham, and others have also found responsive crowds in Norway.

FINLAND UNDER A SHADOW

"There is no heart in Finland which cannot be approached by the good tidings of Christ if only the approach is right."

—BISHOP E. G. GULLIN
The Lutheran Church of Finland

Salute to Suomi. When people think of Finland, they instantly recall scrupulously paid war debts and plucky defense against invaders. Personalities are likewise remembered: Paavo Nurmi for the marathon, Marshall von Mannerheim of the military, and Jean Sibelius in music. The endurance, cleverness, and self-expression represented respectively in these three typify the Finns. But of these stars of sport, strategy, and symphony, perhaps the last man best represents the spirit of Finland. Sibelius, the lonely genius of Ainola, sang through his music the sad majesty of Finland's history. *Finlandia*, his celebrated tone poem, written while his country was still under Russian rule, utters protest and promises resistance. It is said that when *Finlandia* came out, the Russians began to wonder why the Finns played it so often. When they finally understood that it was a morale-builder, they banned it! The great Sibelius was truly unique, influenced by no other composer and impossible to imitate successfully. In the creative mirror of his music this most famous of Finns reflects the image of his people, for they too are inimitable.

Finns are considered dour by people who do not know them well. True enough, to know them is geographically more difficult than to know other Europeans, as they are well out of Europe's most worn tourist pathways. But those who visit this least-known Scandinavian country find that Finnish reserve masks a depth that is admirable and a kindliness which warms the heart. Here are no puppets to be pitied, in spite of their troubles. Independent, tough, and intelligent, these people have always compelled the world's attention for what they call *sisu*, or the courage to see it through. They need this quality, for *Soumi* (the Finnish name for the country) is a land of many problems, not the least of which are an eight-hundred-mile frontier with Russia and restrictive military and commercial treaties with the East.

Thousands of lakes and great forests of birch and evergreen cover much of this country which is roughly the size of Illinois. Since the economy is based primarily on wood, the "green gold" of Finland's trees is precious to her. Most of the population of about four million live in the more fertile south; in the far north, where a third of Finland reaches above the arctic circle there are not many inhabitants. Few mountains rise above the plains—Europe's most heavily-wooded—which blanket two-thirds of the whole land.

Finland is young as a sovereign nation, even though her people have lived there for more than two thousand years. Only since 1917 has she been a united, independent state. United with Sweden for six hundred years and under autonomous Russian rule for over one hundred more, the Finns have nevertheless maintained their individuality. Though they speak a strange eastern tongue, they are racially and culturally true Scandinavians. Still, their foreign rulers contributed to what they are. Sweden gave them Western culture and law, while Russia contributed to the somberness that differentiates them from their northern cousins.

More recently Finland has struggled in warfare as a midget against

giants. Actually she has been involved in three series of wars. The tragic
Winter War of 1939-40 with Russia broke out again in 1941 and continued until 1944. Then the Finns, under the oppressive Russian armistice
terms were forced to turn about and drive out their former pseudo allies,
the Germans. In these struggles the Finns lost 13 per cent of their territory
and suffered overwhelming material destruction. Besides, 85,000 people,
mostly youth, died for their country. They left behind 30,000 widows,
50,000 orphans, and 50,000 permanently disabled men. Expressed differently, every sixteenth young adult today is an invalid, every seventeenth
married woman is a widow, and every twenty-fourth child is a war orphan.
From the ceded Karelia area, 400,000 people had to be resettled in the
shrunken remainder of the land. Characteristic of their sacrificial character, many Finns have been wearing lead and tin rings as cherished substitutes for the gold wedding rings they voluntarily turned in to help pay the
staggering war reparations demanded by Russia.

Finland's largest city and capital is Helsinki on the Gulf of Finland,
with a 400,000 population. Next in size are Tampere and Turku, with about
100,000 people each. Due to a movement of the people toward urban
areas, about one-third of the population now live in towns. Sixty-five
towns and cities contain most of the people in the southern half. With an
average density of only twenty-three people to the square mile, Finland is
one of the most sparsely settled countries in Europe. Though as big as
England, she has only four million people, in contrast to Britain's fifty million. The warm currents of the Gulf Stream and other factors keep Finland from too extreme winters, although she is located in the same latitude as Alaska. Short, dark winter days and nightless summers are
typical here as in other Scandinavian regions.

Finns make wonderful friends. Foreigners who settle in their midst are
taken in without prejudice, swamped with coffee and with party invitations, and made to feel very much at home. Political certainties and economic growth these people may lack, but their greatest need of all is for
the salvation message of Jesus Christ. Therefore the deepest kindness
anyone can do them is to tell them how they can join the heavenly, universal family of those redeemed by the blood of Christ. To this message
they readily respond.

Life on a Political Tightrope. A surprising number of ill-informed
people think that Finland is behind the Iron Curtain with the Baltic
nations. Such is definitely not the case, though Soviet pressure increases.
There have been centuries of active dislike between Finland and her
husky neighbor, Soviet Russia. Before the recent wars Finland had already fought the East more than twenty times. But in spite of her feelings

the smaller country has met her strangling treaty obligations to the very letter. Though the final cash payments of many millions of dollars were made by 1952, further economic pressure has forced Finland to increase her trade with the eastern bloc to almost 30 per cent while reducing it proportionately with the West. A new agreement with the East calls for a 15 per cent increase immediately. Thus it can be seen that Russia seems perfectly willing for Finland to retain her sovereignty and her Western ties so long as she can be slowly drawn into economic enslavement. All the while the Soviets hypocritically continue to insist that this relationship shows how a Western-style capitalistic state can and does live in peace next door to her.

Finnish Communists, after being frozen out of the government proper for seven years and winning less than a quarter of the vote, have recently improved their position. As this is written, the People's Democratic Union, a Communist-dominated coalition, is supported by a number of leftist groups and controls forty-three of the two hundred seats in the Diet or single-chamber legislature. Unfortunately intelligence reports indicate that Communist influence is much greater than this surface position indicates, for its infiltration into administration, army, and trade unions provides a wide espionage network.

When we pray for the Finnish people, we should ask our almighty Lord to keep doors to the west open as long as possible. Surely nothing can happen to this little land that is not in His directive will. But this constant political peril makes the preaching of the Gospel more urgent than ever. The Finns are not frightened, and Christians there are surprisingly unafraid, putting their trust in Him who ordereth all things after the counsel of His own will.

How Christianization Came. Early Finns did not take their forcible conversion from paganism to the Catholic faith lying down. Three crusades from Sweden were needed to force the people by battle to accept baptism. The first genuine historical document relating to the Finns is a bull addressed on September 9, 1172, to Bishop Henry of Uppsala, Sweden, by Pope Alexander III. In this letter the Pope complains that the Finns are difficult to convince and contain. Also the failure of King Eric IX of Sweden to Christianize the Finns is lamented by the Holy Father. The real pioneers of the faith in Finland were English missionaries like Bishop Henry of Uppsala. He was killed in 1157 by a pagan Finn he had excommunicated, but was canonized the next year by Pope Adrian IV, and became Finland's patron saint. The first governing Bishop, Thomas, was also British. The seventy stone churches built during the Middle Ages are still being used in the north country as Lutheran churches. One seven-hundred-year-old shell of granite and brick, overlooking the lake in the province of Häme, remains as a kind of cathedral built during the days of Swedish Catholic domination. On its inside walls the vegetable-dye paintings of Bible stories still speak of days when worshipers could not read.

Finland switched quite peacefully to Lutheranism with the Swedes in 1527. Michael Agricola, who died in 1557, was the leader of this change-over. The former farm boy and student of Luther abolished most of the Catholic features of worship and also translated the first Finnish New Testament in 1548. Amazingly, the ability to read was quite common here, even in the seventeenth century, since the church made it a condition for communion and marriage. An immediate and beneficial effect was that the people were able to read the Bible.

A Purer Lutheranism. Like the other Scandinavian states, Finland is so predominantly Lutheran that the free or nonestablished churches form only an insignificant minority numerically. The Archbishop at Turku oversees from his St. Thomas Cathedral six dioceses, one of which has a Swedish-speaking bishop grouping Swedish Finns under his care. Another bishop is attached to the tiny army. About six hundred priests serve fourteen hundred parishes. Although the Finnish bishops encourage the expression "People's Church" instead of "State Church," the organization is very much a part of the state. The president of Finland appoints each bishop from among the three candidates who receive the most votes. The Diet, or Parliament, in addition to setting pastors' salaries, approves or rejects—but cannot alter—all church laws. Ecclesiastical finances are met by public taxation, but local congregations pay their own priests' wages. The state also underwrites Lutheran teaching in all elementary and secondary schools. Any sizable group of a differing faith is provided a teacher of that persuasion. The importance of the bishops in public life is evident in the choice of one of them to open or close Diet sessions with a special sermon.

Several good features set apart the Finnish church from other Scandinavian Lutheran churches. A wider internal representation and autonomy are practiced. But more important, there is less extreme liberalism. One priest, orthodox himself, told the writer, "We dislike the influence of Lund (Sweden) teaching, and accept little of it here where Christ is more real." Very creditably the government sets aside four days every year for general prayer for the land, at which time all public entertainments are forbidden. Finns are hungry for spiritual blessing. A poll in 1955 showed that more than a million—one quarter of the population—listened regularly to morning prayers on the radio, an amazing fact in a country where there are only one million radio receivers. One local

Communist group is even said to have started its meetings with prayer! Bishop E. G. Gulin, who addressed a Communist leadership training school, was asked to return. On the other hand, an American evangelist preaching in a Red-tinged southern town was labeled by the party as "the devil's propagandist and spy from America."[23]

Revival Touches. The greatest renewals within the churches of Finland have come from the periodic rediscovery of a personal relationship with Christ. Pietistic influences had arrived from Germany during the sixteenth century, and twice during that century these were enlarged into revivals. The second revival was known as "ecstasy pietism" because of its emotional overtones. Whole provinces were affected with the trend to discard cold church life in favor of warm personal faith in Jesus Christ. This revival died down after a time, but reawoke in the nineteenth century.

Four main movements, all still inside the church, are alive today. One, called "the Awakened," counts tens of thousands of members. At an annual summer encampment 15,000 gather. This particular group was formed through the peasant Paavo Routsalainen, who in turn was influenced by the English work, *The Costly Honey Drop,* by Thomas Wilcox. Another movement is Laestadionism, named after its fiery founder, Pastor Lars Laestadius, who lived and preached in the north one hundred and fifty years ago. Clergy and laity who are under the influence of this group regularly assemble in their own prayer meetings, besides attending the usual Sunday services. At the annual summer conference of the group, the atoning work of Christ and a living trust in it are kept central. In the words of Bishop O. K. Heliovaara of Oulu—a region where pietism is still strong, "Sometimes it is said that the time of these revivals is past. This is not the case. These movements are alive, and one who travels here can feel it."[24]

The origin of one of the other nineteenth-century revival waves is interesting. A group of priests were sharing a bottle of brandy, when a parishoner interrupted them to announce that a member of his family was at the point of death. Only one of the priests was sober enough to respond. Although he was too late to help when he arrived at the cottage, the priest was broken up by the immensity of his responsibility and the infidelity of his ministry. Later he was greatly used of God to call back the people of this area to the truth. Simultaneously in other parts of Finland the Holy Spirit fell and numbers turned to the Lord. Today some within the Inner Mission of the Lutheran Church and the People's Bible Society help keep the revival fires burning. During summer months they hold tent meetings, camps, and conferences.

The free churches, too, have had their visitations from heaven. About 1880 a coldness began to settle over church life everywhere. A few here and there cried mightily to the Lord for spiritual renewal. In answer to this, an awakening called "The Congregational Revival" fell. The better educated people in the free churches were especially affected. About fifty years ago the first Pentecostal churches entered the country, bringing their own heartfelt faith into the scene.

The Threat of Secularism. But all is not as it should be in this little land. Heavier drinking and juvenile delinquency are problems which plague the country. Not many go to church. An official church publication honestly admits that "only a small part of the population (on the average 5 per cent) regularly attends divine service and other parish functions."[25] In a large city a traveler reported seeing thirty-eight people worshiping on a Sunday morning in a State church seating 1,800. Often the catechism classes are only a formality. An average of 57,000 fifteen-year-old children pass through them annually, studying Luther's Small Catechism and a short book on popular dogmatic ethics, but little of the Bible itself. An eighteen-year-old girl who was asked to trust Christ as her Saviour said, "I am too bad to be saved." She added the revealing words, "My parents told the Lord that if He would give them a child, they would raise it for the Lord. I am that child. I have attended catechism classes and have been confirmed. But I am not saved." All too frequently such is a common story in this, another Lutheran land. Happily, in this case the girl came to a saving knowledge of Christ. "Secularism is widely spread,"[26] confesses the State Church. A bishop adds that some "have left the church and signed the civil register."[27] The civil register is the roll of those who have formally left the church, some for other faiths but others to repudiate all faith. Communism, based as it is on materialism, naturally plays a part in this, in spite of the exceptions alluded to. But the worldly spirit of the age also plays a part. In Turku a college student said, "We college men need to realize that life means more than the gaining of material riches and power and the satisfying of our lusts. Our religious life is so low. If only there were more to tell us of God!"[28] One reason for the successes of secularism is the failure of the churches to mount a counterattack of evangelism, a need epitomized in the testimony of a new convert, "I knew Jesus Christ died for the whole world, but I never realized before that He died for me personally." The city of Rauma, an old west coast center with narrow streets, had not seen an evangelistic effort for twenty-five years. A campaign held there was so successful that many came to know the Saviour. Scores of other such cities and towns, as well as the isolated country districts, need a like presentation of the living Christ. Will they ever hear?

Challenge from Outsiders. The Orthodox Church with 70,000 members, is the largest religious body outside the Lutheran confession. There is little chance, however, of its growth apart from a natural rise with the population trend. Largest of the free churches is the *Pentecostal* church, which dominates the evangelical scene in many ways. Of a conservative type, which came to Finland about fifty years ago, this group has been responsible for winning may souls to Christ. Services offer a warm contrast to the ritual of the state churches. In the free churches generally foreign evangelists and workers are more welcome. Eighteen free groups in all are listed in the latest census, but they do not total more than 20,000 together. *Baptists* and *Methodists* claim about 2,000 members each. Within these groups there is some spiritual understanding, but an appalling lack of teaching of the deeper things of the Word of God. Worldliness is common, as well as ignorance of the life of victory in Christ, and of witness for Him through the Holy Spirit. The *Seventh-day Adventists* are the largest and fastest growing sect, with the *Mormons* close behind.

Can Foreigners Help? Whenever the Gospel is preached with clarity and power, the response is very encouraging. When a non-Lutheran American evangelist uplifted Christ in Helsinki's principal State church where the President and other government officials habitually attend, a medical doctor testified, "I have been coming here to learn the English language, but instead have learned a heavenly language, as I have given my life to Christ." A pastor elsewhere who had been blessed said fervently, "I have read and heard of evangelistic meetings, but have never known, until now, what it means to lead a soul to Christ." One young school teacher who accepted Christ went on to memorize more than 100 verses of Scripture. Later she wrote the evangelist, "Please pray for me that I may be able to teach my students about my Lord." A 23-year-old lady confessed, "I am known among the young people as a Christian, but I am not a saved girl, nor am I ready to meet the Lord." One wonderful case was that of "the law" fiinding grace! A middle-aged police chief who later came to Christ said, "My wife was converted here at these meetings and she has been telling me that I must come. I am not saved, but I want to be. I also have six children whom I want to see saved." In another meeting a pastor brought a note to the evangelist from four young women in the audience between the ages of 20 and 23. "We have never known how to be born again," it said. "How does Jesus become our personal Savior? How can we accept Him?" When the questions were answered from the Bible, all four came to the Lord.[29]

Christians are grateful for the work of foreigners in their midst, though these are few. "I am glad America has sent us something else than their filthy movies," said one. "Thank you for coming such a long way to tell us about your Jesus," added another. Other ties Finland has with America have helped open the way for Christian work. There are many thousands of Finns and those of Finnish origin in the United States. The country is grateful, too, for financial aid in her time of crisis. In return the American public has always admired the sturdy little land on the edge of the Soviet Union. In Imatra, just three miles from the sinister frontier with Russia, an American woman worker's toil with children has been much appreciated. A father there joyfully reported that his children, saved through this worker in 1951, have been faithfully reading their Bibles and growing in grace ever since. It is often much easier for dedicated foreign workers to preach in the State churches here than in those of the other Scandinavian countries, due to the comparative openness of the clergy and their more orthodox theological views. If a tactful, uncritical approach is made, some priests are glad to receive more light for both themselves and their people. Recently the World Lutheran Crusade of America has sponsored the printing and distribution of 1,500,000 tracts. Pastor Kai Antturi, who is in charge, says that about half of the distribution is finished already by the free churches of Finland. The Finnish version of the Light of Life correspondence course in the Gospel of John is offered to all who receive the literature.

We began our survey of Europe in France, at the western edge of this continent. We close it in Finland, where the free West meets the imprisoned East. That thought raises several questions. How long will free, Western Europe remain politically free? When will the Church of Jesus Christ in the West fully evangelize the pagans within her own homelands? Can North Americans, who have the knowledge and ability to witness to Europeans, refuse the challenge? Most important of all, dare we disobey God in failing to bear His glad word to this "overlooked continent?"

$\mathcal{Appendices}$

APPENDIX 1

MISSIONARY AGENCIES SERVING EUROPE

Listed here are only those missions which are members of the Interdenominational Foreign Missions Association, the Evangelical Foreign Missions Association, and the Associated Missions of the International Council of Christian Churches. Within these three bodies are missions of differing theological emphasis and missionary method, but all are evangelical in doctrine. Some which are not primarily sending societies provide finances. Others are mainly service organizations, with specialists working within a restricted field. Again, one society may be denominational, the other independent.

Whether European nationals should be listed as North American missionaries, even though they are supported from abroad and are usually under foreign leadership, is an open question. If they are not so counted, then the workers sent to Europe by North America are considerably fewer than the total figures indicate.

The prospective missionary to Europe can learn the theological position, geographic scope, special emphasis, and methods of any listed society by writing for information to the addresses given. I need hardly add that much prayer by the individual, as well as guidance from the Lord, should precede any choice of country or missionary society.

Because changes occur in mission titles and addresses, the most accurate guides to evangelical missionary societies for Europe at any given time are the three evangelical missionary associations named above. Of course, some good societies have not joined any association, and a number of individual missionaries are not sponsored by any organization. The Directory of North American Protestant Mission Agencies, published by the Missionary Research Library, 3041 Broadway, New York 27, N.Y., lists member societies of the Division of Foreign Missions, National Council of Churches of Christ, as well as those of the three associations we have used.

Interdenominational Foreign Missions Association
54 Bergen Ave., Ridgefield Park, N. J.

1. Belgian Gospel Mission
   1505 Race St.
   Philadelphia 2, Pa.

2. Bible Christian Union
   1101 E. 35th St.
   Brooklyn 10, N.Y.

3. Bible Club Movement
   1505 Race St.
   Philadelphia 2, Pa.

4. Gospel Missionary Union
   1841 E. 7th St.
   Kansas City 24, Mo.

5. Greater Europe Mission
   214 N. Hale St.
   Wheaton, Ill.

6. Pocket Testament League
   49 Honeck St.
   Englewood, N.J.

7. Slavic Gospel Association
   2434 N. Kedzie Blvd.
   Chicago 47, Ill.

8. The Evangelical Alliance Mission
   2845 W. McLean
   Chicago 47, Ill.

9. Trans World Radio
   354 Main St.
   Chatham, N.J.

10. World Radio Missionary Fellow-
    ship
    58 Elm Hill Rd.
    Talcottville, Conn.

11. Worldwide European Fellowship
    35 Cameo Place
    Levittown, Pa.

Evangelical Foreign Missions Association
1405 G Street N.W., Washington 5, D.C.

12. Assemblies of God
    434 W. Pacific St.
    Springfield 1, Mo.

13. Christian Literature Crusade
    Ft. Washington, Pa.

14. Church of God Foreign Missions
    1080 Montgomery Ave.
    Cleveland, Tenn.

15. Church of the Nazarene
    6401 Paseo
    Kansas City 10, Mo.

16. Conservative Baptist Foreign
    Mission Society
    P. O. Box 5, Wheaton, Ill.

17. Eastern European Mission
    164 N. Euclid Ave.
    Pasadena 1, Calif.

18. Evangelical Free Church of
    America
    2950 Nicollet Ave.
    Minneapolis 8, Minn.

19. International Child Evangelism
    Fellowship
    44 Ionia Ave., S.W.
    Grand Rapids, Mich.

20. International Church of Four-
    square Gospel
    1100 Glendale Blvd.
    Los Angeles 26, Calif.

21. Mennonite Brethren Church of
    North America
    315 S. Lincoln St.
    Hillsboro, Kan.

22. Oriental Missionary Society
    850 N. Hobart Blvd.
    Los Angeles 29, Calif.

23. United World Mission
    Box 10,000
    St. Petersburg 33, Fla.

24. World Radio Missionary Fellow-
    ship
    Talcottville, Conn.

25. Worldwide Evangelization
    Crusade
    Box A, Fort Washington, Pa.

26. Youth for Christ International
   1 N 310 Main St.
   Wheaton, Ill.

Associated Missions of the International Council of Christian Churches
210 Kennedy Bldg., P.O. Box 188, Johnson City, N. Y.

27. Baptist Mid-Missions
   1720 E. 12th St.
   Cleveland 14, Ohio

28. Bible Methodist Missions
   410 Fifth St.
   Altoona, Pa.

29. Independent Board for Presbyterian Foreign Missions
   246 W. Walnut Lane
   Philadelphia 44, Pa.

30. Independent Faith Mission
   Box 516, Northwestern Station
   Detroit 4, Mich.

31. International Christian Missions,
   Inc.
   Kingston Bible College
   Kingston, Nova Scotia, Canada

32. World Baptist Fellowship
   4449 Camp Bowie Blvd.
   Fort Worth, Tex.

Appendix 2

DISTRIBUTION OF MISSIONARIES BY CONTINENTS AND AREAS

(Sources: Missionary Research Library, New York City, and United Nations Statistical Yearbook, 1961)

	Number of North American Missionaries	Percentage of Total Missionaries	Percentage of World Population
Asia and Oceania	6,912	35.31%	63%*
Africa (incl. N. Africa)	6,356	32.46%	8%
South America and the Caribbean	4,825	24.64%	5%
North America**			9%
Europe	416***	2.12%	15%

*Inclusive of Middle East, and Asian USSR.

**North America includes missionaries to the native Indians, Eskimos, and other minority groups reported by some boards.

***This figure differs slightly from our own on the high side.

APPENDIX 3

THE RELIGIONS OF FREE EUROPE (BY PROPORTION)
(Based on the sixteen-nation survey covered in this book)

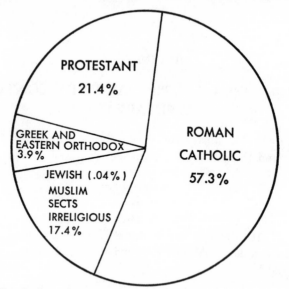

FIG. 1.—General Divisions   (Note: Non-Protestants total 78.6%)

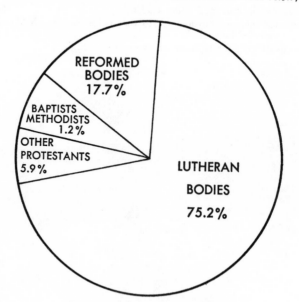

FIG. 2—Principal Protestant Groups

APPENDIX 4

THE RELIGIONS OF FREE EUROPE

Country	Population[1] (in thousands)	Roman Catholics[2] (in thousands)	Catholic Ratio in Population	Protestants[3] (in thousands)	Protestant Ratio in Population	Jews[4] (in thousands)	Orthodox Church (in thousands)
Austria	7,049	6,303	89.6	420	6.	11,500	
Belgium	9,104	8,776	95.9	24	.20	35,000	
Denmark	4,547	26	.6	4,185	93.	6,000	
Finland	4,416	2	.05	4,208	95.	1,800	
France	45,097	37,409	82.2	707	1.5	350,000	
Germany[5]	52,785	26,601	47.8			30,000	7,000
Greece	8,258	66	.8	2	.02	6,000	
Ireland[6]	2,846	2,683	94.			5,400	
Italy	49,052	48,539	99.5	200	.4	31,000	
Luxemburg	324	312	96.9	3	.93	1,000	
The Netherlands	11,346	4,462	39.	4,162	36.	25,000	
Norway	3,556	6	.2	3,222	90.	1,000	
Portugal	9,052	8,120	89.7	12	.13	.7	
Spain	29,894	29,814	99.7	25	.08	3	
Sweden	7,454	26	.4	7,083	95.	13	
Switzerland	5,240	2,169	41.2	2,752	58.		

[1]United Nations Statistical Yearbook, 1960; [2]National Catholic Almanac, 1961 (figures include children); [3]World Christian Handbook, 1958; [4]Handbook of the World Jewish Congress, 1961; [5]German Federal Republic only, including West Berlin; [6]Republic of Ireland (Eire) only.

Note: **According to the National Catholic Almanac, 1961, the Roman Catholic Church claims 186,241,000 people in western and southern Europe.**

Appendix 5

THE CHIEF EUROPEAN LANGUAGES

Language group	Language	Number of speakers*	Chief countries in which the language is spoken
Celtic	Gaelic	140,000	N.W. Scotland
	Welsh	800,000	Wales
	Erse	500,000	Ireland (Eire)
	Breton	—	Brittany
Romance	French	46,000,000	France, S. Belgium, W. Switzerland
	Spanish	26,000,000	Spain, Spanish Morocco
	Portuguese	8,300,000	Portugal
	Romanian	13,000,000	Romania
	Italian	47,000,000	Italy, S. Switzerland, S.W. France, Corsica, Yugoslav coast
Germanic	German	76,000,000	Germany, Luxemburg, E. Switzerland, E. France, Austria, N. Italy
	Norwegian	3,000,000	Norway
	Swedish	7,000,000	Sweden, Finland
	Danish	4,000,000	Denmark, S. Schleswig
	English	53,000,000	Great Britain, Ireland
	Dutch, Flemish	14,500,000	Netherlands, N. Belgium
Slavonic	Polish	26,000,000	Poland, U.S.S.R.
	Czech	7,500,000	Czechoslovakia
	Slovak	3,000,000	Czechoslovakia
	Slovene	1,000,000	Yugoslavia, Austria
	Serbo-Croat	11,000,000	Yugoslavia
	Great Russian	92,000,000	U.S.S.R.
	Ukrainian	35,000,000	Ukraine, U.S.S.R.
	Bulgar	7,000,000	Bulgaria
	Macedonian	750,000	Bulgaria, Greece, Yugoslavia
Classical	Greek	8,500,000	Greece, Albania, Cyprus
Others	Basque	700,000	N. Spain
	Albanian	1,000,000	Albania, Yugoslavia, Greece
	Lithuanian	2,500,000	Lithuanian S.S.R.
	Finnish	4,000,000	Finland, Karelo-Finnish S.S.R.
	Estonian	1,250,000	Estonian S.S.R.
	Hungarian	10,000,000	Hungary, Czechoslovakia, Romania, Yugoslavia
	Turkish	16,000,000	Turkey, Bulgaria

*Totals are only approximate. For few countries are there postwar statistical data on languages spoken. Many people, e.g., most of those speaking Celtic and Basque, are bilingual.

Source: Norman Pounds, *Europe and the Mediterranean* (New York: McGraw-Hill, 1953).

Notes

CHAPTER 1

THE OVERLOOKED CONTINENT

1. From a letter quoted in *His* (Inter-Varsity Christian Fellowship), October, 1958, p. 19.

2. V. R. Edman, *The Light in Dark Ages* (Wheaton, Ill.: Van Kampen Press, 1949), p. 47.

3. W. O. Carver, *The Course of Christian Missions* (N. Y.: Fleming H. Revell Company, 1932), p. 283.

4. Roland H. Bainton, *Here I Stand, A Life of Martin Luther* (N. Y.: The New American Library, 1950), p. 242.

5. *Ibid.*, pp. 244–245.

6. James W. Thompson, *The Literacy of the Laity in the Middle Ages* (Berkeley: University of California Press, 1939), Preface.

7. John C. Thiessen, *A Survey of World Missions* (Chicago: Moody Press, 1961), pp. 423–442.

8. David H. Adeney, *The Unchanging Commission* (Chicago: The Inter-Varsity Fellowship, 1955), p. 42.

9. Billy Graham, American Broadcasting Corporation broadcast of "The Hour of Decision," recorded at the European Bible Institute, Paris, France, June 19, 1955.

10. Graham, "Our Supreme Task," *Sword of the Lord* (Sword of the Lord Publishers, Wheaton, Illinois), Vol. XXI, No. 30, Sept. 23, 1955, p. 6.

11. Graham, personal letter to President Dwight D. Eisenhower from Geneva, Switzerland, June 19, 1955.

12. Graham, at the Prayer Breakfast, Hotel Mayflower, Washington, D.C., Feb. 3, 1955, as reported in *Leadership* (International Council of Christian Leadership, Washington), August, 1955, p. 11.

13. John C. Winston, *Flanders' Fields* (publication of the Belgian Gospel Mission; Philadelphia), Autumn, 1950, p. 2; Summer, 1952, p. 6; Winter, 1949, p. 3; Autumn, 1948, p. 7.

14. Donald Grey Barnhouse, *Eternity* (Philadelphia), Sept., 1955, p. 6; *Revelation* (Philadelphia), Oct., 1948, p. 12.

15. Russell Hitt, *Christian Life* (Chicago), September, 1953, pp. 34, 56.

16. Harold B. Street, "Europe in the World Literature," *Missions Tomorrow* (Chicago, 1957), p. 16.

17. Harold J. Ockenga, personal letter to the writer, April 1, 1959.

18. Kenneth Scott Latourette, *The Christian World Mission in Our Day* (N. Y.: Harper & Bros., 1954), pp. 74, 75, 97, 90, 131, 157.

19. Robert C. Mackie, *World Dominion* (London, England), Vol. XXIX, No. 1, Jan.-Feb., 1951, p. 25.

20. Alexander McLeish, "Are there Still Unoccupied Fields?" *World Dominion* (London, Eng.), Vol. XXIV, No. 3, May-June, 1946.

21. As quoted in *The Prairie Overcomer* (Prairie Bible Institute; Three Hills, Alberta), June, 1955, p. 208.

22. McLeish, *Europe in Transition* (booklet; London: World Dominion Press, no date), p. 23.

23. As quoted by David L. Cooper, Jr., in his *World Evangelization in This Generation* (Los Angeles: Biblical Research Society, 1951), p. 289.

24. Dennis Pape, "The Neglected Continent," *His* (Chicago), January, 1958, pp. 5, 6.

25. A. J. Dain, (ed.), *Mission Fields Today* (Chicago: Inter-Varsity Press, 1956), pp. 114, 127.

26. René Pâche, "Christianity in Europe," *Moody Monthly* (Chicago), Oct., 1956, p. 4.

27. As quoted by Arthur G. Ingleby in *Lines of Communication* (Parede, Portugal), July, 1952, p. 4.

28. Hans Lilje, *Luther Now* (Philadelphia: Muhlenberg Press, 1952), pp. 76, 84, 93.

29. Franz Etzel, Minister of Finance of the Federal Republic of Germany, at Conference of International Council on Christian Leadership, Noordwijk, Holland, Sept., 1956.

30. *Ibid.*

CHAPTER 2

GIANTS IN THE LAND

1. As quoted by Henry M. Woods, *Our Priceless Heritage* (Harrisburg: The Evangelical Press, 1953), 3rd ed. (orig. ed., 1941), p, 32.

2. Paul Blanshard, *American Freedom and Catholic Power* (Boston: The Beacon Press, 1949), p. 44.

3. *Newsweek*, October 27, 1958, p. 38.

4. Hilaire Belloc, *The Contrast* (London: J. W. Arrowsmith, 1923), p. 160.

5. Bishop of St. David's *Charge to the Clergy* (London: 1872), p. 17.

6. As quoted in *Out of the Labyrinth* (N. Y.: Agora Publishing Co., 1947), p. 149.

7. *Newsweek*, October 27, 1938, pp. 38, 39.

8. Stewart W. Herman, *Report from Christian Europe* (N.Y.: Friendship Press, 1953), pp. 97, 98.

9. Frédéric Hoffet, *L'Impérialisme Protestant* (Paris: Flammarion, 1948), p. 189.

10. *Ibid.*, p. 182.

11. *Ibid.*, pp. 190, 191.

12. *Ibid.*, p. 191.

13. *Ibid.*, p. 88

14. *Ibid.*, p. 116

15. *Lenin and Stalin on Youth* (Little Lenin Library), from Lenin's address to the Third Congress of the Russian Young Communist League (London: Lawrence and Wishart), p. 26.

16. Friedrich Engels, *Anti-Düring* (1877) in Marxist-Lenist Classics (London: Lawrence and Wishart, 1929), p. 109.

17. R. N. Carew Hunt, *The Theory and Practice of Communism* (London: Geoffrey Blas, 1950), p. 210.

18. *Time*, December 8, 1961, p. 77.

19. Emil Brunner, *The Word and the World* (London: Student Christian Movement Press, 1953), p. 38.

20. Quoted in C. C. Ryrie's *Neo-Orthodoxy* (Chicago: Moody Press, 1956), p. 51.

21. Paul King Jewett, *Brunner's Concept of Revelation* (London: J. Clark, 1954).

22. David Hedegard, "What Does Barthianism Really Teach?" *Moody Monthly*, June, 1958, p. 30.

23. René Pâche, "Christianity in Europe," *Moody Monthly,*, October, 1956, p. 4.

24. Charles Hodge, *Systematic Theology* (Grand Rapids: Wm. B. Eerdmans Pub. Co., 1952), Vol. II, p. 414.

25. P. Gennrich, *Die Lehre von der Wiedergeburt* (Leipzig: Dunker, 1907), p. 136.

26. Werner Elert, *Morphologie des Lutherums* (Munich: C. J. Beck, 1932), Vol. I, p. 256.

27. William A. Mueller, *Church and State in Luther and Calvin* (Nashville: Broadman Press, 1954), p. 23.

28. B. P. Chavannes, "Introduction à la Pensée de Rudolf Bultmann." *Bulletin du Centre d'Information* (Paris: Centre Protestant d'Etudes et de Documentation), Sept.-Oct., 1955, p. B4.

29. Bernard Ramm, "Bultmann's Theological Dust Storm," *Eternity* (Philadelphia), August, 1957, p. 2.

30. *Ibid.*, p. 22.

31. G. C. Berkouwer, "Changing Climate of European Theology," *Christianity Today*, October 15, 1956, p. 6.

32. Pâche, *op. cit.*, p. 4.

33. Herman, *Report from Christian Europe* (N. Y.: Friendship Press, 1953), p. 75.

34. Arnold Ussher, *Journey Through Dread* (N. Y.: Devin-Adair, 1955), p. 9.

35. *Idem.*

36. Ussher, p. 10.

37. *Ibid.*, p. 11.

38. *Idem.*

39. Ussher, p. 9.

40. Jean-Paul Sartre, *L'Etre et le Néant* (Paris: Gallimard, 1943), p. 669.

41. *Ibid.*, p. 713.

42. David E. Roberts, *Existentialism and Religious Belief* (N. Y.: Oxford University Press, 1957), p. 5.

Chapter 3

THE MISSIONARY TO EUROPE

1. *Newsweek*, July 14, 1958, p. 10.

2. Jacques Maritain, *Reflections on America* (New York: Scribner's, 1958), p. 84.

3. *Newsweek*, Nov. 4, 1957, p. 23.

4. Alexander McLeish, *Europe in Transition* (London: World Dominion Press, 1955), p. 51.

Chapter 4

FRANCE, THE SMOLDERING FIRE

1. David Schoenbrun, *As France Goes* (N. Y.: Harper & Bros., 1957), p. 7.

2. *Ibid.*, p. 5.

3. *Idem.*

4. Schoenbrun, p. 20.

5. *Time*, May 30, 1955, p. 24.

6. Donald C. McKay, *The United States and France* (Cambridge: Harvard University Press, 1951), p. 32.

7. Herbert Luethy, *France Against Herself* (N. Y.: Meridian Books, 1957) p. 23.

8. *Ibid.*, p. 22.

9. Attributed to Napoleon in *Popular Quotations for All Uses* (Garden City, N. Y., 1950), p. 132.

10. *Newsweek*, August 17, 1959, p. 18.

11. *Newsweek*, January 16, 1956, p. 20.

12. *Idem.*

13. *Reader's Digest*, May, 1954, p. 118.

14. *Time*, July 10, 1955, p. 25.

15. *Idem.*

16. Luethy, "Why France Is Seldom Free from Crisis," *Life*, May, 1957, pp. 58, 60, 63.

17. André Lamorte, "The Moral Sag in France," *Christianity Today*, June 24, 1957, p. 11.

18. Quoted by David L. Cooper, *World Evangelization in This Generation* (Los Angeles: Biblical Research Society, 1951), p. 2.

19. *Idem.*

20. From message delivered in Manchester, England, July 2, 1950.

21. Quoted by David L. Cooper, *op. cit.*, p. 3.

22. As quoted by Pierre Mailland in *France* (London: Oxford University Press, 1943), p. 42.

23. Luethy, *op cit.*, p. 34.

24. Pierre Mailland, *op. cit.*, p. 37.

25. Ruben Saillens, *The Soul of France* (London: Morgan & Scott, 1926), p. 137.

26. Luethy, *op. cit.*, p. 59.

27. *Idem.*

28. Luethy, p. 51.

29. Schoenbrun, *op. cit.*, p. 20.

30. *Le Figaro* (Paris), February 8, 1954, p. 3.

31. *New York Herald Tribune* (European ed., Paris), July 6, 1960, p. 4.

32. André Tardieu, *France and America* (Boston & New York: Houghton Mifflin, 1927), p. 297.

33. Schoenbrun, *op. cit.*, p. 199.

34. Tardieu, *op. cit.*, p. 298.

35. *Time*, May 30, 1955.

36. *Idem.*

37. *Idem.*

38. From message delivered in Paris, April 30, 1954.

39. Quoted in book report in *Chicago Sun-Times*, January 24, 1959, p. 6.

40. R. P. Brouillard, S. J., *Petite Revue du Clergé* (Paris), 1935, p. 389.

41. G. Abbé Jacquemet, "Faut-il se fier aux Guerisseurs?" *Ecclesia* (Paris), No. 118, (November, 1958), p. 131.

42. David Barnes, "*Has France Had Her Chance?*" (Chicago: Evangelical Alliance Mission, 1953), unnumbered leaflet.

43. Emile R. Dallière, *The Voice of Faith* (Yorkshire, England: Christian Fellowship, Bradford House), April-May-June, 1960, p. 9.

44. The doctor, whose name is in our files, asked that his name be withheld.

45. *Time*, May 30, 1955, p. 25.

46. *Le Figaro* (Paris), April 21, 1955, p. 7.

47. Paul Blanshard, *American Freedom and Catholic Power* (Boston: Beacon Press, 1949), p. 286.

48. V. R. Edman, *The Light in Dark Ages* (Wheaton, Ill.: Van Kampen Press, 1949), p. 80.

49. Saillens, *op. cit.*, p. 82.

50. Emil Ludwig, *Napoleon* (N. Y.: Random House, 1915), p. 224.

51. C. A. Beard, *Readings in American Government and Politics* (N. Y.: The Macmillan Co., 1909), p. 229.

52. Adolf Keller, *Christian Europe Today* (London: The Epworth Press, 1942), p. 270.

53. Vincent Hopkins, "France," *Catholic Encyclopedia* (N. Y.: The Gilmary Society, 1954), Supplement II, unnumbered.

54. Maisie Ward, *France Pagan? The Mission of Abbé Godin* (N. Y.: Sheed & Ward, 1949), p. 173.

55. *Ibid.*, p. 174.

56. *Ibid.*, p. 79.

57. *Ibid.*, p. 68.

58. Claire Huchet Bishop, *France Alive* (N. Y.: Declan X. McMullen, 1947), p. 16.

59. *Ibid.*, p. 26.

60. Ward, *op. cit.*, p. 69.

61. Evangelical Press Association dispatch, October 14, 1954.

62. Henri Dubois, *Excommunication*, privately published in Albi (Tarn) France, 1954, unnumbered.

63. Anonymous letter of an ex-priest, furnished by Mlle. Léone Shigo, Paris.

64. Léone Shigo, *Témoinage d'une Chrétienne* (privately published leaflet, no date, Montfermeil, S/O, France), p. 3.

65. *Idem.*

66. *Ecumenical Studies: Evangelism in France* (Geneva: Secretariat for Evangelism, World Council of Churches, 1952), p. 6.

67. Ward, *op. cit.*, p. 65 (Part II contains an English translation of parts of Henri Godin and Yvan Daniel's *France, Pays de Mission?*).

68. *Ibid.*, p. 67.

69. *Time*, May 7, 1956, p. 84.

70. *Idem.*

71. Jerôme Carcopino, *Souvenirs de Sept Ans* (Paris; 1953), p. 318.

72. Saillens, *op. cit.*, p. 91.

73. John Calvin, *Institutes* (Philadelphia: Presbyterian Board of Christian Education, 1960), Bk. I, Ch. 7, p. 85 (originally published 1509–1564).

74. Donald Grey Barnhouse, *Eternity* (Philadelphia), September, 1955, pp. 9-10.

75. Lamorte, *op. cit.*, p. 11.

76. As quoted by Emile Léonard, *Le Protestant Français* (Paris: Presses Universitaires de France, 1953), p. 1.

77. *Ibid.*, p. 2.

78. Lamorte, *op. cit.*, p. 12.

79. T. H. Patterson, *The History of Christian Preaching* (Philadelphia: The Judson Press), 1903, p. 222.

CHAPTER 5

THE TRUTH ABOUT SPAIN

1. Quoted by Donald Grey Barnhouse, "The Gospel in Latin Europe," *Eternity*, September, 1955, p. 10.

2. Roy Wyatt, Jr., *This is Spain* (Richmond, Va.: Department of Education and Promotion, Foreign Mission Board, Southern Baptist Convention, 1957), p. 2.

3. Samuel Vila, in *Spaingrams* (Spanish Christian Mission), Toronto, Jan., 1957, p. 1.

4. Vila, *An Easter Letter from Spain*, Tarrasa, Spain, March, 1959, p. 1.

5. Harry Robinson, *The Missionary Challenge of Spain and France* (London: Spanish Evangelical Society, 1955), p. 1.

6. Nicholas B. Adams, *The Heritage of Spain* (N. Y.: Henry Holt, 1959), p. 9 (Introduction).

7. Lucy H. Crockett, *Kings Without Castles* (N. Y.: Rand McNally, 1957), p. 104.

8. *Ibid.*, p. 11.

9. Domingo de Arrese, *La España de Franco* (Madrid: Publicaciones Espanolas, 1946), p. 18.

10. Quoted by Lawrence Fernsworth, *Spain's Struggle for Freedom* (Boston: Beacon Press, 1957), Intro., p. viii.

11. *Ibid.*, p. 236.

12. Quoted in *Christian Heritage* (Christ's Mission; Sea Cliff, N.Y.), Sept., 1959, p. 5.

13. V. S. Pritchett, *The Spanish Temper* (N. Y.: Alfred A. Knopf, 1954), p. 6.

14. Alan H. Broderick, *Pillars of Hercules: The Iberian Scene* (London: Hutchinson, 1950), p. 11.

15. *Newsweek*, Nov. 23, 1956, p. 60.

16. Fernsworth, *op. cit.*, p. 32.

17. *Time*, June 15, 1959, p. 10.

18. Norman J. G. Pounds, *Europe and the Mediterranean* (N. Y.: McGraw-Hill, 1953), p. 335.

19. Robinson, *op. cit.*, pp. 14-16.

20. Ludwell Denny (Scripps-Howard Foreign Director), dispatch dated October 19, 1958.

21. *Chicago Tribune*, Feb. 2, 1959, Part 2, p. 3.

22. Irving Wallace, "Will the Spanish Town Live Again?", *The Saturday Evening Post*, July 5, 1947, p. 87.

23. Crockett, *op. cit.*, p. 112.

24. *Idem.*

25. Wallace, *op. cit.*, p. 87.

26. Pritchett, *op. cit.*, p. 22.

27. Quoted by Broderick, *op. cit.*, p. 11.

28. Quoted in lecture by Taberner, Fernando Valls, "La revalorización de la vida religiosa en España," University of Barcelona, *Aspetos y Problemas de la Nueva Organización de España* (Barcelona, 1939), p. 134.

29. Emmett John Hughes, *Report on Spain* (N. Y.: Henry Holt, 1947), p. 75.

30. Jaime Balmes, *El Protestantismo Comparado con El Catolicismo en Sus Relaciones con La Civilización Europea* (Paris: Libreria de Rosa y Bouret, 1854); fifth edition, I, 466.

31. Pedro Cardinal Segura (Archbishop of Seville), pastoral letter, March, 1952.

32. Quoted by Eugene Fodor (ed.), *Spain and Portugal* (Fodor's Modern Guides; N. Y.: David McKay, 1959), p. 62.

33. Quoted in "Spanish Outlook," by Onlooker (an anonymous missionary in Spain), *World Dominion* (London), Jan.-Feb., 1940, p. 38.

34. Quoted in Delpech, Jacques, *The Oppression of Protestants in Spain* (Boston: Beacon Press, 1955), p. 15.

35. Quoted in "Spanish Outlook," by Onlooker (an anonymous missionary in Spain), *World Dominion* (London), Jan.-Feb., 1940, p. 37.

36. *Idem.*

37. Quoted in *Life*, July, 1949, p. 34.

38. Fernsworth, *op. cit.*, p. 9.

39. "Spain," *Encyclopaedia Britannica* (Chicago: Encyclopaedia Britannica, 1959), XXI, 142.

40. Fernsworth, *op. cit.*, pp. 280–281.

41. *Coronet* magazine, Jan., 1957, p. 112.

42. Fodor, *op. cit.*, p. 63.

43. *Ibid.*, p. 64.

44. *Travel* magazine, April, 1957, p. 21.

45. *Ibid.*, p. 23.

46. Jaime Balmes, *op. cit.*, p. 427.

47. John D. Hughey, Jr., *Religious Freedom in Spain* (Nashville: Broadman Press, 1955), p. 14.

48. Juan Orts Gonzalez, "Spain," *The New Schaff-Herzog Religious Encyclopedia* (Grand Rapids: Baker Book House, 1950), XI, 26.

49. Antonio Carraso and Felix Moreno Astray (Spanish Christian Church), "Al Pueblo Espanol," *La Luz* (June 1, 1872), p. 117.

50. Everett Gill, *Annual of the Southern Baptist Convention, 1923* (Nashville: Southern Baptist Convention), p. 114.

51. John D. Hughey, Jr., *op. cit.*, p. 116.

52. *Ibid.*, p. 130.

53. *Ibid.*, p. 136.

54. Ambrosio Celma, quoted by Everett Gill, *Annual of the Southern Baptist Convention, 1934* (Nashville: Southern Baptist Convention), p. 224.

55. John D. Hughey, Jr., *op. cit.*, p. 137.

56. W. E. Garrison, "Religious Liberty in Spain, II. Freedom of Religion, Spanish Style," *The Christian Century*, October 18, 1950, p. 1233.

57. W. E. Garrison, "Religious Liberty in Spain, IV. The State of Spanish Protestantism," *The Christian Century*, Nov. 1, 1950, p. 1290.

58. Donald Grey Barnhouse, *op. cit.*, p. 8.

59. *Spaingrams*, publication of the Spanish Christian Mission, Toronto, January-February, 1956, p. 3.

60. *Ibid.*, January, 1957, p. 6.

Chapter 6

THE AWAKENING OF PORTUGAL

1. J. F. Swanson (ed.), *Three Score Years—and Then* (Chicago: The Evangelical Alliance Mission, 1950), p. 362.

2. *Time,* Nov. 18, 1957, p. 31.
3. *Ibid.*
4. *Spain and Portugal* (Fodor's Modern Guides; N. Y.: David McKay, 1953), p. 305.
5. Theodor G. Tappert, "Portugal," *The New Schaff-Herzog Encyclopedia of Religious Knowledge* (Grand Rapids: Baker Book House, 1955), II, 894.
6. Alexandre Herculano, *History of the Origin and Establishment of the Inquisition in Portugal* (Stanford, Calif.: Stanford University Press, 1926), p. 564.
7. Gordon Cooper, *Your Holiday in Spain and Portugal* (London: Alvin Redman, Ltd., 1952), p. 227.
8. *Ibid.,* p. 228.
9. Eduardo Moreira, *The Significance of Portugal* (New York: World Dominion Press, n.d.).
10. Excerpt from letter of Rev. Arthur S. Brown, missionary to Portugal, in *Gospel Echoes* (First Baptist Church, Pontiac, Mich.), July, 1956, p. 7.
11. Luiz Cardoso, "Liberty to the Captives," *Christian Heritage* (Christ's Mission, Sea Cliff, N.Y.), April, 1954, p. 16.
12. *Ibid.,* p. 17.

Chapter 7

ITALY, LAND OF HEARTBREAK

1. Lord Byron, *Childe Harold, Canto* IV.
2. Hanson W. Baldwin, "Perils in Rome Crisis," *New York Times* (International Edition), Jan. 10, 1954, p. 6.
3. *Life,* Oct. 4, 1954, p. 73.
4. Massimo Salvatori, and Michele Contarello, *Italy* (N. Y., Foreign Policy Association; Headline Series), No. 51, p. 8.
5. Arthur Wiens, Modena, Italy: Prayer Letter 63, October 1, 1955.
6. Sean O'Faolain, *Autumn in Italy* (N. Y.: Devin, 1961), p. 39.
7. Captain R. M. Stephens, "Sardinia, the Forgotten Island," *The Christian* (London, England), May 1, 1953, p. 4.
8. *Life,* Oct. 4, 1954, p. 73.
9. G. K. Brown, *Italy and the Reformation to 1550* (Oxford: Basil Blackwood, 1933), p. 57.
10. Emmanuel Rodacanachi, *La Réforme en Italie.* 2 vols. (Paris: Hachette, 1914), I, 179.
11. *Religious Freedom in Orthodox, Moslem and Roman Catholic Europe* (London: World Dominion Press, 1945), p. 37.
12. Albert Hyma, "The Reformation in Italy," *The New Schaff-Herzog Encyclopedia of Religious Knowledge* (Grand Rapids: Baker Book House, 1955), I, 584.
13. *New York Herald Tribune* (European Edition), Dec. 6, 1949, p. 1.
14. Lord Byron, *The Age of Bronze,* st. 3.
15. "The Vatican Council," *Encyclopaedia Britannica* (14th ed.; Chicago: Encyclopaedia Britannica, 1949), XXIII, 11.
16. Quoted by Avro Manhattan, *The Vatican in World Politics* (N. Y.: Gaer Associates, 1949), p. 2.
17. Samuel Langhorne Clemens (Mark Twain), *The Innocents Abroad* (London: Collins, 1954), p. 159 (originally published in 1869).
18. *Ibid.,* p. 283.
19. Quoted by J. Sidlow Baxter, "Papal Rome, a New Pose," *Flanders' Fields* (Brussels: the Belgian Gospel Mission), Winter, 1949/1950, p. 3.
20. Herbert Kubly, *American in Italy* (N. Y.: Simon & Schuster, 1955), p. 15.
21. J. H. Merle D'Aubigné, *History of the Reformation,* 2 vols. (N. Y.: Robert Carter & Bros., 1857), Revised Edition, Vol. 2, p. 69.
22. *The Holy Stairway* (a Catholic guide book sold at the Holy Stairs in Rome; Rome: Scala Santa, 1955), p. 2.
23. *Idem.*
24. Lord Byron, *Letter to Thomas Moore,* March 8, 1822.
25. Quoted by J. C. Macauley, *The Heresies of Rome* (Chicago: Moody Press, 1946).

26. *The Holy Stairway* (a Catholic guide book sold at the Holy Stairs in Rome; Rome: Scala Santa, 1955), p. 3.

27. *Idem.*

28. *Idem.*

29. Attributed to Percy Bysche Shelley by Cecil Roberts, *And So To Rome* (N. Y.: Macmillan, 1950), frontispiece.

30. Quoted by *Time*, November 8, 1954, p. 34.

31. *Idem.*

32. *Newsweek*, August 28, 1950, p. 28.

33. *Catholic Freedom in Orthodox, Moslem and Roman Catholic Europe* (London: World Dominion Press, 1945), p. 7.

34. *Ibid.*, p. 7.

35. Salvadori and Cantarello, *op. cit.*, p. 7.

36. Luigi Barzini, "Italy's Creeping Communism," *Harper's*, New York: October, 1954, pp. 35-45.

37. Carlo Sforza, *Italy and Italians* (N. Y.: E. P. Dutton, 1949), p. 73.

38. Joseph N. Moody, "Milan on the March," *America* (National Catholic Weekly Review) Sept. 22, 1956, p. 586.

39. Renato Tulli, "Roman Catholicism in Italy," *Christianity Today*, Washington, April 28, 1958, p. 13.

40. *Idem.*

41. *Idem.*

42. *L'Appel du Maitre* (Lugano, Switzerland), July-August, 1956, No. 4, p. 2903.

43. Gordon D. Jackson, "The Evangelical Front in Post-War Italy," *World Dominion* (London), Vol. XXV, No. 3 (May-June, 1947), p. 150.

44. *Time*, August 3, 1946, p. 8.

45. Quoted by Salvadori and Cantarello, *op. cit.*, p. 8.

46. *Idem.*

47. *New York Herald Tribune* (European Edition), Paris, Dec. 17, 1949, p. 1.

48. *Life*, pp. 68-78.

49. E. J. Jacques, "Christian Literature in Italy," *Report of 21st Annual Bible and Missionary Conference* (sponsored by Calvary Independent Church, Lancaster, Pa., March 11-18, 1956), p. 17.

50. *Idem.*

51. *Idem.*

52. *Idem.*

53. Oswald J. Smith, *The People's Magazine*, Toronto: The Second Quarter, 1956, p. 3.

54. Attributed to Pope Pius XI by P. J. Zaccara, "Italy," *Christianity Today*, ed. Henry Smith Lieper (N. Y.: Morehouse-Gorham Co., 1947), p. 75.

55. Attributed to Louis Veuillot by Adolf Keller, *Christian Europe Today* (N. Y.: Harper & Bros., 1952), p. 113.

56. *Lines of Communication*, ed. Arthur G. Ingleby (Plymouth Brethren, Parede, Portugal), p. 8.

57. *Youth for Christ* (Wheaton, Illinois: Youth for Christ International), p. 13.

58. *Confidential Report* (Youth for Christ International), Wheaton, Illinois, July, 1956.

59. *The Voice of Europe* (The European Evangelistic Crusade; Philadelphia), May-June, 1955, p. 4.

60. Oswald J. Smith, *The Passion for Souls* (London: Marshall, Morgan and Scott, 1950), p. 64.

Chapter 8

BLINDNESS IN BELGIUM AND LUXEMBURG

1. *Flanders' Fields* (Belgian Gospel Mission, Brussels, Belgium), Summer, 1949, p. 6.

2. *Ibid.*, Autumn, 1948, p. 3.

3. *Idem.*

4. *Flanders' Fields*, Autumn, 1955, pp. 1-2.

5. *Idem.*
6. *Idem.*
7. *Idem.*
8. *Flanders' Fields*, Winter, 1956/1957, p. 6.
9. *Idem.*

Chapter 9

AUSTRIA FORGOTTEN

1. G. E. R. Gedeye, "The Austrian Way of Life," *Austria 1956* (Fodor's Modern Guides; N. Y.: David McKay, 1956), p. 42.
2. Erik Von Kuehnhelt-Leddihn, "How Pagan is Europe?", *The Catholic World* (Paulist Fathers; New York, Sept., 1953), p. 443.
3. Penner, Leander, *Survey Report on Austria*, a study prepared for the Greater Europe Mission (Chicago, Illinois, Nov. 20, 1959), p. 1.

Chapter 10

THE ENIGMA OF IRELAND

1. F. Rupert Gibson, in his letter to the editor, *Christian Heritage* (Christ's Mission, Sea Cliff, N.Y.), June, 1959, p. 29.
2. Paul Blanshard, *The Irish and Catholic Power* (London: Derek Verschoyle, 1954), p. 322.
3. *Ibid.*, p. 221.
4. Temple Fielding, *European Travel Guide, 1949* (N. Y.: William Sloane Associates), p. 322.
5. Quoted in Blanshard, *op. cit.*, p. 150.
6. Charles Duff, *Ireland and the Irish* (N. Y.: Putnam & Sons, 1953), p. 124.
7. E. Estyn Evans, *Irish Folk Ways* (N. Y.: Devin-Adair, 1957), p. 256.
8. Conrad M. Arensberg, *The Irish Countryman* (N. Y.: Peter Smith, 1950), p. 82.
9. Sean O'Faolain, *The Irish: A Character Study* (N. Y.: Devin-Adair, 1949), p. 18.
10. Duff, *op. cit.*, p. 139.
11. Blanshard, *op. cit.*, p. 59.
12. Cornelius Lucey, *The Irish Times*, May 28, 1952.
13. Blanshard, *op. cit.*, p. 64.
14. Arensberg, *op. cit.*, p. 25.
15. *Idem.*
16. Anne O'Neill-Barna, "When Leprechauns Get Their Irish up," *Coronet*, March, 1959, p. 137.
17. *New Schaff-Herzog Encyclopedia of Religious Knowledge* (Grand Rapids: Baker Book House, 1955), VIII, 384.
18. Michael W. Devar, in *Christianity Today* (Washington), March 4, 1957, p. 3.
19. Raymond L. Cox, "The Phantom Saint," *Christian Heritage* (Christ's Mission, Sea Cliff, N. Y.), March, 1959, p. 19.
20. V. R. Edman, *The Light in Dark Ages* (Wheaton, Illinois: Van Kampen Press, 1949), p. 163.
21. Fulton J. Sheen, *New York Times*, April 21, 1952.
22. James H. Cotter, *Irish World* (Dublin), Dec. 12, 1945.
23. Arland Ussher, *The Face and Mind of Ireland* (N. Y.: Devin-Adair, 1950), p. 102.
24. *Idem.*
25. *The Irish Ecclesiastical Record* (Dublin), Sept., 1938, p. 260.
26. Quoted by Blanshard, *op. cit.*, p. 68.
27. O'Faolain, *op. cit.*, p. 153.

28. *Ibid.,* p. 139.
29. John K. Cartwright, *The Catholic Shrines of Europe* (N. Y.: McGraw-Hill Co.), 1955, p. 181.
30. *The Rosary and How To Say It* (Dublin: The Catholic Truth Society, 1950), p. 18.
31. Sub-heading to an article by James Stewart-Gordon, "The Odds? 450,000 to One," *Reader's Digest,* April, 1959, p. 93.
32. *A Catholic Dictionary,* Donald Attwater, ed. (N. Y.: The Macmillan Co., 1961), pp. 53-54.
33. "Ireland," *Oxford Dictionary of the Christian Church* (London: Oxford University Press, 1957), p. 700.
34. F. Rupert Gibson, *op. cit.,* p. 29.
35. *Idem.*
36. Blanshard, *op. cit.,* p. 185.

CHAPTER 11

GREECE'S UNKNOWN GOD

1. G. P. Raud, *Inside Facts on Europe* (Brooklyn, N. Y.: European Christian Mission), 1946, p. 171.
2. Will Durant, *The Life of Greece* (N. Y.: Simon and Schuster, 1939), Preface.
3. *Confessio Disithea,* Decretum 2.
4. Julius Richter, *A History of Protestant Missions in the Near East* (N. Y.: Fleming H. Revell, 1910), p. 164.
5. David L. Cooper, *World Evangelization in This Generation?* (Los Angeles: Biblical Research Society, 1951), p. 84.
6. George Kladis, "Thessalonica and Berea Again," *Bible Society Record* (American Bible Society; New York), April, 1949, p. 58.
7. Stewart Herman, *Report from Christian Europe* (N. Y.: Friendship Press, 1953), p. 126.
8. *The Greek Evangel* (Greek Evangelical Mission; Boston), Jan.-March, 1953, p. 2.

CHAPTER 12

CHANGING HOLLAND

1. *De Rotterdamer,* Rotterdam, May 12, 1956. All the interpretations in this section are based on this issue and that of April 28, 1956, as well as on the *Dordtsch Dagblad,* April 21, 1956. The articles on this subject in these newspapers by Jan J. van Capelleven were supplemented by personal conversations with this journalist.
2. *Time,* July 27, 1959.
3. G. Van Leeuwen, *Orn de Jeugd of Om de Kerk!* (The Hague: D. A. Damen's, 1953), p. 19.
4. Hermann Van Brummelen, of Child Evangelism Fellowship International, Hilversum, in personal conversation with the author, August, 1955.
5. I. Gadourek, *A Dutch Community* (Leiden: H. E. Stenfert Kroese, N. V., 1956), p. 455.
6. Records of the Navigators (Kon. Wilhelminalaan 13, Voorburg, The Hague).
7. Recounted to the author by Mr. Jan Reuse, who was present during the conversation.
8. Dick Van Katwijk, *How to Win Others for Christ* (Washington: International Council for Christian Leadership, no date), p. 4.
9. E. Emmen, in *Christianity Today* (N. Y.: Morehouse-Gorham, 1947), p. 11.
10. *E55 Katholicke Gids,* Rotterdam, 1955 (A Catholic Guide).
11. E. Emmen, *op. cit.,* p. 12.

12. A. W. Van Lennep, Assistant General Secretary, Netherlands Bible Society (Nederlands Bijbelgenootschap), Amsterdam, during interview with the author, August, 1955.

CHAPTER 13

WHITHER GERMANY LEADS

1. Richard C. Hottelet, "New Look for Germany," *Reader's Digest*, Sept., 1957, p. 69 (condensed from *The New Leader*, New York, July 15, 1957).
2. George P. Fisher, *History of the Christian Church* (N. Y.: Scribners, 1945), p. 145.
3. *Idem.*
4. Viet Valentin, *The German People* (N. Y.: Alfred A. Knopf, 1952), p. 682.
5. Adolph Keller, *Protestant Europe, Its Crisis and Outlook* (N. Y.: George H. Doran, 1927), p. 28.
6. Wallace Emerson, *Outline of Psychology* (Wheaton: Van Kampen Press, 1953), p. 25.
7. William Loos (ed.), *Religious Faith and World Culture* (N. Y.: Prentice Hall), 1951.
8. Stewart Herman, *The Rebirth of the German Church* (London: SCM Press, 1946), p. 29.
9. *Ibid.*, p. 61.
10. *Das Zeugnis Eines Boten* (Geneva: Oikumene Press, 1945), p. 72.
11. Ernest Klassen, Prayer Letter from German Bible Institute (Greater Europe Mission), Jan. 25, 1956.
12. Paul Hazard, *The European Mind, 1680–1715* (London: Hollis & Carter, 1952), p. 153.
13. *Licht und Leben,* Circular letter of The Society for a Living Church, Oct., 1955, p. 2.
14. Levi Reimer, *The Voice of Europe* (European Evangelistic Crusade; Philadelphia), Sept.-Oct., 1959, p. 8.
15. *The Greater Europe Mission Reporter,* Chicago, October, 1959, p. 2.
16. Personal interview with Emil Diehl, Stuttgart, April 14, 1955.
17. Hans Lilje, *Luther Now* (Philadelphia: Muhlenburg Press, 1952), pp. 140-1.
18. Quoted by *Moody Monthly* (Chicago), Sept., 1957, p. 5.
19. Baron F. von der Ropp, "The German Problem," *World Dominion* (London), Sept.-Oct., 1946, pp. 259-261.
20. *Young Germany: Apprentice to Democracy*, Washington: U.S. Department of State, Division of Publications, Office of Public Affairs, Sept., 1951, Publication 4251, foreword, unnumbered.
21. *Time*, May 7, 1956, p. 83.
22. *Newsweek*, Nov. 18, 1957, p. 50.

CHAPTER 14

SWITZERLAND: NO PARADISE WITHOUT GOD

1. Quoted by Daniel Buscarlet in *St. Peter's Cathedral* (Geneva, a guidebook, no date), p. 2.
2. John D. Hughey, Jr., personal interview at Oerlikon, Switzerland, December 3, 1959.
3. *New York Herald Tribune* (European Edition; Paris), December 14, 1959, p. 5.
4. Adolph Keller and George Stewart, *Protestant Europe, Its Crisis and Outlook* (N. Y.: George H. Doran, 1927), p. 235.
5. *New York Herald Tribune* (European Edition; Paris), March 23, 1950, Section 2, p. 23.

6. Merle J. H. D'Aubigné, *History of the Reformation of the Sixteenth Century* (N. Y., Robert Carter and Brothers, 1857), p. 274.

7. *Swiss Constitution of 1847*, Article 51 (Bern: Swiss Federal Republic Archives, unnumbered).

8. *Letter from Geneva*, Le Roc, Coligny (Geneva), Oct., 1956, No. 9, p. 3.

9. *Time*, January 11, 1960, p. 38.

Chapter 15

SCANDINAVIA IN SILHOUETTE

1. Sören Kierkegaard.

2. Carl C. Rasmussen, *What About Scandinavia?* (Philadelphia: The Muhlenberg Press, 1948), p. 6.

3. *Ibid.*, p. 10.

4. *Ibid.*, p. 11.

5. *U.S. News and World Report* (Washington, D.C.), Aug. 8, 1960, p. 8.

6. Agnes Rothery, *Sweden* (N. Y.: The Viking Press, 1934), p. 163.

7. "Sweden by Car" Kingliga Automobil Klubben, Trollhättan: Trollhätans Tryckert, 1956, p. 13.

8. Hudson Strode, *Sweden, Model for a World* (N. Y.: Harcourt, Brace, 1949), p. 250.

9. Joe David Brown, "Sin and Sweden," *Time*, April 25, 1955, p. 29.

10. *Ibid.*, p. 29.

11. *Ibid.*, p. 29.

12. Quoted by Joe David Brown in his special *Time* article, p. 29.

13. *Ibid.*, p. 29.

14. *Ibid.*, p. 29.

15. Edward M. Korry, "Sex Education in Sweden," *Look*, 1956, p. 34.

16. *Scandinavia 1956* (The Hague, Fodor's Modern Guides; N. Y.: David McKay, 1954), p. 275.

17. Carl C. Rasmussen, *op. cit.*, p. 54.

18. Richard M. Bracket, "Second Spring in Sweden," *America* (New York), March 27, 1959, Vol. 90, p. 679.

19. *Continental Key* (Paris, France), July, 1960, p. 12.

20. Max Eastman, "Norway: Case History in Social Experiment," *Reader's Digest*, May, 1956, pp. 133-134 (condensed from *National Review*, N.Y., April 18, 1956).

21. Paul Gullans (Greater Europe Mission) Prayer Letter (Helsinki, Finland), May 15, 1957.

22. Iver Iversen, "Norway," *New Schaff-Herzog Encyclopedia of Religious Knowledge* (Grand Rapids: Baker Book House, 1955), II, 807.

23. Enos Zimmerman (Greater Europe Mission), Prayer Letter, Oct., 1954.

24. *The Hour* (Eastbourne, England), November, 1961, No. 12, p. 6.

25. *The Church of Finland*, Finnish National Committee, World Lutheran Federation, 1949, p. 14.

26. *Ibid.*, p. 24.

27. Bishop E. G. Gullin, "The Gospel in Finland Today," *World Dominion* (London), Vol. XXVII, No. 1, January-February, 1949, p. 35.

28. Zimmerman, *op. cit.*

29. *Ibid.*

Bibliographic Essay

Since many of the sources used in this book are indicated either in the text or the footnotes, we will comment here only on works of particular value, first on Europe in general, then on a few of the individual countries.

Only one book in this generation surveyed spiritual conditions in Europe as a whole and from the evangelical standpoint. This was *Inside Facts on Europe*, by G. P. Raud, published in 1946 by the European Christian Mission (now the National Bible Christian Union). Raud's book was of an outline character and dealt largely with Eastern Europe, with which he was particularly familiar. Now out of print, the book's general insights are still of some value.

Several have discussed European Christianity from the ecumenical viewpoint during the last two decades. One is Adolf Keller, who wrote *Christian Europe Today* in 1942 (London: Epworth Press). Both this and *Report from Christian Europe*, written by Stewart Herman in 1953 (New York: Friendship Press), contain useful information about European Protestantism. The booklet edited by Alexander McLeish, *Europe in Transition* (London: World Dominion Press, no date), gives added information along the same line, as does his own work, *The Church in Post-War Europe* (London: World Dominion Press, 1949). His survey called *Religious Freedom in Orthodox, Moslem and Roman Catholic Europe*, issued in London by the World Dominion Press in 1945, still has value because some issues it discusses have changed little with the years.

Perhaps the best scholarly treatment of the history of European church life between 1914 and 1955 is *The Twentieth Century in Europe*, the fourth of a five-volume series, "Christianity in a Revolutionary Age" (New York: Harper and Bros., 1961). Latourette devotes 213 pages to continental Roman Catholicism and 154 pages to Protestantism. Much factual material, particularly on Roman Catholic trends, distinguishes the book.

The Baptists have documented their missionary efforts in Europe better than any other American denomination. A good older example is *Believers and Builders in Europe* (Nashville: Broadman Press, 1939). *Europe—Whither Bound?* (Nashville: Broadman Press, 1951) is a symposium edited by A. F. Weeks on Southern Baptist work in Europe, and is written by five men with experience there.

521

Most modern evangelical missionary surveys of the world have not included Europe. A happy exception is *A Survey of Missions,* by John Caldwell Thiessen (Chicago: Moody Press, 1956, second edition). Good brief comments on this continent can be found in David H. Adeney's *The Unchanging Commission* (Chicago: Inter-Varsity Press, 1955), in *A Glimpse of World Missions,* a booklet by Clyde W. Taylor (Chicago: Moody Press, 1960), and in *Mission Fields Today* (Chicago: Inter-Varsity Press, 1956), edited by A. J. Dain.

France

The Soul of France (London: Morgan and Scott, 1926) by Reuben Saillens, skillfully traces the testimony of the believing remnant throughout French history. Two books give the Catholic viewpoint of the postwar missionary renaissance of that church in France. These are *France Alive,* by Claire Huchet Bishop (New York: Declan X. McMullen, 1947) and *France Pagan? The Mission of Abbé Godin,* by Maisie Ward (New York: Sheed and Ward, 1949).

Spain

An official Spanish government document, *The Situation of Protestantism in Spain* (Madrid: Diplomatic Information Office, 1955, second edition, mimeographed) is difficult to locate now, but valuable. It must, however, be interpreted in the light of today's more recent liberal attitudes toward Protestants. The same would hold true for *Secret Journey Through Spain,* by Bjorn Hallstrom (London: Lutterworth Press, 1948), and *The Oppression of Protestants in Spain,* by Jacques Delpech (Boston: Beacon Press, 1955). *Religious Freedom in Spain,* by John D. Hughey, Jr. (Nashville: Broadman Press, 1955) is a valuable historical treatment. In 1957 Lawrence Fernsworth dealt with religious liberty, as well as other freedoms, in *Spain's Struggle for Freedom* (Boston: Beacon Press, 1957). The latest book-length discussion of the Catholic situation in Spain is *Freedom and Catholic Power in Spain and Portugal,* by Paul Blanshard (Boston: Beacon Press, 1962).

Portugal

The book by Paul Blanshard, *Freedom and Catholic Power in Spain and Portugal* (Boston: Beacon Press, 1962) devotes less space to Portugal than to Spain, but documents some abuses of religious liberty there. Mission reports are often fruitful sources of information. A typical one is the section on Portugal in *Three Score Years—And Then,* by J. F. Swanson (Chicago: The Evangelical Alliance Mission, 1950).

Belgium

The origin of this country's largest Protestant work is well recounted in *Ralph Norton and the Belgian Gospel Mission* by Mrs. Edith F. Norton (New York: Fleming Revell, 1935) and in *A New Invasion of Belgium* by Philip E. Howard (Philadelphia: The Sunday School Times, 1924).

Ireland

The best objective interpretation of Roman Catholic influence on the Irish people is *The Irish and Catholic Power,* by Paul Blanshard (London: Derek Verschoyle, 1954).

Germany

Anyone who wants an understanding of the German churches' predicament before and during World War II should read *The Rebirth of the German Church,* by Stewart Herman (London: SCM Press, 1946). An outstanding analysis of the German mentality has been written by a German, Viet Valentin, in *The German People* (New York: Alfred A. Knopf, 1952).

Scandinavia

In 1948 Carl C. Rasmussen, an American Lutheran minister and professor, wrote *What About Scandinavia?* (Philadelphia: The Muhlenberg Press). Rasmussen's conclusions about the dormant state of Scandinavian church life then remain valid today.

Index

A

Adeney, David, 32
Adolphus, Gustavus, King of Sweden, 471
Adrian IV, Pope, canonizes Finland's patron saint, 495
Age of Reason, in France, 125-7
Agricola, Mikael, 455, 496
Alcoholism, in France, 140-1
Alexander III, Pope, addresses bull to Finns, 495
Alexander, Hugh E., 444
Alva, Duke of, 303, 366
Anabaptists, the, in Germany, 24, 414
  in Holland, 366
André, Jean, 446
Arensberg, Conrad, 331
Assisi, St. Francis in, 266
  St. Claire in, 266
Aubigné, J. H., Merle d', 175, 264, 436

B

Bainton, Roland, on Luther's view of the church, 24
Baldwin, Hanson W., 249
Balmes, Jaime, 202, 213
Baptist Mid-Missions, 384
Baptists, Southern, in Spain, 216, 219
  in Portugal, 240
  in Italy, 281
Barbarossa, Frederick, 393
Barnes, David, 138
Barnhouse, Donald Grey, on Europe, 33
  on French Protestantism, 166
  on needs in Spain, 225
Barth, Karl, 70-73, 80, 304
  influence of, in France, 166
  influence of, in Holland, 370
  influence in Germany, 400
  influence of, in Switzerland, 436
  influence of, in Belgium, 304
Basques, Spanish, 198
  their languages, 201
Bayon, Noel, 136
Beatenberg Bible School, 414, 438-9
Belgian Gospel Mission, 11, 32, 303, 306-9
Belloc, Hilaire, 238
Berdyaev, Nikolas, 70, 80
Berggrav, Bishop, of Oslo, 462
Berkouwer, G. C., 76, 361
Bernadotte, Folke, 471
Bible Christian Union, 12
  in Italy, 283, 384
Bible Club Movement, 384
Bismarck, Otto von, 393
Black Mass, the, in France, 138
  in Italy, 274
Blanshard, Paul, on state and church, 49
  on French Catholicism, 144
  on Irish Catholicism, 327
Boegner, André, 169

B (continued, right column)

Borman, Dr. Thorlief, on Norway's spiritual need, 484
Bonaparte, Napoleon, 27, 42, 121-2, 127, 146, 260, 293
Bonhoeffer, Dietrich, 405
Boniface VIII, Pope, 49
Booth, Catherine, 444
Booth, William, 444
Borrow, George, 214
Boulard, Abbé, 148-9, 153
Boyer, Eugene, 36, 167, 173
Bradley, Francis, 398
Brazil, compared to Italy as mission field, 246
British and Foreign Bible Society, the, in Spain, 214, 216
  in Belgium, 300
  in Greece 355-6
Brousson, Claude, 161-2
Brunner, Emil, 70, 73, 80
  influence in France, 166
  influence in Switzerland, 436
Buber, Martin, 70, 80
Buffard, Percy J., 35, 216
Bultmann, Rudolph, 75, 76, 80
  influence of, in France, 166
  influence of, in Holland, 371

C

Calvin, John, 22, 24, 109-10, 150, 160, 165, 353, 434-6, 443
Carranza, Bartholomé, 213
Catherine the Great, of Russia, 126
Catholicism, Roman, 19, 21-6, 28-9, 35, 41, 47
  and American Protestants, 48
  historical objectives, 49-50
  as a half truth, 50-1
  numerical strength in Europe, 51-3
  practice of, in Europe, 53-4
  national aspects of, 54-5
  European missionaries of, 55-6
  mentality, 56-9, 65, 67, 69, 78, 83
  in France, 124-5, 139-40, 144-159
  in Spain, 16, 187-8, 201-11, 217-8, 222-4, 228-9
  in Portugal, 234-9, 241-2
  in Italy, 16, 258-76, 279, 282, 283-7
  in Belgium, 294-301
  in Luxemburg, 311-13
  in Austria, 319-22
  in Ireland, 327-9, 332-3, 335-345
  relation to Greek Orthodoxy, 352-3
  in Holland, 361, 365-8, 373-5, 377-81
  in Germany, 400, 403, 405-6, 415-18, 424, 427
  in Switzerland, 433, 440-3, 445
  in Scandinavia, 449, 455, 457-8, 465-7, 490, 495-6
Charlemagne, 42, 364, 393
Charles, Jerome, 135

Charles V, Emperor, 185, 200, 212, 213, 305, 365-6, 393
Child Evangelism Fellowship, International, in Holland, 384
in Switzerland, 446
in Denmark, 463, 467
Christian Business Men's Committee, International, 384
Claudel, Paul, 154
Clement XI, Pope, issues bull against Jansenism, 150
Coligny, Gaspard de, Admiral, 160
Colinson, Maurice, 136
Columbus, Christopher, 185
Communism, 29, 47
relation to Catholicism, 56-7
European origin, 59
early history of, 60
principal thesis of, 60-1
attitude toward moral law, 61-2
general strength in Europe, 62-5
why Europeans accept, 66
conversions to Christ from, 66-7
Portuguese Protestants accused of, 236
in Italy, 16, 251, 276-9
in East Germany, 426-8
in Scandinavia, 449
Finland's relation to, 494-5
Compte, Jean de la, 440
Condillac, Etienne de, 125-6
Conservative Baptists, in Portugal, 240
in Italy, 283

D

Dain, A. J., 35
Daniel, Yvan, 145
Daniel-Rops, 149, 154
Dansette, Adrien, 149
DeGaulle, Charles, on Catholic schools, 63, 156
Delitzsch, Franz, 399-400
Delpech, Jacques, 223
Demonism, in France, 137-40
Descartes, René, 126
Devlin, John, Jr., 205
Dibelius, Bishop Otto, 12, 477
Diderot, Dennis, 125-6
Diehl, Emil, 422
Donatists, the, 145
Druids, vestiges of worship in France, 137-140
in Ireland, 333
Durant, Will, 348
Dutourd, Jean, 122

E

Eastern European Mission, 357
Edict of Nantes, 160
Revocation of, 111
Edman, V. Raymond, on early Christianity, 22
on France, 144
on Ireland, 336
Eisenhower, Dwight D., on American power, 31
letter from Billy Graham to, 32

on French religious practice, 153, 202
on results of Scandinavian socialism, 469
Emmaus Bible Institute, 439, 445
Emerson, Wallace, 401
Engels, Friedrich, 60, 62, 398
Enlightenment, the, in France, 125-7
in Spain, 191
Erasmus, Desiderius, 258, 302-3
European Bible Institute, 109, 141, 171, 172, 176, 386
European Evangelistic Crusade, 11, 357, 384
Evangelical Alliance Mission, the (TEAM) in Portugal, 243

F

Farel, Guillaume, 435, 443
Fatima, shrine of, in Portugal, 239
Feisser, John Elias, 369
Fèvre, Lucien, 166
Fichte, Johann, 398, 402
Fliedner, Fritz, 214
Franco, Generalissimo Francisco, 27, 179, 186-8, 199, 201, 203, 223
Franke, August, 413
Franson, Frederick, 492
Frederick the Great, of Prussia, 126, 393, 402
Frederick the Wise, of Saxony, 455
Freud, Sigmund, 80, 400-1
Fuglsang, Damgaard, Bishop of Cophenhagen, 462

G

Garrison, W. E., 222
Gasperi, Alcide de, 276, 279, 286
Gasset, Ortega y, 80
German Bible Institute, 420
Gibbons, James Cardinal, 204
Gibson, E. Rupert, 344
Gide, André, 155
Gipsies, 193
Gladstone, William E., 50
Godin, Abbé Henri, 145, 148-50, 152, 154
Graham, Billy, on Europe as a mission field, 32, 36
evangelism in Paris, 167, 173
on need of France, 177, 240
in Holland, 371, 375, 383
on German attitudes, 390
in Germany, 414
in Switzerland, 434, 437-8
on Scandinavian response, 449
in Denmark, 465, 467
in Sweden, 468, 483
on Swedish morals, 475
in Norway, 492
Greater Europe Mission, 11, 141, 176, 169, 288, 289, 323, 313, 384, 411, 420
Gregory XI, Pope, 269
Gregory of Tours, 159
Gullin, Bishop E. G., of Finland, 492, 497

H

Hallesby, Ole, 487, 490

Hamilton, Alexander, 126
Hauge, Hans Nielsen, 491-2
Healers, in France, 136
Hedegard, David, on Karl Barth, 73
Hegel, Georg W. F., 59-61, 398-9
Heidigger, Martin, 75, 80-1
Heliovaara, Bishop O. K., of Finland, 497
Henry, Bishop, of Uppsala, Sweden, 495
Henry, Carl F. H., 12
Henry IV, of France, 120
Herder, Johann, 402
Herman, Stewart, 52, 77, 355
Hindenburg, President von, 393
Hitler, Adolf, 42, 147, 293, 318, 322, 393-4, 402-3, 408, 426
Hitt, Russell, 33
Hobbes, Thomas, 126
Hocking, W. E., 398
Hoffet, Frédéric, on French character, 57-8
Hoffman, Arthur and Agnes, 446
Holy Stairs, at Rome, 263-4
Holy Week, observances in Spain, 208-11
Hughes, Emmet John, 202
Hughey, John D., Jr., 11, 213, 217-18, 436, 445
Huguenots, French, 161-3
Humanism, 381-2

I

Ibert, Jean Claude, 135
Index, Roman Catholic, in Ireland, 338
Innocent III, Pope, 54
International Council for Christian Leadership, 384
Inter-Varsity Fellowship, 467
Irenaeus, in France, 159
on Germany, 392

J

Jacques, Edwin, 11, 278-9
Jansenius, Cornelius, 150
Jansenism, in France, 150
Janz, Leo, 12
evangelistic efforts of, 36
on need of Switzerland, 431
campaigns in Switzerland, 437, 445
Jasper, Karl, 79-80
Jay, John, 126
Jefferson, Thomas, 50
Jesuits, the, in France, 125, 136, 150
in Spain, 187, 217, 228
in Portugal, 235
in Austria, 320
in Switzerland, 442-3
in Norway, 490
Jewett, Paul King, 71
John XXIII, Pope, 158
Joyce, James, 340
Jung, Carl, 436

K

Kant, Immanuel, 391, 397-8
Keller, Adolf, 147
Kernan, Thomas, on French personality, 124

Kierkegaard, Sören, 70, 72, 399, 410, 458, 463, 465
Kiss, Ferenc, 37
Kladis, George, 12, 355-6
Kobner, Julius, 369
Kuiper, Abraham, 369

L

Laestdadius, Lars, 497
Lamorte, André, 82, 123, 167
Languages, of Europe, divisions of, 28, 508
learning of, 95-6
Latourette, Kenneth Scott, on dechristianization of Europe, 34, 69
on Swedish church attendance, 478
Lebras, Gabriel, 153
Lefèvre d'Etaples, 160
Leo III, Pope, 260
Leo X, Pope, authorizes showing of the Robe of Trier, 418
Léonard, Emile, 166, 168
Lenin, Nikolai, 60, 62
Leprechauns, 334
Lilje, Hans, Bishop, 12
on spiritual need of Europe, 38, 68, 389
on Bible ignorance in Germany, 423
Literacy, during Reformation, 24-5,
in Europe, 27
in Portugal, 234
in Spain, 183, 192
Locke, John, 126
Lotze, Hermann, 398
Louis XIV, King of France, 121
Lourdes, 15, 155, 156-9, 239
Loyola, Ignatius, 198, 213, 320
Ludwig, Emil, 146
Luethy, Herbert, on France, 121-3, 125
Luther, Martin on territorial principle, 23-4, 41, 73
theological difficulties with baptism, 74, 76, 150
remarks on Rome, 263
mounts Holy Stairs, 264, 300
jubilation over Belgian Reformation, 302, 321, 389-90, 404, 496

M

Macaulay, Lord Thomas B., 261
Madison, James, 126
Magic, Black, 339-40
Mailland, Pierre, 124
Malan, César, 175
Malraux, André, on French character, 122
Mangs, Frank, 492
Marcel, Gabriel, 80
Maritain, Jacques, 97
Marx, Karl, 41, 59-62, 385, 398
Mary, the Virgin, 29
cult of, centered in Rome, 269-71
veneration in Luxemburg, 312
Spanish shrines to. 203, 207
in Spanish Holy Week, 209-10
Irish shrines to, 339
as viewed by Greek Orthodoxy, 352
in Belgium, 297-8

Massin, Abbé, 151
Mauriac, François, on French character 122-3
  advocates Christian socialism, 154
McKay, Donald C., 121
McLeish, Alexander, 34, 35, 99
Medina, Dr. Gladys, 136
Melanchthon, Philip, 24, 353
Mennonites, American, as missionaries to Luxemburg, 313
Merlin Act, the, on Italian prostitution, 257
Messequé, Maurice, 136
Monod, Frédéric, 175
Montesquieu, Baron de, 125-6
Montfort, Simon de, 160
Montini, Giovanni Cardinal, 273
More, Sir Thomas, 305
Mueller, William A., 75
Müller, Johannes, Catholic Bishop of Sweden, 458
Mussolini, Benito, 282, 284-5

N

Nationalism, of non-Europeans, 39-40, 100-1
  of Europeans, 96-100
  of French, 115-16
Navigators, the, 78, 384, 467
Neumann, Thérèse, 416-17
Newton, Isaac, 126
Nicholas III, Pope, Dante's description of, 272
Nida, Eugene, 96
Niebuhr, Reinhold, 70, 80, 371
Niemöller, Martin, 12, 415
Nietzsche, Friedrich Wilhelm, influence in Germany, 402
  influence in Switzerland, 436
Norton, Ralph, founds Belgian Gospel Mission, 306

O

Ockenga, Harold J., 15, 33
Orthodoxy, Greek, 347-8, 351-6
O'Connell, Daniel, 340
O'Faoláin, Seán, 331, 338

P

Pâche, René, 12
  on non-Protestant Europe, 37
  on European theology, 76
  on missionaries for Europe, 91
Pape, Dennis, 35
Paris, importance of, 120-2
  University of, 142-3
  Catholic growth in suburbs of, 155
Pascal, Blaise, 107, 126, 146, 150, 154
Payne, Homer, 445
Philip, II, 185, 213, 365-6
Peck, Royal 11
  tent campaign in Marsciano, 288
  leads Italian Bible Institute, 289
Pedrosa, Don Luis, 228
Pétain, Marshall Henri, 122, 147, 155
Petri, Olavus, 454
Pietism, 413

Pius VIII, Pope, bans Masonic rites, 274
Pius, IX, Pope, announcement of Immaculate Conception
Pius X, Pope, on relation of church and state, 147
Pius XI, Pope, on winning of laboring class, 148
  signs Vatican concordat with Italy, 284
Pius, XII, Pope, congratulates Franco on victory, 186
  at Holy Year ceremonies, 259
  announcement about St. Peter's body, 262
  encyclical on Mary Queen of Heaven, 271
  warns Italian voters, 274
  excommunicates Catholics espousing Communism, 276
  encourages Danish Catholics, 457
Population, increase of, in Europe, 29
Pounds, Norman J. G., 191
Prostitution, in France, 134
  in Italy, 257
Price, Frank W., on the word "unevangelized," 19
Pritchett, V. S., 188, 200
Pyt, Henri, 164, 175

R

Racine, Gaston, 135
Ramm, Bernard, 69, 76
Raud, G. P., 348
Relics, Roman Catholic, in Italy, 267-8
Reapers' Fellowship, the, 384
Reformation, the Protestant, limitations of, 22-5
  territorial principle in, 23-4, 33, 40, 67
  in France, 132, 160-1
  in Spain, 191, 212-14
  in Portugal, 234-5
  in Italy, 257-8
  in Belgium, 302-3
  in Austria, 320
  in Ireland, 342
  relation of, to Greek orthodoxy, 253
  in Holland, 365-7
  in Germany, 393, 396-7
  in Switzerland, 440-1
  in Scandinavia, 454-6, 465, 486, 495-6
Ritschl, Albrecht, 398
Roberts, David, 82
Rosenberg, Alfred, 403
Rousseau, Jean Jacques, 64, 125-7, 154, 434
Royce, Josiah, 398
Rudolph of Hapsburg, 393
Rüth, Johannes, Catholic Bishop of Oslo, 457
Ryrie, Charles, 71

S

Saillens, Reuben, 107, 110
St. Bartholomew's Day, Massacre of, 160
St. Bernadette, see Lourdes
St. Boniface, 364

St. Bridget, 333
St. Christopher, Veneration in Belgium, 298
St. Claire, shrine of, 266
St. Francis, of Assisi, 266, 417
St. George, veneration in Belgium, 298
St. Hubert, 312
St. Januarius, of Naples, 265
St. John Lateran, church of, 261, 263
St. John's Eve, observances in Belgium, 299
St. Joseph, veneration in Spain, 207 in Belgium, 298
St. Patrick, 335-6, 339
St. Peter's Church, Rome, see Vatican City
St. Willibrod, 312
Salter, Cedric, 203
Santayana, George, 204
Sartre, Jean Paul, 62, 80-2
Sasse, Hermann, 404
Savonarola, Girolamo, precursor of the Reformation, 22
on Italy, 245
in Italian Reformation, 257-8
Scala Santa (see Holy Stairs)
Schaeffer, Francis and Edith, 445
Schoenbrun, David, 111, 114, 133
Schjelderup, Bishop Kristian, of Norway, 490
Schleiermacher, Friedric, 398
Schools, Roman Catholic, controversy over, in France, 155-6
in Belgium, 301
in Ireland, 337
Schumann, Robert, 122
Schuster, Ildefonso Cardinal, of Milan, 274
Segura, Pedro Cardinal, 202-3
Shaw, George Bernard, 331, 340
Sheen, Fulton J., Bishop, 336
Siegfried, André, 40, 48
Simons, Menno, 366
Spener, Philip Jacob, 413
Spengler, Oswald, 398
Sorcery, 15
in France, 136-40
Sorokin, Pitirim, 44
Stern, Wilhelm, 400
Stendahl (Marie Henri Beyle), 124
on Italy, 250
Street, Harold B., 33
Streicher, Julius, 403
Suhard, Cardinal, Archbishop of Paris, 145, 147
Suicide, in Austria, 321
in Denmark 16, 461-2
in France, 141
in Switzerland, 433-4
in Sweden, 473
Sweepstakes, Irish Hospitals, 341

T

Tardieu, André, 132
Tausen, Hans, 455
Taylor, Clyde W., protests Greek persecution, 355

Tacitus, 471
Tennent, Gilbert, 413
Thiessen, John Caldwell, 31
Tillich, Paul, 70, 80
Toulouse, Council of, 282
Touquet, Robert, 136
Trend, J. B.
Trent, Council of, 213, 367, 269, 282, 320, 366
Tulli, Renato, 273, 288
Twain, Mark, 261
Tyndale, William, translates Bible in Belgium, 300, 305

U

Urban VIII, Pope, 262
Ussher, Arland, 337

V

Valdés, Alfonso de, in Spanish Reformation, 212
Valdés, Juan de, in Spanish Reformation, 212-13
in Italy, 258
Van Steenberghe, O., 297, 299-300
Vasa, King Gustavus, 454
Vatican City, description of, 260-4
Dutch gift of radio transmitters to, 380
Vinet, Alexander, 107
Voltaire, 65, 125-6, 154
Von Clausevitz, Karl, 44
Von Molke, Helmut, 402
Von der Ropp, F., Baron, 424

W

Waldo, Peter, 110, 160, 164
Wallace, Irving, 193
Wasserzug, Gertrude, 438
Waugh, Evelyn, 460
Wellington, Duke of, 200
Wesley, John, 413
William the Silent, 365-7
Winston, John, Jr., 308
Winston, John C., Sr., 11
on Europe's spiritual need, 32
on Belgium, 291
Witchcraft, 15
Worker priest movement, in France, 145-6
World Council of Churches, 219, 439
World Health Organization, on French alcoholism, 140-1
Wundt, Wilhelm, 400
Wyatt, Roy, Jr., 181

X

Xavier, Francis, St., 198, 339

Y

Youth for Christ, 384, 467

Z

Zinzendorf, Count von, 353
Zoé movement, 353-4
Zopfi, Kermit, 420
Zwingli, Ulrich, 22, 24, 366, 435, 436, 441